NEW HORIZONS FOR ACADEMIC LIBRARIES

Papers Presented at the First National Conference
of the Association of College and Research Libraries
Boston, Massachusetts
November 8–11, 1978

Edited by
Robert D. Stueart and
Richard D. Johnson

K. G. SAUR PUBLISHING INC.
New York · München · London · Paris

1979

K. G. Saur Publishing Inc.
175 Fifth Avenue
New York, NY 10010
Tel: (212) 477-2500

K. G. Saur Ltd. &
  Clive Bingley Ltd.
Commonwealth House
1-19 New Oxford Street
London WC1A 1NE

K. G. Saur Verlag
Pössenbacherstr. 2
Postfach 71 10 09
D-8 München 71
Tel: (089) 79 80 01

K. G. Saur Editeur
38, rue de Bassano
F-75008 Paris
Tel: 72355-18

LIBRARY OF CONGRESS CATALOGING IN
PUBLICATION DATA

Association of College and Research Libraries.
  New horizons for academic libraries.

  1. Libraries, University and college—Congresses.
I. Stueart, Robert D. II. Johnson, Richard David,
1927-   III. Title.
Z675.U5A73 1979 027.7 79-12059

ISBN 0-89664-093-0

BRITISH LIBRARY CATALOGUING IN
PUBLICATION DATA

Association of College and Research Libraries.
  National Conference, 1st, Boston, Mass., 1978
  New horizons for academic libraries.
  1. Libraries, University and college—United
States—Congresses I. Title II. Stueart, Robert
D. III. Johnson, Richard D.
027.7'0973 Z675.U5 79-40537

ISBN 0-89664-093-0

CIP-KURZTITELAUFNAHME DER
DEUTSCHEN BIBLIOTHEK

New horizons for academic libraries: papers
presented at the 1. national conference of the
Assoc. of College and Research Libraries,
Boston, Massachusetts, November 8-11, 1978/
ed. by Robert D. Stueart and Richard D.
Johnson.
New York, München, London, Paris:Saur, 1979.

  ISBN 0-89664-093-0 (New York)
  ISBN 3-598-40002-0 (München)

NE: Stueart, Robert D. [Hrsg.]; Association
of College and Research Libraries

Printed and bound in the United States of America by Edwards Brothers, Inc.

ISBN 0-89664-093-0
ISBN 3-598-40002-0

CONTENTS

Introduction   vii

PART I: THEME PAPERS   1
  Mary F. Berry   Higher Education in the United States: The
                                     Road Ahead   3
  Warren J. Haas   Managing Our Academic Libraries: Ways and
                                     Means   10
  Joe B. Wyatt   Technology and the Library   23
  Barbara Evans Markuson   Cooperation and Library Network
                                     Development   30
  Richard W. Boss   The Library as an Information Broker   43
  Jay K. Lucker   Library Resources and Bibliographic Control   50
  Millicent D. Abell   The Changing Role of the Academic Librarian:
                                     Drift and Mastery   66

PART II: CONTRIBUTED PAPERS   79

  Section I: Administration and Management   81

  Providing Knowledge and Client Links
    Ken Balthaser   81
  Dealing with the Fear of Change through the Self-Study Process
    Joseph A. Boissé   86
  Management Control in Academic Libraries
    Miriam A. Drake   91
  Academic Libraries, Participative Management, and Risky Shift
    Richard Eggleton   96
  State Systems of Higher Education and Libraries
    Isaac T. Littleton   102
  Cost Allocation and Cost Generation
    Richard Lyders, Diane Eckels and Maurice C. Leatherbury   116
  The Role of the Academic Librarian in Library Governance
    Marion T. Reid, Anna H. Perrault and Jane P. Kleiner   123
  Growing Pains: An Administrator's Viewpoint on Drafting Library Faculty
    Bylaws
    Ralph E. Russell   132

The Plethora of Personnel Systems in Academic Libraries: A Phenomenon
of the 1970s
Billy R. Wilkinson   138
Win Some, Lose Some: Writing Bylaws for an Academic Library
John R. Yelverton   147

Section II: Bibliographic Control and Automation   153

The Dutch-Door Circulation Desk
Joseph W. Barker   153
The Technical Services Budget—1980 and Beyond
Ritvars Bregzis   160
The Future in Our Grasp: An On-Line Total Integrated System for Library
Service
Elizabeth J. Furlong and Karen L. Horny   170
Interfacing Independent Automated Library Systems: A Sampling of
Existing Attempts
Jean L. Graef   175
Erasing the Past: Technological Shifts and Organizational Renewal
Charles Martell   189
The Evolution of an On-Line Catalog
Susan L. Miller   193

Section III: Bibliographic Instruction   205

Bibliographic Instruction in the Graduate/Professional Theological School
John A. Bollier   205
Marketing Library Services: A Case Study in Providing Bibliographic
Instruction in an Academic Library
Jean L. Graef and Larry Greenwood   212
The Neglected Horizon: An Expanded Education Role for Academic
Libraries
Patricia Senn Breivik   229
Curriculum Reform: A Role for Librarians
Michael John Haeuser   236
The Undergraduate Library and the Subject-Divisional Plan: Problems
and Prospects
Edward R. Johnson and Richard D. Hershcopf   241
Course-Related Library and Literature Use Instruction: An Attempt to
Develop Model Programs
Thomas G. Kirk   253
Teaching the Faculty to Use the Library: A Successful Program of In-Depth
Seminars for University of California, Berkeley, Faculty
Anne Grodzins Lipow   262
The Origins of Bibliographic Instruction in Academic Libraries, 1876–1914
John Mark Tucker   268

Section IV: Cooperation   277

Perspectives on Cooperation: The Evaluation of a Consortium
Anne C. Edmonds and Willis E. Bridegam   277
The Fourth Generation: Research Libraries and Community Information
Beverlee A. French   284

Individual Autonomy and Successful Networking: A Canadian Experience
    Virginia Gillham and Margaret Beckman   291
The Universtiy of Washington's Participation in PACFORNET as a
   Contractor
    Barbara B. Gordon   296
Participants' View of an Academic Library Consortium
    Glenn W. Offermann   301
Managing for Results—A Case Study in Coalition Building
    Elizabeth J. Yeates and Laurie E. Stackpole   311

Section V: Economic Aspects   324

A Backward Glance into the Future of University Library Support
    Arthur T. Hamlin   324
The Politics of Book Fund Allocation: A Case Study
    K. Suzanne Johnson and Joel S. Rutstein   330
Budgeting for Non-Print Media in Academic Libraries
    David B. Walch   341
Budgetary Priorities in the Administration of Large Academic Libraries
    Herbert S. White   352

Section VI: The Librarian's Role   357

Compensation Plans for Library Faculty Members
    Martha J. Bailey   357
Interdepartmental Swap-Off by the Buddy System: Report of a Staff
   Exchange Program
    Phyllis Dougherty   365
A Woman's Profession in Academia: Problem and Proposal
    Joanne R. Euster   370
Academic Library Research: A Twenty Year Perspective
    Soon D. Kim and Mary T. Kim   375
Librarians as Risk Takers: Design for Self-Measurement
    Christina Wolcott McCawley and Scott Bruntjen   384
The Academic Reference Librarian: Roles and Development
    Robert J. Merikangas   395
The Future Role of the Academic Librarian, as Viewed Through a
   Perspective of Forty Years
    Jean M. Ray   404
Faculty Status in Academic Libraries: Retrospective and Prospect
    C. James Schmidt   411
Prospects of Community College Librarianship
    Damaris Ann Schmitt   418

Section VII: Resources   424

Toward an Information System for Responsive Collection Development
    Mary H. Beilby and Glyn T. Evans   424
The Compleat Collection Developer
    C. Roger Davis   432
Subject Specialists in Academic Libraries: The Once and Future Dinosaurs
    Dennis W. Dickinson   438

Government Publications in Humanistic Research and Scholarship
    Barbara J. Ford and Yuri Nakata   445
Documents to the People in One Easy Step
    Selma V. Foster and Nancy C. Lufburrow   453
CAP: A Project for the Analysis of the Collection Development Process in
Large Academic Libraries
    Jeffry J. Gardner   456
Women's Studies Resources for College and Research Libraries
    Barbara Haber   460
Rare Book and Special Collections Libraries: Horizontal Consolidation
    Richard G. Landon   467
A Zero-Base Budget Approach to Staff Justification for a Combined
Reference and Collection Development Department
    Diane C. Parker and Eric J. Carpenter   472
Approval Plans One Year Later: The Purdue Experience with Separate
School Plans
    Edwin D. Posey and Kathleen McCullough   483
Collection Analysis Project in the MIT Libraries
    Jutta R. Reed   490
The Collection Analysis Project at Arizona State University Library: An
Exercise in Staff Development
    George J. Soete   496
Applications of an Operations Research Model to the Study of Book Use
in a University Library: Implications for Library Management
    Sandra Spurlock and Ellen Yen   502
Sources for the Humanities: Measuring Use and Meeting Needs
    Stephen Wiberley   516
Microforms: Changing the Conceptual Polarity from Negative to Positive
    Charles Willard   523

Section VIII: Services   529

Academic Libraries and Part-Time Adult Students
    Raymond K. Fisher   529
Access to Information: A Reconsideration of the Service Goals of a
Small Urban College Library
    Edmund G. Hamann   534
The On-Line Library: Problems and Prospects for User Education
    Gail A. Herndon and Noelle Van Pulis   539
The Independent Learner and the Academic Library: Access and Impact
    Leila M. Hover   545
Development and Administration of a Large Off-Campus Shelving Facility
    William J. Hubbard   550
The Query Analysis System: A Progress Report
    Ward Shaw, Patricia B. Culkin and Thomas E. Brabek   556
Off-Campus Library Services: Those Inbetween Years
    Aline Soules   568
The Urban University Library: Effectiveness Models for 1989
    T. Philip Tompkins and Gary D. Byrd   577

INTRODUCTION

The fortieth anniversary of the Association of College and Research Libraries, a division of the American Library Association, served as the occasion for the first national conference of academic librarians. Held in Boston, Massachusetts, November 8–11, 1978, this conference attracted over 2,600 librarians and friends to its various sessions.

This volume includes the major papers presented at that conference—seven theme papers and sixty-six contributed papers.

In preparing for the conference, the planning committee decided not to use the anniversary event as a time for retrospection but rather for looking ahead. They selected as the conference theme "New Horizons for Academic Libraries" and invited a group of outstanding librarians and educators to present in plenary sessions a series of theme papers—each focused on one aspect of the future of academic and research library programs in the United States.

Mary F. Berry, Assistant Secretary for Education, Department of Health, Education, and Welfare, began the conference by looking at the road ahead for higher education in the United States and the role of the federal government. Warren J. Haas, President of the Council on Library Resources, presented an overview of the ways and means in the future of academic library management.

Joe B. Wyatt, Vice President for Administration, Harvard University, spoke on technology and the library; and Barbara Evans Markuson, Executive Director, Indiana Cooperative Library Services Authority, summarized the contributions of networks to academic libraries.

Richard W. Boss, Management Consultant with Information Systems Consultants, Inc., spoke of the future of library services in which the library will function as an information broker; and Jay K. Lucker, Director, Massachusetts Institute of Technology Libraries, discussed the future for library resources and their bibliographic control.

Millicent D. Abell, University Librarian, University of California, San Diego, concluded the theme sessions with her paper on the changing role of the academic librarian and the choice between "drift and mastery."

These theme papers present the speakers' views of the future from the vantage point of the autumn of 1978, a time when many librarians looked to national plans and programs and a national information policy. State conferences were underway to prepare for the White House Conference on Libraries and Information Science in the fall of 1979; reports and announcements from the National Commission on Libraries and Information Science received continuing attention; several months earlier the Council on Library Resources had published its technical development plan for a national periodicals center; and only a few weeks before the conference several national groups had announced their support for a national library agency. Development such as these served as a focus for comments by the speakers.

An important feature at this first national conference was the presentation of sixty-six contributed papers in a series of concurrent sessions during three days of the meeting.

Because of the many sessions and the fact conference participants could attend but a sampling of them, microfiche copies of all contributed papers were given to conference registrants. These copies presented the authors' manuscripts as they were submitted for review several months earlier. At the conference authors were invited to update their papers on the basis of new information they had gained since they had originally submitted them. Many authors took advantage of this opportunity, and this volume includes the papers in revised form.

The contributed papers present the thoughts and concerns of academic and research librarians on a broad array of subjects; and they are arranged in this volume in eight sections: Administration and Management; Bibliographic Control and Automation; Bibliographic Instruction; Cooperation; Economic Aspects; The Librarian's Role; Resources; and Services.

We extend our thanks to authors of the eighty-three papers included here for their contribution to this first national conference and to all the registrants who made the conference such a memorable occasion for academic librarianship.

Robert D. Stueart
Richard D. Johnson

January 1979

PART I

THEME PAPERS

Mary F. Berry

HIGHER EDUCATION IN THE UNITED STATES: THE ROAD AHEAD

Achievements of the federal administration in education during the 95th Congress are summarized as well as plans for the 96th Congress. Considering the future of higher education in the U.S., the author looks at possible changes and what they may mean. Elements discussed are the composition of the student body and of the teaching faculty, use of campus facilities, financing of higher education, kinds of academic programs offered and their quality and the role of the federal government.

I am delighted to join you here on the anniversary of your organization. I understand that the association celebrates a "big" birthday as you meet here in Boston this week. So congratulations on reaching your fortieth anniversary and best wishes for many more.

I am told that this is the first national conference for this particular body of the American Library Association, the Association of College and Research Libraries. I am happy to join you on what apparently has resulted in a very successful first voyage in this effort, too.

THE PRESENT RECORD

Though I have come here to speak on the future of higher education, let me take a few minutes to share with you some recent events that make these exciting times in our nation's capital, especially for those of us in education.

Since April 1977 those of us at the federal level have been bringing messages that were predictive in nature—telling our audiences what this administration intended to do in the field of education. Today I can come before you with enthusiasm and with much sense of accomplishment in the successes which we achieved during the 95th Congress.

Let me say at the outset that:
— If ever there was a champion of education;
— If ever there was the embodiment of a commitment to education;
— If ever there was a friend of education;

Mary F. Berry is assistant secretary for education, Department of Health, Education, and Welfare, Washington, D.C.

That person is Jimmy Carter.

Having experienced a dearth of that kind of commitment in recent administrations, those of us in education are beginning to be "born again" in the belief that education is rightfully gaining its due as a number one priority in this society.

President Carter requested—and got—the largest single increase in education services in our nation's history. Education appropriations were signed in October.

The reauthorization of the Elementary and Secondary Education Act of 1965 comprised the most significant rewrite of that legislation since it was enacted.

The centerpiece of that legislation is on the development of basic skills—an indication of the president's heartfelt commitment to provide our country's children with the basic tools to function in this society.

This legislation:

1. Reaffirms and strengthens the commitment established thirteen years ago to programs which ensure access and equal educational opportunity to poor and educationally needy children.

2. Ensures that all children in the nation's schools master basic skills of reading, writing, and arithmetic.

3. Creates a new federal, state, and local partnership to help carry out these priorities while reducing the paperwork burden.

Specifically, this legislation authorizes about fifty programs, including a dozen major new ones, and provides for spending of more than $55 billion over the next five years. We hope this will mean more students entering higher education institutions who know how to read, write, and think and who will be able to use the library, that most important facility, from the start.

In higher education, we are proud of the Middle Income Student Assistance Act which was signed just this last week and which represents a landmark commitment to aiding families with children in colleges and universities.

This bill authorizes several significant changes in the student assistance programs. The changes will provide more generous grants to low-income students and make eligible students from families with incomes up to $25,000. In fiscal year 1978, about 2.1 million students from families with incomes up to $15,000 were eligible for Basic Educational Opportunity Grants. An additional 1.2 million students from middle-income families will now be eligible. This marks the largest infusion of funds for middle-income students since the 1944 GI Bill.

The bill also expands the Guaranteed Student Loan Program so that any student, who has the need, will be eligible for federally-guaranteed and heavily-subsidized loans of up to $2,500 a year. No interest will be charged on those loans while the student is in college.

This particular legislation, passed in the final hours of Congress, was the president's alternative to various tuition tax credit proposals which failed in the 95th Congress.

Ultimately, we came through the 95th Congress with the largest education budget in history—$12.4 billion. Elementary and Secondary Education Act appropriations were well over the $3 billion mark with an increase of over $358 million in the previous year. Financial aid to students totaled nearly $4 billion with an increase of over $668 million. The total Education Division appropriations increased by over $1 billion in the previous year.

While we were not successful in the passage of legislation which would establish a separate Department of Education, we are determined that we shall not fail in that goal come the 96th Congress.

President Carter has reiterated his commitment to this goal in recent days. He will send that bill back to Congress in the coming session. The Senate, as you may recall, passed the bill, but the clock ran out on the House side, and the bill did not come to a vote. Vice President Mondale has recently stated that President Carter will have a signing ceremony on this bill before the 96th Congress adjourns. I plan to be there for that ceremony.

I believe this is an education record of which we can be proud, and we are hopeful that our proposals for the reauthorization of the postsecondary education programs will fare as well in the 96th Congress.

HIGHER EDUCATION AND LIBRARIES

If there is one fact about colleges and universities, it is that they have changed at a faster rate than ever before in the sixties and seventies.

Our student bodies are more diverse than ever before. Students who once would not have attended colleges are attending. Unfortunately, there is not much diversity in faculties and administrations. Enrollments have increased. Our curriculum has been influenced by our changing society, technology, and the needs which we perceive as a nation.

In recent decades, academic libraries have managed to maintain the changing pace necessary to provide the essential resources which these times demand. The key to that adaptability has been in their ability to discern trends of importance before they occur. But the challenges may be even greater for academic libraries today and in the future.

Reading skills of college students are not what they once were. Where yesterday's college student came to college predisposed to reading and libraries and took pleasure in them, today's college freshman is said to arrive on campus with an experience of 15,000 hours of television viewing. One does not dare to speculate how much reading accompanied that student to the campus. We hope our new legislation will remedy this, but, for now and the next few years, you will see the disinterested reader in your institutions.

Today we are faced with extremely varied student bodies, with extremely diverse skills and needs. Demographic patterns will continue to alter the composition of the student body in the decades to come. Indeed, the challenge of the future may be in serving the same individual at different periods in his or her life.

But the test for all academic libraries will be in serving all of these students adequately. Libraries need to use new technologies that make reading seem as much fun as television viewing. They must find resources to fund technological improvements and book purchases. And they must be creative in finding ways to store and retrieve materials consistent with realistic space demands. They must persuade presidents, foundations, and legislators to increase their budgets.

Federal support for college library resources in fiscal year 1979 totals $9,975,000 and $6 million for research libraries. And we are requesting an additional $2 million in supplemental funds for library demonstration projects. In the reauthorization, we will fully consider what, if any, changes need to be made in our efforts.

LOOKING AHEAD

What do we foresee in higher education? While predictions are guesswork at best in this fast changing society of ours, we can point to some developing patterns that every institution must keep in mind when decisions are made about the future.

THE STUDENTS

The profile of the traditional student will continue to change in the years ahead. The

1980s will see a decrease in the numbers of traditional college-age youth (18-24). An older population, those between 25 and 31, will continue to rise at least until 1988.

While the traditional college-age group will decline in the next decade, that will not be the case for blacks, Hispanics, or Hispanic-blacks until a few years later, since these groups have younger populations.

During the early seventies, higher education experienced an increase of 145 percent in students who were over thirty. We found many traditional college-age students stopping after high school to take jobs, secure incomes, and pursue other endeavors before continuing their educations.

We knew male students would enroll—as an alternative to the draft, at least during the Vietnam War. Now we have a lottery system and a change to an all-volunteer military. We also have a phase-out of the GI Bill.

The narrowing of the earnings gap between those with and those without college diplomas may have discouraged potential college-bound youth.

An older student population will need flexible postsecondary educational opportunities—at the undergraduate and graduate level and in experimental non-degree programs.

The combined forces of demography and attendance of traditional and nontraditional students are anticipated to have an overall stabilizing effect on enrollment.

What will be the impact of these factors?

1. Part-time education will become increasingly popular, particularly as institutions make strong efforts to attract those in the 25 to 44 year-old age groups.

2. The rising trend in enrollment for graduate study is likely to continue but at a lesser rate than during the current and past decades.

3. The slackening of the high-pay job opportunities for college graduates, the narrowing gap between earnings of those with college diplomas and those without, the sluggishness in the wage increases of the college graduate are likely to continue if we do not solve our economic problems.

It is hard to determine the extent to which these perceptions of the future will affect the current college going decisions of youth.

It could mean that college-age students will be more selective about education in anticipation of job and earning opportunities. It may be that the college graduates not able to find suitable jobs will be inclined to continue their education. Maybe the new higher education standard will become graduate degrees. The impact on society, in general, may be that we have captives in school who shouldn't be there. Another approach could be to maintain current standards with a focus on quality and the scaling down of the academic enterprise. But, of course, we are experiencing a period of expansion.

THE FACULTY

We know that personnel costs account for more than one-half of budgets. Although salary opportunities have not increased, the percent of college and university faculty organized by unions in recent years has increased from less than 1 percent in 1967 to almost 12 percent by 1976. There has been a rapid emergence of collective bargaining through unionization. Not unexpectedly, a high priority of faculty unions is to save and preserve the security of the experienced professors.

There was the rapid tenuring of the faculty. Between 1970 and 1976, the proportion of all full-time faculty that were either full or associate professors grew from 40 percent to about 47 percent. In 1977 the percent with tenure had grown to 56.4 percent.

A sharp decline in new faculty job openings and the strengthening of the tenure system have resulted in an older faculty, which likely will continue to age as fewer people leave and fewer are hired. Median age of full-time faculty was 38.5 in 1970 and 40.6 years in 1975. No new blood in the faculty can have a devastating effect on quality.

Since 1959 pay for professors and administrators has gone up about 6 percent annually, while pay for other workers has increased by 8 percent. The lag may be attributed to an adjustment after the rapid surge of the sixties. On the whole, however, there has been a worsening of faculty wages, and pressures to correct this are likely to increase in the future.

Also significant is the increase in part-time personnel. Between 1973 and 1977, full-time faculty grew by 9 percent compared to 38 percent in part-time faculty. The growth of part-time faculty in two-year schools is even more dramatic at 80 percent. For many institutions, hiring of part-time faculty circumvents costly fringe benefits, provision of office space, and making hiring commitments leading to tenure decisions. What effect will this have on part-time personnel? The effects could be positive if there were job sharing and tenure, but there might be a negative impact on productivity. We must watch this development very carefully.

It is premature to speculate on the impact of no new faculty on quality educational services or the rise in the numbers of part-time teachers on the learning environment of institutions.

THE CAMPUS

What happens to the campus physically will be determined by the growth or decrease in student populations.

Plant utilization and growth will be put to the test not only by financial constraints which have always accompanied higher education, but by new constituencies such as the handicapped which we are legally obligated to serve.

Facilities sharing may become an attractive option. Some of this already is occurring in consortia-like arrangements.

FINANCES

A number of factors have begun to adversely affect revenues of institutions. They include depressed wages, higher tuitions, cutting operating costs, and deferring maintenance and investment in plant and equipment. Though these actions are necessary to meet current financial situations, we do not believe that they are a permanent solution to budget problems.

Further, most private institutions have had to devote a larger share of their revenues to student aid, partly to offset the low-tuition advantage of public institutions. But relief to this situation will be provided by the Middle Income Student Assistance Act.

Additionally, endowment income to finance private educational expenditures has steadily declined, and there is no prospect for a reversal of this trend.

Other serious threats to private liberal arts colleges and to liberal arts programs in all institutions are the reduction in the attractiveness of the liberal arts education and the perception, of students and sponsors alike, that the weight placed on a liberal education may not be warranted.

In 1970 one in six of all students enrolled in postsecondary schools for the first time selected a vocational program that did not lead to a degree. The ratio went up to one in four in 1975. Choice of vocational subjects is prevalent in two-year colleges.

These factors raise legitimate questions about the appropriate source of funding for the continued existence of some of our postsecondary institutions. Who should pay to keep them going?

PROGRAM OFFERINGS AND QUALITY

In the face of financial difficulties and stable or even declining enrollments, institutions have continued to increase the number and diversity of the programs which they offer, in part, to stem the tide of declining enrollments.

The response has not necessarily been to the potential demand from new clients. In many cases we can see that "old wine is being offered in new bottles" under different and more attractive labels.

Judgments on the quality of students, institutions, and programs are difficult to determine and may not be appropriate for us as federal officials. But there is a general presumption that standards of college education have been eroding. There is general agreement that entry standards are declining as measured by the long-term decline on SAT scores.

Current attempts are being made to assess the quality of institutions and their programs in a number of states.

In the future we are likely to witness a growing interest and movement within higher education institutions toward minimal standards for college education and stricter justification for offerings in terms of size and quality.

A related development is the renewed interest in "core" curriculum or a reinstitution of general education requirements. The proliferation of courses of little or no academic value and the enormity of course choices allowing a student to opt for less structure and diluted content have prompted debate on alternative means of tackling the problem. Some institutions have already put a back-to-the-basics or an almost-back-to-the-basics emphasis into effect.

One set of proposals involves prescribing that students take an agreed group of courses before graduation. A second alternative goes a step further by attempting to define a set of testable knowledge skills as a requirement for graduation.

THE FEDERAL ROLE IN THE FUTURE

The overriding premise of federal support in the past has been that qualified students should have an opportunity to attend postsecondary education and that the responsibility for financing education should be shared among parents, students, the private sector, and various levels of government. That premise has resulted in the development of a commitment to:
— Reducing financial barriers to postsecondary education through entitlements for students in need of financial assistance. Passage of the Middle Income Student Assistance Act is the most recent example of this continued commitment.
— Enhancing the capacity of students to finance their own education through loans and incentives for part-time employment opportunities.
— Assisting in meeting the needs of specially disadvantaged groups such as minorities, women, and the handicapped.
— Providing selective support for improving the physical, financial, and intellectual capacity of postsecondary institutions, in particular those that serve special purposes.
— Finally, there has been a commitment to stimulate the supply of some specialized skill areas and research in selected fields that are of national interest.

During the reauthorization of the higher education legislation we need to reexamine our role in education.
— We need to reconsider the premises and the commitments to which the federal government has adhered in the past.

— There are some who would argue that the current patterns of financing higher education are totally irrational from an economic standpoint.

— There are arguments that there is a surplus of college graduates and that any future student subsidy will merely contribute to the unemployment rolls of college graduates.

— Do we continue to provide financial stress aid to developing institutions and how?

— Should the needs for changes in physical facilities in higher education required by law be met through federal assistance? How much aid should we provide to institutions?

All of these issues will challenge the federal role in the immediate future.

As one observer put it: "The next decade will try the souls of those connected with colleges and universities. Enrollments are projected to go down. Funds for instruction will grow more slowly than in any period since World War II. The 1980s may well become the Dark Ages of higher education as college graduates will find it increasingly difficult to land jobs which utilize the training they received."

The decades ahead will, of course, be trying times for policy analysts, for planners, for educational providers, for administrators, for those who work in higher education, and for the society they will shape. Going into that time frame with a budget cutting mentality will make it no easier. The point is that innovation and adaptability will be necessary in meeting the challenges of the future.

At the federal level a sensitivity, concern, and commitment to education, as that more recently illustrated by the Carter administration, will serve as a positive environment in which to seek the solutions. No less important will be the role of those in higher education to define, shape, and help us determine that policy which will ultimately affect us all.

Warren J. Haas

MANAGING OUR ACADEMIC LIBRARIES:
WAYS AND MEANS

There is a new library ecology in which interdependence is the dominant force, and the establishment of new operating mechanisms (such as a national periodicals center and a national library agency) is discussed. Funds in the amounts required to meet libraries' traditional needs will not be forthcoming, and thus libraries must transform themselves and make substantial changes in their operations. There is also the need for better ways to set basic policies that determine a library's capabilities, costs, and services. In their management academic libraries have not done as well as their parent institutions in developing reliable data and in putting it to use. But while libraries need the attributes of scientific management, they must not make the mistake of thinking library management is only *a science.*

To begin, I want to underscore the importance of this meeting and acknowledge the efforts of the many individuals who have made it possible. There are many specialties in librarianship. In recent years it has been increasingly apparent that those responsible for library performance in the context of higher education, research, and scholarship have a distinctive set of obligations and need a substantial and expanding arsenal of skills.

It is good that a way has been found to concentrate for a few days on the substance of this specific segment of our large and diffuse profession. This should be the beginning of an important new approach to expand our professional perceptions and capabilities.

For those who are interested in being part of a dynamic, demanding, purposeful, and useful enterprise, this is a good time to be a librarian in the academic and research community. To be sure, there are financial problems too large to ignore, there is the abundant and inevitable confusion that arises when neither ends nor means are unambiguously defined, and there is much uncertainty about who is responsible for doing what. But despite such minor annoyances, we have, individually and collectively, an opportunity at this particular time to test our capabilities and to find our horizons.

If we are actually to do what seems to need doing, large measures of skill, energy, persistence, understanding, and luck will be essential. Success will also require effective management, about which I agreed, in October 1977, to talk here today. But a great

Warren J. Haas is president, Council on Library Resources, Inc., Washington, D.C.

deal has happened in the year since I committed myself, and I see the subject in a somewhat different light now.

I hope that the program planners won't be too upset if I concentrate more on the music to which academic and research librarians are likely to be dancing, instead of on the words concerning the details of the management process itself. There are admitted limits to my knowledge of dancing, so my terminology may be inexact, but to give some sense of my theme, I will be concentrating more on the "hustle" than on the "waltz."

I want to consider the backdrop against which we and our actions are likely to be silhouetted in the years immediately ahead. The importance of that backdrop is becoming more and more apparent each day, and against it both successes and failures will be magnified. The prerequisites for either a smash hit or a spectacular flop are all here.

THE NEW LIBRARY ECOLOGY

Traditionally, and for good reason, academic and research libraries have been considered almost personal enterprises, and operated, by and large, as self-contained organizations. Those who are responsible for their growth and maintenance and those who are their most intensive users take pride in, and are strongly protective of, what they have built and come to know. Distinctive subject collections are typically personal achievements. Reputations for service of high quality are built over time by many skillful people who realize that neglect quickly erodes performance. Exceptional library buildings are a source of institutional pride, perhaps because they are powerful reminders of aspirations as well as reflections of past achievements.

All in all, where collections, services, traditions, and support are of the highest order there has been consistent, skillful, and intense involvement by many individuals.

Interdependence

But there is now a fundamental conflict between what some might call an "idyllic" view of libraries and another set of characteristics that, while always present, have in recent years, become more prominent. The concept of functional independence, attractive and powerful as it is, is really inconsistent with the character of knowledge itself.

The idea of self-sufficiency implies containment, walls which curtail outward as well as inward flow. And finally, there are the hard facts of our time—rising costs that consistently outreach rising income, a persistently growing volume of publications from which we must pick and choose, and a set of new technologies that have, for one reason or another, pressed themselves on us, bringing new intellectual and fiscal challenges.

Valuable traditions, valid philosophies, and long-established methodologies are now being tested by expanding perceptions of library obligations and this new set of present-day realities.

Something has to give. The question is not whether libraries will change—that process is already underway—but rather how and to what ends that change will be controlled and guided. Can libraries as organizations expand capabilities and still be intellectually and financially viable, and can librarians build the substance of this profession and still maintain the pride of personal accomplishment in the process? This is a key question facing our profession.

It is clear, as we search for alternate ways to do traditional things, that the fact of interdependence is the dominant force in our future, interdependence not only among libraries but between libraries and the other components in the chain of scholarly and intellectual communication. The walls are down, and a new ecology is slowly developing.

Few topics in library annals can match "cooperation" for staying power as a subject for study and discussion. Unhappily, the correlation between useful results and the volume of that discussion has moved from zero upwards more slowly than one might have hoped. In part, this has been because the programs proposed were sometimes poorly thought through. Sometimes the methods chosen were not appropriate to the task. Also, librarians and library users alike have not, at all times, had the courage to act in ways that fully supported their expressed convictions.

Cooperative collection development programs have worked best in "no-conflict" areas—that is, Library "A" is encouraged to collect comprehensively in a given subject field by Libraries "B" and "C" because "B" and "C" have no perceptible interest in the field. Cooperative preservation projects have been much discussed, but self-preservation has understandably prevailed. Even interlibrary loan, the cornerstone and corollary of cooperative collecting, is still a cumbersome and frequently frustrating process.

But cooperation of another kind has fared better. When libraries have worked together to establish a new and clearly needed service, along with the necessary structure, the results have sometimes been spectacular. OCLC is an example, as is the National Program for Acquisitions and Cataloging, promoted by the Association of Research Libraries and implemented at the Library of Congress.

This recent experience suggests that an approach based on providing needed services for libraries through new operating mechanisms is likely to have greater impact and stand a better chance of success than more cautious, more traditional cooperative ventures that tend to be limited in both commitments and aspirations.

A National Periodicals Center

There are several prospects for dramatic change on the horizon, one of the most promising being a national periodicals center.[1]

In the fall of 1977 the Library of Congress asked the Council on Library Resources to prepare a technical development plan for a U.S. national periodicals center. The need for such a facility was formalized by the National Commission on Libraries and Information Science in its 1977 document *Effective Access to Periodical Literature*, which recommended that the Library of Congress assume responsibility for developing, managing, and operating the center. LC and the council agreed that the plan would be prepared in such a way that it could be used by the Library of Congress or any other agency prepared to assume responsibility for the creation of a major periodicals facility. Several foundations contributed to the cost of preparing the plan, which was completed in August 1978.

The goal of the national periodicals center is to improve access to periodical literature for libraries and thus to individuals using libraries. The intent of the plan is to assure that the NPC will accomplish this goal (1) by providing an efficient, reliable, and responsive document delivery system for periodical material, (2) by working effectively with the publishing community, and (3) by helping to shape a national library system through NPC operating policies and procedures.

The specific operating objectives of the NPC follow logically from this goal. They are:

1. To provide a reliable method of access to a comprehensive collection of periodical literature.

2. To reduce the overall costs of acquiring periodical material by interlibrary loan.

3. To reduce the time required to obtain requested material.

4. To assure that for any document delivered through the NPC, all required copyright fees and obligations will have been paid.

5. To act, under appropriate conditions, as a distribution agent for publishers.

6. To provide libraries with additional options as they establish their own collection development and maintenance policies.

7. To promote the development of local and regional resource sharing.

8. To contribute to the preservation of periodical material.

9. To provide a base for the development of new and imaginative publication strategies.

10. To provide a working example of a national access service that might be extended to other categories of materials.

These operating objectives make it clear that the national periodicals center will link in new ways the collecting and distribution functions of libraries with the distribution activities of at least some kinds of publishing.

As proposed in the plan, the national periodicals center will contain a centralized collection of periodical literature directly accessible to libraries throughout the nation. Initially projected at 36,000 titles, subscriptions for which would be generated as quickly as possible, the collection would continue to grow prospectively (adding more titles) and retrospectively (acquiring back files) according to an established strategy and in as timely a fashion as possible. All subject areas would be included with the initial exception of clinical medicine.

Eventually the collection may number in excess of 60,000 current titles, but it will never contain all of the estimated 200,000 currently published periodicals. Though few of those not held by the NPC are likely to be in great demand, it is planned that the NPC would provide access to many of them through a system of referral libraries. The NPC will contract with these libraries to provide service to requesting libraries that desire specific titles not in the NPC collection. All requests would be channeled through the NPC to assure uniformity of procedure and to provide the means to monitor system performance.

The NPC will develop and make available a finding tool to identify the titles and holdings to which the NPC can provide access. The finding tool will be organized by key titles and International Standard Serial Number (ISSN) and will include titles available from both the NPC collection and the referral system libraries. For the first several years libraries will be required to request only listed material.

The most important question for many librarians is which libraries will be able to go directly to the NPC. After a breaking-in period for the NPC and after the collection is well established, all libraries will have access. The decision to use the NPC or alternatives such as local, state, or regional resources should be based upon the actual dollar cost of the transaction (a system of service charges is projected) and the reliability of access or delivery.

Librarians using the NPC will be assured that for any item received from the center, the appropriate fees will have been paid. This will relieve libraries of some of the requirements established by the CONTU (National Commission on New Technological Uses of Copyrighted Works) guidelines.

Quite apart from the procedures to comply with the copyright legislation, it is imperative in the interest of efficient scholarly communication that the NPC develop effective relationships with the publishing community. It is proposed that the NPC become a kind of service and fulfillment outlet for at least some publishers. Thus the NPC might provide a back-issue service (probably in microform), an article sales service (so long as the article remained protected by copyright), an outlet for on-demand publishing, and/or a source for the full text of material published in synoptic form.

All of these services would generate some income for publishers while providing the access to material that library users need. It is recognized that a relationship of this kind may tend to modify traditional information production and/or distribution functions.

But each element of the information chain has a unique and valuable role to play in serving the needs of inquiring scholars, and each must be supportive of the other.

I won't take time to describe internal operations other than to note that prompt and reliable response is the dominating objective. Further, the cause of long-term preservation of this major segment of literature is significantly advanced. The capital requirements for a building and the initial collection are substantial but, it is hoped, not insurmountable items. Requirements for an annual operating subsidy, the difference between costs and income, is projected at $3,000,000.

The creation of a national periodicals center will require the cooperative action and support of librarians, information scientists, publishers, politicians, and foundation trustees. One thing is clear. Society has everything to gain from an improved capacity to retrieve and use the information generated by its members. A coherent national periodicals program should provide such an improvement. A national periodicals center is the first step.

Bibliographic Control

In another arena, that of bibliographic control, plans are moving ahead to carry further the already substantial progress that has been made in transforming methods and procedures. Funds for a substantial development effort have been assured by a number of foundations. With the participation and assistance of LC, NCLIS, and a substantial number of institutions and individuals directly concerned with the quality and performance of libraries, the Council on Library Resources plans to continue and even expand its efforts to promote establishment of a functionally sound and cost-effective computerized bibliographic system for libraries.

The council's role is (1) to assist in the coordination of pertinent activity now under way on many fronts, (2) to identify specific additional work that needs to be done and to see that it is accomplished, and (3) to promote development of the necessary permanent entities having the credibility, responsibility, and means to assure continuing operation of fundamental system elements.

In essence, the projected bibliographic system is envisioned as a set of coordinated activities to establish and operate a computerized bibliographic record service and a parallel set of independent activities by individual libraries, groups of libraries, and function-oriented networks (e.g. bibliographic networks, resource sharing networks, etc.) to develop systematically their own individual and collective capacities to use the files and products of the central service and, when appropriate, to contribute to that service.

The general objectives of the entire enterprise are focused, first, on meeting needs of individual library users and second (but not secondarily), on the operating efficiency of libraries. Among the criteria that must be met by the projected bibliographic system is that of economic viability. The intent of those involved in this work is not to create a formal, prescriptive, and tightly structured monolithic system but rather to establish a comprehensive and reliable bibliographic base which can be put to use in appropriate ways by individuals, libraries, and library systems as they seek to meet needs that they, themselves, perceive.

The links between the library components of the bibliographic system and other components of the broader information sphere will require careful attention. Further, simply because bibliography is the keystone of the process of scholarly communication, future bibliographic system capacities will have to be sufficiently broad to accommodate any modifications of traditional publishing systems, such as more extensive use of on-demand publishing techniques; that is, the system will have to record what is potentially available, whether formally published or not.

Equally interesting is speculation about the effect that new and effective links among libraries or even groups of library users with similar missions or interests might have on the way these institutions and individuals work. There is no intent to prescribe any specific course of action in these tangential areas. Rather, the goal is to reduce constraints on making change so that imaginative and constructive future action might be made more possible.

Bibliographic structure and procedures are but part of the equation for successful library performance. Availability of the material itself, purposeful development of local and national collections, preservation of existing resources, effective library management including mission-oriented research and analysis, and, for academic and research libraries, the productive involvement of libraries in teaching and their effective support of research and scholarship are all essential elements. But, in the final analysis, the bibliographic system is the balancing factor, and it thus justifies the time, expense, and skill that are required if the future needs of libraries and their users are to be met.

Other Forces at Work

There are many other forces at work that will affect the obligations and operation of libraries.

The American Council of Learned Societies is sponsoring the National Enquiry into Scholarly Communication which is considering the process of scholarly communication in a systematic way by exploring the links between all parts of the system—journal publishers, university presses, libraries, abstracting and indexing services, and scholarly organizations and associations. A new Commission on the Humanities was recently established by the Rockefeller Foundation. It will inevitably touch on library matters.

The White House Conference on Libraries will consider many topics of concern to academic libraries, not the least of which is the form of future federal funding.

Major national agencies such as the National Endowment for the Humanities and the National Science Foundation are rethinking the library support components of their programs. The prospects seem strong that a Department of Education will be established by the next Congress, and the placement of library programs in that restructuring is a topic worthy of attention.

For academic librarians, one important question is whether support programs for libraries of all kinds should be held together in a single unit, as is now the case, or whether there should be full or partial distribution of such programs to major educational divisions, such as the one focused on post-secondary education.

The prospect of a periodicals center and the possible subsequent development of collections of other categories of material, the probable characteristics of a national, integrated, nationwide computerized bibliographic system, the persistent and still unresolved problem of establishing a national strategy and developing realistic tactics to address the chronic problem of preservation of the nation's resources for research, all raise the same questions. Who is going to assume the responsibility for turning plans into action? Where does the operating and funding responsibility rest?

A National Library Agency

Something we do not now have is clearly needed. There seems to be slowly growing the recognition that some kind of an operating agency is essential if those relatively few, but absolutely necessary, library service programs that are logically nationwide in character are to be established and become functional on a permanent basis.

Federal support at a reasonable level, programmatically targeted, seems essential. But there are hazards that must be avoided. Joseph A. Califano, Jr., Secretary of Health, Education, and Welfare, has warned against undue dependence by our schools on the federal government, and I suspect the warning could be extended to libraries.

Califano asserts, "We must be vigilant against the threat of federal domination," and goes on to say "If I have seen anything made plain in the last year and a half, it is that when programs and dollars multiply, bureaucracies and regulations multiply also; paper work and reporting requirements multiply; the temptation to interfere, however well-meaning, grows. And thus the danger grows that the job we are trying to do with our programs will ironically be made even more difficult—by the unwieldy requirements and burdensome procedures these programs bring." He concluded his remarks with the words: "So I would ask you to be vigilant and vocal—as individuals and as a strong national force to fight for federal dollars—but against federal domination. You must not leave the battle for your independence to be fought by others; you must fight it yourself . . . ."[2]

The discussion about the appropriate form for an operating agency—one that would have a sufficiently broad operating mandate and would still maintain the independence from government, *per se*, that our library and information system seems to require—is just now assuming national proportions.

The NCLIS/University of Pittsburgh conference held November 6–8 addressed the question of governance as a preliminary to the White House Conference deliberations. Equally important is the initiative taken by several organizations and individuals to move ahead quickly with the national periodicals center.

In the last two weeks, both ARL and the executive committee of the Association of American Universities have endorsed a "Statement of Principles for Congressional Action to Establish a National Library Agency." That statement reads in part:

"FINDINGS

"1. Research and education in all disciplines depend upon libraries to collect, organize, and preserve the information of potential use to the scholars of the world.

"2. Although libraries have been growing at exponential rates in recent decades, because of the rapid growth in cost and volume of publications, each library is becoming increasingly less able to satisfy the research and educational needs of its patrons. This experience is documented in studies of interlibrary loan and of access to the periodical literature which have been sponsored by several professional and scholarly organizations including the Association of Research Libraries, and by the National Commission on Libraries and Information Science.

"3. The solution to this problem requires the establishment of an operating library agency at the national level.

"PURPOSE

"A National Periodicals Center (NPC) would be the first operating program of a national library agency. However, the NPC is inseparably linked to the nation's bibliographic structure, the evolving library communications network, and the complex processes of resource development and preservation. The purposes of a national library agency need therefore to include the following:

"To coordinate bibliographic control for the significant scholarly and research literature of the world so that library patrons, scholars, and research personnel are not restricted in their work only to publications in their own libraries;

"To facilitate the development, dissemination, and acceptance of national and international standards for bibliographic description and communications and networking;

"To assure access, through lending or reproduction consistent with applicable laws, to published information of all kinds and formats which are needed by scholars but which their libraries are unable to acquire or retain;

"To assure a program for the preservation of published information through conservation techniques and maintenance of depositories for infrequently used materials in order that the accumulated experience, knowledge, and literature of the past will not be lost but remain available to our own and future generations as a base for continued progress.

"ESTABLISHMENT

"In order to fulfill these purposes an independent national library agency will be established with the appropriate authority, responsibility, and funding. The first operating responsibility of such an agency will be a National Periodicals Center.

"GOVERNANCE

"A national library agency should be governed by a body with the responsibility and authority to establish, fund, coordinate, operate, or contract for the programs and services required to carry out the purposes of the agency, to determine operating policies and evaluate and review management performance.

"Irrespective of form of organization, the governing body should be designed and its membership selected with care and with the same sensitivity to the subject of government presence which has shaped the character of the National Science Foundation, and the National Endowments for the Arts and Humanities. Persons nominated should be drawn from the ranks of scholars, scientists, university trustees and officers, head librarians, and public figures with demonstrated broad intellectual interests. In making his nominations the President is requested to give due consideration to recommendations for nomination that may be submitted to him by the American Council of Learned Societies, the American Library Association, the Association of American Universities, the Association of Research Libraries, the National Association of State Universities and Land Grant Colleges, and other organizations concerned with education, research, and libraries.

"A national library agency should not have prescriptive authority over the activities of the nation's libraries. Such agency should be limited to organizing and directing national services to augment local capabilities and cooperative efforts in order to permit these to operate more effectively and efficiently."

This present intense level of activity on the national scene is, as many of you know at first hand, often matched on state and local levels. Even internationally, the pace of change is brisk. The challenge for the profession, individually and collectively, is to be in control rather than to be controlled. College and university librarians need to find more effective ways to be heard. They also need to demonstrate that they are willing and able to rethink their ways and means, in the context of the new library ecology.

It is with this concern in mind that CLR, the ARL Office of Management Studies, and the leadership of ACRL moved to establish the new Academic Library Program. The intent of this effort is to train a large number of librarians to serve as specialist consultants to academic libraries, including two- and four-year liberal arts colleges and universities. These individuals, using specially prepared materials will, after training, be available to libraries which are willing and ready to assess their own performance and methods in the context of a changing environment.

The intent, over time, is to develop a strong corps of trained consultants who are also experts in special fields, including instructional programs, management methods, collection development, and computer applications. The premise on which the program is based is that more trained manpower is essential if our three thousand academic libraries are to be assisted in responding wisely to change.

THE MONEY PROBLEM

A recently distributed NCLIS brochure[3] draws on data included in the commission's *National Inventory of Library Needs*, which was first published in 1975. The document asserts that the present level of $2.4 billion in annual expenditures for libraries of all kinds must be increased by an additional $6.3 billion to achieve minimum levels of service. The great portion of this awesome increase is for public school library media centers. For academic libraries alone, it is asserted that an additional $621 million is required to supplement the current $1 billion expenditure level, a 60 percent increase.

According to the report, an additional 10,000 professional librarians are needed in the 3,000 college and university libraries; the stock of library materials should be increased by 158 million items over the present 612 million total, which works out to an average of 53,000 additional items per academic library.

The commission is currently having papers prepared to identify and assess possible funding strategies for consideration in late 1979 by participants in the White House Conference.

These are big numbers. In at least some instances, one can wonder how carefully they were developed and how tightly drawn were the underlying assumptions. But even if the needs established can be readily defended, the present level of public enthusiasm for tax increases and more public spending doesn't generate much optimism.

There is no doubt that most academic libraries are hard pressed financially. Many operate under marginal conditions, having known the recent decade of educational affluence more as a rumor than as a fact. Many other libraries, probably the majority, are faced with a slow erosion of briefly glimpsed distinction. Inflation-driven book and journal prices, salary scales that are often a matter of professional embarrassment, the high cost of technology, and new obligations assumed in the belief that an initially soft money base would somehow harden, are all issues that are more pressing each fiscal year.

The hard truth is that, despite the validity of the library case, the funds required to continue to meet traditional needs in traditional ways are unlikely to be forthcoming in anywhere near needed amounts.

How are libraries accepting the gradually tightening belt? In some cases the approach is to maintain a myth of business as usual, which in fact means erosion in salaries and collections and a subtle deterioration of overall library performance. Others will face up to the problem by cutting hours, consciously reducing acquisitions in specific areas, and hedging on the quality of binding. But such actions simply defer the day of reckoning and this is clear to those that are responsible for providing the funds.

There is already strong and rapidly growing conviction that is increasingly evident in meetings of university presidents that libraries, individually as well as collectively, must be fundamentally transformed if they are to meet their current and future obligations with the necessary distinction at an acceptable cost.

Those who are concerned are not naive. They see the problem as a complex and difficult one, one that will not be solved overnight. They realize that each library must be strong enough to carry its own weight in primary areas of responsibility, and the best of them see libraries as active, essential elements in the processes of teaching and learning.

They also see substantial expenditures for material of marginal importance, they see redundancy in bibliographic activities, and they see development of collections in new subject areas that go beyond institutional aspirations. Most important, they are less and less persuaded by the obvious logic in the library case for more funds because they are more and more aware of the fiscal realities with which they live.

The pressure is mounting for a major transformation that will require a new understanding of libraries both by librarians and their users. Each library will have to define with much precision the scope of local resources and the extent of local services, especially technical services. Libraries will have to view periodical centers and other possible national resources as integral and inseparable parts of themselves, not as remote appendages. Those who will be planning cataloging and other bibliographic services at regional or national levels must be pressed hard by all librarians to assure that newly developed services will result in a substantial reduction or even the elimination of local costs wherever possible. There must be an unstinting insistence that the application of computers to processing in fact cuts costs, rather than redistributes them.

All academic libraries and especially academic research libraries are already embarked on a period of unprecedented change. Financial prospects make this inevitable. The form that change will take is still uncertain. One hopes it will be determined in substantial part by fiscally aware librarians who are concerned first and foremost with educational performance and not by fiscally responsible officers who might not be fully aware of library obligations.

An unanswered problem lurks behind all of this. Making change, especially substantial change, costs money. Retraining staff, reorganization of existing space and purchase of new equipment all carry new costs, as do payment of service charges for an increased number of interlibrary loans, for database searches, and for communications. Additional one-time funds and the capacity to redeploy already budgeted funds along more broadly defined functional lines are essential.

Librarians are faced with financially motivated pressures to make substantial changes in their operations which in turn require these new expenditures and a greater fiscal burden. How to budget for transition could well be the real dilemma at the heart of the money problem.

POLICY FORMATION

The process of setting policy has received some attention in libraries in recent years, but it is my contention that, by and large, the changes that have occurred have not gone far enough or, in at least some cases, even in the right direction.

When I use the word "policy," I am referring only to what might be called fundamental or "primary" policies, those that govern the character and growth of a library's collection; those that govern retention practices, even those that relate to cataloging codes.

I would also include policies that determine the physical condition of collections; those that establish the patterns of staff composition; those that set the quality and scope of library service; and those that establish the degree of dependence or interdependence of a library on other libraries or on externally provided services. In short, the policies that determine library capabilities, library costs, and library character.

I am not concerned with what might be called "secondary policies," (loan codes, for example) that are designed to explicate primary policies. I am even less concerned with the process of administration, or policy execution, important as that is.

I want only to consider the process of setting primary policy, and I do so for several reasons. Clearly, these policies determine current and future library costs. Equally important, they determine the quality of library performance, in effect the value of the library to its parent institution. Given the centrality of these policies, it follows that the process of setting them deserves attention.

To be specific and direct, there are signs that something is wrong. Primary policies are too important to be set by library administrators or even by all librarians acting in isolation. We have not always recognized this fact, and even when we have, we have not normally done as well as we might in finding a better way. All librarians, not only library administrators, have the inescapable obligation to take part in stating the issues that underlie each policy question, accurately and perceptively, for their own library and for their own institution.

Just as there are no pat answers, there are no pat questions. Once the question is asked, consideration and response should involve not only librarians but faculty, college and university administrative officers, trustees, and, when useful, students. We seem to have trouble with this process.

Key questions are sometimes not raised purposefully, policy issues are often addressed in a crisis context, issues are often poorly or incompletely stated, and the involvement of the necessary parties is more often than not in the form of ineffective faculty committees, senate library committees, poorly used visiting committees, easily divered school and departmental committees, and budget meetings where the real objective is not policy formulation but rather cost containment.

Libraries are often more isolated, and possibly more insulated, than they should be from the heart of academic administrative activity. Ways must be found to air key topics routinely and thoroughly by all who should be concerned. This may be heresy in the minds of those who find comfort in a low profile, but I might go so far as to suggest establishing a "library cabinet" to consider only these primary issues. Individuals from all essentially concerned components would be included and would have their say.

Purposeful exploration and decision on key topics would in the end provide librarians with a new level of confidence in their actions and would help build an informed and probably more supportive constituency. Policies would be better understood, program and funding would perhaps become more clearly related, and the prospects for long-range planning improved.

There is no half-way point in this approach. It requires professional skills of the highest order, it requires some sublimation of personal ego, and it requires a great deal of work. But the nature of college and university libraries is such that the wisdom of many is required to build a proper foundation for action. Each librarian needs to take the time now to assess the process of policy formulation and to take action if all is not as it should be. I see this as a matter of great importance.

MANAGING LIBRARIES—WAYS AND MEANS

I will turn finally to my assigned topic. True to form, there will be no organized treatment. Rather, I have a few observations, possibly unrelated, and I offer them with the simple objective of promoting the idea that the process of library management is a means to an end, and not an end in itself.

The study of management as a discrete discipline is something that has developed in our lifetime (at least my lifetime) and has really flourished only since World War II. Scientific management, or, more specifically, the development and use of a wide range of analytical techniques to improve managerial behavior and performance, has dominated business and industry and, more recently, has been extensively employed in the public service sector as well, including colleges and universities.

Personnel compensation plans, space utilization schemes, strategies to reduce fuel consumption, income projection, and other phases of institutional management have been closely examined for the purpose of improving procedures. Comprehensive planning models have been developed at a number of universities (Princeton and Stanford are examples) and are used, not to make decisions, but to assess the financial impact of alternative courses of action.

Libraries, in general, have not done as well as their parent institutions in developing reliable data or in putting what little we do know to use. Not enough is known (and we have problems accepting what we know) about almost everything we do.

For example, who really uses the more obscure components of a bibliographic record? Does availability of a sophisticated, comprehensive bibliographic record system generate additional demand for material? How much? What prompts individuals to buy books and journals rather than borrow them? What factors most heavily influence library budget decisions in universities and colleges?

The list of basic questions is long and the answers are of great importance, especially as work proceeds at the national level on many of the major undertakings on the agenda we all have before us.

For example, I wish we had an imaginatively constructed economic model of the bibliographic structure of the country available for use now as we begin to assess alternative approaches to building standardized data bases. Substantially better data and more credible analytical techniques than we have are badly needed.

Even more important is the wisdom to interpret the data collected. For example, a recent report from a liberal arts college indicated that about two-thirds of the titles recommended in *Books for College Libraries II* and included in the library collection were apparently not used during 1976/77. What does this information mean? Does it say something about the student body? About the teaching methods of the faculty? About *Books for College Libraries?* About the performance of the library itself? I don't really know. The point is that gathering information for use in managing enterprises such as ours doesn't automatically point the way towards the solution of a problem. That, in the end, is up to people, not systems.

A few days ago a friend who was properly concerned about the questionable effectiveness of my own indecisive and vague management style sent me (for my private and personal use) a photocopy of an article published in the *Harvard Business Review* entitled "Zen and the Art of Management."[4]

The author, Richard Pascale, reflects on the differences between Japanese and American decision-making processes and finds much similarity in methods and results. Two differences, however, are evident:

"1. Three times as much communication was initiated at lower levels of management in the Japanese companies, then percolated upwards.

"2. While management of Japanese companies rated the quality of their decision-making the same as did their American counterparts, they perceived the quality of *implementation* of those decisions to be better."

At the heart of the difference between the two styles of management is the manner in which issues are raised, and the acceptance of ambiguity as a part of the management process. There are, in the view of the author, "certain situations (where) ambiguity may serve better than absolute clarity." There are many topics where the issue is more complicated than the bare facts, especially, the author notes, those issues where human feelings are aroused.

The substance of our professional effort is of tremendous importance, because we are really trying to improve the way recorded information and the products of intellectual creativity are put to use by individuals. This is an awesome responsibility, and there are many reasonable points of view as to how this should best be done. Within every library, many actions and decisions affect individuals in many different ways. In such situations, progress towards established policy objectives requires tentative approaches and the facility to adjust direction as new evidence develops.

In assessing the Japanese style, the author finds ambiguity a useful concept in dealing with others and with "legitimatizing the loose rein that a manager permits in certain organizational situations where agreement needs time to evolve or where further insight is needed before conclusive action is taken."

In short, we need the techniques and information that scientific management provides, but our responsibility and the nature of our assignment are such that absolute answers are, almost by definition, suspect. We need the attributes of scientific management, but let us not make the mistake of thinking that library management is only a science.

REFERENCES

1. The description of the national periodicals center is drawn from the summary: *A National Periodicals Center: Technical Development Plan* (Washington, D.C.: Council on Library Resources, 1978).
2. As quoted in *Higher Education and National Affairs* 27:1-2 (Aug. 25, 1978).
3. *Our Nation's Libraries: An Inventory of Resources & Needs* (Washington, D.C.: National Commission on Libraries and Information Science, 1978).
4. Richard Tanner Pascale, "Zen and the Art of Management," *Harvard Business Review* 56:153-62 (March-April 1978).

Joe B. Wyatt

TECHNOLOGY AND THE LIBRARY

Technology has dramatically changed our environment and lifestyle, and more specifically information technology plays a role both in library administration and in use of informtion resources. Viewed in historical perspective, the "computer era" is just beginning, and the prospect of "the electronic book" is good. Librarians must be computer-literate and lead students and the public in the use of new information technologies.

"As the most technologically advanced great nation in the late twentieth century we are a center from which radiate the forces that unify human experience. Ideology, tribalism, nationalism, the crusading spirit in religion, bigotry, censorship, racism, persecution, immigration and emigration restriction, tariffs, and chauvinsim do interpose barriers. But these are only temporary. The converging powers of technology will eventually triumph. They triumph for a host of reasons which we are only beginning to discover."[1]

I found this quotation an interesting introduction to a discussion on the role of technology and the library for two reasons. First, it comes from a distinguished historian, not a scientist. Second, it states a ringing challenge for every person engaged in the information sciences. It comes from the foreword to a new book, *The Republic of Technology*, by Daniel Boorstin, Librarian of Congress.

I want to use this occasion to briefly explore the hypothesis that technology, more specifically information technology, will have a more far-reaching effect on our society and other societies of the world than we can now imagine. I want you to consider the proposition that as professional librarians, one of the premier professions in the information field, you stand at the entrance to a gateway of opportunity that few professionals have ever experienced. In the vernacular of the current White House, you have the opportunity to be "born again."

I should warn you that the opportunity includes the obligation of an intellectual change not unlike the move from the sheltered womb to the rigors and demands of the earthly environment. But opportunity as exciting and rewarding as you have before you usually carries the price of change.

Joe B. Wyatt is vice president for administration, Harvard University, Cambridge, Massachusetts.

TECHNOLOGY IN OUR LIVES

Technology has played a major role in the lives of Americans for several decades, and it continually dramatically changes our environment and our lifestyle. Permit me to characterize this personally in a brief anecdote.

I am professionally engaged as a teacher, researcher, and practitioner of computer science and technology. But I was born and raised on a small farm in Texas. When I was a youngster, we heated the house and cooked with wood that we cut and split. We had no electrical power. We had no telephone. We had no running water. As time passed, we got electrical power and the benefits of the electric light. It was a long time before I had to stop drawing water out of the well. We didn't get a telephone until I was a teenager. In other words, technology was minimal in my beginnings, and I do know how it feels to move "from the land to the machine."[2] (I may be one of the only computer scientists in the world who can harness and plow a mule.)

This anecdote is clearly personal, but it characterizes the kind of change that my generation is experiencing. I think it important that you consider for a moment those changes that technology has brought to your own lives. Many people have viewed changes wrought by technology very negatively. Henry David Thoreau said in the late nineteenth century that "men have become the tools of their tools." But even Thoreau, whose writings lashed out at technology and societal change, had a personal attitude toward technology that differed from his oft-recorded view. First, he was an accomplished land surveyor and, as such, was a practitioner of technology. His surveying instruments can still be viewed at the Antiquarian Museum in Concord, Massachusetts. Second, I am told on the best of authority that Thoreau, while ostensibly at Walden, occasionally sneaked back through the woods after dark to the Emerson house for some high technology cooking!

FUTURE EFFECTS OF TECHNOLOGICAL CHANGE

As you may have already guessed, I view the prospects of technological change with great enthusiasm and hope. I do not long to return to a world in which there are no electrical power, no convenient water supply, and no telephone—not to mention the other conveniences offered by technology that free us for intellectual activity. I look forward to the contribution that technology can make to overcome societal problems in the future.

For this discussion I would like to couch my enthusiasm in terms of the opportunities represented by information technology. I have spent a professional career in the field. I think that technology represents a great opportunity for those engaged in the information professions such as yourselves. My discussion of the role of technology in the library will be divided into two parts. The first part concerns the use of technology in the administration of libraries. The second part concerns the effect of information technology on the resources that will be a part of the library collection. After a brief visit to the first area, I will dwell on the second.

TECHNOLOGY IN LIBRARY ADMINISTRATION

The use of computer and communications technology in library administration has received substantial attention over the last two decades. Their effect on one of the largest and most difficult of the administrative tasks, that of cataloging the collection, has been attacked exhaustively in the last few years. One might even say exhaustingly. But much progress has been made. Several systems are in operation now, and they continue to be developed and refined. I am very enthusiastic about that problem being licked, with all due respect to those who are continuing to work away on it. The major conceptual and technological barriers are now passed, and it is time for refinement of systems and standards.

TECHNOLOGY AND THE LIBRARY'S INFORMATIONAL ROLE

So much for the brief visit to the issue of information technology and library administration. Now for the issue of information technology and the informational role of the library.

The Perspective of Time

First, consider the perspective of time. In the history of mankind there have been four great inventions relating to information communication. The first was writing, begun by the Egyptians and Accadians about 5,000 years ago. Second was the development of an alphabet by the Greeks about 3,000 years ago. The third was the invention of movable type by the Koreans about 700 years ago and developed independently by Gutenberg about 500 years ago. The last of the great inventions is the stored program computer conceived by John Von Neumann about thirty years ago.

Think for a moment about the time line that these four great inventions represent. It was 2,000 years between the invention of writing and the alphabet. About 2,000 years elapsed between the developments of the alphabet and movable type. And 500 years passed between the invention of movable type and the computer. But only thirty years have elapsed between the invention of the computer and today. Although the changes wrought in those thirty years are mind-stretching, if one looks at the perspective of time, the "computer era" is just beginning. The thirty years are only a tiny fraction of any of the other historical intervals.

Early applications of the computer to information problems occurred in laboratory environments with objectives like calculating artillery tables and predicting the weather. (In the first case it was very successful, and in the second case it's making progress.) These computers were housed in large and expensively air-conditioned rooms. They were manifested in massive electronic and mechanical devices as late as 1955. And each one cost millions of dollars.

Yet today the power of these devices, even computers more powerful than those early computers in every way, can be held in my hand, carried in my pocket, and used wherever I go. Moreover, these devices that I can hold in my hand have brothers and sisters, through the genealogy of large scale integrated circuit chips, that continually find expanded roles in almost every human endeavor, particularly in the communication and processing of information.

For example, I walked over to the Harvard Coop early this morning to see a new gadget called "Speak and Spell" (a registered trademark of Texas Instruments, Inc.). It is a little box that ostensibly helps to teach youngsters spelling. It has a typewriter keyboard and a "vocabulary" of 200 words or so. (According to the salesman, it will soon have a vocabulary of several thousand words.) The vocabulary is interchangeable by switching small magnetic memories. Plans include a vocabulary of foreign languages. It is portable, battery operated, and costs $50.00. At its heart is a voice synthesis chip, a key invention. It means that a small collection of LSI chips can take words spelled out in digital form, as from a computer, and convert them to high-quality audio output at a very low cost. To begin the process of getting your mind around where this little toy and its kin may be going, drop into your local electronics store and take a look.

For those of you who haven't been there lately, your future holds a treat. You will find numerous examples of information technology that you can buy for your personal use at prices well under $1,000, that only a few years ago were not available outside the laboratory and cost tens and hundreds of thousands of dollars. You may even begin to believe as I do that the "electronic book" is not just science fiction.

The Information Industry

Consider another perspective on the information issue. In 1860 over 40 percent of the work force in the United States were farmers, and under 20 percent worked in factories. By 1950, at the peak of what we have come to call the industrial society, over 40 percent of the work force had moved to the factories, and only 10 percent stayed on the farm. Today half of the work force in the United States are employed in what is called the information industry: processing, communicating, researching, developing, and administering information in one form or another.

Let me describe briefly an economic characterization of that information industry. In terms of a U.S. gross national product of 1,295 billion dollars in 1973, broadcast television accounted for 3.5 billion, cable television another .5 billion, radio a billion and a half, newspapers 8.3 billion, books 4 billion, periodicals 3.7 billion, telephone 25.5 billion, postal service 8.3 billion. Computer software in 1973 was already at the level of 3.7 billion (not hardware, just software). And libraries accounted for 3.5 billion. When one adds in computer hardware, advertising, education, and other information enterprises, it comes to over 300 billion dollars. Banks, law firms, and a number of other "information businesses" would include a marketplace that approaches 500 billion dollars.

Every one of these segments of the information industry was growing then and is continuing to grow now. In this marketplace it is very clear that information distribution is becoming more decentralized and more personalized.

Information Literacy and Information Growth

The media are becoming more complex. Information literacy has become a problem along with information overload. As children some of us read everything we could get our hands on, but we couldn't get our hands on much to read. If a child of today tried to read or otherwise absorb all of the information that is available, it would be absolutely impossible. In today's society and even more in the future, it is a necessity to be both selectively literate and multi-technology literate to take advantage of available information resources.

Kas Kalba, who heads a consulting firm that specializes in the information technology field, recently gave a partial list of the kinds of literacies that one needs: computer literacy, CB radio literacy, newsletter literacy, graphic arts literacy, on-line retrieval literacy, legal literacy, consumer information literacy, pocket calculator literacy.[3]

Obviously, the list is not exhaustive in terms of the kinds and types of information that is not only available to us but is often thrust on us. I believe that if libraries are to remain active information resources then librarians must not only become multi-literate but most also bear a major responsibility for leading students and the public to multi-literacy in these new information technologies.

About a year ago Richard Atkinson, the director of the National Science Foundation, asked me to chair a multi-disciplinary committee to review the National Science Foundation's programs on information science, science information, and the like. It was one of the most productive such efforts that I have ever experienced. I know those of you from universities are likely to be engaged in endless task forces. This one, of course, produced a report that was added to all those other reports that line the shelves. But our report was only nineteen pages in length. It recommends, among other things, that the National Science Foundation establish a new basic research program in information science and technology.

The recommendation is being followed. A new Division of Information Science and Technology has been established. Its new director, Howard Resnikoff, has begun work. I will paraphrase a statement of the information problem that he first mentioned as a member of the committee and has more recently refined. Resnikoff relates his perspective to the work of Thomas Robert Malthus, who, in 1798, wrote his *Essay on Population* relating to the growth of human and animal populations.[4]

Like people, information is a rapidly growing resource in contrast to almost every other resource on earth. That is, most other resources are diminishing and being used up. Information is not being used up; it is growing. Like people, information must be sheltered and cared for. But sheltering and caring for information in its traditional printed form consume other more scarce and diminishing resources. Moreover, it leads to a Malthusian struggle for existence, analogous to that which afflicts the human population. Darwinian evolution may even play a role in this struggle in that only the fittest information may survive.

Clearly, the population pressure of information will continue to test the capacity of society to contain it. Zero population growth for information is even less plausible than one can imagine for human zero population growth. So as Resnikoff puts it, "we find ourselves between the hammer of information population pressure and the anvil of societal need for information." He goes on to say that "we do not yet know how to do what must be done." Therein lies both the problem and the opportunity to those engaged in the information professions.

I certainly don't know what the future might hold for our information society. It is almost reckless to predict. But one might imagine a world in which our present libraries become information museums, collections for retrospective research and historical significance—a world in which every home, perhaps each person, can be instrumented with information technology so as to communicate freely with the rest of the world.

I feel safe with only one prediction. Whatever the future does hold in the development of new information technology will, if we remain a free enterprise society, happen almost spontaneously just as it has in the last three decades. No bureaucracy is in control of the basic ingenuity and entrepreneurial spirit that characterize the development of new technology, thank God. And you are stake holders. Virtually everything that you encounter as professional librarians is affected by this spontaneous and rapid change including the media, the economics, and the public policy of information technology.

THE LIBRARIAN'S RESPONSE

In conclusion, I suppose that it is fair to suggest how you as librarians might deal both personally and as a profession with the issues that I have raised. I have an idea. It falls into the category of a recycled idea rather than a new one. But it seems to work in its other contexts.

I have long been interested in academic programs to train practicing computer professionals for business and government, curricula that combine in-depth knowledge about computer technology with in-depth knowledge about business and government.

At Harvard we have established such a program jointly between the Division of Applied Science (in the Faculty of Arts and Sciences) and the Harvard Business School. We started admitting students four years ago in groups of eight. We were immediately oversubscribed. The experimental program was enormously successful, and it has now become a regular option in the MBA program of the Harvard Business School. It currently engages about ninety students.

Also at Harvard the John F. Kennedy School of Government has a professional program in public administration leading to the MPA. The program admits those who have practiced in the public administration area and who plan to return. I teach a course in the Kennedy School called Management Information Systems in Government that is a part of this Program. The course is heavily subscribed. Case material on information technology and its use in government make an important contribution.

For example, one of my cases concerns a computer-based information system in the United States Congress, the House of Representatives to be specific. Those of you who know the Library of Congress know that the House members often ask for information from the Library of Congress. You would probably safely predict that they will ask more and more and more. In addition, many members of the House have already instrumented their own offices with computer terminals or small computers. And more than one member now employs a computer programmer as legislative aide.

In dealing with information technology policy, these members of Congress are not only becoming familiar with the technology through the normal legislative information process but also through personal experience as users. So we can expect a more broadly informed legislative branch both making and questioning information technology policy.

I suggest that you review and reconsider your academic programs in library science, including mid-career programs. Demand enlightened curricula that include basic material from the information technologies. This includes computer-based system design, development, management, and use—their complete understanding.

Every librarian should be computer literate—to be able to read and write computer programs for a variety of information applications. To avoid doing so will, over time, result in a growing lack of understanding for both the new material that you will find in your collection and the computer literate clients who wish to use it. And to avoid doing so is to eventually become a follower and not a leader in our information centered society.

I will end this discussion, as I began it, with a quotation from Boorstin:

> "We must be willing to believe both that politics is the Art of the Possible and that Technology is the Art of the Impossible. Never before has a people been so tempted (and with such good reason) to believe that anything is *technologically* possible."[5]

REFERENCES

1. Daniel Joseph Boorstin, *The Republic of Technology: Reflections on our Future Community* (New York: Harper and Row, 1978), p. xv.
2. Chapter 3 of Boorstin's book is titled "From the Land to the Machine."

3. Kas Kalba, "Libraries in the Information Marketplace," in *Libraries in Post-Industrial Society* (Phoenix, Ariz.: Oryx Press, 1977).
4. Howard L. Resnikoff, "Remarks on a National Information Policy," presented at the Conference on Federal Support of Library and Information Services sponsored by the National Commission on Libraries and Information Science, September 1978.
5. Boorstin, *The Republic of Technology*, p. 34. Italics in original.

Barbara Evans Markuson

COOPERATION AND LIBRARY NETWORK DEVELOPMENT

Networks function as change agents for libraries because they provide three critical services—research and development, capital acquisition, and technology transfer mechanisms. Areas in which network participation has an impact on the academic library include the management of change, economic and attitudinal change, and cost accountability. Because of their early successes, networks have given rise to increased expectations for solutions to many critical library problems and for the equally rapid development of a national library network.

When the new journal, *College & Research Libraries*, was issued in December 1939, a new era and new horizons for academic libraries, based on cooperation, improved bibliographic control, technology, and legislation seemed imminent.

Forty years have passed. We still seek improved technology. We still propose legislation. We still fund cooperative projects at a level that would have disgraced the board of a backward eighteenth century poor relief society. As for bibliographic control, we still hope that someone will invent a bibliographic Cuisinart that will automatically chop, mash, puree, and blend national standard bibliographic records into an inexpensive and tasty dish seasoned to the local palate.

Having achieved at least a national, standard, machine-readable bibliographic record, after enormous expenditure of effort, local catalogers reverse the effort by working their exquisite local petit point, having refined bibliographic embroidery to a high art form. In many of our libraries we still treat users with benign neglect, as we concentrate on amassing collections accessible by methods with which Mr. Cutter would be thoroughly familiar.

Nevertheless, there are glimpses of a new horizon. If we subscribe to Ivan Illich's tenets, our salvation may rest in our failure to get exclusive rights as purveyors of information.

When physicists, engineers, mathematicians, programmers, and other strange folk invaded our field after World War II, we couldn't have them arrested for practicing with-

Barbara Evans Markuson is executive director, Indiana Cooperative Library Services Authority, Indianapolis.

out a license. After setting up camp, they made forays into the bibliographic jungle. Then after having surveyed our manual control mechanisms, our massive collections, and our primitive file access, they called us dinosaurs doomed to extinction. The dinosaurs continued, with ponderous movements, to graze the ancient feeding grounds, so the interlopers decamped and invented what is now called the information industry.

Finally, the dinosaurs, nibbling through the midden, found such food for thought as data processing, information as a national resource, work flow analysis, cost effectiveness, and user service on demand. It was not easy to adjust to this strange diet; and, unfortunately, the interlopers decamped so hastily that they failed to leave the formula for changing dinosaurs into ecologically efficient beasts.

When Fred Kilgour hit on a way to pry enough money loose from academic library budgets to form a large-scale cooperative, decently funded and technically oriented, it was an historic moment in American librarianship. I am convinced that we now have at least part of the formula for change.

Expanding on this theme, the following sections review networks as change agents and coping with change, and the final section scans the new academic library horizon, taking brief notice of a few cloudy issues.

NETWORKS AS CHANGE AGENTS

The rapid development of cooperative computer-based library networks, in which academic libraries played a seminal role, is a phenomenon yet to be adequately investigated. Whether networks will become permanent components of the library environment or whether they are an expedient and ad hoc structure is uncertain. Despite these unknowns, a present attempt to rationalize network development is both a matter of immediate concern and of permanent professional interest.

To this end, I hypothesize that networks provide three critical services: research and development, capital acquisition, and technology transfer mechanisms. The permanence of networks will largely depend on their ability to provide these services until more efficient technology change agents are provided.

Research and Development

Any institution's survival depends upon its response to social, economic, and technical change in its environment. Since World War II, libraries, as well as other institutions, have attempted to accommodate to almost continuous change. The effort to adjust to technical change in the library field has been difficult due to the nature of technical change and the inadequate library mechanisms for technical planning, assessment, and transfer.

Technological developments spawn new developments like yeast spores, multiplying rapidly, mindlessly, and endlessly. Banks turned to computers, and we now have automated tellers; transistors were invented, and now even school children have their own personal calculators. Soon videotape recorders will be as prevalent as television sets. Unfortunately, the library profession's mechanisms for assessing these technologies have, until recently, not advanced much beyond those used by Melvil Dewey and his peers, who sat around and swapped tales of staff resistance to, and the relative efficiencies of, the Hammond, Sun, Calligraph, and other variants of the typewriting machine.

Beyond our grudging annual widow's mite to the American Library Association and similar groups, we support no permanent organizations to assume responsibility for library research and development; we have no library think tanks gathering data and formulating long range strategies; we have no laboratories testing new equipment and alerting us to its potential impact, cost, and benefit.

None of this would matter if each library's budget provided for technological assessment and planning. Not only is this far from true, but the limited research and development funding available to the library field is sporadic, limited to areas of concern to funding agencies, geared to short-term projects, and inadequate. Moreover, the political realities in the distribution of funds generally result in small-scale efforts, since not only the politicians but the librarians as well complain if large grants are given to only a few.

An additional problem arises as library budgeting mechanisms rarely allow forward funding, permit massive equipment and system replacement, provide for amortization of long-range development efforts, or allow the establishment of "risk" capital or depreciation funds. Inevitably, long-range advance planning for continuous absorption of technological change is virtually nonexistent in libraries.

This lack of technical research and development was not so important when the technology was simpler. If one bought an inefficient copier or microfilm reader that was condemned after consumer testing, the impact was localized, and the defect was remedied with a reasonable outlay of cash. Attempts to use computer technology revealed for the first time and on a large scale, lack of appropriate agencies and mechanisms for massive technological retooling of library operations. The manpower and funding required if literally hundreds of libraries were to convert to computer based operations made evident not only serious flaws in the library economy, but the essential lack of structure in the library community.

Furthermore, the forces that made computer technology of particular relevance to libraries continued. It was unthinkable that a field besieged by an information explosion, more sophisticated user demands, and cyclic financial retrenchment would be unable to use a machine that processed, retrieved, and transmitted data rapidly; offered potential for increased staff productivity; and expanded the range of user services.

Thus, while it is generally assumed that the raison d'être for networks stems largely from our tradition of interlibrary cooperation, an equally compelling argument can be made that networks are largely a response to our lack of techniques to deal with innovation and change when these involve complex technologies.

Although many networks have done little in the way of significant research and development, although many do not yet have research projects as budgeted line items, and although networks themselves are still largely dependent upon uncertain funding sources to support research and development, a potential exists for a permanent research and development program.

This year, for example, OCLC, Inc., announced the formation of a research department within its research and development division. Projects include a study of machine/machine interface, the efficient response time for different terminal operations, the potential of the home television set as a remote catalog access device, and the problems of subject access to very large files of catalog records.

By assessing a tiny research and development "tax" on each operation, networks could aggregate funds to support permanent research and development projects. This internal funding of research to supplement our limited external funding could increase our ability to use new technology efficiently and to develop new techniques for information handling.

Capital Acquisition

The library literature generally concentrates on the operational aspects of library technology; rarely are we given insight into how a given library acquired the capital for the new technology. Computer technology has, perhaps, been the most capital intensive of any introduced on the library scene. In addition, computer systems tend to be upgraded on a regular basis, requiring more or less continuous funding for modification and maintenance. It is important that libraries understand the role networks play in transmission of technology because of their ability to assist in the acquisition of capital required for change.

A recent OCLC financial statement indicates that over $13,000,000 in land, buildings, computers, and other equipment is owned by OCLC, and almost $10,000,000 is owed in current and long-term debt for computer equipment and other resources. Assets as of September 30, 1978, totalled $27,785,070, corporate equity was slightly over $9,000,000, and liabilities were about $18,500,500.

Over and above these central costs, there are some 2,000 terminals purchased by library networks or individual libraries representing, ignoring depreciation, an aggregate investment of about $7,400,000. A conservative estimate of the current budget for the OCLC, Inc., and its associated networks would be in the neighborhood of $30,000,000—roughly about $23,000 per library.

Melvin Day, formerly deputy director of the National Library of Medicine, recently noted similar features of the NLM on-line network. Over 2,000 terminals in 1,000 health science libraries use the system for more than a million literature searches annually. This allows the large capital investment that NLM has made to be amortized over a high volume of use. Commercial information retrieval services, such as SDC and Lockheed, follow a similar strategy.

It seems reasonably clear that only large firms, the federal government, a few large states, and large library networks will be able to undertake the capital investment needed to support complex, large-scale, on-line networks and to provide the continuing research and development needed to mount new services. In the library community the network provides the structure required to concentrate needed capital. Networks can also employ various entrepreneurial strategies, such as indebtedness, that are unavailable to many libraries. It is important that network organizations have a legal basis which allows maximum flexibility in funding strategies and that member libraries honor contractual commitments which the network has incurred on their behalf.

Technology Transfer

Networks are an efficient mechanism for comprehensive, rapid, and wide-spread technology transfer at a reasonable cost. Networks facilitate this transfer by centralized contracting with commercial firms, by centralized acquisition of equipment by contracting for development of specialized services and by contracting with other networks.

Networks can also effect rapid change by centralizing a specialist staff whose skills are made available to many libraries. As new technologies require increasingly skilled and specialized staff, this feature of networks will become critical to continued development, especially as salaries of specialists increase. Job descriptions which appear in network newsletters, such as the one published by BALLOTS (now RLIN, the Research Libraries Information Network), give insight into the range of skills required to develop and maintain large scale on-line systems.

The economics of this centralization of staff is made evident by an analysis of the OCLC system. A library using OCLC supports about one-fifth of an OCLC staff member's time a year and obtains skills, such as electrical engineering, cost accounting, programming, computer operation, telecommunication planning, and systems analysis. Few libraries can acquire even some of these specialists on their local staffs.

Networks also facilitate rapid change by role specialization. Networks such as RLIN, Washington Library Network, and OCLC concentrate their efforts on the development, installation, and management of central computer-based systems and services. Affiliated networks such as CLASS, AMIGOS, SOLINET, INCOLSA, and MINITEX concentrate their skills on marketing, user education and training, and assisting with local installation of network services.

Although this development in role specialization was largely unplanned, it has proved to be an effective and efficient means of rapid technology transfer, has allowed an equitable access to network services on a nation-wide basis, and yet has permitted some differentiation in services and governance as the needs vary in different parts of the country.

THE ACADEMIC LIBRARY IN THE NETWORK ENVIRONMENT

No one has yet detailed the total impact that network participation may have on the academic library. Areas of special importance are the management of change, economic change, attitudinal change, and cost accountability.

Management of Change

For many academic libraries, participating in network services and connecting to on-line cataloging may well be the first major change in library operations. Many library administrators are not experienced in the management of change. It seems inevitable, however, that, once a library embarks on an automation program through network participation, change becomes a permanent way of life.

There are macro changes (for example, the impending introduction by OCLC, Inc., of automated interlibrary loan) and micro changes (for example, the change in a field of the MARC serials format). In addition, there are local changes that result from network participation, for example, the decision to shift to a computer-output-microform catalog using machine-readable records generated via the network.

Each of these changes involves external communications, internal communications, and perhaps endless committee meetings. Professional librarians must find efficient ways to cope with change to facilitate the decision making process. Librarians must begin to consider themselves as information resource managers rather than guardians of time-honored local routines. As managers, they need to be concerned with costs, increased productivity, increased success for the library user, and quality.

Library staff rarely begin a discussion of the potential use of on-line cataloging by stating, "Our goal is to reduce our costs by 'x' dollars per title and to increase our annual output by 'y' units without reducing quality." Instead, they are more likely to ask something like, "Will the system be able to print the location symbol for reference books under the call number as we now do?" We need to emphasize that technical processing is an internal service supporting the library's public service just as the network is an external service supporting the library.

Management needs to exert more efforts toward alerting the entire staff to its goals, objectives, and plans if the management of change is to be effective. Effective use of technology usually results from group action rather than individual action because technology inevitably affects a wide range of library operations. Group decision making is often slow. Management should encourage staff decision making based on objective data, gathered from sampling, performance analysis, costs, and so on, rather than on opinions. My experience has been that this speeds up decision making and settles arguments more objectively.

Time for planning and training must be made available if systems are to work well in the local library. Inevitably time will be lost in attending network meetings and in reading network communications, but, overall, increased efficiency and understanding should result. Librarians also need to give attention to more effective ways of transmitting information internally so that network and cataloging documentation is rapidly disseminated to those whose work is affected.

Economic Change

Academic libraries will need to automate operations as rapidly, comprehensively, and economically as possible to meet increased demands within budget limits, and, because of these limits, the success in meeting this goal for the majority of libraries will depend largely on network capabilities.

Inflation and increased labor costs are a reality. If we cannot improve production, we may face future hostile confrontations from users and funders. Other professions are under attack for outrageous fees. We feel intuitively that $75.00 is too much to pay for having one's teeth cleaned. Others may feel that it is also too much to pay to get a book on the shelf. Even if we are below that cost today, a combination of inflation and increases in wages, benefits, and supplies could get us there in a few years. We can argue that these are inflated dollars, but we, too, can reach the tolerance level, especially for internal services which are politically vulnerable.

The manual operations will not only increase in cost, but it will be increasingly difficult to offset these costs by benefits. Even if automated systems cost more, benefits are such that it is at least evident that the library is getting more for its money.

Although commercial vendors and locally developed automated systems are alternatives to network services, they may not be feasible for many academic libraries. Small libraries may be barred from these alternatives due to lack of capital; very large libraries may be barred due to the complexity of their operations, the size of their files, and the large investment required to bring about a satisfactory system. Although millions of dollars and hundreds of staff years have been spent, it is remarkable that few large academic research libraries have achieved anything close to a total local automated system, and most large research libraries have now affiliated with networks.

Two years ago interest in closing the card catalog was high. Recently one hears less of this partly because the initial assessment of the cost of local development and installation of on-line catalogs has been sobering. One suspects that the inauguration of the Research Libraries Information Network results from the interest, particularly in large research libraries, in on-line catalogs, the difficulty in finding an adequate solution on an individual basis, and the hope that the RLIN can solve the problem in a network environment.

Attitudinal Change

We continually say that information is power, but when we say this we usually are thinking about our library users rather than our staff. However, library operational information is also power. Manual files allow minimal file access and, thus, minimal knowledge throughout the library of certain file-centered operations. This fact gives rise to the familiar "my file" and "my collection" syndrome. If we view the library as a micro network, it is obvious that some "members" of the "micro network" have very restricted access to information.

On-line files, whether locally maintained or centralized in a network, will become "our files," and collections will become "our collection" because they will be accessible to more library staff. Micro and macro networks may eventually allow access throughout the library, including its branches and departments, to serial check-in files, circulation files, cataloging and in-process files, acquisitions and subscription files, authority files, union list files, and management information files. Information about library operations will then be available on an equitable basis.

Among the changes resulting from on-line access, observers have noted the following: (1) File access takes less time and personal efficiency is increased; (2) traffic patterns are altered; (3) the feeling of a community of purpose is strengthened; (4) pride in the total effort is fostered; and (5) equitable access to information and resources is available to staff and, in many cases, to users.

However, the "my file" and "my collection" syndrome shifts from the micro network to the macro or central network. Librarians are not at all certain which of their files should be accessible by other libraries. For example, should an order file or a serial check-in file be available for search by another library? At present, we have some vague feeling that access to operational files would be pernicious, but as yet I have seen no well reasoned arguments to show why this is so. (Exception, of course, would be made for access that could permit surveillance of an individual's reading habits.)

The need to view each library's catalog as a subset of the network catalog is important conceptually if quality is to be obtained and if benefits of cooperation are to be realized. Many people talk about the supposedly bad quality that resides in cooperative network data bases. I take the opposing view that network participation has done more to raise the quality and standardization of cataloging than any other event since the beginning of the Library of Congress card service. Within the past five years hundreds of thousands of hours of work have gone into training on AACR, MARC formats, CONSER standards, quality control, and error reporting and correcting. Librarians are showing an increasing concern for quality work on initial network input to benefit others.

There are, of course, libraries that still regard networks as a machine for their local convenience; but where this obtains, the fault should rest with library management and not with the catalog departments.

Increasingly, the fear of putting one's data on-line for all to see is giving way to those attitudinal changes noted above: a strengthened commonality of purpose (we are not just "cataloging" but, rather, creating a national bibliographic entry which will serve many purposes) and a pride in the total effort.

To achieve these benefits, networks need to establish even greater communication channels with the Library of Congress to ensure a more cost effective flow of information about changes of cataloging rules, subject heading changes of interpretation, etc., so that we build an efficient information network which will support our efforts to develop an efficient bibliographic network. I should note in passing that the library field's dissemination of documentation and rules relating to bibliographic control must surely be one of the most primitive now extant on the national scene.

The wider distribution of information and improved access to information on-line, will be an increasing phenomenon as networks mature and as more functions are available through networks. The impact of these changes on academic libraries has already been seen, but even more far-reaching changes should be in store for us over the next decade.

Cost Accountability

The lack of library cost data is endemic. Despite exhortations from the pulpit and press, we still fail in fiscal matters. Many believe we may even be afraid of what such data would reveal. Networks may be able to exert a beneficial influence by emphasizing the profession's need for accountability and by the network's own emphasis on accountability to its members. In perhaps no other segment of the library community is cost and budget information so widely distributed and so openly discussed. Some networks are encouraging their members to gather data to support cost accounting, collection development analysis, and statistical reporting efforts.

Because of cooperative funding and governance, many computer-based networks are required to maintain cost accounting and audit information. Cost decisions made by networks have a direct impact on library budgets so that library management is keenly interested in network costing. There is also interest in cost comparisons between networks. It is obvious from some of the literature that many libraries are not yet used to paying overhead to support both operations and research and development activities. Because of this mutual relationship—with the network exhorting the library to be more cost-effective and with the libraries monitoring networks—services should be beneficial to our public, keep us all honest, and promote maximum return from the funds invested in library and information services.

NEW HORIZONS

Networks have perturbed the structure of the library field. The typical library indicia of status—size of staff, collection, and budget—which have in the past been the measure of influence, power, and importance are not appropriate for networks. This has tended to disturb balances of power in the field. On the other hand, networks, by the rapidity of their early successes, have given rise to expectations of an equally rapid development of a national library network and cost-effective solutions to many critical problems.

This section deals first with raised expectations and then with national developments.

New Services and Systems

Networks and other on-line systems have whetted appetites for transferring more library functions to on-line operations. We want, among other on-line authority files, catalogs and management data.

Much of this interest was generated by the alarm created by the second edition of the *Anglo-American Cataloging Rules* (AACR 2) and the initial stampede toward the closing of catalogs. Some are now beginning to realize the paucity of research and development concerning the requirements and specifications for an on-line catalog. It is inevitable, of course, that a first conception of an on-line catalog is that it will be like our present manual file, except that records would be viewed via a CRT display.

However, the opportunity to begin our central access file using a new technology should cause us to rethink the functions of the catalogs. The on-line retrieval systems are probably a closer model than is our manual catalog structure. Efficient use of catalog records will probably require more subject indexing and content analysis to allow the user to select the records of interest more economically.

One approach might be similar to that used by NLM in creating records that would be used both for printed display and for on-line retrieval. More access points were added, and codes were used to identify subject terms to be used only for on-line retrieval. This technique would allow LC to generate catalog records for both manual and on-line systems.

The need for research and development will delay the transition to on-line catalogs; but since these catalogs have real merit for improved library operation and user access, we should begin to provide increased funding now if we are to achieve our goal within the next decade.

The transition to on-line catalogs will also require a massive retooling which will make what we are now doing seem very simple. The capital and equipment acquisition will need to be planned and budgeted well in advance.

For example, if we needed only an average of five terminals for each library now using an on-line network to provide public access to an on-line catalog, we would require at least 15,000 terminals; but if we are thinking about on-line catalogs for all libraries, accommodating users in remote locations, branches, department libraries, units of the library, etc., we might be in the range of a million terminals at a total cost of a billion dollars if the cost were about $1,000 per terminal. Obviously, it will be a long time before on-line catalogs will be generally available to the public.

Interest in AACR2 and on-line catalogs has also stimulated interest in on-line authority control. In some quarters there is the belief that, unless a network can provide this service, on-line cataloging will be deficient. However, it is not yet clear how a large on-line network can provide authority control at a reasonable cost, unless we alter our concept of authority control.

I suspect that most libraries conceptualize network authority control as a system which would maintain, for each, an on-line version of its present manual authority file, thus maintaining a link between the records it has used and the authorities relevant to each record. Conceptually, this approach mirrors present manual practices in which cross references and see also cards are interfiled with catalog cards for items in the collection, although the functions of the two records are totally different. As a result, the relevant subset of the authority file needed for each library is not only unique but literally changing constantly (which explains why most libraries do a less than adequate job of coping with this operation). How this approach can be accommodated in a large network with millions of records used by hundreds of libraries is not obvious.

A more feasible approach may require us to think about the authority control system as functionally different from the system which describes the contents of the collection. Thus each network might maintain a single authority file for all users of the network against which all proposed input would be screened and not maintain links to each record used by each library. The authority file would become more comparable to the thesaurus in on-line retrieval systems which is used to develop the search strategy before the catalog file is accessed.

This approach prepares the way for on-line catalogs. It also eliminates the screening of information that the present systems perpetuate. Users may wish to have information on all subjects relevant to their inquiry, not just the subset that matches the particular collection at hand. In other words, it is possible that a system that would respond with a message such as, "We have no materials on the following subject; if you wish to pursue this subject, please see the reference staff," would be a positive rather than a negative service to users, since it could well be that information is available in journal articles, through interlibrary loan, etc.

If libraries can agree on a centralized authority system for each network, then networks will be able to find solutions much more rapidly, and the access strategies for library catalogs and to information retrieval services will become more comparable.

The limits to network capabilities are not yet defined. There is an intuitive feeling that networks will not be able to support both on-line catalogs and circulation because of the volume of traffic and the local nature of the use of such systems. However, because of limited funding available for research and development, networks may design local catalogs that are linked to the network data base. Such an approach would allow full data to be kept in the network file and available on demand while briefer records are stored locally.

At present, OCLC, Inc., can be viewed as our closest approximation to an automated national union catalog. It supports the two major functions that the NUC provides, namely access to catalog data and holding information. Through automation it has made both the generation of cataloging records and the transmission of interlibrary loan requests an integral operation. At the present stage of networking, the local catalog itself is still maintained largely as it was before networking, although some filing labor has been eliminated.

We need to mount research and development efforts so that the catalog itself will become an integral operation as well. It appears that most national research and development efforts will be expended toward linking present networks, or developing competing networks, rather than providing networks funding to extend the range of automation that they can offer.

Academic libraries can be assured of continual refinement of present network services and extension of network services into additional areas, but it may be some time before their own files will become linked to the network data bases. OCLC's present investigation of automated circulation systems should give us further information about the economic feasibility of decentralization of network services. In the long-range network plan, it may also someday be economically feasible to achieve further decentralization, allowing users, in their homes, to access a library's on-line catalog and, in turn, the central network files.

It is a truism that we generally tend to overestimate what can become technically feasible in the short-term and underestimate the long-term potential of technology. For this reason, I believe that we will have no dramatic changes in network services, e.g., local on-line catalogs, within the next two or three years. But within the next decade we can expect significant changes in library operations, and almost all library support functions will be automated.

National Developments

The number of reports describing the national library network, national network plans, etc., might mislead a naive observer into thinking that our present network structure results from such directives and plans. Nothing could be farther from the truth.

Present networks have developed from local initiatives. BALLOTS (RLIN) began from a private academic library automation program, Washington Library Network from a state plan, and OCLC, Inc., as a consortium of academic libraries in Ohio. Affiliated networks such as NELINET, BCR, COWL, and PALINET also stemmed from local, state, or multi-state initiatives. If anything, it could be argued that national planning is now being based on achievements at the local, state, and regional level.

The interest in national networking might also mislead some to believe that networks receive large amounts of federal funding. This also is untrue. Most networks are supported by transfer funds from local operating budgets of member libraries supplemented, in some areas, by state tax funds.

While federal funds, particularly U.S. Office of Education funds distributed through the Library Services and Construction Act and the Office of Libraries and Learning Resources grants, have been valuable in stimulating network development and expansion, federal funds have continued to be a small portion of the total network budget.

Similarly, private foundation funds have been instrumental in expanding networks, particularly the Kellogg Foundation grants to enable small academic libraries to join networks. Up to now, however, these funds have also been a small portion of the total funding. As far as I am aware, the only federal funding especially earmarked for networking is the small LSCA Title II grant allocated each state and territory.

Another view of national library network directions could stem from the belief that present networks are struggling with problems of governance and organization and need help from above. This can also be challenged.

Present network structures have accommodated to political realities in various parts of the country. Without federal direction networks have already cooperated, coordinated activities, and have undertaken several jointly funded projects. Much of the present network achievement rests in the organizational flexibility which allows entrepreneural strategies and the development of pilot projects with a minimum of paper work. Network role specialization has allowed present resources to be used effectively to benefit many libraries. The local support of state agencies and large academic libraries has also allowed additional stimulus to foster network growth.

Virtually without federal or even much state planning, many networks have evolved from the professional drive of committed librarians. A recent informal study by Thompson Little, Associate Executive Director of OCLC, Inc., indicates that, if the data reported in *Library Statistics of Colleges and Universities* to the U.S. Office of Education are reasonably accurate, then we have already reached the point where in the OCLC network alone, about 60 percent of current academic library cataloging is being done on-line. If we include other networks then this total may be up to 75 percent. This does not mean, of course, that 75 percent of all of the 2,831 institutions reported to USOE are now on-line, but rather that the academic libraries using on-line networks account for the bulk of the total academic library cataloging annually.

The impact of this development on academic library collection management and sharing is enormous, and we are just beginning to understand the potential benefits that might accrue. Whereas researchers have tended to rely on resources in large academic libraries, we are beginning to unveil a vast decentralized research library of unparalleled richness through network data bases. Many special collections in small colleges, seminaries, and state and public libraries will come to light and will supplement the holdings of the large research libraries in support of access to resources. This knowledge will create demand for better strategies for resource sharing and document delivery, areas which many networks are just beginning to address.

To this richness of data, the addition of on-line holdings of serials to network data bases, will add more specific location data for serials, plugging a gap that has existed since the final edition of the *Union List of Serials* almost two decades ago.

It is unfortunate that many of the national plans that have been published fail to take these developments into account. For example, the national periodicals center plan, recently released by the Council on Library Resources, suggests transmission of requests via TWX, when, out in the field, many libraries are preparing for electronic mail box transmission of interlibrary loan. Such networks are already in place and available at virtually no additional cost.

Several proposals are now afloat concerning aspects of the national library network. This year, for the first time, suggestions are being made that we need a national library agency or national library board. The CLR report on the national periodicals center espouses such a view, and one argument advanced is that we can't have the center without the agency. Why this is so is not fully demonstrated, particularly when organizations such as the Center for Research Libraries and the Universal Serials and Book Exchange (formerly U.S. Book Exchange) have provided somewhat similar services for years as non-profit cooperatives managed by participating libraries (the governance of the exchange includes some 1,600 members electing an executive board).

Potential services of the national library agency or board (also called the "capping" agency) vary in the different plans being advanced. Among them are: setting standards, determining network fees, reimbursement for interlibrary loan, developing national tele-communications channels, linking existing networks, administering the national period-icals center, establishing national library information policy, determining protocols for inter-computer communications, and preservation of materials.

Since such a capping agency would affect all libraries, it should be a professional responsibility for each of us to be thoroughly familiar with such proposals. We need to decide whether we want to expend the limited federal dollars that libraries obtain for such an agency or whether such an agency would increase our ability to obtain federal dollars. We need to understand whether such an agency would actually forward our ability to reach national goals or whether we can reach these through cooperation and networking. We particularly need to know how the directors and staff of such an agency would be selected and to whom they would report. What input would we have either as individual libraries or networks? How would such an agency relate to the Library of Congress, the National Library of Medicine, and existing library funding programs, such as the U.S. Office of Education Library support programs?

A recent report states the premise that a most critical problem facing libraries in this country is the need to develop a coherent national network system. Whether this is true or not, only a survey of libraries could reveal. Many of the libraries with which I deal worry more about getting funding to use the network services already available. Even for many large libraries, present networks are filling 95 percent of their need for cataloging data. A major feature of a coherent national system might be an improved facility to access the total national resource. It may well be that, for the majority of libraries, this is not a critical need. They might rather see funds diverted to the development of a local operating system tied to existing systems than improving their capability to operate better libraries.

We do need, however, to encourage all Library of Congress efforts to improve our coverage of current cataloging of non-book materials, to support LC's efforts to develop standard formats for analytics and technical report literature, and to encourage LC's continued interest in and support of network developments in the field.

Another argument recently advanced is that the national network must be designed to meet the needs of our largest research libraries. This may be true, but it has yet to be demonstrated. Perhaps the internal operating needs of large research libraries are different from the needs of networks. What we may need is not to skew network services to a few libraries but to mount an extensive research program aimed at developing cost effective systems. In this way large research libraries could operate independently of the network but still be linked to it. Skewing the entire network to the needs of a few could make it uneconomic for many libraries particularly if we review the past history of systems developed in several such libraries.

We should also decide whether it is politically wise to mount a federal program geared principally to solving the operational problems of libraries. Surely these problems have limited political appeal, and it is dubious whether a strong case can be made that they are federal concerns. Shifting to programs in user services would be wiser, but public service librarians do not seem to exert their interests as effectively as technical service librarians. Support for user access to federal and government data banks, national information de-livery systems, improved distribution of government documents, and subsidies to allow small libraries to enjoy network participation may be more politically appealing than bibliographic control.

In any case, all of the planning groups invite your comments and suggestions. The Library of Congress, the National Commission on Libraries and Information Science, the Council on Library Resources, and other groups disseminate their reports widely and encourage comments. I recommend ACRL take steps to ensure that reports from each of these agencies be brought to its members' attention and that reviews be published and comments invited. This association could take a leadership role in ensuring that users of academic libraries are well served.

When this association was founded, the technical support of cooperation was primitive; for example, improved microfilm cameras were described as advancing cooperative efforts. Many of the greatest cooperative ventures then underway were labor intensive, and the labor was frequently a labor of love.

Today advanced technology and networks play a role in helping the association achieve the goals it espoused almost forty years ago. The continuing interaction of academic libraries with other libraries in multi-type library networks can benefit all. Such interaction should also gain additional political support to improve the funding for research and development of improved services to academic library users. Each of you can help shape the direction of local, state, multi-state, and national library network planning.

Richard W. Boss

THE LIBRARY AS AN INFORMATION BROKER

Since the late 1960s research oriented to broad, complex issues has given rise to information brokers, who package, validate, and evaluate data for clients on a cost effective basis. They employ all forms of technology—from the telephone to on-line searching. Such technology is now entering the home through home computers and video. Librarians should familiarize themselves with these new trends, benefit from them through their use, and seek the development of a national information policy.

We are all painfully aware that prices for library materials, labor, and the construction and maintenance of physical facilities are rising dramatically. It isn't necessary to wait for an annual summary issue of *Publishers Weekly* or *Library Journal* to confirm these trends because library administrators are coping with the fiscal and statistical evidence on a daily basis. There are two other trends that are less obvious:

1. The importance of information in our society is increasing:
   — More than 50 percent of the working population is involved in information handling in such information industries as education, broadcasting, telephone, publishing, libraries, and the postal service.[1]
   — The information industries represent expenditures of $1/3 trillion annually.
2. The users of information are approaching their needs differently from before.
   — A recent Arthur D. Little, Inc., study for the National Science Foundation described the changes under the catchy title, *Passing the Threshold into the Information Age.*[2] It portrays three information eras: Era I, that of discipline-oriented research; Era II, that of mission-oriented research; and Era III, that of problem-oriented research.

THREE ERAS

Era I was dominant through World War II and remains very significant even today,

---

Richard W. Boss is a management consultant with Information Systems Consultants, Inc., Boston, Massachusetts.

especially in academic institutions. The attitude might be described as knowledge for knowledge's sake.

Era I information is customarily disseminated through books, journals, and professional meetings. The "invisible college" is also a significant factor. It is the exchange among a limited number of persons in a field through conversation, correspondence, and the exchange of pre-prints. It is possible because the producers and users of information are usually trained in the same discipline.

Information access is often subsidized both at the production end and at the user end, the latter through libraries.

The development of Era II was promoted by the grantsmanship of mission-oriented federal agencies such as NASA and AEC, according to the Arthur D. Little study. It involves the organization of vast resources to accomplish a fairly well defined task.

Era II research involves information from a variety of related disciplines. The service agencies of Era I, such as libraries, are used, but additional sources are tapped. Private systems for repackaging information are characteristic of Era II. Many of these were developed in-house with research grant funds, while others were begun as speculative commercial ventures. Over 3,000 indexing and abstracting services are a major development of Era II.

The "invisible college" is less of a factor in Era II because the producers of information are often in a different discipline than that of the user.

Era III emerged in the late 1960s as society began to grapple with broad, complex issues such as energy, environment, and health. Topics such as these require the use of information from many varied disciplines such as law, economics, engineering, and sociology.

More than ever, decisions must be reached quickly and they must be of high quality. That requires suitable information in usable form.

The Arthur D. Little study for NSF characterized many end users as limited in their skills to cope with information flow and suggested that information can best flow through various expert intermediaries, consultants, and secondary information channels.

The view is justified by the fact that producers and users of information are quite separated. There is no "invisible college."

Users often don't know the vocabularies, biases, and methods of various disciplines. Conflicting information is common. Users need to have information repackaged. They often needed to have it validated and evaluated.

Newsletters, data base publications, and on-line services are common to Era III. On-line services alone now may serve as many as 5,000 customers with more than 100 data bases.

THE INFORMATION BROKERS

Information brokers are a phenomenon of Era III. They are individuals or firms who search out and organize information for users. The principal concern is to be of value to the client whether within the same parent organization or outside it. They locate and interpret information in light of the problem the client seeks to solve.

Until the late 1960s, according to the study, the distributors of information have generally tended to be within an organization and have operated almost as "servants." In contrast, information brokers of the 1970s are using a business venture approach, billing even within a parent organization.

There are, of course, counterparts in academe and government. The NASA sponsored information access centers in universities are an example.

Brokers may provide highly specific information. They may or may not validate or evaluate the information. The trend appears to be toward validation (by information search services) and evaluation (by consulting services).

Brokers may undertake broad research questions. This is often sought by clients to overcome the lack of standardization of access mechanisms—vocabularies, index terms, formats, computer file structures, languages, protocols, etc.

Another reason for validation and evaluation is that much conflicting information is found when one is dealing with problem-oriented research.

There are at least seventy-five for-profit information search or brokerage firms in the United States. Information brokerage costs from $20 to $75 per hour, with $40 the most common figure quoted by persons contacted recently. The complexity of the research accounts for the range, rather than arbitrary pricing practices.

Who is buying such services? Not those the pioneers in the field first approached. The founders of Warner-Eddison in Cambridge thought they would be serving small companies without libraries, but they have discovered that large companies and government agencies are the principal clients, not only for searching but also for information management—including the creation of special subject headings and indexes to meet special needs.

Other information brokers have reported that they serve marketing departments of corporations or market research organizations. The Congressional Research Service has developed into an information broker for Congress. Citizens groups and planning organizations buy such services as do the regulatory agencies of state and national government.

The users have the resources. There are undoubtedly many more who would use these services were the agencies of Era I or Era II to offer them without charge. The unanswered question is, does it take more money to offer Era III services or is it a matter of allocation of resources? A closer examination of the actual practices of information brokers is warranted. I have visited several and have the following impressions:

TECHNIQUES OF THE BROKER

The emphasis on information as a commodity with monetary value and the need to satisfy clients with cost-effective service make the information brokers very conscious of the costs of accessing information and alert to altenative ways of gathering information.

I was struck by the emphasis on the use of the telephone to gather or validate information. I was told repeatedly that experts in a field are flattered to be sought out for help. When I raised the objection that wide-spread reliance on this technique of information gathering would jeopardize its success, the response was "then we'll pay them for their response." There is no question, but that timely information can best be gotten in this way—and at a very low price.

USE OF TECHNOLOGY

The use of technology is widespread, with the computer terminal for access to on-line data bases almost universal. When I inquired about cost effectiveness, several referred me to Dennis R. Elchesen's recent article: "Cost-Effectiveness Comparison of Manual and On-Line Retrospective Bibliographic Searching."[3] Let me summarize from that article.

On-Line Searching

Over one million on-line retrospective searches were performed in the United States and Canada in 1977, according to Martha Williams. Over 800 organizations now use such searching, of whom 600 use both manual and on-line. (On-line vendors estimate over 2.5 million searches in 1978.)

The current study employs cost-effectiveness analysis—to learn which search mode is generally faster, less costly, and more effective in scientific and technical organizations.

The study was to find which search mode was more effective in handling broad queries, narrow queries, phrase searches, free-text searches, and searches that aim at high recall or high precision.

The study attempted to account for all components of the total cost: labor, information, reproduction, equipment, space, and telecommunications.

The searches were done by members of the Lawrence Livermore Laboratory Research Information Group at the University of California, Livermore. A supervisor selected manual and on-line searchers of comparable subject expertise and searching experience and gave each an identical description of the search topic. The supervisor also chose the information sources to be used. Forty topics were selected.

On the average, five on-line searches may be conducted in the same amount of time required to perform a single manual search. For both search modes, the most time-consuming task was searching itself.

The mean composite cost of a manual search was somewhat higher than the corresponding on-line search.

On-line searching becomes more economical than manual searching as searcher skill increases.

For manual searches the most expensive areas were searcher labor and information. For the on-line searching the most costly component was information, with the cost of searcher labor and reproduction divided almost equally.

The cost of on-line retrospective searching is decreasing.

On the average, the on-line searches retrieved more citations per search than the manual searches, although wide variations were observed among the data bases.

For manual searches, all citations retrieved were considered relevant since the searchers made their own relevancy judgments during the searches. In the case of on-line searches, relevancy was usually determined after receipt of the print-out hence a relevance rate of 84 percent.

The average cost per relevant citation retrieved manually was 86 cents, compared to 65 cents for the on-line mode.

On-line searching is generally more effective than manual searching for both broad and narrow topics. There are some other studies in this area with contradictory results, however.

Certain extremely general or extremely specific searches are best supplemented by the use of printed tools and personal contacts.

The Future for On-Line Systems

The time and cost advantages now enjoyed by on-line system users are likely to grow in the future. Recent studies by Arthur D. Little, Inc., indicate that by 1983 costs for central processing will be less than half of today's, communication costs will have decreased by two-thirds, and the cost of an intelligent CRT terminal will have decreased by 80 percent. They further predict that in the 1980s it will be cheaper to store information in random access memory than to print, distribute, and store hard copy publications.

Technology in the Home

There also appears to be a high level of awareness that home computers and home video may change the way people will access information in the future.

Entertainment technology is a higher priority for the television industry at this time than information technology, but it is reasonable to assume that home computers and home video will be adapted to other than entertainment applications. Makers of home computers have already augmented their offerings of games with programs for home bookkeeping and the teaching of mathematics and spelling to children. Videocassette rentals of educational materials are increasing rapidly.

The mass market for entertainment can support home systems costing thousands of dollars and software that costs from $40 to $400 per hour of programming. The information market will probably not mature until a moderately priced keyboard terminal can be attached to any television set and the videocassette is augmented with the lower cost videodisc.

Videodisc technology is of particularly great interest to those with whom I spoke even though the first marketing is not to be undertaken until December 1978. At that time North American Philips and MCA are to introduce a player and a catalog of more than 200 entertainment programs. The cost of producing a single disc when several hundred thousands are stamped from a master is less than $1.50. The total production cost is less than six dollars when at least 2,500 copies are made. The cost of producing fifty copies would be less than forty dollars each, still much less than the least expensive videotape.

More than 54,000 images can be stored on a single side of a disc. The use of both sides gives 108,000 still images or one hour of playing time for a program taken from film or videotape. Slides, photographs, and the printed page can also be stored on videodisc.

MCA has already entered the industrial market with Universal Pioneer of Japan. The MCA 7280 Video Disk Viewer is already being sold selectively. The CIA has bought at least thirty units and has acquired pictorial data on disc through MCA.

It is clear that it is possible to produce entire libraries at very small cost, thus further adding to the resources of the information broker. The greatest hurdle is probably that of copyright. Several of those with whom I spoke are convinced that payment for use, rather than payment for acquisition of information, is the key to the resolution of this issue.

RISK AND UNCERTAINTY

There seems to be a willingness to deal with risks. The field is still small, and the presence of so many independent-minded entrepreneurial types may be only a temporary phenomenon.

I got into a very interesting conversation with one person about the difference between uncertainty and risk. We agreed that uncertainty is the situation in which there are many possible outcomes, but we neither know them all, nor do we know the probabilities of the outcomes of which we are aware. Risk, on the other hand, is measurable uncertainty. We know the possible outcomes because we have researched them and we make a careful estimate of the probabilities of each. We just don't know what will happen in a specific case. It is the willingness to move forward in the face of this risk that is a key to the success of the information brokers to whom I talked.

Allow me a tangent: I think most of us don't take as many risks as we might because as R. Kent Wood says: "In our society we are conditioned to avoid more than casual mention of failure, let alone set about to analyze it. . . ."[4] In reality we should analyze possible modes of failure in our systems for the very positive reason of increasing the probability of success.

A RESPONSE BY LIBRARIANS

Information brokers have developed techniques and attitudes to meet the needs of the Era III user. They have created a new growth industry. I believe librarians can and should increase their awareness of future trends by visiting one or more such organizations in their areas.

I believe libraries should move away from a book and journal orientation to an information needs of users orientation, with information stored and accessed economically utilizing the new technologies.

I am not saying they should become information brokers for all of their users, because there are Era I, Era II, and Era III users. But the Era III users should be served. I am painfully aware that the addition of new demands does not mean a diminution of the old demands. The old demands remain and continue to grow. One of the advantages enjoyed by the for-profit information brokers I have described is that they can select a segment of the market at which to direct their services. Not many academic libraries have that option.

Librarians can't accomplish major changes in their respective libraries by just reallocating resources. There are too many faculty and staff who will seek to protect the library materials and personnel budgets against any reallocation to something untried. Publishers may protect their interests in the traditional methods of book and journal publishing. Major federal funding agencies and foundations are committed to basic and applied research and opposed to funding research applications, even though the diffusion rate of sponsored research is one of our major problems.

What is needed is a national information policy to increase awareness, provide forums for different sectors of the information system to come together, and stimulate a reshaping of foundation and federal agency attitudes about the funding of research applications.

Librarians should seek the development of such a policy by approaching the legislative and executive branches of government through their professional organizations.

Can librarians do this alone? No. There are too many vested interests and the various components of the information industry are too interdependent. The suggestion of a national library board advanced in the recently published Council on Library Resources technical development plan for a national periodical center has already drawn the ire of the publishing and information industries.

Can information brokers do it alone? No, and they don't think they can. They have already decided that what is needed is a national information policy. In May 1977 the board of directors of the Information Industry Association decided to draw up a position paper setting forth the industry's viewpoint on such a national information policy.

Can a single national agency do it? No. The National Science Foundation, an agency that funded 90 percent of the federally supported information science research in this country in 1976, has had such a recommendation from task forces, consultants, and staff for more than two decades, but no such policy statement has been forthcoming.

What is needed is a joint planning effort among the various components. Information transfer has been a low priority for national attention because the components of the system have been fragmented. Conflict resolution can best be undertaken with the various interests around the same table. We all exist to serve the end users of information.

REFERENCES

1. Harvard University, Program on Information Resource Policy, *Information Resources, Arenas, Players, and Stakes.* Annual Report, 1965–1976.
2. Reprinted, in abbreviated form, as *Into the Information Age: A Perspective for Federal Action on Information* (Chicago: American Library Assn., 1979).
3. Dennis R. Elchesen, "Cost-Effectiveness Comparison of Manual and On-Line Retrospective Bibliographic Searching," *Journal of the American Society for Information Science* 29:56–66 (March 1978).
4. R. Kent Wood, "Success is Easy When You Know How to Fail," *Audiovisual Instruction* 23:22 (Oct. 1978).

Jay K. Lucker

LIBRARY RESOURCES AND BIBLIOGRAPHIC CONTROL

The future of academic libraries is discussed from the perspective of their resources and bibliographic control. Emphasis is focused on collection philosophy, book selection, the collection itself, resource sharing, adequacy of library space, preservation, new cataloging rules, a national bibliographic data base, and subject access. To provide a better forum for discussion of these matters and to assist in the solution of related problems, the author sees the need for a national library agency.

I have long maintained the view that the human mind, or at least my own, is capable of dealing with only a limited number of problems at any given time. In other words, I can cope with a relatively small number of major concerns with any hope of success.

Now I am not talking about the relatively unimportant matters that might concern me: the future of mankind, the possibility of nuclear war, pollution of the environment, alternate energy sources, and the like, nor the more personal issues such as whether or not I will ever be able to grow a decent lawn, or whether I should buy a snow blower, or whether it is possible to own a car that does not own you.

I can handle all of these, mostly by not thinking too long about them. My limitation on worrying is principally connected with my professional life. A few months ago I was asked by an old friend in the library education field to list the ten most important concerns that face me as an academic librarian today. After some cogitating, I began to compile the list. You will not be surprised, I am sure, to hear that the list contained the following, in no particular order of priority: financial support, cooperative activities, personnel issues and staff development, bibliographic control, automation and the new technology, space, educating library users, governance and management, access to new forms of information, preservation, and collection development.

Most of you will quickly recognize that my list of concerns contains eleven rather than ten elements. Actually, the only significance that has is that I stopped listing topics because I realized I had reached the limit of my worrying capacity not because I had run out of ideas. A list of major concerns could well be twice the size of the above or, given

Jay K. Lucker is director of libraries, Massachusetts Institute of Technology, Cambridge, Massachusetts.

the marvelous capacity of the human intellect to create problems even where they do not exist, even greater. Fortunately, my assignment for this conference is to discuss only a subset of the list I generated, but I shall try to do that in the perspective of the future of academic libraries in general.

The future of collections in academic libraries and the concomitant question of bibliographic access to these resources is by no means clear. What is apparent, to me at least, is that present trends cannot continue indefinitely. Present trends mean continued inflation in the cost of acquiring and processing materials; reduced financial support for libraries of all types; limitations on size, expandibility and flexibility of the buildings in which we house our collections; the physical deterioration of books, manuscripts, and other information sources; and the apparent lack of coordinated, cooperative planning to attack these problems.

I certainly do not mean to imply that nothing has been done; what I do believe is that much more needs to be done by individual libraries and librarians, by professional organizations, and by government at all levels. We are spending more and buying less, we are cataloging more and finding less, we are cooperating more but with limited results.

It would be presumptuous for me to suggest I have the complete answers for even some of these questions, but perhaps I can offer a few insights into how we might begin to attack them. Predicting the future is both hard and easy. It is hard for the obvious reason that there are many more unknowns than certainties. It is easy because we, or at least I, will probably not be around when the time comes that proves I was wrong. With these caveats behind me, let me try to anticipate what I think will be happening in academic libraries in the areas of resources and bibliographic control.

I recognize that this conference attempts to respond to the concerns of academic librarians from all types of institutions: public and private; research libraries, college libraries, community college libraries; small specialized collections and large general ones. I also realize that no set of principles, no formulas, no prescriptions for how to do it or how not to do it will work for everyone. The best I hope for today is that I can provide some ideas, some stimulation for further thought, some provocation—that is what I shall try to do at any rate.

LIBRARY RESOURCES

In the beginning there is book selection. Or is that the beginning? Flow charts of technical processes operations usually begin with selection and acquisition, but I believe collection development starts much earlier with the establishment of a collection philosophy. In my view, academic library collections of the future will be more specifically developed around a particular set of institutional needs.

Except for the largest research collections, buying for speculative or anticipated needs will inevitably be greatly reduced. This is a function both of financial necessity and accountability. Most of us do not have nor will we ever again have the resources to buy most or even a part of what our patrons might need. We will have to do a much better job of defining and obtaining what they will need.

A Collection Philosophy

Establishing an overall collection philosophy requires a number of steps. Certainly the first is to identify the institutional objectives that the library or learning resources center is supporting. What are the instructional, research, and extra-curricular programs that require information resources? What are the levels of needs of each of them and what are the institutional priorities?

In the past, most of us have not had to face the situation where programs are curtailed or cancelled. Conversely, many have had to face the question of how to deal with new programs and new courses, new research interests, new centers, and, perhaps most commonly, new faculty, usually with the same total acquisition budget.

In the light of projections regarding student enrollment in the next decade and in the absence of a massive infusion of additional support for libraries, I am willing to predict that many more of us will be required to adjust library acquisition programs to a smaller set of institutional programs. It is essential, therefore, to identify in collection development terms not only the individual programs being supported, whether they be departments, schools, centers, or the like, but also the amount of resources assigned to each.

I would also suggest that the kind of gross allocation of funds, traditionally by academic department, that we have been using up to now will be inadequate for future planning. Think if you will of a number of not so hypothetical cases.

One, a college or university decides to discontinue a graduate program but to maintain an undergraduate major in that field.

Two, an institution decides to drop an undergraduate major but to maintain a small number of service courses.

Three, a school decides to suspend a program, but with the strong possibility that it may be revived in the future.

How do we as librarians respond? In order to be able to act effectively in response to changes in institutional directions, we must define our collection policies in terms of overall goals and objectives and also be able to identify resources accruing to specific programs.

Let me relate two specific cases.

About ten years ago, MIT decided to eliminate its program in mining engineering, a field in which it had been intensely involved for many years. Aware of this change, the libraries decelerated the acquisition program primarily as a result of fewer requests for new books and journals from the faculty and research staff and, of course, as a result of reduced needs for course-related materials. Today, with a renewed national interest in alternate sources of energy, including coal, we are back in the mineral resources business. The problems are several: What shall we buy to support the new program, what did we miss in the past ten years that we will need for the present and future, and most important, what will this all cost?

At Princeton, in the early 1970s, a decision was made to discontinue the graduate program in Slavic languages and literatures. The undergraduate program, however, was to continue, but on a reduced basis. How, we were asked, will the library respond? How much money can be saved? While we knew the total cost of materials in this field, it was extremely difficult to identify that portion accruing to the graduate program. The situation was compounded by the fact that graduate programs in Russian history, economics, and political science were continuing. Without going into details, I can report that in both these situations, decisions were made with less than the optimal amount of information.

I think we need better methods for accounting for library expenditures not only for the reasons given above but in the event of more salutary changes. When new programs are established, when new centers are built, and when new faculty are hired, libraries should be able to respond rapidly and accurately with what perhaps might best be described as environmental impact statements.

If we are going to be more responsive to institutional needs, and I believe we have to be, librarians must be more systematic in allocating resources among competing needs. I recognize that this process in many instances may involve others including faculty and administrators, but I am sure you will agree that it is our responsibility to take a leadership position.

While intuition, tradition, persuasion, and collective action may have been and may continue to be ingredients in the allocation process, quantitative information is essential. We should certainly not become slaves to our victims of formula budgeting, but we do need hard data to support our recommendations and to enable us to compete for the institutional dollar.

Enrollments, size and composition of faculty, research interests and programs, and information on publishing trends and costs should all be part of the allocation process. Data on collection use should be assembled and fed back into the allocation process. We should view this process as a positive and productive means for ensuring equitable utilization of resources, not as a defense against discontent.

Book Selection

Book selection is an imperfect science at best, if it is a science at all. I firmly believe that book selection belongs in the first instance in the hands of those who should know the most about it—the professional librarians. I also believe it cannot be done in a vacuum. Only with maximum information on institutional needs, on faculty and student interests, and on the use of existing collections can we select new books and serials for our libraries.

Developing knowledge about what we need requires that librarians become intimately involved in the educational process. Serving on faculty and administration committees, answering reference questions, providing formal and informal instruction; in total becoming an integral, dynamic, functioning member of the academic community is the best way of becoming an effective selector. Academic libraries need to have more staff involved in the selection process, and we need to develop a high level of subject competence among as many of them as possible. Faculty and student input is necessary and it is good, but as we all know it is uneven, often provincial, and frequently unreliable.

The importance of evaluative mechanisms in book selection cannot be overlooked. As we continue to be faced with the necessity for making harder and more complicated decisions about what to buy and what not to buy, we need all the help we can get. The availability of critical and authoritative reviews not only for books and serials but for large microform sets, films, videotapes, records, cassettes, maps, and other publications is not only desirable, it is essential, and we, as librarians, must be an integral part of the process.

Sharing resources, in my view, means not only physical resources but intellectual ones as well. Let me go one step further. I think librarians ought to take a more aggressive role in identifying what needs to be published as well as reacting after the fact to what has been published. I would urge a stronger partnership between the library profession and the publishing community for the benefit of both.

Library Collections

What of library collections themselves? What will they look like in the next decade and beyond? For the immediate future, I do not foresee any revolutionary changes in academic library collections. I do see a continuation of a number of trends that have occurred during the recent past. We will continue to buy books, and they will be the principal means by which we collect information. Except for large research libraries, we will be buying mostly new books and few older ones.

Libraries having to acquire retrospective materials will be relying much more on microforms than in the past not only because of cost but also because of space limitations. I assume in connection with microforms that the quality and diversity of reading and reproducing equipment will improve, and the unit price of such equipment will decrease. Original publication in microform will continue to expand. The dominance of this medium that has occurred with theses and technical reports and is now extending to U.S. government documents will in all probability have a substantial impact on publishing of state and local documents, legal materials, and, perhaps of greatest potential, serials.

Resource Sharing

If anything produces a crack in my already clouded crystal ball it is when I start thinking about the potential impact of resource sharing on collection development. Nothing I know of holds such great potential for academic libraries, yet nothing is so full of complications and pitfalls.

Let me start out by saying what I think resource sharing is not. It is not a substitute for collection development in individual libraries. Each of us has the responsibility to do everything possible to provide as much information in our own libraries as is feasible for the present and anticipated needs of our primary constituency.

It is clear, of course, that we cannot provide everything that our users need or may need, and it has become apparent in the light of present financial trends, inflation, and the steady increase in the total amount of information published, that the percentage of that elusive "everything" is steadily decreasing. Defining what is a reasonable level of local fulfillment of needs is both necessary and difficult. Most faculty members would, I am sure, be quite willing for their institutions's library to establish a goal of less than 100 percent as long as it is for someone else's discipline.

Leaving the obvious aside for the moment, however, I would suggest that this can be done in an approximate if not absolute manner. As part of the Collection Analysis Project undertaken at MIT last year and continuing through the present, we are attempting to establish levels of collection comprehensiveness for more than seventy-five subject areas.

While we will start with the general categories familiar to all of you—comprehensive, research, etc.—I expect we shall be able in the end to be considerably more precise. The ability to define these levels in a qualitative as well as quantitative manner will be extremely valuable as we enter into bilateral and multilateral resource sharing arrangements.

The second thing resource sharing is not—and I am really speaking here to our administrators—is a means of cutting library budgets. It should, however, enable us to be more effective with the funds we have. The ideal resource sharing arrangement would permit a library to cancel subscriptions to less used journals and not to order certain monographs, releasing those funds for more substantial development of fields where there is strong local interest.

Resource sharing is not a one way street. There must be identifiable and visible benefits to all participants. Libraries should cooperate in areas and at levels where there is the potentiality of reciprocity. This argues for sharing within disciplines rather than among disciplines. Each library engaged in a resource sharing arrangement should undertake to supply the basic needs of its own user community.

The sharing takes place when the cooperators can agree to apportion acquisitions above that basic level with each taking responsibility for a portion of the subject field. This guarantees borrowing in both directions and avoids imbalance. It also promotes understanding among all users and avoids a situation where faculty and students in a subject field see only a one way flow.

Finally, resource sharing is not a panacea for all that ails our collections. We still have to battle for more resources and we still have to be able to justify our acquisitions decisions. Resource sharing is an adjunct to collection development, essential for the long-term survival of academic libraries, but even in its most ideal form, one of several means for improving service to users.

Resource sharing begins at home, or at least it should on multilibrary campuses. While it is perhaps erroneous to speak of intralibrary loans and intralibrary cooperation, this is no small problem in many academic institutions. I have often thought that if there were some horrible catastrophe and only two scholars were left in the world, each would want a departmental library.

Let me assure you: I do not propose to sermonize about the pros and cons of departmental libraries. As a matter of fact, I support the concept both theoretically and pragmatically. I do believe, however, that we must find ways to insure that our dispersed collections are based on sound philosophies of collection development and that we implement this through coordinated collection development. This is no mean feat given the growth and complexity of interdisciplinary studies and the fuzzing of traditional departmental scholarly lines.

How, then, can resource sharing be used as a positive force in collection building? In the case of research libraries, there are many examples of bilateral and multilateral cooperation. I would include as examples the Center for Research Libraries, the Research Libraries Group, the National Program for Cataloging and Acquisitions, and the Farmington Plan, as well as a number of compacts involving two or three institutions.

In looking ahead, I anticipate that the number and diversity of such programs can only increase and that they will involve more libraries and many libraries not presently involved in these ventures. The prospect of a national periodicals center or national periodicals system could have a tremendous impact on every academic library in this country, and I will have more to say about this program shortly.

First, however, let me move away from research libraries and national programs and talk about the link between collections and cooperation in the arenas of smaller academic libraries—those of two- and four-year undergraduate institutions. None of us needs to be reminded of the great progress that has been made in resource sharing through the advent of cooperative cataloging networks like OCLC, WLN, BALLOTS, and others with which we are familiar.

The availability of holdings information in these data bases has had a remarkable effect on load leveling of interlibrary lending. As the administrator of a library that fits into the category of "net lender," I applaud and welcome this shift. I am delighted to know that the flow of materials among smaller academic and public libraries has increased dramatically, and I am equally pleased that the larger research libraries are able, as never before, to call upon some of these same institutions.

I would argue, however, that the impact of cataloging networks on collection development has been minimal. The reason for this is, in my view, that we have been only passive users of the capability available to us. Given the challenge of diminishing local resources, we shall have to be more aggressive, or surely we will not succeed. I have no illusions, however, of the inherent difficulty in such a philosophy.

Cooperation in collection development is extremely problematical in the absence of institutional compacts. In order for two libraries, any two libraries, to undertake a program that calls for the delegation of acquisition responsibility, there ought to be some agreement between the schools they serve. I think we will not see a major shift in collection development practice until there is a change in the way that colleges and universities establish and disestablish teaching and research programs.

Pessimistic as this must seem to all of you, experience has indicated to me at least that this is the case. Let me provide an example.

The libraries of Brown University and Massachusetts Institute of Technology are engaged today in trying to develop guidelines for cooperative acquisitions in one or more subject areas. We know already that we will have to find such areas among the disciplines in which both institutions are deeply involved. Let us suppose that we find some subjects or parts of subjects that qualify. Let us suppose further that we can actually identify a body of information that because of various factors—language, cost, and, principally, patterns of past use—would qualify as being needed in only one of the two libraries. Let us assume further that we can agree as to which library will buy what serials and monographs.

The key question still remains: Can we proceed without some sort of cooperative agreement between the two parent institutions? I wish I could tell you that I have an answer to this question. I do not. All I can say right now is that we are going to do the best we can with what we have and what we know. I can also say that I am doing everything I can within my own university to link cooperative programs to library collection development.

The above notwithstanding, I do think a great deal has been accomplished with regard to cooperative collection development. Many libraries are involved in networks where union lists of serials are used not only for interlibrary loan but also for acquisition decisions. Groups of libraries have gotten together to share the acquisition of large sets or expensive materials. Libraries are beginning to think about cooperative retention of serials and older monographic material. We are also talking about working jointly in connection with preservation.

My personal view is that in the long run these programs may have a greater impact on library budgets and may be a more practical way of shared collection development than attempting to develop agreements on acquisition policy where colleges and universities continue to try to teach everything to everyone.

A National Periodicals Center

If you have not already read the report of the Council on Library Resources on a national periodicals center, I commend it to you. If you have read it, I will not attempt to summarize its contents; but I would like to reflect a moment on why I think this program is important and, yes, essential, for college and university libraries. Periodical subscriptions continue to take a bigger and bigger bite out of our acquisition budgets. We have to add substantial sums of money merely to keep up with current subscriptions while the number of new titles appearing each year continues to haunt us. Where will it all end? Not, I hope, with the collapse of libraries as we know them, and not, I am sure, with the demise of the publishing industry.

A national periodicals center is a viable answer to this problem. It would, if established, provide, in the words of the CLR report, "an efficient, reliable, and responsive document delivery system for periodical literature." More important for us, such a center would enable individual libraries to make more effective decisions on binding and preservation of existing collections and on the acquisition of titles not currently held.

The center would also promote local and regional resource sharing arrangements for the periodical literature. Individual library decisions on the acquisition of titles would still be made on the basis of local needs, but the impact on binding and microfilming budgets of such an operation could be substantial.

Beyond its immediate impact on individual library development, a national periodicals center as envisioned in the CLR report could have some additional effects on the future of academic library collections.

First of all, the center could have an influence on the actual publication of periodical articles. Two possibilities are provided in the report: One would be the publishing of abstracts or synopses with an article distribution service; the second, the possibility of on-demand publishing. Implicit in this type of operation and in the rest of the recommendations made in the report is that publishers' rights and interests will have to be protected not only in terms of copyright but with regard to economics. Think, if you will, however, of what on-demand publishing might mean in terms of space requirements and binding budgets. Think also of how much more information could be acquired under such a system.

The second exciting possibility that the national periodicals center offers is that it might be a prototype of similar centers for other types of material. Collections of monographs, state and federal documents, microforms, and technical reports appear to be possible candidates. This is not a paid or even unpaid endorsement of the CLR report on my part. I do think, however, that it behooves us as responsible members of the library community to read it, to discuss it, and to respond.

Interlibrary Loan

Before leaving the subject of resource sharing and the future of collection development, I would like to speak briefly about a matter of more immediate concern. As most of you know, the National Interlibrary Loan Code, last revised in 1968, is being reviewed by a committee of the American Library Association. A great deal has happened in the library world since 1968 that justifies a major expenditure of effort in proposing changes in the code: the rise and growth of library networks, the use of telecommunications and computer technology in the lending process, and a new copyright law, to mention only the most significant.

In addition, a number of other questions arise in any discussion of interlibrary loan. To what extent should interlibrary lending at the national level take into account the needs of undergraduates as well as the needs of the non-university connected researcher? How can we strike a balance between resource sharing and the need to serve our primary constituency? How can the code promote the development and use of interlibrary lending at the level of local and regional consortia? Is the scope of materials as defined under the code too narrow? Or is it too broad? Is the concept of "in print materials of moderate cost" obsolete? What about the lending of genealogical materials?

The new code should, of course, reflect the requirements of the new copyright law and should, in addition, cover a wider range of materials than before such as films videotapes, and audio transcriptions. As a member of the committee responsible for drafting a revised code I can tell you that all these questions and many more concern me and we will try to develop responses to as many of them as possible.

Some of you who are involved in interlibrary loan have already been contacted for suggestions and comments about the code. I want to use this opportunity to extend an invitation to any of you who have not been contacted to date and who have ideas as to how a revised interlibrary loan code might improve the sharing of resources, to write to me at the MIT Libraries. I will not promise that we will adopt all of your suggestions, for I have seen already that there is a wide range of views, even among ARL interlibrary loan librarians, on some of the issues described above, but I will see that they are all considered by the committee.

SPACE AND LIBRARY RESOURCES

In looking back at my original list of concerns, I see two other topics that I would like to relate to the matter at hand—the future of library resources. The first is space. No one would deny that space is a resource, and I can tell you from recent experience that it may be a more valuable resource than money, particularly on an urban campus.

If some of the library directors in the audience are not worrying about their buildings, it is either because they are among that ever-diminishing group who have managed to convince their administrations that a new building or a major renovation or expansion has a higher priority than other pressing needs or because they have given up all hope.

It seems to me that it has been and will continue to be increasingly difficult to justify and support indefinite expansion of academic library buildings. This is not to say that many of our facilities are not outmoded, overcrowded, and inefficient. It is also not to say that, in some cases, new buildings or renovations are necessary. I am concerned, however, that the supply of capital funds for library buildings is limited.

Despite all the inhibiting factors that we have noted for years, library collections continue to grow. They are growing, in many cases, at a slower rate than in the glorious sixties, but growing nonetheless. I do not know if I have a universal solution for this problem, but let me for a few minutes share some personal views about what might be the way to approach the next few decades.

Collection Size vs. Collection Use

Painful as it may be, we must recognize that not everything in our collections is used to the same extent. Some books are used heavily when first acquired and seldom thereafter. Some books are not even used when first acquired, but I think we are doing a better job in book selection and are becoming less vulnerable to criticism in this area.

Now I am not talking here about the very large research collections that build for the future as well as for the present, but even such libraries are becoming more cognizant of the need to relate current acquisitions programs to current teaching and research. For the majority of libraries represented at this conference, however, the problem of collection size versus collection use is a real one. It does seem to me that there are positive prospects on the horizon to help us face this situation.

A national periodicals center could have significant impact on the size of academic collections by enabling libraries to discard or transfer files of seldom used back files of journals.

As a corollary, I envision the growth in number and importance of regional depositories of serial collections. While it is only in the thinking stage at present, I can tell you that there is some possibility of such a facility being established for the Boston Library Consortium. This prospect, however, is not without its difficulties. Among the obstacles to such an arrangement are questions of ownership, institutional prestige, access and delivery, and relation to other regional and national programs.

On-Campus Storage

Another approach we are taking at MIT is the establishment of an on-campus resource sharing center. While similar in many ways to storage facilities already in existence at other universities, our approach to this concept does have some unique features. To begin with, we are going to develop our facility in two stages.

The first, with support from the Booth-Ferris Foundation, will be to set up a model facility in a smaller building where we will endeavor to develop policies and procedures and to set up operations in a laboratory mode, thus enabling us to make changes without causing perturbations in a large system. The MIT Resource Sharing Center will be on the campus, fully accessible to users, but with the emphasis on quick delivery. We envisage a facility that will handle the increase in our collections for from fifteen to twenty years with the view that during that time the effects of such things as the national periodicals center, new forms of publication, and technological advances might provide an even longer-range capacity to handle the growth of the libraries. The possibility of local and regional cooperation in storage of older materials is another factor that could increase the time before this building becomes full.

Space and Resource Sharing

If space is at such a premium, why haven't we done more to cooperate in the sharing of older resources? The answers are complex, and it is perhaps unnecessary to dwell on the past. I do believe we must begin thinking more imaginatively about this matter, and, to me, the "we" means all of us.

One avenue that appeals to me is to discard any preconceived notions about cooperating only among libraries of the same type. I wonder if we would not serve ourselves and our users more effectively if we started thinking about sharing space among libraries of many types—public, school, academic, and special. Is there not some value in a partnership of all kinds of libraries, joined together with the common goal of sharing?

Would not special libraries be willing to support a local or regional storage facility that would provide back files of serials and older monographs? Are there not city councils or library boards who could be convinced of the economics of supporting a regional resource sharing center that would have the effect of inhibiting the physical growth of local public libraries? Surely state libraries and library agencies have a major stake in seeing that public funds are used for collection development and improved library service rather than for the housing of copies of little used and redundant material.

The coordination of local and regional centers with national resources like the national periodicals system could conceivably provide a solution to the long-range space needs of academic and non-academic libraries.

PRESERVATION

A second topic I should like to mention briefly is that of preservation. We are faced today with the specter of accelerating deterioration of our collections, many of them representing unique materials.

It is obvious that there is not enough money available for all libraries to preserve even a major portion of their collections. If we are to preserve the record of the past, we are going to have to do this collectively. I feel strongly that the time for a national program for preservation of library materials is now.

This program should include the identification of those collections or portions of collections that represent a national resource. The program should be coordinated with national centers like the Library of Congress and the national periodicals center. Training programs for library staffs and research in the scientific and technical aspects of preservation should be supported and funded.

I would be remiss at this point if I did not recognize the tremendous support that libraries and archives have received in recent years from the National Endowment for the

Humanities and the National Historical Publications and Records Commission. Much more remains to be done and we academic librarians must take a major role in this area.

BIBLIOGRAPHIC CONTROL

We are entering a period of great change and considerable uncertainty in terms of the future of bibliographic control in academic libraries.

AACR 2

There is certainly no one at this conference who is unaware of the significance of the date January 1, 1981. It is almost as certain that most of us are relieved that that date has recently been changed from January 1, 1980.

In either case, however, the impact of the decision of the Library of Congress to close its catalogs and to adopt the second edition of the *Anglo-American Cataloguing Rules* (AACR 2) will be far-reaching, expensive, and complicated. The very fact that the date of this conversion was delayed after a meeting of representatives of major library organizations with the Library of Congress is in itself significant and worthy of comment. I do not propose to dwell here on the arguments for or against delaying the implementation of AACR 2. The decision has been made and I, for one, welcome the additional time available to develop plans to cope with the change.

What is important to me is that the manner in which the library profession approached the question indicates the need for a higher level of coordination of bibliographic control on a national basis. There is at present no organization, no agency, indeed no mechanism for the consideration of questions like AACR 2 that brings together all the concerned parties.

For this reason alone, but also for the reasons I have stated earlier, the prospect of a national library agency as envisioned in the CLR report on a periodicals system holds a great deal of attraction for me. Had we had such an organism in place last summer, I believe the difficulties encountered in considering the time frame for AACR 2 and concomitant problems would have been avoided or at least lessened.

A national library agency could also provide an umbrella for research, planning, and developing of such activities as a national bibliographic data base, national programs for cooperative collection development, a national preservation program, resource sharing, and regionalization.

Leaving the events of the past few months behind us, we must still face the inevitable. AACR 2 will be upon us in a little more than two years. Libraries will have to decide, and soon, whether they will close their card catalogs and start new ones, whether they will try to integrate cataloging produced under the new rules with those produced under AACR 1, or whether they will establish new bibliographic apparatus like on-line catalogs, COM catalogs, or some combination thereof.

I am not an authority or even a knowledgeable amateur in this complex and intriguing field. Unraveling the intricacies of cataloging rules requires experience and knowledge that only years of working with them provides.

On the other hand, there are going to be shock waves resulting from these momentous changes that will have impact on other facets of library operations beyond technical services. From personal experience I cannot emphasize too strongly the necessity for close cooperation within academic libraries to meet the challenge.

It is important for library directors to become as aware as possible of the financial and political implications of the impending changes. Reference and information service specialists must be intimately involved in the planning and implementation of these changes not only because they will have to interpret them for the library's public and teach patrons how to work with a whole new set of access principles, but, more important, because these staff members know, as well as anyone can know, how users approach and interact with the bibliographic tools available.

A National Bibliographic Data Base

Beyond the immediate prospect, or some might say, specter, of AACR 2, however, lies another goal: the potentiality of a national bibliographic data base.

The principle embodied here is not very complex; the planning and implementation certainly are. What is being proposed by the Association of Research Libraries in close cooperation and consultation with the Library of Congress is a system of decentralized input to a national bibliographic data base under a set of carefully conceived and well developed rules with the objective of sharing responsibility for providing original cataloging information and offering access throughout the country to a wider range of library materials.

In some ways this program might be visualized as a Farmington Plan for cataloging. Individual research libraries would accept responsibility for inputting records in subject areas or languages for titles not already in the MARC data base. They would necessarily have to agree to a set of cataloging standards that cover not only individual descriptive elements but also the general framework of the data base.

At present, the plan calls for a group of six sets of standards that would be applied to all records entered by cooperating libraries. For overall descriptive cataloging, AACR 1 would apply to original cataloging prior to 1981 and AACR 2 after 1981.

While a single classification system is not prescribed, numbers would have to follow standards set by the Library of Congress for the LC and DDC classifications, by the National Library of Medicine, or by the National Library of Agriculture. Subject headings input at the national level would likewise have to be consistent with Library of Congress subject headings, the Medical Subject Headings (MESH), or the NAL subject headings.

The appropriate fields in the machine-readable record format would have to follow the national standards, but libraries could also include subject headings from other systems such as Sears as long as the records were tagged accordingly. Name headings following the LC form or a national authority system assuming such were developed are the fourth standard. Anticipating an authority system for series headings, this would be the fifth element. The final mechanism for insuring consistency is the MARC format for machine-readable records.

It is obvious that the concept of a national bibliographic data base is not only extremely complicated but also requires a tremendous amount of coordination and planning. We should all be heartened to know that the Council on Library Resources has received financial commitments from various sources to work on establishing the machinery and begin putting together all the elements required for a national bibliographic system.

It is not difficult to find positive implications in this program for all our libraries. The availability of cataloging information for more books and other materials must, in time, lower the cost of cataloging for individual libraries. Second, the existence of bibliographic information in the several cataloging systems already in existence has proved to be a strong positive force in the sharing of resources; increasing the amount and diversity of this information can only improve the situation.

Subject Access

I would like, at this point, to move from one aspect of bibliographic control that is strongly oriented toward the descriptive to another that emphasizes the intellectual content of the material being indexed, namely subject access. We are in the midst of exciting changes that affect the ways in which we and our users approach information from the context of its subject content. The growth in number and extension in coverage of on-line data bases is something of which we are all aware. The ability to search extensive files of information using multiple access points and combinations of subject descriptors has revolutionized the literature searching process.

We have developed a whole new field of library service and in the process have become more aware not only of the power that the computer provides in literature searching but also of the inadequacy of some of our more conventional approaches to subject access by comparison.

Let me, for a moment, share with you some of the issues facing librarians and others in connection with subject access and some ideas about how they might be attacked. The substance of what I have to say comes from a recent meeting on subject access sponsored by the Committee for the Coordination of National Bibliographic Control held in Springfield, Virginia, in October 1978.

This committee is supported by the National Science Foundation, the National Commission on Libraries and Information Science, and the Council on Library Resources. Participating in this workshop were representatives from libraries—academic, public, and special; abstracting and indexing services, information dissemination centers like BRS, Lockheed, and the University of Georgia; publishers; and users of subject access systems.

To begin with, I should define subject access. Prior to the workshop the planning committee of which I was part asked each participant to provide a definition of the term. As you might expect, the responses were diverse and interesting. In the interest of time, however, let me use the definition that the planning committee put together: by subject access is meant the use of words, phrases, or symbols to represent the intellectual content of recorded knowledge for purposes of organization and research.

In assessing the current state of subject access, we attempted to describe the present situation within a framework of four groups that are either involved in the production of subject systems or are distributors or users of them. These were the Library of Congress, abstracting and indexing services, information dissemination centers, and publishers. One of the major concerns of the planning group that set up the workshop was the matter of subject control of monographic literature.

The problem can be put in perspective when one compares the multiple subject access points available in a system such as *Chemical Abstracts* or MEDLINE with those available in the conventional subject catalog found in most libraries, whether through a card catalog or a computer-produced display of a card catalog. A non-fiction monograph cataloged by the Library of Congress may carry two or three or occasionally four subject headings; the average for monographs cataloged by *Chemical Abstracts* is between 5.5 and 7.5 and the average there for papers is 9, with some having as many as 25 subject descriptors.

The problem, however, is not only with numbers. The Library of Congress subject heading system, with which we are all familiar, has a number of strengths: it is relatively universal at least among academic libraries in North America; it is large—almost one third of the 21 million cards in the LC main catalog are subjects; it is authoritative; it is documented.

This list also has a number of weaknesses: there is no underlying code or theoretical basis as, for example, with the Anglo-American Cataloguing Rules for descriptive cataloging; it is difficult to change because of the tremendous amount of work involved in correcting existing records; it is inconsistent in the formulation of headings, in the use of phrases or subdivisions, and in punctuation. Some say the list is biased. Some say it is changing too much; others, too little. If these problems were not enough, just consider the effects on subject catalogs of the LC decision to close.

The question of subject access to monographic literature and the related matter of LC subject headings are only a small portion of what has been identified as the "subject access problem." There are several other issues that developed during the workshop. It is interesting to note that while most of the participants and most of the discussion concentrated on on-line data bases, there are in most instances correlations and implications for subject access through library catalogs.

A major concern was the diversity of subject access vocabularies. There is almost no carry-over from one data base to another. Subject terms used in one discipline may not be used in another, or if they are, they may have an entirely different meaning. An example used was the term "bridge." Think of the many ways this descriptor might be used in dentistry, civil engineering, electrical engineering, philosophy, semantics, music, and so on.

Another group of questions involves the user of subject access systems. For a given tool, whether it be a printed index, on-line data base, or subject catalog, there are a variety of users in terms of education, interest, and approach, and each user may be querying the system for a different purpose. It is clear that we do not know enough about how people use subject indexes, and, beyond that, we know even less about how questions are formulated.

A third general area of concern is economics. How can we measure the cost effectiveness of a subject system? Can a system ever be too large? How do we remove or purge seldom used citations or subject entries from a system, and should we? Is there some way to provide a qualitative indicator for indexed information, and is there some relationship of this question to that of user feedback? How can users of a system influence its future direction, and is there any value in having a dynamic system that contains the results of previous searches accessible to later users?

Other issues are equally important but do not fit neatly into the categories listed above. Can we improve direct user interface with on-line retrieval systems? How do we improve bibliographic coverage, particularly of the periodical literature, in the humanities? How, indeed, do humanists use the subject approach; if it is different from the way in which scientists and social scientists and engineers do it, what are the differences and how can they be reflected in the design of subject indexing systems?

Finally, there is an issue that many librarians have puzzled over for a long time: how can we relate library subject catalogs to on-line retrieval systems both for searching purposes and for item identification?

It would be exciting if I could tell you at this point that we solved all or even a few of these problems. We did not. We have, however, made a good first step by bringing together a group of specialists with diverse backgrounds to identify the issues involved in subject access and to suggest ways in which they might be attacked. The specific suggestions that will come from the Workshop on Subject Access are still being written. These ideas, along with a summary of the proceedings, will be available in the near future.

In advance of that, however, let me list some of the possible directions that future research and development might take:

1. Improving multi-file subject access through building composite indexing records from several sources.

2. Increasing cooperation between the abstracting and indexing services and national libraries to work toward more consistent subject vocabularies in areas of mutual interest.

3. Increased support for the development of subject access systems in the humanities.

4. Research on the effectiveness of various subject access schemes including card catalogs, vertical files, on-line data bases, printed abstracts and indexes, and back-of-the-book indexes.

5. Research on the question-asking process.

6. Improved subject access for specialized types of material: maps, audio-visual, manuscripts, materials for the handicapped.

Scope of the Catalog

In thinking about the future of bibliographic control, I am concerned that we may have been tied too much to the concept of catalogs being designed primarily to reflect an individual library's holdings. One thing I hope for in the catalog of the future, regardless of what form that mechanism takes, is that its scope extend as far as possible beyond what is in a particular library.

Let me provide a local example. If Brown University and MIT cooperate in the future in collection development and if one library agrees to forego materials because the other library acquires them, why shouldn't a record of the book or serial or other material appear in both catalogs? In my opinion, library catalogs should, insofar as possible, reflect the totality of what is available to a user, not just what is on the shelves or supposed to be on the shelves.

CONCLUSIONS

I would like to conclude by offering a few generalizations on the future of resource development and bibliographic control with the full knowledge that I might, at some point in the future, be confronted with a set of unrealized predictions.

1. Academic library collections will be more diverse in terms of format but more specific in terms of relevance to teaching and research programs.

2. Collection development will take place in an atmosphere of limited funds, limited space, and a steadily increasing publishing output.

3. Cooperation in collection development will grow but will not supplant or even substitute for a significant portion of individual library collection building.

4. National centers containing information needed by library users and having the potentiality for providing this information quickly and economically will play an increasingly important role in local library decisions on acquisitions and on retention of older materials.

5. New forms of publication, such as publishing on demand, and new means of supplying information, like videodiscs, will affect collection development in academic libraries but will not solve the overall problem of physical growth.

6. Library card catalogs as we know them today will slowly go out of existence and be replaced, first by physical substitutes created through computerized cataloging and later by on-line catalogs.

7. Academic libraries, including those of many colleges and universities as well as the large research libraries, will play an increasingly important role in the creation of a national bibliographic data base.

8. AACR 2 is not the end. It is not even the beginning of the end. There will be an AACR 3, and probably an AACR 4. One would expect, however, that prior to that inevitability there will be a national library agency to coordinate library services and programs to the benefit of users and librarians alike.

I have been involved with academic and research libraries for almost twenty-five years. During that time I have never given serious thought to doing anything else. Like many of you, I have sometimes been depressed by a seeming lack of progress. Like many of you, I have often been encouraged by the tremendous advances that have taken place in academic libraries both in terms of physical resources and human resources. I am optimistic by nature, and I am completely optimistic about the future of academic libraries.

Today is a great time to be a librarian; the challenges we face will stimulate our imagination and test our flexibility, but the prospects are unlimited. The first national meeting of the Association of College and Research Libraries is significant for many reasons, but it is most significant for me in that it comes at a time when all of us are facing some of the most difficult and complex problems librarians have ever encountered. I believe we will solve these problems and others to come because we have done it before.

Millicent D. Abell

THE CHANGING ROLE OF THE ACADEMIC LIBRARIAN: DRIFT AND MASTERY

There are elements of both stability and change in the academic environment. Hence, although the traditional functions of the library will persist, librarians are increasingly confronted with opportunities and requirements for the improvement of library services. Their success depends on librarians' ability to escape a working pattern of routine and reaction and to master the professional role. Crucial to this mastery are awareness of the library's dynamic environment, the exercise of individual initiative, and the willingness to engage in critical analysis and evaluation of the performance of the library and the profession.

More than sixty years ago Walter Lippmann entitled one of his works, *Drift and Mastery: An Attempt to Diagnose the Current Unrest.* Drift and mastery is a theme which suggests a constantly recurring set of options. We have a choice. We can drift with environmental changes or we can try, and occasionally succeed, in mastering them. As a profession, our development and effectiveness have ebbed and flowed through the years. Broadly speaking, we are now working in an era of extraordinary opportunity to shape the flow and utilization of information and ideas and to play our roles in the academic enterprise more effectively than ever before.

As we have sought over the years to exercise our full potential as academic librarians, our professional leaders have often clearly articulated the issues of librarianship and higher education—and sometimes even the means for resolving these issues. One of the most difficult professional challenges has been to escape the drift of routine and reaction and to raise our level of performance to match more precisely the historical aspirations of academic librarianship. In this effort to gain mastery of our particular role in academe, we have manifested a variety of stages which might be labeled: groping, coping, and hoping.

In this paper I shall try to identify and project the main elements of the role of the academic librarian and the professional abilities embedded in it. Several of our professional forebears and contemporaries will be cited to illustrate the constancy of the principles of academic librarianship and our primary mission.

Millicent D. Abell is university librarian, University of California, San Diego.

GROPING: THE ISSUES

In this decade it seems to be incumbent on all writers and speakers in librarianship and in higher education to demonstrate that they understand—or can at least identify—the principal issues before getting to the point of the paper. Nevertheless, were the history of issue identification not a key to my contentions in this paper, I would be tempted to utilize the technique of Steven Muller, who, in a recent paper on "A New American University?" states in his last footnote: "I am conscious of having avoided almost the whole of the current agenda of problems confronting higher education. . . ." and then explains why he has done so. He completes the footnote by listing a dozen or so broadly encompassing problems, so that you know that he knows them, ending with the classic weasel words: ". . . and a host of others."[1]

A particularly comprehensive statement of issues for libraries in higher education appeared in an article published by *College & Research Libraries* in 1973. It is the widely-cited piece by McAnally and Downs, "The Changing Role of Directors of University Libraries."[2] In trying to account for the recent instability of directorships, the authors surveyed a number of librarians who had recently experienced changes of position and through them identified some all too familiar critical issues.

Among background factors they list the following: growth of enrollment, changes in institutional presidency, proliferation of university management positions, changes in the world of learning and research, the information explosion, hard times and inflation, changes in planning and budgeting processes, technological disappointments, changing theories of management, unionization, increasing control by state boards, and no national system for information. Their explication of the last issue is well worth reviewing in light of the positive steps toward resolution of some national issues now being undertaken.

In the few years since publication of this article other specters have loomed on our changing horizons, such as the increasing demands for accountability from a variety of agencies, declining enrollments, stabilized or declining budgets in the face of continuing increases in costs, and the ill-understood effects of initiatives like California's Proposition 13.

To continue the depressing litany, among the internal problems cited by McAnally and Downs are the following: greatly intensified pressures from various sources; the declining ability of library to meet needs; lack of goals and planning; inability to accommodate to educational changes quickly; decline of the status of the director and hence of the library; and prevalence of traditional authoritarian styles of management.

In a somewhat lighter tone with similar effect, David Kaser has recently written:

> The revolution of 1969–1970, at least as it affected libraries, was aggravated by perhaps only one atypical characteristic—only one factor that was different from those of previous revolutions. This was the frustration of unrealized expectations—expectations that had for the most part been unrealistic in the first place. It is difficult today to reconstruct the total sense of unbridled optimism that permeated the "Great Society" days of the early and mid-1960s. Somehow we had come to believe that we held all the aces, that we knew what society needed, that we knew how to deliver it, and that we had the resources to get the job done. As regards libraries, the press and public expected them to purvey extended services through instant computerization. University presidents expected them to cut costs. Faculty expected them to deliver everything they needed. Students expected them to stay open all night. Staff expected that work should never be dull and that salaries should rise 10 percent per year."[3]

In yet another cut at problem definition, a colleague produced the following:

> There is a law affecting the growth of libraries not unlike that of geometric
> progression. By the principle of *noblesse oblige*, a library which has attained
> a certain size is called upon to grow much faster than when it was smaller.
> Each year's additions result in a good many books which are but beginnings
> of series to be indefinitely continued; or the enlargement of the scope of the
> library by the purchase of books in some departments hitherto neglected
> makes it necessary to cover the increased ground every year thereafter. Not
> long ago the trustees of the Astor Library (now the NYPL) complained that
> they could hardly use any of their large income for the purchase of really
> new books, on account of the demands for continuation of series already
> commenced. So with Harvard University Library, where it is reported that
> over $7,000 is required annually for subscriptions to serials and for other
> standing charges entered against the income as liabilities to be met before a
> dollar can be appropriated for new books.
> As our numerous libraries grow, this tendency to demand largely increas-
> ing funds and to require larger and still larger buildings gives serious occasion
> to pause and look the matter over to see what can be done by way of relief.[4]

This gem, mined by Edward Holley, appeared in 1894 in a book by William I.
Fletcher. Holley further reports that "... Fletcher suggested that library cooperation
between libraries in one locality might be a partial remedy."

This remembrance of things past and present pertains not only to issues. We can also
trace the history of exhortations.

Once again Edward Holley located reminders that there is little new under the sun.
More than 102 years ago, Otis Hall Robinson stated the following:

> A librarian should be much more than a keeper of books; he should be an
> educator ... the relation ... ought especially to be established between a
> college librarian and the student readers. No such librarian is fit for his place
> unless he holds himself to some degree responsible for the library education
> of his students. ... Somehow I reproach myself if a student gets to the end
> of his course without learning how to use the library. All that is taught in
> college amounts to very little; but if we can send students out self-reliant in
> their investigations, we have accomplished very much.[5]

There follows a more recent quotation from Justin Winsor, published only 100 years
ago:

> A collection of good books, with a soul to it in the shape of a good librarian,
> becomes a vitalized power among the impulses by which the world goes on
> to improvement. ... the object of books is to be read—read much and often
> ... At the average college it is thought that if anybody gets any good from
> the library, perhaps it is a few professors; and if anybody gets any amuse-
> ment, perhaps it is a few students, from the smooth worn volumes of Sterne
> and Fielding. What it is to investigate, a student rarely knows; what are the
> allurements of research, a student is rarely taught.[6]

The foregoing exhortations to librarians to fulfill their proper role laid the groundwork
for the struggle to achieve recognition of that role with the conferral of some variety of

academic status. An instructive, and occasionally discouraging review of this struggle was provided by Robert Downs in his ALA Centennial Article, "The Role of the Academic Librarian, 1876-1976."[7] Downs reports that H. A. Sawtelle proclaimed in 1878 that the college librarian ought to work closely with the students and provide guidance in the development of literary taste. Sawtelle ". . . concluded that such college librarianship as he described ought not to be annexed to a professorship, but be itself a professorship."[8]

As documented by Downs and others, this search for role and status—for the academic librarian's particular mission as differentiated from other academic actors, including the so-called teaching faculty and the educational technologists, and from other library workers—has occupied librarians for over a century. The search often seems as plaguing today. No issue better exemplifies our groping than this one. To some extent, we have been so concerned with defining our status that we have lost sight of the purpose of the effort. Surely the single most compelling reason for seeking and maintaining academic status for librarians is not to gain a reward or to establish a symbol, but rather to provide an organizational tool to stimulate and facilitate the efforts of librarians to make their activities directly relevant to the dynamic educational process.

The groping occasioned by role confusion has not been limited to the faculty status quest. As librarians, we have sometimes neglected, overlooked, or relegated to secondary importance the roles of other persons, particularly library assistants under whatever label, without whom librarians, libraries, and our clientele would be unable to function. For too long, too many library assistants have had good reason to ask why they should do the same work as librarians for different status and different pay. This issue will be noted again in the discussion of the specific elements of the role of the librarian. Other issues with which we grope are those of participative management, whatever that means, and the sometimes related issue of collective bargaining.

These issues have intensified in an era of burgeoning organizations, new campuses, spectacular institutional growth, and, however suddenly, confrontation with dismal fiscal realities. These issues will not be discussed here in detail because most of them appear to be profoundly affected by two factors which make it impossible to generalize adequately in so short a presentation.

First, the environment in which one deals with an issue like faculty status or collective bargaining has such influence on the options and the choice among them that attempts at generalization are frequently misleading. As one reviews the debates on these issues, it is apparent that two diametrically opposed viewpoints may be equally valid when each is assessed within the particular context from which it has arisen. The elements of status that are feasible for the Virginia community college librarian are different from those appropriate to the University of California librarian and different again from the elements meaningful at an Illinois state college. Recognition of these differences is, of course, what led the drafters of our standards and model statement on faculty status to relate the elements of a given librarian's status to parallel elements for the faculty in the same institution.

The second consideration is that many of these issues of role confusion can be clarified by individual initiative, confidence, and the will to assume a more professional attitude with concomitant effect on performance.

Environment and initiative are the key words.

COPING: THE EFFORTS TO RESPOND

In spite of the rapidly increasing complexity of the environments in which we function, many of our contemporaries have demonstrated well the ability to identify the salient forces and trends—scholarly, technical, political, economic, demographic, and social—with which we must deal. On the national level, there are numerous well-edited and widely distributed journals through which professional intelligence is communicated. The divisions of the American Library Association and other professional associations and cooperating agencies have sponsored a number of regional workshops across this country on topics of current urgency.

Several efforts, aimed at improving the ability of an individual library to cope with its changing conditions, have been mounted in the last ten years. These include the institutional efforts at Michigan, Cornell, and Columbia, and, stemming from the latter experience, the work of the Office of Management Studies of the Association of Research Libraries.

Through the Management Review and Analysis Program (MRAP), the Academic Library Development Program (ALDP), the Collections Analysis Project (CAP), the publications, and the workshops, many of which are drawn together in the new Academic Library Program (ALP), libraries are being provided with an impressive array of tools for coping. Moreover, with a bit of perspective on the efforts of this program, one can perceive that one of the effects is the upgrading of the ability in libraries to anticipate, cope with, and even effect change. But this is in anticipation of the third section of this paper— what we are hoping will be manifest in the changing performance of the academic librarian.

On the other hand, coping all too often signifies something far different from the thrill of victory. It signifies pain, alienation, reversion, or defeat. Pain has come through cutting and closing—cutting budgets and staff, closing libraries. Many who are here have shared these experiences. Even more colleagues, not present here, have done so.

To demonstrate the loss of staff within a limited group of libraries I tracked the changes in staff size and mix in the eighty-eight university libraries which were members of the Association of Research Libraries in 1974–75, and these are shown in table 1.

Table 1.   Changes in Staff Size in Eighty-Eight ARL Libraries

Category of Staff	Year		
	1974/1975	1976/1977	Difference
Professional staff:	6,946	6,826	−120
Nonprofessional staff:	13,920	13,851	− 69
Student staff	5,188	5,328	+140
Total staff	26,054	26,005	− 49

The total FTE employed in these eighty-eight libraries declined by forty-nine during this two-year period. You will note that the overall reduction in regularly appointed staff is masked by the increase in student FTE. These intriguing data deserve a far more careful and complex analysis than can be provided here. Suffice to say for the moment that they reveal some thoughtful administrative coping and provide stimulus for reflection on the core activities of academic librarianship.

The preceding were raw and generalized figures. In part, they reflect the fiscal condition of the research university library. While inadequacy of resources is hardly a novel phenomenon in research-oriented universities, austerity is a condition which has been understood and endured by the private sector, undergraduate colleges for many years. It may now be visited on our community college colleagues.

Two environmental agents are at work. The first is the declining birth rate which has caused academic institutions on all levels to scramble for enrollments. A crucially important corollary factor is the potential effect of initiatives like California's Proposition 13. The effect of Proposition 13 may well be to undermine the ability of California's community colleges to provide education at a nominal, or even significantly lower, price than can be provided by other educational institutions within the state.

Perhaps more profound in impact is the likely shift of policy control from the local to the state level. Should this phenomenon spread and the community college become a state supported or pay-as-you-go enterprise, this segment of higher education will be forced to cope with its mission in new ways and may be forced to rethink its assumption of general education responsibilities. The implications for libraries in turn are profound.

Economic pressure can lead to alienation. The potential for alienation lies between types of libraries, between librarians and the others in the academic community, between librarians and other employees within the library. It is critical that we be aware of this threat and move to cope with it by rethinking our common, as well as our distinct, missions and roles.

One of the most disturbing of all symptoms of coping is the tendency of a segment of our profession to opt for a reversion of status. C. James Schmidt has described how well academic librarians have succeeded in recent years in gaining more appropriate recognition of our role in higher education even in the face of declining resources. He observed that the proportion of librarians with faculty status increased from 50 percent of the academic librarians to 75 percent in the years between 1966 and 1975.[9]

However, without naming names or places—too many of you can probably supply details—there are now those among us who would opt to denounce academic status and criteria and to revert to that passive, strictly hierarchical form of review which is solely dependent on a supervisor's evaluation of how well assigned tasks are performed.

Should this reaction prevail, it would be a terrible blow to the quality of academic librarianship. Performance reviews under conditions of academic status entail review of professional growth and contribution which may be manifest in many ways, including professional activity, research, and writing. This activity extends beyond "doing the job good," the invariable essential element of acceptable job performance. As an academic, the librarian is expected to perform his or her work in terms of the future, as well as the past, to seek ways to further the state of the art of the profession, as well as his or her own job. In my experience, the performance expectations associated with academic status have extended our performance and have moved the profession toward a higher standard of excellence. We do not want this quest for high standards to be diminished.

It is also essential that we monitor ourselves to avoid reacting to crises in a fashion that is constraining for us all. In several of these United States, I have witnessed the debilitating effects of anxious administrators responding to declining resources or the need for action by seeking to exercise ever greater control and more homogenization of practice. No level of administration is exempt from this tendency—national leaders, federal and state departments of finance and educational commissions, boards of trustees, central university administrations on statewide or local levels, library administrators, department heads, supervisors.

Some such managing is essential, if novel. In an address last year a University of California official stated that ". . . Too many people in the academic sphere felt the idea of managing a University was almost an insult. They are used to the idea that a University does not get managed, it just sort of happens."[10] In the same tone this speaker had stated earlier: ". . . an increasing proportion of our resources has to be taken up with institutional defense—we have to try harder to stay more or less in the same place."[11]

The danger, of course, is that we lose sight of the fact that to stay in the same place is to lose ground in a changing world. We must fight for opportunities to exercise individual initiative and innovation, the marks of professional endeavor and part of the very essence of the scholarly enterprise.

HOPING: THE VIEW AHEAD

To succeed at a level beyond coping requires clear objectives, an understanding of our environment, and personal initiative. We need to establish our direction and what we seek to accomplish. We need to implement mechanisms to enable us to remain aware of both stable and changing forces in our environment. We need to exercise the initiative required not only to respond to change, but to effect change. The fundamental mission of the academic library will not change substantially within the foreseeable future. It is the means for moving toward our goals that are marked by rapid change, change which has been amply described at this conference and elsewhere in recent months.

The mission of the academic library, which largely shapes the role of the academic librarian, is to contribute to the goals of the college or university of which it is a part and to the wider scholarly community. Those goals pertain to teaching, learning, research, and public service in some combination. The enduring, traditional, and widely accepted function of the academic library is to provide bibliographical and physical access to the books and other information resources required to support the diverse missions of our various academic and research institutions. Adoption of other functions, including those of direct provision of information and of instruction in the use of libraries, has proved far more controversial within our profession and is deserving of more profound consideration and debate than has typically been generated in recent years.

Robert Hayes expressed a conservative viewpoint in a delightful paper presented in the Chemist's Club Library Seminar in 1974, rephrasing the historical question: "Is the role the library—and thus of the librarian and of the catalog, as the principal tool of the librarian—to provide access to the books in the library or to the content of those books?" In this paper, Hayes credits Panizzi, librarian of the British Museum in the mid-nineteenth century, with arguing for a form of catalog that led to the decision that ". . . the crucial function served by libraries is to provide access to the books, and that decision set the tone for libraries ever since." Hayes goes on to note:

> . . . the fact that if a record is not preserved and if access to it is not available, it is impossible to provide access to the content. If the book or journal is not available, nothing in it is available (unless it has been transferred to some other record, which simply changes the record to be preserved, not the fundamental issue). This elemental fact has implications of overwhelming importance, because it establishes the role of the library *vis-à-vis* other institutions; it determines the ways in which the library allocates its resources; it establishes the context within which the librarian's role is identified; it predetermines what the content, form, and organization of library records will be.[12]

Certainly, the provision of bibliographical and physical access to the intellectual record is an essential and exciting pursuit; one in which librarians have been engaged with distinction for years; one in which the challenges are as great today as they ever were. It is a task that takes brains, courage, imagination, and energy. Furthermore, it can be argued that it is the ideal complementary role to be played *vis-à-vis* our clientele in an academic setting. It is the students and scholars who are learning, mastering, and utilizing the techniques of intellectual discrimination.

A different point of view on the provision of information has been presented by a number of academic librarians, notably Samuel Rothstein and Anita Schiller. Like many of you, I first encountered in library school Rothstein's 1960 paper, "Reference Service: The New Dimension in Librarianship," with its memorable distinctions among minimum, middling, and maximum theories of reference service. You will remember that he characterizes the maximum theory as one which leads to the direct provision of needed information, not simply information about information, such as where and how to find it. Rothstein recognizes the practical difficulties of introducing such service on a broad scale, but concludes:

> ... I would remind you that practical solutions are always a secondary matter; what comes first is conviction. If we can achieve a clear cut decision on direction and policy, if we can settle on ends, I have no doubt that we can find some of the means.[13]

Anita Schiller joined the fray with a brilliant analysis of conflicting values, goals, and attendant rationalizations within the profession. Published in *Library Quarterly* in 1965, her article, "Reference Service: Instruction or Information," provided a clear delineation of the functions of the reference librarian in pursuit of the library's goals.[14]

Schiller's particular focus is on the antagonistic relationship between the minimum and maximum philosophies of service. The antagonism is frequently suppressed or overlooked. This failure to confront the issue directly has contributed to the library user's confusion in that he or she does not know what to expect of the librarian. In the application of the minimum philosophy, the library user is expected to learn how to help oneself in extracting information from the library's resources. Instructional services are intended to facilitate this process. Schiller contends, however, that the maximum view, with the goal of providing comprehensive and accurate information, leads to a more direct, and hence more effective, type of service.

The choice we make, personally, institutionally, and professionally, is certain to have far reaching effects on the librarian's role and environment. Failure to understand or deal with the issue is likely to leave us in the middle, or the muddle—groping again.

Such groping would seem to be decreasing as a sign of the times. The librarian today has opportunities to function at a level of professionalism higher than ever before possible. These opportunities influence in extraordinary ways the work of the librarian as well as recruitment and education, the governance of libraries, and our leadership patterns.

Inadequate fulfillment of the academic librarian's potential role has been widely observed. In 1970 Eldred Smith described this underutilization of professional capacities:

> The ... functions that librarians perform are, more often than not, so circumscribed by regulation and routine, so lacking in autonomy, individual judgment, and expertness, as to qualify far more as bureaucratic rather than professional activity. There is little professional about an acquisition librarian who spends his time on bibliographical verification or even on the routine review of a national bibliography or blanket order shipment; there is little professional about a cataloger who rather automatically applies the principles of the Library of Congress or Dewey to a given number of books each day— usually trying to maintain an acceptable volume of productivity—without real knowledge of the field in which he is cataloging or of the needs of the library's clientele and how they use the catalog; there is little professional in a reference librarian who answers routine and substantive questions with

equal indifference to and lack of knowledge of the questioner and his library needs. Such librarians are guided primarily by institutional routines, regulations, and values. Their relations to their clientele are, at best, indirect or fragmentary. Their involvement with any subject or area of the collection is incidental and usually through the medium of book trade lists or cataloging rules.[15]

The current climate of austerity and retrenchment, a climate we expect to prevail for the foreseeable future, has provided us with an opportunity both to seriously reexamine the functions of various types of staff within the library and to take action on the basis of that reexamination.

As indicated earlier, in many academic libraries staff size has declined, at least relative to the workload. Furthermore, there has been a major shift in proportions, marked by the use of greater numbers of student staff, especially for those tasks characterized by minimum training and maximum routine. That is the result of necessary steps taken by many library administrators across the continent.

An accompanying trend in academic libraries in the last several years has been the increase in use of clerical and paraprofessional staff in supervisory positions and in a variety of complex library activities. In this respect, as in many others, the larger libraries lag behind the community college and college libraries. Examples abound. High grade library assistants are frequently found managing circulation departments. In some branch libraries, senior library assistants bear the title of branch manager, thus freeing the professional staff in those branches from the tasks of recruitment, training, and operational supervision of non-professional staff. Preorder search sections are often staffed entirely by library assistants. Each of you could add to this list of tasks, once thought to be primary professional responsibilities.

In many such conversions thousands of dollars are being saved in individual library budgets. Moreover, in many instances the tasks are being performed more effectively. One can speculate on the reasons for better performance by library assistants. Certainly, their quality of performance is related to the extensive experience in operations and supervision which library assistants bring to their management positions. Where previously there had often been an inexperienced, freshly minted holder of an MLS or a frustrated old-timer, supervision was less likely to be effective. Librarians have, or should have, different expectations for themselves from the handling of these kinds of responsibilities.

As noted earlier, another way in which libraries have been increasing production or handling greater work loads with fewer dollars is through development of greater reliance on student staffing. In many instances almost all circulation and stack maintenance functions are handled by students. Students are also widely used for routine technical processing and searching operations, special projects of all descriptions, and not infrequently, they have worked their way into the reference team while shelving in the reference stacks on a busy day.

Libraries have produced many more staff hours for the dollar wherever such ways can be found to shift functions, dollars, and attitudes in that direction. Certainly the prospect of increasing workloads with stable or decreasing staff resources makes managers and librarians on all levels at least more open minded to the possibilities.

What is the outcome? If the operation and supervision of the library are turned over to students, clerks, paraprofessionals, and some other non-librarian specialists, where does that leave the displaced librarian? Out on the streets, if you believe that these activities are the core of librarianship. In a position with unprecedented promise, if you believe that the making of library collections and services dynamically responsive to user needs is the core activity of librarianship. Librarians are being freed for essential interaction with the library's clientele.

Of course, many librarians have functioned in this way for decades. What seems to be new is a climate which encourages and requires the majority of academic librarians to perform in this fashion. At the heart of the effort is the necessity to understand, respond to, and influence faculty and students; other users; educational administrators; the producers and vendors of library materials, services, and equipment; legislators; and our own professional leaders.

For effective performance it is necessary the librarians be aware of the changes such as those which have been described during this conference and which have invigorated our professional literature in the past couple of years. These are: (1) changes in higher education; (2) variations in management and governance; (3) changes in scholarly communication; (4) changes in technology; (5) changes in patterns and effectiveness of cooperation; (6) changes in disciplinary and individual scholarly interest; and (7) changes in the ways services and resources are provided.

These changes constitute a massive stimulus to the professional body. To maintain a sufficient level of awareness and interaction the librarian must not be ensnarled in circulation transactions. It further requires in many libraries a deliberate orchestration of professional activity to assure an effective harmony among diverse individual interests and organizational needs.

The individual librarian must work toward acquiring simultaneously more specialized knowledge and more versatility. This paradox can best be resolved if we recognize that our eduction must be built on a foundationof principles and not be limited to current techniques. The choice is, as Steven Muller has put it, between higher education and higher skilling.[16]

What then are the principal functions of the academic librarian today and in the foreseeable future? They are the planning, provision, and evaluation of service that is designed to meet the needs of the particular clientele group that is primary to the given academic library.

This responsibility entails developing collections which as a whole respond to the needs of the local scholars and designing or adopting flexible and efficient alternatives for bibliographic access to those and other collections. It also requires an ability to reexamine the library's priorities and operations critically, to develop means to evaluate the effect of those services, and to be aware of new alternatives which will enable the library to deliver those services more effectively.

Beyond that, it requires the librarian to help students and faculty members find ways in their learning, teaching, or research which can take better advantage of the services, including direct and indirect provision of information, that the library has to offer. It is also the librarian's responsibility to interpret clientele needs to vendors and producers in order to ensure timely delivery of satisfactory products.

Earlier, I indicated two keys to my remarks—environmental awareness and initiative. I shall now offer a third—critical analysis and evaluation of our efforts. Just as we have passed the point in libraries where we can afford to compensate for individual poor performance by hiring a second person to do the job without removing the first, so too I think the time has come to examine some sacred cows and calves.

For example, library instruction is currently a flourishing activity. As an early practitioner in its most recent revival, I am well aware of the positive impact and the personal satisfaction for teacher and learner which such activities provide. I am also well aware of the immense amount of time required to prepare and teach well, especially to teach in traditional classroom settings through traditional credit courses.

We must rigorously reevaluate that mode and other types of instruction in which we so wholeheartedly engage, to ask whether the typical payoff—a minority of students deeply instructed in the use of libraries in their present form—is indeed the most appropriate or productive use of anyone's time. Does library instruction provide the student with tools for lifelong learning in this era of changing information needs and means for satisfying those needs? How much such instruction is provided in order to help library users compensate for limitations in the library's operations and services? Finally, remember Schiller's suggestion: Is instruction based on a philosophy which ultimateiy shortchanges the clientele? These remarks constitute not a negative judgment of library instructional activities but a plea for thoughtful analysis and criticism of their effectiveness for the users.

Other sacred cows which have come dangerously close to consuming the entire pasture include the seemingly endless debates over issues of status and governance. I confess that I have been a hyperactive participant in these activities as well. But the librarian I foresee dominating the scene in the years to come is more turned on by the analysis of user need than reflection on the professional navel. Such librarians are influencing decisions in academic libraries everywhere through sheer depth of special knowledge.

What is the source of such librarians? The question of recruitment is very much intertwined with that of the education of librarians. To the extent that we are unable to educate librarians through our professional education programs with the rigor, breadth, or depth required, then we must seek compensating influences in their other educational experiences.

I would argue that graduate education in a subject discipline is a highly desirable, if not necessary, qualification for an academic librarian. Some of the best and brightest among us do not have such a qualification, but they would be better for it. To experience a library, as a subject oriented scholar does, is quite different from the way that a librarian experiences it. Even as a graduate student, one senses a rigor, a multiplicity of values, an environment of stress and demand, a narrowness of focus, from which many of us in libraries are insulated. Furthermore, for many librarians, subject knowledge establishes a basis for rapport with their clientele for which even the most pleasant personality or extensive case study exposure is not an adequate substitute.

William Moffett and Rush Miller have written within the last six years in *College & Research Libraries* about our opportunitites to upgrade the profession through the attraction of subject PhD's.[17] Although we have responded to a limited extent, libraries and library schools alike are still insufficiently aggressive in this regard and in raiding other types of graduate programs on other levels.

It is, of course, perennially fashionable to ascribe our professional inadequacies to failures in our library schools. I would prefer to stress the elements of professional education which might lead to a strengthening of the qualifications of the individuals I hire and on whom the quality of library service depends. What is required is hardly news. As Lester Asheim has phrased it:

> ... the problem of educating for the future is not essentially different from the problem that has faced educators in the past: how to establish the proper mix, the theoretical and practical—the why and the how—so as to turn out practitioners who will be flexible; who can evaluate practice and introduce needed change; who are hospitable to new approaches but sensitive to the values in tradition; who are capable of gathering, organizing, and interpreting pertinent data on which to base innovation, but who can also make responsible decisions when the hard data are not available.[18]

This is neither the time nor the place to describe the ideal curricular content of our professional education, except to urge that principles and theory be emphasized over the application of current techniques. Indeed, a variety of skills must be taught, but not necessarily those involved in pursuing great masses of reference questions or cataloging particular books. Rather, we urgently need the skills required for intelligently analyzing our environment; for conducting research, including the manipulation of numerical data; for interpreting various clientele needs; for applying new technology; and for interacting effectively with other members of the team that provides academic library service. Finally, a deep appreciation for the importance of understanding the environment in which we operate is required.

The missions of various types of higher educational and research institutions must be understood. An appreciation of the sociology, politics, and economics of higher education is invaluable. It is far easier to teach the elements of cataloging a book into a particular collection on the job than to teach these more fundamental and enduring concepts and attitudes.

Even with this kind of educational base, a librarian's needs for continual updating are intense. Fortunately, opportunities abound. There are numerous workshops and stimulating articles in the librarian's professional literature and that of higher education and organizational behavior. Hence, one might question the effort which is being invested in trying to build comprehensive, formal structures in librarianship for this purpose. The primary unfilled need is for the kind of intensive mid-career educational update from other segments of the knowledge industry, such as that suggested by Wyatt in his earlier paper. Otherwise, with some personal initiative, and sometimes a little extra mutual tolerance and support by colleagues, most of us have more opportunities to learn and to grow professionally than we can possibly handle.

All of this opportunity, all of this change, all of this challenge has resulted in very complex organizations. One of the consequences is that some form of shared leadership and governance is inevitable, simply because it is impossible for one, or a very few individuals, to comprehend it all. Particular leadership styles are so affected by the individuals involved, by the academic environmental traditions, and by the situation that generalizations are very risky. However, I will venture one prediction: As librarians become ever more expert in identifying and analyzing change and in establishing relationships within either the consumer or the vendor community, those librarians will inevitably have greater voice in the determination of the policies of any given library.

What is described here is a climate which facilitates increasingly widespread peer influence and leadership. However, in order to be fully effective, all participants will need the courage to make tough judgments—to evaluate their own and each others' accomplishments and potential in terms of the library's mission—and the needs of students, scholars, researchers.

Also required is an individual commitment to the notion that our profession does play a critical role in higher education and that the quality of our performance and contribution to this enterprise is our greatest concern. We cannot leave our future, or even our rapidly changing present, to a few articulate and powerful professional leaders—our stars, if you will.

It remains the responsibility of individual librarians to monitor the probable consequences of the decisions that are being made today and to provide the vital linkage and feedback that will enable those who plan big also to plan right.

The choice between drift and mastery for the person and the profession, dear colleagues, is not in our stars, but in ourselves.

REFERENCES

1. Steven Muller, "A New American University?" *Daedalus* 107:45 (Winter 1978).

2. Arthur M. McAnally and Robert B. Downs, "The Changing Role of Directors of University Libraries," *College & Research Libraries* 34:103-25 (March 1973).

3. David Kaser, "The Effect of the Revolution of 1969-70 on University Library Administration," in Herbert Poole, ed., *Academic Libraries by the Year 2000: Essays Honoring Jerrold Orne* (New York: R. R. Bowker Co., 1977), p. 64-65.

4. William I. Fletcher, *Public Libraries in America* (Boston: Roberts Brothers, 1894), p. 116. This and phrase which followed appeared in Edward G. Holley, "The Magic of Library Administration," *Texas Library Journal* 52:58 (May 1976).

5. Otis Hall Robinson, "Proceedings," *American Library Journal* 1:123-24 (Nov. 30, 1876), as quoted by Edward G. Holley, "What Lies Ahead for Academic Libraries," in Herbert Poole, ed., *Academic Libraries*, p. 17-18.

6. Justin Winsor, "The College Library and the Classes," Library Journal 3:5 (March 1878) as quoted in Edward Holley, ibid., p. 18.

7. Robert B. Downs, "The Role of the Academic Librarian, 1876-1976," *College & Research Libraries* 37:491-502 (Nov. 1976).

8. H. A. Sawtelle, "The College Librarianship," *Library Journal* 3:162 (June 1878), as quoted in Robert B. Downs, ibid., p. 492.

9. C. James Schmidt, "A Letter to H. W. Axford," in H. William Axford, ed., "The Three Faces of Eve: or The Identity of Academic Librarianship; a Symposium," *The Journal of Academic Librarianship* 2:281 (Jan. 1977).

10. Frederick E. Balderston, "Keynote Address: Managing Tomorrow's University," in Craig L. Michalak, ed., *Managing Tomorrow's University: Proceedings of the 1977 University of California Business Officers Conference* (Berkeley: University of California Business Officers, September 1977), p. 9.

11. Ibid., p. 6

12. Robert M. Hayes, "The Changing Role of the Librarian," *Journal of Chemical Documentation* 14:118 (1974).

13. Samuel Rothstein, "Reference Service: The New Dimension in Librarianship," *College & Research Libraries* 22 (Jan. 1961): 11-18.

14. Anita R. Schiller, "Reference Service: Instruction or Information," *Library Quarterly* 35:52-60 (Jan. 1965).

15. Eldred Smith, "Service and Housekeeping: Changing Professional and Nonprofessional Responsibilities in the Academic Research Library," in *Papers Delivered at the Indiana University Library Dedication, October 9-10, 1970* (Bloomington: Indiana University Library, 1971), p. 59-60.

16. Steven Muller, "Higher Education or Higher Skilling?" *Daedalus* 103:148-58 (Fall 1974).

17. Rush G. Miller, "The Influx of Ph.D.'s into Librarianship: Intrusion or Transfusion?" *College & Research Libraries* 37:158-65 (March 1976), and W. A. Moffett, "The Academic Job Crisis: A Unique Opportunity, Or Business as Usual?" *College & Research Libraries* 34:191-94 (May 1973).

18. Lester Asheim, "Education of Future Academic Librarians," in Herbert Poole, ed., *Academic Libraries*, p. 129.

PART II

CONTRIBUTED PAPERS

The contributed papers of the Conference fall into eight broad categories—Administration and Management; Bibliographic Control and Automation; Bibliographic Instruction; Cooperation; Economic Aspects; The Librarian's Role; Resources; and Services. Although some of the papers in each category address a number of issues in a variety of subjects, each one has been assigned its most appropriate chapter. Papers, within those categories, are then arranged alphabetically by the last name of the author, or in case of multiple authors, the last name of the first author.

In addition, a special session on the Community College Library was developed around a theme paper with a reactor panel. That paper has been incorporated into the chapter on the Librarian's Role.

Ken Balthaser

Indiana University–Purdue University at Fort Wayne

PROVIDING KNOWLEDGE AND CLIENT LINKS

Directors of college and research libraries serve as the primary links between recorded knowledge and their respective client systems. The responsibilities associated with that linkage center on directors' roles as change agents. The library director of the future must be a leader who is a technologically-oriented, innovative, change agent. As a change agent and recognizing the challenges of the future, that individual will help provide the optimum link between recorded knowledge and the client system.

The thesis of this paper is that the directors of college and research libraries serve as the primary means of linking the client system of their own library with the recorded knowledge available from that library.

The library director has the organizational responsibility as the primary link; that responsibility has stood the test of time, and there are many excellent definitive works related to it that elaborate upon library management. However, very little is known about the director's responsibility as the primary link between recorded knowledge and the client system. General library science works related to library directors' responsibility in linking recorded knowledge and client systems are meager. Any works of the excellence and quantity of those related to library management responsibilities, for example, are very difficult if not impossible to find.

Some writers, outside the field of library science, have come very close to describing the library director's linking responsibilities. Ronald Havelock, writing on the topic "linking roles," was one. He, although addressing himself to matters other than the relationship between the library director and the client system of the library, had some comments that are very relevant to the linking responsibility purview of the library director. He wrote, for example, that a natural starting point for a general discussion of linking roles is a birdseye view of what he termed "the knowledge gap," the situation as he saw it for which linkage is required.[1] Surely "the knowledge gap" is a phrase well-describing the gap between recorded knowledge available from a library and clients' awareness, utilization, and incorporation of it. Another close relation to the linking responsibility of the library director was that the person filling the linking role proceeded in certain ways to provide knowledge to the user of the knowledge. In accomplishing this particular end, the person filling the role worked with the recipient of the knowledge in a meaningful sequence of steps. This sequence was designed to help the recipient by making the recipient more expert, more open to ideas, and more adaptive. Surely these same steps are taken by the library director. They are now taken through the implementation of organizational procedures through the administrative entity that is the library and the following of management philosophies therein. Effecting a closing of the knowledge gap and proceeding in certain ways to provide knowledge to a client while working with the client in a close or distant relationship are all functional characteristics related to library directors' linking responsibilities.

What's the generic name of the library director who effects this linking role? Linker? As Havelock and I see it, the name is "change agent."[2] Certainly many of the characteristics of a change agent are strikingly similar to the direct and integral responsibilities of a college and research library director. For example, a change agent's social position is located midway between the bureaucracy to which there is responsibility, and the client system with whom work is effected to provide closure of the knowledge gap. Thus the change agent is subjected to various role conflicts. One such conflict is that the change agent is sometimes expected to engage in certain behaviors by personal tendencies, administrative fiats and/or by professional systems. At the same time, the change agent is expected by a client system to carry on sometimes quite different actions.[3]

The idea of academic and research library directors being change agents is not a new one. It is one whose time has not been, but may now be here. Many library directors have been change agents as such, primary links between recorded knowledge and a client system. Those change agent directors were rarities in their time. The library director of today and the future should be a change agent and as such should cease being a rarity. The term "library director" should become synonymous with the term "change agent."

Being a library director/change agent requires that the person possess at least six characteristics. First, it requires that the director be a leader. Are library directors now generally leaders? Who knows? What we do know is that significant qualities of library leadership have not really been considered in research or other publications in library science, and that such qualities are elusive, defying quantification or written elaboration in the library environment, as they have in every other professional environment. At least one writer has wondered whether library director leadership is in fact an inscrutable mystery.[4]

A second characteristic is that the library director/change agent be an innovator. What do we know about innovations as they might relate to a college and research library setting, when an innovation is an idea perceived as new by the client? First, we know that academic librarians can be and have sometimes been, leaders in educational innovation, even among client systems reluctant to change.[5] Second, we know that a client's position in the academic system—for example, academic rank, which is usually closely related to job security—bears some relationship to receptivity to innovation. This position in the academic system concept, in fact, may represent one of the major keys to understanding the acceptance or rejection of certain kinds of innovations in the college and research library community.[6] Third, we know that it matters little whether or not an innovation has a great degree of advantage over the idea it is replacing. What does matter is whether the client perceives the relative advantage of the innovation.[7] Fourth, it is the potential innovation adopter's, that is, the client's, perceptions of the compatibility, complexity, divisibility, and communicability of the innovation that affects its rate of adoption.[8] Fifth, we know that the innovation must be presented in an overt fashion. It must be presented, diffused, and adopted in order to have the long-term benefits that are essential. Finally, we know that if the innovation is to be more than a game of musical chairs—that is, if genuine innovation is to occur and become institutionalized—long-term programming of continuing reinforcement needs to become an integral part of the innovation-receiving system. Accidental or trial-and-error support for innovations results in occasional short-term adoption. However, significant change seems unlikely to occur in a higher education setting if long-term innovation benefits are not sought.[9] As Evans indicated, the most successful librarians will be those who combine management knowledge with a true interest in people and their needs.[10] The successful management knowledge/people combination is at least partially the result of awareness and utilization of the six innovation characteristics just stated.

The concept of innovation tends, today, to be inextricably linked with the concept of technology. Today an innovation is almost always related in some way to technology, so I must consider the innovation/technology paradigm. What do we know about technology as it relates to the library director? Probably too much. Every time a library director turns around, there is some representation of technology facing in such a way as not to be avoided. As related to the library organizational structure, for example, computers abound. Educational media shines on the library director with bright spots of light and silently records ageless verbiage. Microforms are constantly underfoot. So quite a little bit is known about technology as it relates to the academic and research library.

What does all of this mean for the change agent, innovator, technology-oriented future college and research library director? It means that the library director of the future must be a leader who is a technologically-oriented, innovative, change agent, in order to best meet client needs of the client system in the particular library directed. It means that the library director must be the primary linking agent between recorded knowledge and the client system. To repeat, the library director has this responsibility as part of the scope of responsibilities related to the library as an administrative organizational entity. If the library director is this type of change agent, does that mean linking is automatic? That the director's success as the primary linking agent is assured? It might well be. Consider this: we know that the client systems utilizing college and research libraries are intellect-oriented and that their subsequent social status is high. Commensurate with that is the knowledge showing change agents reaching the upper social status portion of their clientele disproportionately more than the lower strata.[11] We also know that the concept of innovation is really not a simple one, and that variables exist within that concept. Interestingly enough, the typical variables of an innovation—including technical, social, and economic[12]—are exactly those of greatest importance to today's library director. Finally, there exists a need for the library director to serve as the primary link. The need is demonstrated by the knowledge that some professors are very selective about the kind of innovations they are willing to accept.[13] The library director as a leader who is technologically-oriented, innovative, and a change agent should easily fit into the change agent role of controlling and influencing the degree to which innovations are presented to and adopted by the various library clients.

What else must a library director do? Among other activities is the one of promoting the library. The extent of promotional efforts by change agents is directly related to the rate of adoption of an innovation. The greater the promotion, the quicker the adoption. The relative advantage of an innovation over the idea it supersedes may be emphasized by the promotional efforts of change agents.[14] Of course, writers have noted that the following ideas have not caught on with most academic librarians: "selling" the library and its services to college and university faculty and working with faculty colleagues, not just teaching their students how to use the library, but also assisting them in preparing and improving their own particular materials.[15]

Most important of all for the future of college and research library directors, the library director must grasp and utilize every form of relevant technology that can possibly be used to better effect the adoption of innovations and the subsequent closing of the knowledge gap. Drucker defined the word "technology" and related it very well to academic libraries. He considered that technology—that is, the application of the physical sciences to work—is one form of knowledge. In no one enterprise is it the only necessary knowledge. There are many successful enterprises in highly technological fields, for example, that do not excel in technology. Such enterprises must be technologically competent, of course, but their specific strength lies elsewhere.[16] One such enterprise must be academic libraries. Certainly the strengths of academic libraries must lie elsewhere than in technology, but the available forms of relevant technology must be used by library directors to their greatest advantage. What better way to use technology, a form of knowledge, than as a tool to effect diffusion of knowledge through a client system?

Technology has been a constant topic in recent professional publications relating to college and research libraries. At least one writer has expressed the thought that many experts predict very rapid technologically-oriented changes in libraries.[17] However, at least one other writer has felt that new technology is bound to change libraries incrementally, but slowly. Slower, as the writer says, than the bright-eyed and bushy-tailed electronics-oriented reformers predict.[18]

In any event, the library director should be ready to seize every opportunity to use each new technology-based tool as it develops.[19] The ability to control and influence the diffusion of knowledge and to provide the link between knowledge and the client system is enhanced through the use of innovations and technology. In this vein, the relevant emerging technologies will become a major factor in determining the role of librarianship in society.

If the events of the past and the needs of the present are any indication, we can expect that the college and research library of the future will undergo several changes.[20] These changes should be controlled and influenced by library directors who are the type of change agents already described. Perhaps the most significant of these changes which will be undergone includes the expanded technological environment, structural changes within the library, and increasing interaction between the library, its client system, and the rest of society. All of these changes should be effected by the library director. That will happen when the library director realizes that the change agent role is a necessary and primary one.

Curious phenomena will result from the library director's role as a change agent. For example, the library director will be required to devote more and more resources to technological advances about which less and less is understood, given the state of technology in this present day and as we can see that state being in the future.[21] As Shera pointed out, advanced computer technology, telecommunications and micro-recording, and the nonprint audiovisual materials gives libraries a much wider choice of ways to serve their users, to communicate with each other, and to perform their daily work.[22] Along with this wider choice must come greater dependency on technology and upon those individuals who accept allocated resources to perform their technologically-oriented functions. So the library director as change agent, while having a potential plethora of tool possibilities at hand, must judiciously and correctly devote monetary resources to advances about which the director's own knowledge might be somewhat superficial.

Surely, then, the challenges for the future are evident—how to best use the technologies, how best to be an innovator, how best to function as a change agent, and how best to be a leader. The continuing resolution of these challenges must be directed toward providing the optimum link between recorded knowledge and the client system. The successful college and research library director will provide that optimum link.

REFERENCES

1. Ronald G. Havelock, *Planning for Innovation Through Dissemination and Utilization of Knowledge* (Ann Arbor, Michigan: University of Michigan, 1971), p. 7-1.
2. *Ibid.*, p. 7-33.

3. Everett M. Rogers, *Diffusion of Innovations* (New York: The Free Press, 1962), p. 256.
4. David Kaser, "The Effect of the Revolution of 1969-1970 on University Library Administration," in Herbert Poole, ed., *Academic Libraries by the Year 2000: Essays Honoring Jerrold Orne* (New York: R. R. Bowker, 1977), p. 71.
5. Damon D. Hickey, "The Impact of Instructional Technology on the Future of Academic Librarianship," in Herbert Poole, ed., *Academic Libraries by the Year 2000: Essays Honoring Jerrold Orne* (New York: R. R. Bowker, 1977), p. 44.
6. Richard I. Evans, *Resistance to Innovation in Higher Education: A Social Psychological Exploration Focused on Television and the Establishment* (San Francisco: Jossey-Bass, 1968), p. 156.
7. Rogers, *op. cit.*, p. 124.
8. *Ibid.*, p. 124.
9. Evans, *op. cit.*, p. 155.
10. Edward G. Evans, *Management Techniques for Librarians* (New York: Academic Press, 1976), p. 270.
11. Rogers, *op. cit.*, p. 257.
12. Evans, R. I., *op. cit.*, p. 152.
13. *Ibid.*, p. 153.
14. Rogers, *op. cit.*, pp. 257-258.
15. Hickey, *op. cit.*, p. 45.
16. Peter F. Drucker, *Managing for Results* (New York: Harper & Row, 1964), p. 114.
17. Richard M. Dougherty, "Personnel Needs for Librarianship's Uncertain Future," in Herbert Poole, ed., *Academic Libraries by the Year 2000: Essays Honoring Jerrold Orne* (New York: R. R. Bowker, 1977), p. 114.
18. Stephen K. Bailey, "The Future of College and Research Libraries," *College & Research Libraries* 39:5 (January 1978).
19. Dougherty, *op. cit.*, p. 115.
20. Evans, E. G., *op. cit.*, p. 267.
21. *Ibid.*, p. 267.
22. Jesse H. Shera, *Introduction to Library Science* (Littleton, Colorado: Libraries Unlimited, 1976), p. 103.

Joseph A. Boissé

University of Wisconsin—Parkside

DEALING WITH THE FEAR OF CHANGE THROUGH THE SELF-STUDY PROCESS

Organizations have historically confronted problems in bringing about change. Not the least of these is resistance on the part of people affected. This resistance is the direct result of the panic of change. This fear has four roots, and, if change is to occur successfully, these must be dealt with. In attempting to deal with this fear and its roots, the University of Wisconsin— Parkside turned to the self-assessment process exemplified by the Academic Library Development Program. By involving staff from the very beginning and by contributing to their development, the process destroys the ignorance, lack of self-confidence, and uncertainty which are the four roots of fear of change.

To state that the modern world is, above all else, a world of rapid and near-constant change, is to state the obvious. While there are probably few people who would take issue with the preceding statement, most of these same individuals are not entirely certain just what the statement means. Nor are they certain about what its consequences are. In a book on the dynamics of change, published nearly two decades ago, the authors reflect briefly upon that statement:

What does it mean? Many things, of course; but perhaps its primary meaning lies in its effect upon people. It means that people, too, must change, must acquire an unaccustomed facility for change, if they are to live in the modern world . . . It means that if we are to maintain our health and a creative relationship with the world around us, we must be actively engaged in change efforts directed toward ourselves and toward our material, social, and spiritual environments.[1]

The authors are obviously making their observations while considering the world at large. Every organization is a world in itself, however, and feels the same pressures, internal and external, which make change both necessary and inevitable. An organization cannot claim to be dynamic unless it be characterized by a continuous process of change, that is a process of continuous adaptation, adjustment and reorganization.[2]

In most cases, this process does not occur easily; in many cases, it is not accepted willingly. Observation of various types of organizations has shown that a majority of them attach a great deal of importance to stability and continuity. They, consequently, frequently resist change, giving in to it only when the weight of the evidence favoring change literally overwhelms them. All too often, as a result, organizations change only when they are forced to do so by circumstances which they never have controlled or can no longer control. In a word, the majority of organizations are reactive and not proactive in the matter of change.

Academic institutions are not unlike other organizations and consequently have not, for the most part, actively pursued change. Within academic institutions, libraries tend to take the lead from the university administration. Libraries in these institutions only rarely attempted to play an active role in shaping their surroundings and in doing more than reacting to external influences. At least until the last decade or so.

Since the late 1960's, American higher education has been undergoing such an upheaval that libraries have of necessity been directly involved. This general upheaval has received much attention in recent years:

> Critical and fundamental shifts are occurring in American society and in the economy, and colleges and universities will have to cope with their ramifications: changes in public attitude, financial support, student enrollment, and operating procedures.[3]

Because of these pressures, planning in academic institutions has gained a new respectability. Library administrators have also begun to fully understand the value of seriously prepared planning documents in meeting the challenge of the future. Phrases such as "new technology," "increased productivity" and "greater efficiency" have been dealt with by careful evaluations of on-going programs and activities.

These evaluations and analyses have inevitably resulted in change. The change has inevitably impacted heavily on staff with the results frequently being less than felicitous. Individuals have felt threatened, have given in to serious feelings of insecurity and, in many cases, have been something less than cooperative.

There are two questions which will be addressed in this paper:

1. Why is change usually considered to be so threatening?
2. How can the process be made less threatening?

If we can answer these questions, we will have understood the necessity for managing change rather than just letting it occur and we will suggest a procedure for insuring that change in an institution is managed.

In an article in *Management Review*, Robert E. Levinson lists four factors which he assures us account for what he calls "the panic of change."[4] The first is one over which there is probably little disagreement. Individuals, and this includes the director of the library as well as to the bindery clerk or the serials check-in clerk, tend to fear the unknown. Change, more often than not, represents the unknown and, as a result, generates its full share of apprehension and fear. There is a desire among people to understand what is going on around them. Change will disrupt the status quo, "I don't know what will occur and therefore I'm afraid!"

The second cause of this fear has to do with the individual's self-concept. Not knowing whether one has the self-confidence and ability to deal successfully with change—and therefore concluding that "I do not"—further reinforces the fear which is already nascent in the mind.

In the third place, change is feared because one anticipates that it will disrupt a way of life or a collection of procedures with which one is comfortable. To varying degrees perhaps, but without exception, we are creatures of habit. Anything which is expected to disrupt our habits generally does not enjoy our wholehearted support. Change, by its very nature, disrupts habits and established processes and therefore does not generate spontaneous support.

The last of the factors again has to do with how we perceive ourselves. It is not uncommon for individuals to lose sight of the organization as a whole and to attribute to themselves an undue importance in the functioning of the organization. We feel that everything should be done at our convenience and with our approval. If, in fact, one feels that way, any change which is imposed by the organization is interpreted as demeaning.

These then, according to Levinson, are the root causes of "the panic of change." If one wants to bring about changes in an organization—and more specifically in a library —one must deal with these factors. Ignoring them may not in itself destroy the effort but it will certainly make it more painful and minimize its impact.

One strategy for managing change which deals with these potential problems by its very design based on our experience with the Academic Library Development Program at the University of Wisconsin–Parkside.

A word first about the ALDP. It ". . . is a detailed self-improvement strategy for small to medium-sized libraries. It is a program of techniques, methods, and processes that academic libraries may use in evaluating and developing all aspects of their performance."[5] The ALDP is designed to bring about, in a library, those changes which will improve the organization and its services and thereby insure its dynamism.

There were many reasons why, early in 1977, the administration of the Library/ Learning Center at the University of Wisconsin–Parkside began thinking of some kind of comprehensive review of library operations. The institution, established in the late 60's, had gone through a variety of changes. Initially established in the belief that it would have some 20,000 students and a full range of doctoral programs, UW–Parkside was jolted, in the early 70's, by two hard facts. In the first place, the fact that the original enrollment projections had not been founded on adequate data became obvious. In the second place, a major reorganization of publicly-supported post-secondary education in Wisconsin was announced.

By 1973, new and decreased growth projections were made public and the institution saw all prospects for the development of doctoral programs disappear. At about the same time, the first in a series of annual budget reductions was imposed on the campus. These stemmed in part from the revised plans for the institution and partly from the withdrawal of start-up money. The library absorbed its share of the reductions. The years 1975 and 1976 brought about two major phases of campus reorganization. In both cases, the library was affected. In July 1975, the university Archives and its Area Research Center (a unit which acquires and processes local and regional history materials) ceased to exist as separate administrative units on campus and were assigned to the library. In July 1976, the university's Learning Center, which circulated non-print materials and audio-visual equipment on campus and which operated both audio and video production studios, ceased operating as a separate administrative unit and became a division of what was now called the Library/Learning Center. Just as the functions of these units were transferred, so were most of the staff members.

Through this period of upheaval—the word being used advisedly—the administration of the Library/Learning Center made many adjustments. Changes occurred but most were instituted in an atmosphere of intense pressure and, it is probably fair to say, without adequate planning. At no point in time was it possible to step back and try to view the entire picture in an atmosphere of calm. In any institution such a periodic analysis is necessary; in a situation undergoing turmoil such as that described above, it is essential.

At that point in time—early 1977—the choices open to the administration of the Library/Learning Center were: 1) hire an outside consultant, 2) find a way to conduct a self-analysis, and 3) forget the entire matter and continue to "make do." The second alternative was favored precisely because it would involve the staff. There was a belief on the part of the administration that the staff, at least intuitively, knew more than anyone else what problems needed correction and what issues and opportunities existed.

At about the same time the Council on Library Resources was seeking institutions to participate in phase two of its Academic Library Development Porgram. The advantages of the ALDP self-study were readily apparent: all the staff would be involved in some way in the process; the process would constitute a staff development function as well as a self-study task; recommendations resulting from a self-study would have a better chance of being accepted than those of an outside consultant. For these reasons, UW—Parkside applied for and received a grant to conduct the self-study as part of phase two of the ALDP.

One question remains to be answered: how does the ALDP process deal with "the panic of change" and its roots.

In the first place, it involves the staff in the process from the very outset. If in fact, fear of the unknown is a major causal factor of the panic of change, involvement from the outset should counter that fear. The procedures developed by the authors of the ALDP Manual carefully insure staff involvement in the early planning of the study. Established procedures call for their advice in the early planning and in the selection of the actual study team and its task forces. At UW—Parkside the final decision to undertake the study was not made until the issue had been thoroughly discussed in staff meetings and the overwhelming majority favored the project. The study was not being imposed on the staff; it was rather something which they chose to do.

These same procedures which insure staff involvement early in the self-study tend also to create a positive attitude among staff. Again, staff members are aware that, to a certain extent, they can chart the future of the library. They quickly become more positive in how they view change, they develop a proactive rather than a reactive attitude toward change.

As the study progresses, it contributes clearly and positively to staff development. The manual charts the course of the study and step by step explains those processes and procedures to be used. It assists not only the study, but the entire staff, in confronting problems, in analyzing them and in identifying potential solutions. It thereby greatly increases the library's problem solving capabilities. It further expands the staff's knowledge by helping them develop general analytical skills through the "learning-by-doing" approach. Lastly, it fosters development of the interpersonal skills of the staff, thereby insuring more effective work in group situations.

The three remaining roots of fear which were mentioned earlier are all dealt with— indirectly perhaps, but nonetheless positively—by this educative process which takes place among the staff. People begin to develop a keener awareness of their limitations, an interest in improving their skills, a realistic assessment of the overall organization of the library and of their role in it, and an eagerness to improve the organization of which they are a part. Once this process is in motion, the panic of change has been effectively defeated.

In summary then, fear is the major cause of resistance to change and that fear derives from four roots. If a manager wishes to bring about change and have it accepted in the organization without its being too disruptive, he/she must deal with this fear of change. The self-assessment process formalized and explained in the ALDP provides the mechanism for accomplishing that task and, consequently, for successfully managing change.

REFERENCES

1. Ronald Lippitt, Jeanne Watson and Bruce Westley, *Planned Change* (New York: Harcourt, Brace & World, 1958), p. 3.
2. *Ibid.*, p. 4.
3. C. V. Martorana and Eileen Kuhns, *Managing Academic Change* (San Francisco: Jossey-Bass, 1975), p. 2.
4. Robert E. Levinson, "How to Conquer the Panic of Change," *Management Review*, 66 (July 1977):20-21.
5. P. Grady Morein and Duane Webster, *The Academic Library Development Program* (Washington, D.C.: Council on Library Resources, 1977), p. i.

Miriam A. Drake

Purdue University

MANAGEMENT CONTROL IN ACADEMIC LIBRARIES

Management control in academic libraries is likely to change significantly in the future. This paper discusses the future operating environment of academic libraries and its likely effect on management control. A review of the underlying problems associated with the control process is followed by suggestions for creating, acquiring, and reallocating financial and human resources.

Management control has been one of the most complex and difficult areas of management for academic librarians. The process is likely to be more complex in the future as the operating environment continues to change.

Management control is "... the process by which managers assure that resources are obtained and used effectively and efficiently in the accomplishment of the organization's objective."[1] The term resources refers to financial, material and human resources.

The purposes of this paper are to review the critical factors in the future operating environment of academic libraries, their effect on the management control process and to suggest ways to improve the process.

OPERATING ENVIRONMENT

During the nineteen sixties, when library budgets were relatively generous and prices were low, there was little pressure to set operational priorities or allocate resources to achieve specific results. "Bigger is better" and service for all appeared to be the most suitable philosophies. Recent inflation, budget cuts and declining enrollments are contributing to a climate of uncertainty and questioning about priorities for academic libraries. In this uncertain environment, librarians are growing increasingly uncomfortable with resource allocation decisions based on tradition or the reactive squeaky wheel. Technological developments and resource sharing are beginning to offer viable alternatives for many libraries. Integrating them into resource acquisition and allocation decision making, however, is not a simple matter.

The future operating environment of academic libraries will be different from anything we have known previously. In quantitative terms, projections of student enrollment

91

indicate a peak of just over 8 million in 1981 declining to 7.6 million by 1985. There are indications that this trend will continue well into the 1990's because of continuing low birth rates. The declining student population may be offset somewhat by greater emphasis on continuing education and new programs in adult education. The impact of these programs on the library and its user population is difficult to predict.

The number of faculty employed also is expected to decline. In individual institutions, the decline in teaching faculty may be offset by an increase in research faculty. Smaller colleges and universities which emphasize teaching are likely to experience greater declines than large universities which derive substantial amounts of funds through research.

The decline in students will lead to a decrease in funds available for libraries. Total expenditures in constant 1975–76 dollars of colleges and universities will begin to level in the mid 1980's. Individual institutions may be able to compensate for losses in tuition income through increased endowments, gifts and research funds. The impact on library financing is not clear.

Overall, the financial picture for libraries is uncertain. If the library's share of the expenditure dollar keeps pace with past, the funds will not be sufficient to compensate for the reduced purchasing power which is likely to result from continuing inflation. In the recent past, the prices of goods and services purchased by libraries have increased faster than the inflation in total expenditures. This trend is likely to continue even if the overall rate of inflation declines.

EXPENDITURE MIX

During the last ten years there has been a shift in the mix of library expenditures. Purdue University Libraries in 1966–67 spent 35% of its budget for materials and binding and 53% for salaries and wages. By 1976–77 the materials share of the budget had declined to 32% while salaries and wages increased to 64%. The number of people employed at Purdue Libraries declined from 242 FTE in 1966–67 to 216 FTE in 1976–77. Data for universities in the Big Ten show similar shifts. The materials and binding share of budget declined from 35% in 1966–67 to 31% in 1976–77 while wages and salaries increased from 58% to 62%.[2]

RESOURCE UTILIZATION

Expenditures for specific items show only one side of the library's financial resource allocation. The line item budget does not indicate whether these resources were used efficiently or effectively. We are just beginning to see the necessary cost accounting and resource utilization studies which will give us information on how well resources are being allocated and used. The library use study conducted at the Univerity of Pittsburgh is an excellent example of needed studies which relate expenditures and investments to use.[3] The findings of that study raise serious questions about effectiveness of investment in collections as measured by use and user benefit. Given the high cost of books and journals, the cost of acquiring, processing, storing and maintaining a large book inventory and the likelihood of continuing inflation and lower budgets, it becomes essential for most academic libraries to question and examine their use and allocation of financial resources. Librarians need to assure themselves and university administrators that their resources are being used to achieve the desired result.

UNDERLYING PROBLEMS

The problems underlying the acquisition and allocation of resources in libraries are lack of quantifiable goals, objectives, or performance measures and the conflicting interests of funders, users and others who are involved with an academic library. The conventional book and body counts do not indicate whether the library is doing its job or how well its clientele are being served. The delivery of material to the user does not mean that pertinent information has been transferred or that the user is satisfied. The importance of quantifiable goals and information transfer will vary with each institution. In universities where research is expanding, there will be increasing pressure on the library to deliver substantive information at lower cost to support the research activity.

As a result of the intangible nature of library service, many academic libraries, by choice or by constraint imposed from the parent administration, have allocated resources according to tradition or politics. Some libraries have chosen to try to be all things to all people or have tried to provide something for everyone. There has been an understandable reluctance to provide service to one group at the expense of the others. Funders and users do not understand the complexities of library economics or operations and, in some instances, have prevented librarians from eliminating services which are not cost effective or little used. The emphasis on collection building has resulted in librarians being the under-utilized resource in the libraries. Many teaching and research faculty members have failed to tap the library's most important intellectual resources, the human resources. Administrators often have failed to provide librarians with sufficient and proper tools to do their job. University administrators, who readily buy lab equipment and computers for their faculty, are reluctant to buy better reference books and computer-based information services for their librarians.

The problem of obtaining resources or reallocating existing resources in academic libraries is further exacerbated by the fuzzy relationship between money and service. In many situations, it is difficult to demonstrate that more dollars will deliver more value to users or that additional funds will enhance the library's contribution to the educational and research missions of the institution. Given the lack of output targets and priority goals and the difficulties of measuring output, librarians don't really know whether one distribution of resources is better than any other.

When college and university administrators divide the funds, they weigh the library's demand for funds against demands of teaching departments, computer centers, etc. They tend to view the library as overhead. Since most administrators try to keep overhead as low as possible they are reluctant to increase the library's share of funds.

IMPROVING MANAGEMENT CONTROL

The projections discussed earlier indicate that it is likely that the funds available for libraries will not increase rapidly enough to maintain collections and service at current levels. In addition, university and college administrators trying to adjust to the new environment of reduction will be forcing cuts in overhead expenditures. By 1985, many colleges and universities will be operating with fewer students and faculty. Competition for research funds will be more intense. Many academic librarians will find themselves in a different operating environment which will necessitate changes in library operations. Cost cutting will become an everyday activity rather than a one-time affair.

In order to improve the management control process in academic libraries, it will be necessary for each institution to decide what role the library will play in education and research and to define the services to be offered and materials to be acquired in operational terms. Goals and priorities will not be as generalized as they have been in the past. The priorities of a library in an institution serving a large student population and multi-million dollar research efforts will be very different from the priorities of the library in a small largely undergraduate liberal arts college. Little used services may have to be discontinued as well as expensive services which result in small user benefit. Because of the conflicting pressures on the library these decisions will be difficult. The teaching faculties may not adjust as rapidly as the library and the administration to the new era.

The critical problem, in the long run, will continue to be acquisition of sufficient resources to accomplish the library's program. Given a constant or decreasing amount of money, additional resources can be created by cost cutting and investing in resources which result in greater staff and user productivity or by tapping new sources of funding. In the resource allocation process, options which create additional resources or which will result in more effective use of existing resources will need to be considered and integrated into library operations. Investments in services, such as reference, collection development, literature searching, etc., need to be examined in the context of costs vs. use and benefit. Technical services, administration, and other support services need to be examined in terms of their contribution to library effectiveness and in relation to the resources consumed.

Automation is a logical option for long run increases in productivity. While the initial investment is large and may be out of reach for many libraries, the savings in labor cost over a 5–10 year period are likely to be substantial. With labor costs increasing at 6% per year, the costs of operating manual systems in purchasing, cataloging, circulation and bibliographic information retrieval are rapidly becoming unaffordable. In addition to enhancing staff productivity, automation provides a means for increasing the productivity of the library user by providing rapid and up-to-date information on the library's holdings and the availability of specific materials. Obtaining funds for automation will be dependent on demonstrating that productivity increases will result and that unit costs can be reduced.

When possible, libraries should consider the purchase of turnkey systems as an alternative to in-house development. The initial investment and operating costs of such systems are making them increasingly attractive. Working with other libraries on joint systems development projects is another way to reduce costs.

Materials resource sharing is another option which should be examined in the context of unit cost reduction. As emphasis shifts from acquisition to access, priorities in acquisitions will become possible. We need to recognize that this shift will mean inconvenience to users and could cause rebellion in the teaching faculty. In some cases, users will need to go to another library to use materials because it may be cheaper to transport the person than to order and transport a large volume of material. In other cases, the user will have to wait for needed material to be delivered.

Users, both on-campus and off-campus, may be forced to pay for some library services or do without them. User fees represent potential additional income for the library and may be the only way for libraries to finance custom services which increase in cost as usage increases. In most colleges and universities it would be impractical and uneconomic for libraries to charge fees for standard services because unit costs of these services decline with use. Each institution will have to settle on a compromise which is appropriate to its situation.

As libraries attempt to create new resources from existing resources, librarians will need to educate teaching faculties about libraries and, in some instances, work to recruit faculty as active supporters of new programs rather than friendly adversaries. In a sense, we have to play doctor by saying that it may hurt now but the health of the library will be improved.

GOVERNMENT FUNDING

Thus far, the discussion has been limited to resources internal to the library. It is doubtful whether cost effective library service can become a reality without a substantial addition of capital from local, state and federal governments. On the state level, networks and cooperatives need to be enlarged to include all types of libraries. State legislators need to be convinced that they share responsibility for making information available. In addition, the legislators need to be convinced that libraries by themselves cannot provide resource sharing mechanisms, such as document delivery services, on-line catalogs, reference referral, and state-wide telephone services. While LSCA funds can be used for research, development feasibility studies and initiation of service, special funds are needed to provide continuing operational support of state-wide services. Experience in Indiana in obtaining funding for the Indiana Cooperative Library Services Authority has shown that the legislature will respond to documented need and benefit.

The role of the federal government in financing information services is changing. Ideally, the federal government would complement the efforts of state and local governments in providing funding for national networks, interfaces between state, regional and national networks and a variety of national resource centers.

Librarians will need to work hard with all types of libraries at all levels of government to assure that programs and funding are responsive to our needs and that they will enhance delivery of information services rather than create obstacles to effective service.

CONCLUSION

In summary, the components of the management control process, acquisition of resources, allocation of resources, and effective utilization need to be viewed as a whole process in the context of the operating environment of each institution. By 1985, the operating environment is likely to be very different from our previous experience. Increased resources are likely to be created through cost cutting, increased access to resources outside the particular institution and capital from government.

The changes in academic libraries will bring new and difficult challenges. The knowledge and skills of librarians will become more important assets than the collections. In the long run, the change is likely to produce more stimulating and exciting work for the profession.

REFERENCES

1. Robert N. Anthony, John Dearden, and Richard F. Vansil, *Management Control Systems.* (Homewood, Ill., Irwin, 1973) p. 5.
2. Data derived from *ARL Statistics*, (Washington, D.C., Association of Research Libraries, 1966–67 and 1976–77).
3. Thomas J. Galvin, and Allen Kent, "Use of a University Library Collection," *Library Journal*, 102 (November 15, 1977):2318.

Richard Eggleton

University of North Carolina At Greensboro

ACADEMIC LIBRARIES, PARTICIPATIVE MANAGEMENT, AND RISKY SHIFT

Various methods to increase staff participation in the management of academic libraries have been attempted, and most have been applauded in our literature. The use of committees would seem to be the most favored approach and has been used extensively in many libraries. The theory of risky-shift, developed in social psychology, has shown that under certain conditions groups will reach "risky" decisions while under other conditions groups will decide upon a more cautious decision. This research on risky-shift is reviewed, and its implications for committees and decision making in the academic library context are discussed.

There has been a great interest in, and literature published on, participative management in all kinds of organizations. This literature will not be reviewed in this paper because it has been well reviewed, analyzed and synthesized in a number of articles and monographs. Librarians have added to this literature by contributing a voluminous number of reports and articles which discuss its application in libraries.

Kaplan, in an excellent review of the subject, notes that the literature of management has shifted from a simplistic and optimistic assessment of its possibilities.[1] This aptly illustrates one of our major problems. Although we should be masters at finding and using information, we fail badly, at least in regard to management theory. We accept and use second-hand and popularized versions of theory; by the time new insights reach our literature from other disciplines they are years old, and sometimes, even out of favor or greatly changed by the discipline from which they emanate. For example, a theory of motivation developed by Herzberg is repeatedly found in our literature and textbooks and highly touted.[2] Yet, if we had read the literatures of psychology and management, we would know that this theory has been severely criticized for major conceptual faults and that this criticism has continued for over ten years. The theory is now disregarded completely by many in psychology and management.

This paper is a small attempt to remedy this kind of situation. Since committees have been widely used in libraries as a form of participative management, we need to know a great deal more about group processes. One theory of these processes, the risky shift effect, is reviewed for applicability to the library situation.

RISKY-SHIFT

Management theory before the 1960's stated that group decisions would be more cautious or conservative than those made by individuals. The *Organization Man*, by William Whyte, published in 1956, helped to popularize this belief.[3] Whyte implied that groups would make more cautious decisions because members would not want to appear foolish or extreme in the presence of peers and superiors. In 1961, a student at the MIT School of Industrial Management decided to examine this popular notion to complete his masters thesis requirement. This student, J. A. F. Stoner, was to begin a line of investigation which, at last count in 1976, had generated over 300 published research reports and communications. Stoner's research, which found that groups were on average more risky in their decisions than individuals, was reported soon after its completion by two members of the MIT faculty committee overseeing the thesis research.[4] The phenomenon was quickly dubbed the "risky-shift" effect. Since this research refuted an existing theory of management, with serious implications for practitioners as well as theoreticians, a tremendous interest in group decision making was spawned. It is not an exaggeration to state that a whole sub-field of social psychology was given life by this MIT student, who for the most part, has not been involved in any research on "risky-shift" since the completion of his thesis.

A number of years later and after a large number of contradictory studies, it became clear that the term "risky-shift" was a misnomer. Researchers began to note that under various conditions it was possible to produce a "wary" or cautious shift. This is the situation whereby groups will on average come to a more conservative decision than those arrived at by individual group members before group discussion and decision. Various studies were finding "risky-shift" as found by Stoner, while others were finding a cautious shift, just as William Whyte had predicted. The research paradigm of the field faced a crisis and a new perspective was needed. Did groups reach more risky or more cautious decisions than individuals? A broader focus was needed in the research. This new focus is implicit in the euphemism which is now used to describe this group phenomenon —the choice shift effect. Indexing of reports on the topic and popular accounts however still are usually to be found under the conceptually more limited phrase of "risky-shift."

Much of the research completed during the last several years has been aimed at defining the conditions which cause various choice shifts. Specifically, what factors cause a shift toward risk in some problems and what conditions cause a shift toward caution. Again, it should be noted that this shift, in either direction, is the difference between the average scores or decisions of individuals and the decision reached by a group composed of these same individuals.

It does seem clear that the type of problem/decision under consideration has an effect upon the type of choice shift. Research by Cohen,[5] Spector,[6] and Schellenberg[7] note that type of problem is a factor in the kind of choice shift taken by groups, but none are able to offer further explanation of this relationship since in each of these studies type-of-problem effects were not the foci of the experiments. One study has been published which attempted to measure type of problem as a causal variable in producing choice shifts. Blitz and Dansereau report that three factors of problems under consideration would effect the type of choice shift made by groups: (a) Effect, the effect of the decision on others, (b) Salience, the importance of the consequences to these others, and (c) Influence, the amount of influence decision makers would have over the success or failure of the problem *after* the decision had been reached.[8] Various hypothetical decision situations were constructed which varied the amount of these three factors (i.e., S–high, E–low, I–high). These situations were presented to individuals and then to groups composed of these individuals, each in turn making a decision. Results showed a significant move toward a cautious choice shift when the Salience Factor of the problem under consideration was "high." The other two factors under study (Effect and Influence) did not effect choice shift in a statistically significant manner although there was a trend for problems with high Effect, low Influence,and high Salience to lead to the most cautious choice shifts. This research will hopefully encourage others to study type of problem as a causal factor in choice shift and thus extend this line of investigation.

Several other researchers have begun to look to differences in individual personalities as possible explanations for wary or risky choice shifts. Goldman[9] has considered types of choice shifts in terms of a theory of motivation developed by McClelland[10] and Atkinson[11] and commonly called Achievement Motivation theory or nAch (need achievement) theory. Since individuals scoring high in nAch are less likely to yield to pressure to conform, have a low fear of failure and are likely to take moderate risks rather than extreme (low or high) risks,[12] Goldman reasoned that nAch might well be a valuable predictor of choice shift behavior. A study was conducted in which subjects were tested on nAch and placed into either high, low or ambivalent (inconsistent) classifications. As is usual with choice shift research, subjects were asked to make decisions on problems presented by the researcher and then placed in groups to reach a group decision on these same problems. However, these groups were formed in such a manner that some had a majority of those either high or low in nAch. Results confirmed the hypothesis: groups in which the majority had scored high in nAch made significantly riskier choices from previous individual decisions. Groups in which a majority of the individuals had scored low in nAch showed a significant choice shift toward caution as contrasted with previous individual decisions. Groups where "high's" and "lows" were represented in equal numbers showed a slight but non-significant risky choice shift. Goldman believes a "tug-of-war" situation develops in the group situation, the group with the majority exerting social influence over the ambivalent members, pulling these "Walter Mitty" types into their sphere of influence. The trend toward risky choice shift in equalized groups (non-significant) is believed to be related to the persuasiveness of those high in nAch or perhaps the less yielding posture taken by them.

Plax and Rosenfeld, also examining choice shift in terms of the personalities involved, conducted extensive research using a number of standard personality measures.[13] They found that individuals likely to display a risky choice shift could be characterized as "... persistent, effective in communication, confident and outgoing, clever and imaginative, aggressive, efficient and clear-thinking ..." in terms of these standard measures. "Social Presence," as measured by the California Personality Inventory (CPI), was found to be the best single predictor of risky choice shift in individuals. The authors summarize the personality of such individuals as "... dynamic task oriented leader(s) ...". No studies have yet been published in which both, type of problem under consideration, and personality of those involved in the decision process, have been combined in an experiment. This would seem to be the next, and a most useful, step in research.

IMPLICATIONS FOR ACADEMIC LIBRARIES

As noted in the introduction to this paper, academic libraries in particular have found the committee process an attractive means of implementing a form of participative management. If these committees have the power to make decisions, as is true in some cases, or to make a strong recommendation, which is perhaps the more likely situation, then the literature on choice shifts should have important implications for academic libraries and participative management.

Firstly, committees have often been used for various personnel functions such as hiring, evaluation and promotion, choosing leaders, etc. The staff selection process has probably seen the most extensive use of the committee process. The ACRL has published guidelines on the appointment and work of such committees and although not stating so flatly, must be regarded as advocating the use of committees as much as possible.[14] This is not surprising in light of ACRL's support for professorial status for librarians. Peer review and evaluation is also generally accepted as one of the responsibilities of professionals and has also been the subject of an ACRL policy guideline.[15] Finally, the collegial model for library organization, espoused by many librarians, would normally presume that leadership positions would be filled by some group decision process.

Secondly, academic libraries have found the committee structure extremely useful in studying and recommending action on a variety of technological, social, and policy issues facing libraries. A committee offers the advantage of bringing increased expertise to bear on a problem and of making sure that vital viewpoints are integrated into the solution.

Given these two broad areas of committee use in libraries, what might be the effect of choice shift? In terms of the type of problem under review as a variable shaping choice shift (Blitz and Dansereau), personnel problems in particular would seem susceptible to cautious rather than risky shift. Hiring, promotion and similar decisions would have high salience and effect, and low influence, using the taxonomy discussed earlier. A recent article by Harvey and Parr, discussing library search and screen committees, has pointed out the strengths and weaknesses of such committees.[16] Several issues later this article was followed by a letter in reply by Galloway which attacked such committees.[17] Galloway holds that such committees often have quite unrealistic and lofty expectations for candidates and thus discourage many qualified individuals from even applying, leaving the field open for those "with grand notions of their own importance or are desperate enough to apply for anything."[18] Harvey and Parr hint at these problems when they note as weaknesses: "failure to appraise realistically the qualificiations required. . ."; "some committees have deliberately sought candidates less well qualified than the predecessor!"; ". . . may screen for obvious paper qualifications rather than for potential. . ."; ". . . are said to select not the best candidate, but instead, the candidate who displeases no one."[19] Within these committees there would appear to be strong concern for the elaboration of the processes and mechanisms of searching and the rigid specification of criteria for judging candidates. This might be interpreted as an effort to make the decision readily apparent, and self-fulfilling. Such caution in the formation of procedures and criteria would seem to be an attempt to avoid risk, in effect, a shift toward caution through the formulation of procedures and criteria. It might further be assumed that similar difficulties would be faced by committees dealing with other personnel related issues.

Technological and policy issues, when handled by a committee, should be less affected by these "type-of-problem" factors. For example, circulation policies would not seem subject to a cautious choice shift since problems of this type would have low salience and effect. However, even here certain kinds of problems may have high salience and lead to a cautious choice shift when decision making is handled by a group. Any decision involving organization restructuring would have high salience. An automation project which projected the wholesale shifting of personnel would have a great deal of salience and effect and point towards a cautious choice shift. Other problems, of course, might lead to a risky choice shift.

Addressing the second area of research reviewed, personality studies, what might be the effect of personality type on choice shift for academic library committees? As noted earlier, Plax and Rosenfeld found the "Social Presence" scale of the California Personality Inventory (CPI) the best single predictor of risky choice shift for individuals.[20] For librarianship, Clayton, in what is now a very dated study, found that library school students as a group scored significantly lower on the "Social Presence" scale of the CPI as compared to the national norms provided by the test distributor.[21] We do not have any information on how practicing librarians might compare today or how they would compare specifically to the subjects in Clayton's study. Much more research would be needed before any connection could be affirmed.

As discussed earlier, Goldman has found that those high in need for achievement would tend to make risky choice shifts while those low in nAch would make cautious choice shifts.[22] I have undertaken a study of nAch theory as it relates to academic librarians. Although the results of this dissertation research cannot be compared directly to other findings on nAch or to Goldman's work, since different instruments were employed, the findings are suggestive.[23] Results indicated that librarians employed in supervisory positions (supervising the work of at least one other professional) scored significantly higher in nAch than professionals not holding supervisory positions. This would seem to suggest that supervisory librarians would make riskier choices, on average, than other professionals. Hence, the membership character of committees in academic libraries could have a startling effect upon the kinds of decisions we make about our future.

CONCLUSION

It is beyond the purview of this article to discuss the need for either more risky or more cautious decision making in libraries. However, it is a certainty that many decisions about the future of libraries and librarians will be made and that many will be made by a group or committee. Since academic libraries in particular have embraced the committee process as a means of participative management, and as a means of dealing with sensitive and complex issues, this paper suggests that the literature on group processes, developed by social psychologists, is pertinent to decision making by library committees. This short and selective review of the literature indicates that the type of problem being considered and certain personality variables have an important effect upon these decisions. More research is needed to determine the characteristics of decision making by individuals and groups in libraries; it is the hope of this author to conduct such research in the future.

REFERENCES

1. Louis Kaplan, "The Literature of Participation: From Optimism to Realism," *College & Research Libraries* 36 (November 1975): 473–479.
2. Frederick Herzberg, *Work and the Nature of Man* (Cleveland: World Publishing Company, 1966).
3. William H. Whyte, Jr., *The Organization Man* (New York: Simon and Schuster, 1956).
4. M. A. Wallach, N. Kogan and D. J. Bem, "Group Influence on Individual Risk Taking," *Journal of Abnormal and Social Psychology* 65 (1962):75–84.
5. Stephen L. Cohen and Carol Beth Ruis, "Wary Shift or Risky Shift?," *Bulletin of the Psychonomic Society*, 3(1974):214–216.
6. Paul E. Spector, Stephen L. Cohen, and Louis A. Penner, "The Effects of Real vs. Hypothetical Risk on Group Choice–Shifts," *Personality and Social Psychology Bulletin*, 2(1976):290–293.

7. James A. Schellenberg, "Is There a Pessimistic Shift?," *Psychological Reports*, 39(1976):259–362.
8. Robert Blitz and Donald F. Dansereau, "The Effect of Underlying Situational Characteristics on the Risky Shift Phenomenon," *Journal of Social Psychology*, 87 (1972):251–258.
9. Ethel K. Goldman, "Need Achievement as a Motivational Basis for the Risky Shift," *Journal of Personality* 43(1975):346–356.
10. D. C. McClelland, J. W. Atkins, R. A. Clark, and E. L. Lowell, *The Achievement Motive* (New York: Irvington Publishers, 1973).
11. John W. Atkinson and Joel O. Raynor, *Motivation and Achievement* (New York: Wiley, 1974).
12. Goldman, *op. cit.*, p. 348.
13. Timothy G. Plax and Lawrence B. Rosenfeld, "Correlates of Risky Decision-Making," *Journal of Personality Assessment* 40(1976):413–418.
14. "Guidelines and Procedures for the Screening and Appointment of Academic Librarians," *College & Research Libraries News* 38(September 1977):231–233.
15. "Standards for Faculty Status for College and University Librarians," *College & Research Libraries News* 33(September 1972):210–212.
16. John F. Harvey and Mary Parr, "University Library Search and Screen Committees," *College & Research Libraries* 37(July 1976):347–355.
17. R. Dean Galloway, letter in response to "University Library Search and Screen Committees," *College & Research Libraries* 37(November 1976):551.
18. *Ibid.*
19. Harvey and Parr, *op. cit.*, p. 353–354.
20. Plax and Rosenfeld, *op. cit.*
21. Howard Clayton, "Femininity and Job Satisfaction Among Male Library Students at One Midwestern University," *College & Research Libraries* 31(November 1970): 388–398.
22. Goldman, *op. cit.*
23. "Achievement Motivation Theory as it Relates to Professional Personnel at College and University Libraries," doctoral dissertation in progress, Graduate School of Library Science, Drexel University, Philadelphia.

Isaac T. Littleton

North Carolina State University at Raleigh

STATE SYSTEMS OF HIGHER EDUCATION AND LIBRARIES*

This paper reports on a study of the role that state boards and systems of higher education play in the development of public senior academic libraries. Forty-nine states have now established one of three types of statewide systems of higher education: voluntary, coordinating, or governing. Current trends in statewide funding and coordination of senior academic libraries are discussed, including funding formulas now in use. Although the academic library budgets in a number of states were raised significantly when statewide funding formulas were adopted, the author concludes that formulas per se do not raise library budgets unless funds are available and unless budgeting authorities give library support high priority. State systems of higher education are increasingly concerned about the use of resources and technology. A fully developed statewide plan for academic libraries may include, in addition to coordinated funding, the shared use of technology, more effective programs of resource sharing, joint on-line catalogs, improved statewide delivery systems, cooperative acquisitions programs, and joint storage of lesser-used materials.

A major trend in higher education during the 1950's and 1960's was the establishment of boards or commissions in nearly every state to coordinate planning and financing of public universities.[1] Arthur McAnally reported on a study of library budgeting procedures of state systems of higher education in 1963 when these state boards were just beginning to scrutinize campus budgets.[2] At that time only 31 states had statewide agencies for the governance of public colleges and universities and few states had adopted integrated funding plans for academic libraries; those states that did so used mainly arbitrary methods that had little relationship to real needs. In 1972 Kenneth Allen, in a report to the Council on Library Resources, compared the major statewide funding formulas being used at that time.[3] Both the McAnally and Allen studies are significant contributions, but formulas are revised to meet new demands and needs. As Lyman Glenny, Director of the Center for Research and Higher Education, has said: "Experience

---

*Based on Isaac T. Littleton. *State Systems of Higher Education and Libraries: A Report for the Council on Library Resources* (November 1977). Multilithed. (97 pages)

has shown that formulas must be constantly re-evaluated to keep them timely and equitable and to reflect as accurately as possible the changing assumptions which serve as their basis."[4] It is not surprising then, that since Allen's study of 1972, important new formulas have appared on the horizon and old ones have been modified or abandoned. An up-date of the McAnally and Allen studies is needed. The purpose of this paper is to point out current trends in statewide funding and coordination of public senior academic libraries.

PROCEDURE

The observations are based on data and information obtained during the Fall of 1976 and the summer of 1977. A Council on Library Resources fellowship made it possible to visit the staffs of state agencies of higher education in eleven states as well as representative libraries to get librarians' points of view. After the visits, questionnaires were mailed to state agencies in all 50 states. Areas explored in the interviews and questionnaires were: funding, planning for library development, library cooperation, and the role of advisory committees of librarians. Long range plans, reports, surveys, budgeting instructions and formulas were requested.

STATEWIDE AGENCIES OF HIGHER EDUCATION

Forty-nine states have now established some kind of statewide system of higher education, forty-six during the 1950's and 1960's.[5] There were two major reasons for the trend toward statewide higher education systems: first, the unprecedented enrollment increases due to the return of World War II veterans in the 1950's and the sudden increase in college age persons in the population during the 1960's and secondly, an unparalleled growth in the diversity of functions and programs of state colleges and universities.[6] During this time of expansion, there was great concern by state governments that financial resources of each state be used as efficiently as possible to meet the added demands and to insure quality education for the masses of new students. One writer stated that statewide planning and coordination were the twin keys to quality and effectiveness. States were advised to establish coordinating boards as the best approach to statewide planning.[7]

The problems facing higher education in the mid-seventies and eighties are different than in the fifties and sixties but no less challenging. During the 1970's enrollments and budgets are stabilizing and, in some states, declining. The decreased rate of growth is caused by a number of factors, but especially by economic pressures and a high rate of inflation as well as competing needs of other segments of state governments. Enrollments are effected by economic conditions and by a drop in the number of college age persons in the population. Henderson and Henderson say that the wave of growth in the 1960's "has left in its wake a multitude of problems."[8] An era of affluence and growth is changing into a period of austerity and declining enrollments. There is now even greater demand for coordination and accountability by state governments in their efforts to cope with the new problems of the 1970's and 1980's. As far as libraries are concerned, the changing economic conditions have caused increased interest by state systems of higher education in effective resource sharing programs, cooperative acquisitions, joint storage and shared uses of technology.

Vermont is the only state without such an agency, whereas Delaware and Nebraska have voluntary agencies with no legal status.[9] The other forty-seven states have either governing or coordinating boards. A governing board has legal control over a multi-campus university system with the authority to approve systemwide budgets, capital improvement requests, new academic programs, and to appoint institutional chief executives. Twenty states now have statewide governing boards. The other type is the coordinating board which is superimposed over institutional boards of trustees and has advisory and recommending authority only. Coordinating boards are usually charged by state legislatures to make studies, surveys, and long-range plans for higher education and to approve new academic programs. Some coordinating agencies, such as the Ohio Board of Regents, have strong budgetary roles by providing guidelines for institutional budget requests and others, such as the New York Board of Regents have no budgetary role, but strong authority over the registration and approval of academic programs. Both New York and California have a coordinating board and two multi-campus universities with their own governing boards. These two states have the most complex higher education establishments and the most highly coordinated academic library systems in the country. The higher education system in these two states also employ sizeable staffs at the system level for library coordination.

Coordinated funding of public academic libraries was the first area relating to libraries in which state boards of higher education began to operate but overall library planning and the implementation of statewide resource programs are important functions of many of these agencies.

FUNDING

In 1963 McAnally observed that statewide budgeting had come to many academic libraries and, as he correctly predicted, "it is here to stay."[10] In 1977, systematic budgeting procedures for public academic libraries have come to at least 23 states, according to a recent report by the Washington Council for Postsecondary Education.[11]

At the present time, funding procedures for public university and college libraries may be categorized in three ways: (1) traditional: budgeting to the institution by object line based on institutional requests, (2) lump sum budgeting to the institutions, (3) restricted funding for library use based on a statewide funding plan or formula. Although a majority of states still use traditional budgeting methods for libraries, there has been a gradual trend since the 1960's toward the use of coordinated statewide budgeting for public academic libraries. Library funding formulas are used both in institutional lump sum budgeting and in restricted library budgeting. They are used to generate total amounts of library funding for the system and also to divide available funds among libraries.

A large number of states provide lump sum funding to institutions based on formulas in certain cost categories. Library costs are usually included in the category "academic support." The staff of the board of higher education, on the basis of formulas, develops an "asking budget" for the system. The institution is provided a lump sum budget and the institution has *complete autonomy* in deciding how the appropriation is to be allocated. Formulas used for generating library portions vary from state to state, but campus libraries seldom obtain the full amount generated by formulas. The practical benefits of the use of formulas in lump sum budgeting are purported to be that they are *simple* to implement, that they provide *equitable treatment* of institutions and that they provide institutional *flexibility* if used to develop *asking* budgets and not *spending* budgets.

In a very few states boards allocate funds restricted for institutional libraries. These state systems use formulas as vehicles for distribution of available funds and also to provide a more rational approach to library budgeting. Again, this approach offers the advantage of simplicity and equity among institutions; from the library's point of view it may be desirable because an institution's administration cannot divert funds to other purposes as has been done in some states with lump sum institutional budgeting.

McAnally found a wide variety of funding procedures in use in 1963 and categorized them into four types: (1) percentage formulas usually based on a percentage of the instructional and research budgets, (2) formulas that use enrollment as a basis, (3) comparisons of proposed budgets with past or current budgets, and (4) unit cost bases.[12] These basic methods are still in use but there has been a movement toward the use of formulas which include factors that have a direct relationship to library needs.

One of the first methods used to generate public academic library budgets on a systemwide basis is the percentage method. Currently Georgia uses 9% and South Carolina, 10% of the instructional, research and extension budgets as a basis for library support in the asking budget for the system. This does not mean, however, that libraries receive the full percentage from the institutions; in most cases, they do not. McAnally points out that the percentage method is arbitrary and is not based on library needs, nor does it allow institutional variations in programs and other variables that effect library needs.[13]

ENROLLMENT BASES

Enrollment is being used as the basis for library budgeting in a number of states, but differential rates by academic level of students have provided further refinements in the use of enrollment figures as a basis for budgeting. The University of North Carolina Board of Governors adopted a plan for improving libraries in 1973, which consists of two formulas: one for increasing the holdings of all libraries up to the ACRL 1959 college standard[14] and one for increasing the continuing base budgets.[15] The second part of the plan, that for increasing the basic and continuing total annual budgets, includes a basic support figure of $134 for each full-time equivalent (FTE) undergraduate student, twice that amount ($268) for each FTE Master's degree student, and seven times the base figure ($948) for each FTE doctoral and first professional student. Budgeting authorities in North Carolina established the formulas as a goal and agreed to provide funds in annual increments until the libraries' holdings and budgets were raised to the level of the formulas. The library budgeting plan not only has produced more equitable funding for each of the state's 16 senior institutions but it has also increased annual library expenditures. This increase is due largely to the high priority that the staff of the UNC Board of Governors attaches to the improvement of library resources.

The formula for the budgeting of Texas public senior college and university libraries substantially raised library funding in that state when the Coordinating Board of Texas College and University System adopted it in 1965. A differential dollar rate per semester hour is established by academic level.[16] The rate for the Master's level is twice that for undergraduates and the doctoral level is almost nine times the undergraduate level. The formula contains a lower rate for law semester credit hours than for those at the doctoral level. The dollar figures used in this formula have been raised each year since it was adopted to counteract inflation. The library formula along with formulas in 15 other areas of univerity operations are developed biennially by *ad hoc* committees composed of systemwide representatives and fiscal officers. Librarians serve on the Library Formula Committee. The Texas formula is rarely funded fully, but it does serve as a vehicle for equitable distribution of available funds to the institutional libraries. The Texas formula was based on a study of the average costs of providing the facilities and services for undergraduates, graduate students and faculty members at Purdue University which was done in 1961 by Gerald L. Quatman.[17] A number of states in the South, including Arkansas, Alabama and Tennessee, have adopted the Texas model.

UNIT COSTS

McAnally says that "the ideal way to build a library budget should be to build it on unit costs."[18] Planning, Programming, Budgeting (PPBS) is a form of unit-cost budgeting which a number of states are considering. Ann Prentice has given a brief definition of PPBS: "the first steps in (PPBS) budget development are a statement of the objectives of the library and the identification of programs and sub-programs which will achieve those objectives. The cost of each program is analyzed according to criteria of cost benefit, and the program activity that provides the greatest benefit at least cost is selected." PPBS includes a plan for feedback and evaluation which "enables the administrator to determine to what extent program objectives are being achieved and at what cost."[19] Allen summarized the concepts, theory and evolution of PPBS, and concluded that it is difficult to apply PPBS to academic libraries. His survey found that academic libraries generally have a negative and pessimistic attitude toward the practical usefulness of PPBS for libraries.[20]

California has, for a long time, used unit costs as a basis for budgeting. The budget for acquisitions is calculated on the basis of total number of volumes authorized for each of the two systems of higher education. The Department of Finance establishes an average price per volume derived from data published in *Publisher's Weekly* and *Library Journal;* the total acquisitions budget is determined by multiplying the price per volume by the authorized number of volumes. Each system determines the number of volumes required by formula and on the basis of the aggregate experience of the libraries involved.

The Califorha State University and Colleges System uses staffing formulas that have undergone constant change and revision over the past seven years and at the present writing it is not possible to say with any degree of certainty which staffing formulas will be used in the future. However, formulas recommended in the 1977/78–1981/82 plan for library development are based on uniform workload factors and work measurement.[21] The formula adopted is a modification of a SUNY formula. Functions, such as filing cards, advising users, selecting serials, etc., are measured by a set of work measurement units expressed in output terms. The result is a series of "standard times" for performing rather distinct functions both manually and by automated procedures. These functions are all related in a formula to five basic concerns of libraries: holdings, acquisitions, academic year FTE users (faculty and students), head count students, and academic year FTE faculty. The resulting staffing formula is as follows:

$$\text{General staff} = \frac{Aa + Bb + Cc + Dd + Ee}{110,340}$$

Where A = Countable library volumes
   B = Volumes added
   C = Student FTE and faculty FTE
   D = Head count students
   E = Academic year FTE faculty
   a = 2.616 minutes
      (Weighted Standard Time, Technical Services Standards–Holdings)
   b = 139.283 minutes
      (WST, Technical Services Standards–Acquisitions)

c = 178.957 minutes
    (WST, Public Services Standards—Users)
d = 207.517 minutes (WST, Public Services Standards—Enrollment)
e = 174.174 minutes (WST, Public Services Standards—Faculty)

The 110,340 in the above formula represents, in minutes, a man-year figure (excluding sick leave and holidays). Tables are provided that demonstrate how "weighted standard times" are derived. Each WST is calculated in minutes for specific library tasks grouped according to the five basic concerns. A table is also provided to show the total number of staff members that the formula would yield for each of the 19 campuses. If this formula is finally accepted, requests for staff would be made on the basis of the positions yielded by the formula. The new CSUC staffing proposal is an attempt to apply work measurement and scientific management to library personnel budgeting. It is a highly complex formula that will require a large amount of staff time to implement. It has not been actually tried so its effectiveness is difficult to measure but, on the surface, there are a number of pertinent questions that it poses. Will there be uniformity of measurement and accuracy from campus to campus? Can all library work, particularly at the professional level, be mechanized and quantified to this extent? Staff needs and special requirements vary among campuses. Are these taken into consideration?

FORMULAS USING LIBRARY-RELATED VARIABLES

The Clapp–Jordan Formula, devised in the mid-1960's by Verner Clapp, was intended as a quantitative measure of the adequacy of library holdings. It was initially used in a survey of the adequacy of libraries of public senior colleges and universities in Ohio[22] and later published in an article that appeared in *College and Research Libraries.*[23] For the first time, an attempt was made to include in a formula, some of the program and enrollment factors that are known to affect adequacy of holdings. The varibles in the Clapp–Jordan formula are: an "opening day" basic collection, the number of faculty, the number of students, the number of undergraduate major subject fields, the number of masters fields, and the number of Ph.D. fields. Clapp and Jordan estimated the number of volumes required for each variable on the basis of basic lists, specialized subject bibliographies, and professional experience and judgment. The authors point out that the formula is intended to measure only *minimal* adequacy. A number of surveyors have adopted the formula to assess adequacy of library resources and some state agencies have adapted it as a funding formula for acquisitions.

The State of Washington has used a modification of the Clapp–Jordan formula since 1969 as a basis for recommending acquisitions budgets. A separate formula is used for library operations (staffing and binding). The Washington State formulas were first published in 1970.[24] Since then a number of states have adopted them or modifications of them. Perhaps the most notable adoption of the formulas was by the Association of College and Research Libraries as a national standard for assessing the adequacy of holdings and staff of college libraries.[25] The 1975 ACRL standards use formulas that are almost identical to the 1970 Washington State formulas for holdings and staff. In 1975 a library formula task force recommended a modification of the 1970 Washington State formula system and added a number of elements but the new formula was not accepted by the budgeting authorities because it did not give consistent results and it is still under revision.

Librarians and faculty are questioning formulas that are based solely on enrollment and numbers of programs and are looking for more satisfactory approaches to library funding. A recent study by the Faculty Senate Library Committee of SUNY states that it is especially critical to reexamine library allocation practices "at a time when enrollments are stabilizing, particularly if collection growth is tied to student FTE growth."[26] The Committee recognizes that demands on a library collection depend upon a number of factors other than students, faculty and programs which are the elements on which the Clapp–Jordan-type formulas are based. Some of the additional factors are: the differential costs and publication rates among disciplines; the purpose of the collection, i.e., whether it is for teaching, research, or for basic use; and the level and variety of academic programs. Important operational factors are: user population, the size and adequacy of existing holdings, the extent to which holdings are dispersed in branch libraries which determines the degree of duplication necessary, the accessibility to other libraries, the loss and physical deterioration of materials, and the spiraling costs of books and periodicals.[27]

One authority has concluded that, in view of the shortcomings of the Clapp–Jordan-type formulas, that "considerable additional research be undertaken to determine precisely which factors, and the respective weight of each, affect book needs in particular academic situations."[28]

Librarians of research university libraries are concerned about formulas that are applied uniformly across the board both to colleges without graduate and research programs and to research universities. Most of the funding formulas do not take into account the special requirements of research universities. There is a search for better methods for funding research university libraries.

The Voigt formula that was reported in the July 1975 issue of *College and Research Libraries* was designed for the libraries in the University of California by Melvin Voigt, Librarian Emeritus at San Diego.[29] It is specifically for university libraries that must support large numbers of doctoral and research programs. The model is based on the numbers of volumes deemed necessary for doctoral programs in specified subject fields; it also takes into account the special needs of extramurally funded research. The formula also includes a supplement for undergraduate and graduate use based on enrollment and an addition for lack of access to other libraries. The major criticism of the model is that there are no empirical data to support the numbers of volumes used in the formula. Voigt readily admits this but he says "most librarians who have commented on the model believe them (the number of volumes assigned to subject fields) to be of the right order of magnitude."[30] Librarians have also raised an objection to the formula because it depends almost exclusively on doctoral programs with no weight given to master's or professional degree programs. Some administrators have expressed concern that the formula may measure some factors two or three times and some not at all, for example, credit for doctoral programs and research programs in the same fields overlap. Nevertheless, professional opinion is generally favorable. It does provide a uniform method for making comparisons among libraries supporting universities with large doctoral and research programs. Voigt has provided a formula for determining the number of volumes to be added annually as well as for assessing adequacy of the total holdings of a university library.[31] The University of California has used it to determine the number of volumes to be funded by the system.[32]

The Voigt formula is being used in Virginia as a basis for acquisitions budget requests of the two doctoral universities (Virginia Polytechnic Institute and State University [VPI] and the University of Virginia) and it has been accepted by the four graduate universities in the State University of New York (SUNY).

The Virginia budget guidelines for 1978–80 also provide a new type of funding formula for four-year colleges which is based on differential weights assigned to subject disciplines.[33] Weights were derived by calculating the dollar value of books published in the first six months of *Choice* for 1974 and combined with the dollar value of periodicals listed by Katz and Farber.[34] The subject discipline weights are multiplied by weights assigned to program magnitude which is a measure of the number of programs in the Higher Education General Information Survey (HEGIS) classification of the discipline. The total program weight is then multiplied by a dollar value ($15,095 and $15,975 for 1978–79 and 1979–80 respectively). An enrollment weight is then multiplied by the corresponding program funding to determine maintenance funding for acquisitions.

The staffing plan for Virginia senior public institutions of higher education differentiates on the basis of type of institutions.

The guidelines for staffing each of the two ARL institutions (University of Virginia and VPI) in Virginia is established by using the mean level of staffing of the group of 20 ARL institutions with the Virginia institution as its median in terms of volumes held.[35]

Non-ARL doctoral institutions and other universities and four-year colleges are allocated 9 FTE positions as a basic staff regardless of enrollments and one FTE position for every 400 undergraduate annual FTE students. Library positions are also to be added on the basis of the number of graduate students and faculty members.

The acquisitions funding formulas and the staffing formulas recommended by the Virginia librarians and those adopted by the Council, although complex, provide new approaches to library funding. They are attempts to grapple with many of the factors other than enrollment that are important in determining adequacy of library funding and to differentiate between the requirements of different types of institutions.

Unfortunately, formulas, regardless of which are used, are seldom funded fully because of economic or political pressures from the state government. Sometimes when economic conditions worsen significantly, formulas are abandoned. The Florida Board of Regents, which has always advocated strong univerity library resources, provided funding earmarked specifically for libraries in recent years according to a modified Washington State formula—until fiscal year 1976–77. In 1976–77, however, because of severe economic problems, formula budgeting was abandoned by the system and a lump sum based on FTE enrollment was appropriated to each institution. The University administration on each campus determined the amount to be allocated to each campus library. The total amount for public university libraries in Florida decreased by an estimated $1,000,000. Book budgets and staff at many of the institutions were significantly reduced or stabilized. Inflation caused even less purchasing power.

The Florida budget decline reflects a decrease in the rate of increase of total appropriations for higher education in Florida. According to statistics reported in the *Chronicle of Higher Education*, Florida's appropriations for higher education increased only 5% but actually decreased 9% when corrected for inflation for the two-year period from 1975–76 to 1976–77.[36] In 1976–77, the state ranked 48th in percent increase among the 50 states. According to budgeting authorities in Florida, library budgets were cut to save positions and to meet rising salaries and costs in other areas, particularly utilities. The situation in Florida illustrates the breakdown in formula budgeting if budgeting authorities give higher priority to other needs. Unless budgeting authorities, either at the state or campus level, give library needs high priority these needs will not be met in severe economic declines. Under such circumstances libraries must cancel periodical subscriptions. indefinitely delay the purchase of materials to support teaching and research programs, and cut services. A happy footnote (and an important one) is that in 1977–78 Florida provided an appropriation of $10,000,000 to libraries of the nine public senior institutions to make up for the severe budget cuts in 1976–77 and past inadequate funding. The appropriation was allocated to the institutions on the basis of the Washington State formula.

States develop budgeting practices to meet their own political and economic circumstances. There appears to be a trend toward ever more complex funding formulas for both acquisitions and staffing. There may be a danger in developing formulas that are so complex that budgeting authorities and legislatures find them incomprehensible and therefore unacceptable as a funding mechanism. It is clear that formulas are not as important in obtaining adequate library funding as the commitment of state boards of higher education, state budgeting authorities and legislatures to library improvement and development. It may be just as important for librarians to convince state boards of the essential role that libraries play in the educational and research process as to develop ever more complex budgeting formulas.

CONCLUSIONS ON FUNDING

State systems of higher education are under political pressure to provide equitable funding among all public institutions, and, as a result, older funding patterns are changing. There is considerable concern on the part of some of the larger university libraries that a leveling process is occurring, caused by coordinated budgeting procedures.[37] In some of the states, integrated budgeting plans for all public academic libraries within a state system have been successful in raising the general level of library funding. In these states, the staffs of the state boards have been able to deal more effectively with legislative and budgeting authorities on the basis of integrated library funding plans than by separate institutional budget requests. Nevertheless, libraries in over half of the states are still not directly affected by statewide funding programs.

McAnally noted that "there are a great many bases and methods for preparing library budgets . . ., each of which has some virtues and some defects. Which formula may be the best and is likely to emerge or gain general acceptance cannot be foreseen . . ."[38] A wider variety of budgeting formulas is being used today than in 1963 and no "ideal" has yet emerged. However, the general principles established by the Clapp–Jordan formula have been adopted in a number of formulas. The Washington State formulas for both staff and acquisitions have become national standards for assessing adequacy. The Texas model has been adopted by a number of states also. The Voigt formula is being used as a model for acquisitions requirements for doctoral granting universities. The Virginia budgeting program, in addition to enrollment and faculty, includes other variables such as the differential costs of materials by subject discipline. A "best" or "ideal" formula is not likely to be universally adopted because of, first, the variations in the missions and programs of colleges and universities and, secondly, the differences in the economic and political climates among the states. A funding plan or formula that works for one state may be a failure in another state.

Budgeting formulas are very seldom fully funded, but they do serve as vehicles to distribute available funds to institutions on the basis of specified variables. In some cases, the formulas are manipulated by budgeting officials to reflect the funds available. In other states, recommended formulas have been rejected because they generated substantially more funds than the agencies thought politically wise to request. In addition to using formulas as bases for generating asking budgets and for distributing available funds among institutions, state agencies use them as standards for assessing the adequacy of collections and staff. Standard formulas have been used in statewide surveys of library resources to provide data that gave visibility to library needs. If these needs are given widespread publicity the data can serve as a springboard to obtain special appropriations for improving libraries.

McAnally points out that "the coming of systematic budgeting is neither a cause for rejoicing nor a reason for alarm, for there are advantages and disadvantages."[39] Public academic libraries in a number of states have had reason for rejoicing during the late

1960's and 1970's because they have received substantially increased budgets as a result of statewide coordinated funding programs which in turn came about because state agency officials were convinced of the need to improve historically inadequate academic libraries and to provide more equitable funding among institutions in the system.

Some of the state agencies provide funds for special requests to take care of institutional needs not covered adequately by a formula, such as supporting new academic programs or bringing particular libraries up to minimum accreditation standards. Special requests from institutions over and above formula funding should be an important element of any funding program. North Carolina has provided funds to campus libraries over and above formula funding to counteract inflation and to enable the library to keep up with enrollment increases. It has become clear that the formulas which are used are not as important in achieving adequate funding as the strength of commitment of the state system and budget officials to libraries. Formulas per se do not raise budgets unless funds are available and unless budgeting authorities give library support high priority.

STATEWIDE PLANNING

Until recently, if state agencies of higher education were concerned at all with academic libraries, the concern was budgetary. There is a growing trend, however, in overall planning and coordination of academic library resources. We have seen in a few states, notably in the University of California system, a denial of funds for library buildings and increased acquisitions until an overall library plan was developed to ensure the most effective sharing of resources. State agencies of higher education are becoming increasingly concerned about the *use* of resources and technology. Systems of higher education in the larger states (California and New York) employ sizeable staffs dedicated to the development and coordination of library resources on a statewide level. It can be expected that other states will develop systemwide library plans. Most will depend on campus librarians and outside consultants to make surveys and to write planning documents, but if a statewide plan is to be effective, it must be monitored and supported by continuing studies of library operations as is being done in the states with full-time staffs for libraries at the system level.

McAnally pointed to the need for librarians to provide advice to officials of state agencies in developing funding and cooperative programs.[40] In 1963 there were few state committees of librarians. Now most states have either official advisory committees or volunteer committees.

Communications between the staff of boards of higher education and librarians are extremely important, particularly in states in which the boards play a role in library funding and planning. This is done in most states through advisory committees of librarians on either a continuing or an *ad hoc* basis. *Ad hoc* committees may be appointed to advise on a specific matter, such as a budget formula or a binding contract. Committees of librarians are sometimes appointed to carry out statewide surveys of library resources and services.

The most satisfactory relationship is through one or more committees that meet regularly with staff members of the boards. Virginia, Florida, Iowa, North Carolina, SUNY, Georgia, and the two California multi-campus universities are among the systems that have strong continuing advisory boards. These library planning boards advise on various aspects of library operations including funding, cooperative programs, building programs and personnel policies.

In some states, however, the lines of communication between state officials and campus librarians are not open; the formation of official committees is discouraged and even prohibited by either the Boards or the institutions. This is more prevalent in certain areas of the country where institutions are fearful that institutional autonomy will be compromised. In many of these states *volunteer* committees of librarians have been established for the purpose of developing statewide cooperative projects. Some of the most outstanding cooperative projects have been developed in states in which librarians have taken the leadership without systemwide financial backing. OCLC grew out of the efforts of Ohio librarians with little assistance from the Ohio Board of Regents. Another example is the Wisconsin Interlibrary Service (WILS) which was initiated by librarians with little or no assistance from the University of Wisconsin system.[41]

McAnally found little interest in library cooperation on the part of heads of state agencies and he expressed skepticism about the effectiveness of state level cooperation, especially in the development of resources.[42] In 1963 it was difficult to visualize the extensive library coordination at the state level that is now taking place in California, New York and Minnesota. The Minnesota Interlibrary Telecommunication Exchange (MINITEX)[43] and the New York State Interlibrary Loan Service (NYSILL) and its 3R's[44] (Reference and Research Resources) are outstanding statewide resource sharing programs that are funded directly by state legislatures as a result of support from state higher education systems. The shared uses of technology for cataloging, interlibrary loans and joint catalogs have been major factors in the development of state academic library systems. Statewide computerized library networks have been encouraged, and in some cases, funded directly by state legislatures. It is no longer economically feasible for a single library to afford complex local computer-based systems. Statewide programs for sharing these costs have been developed in a number of states. California and Minnesota legislatures have provided funds earmarked for cooperative purchases which are not to be duplicated among campuses. Improved statewide delivery of library materials among campuses is also being planned and funded in California and a number of other states.

Many librarians and faculty members have a fear of statewide coordination, some of which results from parochial interests in collections and institutional jealousies. McAnally listed some of the dangers: "the possibilities of regimentation (resulting in a loss of initiative, flexibility, and diversity), red tape, isolation of supervisory boards from direct contact with academic life, and the fostering of uniform mediocrity in states that finance higher education inadequately."[45] There is some apprehension among university librarians and faculty about statewide coordination because of the fear that university research collections will suffer as a result of the emphasis on resource sharing and joint on-line systems. Higher education agencies, campus administrators and librarians must guard against these dangers as states move in this direction. The "dangers" can be overcome to some extent through improved communications between librarians and officials of state agencies.

The University of California Libraries *Plan for Development, 1978–1988* calls for a "new approach" to meet the needs of users in an era of budgetary austerity and rising costs.[46] The new approach involves a greater dependence on resource sharing through the library system and less dependence on the campus library. But it also includes adequate acquisition rates on each campus. The UC development plan recommends increased acquisitions rates on each campus based on an integrated plan for acquisitions.[47] In addition to systemwide acquisitions programs, a fully developed statewide plan for academic libraries includes the shared use of technology, more effective statewide programs of resource sharing, joint on-line catalogs, improved statewide delivery systems, cooperative acquisitions programs, and joint storage of lesser-used materials.

Although no completely developed state academic library system exists as yet, the two California college and university systems have articulated highly integrated plans and are moving toward full implementation. Boards of higher education in other states, for example New York, Minnesota and Virginia, have elements of integrated systems and other states can be expected to move in this direction. McAnally observed that "an era of individualism in budgeting is drawing to a close for many colleges and universities."[48] In 1977, not only has systemwide budgeting become a fact of life for many colleges and universities but the coordination of other library operations at the state level has also become a reality.

De Gennaro has said "the time has come to shift emphasis away from holdings and size to access and services." He predicts that "more realistic concepts of collection building" and "new patterns of service" will be adopted with greater dependence on a national network and nationally developed resource collections patterned after the British Lending Library.[49] National planners must not overlook the role that state systems of higher education play in the funding and coordination of academic library resources. State agencies of higher education, in many states, can and will take major responsibility for finding solutions to funding and space problems of academic libraries through statewide funding plans and more effective programs for resource sharing. State academic library systems will undoubtedly be key elements in any national plan for library service.

REFERENCES

1. cf. John J. Corson, *The Governance of Colleges and Universities: Modernizing Structures and Processes* (Revised Edition), McGraw-Hill, 1975, p. 50.

2. Arthur M. McAnally, "Budgets by Formula," *The Library Quarterly*, 33 (April 1963): 159-171.

3. Kenneth S. Allen, *Current and Emerging Budgeting Techniques in Academic Libraries, Including a Critique of the Model Budget Analysis Program of the State of Washington*, University of Washington Libraries, April 1972.

4. Washington. Council for Postsecondary Education. *Progress Reports: Review of Higher Education Budget Formulas*. December 1975, pp. 2-3.

5. Rober O. Berdahl. *Statewide Coordination of Higher Education*, Washington, D.C., American Council on Higher Education, 1971; M. M. Chambers, *Higher Education and State Governments*, 1970-75, Danville, Illinois, Interstate Printers and Publishers, 1974.

6. Some of the books on higher education which provide information on the functions of these agencies are: Robert O. Berdahl, *Statewide Coordination of Higher Education*. Washington, D.C., American Council on Education, 1971; Carnegie Commission on Higher Education, *Governance of Higher Education: Six Priority Problems*, New York, McGraw-Hill, 1973; M. M. Chambers, *Higher Education and State Governments, 1970-1975*, Danville, Illinois, Interestate Printers and Publishers, 1974; John J. Corson, *op. cit.*; Olga D. Henderson and Jean Glidden Henderson, *Higher Education in America*, Josey-Bass Publishers, 1974; Eugene C. Lee and Frank M. Bowen, *The Multicampus University*, McGraw-Hill, 1971; D. Kent Halstead, *Statewide Planning in Higher Education*, U.S. Department of Health, Education and Welfare. Office of Education and Welfare. Office of Education (DHEW Publication No. ([OE] 73-17002) 1974; Carnegie Foundation for the Advancement of Teaching. *The States and Higher Education* and *Supplement*, Josey-Bass, 1976; National Commission on the Financing of Postsecondary Education, *Financing Post-Secondary Education in the United States*, Washington, D.C., U.S. Government Printing Office, 1973.

7. A. J. Brumbaugh, *Statewide Planning and Coordination of Higher Education. Southern Regional Education Board, 1963, p. 1.*

8. Olga D. Henderson and Jean Glidden Henderson, *Higher Education in America*, Josey-Bass Publishers, 1974, p. 1.
9. Based on a list of statewide boards, dated July 20, 1976, issued by the State Higher Education Executive Officers.
10. McAnally, *op. cit.*, p. 168.
11. Washington, Council for Postsecondary Education, *op. cit.*, p. 2.
12. McAnally, *op. cit.*
13. McAnally, *op. cit.*, p. 162.
14. "Standards for College Libraries," *College and Research Libraries*, 20 (July 1959): 278.
15. North Carolina. University. Board of Governors. *Long Range Planning, 1976–81*, Chapel Hill, April 2, 1976, p. 300.
16. Texas. College and University System. Coordinating Board. "Formulas Designated by Coordinating Board for the Public Senior Colleges and Universities, 1977–79 Biennium," Austin, February 25, 1976.
17. Gerald L. Quatman. *The Cost of Providing Library Service to Groups in the Purdue University Community–1961*, Lafayette, Ind., Purdue University Libraries, June 1962.
18. McAnally, *op. cit.*, p. 166.
19. Ann E. Prentice, "The Lingo of Library Finance," *American Libraries*, 8 (November 1977): 551–552.
20. Allen, *op. cit.*, pp. 4–18.
21. California. State University and Colleges. *Library Development, 1977/78–1981/82.* Long Beach, May, 1976, pp. 27–28, 56–61.
22. Verner W. Clapp and Robert T. Jordan, *The Libraries of the State-Assisted Institutions of Higher Education in Ohio–Their Maintenance and Development–Guidelines for Policy*, Washington, D.C., Council on Library Resources, 1964.
23. Verner W. Clapp and Robert T. Jordan, "Quantitative Criteria for Adequacy of Academic Library Collections," *College and Research Libraries*, 26 (September 1965): 371–380.
24. Washington. The Interinstitutional Committee of Business Officers. *A Model Budget Analysis System for Program 05: Libraries*, Olympia, Office of Interinstitutional Business Studies, March 1970.
25. "Standards for College Libraries," *College and Research Library News*, No. 9 (October 1975): 277–279, 290–301.
26. New York. State University of New York. "Factors Underlying Library Collection Development," *Faculty Senate Bulletin*, 10:4 (June 1975), p. 5.
27. *Ibid.*, pp. 5–6.
28. W. Kent Halstead, *Statewide Planning in Higher Education*, Washington, D.C., U.S. Department H.E.W., 1976, p. 412.
29. Melvin J. Voigt, "Acquisition Rates in University Libraries," *College and Research Libraries*, 36 (July 1975): 263–271.
30. *Ibid.*, p. 271.
31. *Ibid.*
32. California. University. *The University of California Libraries: A Plan for Development, 1978–1988*, July 1977, pp. 118–122.
33. Virginia. Council of Higher Education. "Budget Manual, Appendix M: Guidelines and Special Requirements for Institutions of Higher Education, 1978–80 Biennium," (January 12, 1977).

34. Evan Ira Farber. *Classified List of Periodicals for the College Library*. 5th ed., West-wood, Mass., F. W. Faxon, 1972; William Armstrong Katz. *Magazines for Libraries*. 2nd ed., New York, R. R. Bowker, 1972.

35. Virginia. Council of Higher Education. *op. cit.*, p. 17.

36. "Analysis of Appropriations," *The Chronicle of Higher Education*, 13 (October 25, 1976): 9.

37. James F. Govan, "The Better Mousetrap: External Accountability and Staff Par-ticipation," *Library Trends*, 26 (Fall 1977): 256.

38. McAnally, *op. cit.*, p. 169.

39. *Idem.*

40. *Idem.*

41. For an excellent history and description see: Alice E. Wilcox and Nancy H. Marshall, *MINITEX and WILS: Responses to Access Needs, RQ*, Summer 1974, pp. 299–307.

42. McAnally, *op. cit.*, p. 170.

43. Wilcox and Marshall, *op. cit.*

44. See E. J. Josey, "Systems Development for Reference and Research Library Service in New York State: The 3R's," *British Columbia Library Quarterly*, 31 (April 1968), pp. 3–21; E. J. Josey, "The 3R's: Reference and Research Library Resources," *Stechert Hafner Book News*, 21:7 (March 1967); Annual Reports of NYSILL by Jane G. Rollins for 1970–71, 1971–72, 1972–73, 1973–74 and 1974–75 in *The Bookmark*, Albany, The University of the State of New York, The State Education Department, The New York State Library.

45. McAnally, *op. cit.*, p. 1

46. California. University. Office of the Executive Director of Universitywide Library Planning. *The University of California Libraries: A Plan for Development*, Berkeley, July 1977, Chapter III: 'The Need for a New Approach," pp. 35–44.

47. *Ibid.*, Chapter VIII: "Acquisitions and Processing of Materials," pp. 111–135.

48. McAnally, *op. cit.*, p. 171.

49. Richard de Gennaro, "Austerity, Technology and Resource Sharing: Research Libraries Face the Future," *Library Journal*, 102 (May 15, 1977): 423.

Richard Lyders, Diane Eckels and Maurice C. Leatherbury

Houston Academy of Medicine–Texas Medical Center Library

COST ALLOCATION AND COST GENERATION

The allocation of library budgets is normally attempted using simple activity or numerical factors alone, such as library usage or user counts. These factors are normally considered in isolation. It is argued here that this simple allocation method does not relate to all costs as they are actually incurred. A method utilizing a combination of factors is discussed as an attempt to come to terms with the complexities of equitable budget allocation. Besides actual usage relating to their direct costs, another allocation factor is suggested as being necessary to handle the library's fixed support costs.

When academic librarians discuss allocating costs or budgets, the picture that presents itself is usually one in which there is a central library with departmental or branch libraries and there are library users who can be defined as undergraduates, graduates, faculty and others. The general purpose of studies on the allocation of costs has to do with actually allocating the library budget to schools or departments within the university or college system; but these studies are used also as aids in budget planning, in explaining department cost comparisons or in providing data to outside agencies.[1] In general, the allocation problem becomes one of studying a single entity (a budget derived from one source), towards the ultimate goal of a well-managed library budget.

The Houston Academy of Medicine–Texas Medical Center Library (HAM–TMCL) is concerned with budget and cost allocation as well, although the direction is somewhat different: from a needed budget back to various budget-granting institutions. Whereas the college or university library would literally determine for each teaching department or school how much of the library's budget it should *allocate* to support that school, the HAM–TMC Library must determine annually how much of the Library's total budget each school must *supply* to the Library. Other than the contention that the latter situation reflects a real problem (if you don't get it, you can't use it), the two situations are working to answer the same question: "How much of the library's operating costs can be attributed to a particular school, or department, or program?"

In her recent article, Miriam Drake reviewed four basic methods for attributing, or allocating, library budgets, all of which were used in the Purdue study reported in the same article.[2] The first two methods divide library costs according to faculty, one by proportionate number of FTE faculty and the other by faculty salaries The third and fourth methods presented for allocating budgets are based on library use. One of the use allocations was based on *intended* use; that is, if X dollars are spent in support of operating a particular department, or school, or subject area library, all of these costs should be wholly attributed to that particular user group. The difficulty with this method, as Drake points out, is that disciplines as they exist today are not separated by such clean lines as they may have been in the past.[3] For example, although one might intend that nursing students use only nursing materials, the students themselves do not have such a limited perspective on their profession's needs and actually use a wide variety of materials outside of what might be considered their professional literature. The fourth method Drake presents for allocating the budget, and the second use-based one, is based on *actual* library use. Data for the fourth method, however, are usually not readily obtainable for many library services. Circulation data are usually the most straightforward and available, particularly now with so many libraries operating automated circulation systems; but there are other library activities and services that should be costed as well—reference services, manual and automated bibliographic services, in-house use of library materials, interlibrary borrowing, photocopy on demand, and user education, for example.

The assumptions that are normally made when discussing these four allocation methods, or any others, for that matter, are that the methods can be applied discretely and that one method is better than another. We contend, however, that a combination of methods must be applied to the cost allocation problem for its proper solution. At the HAM–TMC Library we found that neither the numbers of people served nor the amount of use they made of the Library were enough to explain the Library's total operating costs. A large portion of these costs are in reality unrelated to either of these factors. And since the HAM–TMC Library must use a cost allocation formula to obtain its budget from its supporting institutions, we found it necessary to develop a more complex method of allocating costs—a combination of methods or factors—which is presented below.

Before discussing the method, some background information on the Houston Academy of Medicine–Texas Medical Center Library is necessary to put the problem into perspective. The Library is located within the confines of a large multi-institutional health complex, the Texas Medical Center in Houston, Texas. It is a consortium library, principally funded and governed by five institutions with representation on a Library Board of Directors, and additionally funded by thirteen other institutions. The Library's primary user population numbers just under 10,000 and it supports the teaching, research, and clinical programs of two medical schools (Baylor College of Medicine and the University of Texas at Houston), three nursing schools, a county medical society, four medical school-affiliated teaching hospitals, and various other health science institutions and programs.

THREE FACTOR BUDGET ALLOCATION

According to an operating agreement signed in 1970, the level of support required of each of the user institutions served by the HAM–TMC Library is to be based on 1) an established amount to be assessed against each user institution for the general support of maintaining the Library as a resource of the Texas Medical Center and the Houston medical–scientific community; 2) the size of the faculties and student bodies of the governing institutions as well as the size of the membership of the Houston Academy of Medicine; and 3) the use of the Library by the faculty, students, and clinicians of the governing institutions as determined by usage statistics. All of the Library's supporting institutions are assessed according to these three factors—which may be more clearly delineated as factor one, a basic factor; factor two, head count; and factor three, library use.

Prior to the assessment formulas that were developed through the study that will be discussed below, the allocation process of the Library's budget contained little scientific sophistication. The three factors were used, but in quite a naive manner. For factor two (head count) all library users were considered equal, in that the total numbers of faculty and students from each supporting institution were used, undifferentiated by user type, with the charge per user set arbitrarily. For factor three (library use), statistics were maintained in six usage categories: circulation, reference questions, computerized searching services, interlibrary activities (borrowing and lending to supporting institutions with libraries), and manual bibliographic search services. Unit costs in each category were set according to the best cost information available, whether from the literature or from our own cost estimates.

In contrast perhaps to situations in other libraries, factor three, the usage category, actually offered the least difficulty of the three factors. The Library has gathered rather complete use statistics since 1971 in all public service areas, distinguishing users not only by institution, but by some nine user categories as well. Since, however, it is much more difficult and obtrusive to obtain such detail on users in non-automated areas, only the institutional categories for users were used. Furthermore, we had no basis upon which to say there were significant differences in usage costs among any of the user categories of medical faculty, medical student, resident, nursing faculty and student, graduate student, etc.

The allocation or assessment factor offering the greatest difficulty under the previous allocation method, as might be expected, was factor one, the so-called "basic factor." One might ask why a "basic factor" anyway? Wouldn't the combination of six categories of use plus institutional head counts be sufficient to allocate a library's budget? In fact, a heavy proportion of the operating costs of a library are not dependent upon numbers of people or quantity of usage. For example, the cost of materials for 200 first-year medical students would probably not be substantially more than the cost of materials for 100 first-year medical students. The costs for duplication of titles would increase, but not the costs for different titles. As another example, how could costs of technical processes be allocated equitably to the user? In fact, the cost of technical processes would probably be more equitably allocated on a program basis. Simple usage-based allocation models are actually unfair, then, in that they fail to take into account joint fixed costs, costs which have nothing to do with actual use or numbers of users and which require, therefore, other considerations for equitable allocation. And beyond this, in limiting budget allocation to counts, whether to user head counts or actual usage counts, unless unit costs are increased each year the underlying assumption must be that these counts will go up each year, as the Library's budget must, to keep pace with economic factors. When the counts remain stationary, or begin to drop, the method fails from a practical standpoint, since the library is an essential program and services will need to be financially supported at a level consistent with changes in the economy. Increasing unit costs for direct services ignores the basic issue that only a portion of a library's costs relate to direct services.

For reasons such as these, the HAM–TMC Library found it necessary to apply more than usage and head counts as allocation factors and added the so-called "basic factor" to its allocation method. As this basic factor was defined in the Library's operating agreement, it consisted of amounts to be assessed against each user insitution for the general support of maintaining the Library as a resource of the Texas Medical Center and the Houston medical–scientific community. Those who drew up the agreement either understood the budget allocation process better than many seem to today, or they were just using some good common sense. Although this has been a troublesome factor for us to come to terms with operationally, it has, at the same time, been the factor that has enabled us to maintain equitable assessments to all of our 18 users institutions.

MANUAL FACTOR MANIPULATION DIFFICULTIES

The three-factor procedure for allocating the budget mentioned earlier, while workable, had definite drawbacks. First, it was a complex procedure requiring manual manipulation and the logic for all three factors had to be restructured each year. It was clear that a model or formula was needed that could be used repeatedly over time, that would yield satisfactory results without such laborious manual restructuring. Second, because of the dynamic environment of the Texas Medical Center, any model to be used would have to be flexible enough to incorporate changes external to the Library, such as the addition of new programs and entire schools. In addition, it would have to be able to incorporate changes from within the Library; for example, changing patterns in the demands for the Library's services, changing costs, and new services.

A third difficulty with the Library's manual assessment model was that it did not incorporate current methods of costing. Costs for library services were determined by simple time and motion studies or from "standard" costs as were found in the literature and these costs did not take into consideration joint costs (for instance, a book may be used in any one of several services), or peak loading factors (since many resources of a library are fixed, some provision needs to be made to meet peaks of demand, as opposed to average demand), or economies of scale.

OPERATIONS RESEARCH APPLICATION

Through a fortuitous meeting of personnel from the Center for Cybernetic Studies at the University of Texas at Austin, the administration of the HAM–TMC Library entered into a research project through which it hoped to resolve some of the difficulties it was having with its cost allocation mechanism and, therefore, with the institutional assessment model from which its budget is derived.

Although no attempt will be made to discuss the details of the Library's operations research study, which are covered elsewhere,[4] the discussion that follows concerns some of the non-technical aspects of the Library's basic factor model, factor one of the three factors used to recover library costs.

First, and most important for the HAM–TMC Library, the study of its budget allocation procedures created a fairly comprehensive, computerized operations research model and developed a workable logic to be used in the Library's annual budget allocation procedures. Essentially, the operations research model has enabled the Library to recover its costs through mechanisms that are consistent with the different ways costs are actually generated. The direct costs of library user services and a portion of the library's support costs have been programmed for recovery through the usage factor charges, factor three. Other support costs, those arising from library operations not directly attributable to user services—such as the collections, processing the collections, and administration—are recovered through factor one, the basic factor, which represents about 45% of the Library's operating budget.*

---

*The HAM–TMC Library's total annual budget includes building rent and maintenance charges, which make up about 20% of the *total* budget. These charges are not considered in the Library's operating budget as discussed here and are recovered using the head count factor, factor two.

THE BASIC FACTOR RATIONALE

The logic for distributing costs through the basic factor became an area in the research project where a considerable amount of study was needed, since so little relevant information was available in the literature. The task here was to answer a basic question: "Regardless of the amount of use of the Library, how much money would be saved by each institution that participated in the HAM–TMC Library because it then would not need to have a library of its own?" To answer this, we found we had to come to terms with the kind of library each of the supporting institutions needed.[5] To help answer this question, further questions were asked: "What portion of the HAM–TMC Library's total collection would each of the supporting institutions need to support their programs?", and "What library configuration would each supporting institution need in relation to study space, collection storage space, and library administration?" A search was made of the literature for answers to these questions with little or no success: we were looking for library standards relating to nursing programs, hospital libraries, public health schools, dental schools, medical schools, graduate schools in the biomedical sciences, allied health schools, etc. Without these standards, or without so much as an existing library that we felt could be used as a standard, we used data derived from our experience and knowledge in serving our programs and schools. Of course it became quite clear that it would require the good part of a project itself to derive more accurate data on program needs, but we felt our assumptions were sound enough for the institutional relationship picture needed.*

One of the basic assumptions we made in our study was that, although the library must meet the demands of all the schools or programs it serves, distinct differences in informational requirements and quality and type of library facilities demanded exist among user groups. Such differences are determined by various non-usage related characteristics peculiar to different schools, such as programs offered, accreditation standards, and potential user populations. Our task was: 1) to recover all of the fixed support costs of the Library in this basic factor assessment and 2) to allocate the Library's budget as institutional assessments that were equitable for all, in that what was recovered from each school would closely reflect that school's actual contribution to costs.

The Library's annual fixed support costs are costs that are related to the school's needs to have a certain quality and type of library, as are dictated by their diverse informational requirements and demands for facilities, regardless of any use. Now these institutional characteristics—requiring a library of a certain configuration and quality—can be equated to that set of institutional characteristics used to determine the quality of library that institutions would require in the first place. On this basis, we felt we could safely assume that, for any group of schools, the fixed support costs of operating a library to accommodate each of their requirements would be proportional to the fixed costs needed to set up this particular type of the library in the first place. We further assumed that the relative ranking of institutions would remain the same for both initial set-up costs and fixed annual support costs.

Since certain data bearing on the costs of creating a library were felt to be more easily derived than on-going operating costs, we began a search for this information. However, as with the continuing costs of operating a particular type of library, data relevant to setting up a library were also not documented in a format we could readily apply to our problem. Therefore we assumed that the cost of setting up a library was a function of a combination of the number of volumes needed and the number of people to be served.

---

*We have submitted a follow-on research grant to the National Library of Medicine, a portion of which is directed to this problem.

We turned, therefore, to our collections development librarian for estimates on how much of our collection each school might require and we made estimates based on our expertise in serving our supporting institutions on how much of a physical facility relating to study space each might require. These data were applied to an operations research game theory method for solution, which set forth a hierarchy of the institutions, based on their individual needs for a library, with the largest institution requiring the total library. Their ranking was then carried over and applied to the Library's fixed support costs. The game theory solution method was chosen because it was felt that the notions of game theory could provide us with the analytic formulation of fairness and efficiency that are demanded of our assessment figures.

Table 1 is an example showing some proportionate weights that might be assigned certain types of supporting institutions through the operations research game theory. Medical School A, the standard at weight 1 for both collections required and study space required, is assumed to need all of the Library as it stands. Medical School B, with fewer programs—for example, no attached nursing program—is weighted proportionately less, the assumption being they would not need all of the collections or study space of the library. To account for a new school, or a developing school, or the loss of a school or program, the game theory model is solved again and new weights are derived. The weights are related to the fixed support cost portion of the library's annual budget and actual dollar amounts are derived according to the weight assigned.

TABLE 1

Basic Allocation Factor Showing Relative Weights for Selected Institution Types for Collections and Study Facilities

Institution Type	Relative Collection Weight	Relative Study Facilities Weight
Medical School A	1.000	1.000
Medical School B	0.826	0.878
Medical Society	0.291	0.023
Nursing School A	0.010	0.276
Nursing School B	0.006	0.019
Hospital A	0.010	0.006
Hospital B	0.010	0.008
Hospital C	0.010	0.005
Dental School*	0.002	0.109

*The dental school has its own library, but requires the HAM—TMC Library for support outside dentistry. Their weights have been adjusted accordingly.

The "basic factor," then, in the Library's cost allocation formula, is based on a combination of the proportion of the collection needed to support an institution's programs and the proportion of the building space needed by the institution's users. Game theory solution methods are then employed that take into account the complex interrelationships between the two factors and that produce weights which can then be used to calculate actual dollar figures. The fixed joint costs of the Library's support services that cannot easily be directly related to user services are thus recovered through the basic factor.

SUMMARY

The HAM–TMC Library has used a combination of three factors to allocate its budget to its user institutions since 1970. In the experience of those who have worked with these three factors–1) a basic factor, through which an allocation is determined according to the needs of a school; 2) a head count factor; and 3) a factor based on actual library use–any attempt to allocate a library's operating budget based on usage or head count alone is considered inadequate, since all library costs are not incurred through these variables alone. Fixed support costs of a library are incurred regardless of actual use or persons served and these costs, to be allocated equitably, must be related to the factors responsible for them. One method for determining the portion of the budget a school should pay of a library's fixed support costs is to relate these costs to the fixed costs that would be required by a particular school to set up their particular type of library and, in turn, to relate these costs proportionately to similar costs for the other schools involved in the allocation. A model based on operations research game theory is used for the solution of this relationship.

Since the HAM–TMC Library must use a cost allocation formula to obtain its budget and, ipso facto, to spend it, it must be much more precise in its cost justification formula than the typical college or university library. Nevertheless, the method discussed here, although probably more complex than methods used heretofore by most libraries, does lend itself to use in all libraries.

REFERENCES

1. Miriam A. Drake, "Attribution of Library Costs," *College and Research Libraries*, 38 (November 1977): 514.
2. *Ibid.*, p. 515–519.
3. *Ibid.*, p. 516.
4. E. Bres, A. Charnes, D. Cole Eckels, S. Hitt, R. Lyders, J. Rousseau, K. Russell, M. Shoeman, "Costs and Their Assessment to Users of a Medical Library," *Research Report CCS 303* (Austin: Center for Cybernetic Studies, 1977). This research was supported in part by Grant Number LM02333 from the National Library of Medicine, Department of Health, Education and Welfare.
5. This concept is consistent with the concepts presented by Jasper G. Schad, "Allocating Materials Budgets in Institutions of Higher Education," *Journal of Academic Librarianship*, 3 (January 1978): 329–332. Schad contends that the solution to library materials budget allocation problems is beyond what can be accounted for by formula involving activity measurements, such as usage and enrollment count. We agree with this view, contending further that whatever kind and quality of library an institution or program needs relates to other library support costs as well; that is, to those costs that cannot be attributed to direct services and therefore are not recovered in usage fees.

Marion T. Reid, Anna H. Perrault and Jane P. Kleiner

Louisiana State University

THE ROLE OF THE ACADEMIC LIBRARIAN IN LIBRARY GOVERNANCE

This paper reports the establishment and achievements of a faculty commit-tee involved in policy making in a university library. Elected representatives of the library faculty participate in an advisory capacity to the library admin-istration with authority to recommend alternative viewpoints to the univer-sity administration. The paper is in three parts: (1) history and formation of the committee; (2) major administrative policy revisions initiated by com-mittee actions; and (3) applications of this concept to other libraries. Addi-tional aspects include bylaws and guidelines, documentation of committee activities, opinion surveys, and relationship of this concept to participatory management and unionization.

PART I

The "new horizon" to which many academic librarians look forward today is that of an increased faculty role within the library in managerial participation and outside the library in university activities. The concept of this role is specifically stated in the ACRL "Standards for Faculty Status for College and University Librarians" in the section en-titled "Library Governance:"

> College and University Libraries should adopt an academic form of govern-ance. The librarians should form as a library faculty whose role and authority is similar to that of the faculties of a college or the faculty of a school or department.[1]

This "academic form of governance" is experienced by a *faculty*, which, according to McAnally, is "an association of colleagues banded together by a common interest." He says that

> They establish their own policies concerning themselves and their work, with-in limits, and conduct their own affairs. They usually vote, or a subcommit-tee does, on new appointment, promotion and tenure recommendations. They accept leadership, but they tend to resent authority and to reject dic-

tators. They are not administered though they may be led; they are co-
equals, colleagues, and individualists.[2]

Donald H. Wollett defines the components of such a governance system as the governing body of the institution, the administration, and the employed staff—which may
include both professionals and non-professionals. He points out that this governance depends on shared authority of the governing body, the administration and some staff,
although the governing body has the power to recall the authority of the administration
and staff when appropriate. Academic governance deals with a broad scope of matters,
ranging from salary levels and fringe benefits to tuition and curriculum considerations.
The diffuse nature of such decision-making blurs the employer/employee relationship so
that it is difficult to hold a particular person responsible for a decision.[3]

By its very definition a *faculty* allows for participatory management—in fact, ideally,
it IS governance through participation of the group. It theoretically provides the benefits
of participatory management. Such benefits as

- commitment on the part of the participants to a vocation,
- job satisfaction,
- the idea that the individual is a part of the entire group, not just a subgroup such as
a department within the library,
- reduction of authority problems, since the decisions are group decisions,
- decisions which are often superior to one person's decision, because more input is
allowed and more angles are considered.[4,5]

Juxtaposed to the desire first to attain and then to retain their academic form of
governance, some librarians find unionization. What benefits are they likely to gain from
a union? Indeed, what constitutes collective bargaining?

Wollett enumerates the components of a collective bargaining system. It is a partly
adversarial system, with management on one hand the the organizational representative
of the employee on the other. It is clear who decides what, for the concept of shared
authority is alien. Management governs; employees react to governance through their
union.[6] Unions are generally concerned with matters that can be bargained for and placed
in a contract, rather than with "the elusive quality of the academic environment."[7]

Chaplan and Maxey examined 56 actual faculty bargaining agreements involving librarians. In 46 of these, librarians were included in bargaining units larger than the library
faculty itself; they were categorized with the entire faculty. Implications of this situation
are (1) the organizational representatives, which are elected from the entire faculty may
very likely not include librarians, and (2) "the special interests of the librarians may be
in competition *within the union* with those of other faculty groups."[8]

For some librarians, the point of whether or not to unionize is moot, for most of their
faculty are already a part of a collective bargaining unit. In 1976 Weatherford estimated
"at a very rough guess" that there were 2,000 librarians who were then bargaining unit
members.[9] The lastest Ladd–Lipset survey states that "nearly three-fourths of all professors, and a majority at every type of institution, said . . . that they would vote for a
collective bargaining agent if an election were then held at their institutions."[10] This
implies that in the future more faculty—and hence more academic librarians—are most
likely to become union members. Will such unionization be effective for librarians?
Current library literature indicates not. Tallau and Beede state "Unionization, like
senates, may provide a means for the participation by librarians in overall university or
college affairs, but involvement in decision making within the library is best accomplished
through a library faculty."[11]

In her survey on academic librarians' involvement in collective bargaining, Kennelly found that collective bargaining more often brought "no change" than either "change for the better" or "change for the worse."[12] Indeed, Weatherford states that unless collegial governance is minimal, collective bargaining is of no benefit:

> At one end of the scale of colleges and universities the structures of academic governance are so frail, the spirit of free inquiry so mean, the administration so alien, and the dignity of the professoriate so atrophied, that collective bargaining can scarcely fail to bring improvement. At the other end of the scale, where these traits are reversed, collective bargaining may offer no advantage at all.[13]

The literature, then, supports the collegial model of governance for academic librarians. How do librarians achieve such a model? The remainder of this paper and the next two papers will describe the formation and initial accomplishments of a library faculty policy committee at an ARL library.

First, I will set the stage by defining what type of status we as library faculty had at the university prior to the establishment of the faculty policy committee. Then, as now, we possessed the following benefits: representation on the Faculty Senate; eligibility to participate on Faculty Senate committees; eligibility for sabbaticals and educational leave; eligibility for some local research support; ranks "equivalent to" those of other academic faculty. Appointment, promotion and tenure did not follow a collegial model. Although two librarians had served on the Search Committee for the Library Director in 1973/74, library faculty did not consistently participate in appointment procedures. Promotion occurred principally as a result of one's supervisor's recommendation. Tenure was virtually automatic upon the third anniversary of a person's first workday as a librarian on the staff. There was no provision for colleague evaluation.

During the next portion of this three-part presentation, you will hear how our library faculty policy committee came into being and of some of its initial accomplishments. The third paper will consider some intangible benefits of the committee and offer suggestions on how other librarians might go about forming their own faculty policy committee.

PART II

At L.S.U. determination of educational policy is the purview of the faculty handled through the Faculty Senate, Faculty Senate committees, college policy committees and departmental academic affairs committees. Librarians have long had equivalent faculty status, i.e., sabbatical leaves, senate membership, a rank promotion system. But it is only recently that we have begun thinking of ourselves as FACULTY. The significant event in this change in thinking occurred in February 1975, when the Faculty Senate distributed a memo asking that all faculties of schools and colleges vote on the establishment of faculty policy committees within their academic units. The library faculty voted to form such a committee.

The senior library senator appointed a committee composed of representatives from each library department to draft a set of by-laws. In beginning its work, the committee obtained copies of the by-laws of other policy committees already in existence on campus. These were all very much alike in excluding administrators from membership and in designating the policy committee as the voice of the faculty. They were also alike in that the charges to these policy committees were very broad in scope, having both academic and non-academic matters under their jurisdiction. The call from the Faculty Senate for the establishment of the policy committee gave strong support to these ideas:

These policy committees, when established, should assure that academic matters, over which by statute and university regulation the faculty has control, are controlled by the faculty. The policy committees should also determine and formulate faculty opinion on non-academic matters; on the basis of these determinations the policy committees should give advice to the appropriate administrative officers. College policy committees should be elected by the faculty of that division. Administrators should be excluded from membership on the policy committee.

With these good models in hand, the By-laws Committee got to work. It was clear that there was ample backing for excluding administrators but the question arose, Which administrators? Only the Director? Or including the Associate Director, the Assistant Director? What about department heads? (17 people) Who would then serve on the committee? It was finally decided to specify that administrators would be defined as the members of the Library Administrative Council (presently the Director, Associate Director, Assistant Director for Technical Services, Chief Bibliographer, and Coordinator for Special Services.)

Another point provoking much discussion was the basis of representation on the committee. Would each major library area be allowed a certain number of representatives? Or would some other method be used? Some committee members wanted mandatory representation from each major area of the library. Opponents of this idea argued that emphasizing divisional lines encourages divisiveness. Some librarians made the point that the FPC would be expected to function across divisional lines and unify the library faculty to work together as a whole. Others pointed out that in the past one's influence had been directly proportional to one's years of service and that it had been difficult for new librarians to have ideas accepted. Ultimately, a system of representation was worked out with years of service as the basis. Three categories were established each containing approximately one-third of the librarians on the staff. There were to be two representatives from each category for a total of six members on the committee.

All members of the committee were to be voting members. In the event of a tie vote, the issue would be placed before the entire faculty for resolution. Under this system all levels of experience are assured of representation. By not utilizing a quota system by library area, the Policy Committee emphasizes the common bond of professionalism for all members of the library faculty.

During the writing of the By-laws, committee members began to use the term "library faculty." Faculty in other academic units were described as "non-library" faculty. The University Faculty Handbook became our Bible as we prepared ourselves for more participation in the determination of library policy.

Once the By-laws were completed, the library faculty voted to approve them. The next step was an election to determine the membership of the first committee. The By-laws committee drew up special election guidelines for the first campaign because the terms of office set in the By-laws are two years beginning July 1. Due to the fact that the By-laws were approved late in the Fall semester, however, it was decided to hold the initial election at once and let the terms of the first committee run 18 and 30 months instead of one and two years. This arrangement gave the first committee organization time, a "breaking-in period." Because the first committee and its officers were participating in an activity unfamiliar to them and the library administration, the By-laws committee felt the additional six months would serve as an orientation period.

The composition of membership of the first committee was fortuitous—by chance. This first committee not only drew its membership from all three years of service categories, but from all four administrative units of the library: Public Services, Collection

Development, Technical Services, and Special Services. There was one male and five females, which roughly follows staff apportionment between the sexes. Two of the six elected had served on the By-laws committee, one as chairman. Four of the six were department heads. There was one representative from the University Commission on the Status of Women and three were on university faculty senate committees. (It is interesting to note at this time that all three of these people later became chairmen of those faculty senate committees and one of the three was elected Faculty Senator.) Several of the members of the first committee had been active in library activities on state, regional and national levels and had published in the literature.

The committee began meeting in February of 1976. The chairman of the By-laws committee was elected the first chairman of the Library Faculty Policy Committee. The committee then began the task of organization by drafting procedural guidelines. The "Procedures for Handling Topics" authorizes the committee to discuss an item brought to it by any member of the library faculty. The committee has three options on an issue:

1. Vote to make a recommendation to the appropriate authority.
2. Decide to submit the issue to the full library faculty for a vote.
3. Vote not to take action on an issue.

The guidelines further specify that all recommendations of the committee are to be written and written replies are to be requested. If an unfavorable or unsatisfactory reply is received from the Library Administration or other university authority, the committee can forward the issue to the next highest administrative level for consideration. (It has not been necessary to use this alternative to date.) Copies of all actions forwarded outside the library are sent to the Library Director for his information.

The procedures to be used in requesting the committee to consider an issue are stipulated in the "Guidelines for Placing Issues on the Library Faculty Policy Committee Agenda." These guidelines require that the request be in writing. Sensitive matters can be submitted to one member of the committee in confidence. The Library Administration, Library Staff Council and the University Administration can and do ask the committee to consider matters.

The "Procedure for Halting Consideration of an Issue" provides that any faculty member may ask the committee in writing to discontinue discussion of a topic. The committee still has the option of continuing with the matter.

It was decided that copies of all committee minutes, memos, replies to memos, etc., would be placed in a notebook and kept permanently in the Library Reserve Book Room. An "original" set is kept by the Committee secretary. Minutes of committee meetings are duplicated and distributed to all library faculty members. Prior to each meeting the agenda is posted in the staff lounge. All agendas carry the phrase, "Library Faculty Policy Committee meetings are open meetings."

The committee had been in operation for several months when members began to get the question "When is the FPC going to *do* something?" The committee had been "Doing" a great deal, but no one realized this because memos had not been printed verbatim in the minutes. After the committee voted to include all memos and replies to the minutes (except those pertaining to one individual) everyone was better informed.

As to just what the committee "did do," a brief summary of the most significant actions and accomplishments might be helpful.

As has been previously mentioned, librarians had not participated in selection, appointment, promotion and tenure decisions as a collegial body. At the time of the committee's formation, The Vice-Chancellor for Academic Affairs was asking all academic departments on campus for copies of their appointment, promotion and tenure policies. Subsequently, the Vice-Chancellor asked that the library bring its policies into line with those in the University Faculty Handbook. The FPC submitted a promotion policy to the Library Administration. Appointment and tenure sections were added to this draft by the Library Administration. Some changes were made in exchanges between the FPC and the Library Administration, and the policy went into effect in May, 1977. The Appointmant, Promotion and Tenure policy is the companion event to formation of the FPC in bringing our librarians together as a faculty.

Another major project of the FPC during its first year was concerned with a proposal for library reorganization drawn up by the Library Administration. The FPC distributed a questionnaire, gathered written comments and forwarded all of this input to the Library Administration. The plan was revised and the above process repeated. In conducting these surveys the FPC was carrying out its authorization in the By-laws to survey the faculty and represent faculty opinion.

The Vice-Chancellor for Academic Affairs addressed the Faculty Policy Committee directly in a memo dealing with various aspects of faculty status for librarians. The committee invited the Vice-Chancellor to a meeting to discuss this topic. All library faculty including the Library Administration were invited to the meeting. There was a successful exchange of information and ideas. Since that time the Vice-Chancellor has asked the committee to study changes in the tenure policy for librarians.

Briefly, a few other matters the committee dealt with were continuing education, release time, salaries and library assistant classification. It worked with the Library Administration on performance evaluation and improving communication within the library.

Serving on the FPC is a very time-consuming but rewarding experience. The emphasis in this paper has been factual. The next speaker will discuss the intangible benefits such a committee can bring to a library.

PART III

The organization of the Faculty Policy Committee served as the formal introduction to our university library of a new vehicle developed to open and improve channels of communication between library faculty and library administrators. Members of the first FPC were aware that a breakdown in communications was contributing to misunderstandings among colleagues on procedural matters and misinterpretation of existing administrative policies between the library faculty and the library administration.

The development of a group empowered by the university senate to represent its faculty in determining policy matters on academic and non-academic affairs was sorely needed in the library. Though the librarians had long had faculty status, there was an apparent degree of reluctance among many to accept and exercise their rights and responsibilities as true faculty members.

This reluctance concerning faculty status extended to the membership of the first FPC, but to a lesser degree. Nevertheless, the members welcomed the additional six months accorded the officers and membership of the first elected committee. The initial FPC felt the extra six months would be a learning period for its membership as well as for the library administration.

This decision to extend the first terms of the officers and members proved to be well founded. The organization of any new group takes time if that group is to develop effective goals and work toward the implementation of those goals. It should be emphasized at this point that the FPC was proceeding with caution in its early actions because the group wanted to avoid being considered solely as a grievance committee. This was not the intent nor the charge of the committee. A university Faculty Senate grievance committee exists for that purpose. The FPC will accept individual grievances, but discourages them as the committee prefers to maintain the position of representing the scope of library faculty opinion.

To return to consideration of the value of the additional six month term for the novice committee—the experience at this university strongly substantiates the belief that the added months to the term of the first committee can be critical to the future of such an organization as the FPC. The importance of the time frame is apparent for it is essential that the committee establish itself with the administration as soon as possible as spokesman for the library faculty on all matters pertinent to the library and its faculty's policies. This transition must be accomplished if such a committee is to work amicably with the library administration. In other words, a policy committee should be constituted of representatives as open and honest as Abraham Lincoln (assassinated), yet as diplomatic as Henry Kissinger (not assassinated).

As for the actions of this first committee, an account of each would be too time consuming. The second paper described some of the major actions, but it should be emphasized that those are but a few of the many reviewed and acted upon during the first term. It seems more beneficial at this time to discuss the intangible changes initiated by the first committee or emanating from the members' interaction which are not evident in the 18 months of records and assorted documents resulting from the group's formal activities.

Before the advent of the FPC, members of the library faculty either expressed feelings and opinions as individuals, sought guidance from those with more years of experience and confidence in their position within the administrative hierarchy, or remained silent, the latter seemingly the most preferable of the three. Also, as in any organization where more than two people are involved, factions were formed, librarians divided, and degrees of mistrust existed among colleagues.

The library faculty at this university is not singular in this reluctance to express untried attitudes, nor is it unique in having a divided staff. Differences between public service and technical service librarians are apparent in many libraries.

During this first year and a half of committee operation, this neophyte group, representing all areas of service, shed much of its apprehension and began to develop trust in the opinions and capabilities of all the FPC members and of the remaining library faculty. This is not to indicate that the FPC members unanimously agreed on all points in question. The reality was frequently far from unanimous agreement, and that is as it should be. The members represented different viewpoints in the library and with each additional meeting began to feel freer to express them. After months of working together, the first committee's members began to understand something of the personalities and emotions of one another. Too, all developed a better understanding of one another's professional attitudes as related to librarianship in general and their own positions in particular.

The importance of selecting a library's first policy committee members cannot be overemphasized. Ideally, varying age groups, differing service areas, plus both sexes should be represented on a library's initial policy unit. Too, liberal as well as conservative elements should have voices on this committee. Do not make the mistake of thinking age shapes one's political leanings. This error is one which occurs frequently in public elections. Know or make it a point to learn the nominees' attitudes toward policy making and the administration it must approach.

Additionally, the formation and successful performance of a first committee is too important to an institution to elect representatives on a popularity basis alone. Ask those who wish to be nominated and elected to initial membership to provide a summary of their previous leadership experiences; request a summary of university activities apart from library and professional ones, and, finally, determine a candidate's contacts outside the library or a candidate's ability to develop such contacts. Granted, these candidates are not being nominated for U.S. president or state governor, but these nominees probably will exert more influence on librarians' professional futures at the individual institutions than a president and governor combined.

At this point, many of you may be favoring organizing a policy committee at your institution. You may be thinking that the information presented here is fine in theory but impossible to realize in your situation. The majority of librarians at this session are from academic institutions, most of which have a faculty body involved in varying degrees in the business of recommending policy to their administrations or governing boards. These faculty bodies vary in composition and in degree of importance.

At our university, the Faculty Senate is composed of approximately 50 representatives elected by their academic colleges and/or departments. The senate presently has a voice in matters being considered by the university administration and that voice appears to be gaining in strength. In the event that academic institutions represented at this meeting do not have a similar faculty body, it is recommended that the American Association of University Professors be queried as to the support they could provide in developing a policy committee at your library.

Should all else fail, use your library staff association as an organizational vehicle. Not having a staff association is no reason to cease efforts. The American Library Association has a roundtable for library staff associations and can aid libraries in developing that type of organization.

The only remaining obstacle to organizing one of the described associations could be a library staff's interpretation of an institution's policy of administration. Even this point can be argued. From observation and study, it appears academic or research institutions often lean toward administrative extremes. One library may be structured stringently while another may be so freely administered that anarchy appears to prevail.

Because of such extremes, a policy committee can be as beneficial to a library's administration as it is to its faculty. In a rigidly structured institution, a policy committee serves to open channels of communication. It provides a spokesman for the body of professionals who frequently have been without a voice in establishing policy. Admittedly, a novice committee in a structured administration may confront barriers requiring it to act with a large measure of caution. But strange as it may sound, the official organization of a policy committee may be easier at a library where the administration is rigidly structured because channels of communication exist—possibly ineffective channels, but channels through which a committee like this can begin communicating.

Organizing a representative faculty group in a non-structured situation may be more difficult to initiate than in a structured administration. It could require the added time and ingenuity to nurture and develop viable channels for communication with the library, the institution's administration, and the rest of the academic faculty.

Libraries and librarians are working harder and accomplishing more in achieving faculty status and professional standing at academic and research institutions than ever before. A policy committee like the one under discussion is another motivating factor to achieving stature and understanding among colleagues.

Those of us with experience in this area are not naive enough to believe that conflicting attitudes and feelings of mistrust, which apparently exist to some degree in all libraries, can be totally erased by the efforts of such a committee. Experience has taught us though that in the initial 18 months of working together as library faculty representatives, the committee broadened its perspectives on librarianship and professionalism to such a degree that a healthy climate now exists for the growth of mutual respect and understanding.

Had the committee accomplished nothing other than developing the groundwork for this improved understanding of one another an individuals as well as librarians, the initial term of the FPC would have been successful. It appears, however, that even more than a healthy climate for expressing ideas among one another has taken shape at our university, for the atmosphere of mutual respect among the committee and the library faculty has extended to the library administration.

The appointment, promotion and tenure policy of the university library, distributed in May 1977, is an example of the joint efforts of the FPC and the library administration. The first committee considered acceptance of the new policy after 13 months of negotiations a major step toward opening channels of communication to a freer exchange between the library faculty and its administration.

The new appointment, promotion and tenure policy provides for colleague evaluation and participation in appointments and tenure reviews. It appears to point toward increased cooperation throughout the library, and surely is indicative of the growing climate of respect between the library administration and the faculty.

The development of such a committee is possible at any institution represented at this conference. It is dependent on two factors only—courage and belief in the direction the faculty must take. The beginning requirements are minimal while the results can be maximal. It is a "new horizon" all professional library staffs should seek. The librarians at your university may discover as we did that this is a "horizon" within reach and not one "Somewhere Over the Rainbow."

REFERENCES

1. *Faculty Status for Academic Librarians: a History and Policy Statements;* compiled by the Committee on Academic Status of the Association of College and Research Libraries (Chicago: American Library Association, 1975), p. 32.
2. A. M. McAnally, "Status of the University Librarian in the Academic Community," in *Research Librarianship: Essays in Honor of Robert B. Downs* (New York: Bowker, 1971), pp. 31–32.
3. Donald H. Wollett, "The Nature of Collective Bargaining and its Relationship to Governance in Higher Education," in M. D. Abell, ed., *Collective Bargaining in Higher Education* (Chicago: American Library Association, 1976), pp. 4–6.
4. F. Dickinson, "Participative Management: a Left Fielder's View," *California Librarian* 34 (April 1973): 31–32.
5. M. P. Marchant, "Participative Management in Libraries," in *New Directions in Staff Development* (Chicago: American Library Association, 1971), p. 30.
6. Wollett, *op. cit.*, p. 6
7. A. Tallau and B. R. Beede, "Faculty Status and Library Governance," *Library Journal* 99 (June 1, 1974): 1523.
8. M. A. Chaplan and C. Maxey, "Scope of Faculty Bargaining: Implications for Academic Librarians," *Library Quarterly* 46 (July 1976): 231.
9. J. W. Weatherford, *Collective Bargaining and the Academic Librarian* (Metuchen, N.J.: Scarecrow, 1976), p. 1.
10. Everett Carl Ladd, Jr. and Seymour Martin Lipset, "Faculty Support for Unionization: Leveling Off at About 75 Per Cent." *The Chronicle of Higher Education* 15 (February 13, 1978): 8.
11. Tallau and Beede, *op. cit.*, p. 1523.
12. Jean R. Kennelly, "The Current Status of Academic Librarians' Involvement in Collective Bargaining: a Survey," in M. D. Abell, ed., *Collective Bargaining in Higher Education* (Chicago: American Library Association, 1976), p. 75.
13. Weatherford, *op. cit.*, p. 123.

Ralph E. Russell

Georgia State University

GROWING PAINS: AN ADMINISTRATOR'S VIEWPOINT ON DRAFTING LIBRARY FACULTY BYLAWS

The drafting of a library governance document (bylaws) which provides for input by library faculty into decision-making is described by the library administrator. The site is an urban university library. Principal topics of discussion, major decision points, and compromises in the evolution of the bylaws are discussed. Topics include: evaluation of the library administrator, the reporting chain for standing committees, committee participation in budget formulation and allocation of travel funds, and committee participation in the recruitment and hiring of new faculty. The paper concludes with a personal assessment of the process.

Twice this author has been involved in the discomfiting compromises required to put on paper the game rules for faculty participation in library governance. Call it a code, a constitution, or bylaws—the process caused a few more grey hairs, and some agonizing self-evaluation. Hopefully it produced both professional and personal growth. This paper is a personal recollection of that most recent experience as a member of the committee charged with drafting a governance document for the library faculty and simultaneously the chief library administrator. It was an experience of frustration, chagrin, self-doubt, anger, a sense of achievement, and a respect for the other members of the committee. When the drafting process had concluded, there was not yet a general agreement. However, we were committed to a governance structure which would enhance the library services and collections we offered our clientele.

That clientele is found in an urban university of twenty-thousand students with a faculty of eight hundred. The library and the University have experienced most of their growth since 1960. The library staff consists of ninety full-time positions, of which twenty-seven are faculty appointments. The librarians have faculty rank and are an integral part of the University faculty; they serve with distinction on university-wide committees, in the faculty Senate, and on the major committees in a recent self-study for reaffirmation of regional accreditation.

Within the University organization, the University Library is treated as a college. The University Librarian reports to the Vice President for Academic Affairs, has the status of a college dean, and serves at the pleasure of the University President. When this author interviewed for the position, the President said *unequivocally* that the University Librarian was held responsible for the library and, particularly, for personnel actions. This accountability was one attraction of the job; it was also a cause of frustration in the process of evolving a viable constitution.

In 1975, the University faculty completed statutes for faculty governance which provide for consultation and specify due process procedures. They served as the philosophical and legal basis for the subsequent governance document for the library, the Bylaws.

For several years prior to 1975, some dissatisfaction had been experienced by the library faculty with the library organizational structure. In early 1975, an ad hoc committee of library faculty was formed to study current trends in the governance of academic libraries and to make appropriate recommendations. This committee will hereafter be referred to as the governance committee. Recommendations which resulted were that:

(1) The Library professional staff organize as a faculty and bylaws be drafted to effect this; and
(2) The following major areas of concern be considered by a bylaws committee:
    (a) The University library as a division within the University;
    (b) The University Librarian, his authority, and the library's administrative structure;
    (c) The library faculty;
    (d) Standing committees;
    (e) Representation of non-academic or support personnel in library governance; and
    (f) Interpretation of the bylaws.

The report of the governance committee was submitted on September 18, 1975; just three days after this author became University Librarian.

Examining the questions and issues raised by the governance committee, some troublesome points were identified which could dilute the effectiveness of the library administration and which were antithetical to my own perceptions of the functions of administration, and made specious my accountability to the president. They were:

(1) The suggestion that any committee dealing with personnel matters should report to the faculty rather than the University Librarian.
(2) The utility and desirability of a standing committee concerned with collection development.
(3) The establishment of a staff relations committee to hear grievances and complaints.
(4) The involvement of a standing committee on faculty development in the recruitment of new faculty.
(5) The establishment of a budget committee.

These issues could be generalized to two broad areas of concern: personnel actions and budget. I was concerned by the trend towards committee decisions; my objective was bylaws which mandated consultation between library faculty and the University Librarian and which involved faculty in library-wide concerns.

I was deeply involved on a pragmatic and gut level, having just arrived on the job; whatever emerged as faculty bylaws, I and my successors would have to live with and rationalize continuously to the University administration. It was imperative, therefore, that we produce a document with which we (and that is not magisterial!) could administer the library, achieve the level of services and collections our university required, find professional fulfillment and development in so doing, and rationalize to reasonable critics.

My own managerial style (with or without the prodding of bylaws) leans very heavily on consultation with library faculty and staff. Consultation is crucial for two reasons.

First, it solicits knowledgeable, informed viewpoints on an issue. It has been my experience that in most situations, there is at least one staff member who is *both* more knowledgeable and more concerned than his/her colleagues.

Secondly, the consultative managerial mode stimulates the professional development of the participants which, again, benefits the organization. Likert fans may well ask, "Wouldn't democratic or shared decision-making give more encouragement to one's professional development?" It very well may. In my opinion, however, the individual's benefit is offset by losses because the institution and its library suffers when democratic decision-making is utilized as a norm. Expenditures for personnel increase (because of the augmented number of participants) with no proven, commensurate rise in the quantity or, worse yet, the quality of library services and collections. Variant levels of expertise, commitment, and experience possessed by the library faculty invalidate the "one person, one vote" philosphy. I perceive the library administrator as the individual who orchestrates the diverse backgrounds and talents of the staff, using his/her insight to assess and balance the various contributions a staff and faculty will offer.

The unwary and unlucky manager may be consumed in the bright flames of the democratic process. An administrator's powers of persuasion and sharpest logic may finally be over-ridden by the committee vote. Inevitably, library services depend on the library faculty and staff. It is "power with" as Mary Parker Follett described it, not "power over." They (the Library faculty) do not work *for* me, but *with* me. I cannot afford to alienate them and yet I cannot in good conscience sit back and say, "all right, Gang, anything goes." I am held responsible for their collective actions. Regardless of what that action might be, most people assume that the University Librarian could—or should—do something about it.

So six of us embarked on our drafing mission with high hopes and, I must confess, some trepidation on my part.

The first area for extensive discussion was Article II, "The University Librarian and the Administrative Staff." Some committee members felt that the University Librarian should seek the *approval* (emphasis mine) of the library faculty on library policy matters. I saw no result in such an arrangement other than chaotic working conditions for the University Librarian. Someone would be carping weekly that he or she had not been consulted on a matter which he/she considered policy and I did not; secondly, we would be quibbling over the definition of "policy matters;" and thirdly, not only would the faculty consensus not necessarily be the advisable strategy to follow, but the meetings to explain, discuss, cajole, and persuade would devour much of the work week for many of us. Who would perform the library service functions, the delivering of our product to the consumer?

The matter was resolved satisfactorily with the following statement;

> "When these matters [library policy and development issues] affect the library as a whole, he [the University Librarian] *at his discretion*, shall consult with and seek the recommendations of the library faculty (Art. II, Sect. II) (emphasis mine)."

Another point of discussion with which I felt threatened (and in the process learned something of myself) was the periodic vote by the library faculty on the evaluation of the University Librarian. A full-scale evaluation of the University Librarian is to be conducted by the library faculty every five years, to be culminated with a vote on his/her effectiveness. During lengthy discussions on this I was most uneasy because if I voiced objections to the vote, I could be perceived as afraid to "face the vote of my colleagues." Yet, I felt strongly that such a vote was wrong, wrong, wrong. It was a quantitative measure which might provide, at quick glance, an erroneous conclusion. If the vote is in the favor of the University Librarian, the Vice President for Academic Affairs has a difficult time firing a generally ineffective University Librarian. If the vote is negative, the Vice President is in equally difficult straits in trying to retain a generally competent library administrator. Is it not probable that such voting reflects popularity more than effectiveness?

A complicating element in this issue is the myriad constituencies with which a library administrator deals daily. You know them: the support staff as well as library faculty; the university administration; the teaching faculty; the student body; the university staff; and other library users including city, state, and federal employees, visting scholars, and other libraries and librarians. To term a library administrator ineffective and to determine that assessment by a vote of only one constituent group, the library faculty, is invalid.

I discussed with the Vice President the matter of the vote on the effectiveness of the University Librarian. He agreed that the vote was a superfluous, detrimental device. The retention or dismissal of the University Librarian is an action of the University administration, considering more than just his/her relationship with the library faculty. The performance evaluation, however, is essntial and is transmitted to the Vice President for his information. I vetoed the effectiveness vote, leaving the performance evaluation of the University Librarian otherwise intact.

One of my early and major concerns, a budget committee, did not materialize into the problem I anticipated. I wanted no budget committee and the opposing view wanted a committee to develop and implement the library budget. A compromise was reached: the University Librarian would present the approved budget in lines and amounts as a matter of information to the library faculty. The formulation of the budget request would still be done by the library administration and department heads, consulting with library faculty and staff as required.

STANDING COMMITTEES

The standing committees which we identified as necessary are Bylaws and Elections, Faculty Development and Continuing Education, Communications and Public Relations, Appeals and Grievances, and Faculty Personnel.

The *Bylaws and Elections* committee elicited little discussion and even less controversy. I felt that the initial interpretation of the bylaws should be the responsibility of the University Librarian; the bylaws committee did not. I yielded the argument and the bylaws and elections committee are responsible for the initial interpretation of the bylaws and standing rules.

The *Faculty Development and Continuing Education* committee incited more debate and a little more heat. We discussed the appropriateness of this committee's allocating travel funds. I considered it inappropriate for a committee to allocate the budget when it is clearly the responsibility of the University Librarian. The decision of the bylaws committee was to leave the faculty development committee out of the allocation process except for reviewing annually the guidelines used by the University Librarian in allocating the travel funds. I consider this a reasonable and desirable function for the committee.

The bylaws committee felt that the *Faculty Development and Continuing Education* committee should develop guidelines for staff orientation and for released time. Released time is a particularly sticky wicket in this library. The existence of the term in our lexicon and its absence from the general professional terminology is revealing. Released time is time which does not have to be "made up." Again, this was an issue with explosive characteristics which overwhelmed the newcomer without the background of chafing and shared experiences. The irony of such a term in a faculty governance discussion is striking.

The strongest source of disagreement and distress for me, personally, was the *Communications and Public Relations* committee. Several discussions provided interesting studies in group interaction. I considered the committee superfluous because it dealt with publications, printing, graphics, displays—all these efforts required money, which involved the University Librarian's office. Decisions usually involve weighing priorities and choosing X over Y. Such a committee would require thorough understanding of the budget. Additionally, the university printing office would not accept anything to be printed without clearance from the University Librarian. Yet, it was not quickly decided whether the committee would report to me or to the faculty. As the issue continued to simmer, I learned some background: the library faculty felt effectively stymied by the library administration in the public relations area—they felt that they had not only *not* been consulted, they had been ignored. The reaction I was reaping from the library faculty was based on the precedent of bruised feelings and perceived exclusion. The chairman of the bylaws committee justified the public relations standing committee because "it was important for faculty to be able to propose and voice new ideas and the committee would provide such an outlet." My own (horrified) reaction to that comment was to question whether things were presently in such foul shape that the library faculty had no outlet for new ideas with the existing arrangement. We all agreed that the functions of the committee *vis-à-vis* the library administration should be clearly distinguished. The *Communications and Public Relations* committee should report to the faculty, the bylaws committee stated. I disagreed strongly.

At a subsequent meeting, I tried to dismantle the *Communications and Public Relations* committee but was unsuccessful. I contended that if the committee was to be, however, it should be advisory and report to the University Librarian. That opinion finally prevailed. I objected to the committee generally on at least two more occasions. In the finished bylaws, I lost the struggle regarding the committee's existence. The committee is there. There were some modifications, however, which I considered improvements in the original draft. The committee does not report to the faculty; rather, it reports to the University Librarian. He/she then takes major recommendations to the faculty for reaction or as a matter of information.

In discussing the *Appeals and Grievances* committee, we consulted with the University Attorney, studied the university-wide appeals process, and followed very closely the process provided in the revised faculty statutes. We addressed such questions as what is a grievance, can an aggrieved party be represented by an attorney, how much access should be provided to personnel folders in the library administration office?

A thorny question was the membership of the *Faculty Personnel* committee. At the time, there was only one tenured library faculty member so, obviously, the committee should be comprised of more than tenured faculty. (Subsequent tenure recommendations have added to our number of tenured faculty.) The solution was to have a mixed membership, tenured and non-tenured, with discussion by all; only tenured faculty, however, would vote on tenure recommendations.

There was discussion and disagreement over the *Faculty Personnel* committee's involvement in setting salaries. One faction contended that recommendations for salary increases should begin with this committee. I voiced strenuous objection. The question was tabled for at least one meeting.

(A parenthetical note: In areas which were controversial or sensitive or threatening to any of us on the bylaws committee, we tended to table the matter for at least one meeting. It seemed easier to consider uncomfortable thoughts and to take difficult action if one had viewed the impending decision or action for some days or weeks.)

Should the Faculty Personnel committee be involved in initial appointment of faculty? I recommended that they examine the candidate's credentials and recommend beginning rank and any tenure credit to be assigned. The consitution committee haggled over whether the faculy personnel committee should advise the University Librarian on initial salary for new faculty but decided no. I was advocating negative as hard as I could. The question of salary recommendations surfaced several more times. Ultimately, after several more drafts of the charge for the faculty personnel committee, the word "salaries" was removed from the charge as it relates to individuals; the committee was charged as follows:

> The committee shall seek to develop appropriate salary ranges for adminis-
> trative and academic ranks within the library. In order to accomplish this,
> the committee may investigate and compare evolving salary patterns within
> the profession and within the region. (Section VI, E.)

The discussion regarding tenure dealt, in great part, with harmonizing our document with Board of Regents policy. Tenure has traditionally been the grounds for much litigation in higher education. Such questions as what constitutes denial of tenure required some research on our part and discussions with more informed individuals than ourselves.

From my viewpoint, these were the highlights of discussion in our many sessions. We began implementing these bylaws last September. The standing committees are operational; the Library Administrative Council (three general library administrators, six department heads, and three elected faculty) is organized; the library faculty meets regularly. The Vice President for Academic Affairs approved the bylaws last February. The University President presently has them under review. I am confident that he will approve them.

Was it worth it? Will the processes established by the bylaws be of benefit to the library and the university? The answer to both questions is an emphatic yes. Library administration is made more complex, but that is not necessarily negative. Library faculty—library support staff, for that matter—feel free to question actions and decisions on the part of library administration. The Public Relations and Communications Committee, the standing committee I fought hardest to delete, is productive. In the cold analytical perspective that time provides, my resistance to this committee was based on weak reasoning. I gave a budget presentation to the library faculty last fall which, for the first time, informed them fully of the library budget. Such disclosure can only enhance their involvement and the realization that they are an integral part of the library operation for the university.

Finally, I have learned that my attitudes and perceptions are not what I had assumed. Labels and terminology enjoy cyclical popularity; I confronted the truth about myself and others, and had to discard some self-imposed labels (democratic, liberal) for less vogish, more accurate terminology (elitist, autocratic in some instances). The most important appelation, cutting across other divisions, is that of humanist. Can a manager—and the managed—acknowledge common humanity and establish a work environment sensitive to human needs? It is a gradual evolution but I am satisfied that we are doing it in my institution. Our bylaws are a milestone in our progress.

Billy R. Wilkinson

University of Illinois at Chicago Circle

THE PLETHORA OF PERSONNEL SYSTEMS IN
ACADEMIC LIBRARIES: A PHENOMENON OF THE 1970s

Unlike their predecessors, academic library administrators in the late 1970s must deal with a plethora of personnel systems. The great variety of personnel in academic libraries is noted, ranging from part-time freshmen to librarians with faculty status. Both regulations from outside the institution (e.g., equal employment opportunity and affirmative action guidelines) and constraints from within (e.g., grievance procedures for library faculty, civil service non-academic staff, and students) are enumerated. A prescription of how to manage these different categories of staff under differing sets of personnel systems but with all having the same objective (provision of library services to users) concludes the paper.

Unlike their predecessors in the earlier golden decades of American librarianship, academic library administrators in the late 1970s face a plethora of personnel systems. These administrators are forced into frequent, sometimes hourly, shiftings from one system to another as they deal with the library's staff. They are constantly asking themselves as the next encounter, scheduled meeting, bargaining session, the next confrontation is about the begin, "Under which constitution, contract, and/or constraint are we operating with this group or individual?" Because academic library managers believe they have an undesirable and hampering superfluity of personnel systems, they lament: "Why can't we be one big happy family as we were in the good ole days?"

The main body of the paper lists in a brief, staccato recitative the various kinds of personnel in academic libraries. Rules and regulations imposed from outside the library by the parent institution, by the state and federal governments, and by other regulators will also be enumerated. Examples are given of the complexities of today's personnel management.

The final section is an attempt to sing more sweetly, or at least provide an interlude, on the way to a more harmonious symphony which the next generation of academic library administrators hopefully can conduct. The concluding part also prescribes how academic administrators should manage the different personnel systems but with all having the same objective: the provision of library services for the users and potential users of academic libraries.

138

BACKGROUND

Before cataloging the contemporary scene, the importance of personnel administration should be stressed. An experienced director of university libraries writing in the mid-1970s listed the most important functions requiring administration in the academic library in this order of importance: 1) personnel management, 2) fiscal management, 3) public services, 4) public relations, 5) technical management, and 6) physical property management. "It is important to note the placement of the personnel function first in the list. Ten or twenty years ago it would not have held this position. This is clear recognition of change; in other times personnel management was not seen as such a crucial issue."[1]

In order to emphasize the requirement for excellent personnel management programs, we need only review data on the ninety-four university library members of the Association of Research Libraries which reveal that 71% is the highest percentage for salary and wages expenditures of the total operating costs for one library during 1976-1977. The median for the group was 58% of the costs going to personnel.[2]

Variety of Academic Library Staff Members and Positions

Academic libraries now employ an amazing variety of persons: male, female; young, old; Black, Spanish or Hispanic, Asian or Pacific Islander, American Indian or Alaska Native, White; homosexual, heterosexual, bisexual; with or without undergraduate college and/or advanced degrees; with or without physical or mental disability; economically advantaged or disadvantaged; brilliant or more ordinary in intellect; active or passive in social situations; possessing or lacking supervisory talents; hard-working, lazy; ex-drug addict, non-users of drugs; those who are temporary or more permanent; aggressive in attacking administrations, non-caring and ignoring of all things administrative; honest, dishonest; or any of the myriad other characteristics possessed by humankind.

These persons are in one of a variety of categories of positions which range from student assistant, part-time door attendant, and clerk through technical assistant, bibliographer, reference librarian, and chief of catalog department to top manager of the academic library. They have the corresponding offical titles of Student Aide I, Attendant II, Clerk-Typist III, Library Technical Assistant IV, Bibliographer for the Humanities, Assistant Reference Librarian, Catalog Librarian, or Director of University Libraries.

One of the following ranks usually goes with the position: Associate Professor with tenure; Assistant Professor with tenure (or without); temporary probation (if in first six months of civil service); certified permanent status (after six months of civil service system); voting and dues paying union member; non-voting but contract-consideration-fee-paying staff member; academic or professional category within the college or university (i.e., librarian not having faculty status); service at the pleasure of the Board of Trustees; or one of the other stages of security of employment.

In reciting this great variety of persons, positions, titles, and ranks, mention has not been made of scores of other people: volunteers who serve unpaid in either professional or non-professional positions; other professionals, such as personnel officers and accountants; holders of joint appointments in the library and a teaching department; contract or agency employees who work temporarily in the library; Work-Study students; conscientious objectors assigned to the library for alternative service; library school students on field study work assignments or holding internships; staff on exchange agreements from domestic or foreign libraries; holders of mid-career or minority internships; faculty members under terminal notice assigned from teaching faculty to library faculty; librarians who hold professional degrees, but who take technical or clerical positions because of inability to secure professional positions in current job market; holders of subject doctorates who are appointed to professional or non-professional positions for their subject expertise; staff who have gained professional status via the experience route; library faculty who are organized with a collegial governance system; library faculty members who are part of the bargaining unit with teaching faculty; librarians and library clerks who are in the same bargaining unit; persons who are paid by the federal government under the Comprehensive Employment Training Act (CETA) and assigned to work in either professional or clerical positions.

CATALOG OF CONSTRAINTS FROM OUTSIDE THE COLLEGE OR UNIVERSITY

Library administrators of an earlier era were not constrained by as many rules and regulations from outside the parent institution as are today's library managers. Equal opportunity and affirmative action guidelines are a recent innovation. Opportunities to appeal to the Equal Employment Opportunity Commission have also been created. Fair labor practices as defined by federal or state labor relations laws also guide a contemporary library manager in his daily contact with the staff. Although Civil Service systems for supporting or non-academic staff may not be of recent vintage, they have probably been recently elaborated. For example, the Universities Civil Service System of Illinois began as a law passed by the General Assembly in 1952, with amendments, usually more restrictive upon the employer, being passed throughout the years.

In addition to being subject to the local or state civil service system, public colleges and universities may have the state or city legislatures determining the step plans for salaries, granting across-the-board automatic increments, and in general determining completely salaries for non-professional staff. The wages of part-time student assistants may be determined by the state or federal minimum wage laws.

Another outside agent dictating rules and regulations might be the local union's international office. Locally determined union grievance procedures might be out of sync with those determined to be appropriate by the union's central and higher bureaucracy. It is also possible that consortia to which the academic library belongs or its other affiliations will lessen the operational freedom of the local library administration in its staff relationships.

As the ultimate example in this new era of constraint, consider the clerk or librarian employed on federal funds through the Comprehensive Employment Training Act (CETA) who is constantly late and absent from work, is warned that this is unacceptable and is finally terminated. The employee then files a grievance with the local CETA office charging the library with discrimination because of race, sexual preference, age, or some other reason. (This grievance may finally go to the U.S. Secretary of Labor or his/her designee.) Concurrently, the employee 1) files a grievance under the local union contract which may finally be decided by the American Arbitration Association, 2) appeals to the U.S. Equal Employment Opportunity Commission, 3) files a complaint charging discrimination with the City's Human Rights Commission, and also 4) charges the library with discrimination before the state's Human Rights Commission.

Is it any wonder that one university librarian recently said to a graduating senior who had worked for several years in the library as a part-time student assistant and was about to enter law school, "How about being our house lawyer when you finish?"

REGULATIONS IMPOSED BY THE PARENT INSTITUTION

The locally imposed constraints are easily a match for those from the outside world.

Usually each college and university has a set of elaborate personnel rules and regulations which govern the library's relationships with its clerical and technical staff members. They define in great detail how certain personnel policies are to be implemented which "have been developed in the interest of equitable and consistent treatment of employees and to derive the benefits of efficiencies that result from University-wide applications."[3] No matter how laudable the purpose, they are constraints.

There are also institution-wide and separate grievance procedures for the professional staff, non-professional staff, and students. In addition, the library staff association may have a grievance or employee rights committee which stands ready to hear the staff member's complaints and/or grievances. Local union contracts, in addition to containing grievance procedures, contain other regulations, both trivial and substantial, under which the library management must operate.

EXAMPLE I: PROLONGED HIRING PROCEDURES

In order to describe more fully some of the complexities of personnel management, three examples have been selected to illustrate how efficient and effective personnel programs can be hampered by complex hiring procedures and practices, protracted contract negotiations, and allegations of discrimination.

Colleges and universities in order to comply with federal, state, and/or municipal guidelines and regulations for equal opportunity of employment and affirmative action in the hiring of women and members of minorities have devised elaborate procedures and hired extra staff with titles such as Academic Equal Opportunity and Affirmative Action Officer. Naturally, these procedures and staff members have considerably slowed down the recruitment and hiring of professional members of the academic library's staff. In conducting a search for a beginning librarian for a full-time permanent position with a salary of $12,000, the academic library often may be required to advertise nationally in four or five newspapers or journals, including minority publications, in an attempt to develop a heterogeneous pool of applicants as required by law. The lead time for placement of ads varies greatly from thirteen days for the Sunday *New York Times Book Review* to almost two months for some journals. When the deadline for application has passed and the advisory search and screen committee appointed by the director of the library begins its deliberations, inexperienced staff may delay the search by their unrealistic quest for the perfect candidate, even going so far as to abort the search by declaring none of the applicants qualified to meet the stated requirements of the position when several persons do qualify. Finally, a long interviewing process begins, with too many persons probably brought to campus. Two almost equally outstanding candidates emerge. When the woman is chosen over the white male, the university's affirmative action officer become worried about a lawsuit because of the Bakke case (which at the time of this writing awaited decision by the U.S. Supreme Court). However, the woman is offered the position, accepts, and reports for work. Six to nine months may easily have been consumed in the process. In contrast, it is probable that two correctly placed ads would have reached the same heterogeneous applicants, both minority and non-minority, women as well as men, and one or two administrators could have chosen the same outstanding candidates, interviewed them, and then selected one—all in less than two months.

EXAMPLE II: PROTRACTED, ALMOST ENDLESS NEGOTIATIONS

The librarians of a private urban university were organized in the late 1960s by a strong international union. Lest the management be thought of as being illiberal or in some other unenlightened state there was no demand on the part of management to even see the cards of intent to join the union which the union officials said they had gathered.

The local bargaining unit was easily formed, presented its demands for the first contract, and after a fairly short time, the contract was written incorporating many of the union's demands, including a statement that the current personnel rules and regulations were also incorporated into the agreement.

During the next three years—the term of the first agreement—several librarians were not granted tenured academic status at the end of their probationary periods. The probationary period with retention or non-retention had been the practice for over twenty years. Non-retention had also not been subject to grievance.

The union took as its cause the abolition of the probationary period and management's rights to not grant a permanent, tenured position at the end of the probation. First, it grieved an individual case, and upon receiving a statement from management that the matter was non-grievable, the union filed the case with the American Arbitration Association (the contract provided that appeals from an unsatisfactory decision at Step 4 of the grievance procedure could be brought by the grievant to impartial arbitration).

At the arbitration hearing, although management protested and presented its case that the matter was not grievable, the arbitrator, as is customary in such situations, decreed that he would rule on this question in his written decision, but in case his ruling should be for the union, he wished to also hear the substance of the case at the hearing. The arbitrator finally ruled in favor of management.

The union was undaunted and when the negotiations for the second contract opened in a few months, prominently among the union's 105 demands was one to abolish the probationary period and automatically grant tenure to everyone.

The negotiations lasted for two years. Management refused to change the past probationary system, but it did finally agree to incorporate the system into the contract. Ultimately, the two parties drafted six very detailed pages which included the statement that refusal to grant a tenured appointment shall not be subject to appeal, grievance, or arbitration.

If six months were a reasonable time to negotiate the contract, what were the costs of the additional eighteen months?

EXAMPLE III: ALLEGED DISCRIMINATION

Colleges and universities are attempting to increase the number of women and members of minorities on their academic staffs. At a state university, an Hispanic woman was appointed to an untenured position as assistant professor in the catalog department. She had been working in a senior position in the national library of a Latin American country when recruited by the head of the university's Latin American program. The library's personnel officer recommended to the director of university libraries that she not be hired until references could be checked and some determination be made of her ability to understand English. However, for various political reasons, she was immediately appointed. Her library supervisor, a Latino, found her to be totally inept in cataloging or processing even the simplest Spanish language materials. In addition to following her own cataloging rules, she was disorganized and lazy. When these shortcomings were discussed with her, she responded with long, incoherent memoranda which constantly referred to her holding a major position in the national library of her native country. After a two year period in which the cataloger was given more than ample opportunity to prove that she was capable of performing the duties of the position, the head of the catalog department recommended that she be terminated at the end of the contract year. The director of university libraries approved this action. The head of the University's Latin American program protested and assisted the cataloger in filing a grievance under the local union contract between the faculty and the University. During the grievance hearings, the individual's disorganization and other faults were clearly evident and at each step of the procedure, the termination was sustained. Concurrently with her appeal after the last step of the grievance procedure to the American Arbitration Association, as provided in the union contract, the cataloger filed a charge of discrimination because of national origin against the director of university libraries and the head of the catalog department with the state Human Rights Commission. At the hearing, when the arbitrator was informed that the matter was also before the Human Rights Commission, he adjourned the hearing pending the findings of the Commission. The arbitrator retained, however, jurisdiction over the case.

There is no need to recite the many attempts by the Commission to get the parties to settle the matter without formal hearings, the holding of long and rambling informal hearings, the final determination by the investigatory officer of the Commission to find probable cause of discrimination against the library, the scheduling and then actual holding of the formal hearings, and the ultimate dismissal of the allegation by the Commission. It is sufficient to say that the whole process to this point has taken almost three years and there is one final appeal being made. The retention of jurisdiction by the arbitrator is yet to be technically settled. The costs have been in the tens of thousands of dollars for legal fees and an uncounted cost in the staff time of five, and at times as many as eight, highly paid library and university employees.

PRESCRIPTION FOR FUTURE ACADEMIC LIBRARY MANAGERS

These examples are illustrative of the prevailing personnel environment in which we in academic librarianship now find ourselves. We have devised complex and protective personnel systems and have unthinkingly scattered them everywhere. One university which is under the constraining direction of a state universities civil service system for its non-academic staff members has a group of its own bureaucrats who seemingly wish to create an equally complex and encumbering system for its part-time student workers.

It is a time when directors of college and university libraries believe that the world has been turned upside down and that they, the top administrators, are the only ones who care and constantly worry about library services for students and faculty because staff members are devoting their time and energies to confronting, grieving, negotiating, or attempting to take over the administration of the library.

It is a time in which one university library director shocks his recently retired colleagues when he tells them that he now spends amost 50% of his time preparing for or participating in negotiations, grievances, or some other recently developed mode of personnel administration.

It is a time when the board of trustees of a private university is told by a futurist that if the trustees think that employee relations have been difficult in the late 1960s and early 1970s, they have not contemplated the future. He predicted that a dentist's office would require the services of an arbitrator to settle the personnel problems of the three person staff—the dentist, the hygienist, and the secretary-receptionist. Only shortly after this expert had observed that if the trustees thought marital relationships for couples had been difficult in recent years and predicted a future with mediators and arbitrators entering this area of human relationships, the American Arbitration Association announced its availability to handle marriage disputes and opened a marital arbitrarion office on Long Island.

What are academic library administrators to do? First they should realize that they may be partially to blame for their predicament by their weak office holding. Second, they should probably expect that it will get worse before it gets better. The proliferation of more complex personnel systems with which they must deal will continue and spread. They must, therefore, learn how to manage the academic libraries for which they are responsible by knowing everything possible about each intricate rule or regulation. They should take courses, seek out experts for advice and counsel, hire experts as assistants, and not be afraid to admit they may not be naturally endowed with every skill and knowledge necessary to be an academic library administrator in the late 1970s.

But these are only small steps in managing successfully the different personnel systems. One giant step remains: each academic library administrator must resolve individually to be a true administrator as brilliantly and simply defined by Robert M. Hutchins, former President of the University of Chicago, in his lecture entitled "The Administrator" for the University's "The Works of the Mind" Series.[4] Hutchins stated that the highest function of the administrator is to "define, clarify, or discover the aim of his institution."[5] There are four minimum qualifications—courage, fortitude, justice, and prudence or practical wisdom—for this high function:

> When I say that the administrator should have courage, fortitude, justice, and prudence, I am saying only that he should be a good man. If the administrator is to function at all, he must have prudence or practical wisdom, the habit of selecting the right means to the end. But the administrator's life reveals that, though the virtures may be separated for purposes of analysis, they are one in practice. The administrator cannot exercise prudence without courage, which is the habit of taking responsibility; fortitude, which is the habit of bearing the consequences; and justice, which is the habit of giving equal treatment to equals.
>
> Habits are formed by action. The way to become a good administrator is to administer. But this is also the way to become a bad administrator; for vice is a habit, too. The minimum function of the administrator is to decide, and, since he has to make more decisions than most men, he has the chance to be either an especially good or an especially bad man.
>
> But you will say that most of the administrators you have known have not been especially good or especially bad men. This is because there are three courses, rather than two, open to the man who holds an administrative position. He can practice the four virtues I have named, he can practice their opposites, or he can decline to make decisions . . .
>
> The administrator is a man who decides upon the class of cases commited to his care. If he fails to decide, he may be an office holder; he is not an administrator. The shifts and dodges and downright dishonesty to which administrators will resort in the effort to become office holders are an element of low comedy in the high tragedy of university administration . . .[6]

Hutchins continued his wise advice stressing that the person willing to be an administrator and not just an office holder will discover that the strain is chiefly on his character and not on his mind.

> The strain on the character is very great. The administrator who is afraid of anybody or anything is lost. The administrator who cannot stand criticism, including slander and libel, is lost. The administrator who cannot give equal treatment to equals is lost. In a university, he must give equal treatment to

equals no matter how much it would promote his plans or assuage his feelings not to do so. I would recommend to the young members of the faculty of any university, other than the University of Chicago, that they attack the administration. Their advancement will then be assured; for the administration will have to lean over backward to show that these attacks did not prevent a fair appraisal of the professors' scholarly contributions.

The administrator has all these ways to lose, and he has no way to win . . .

The natural course, then, is to become an office-holder. Your life will be much easier, and you may even become popular. To the administrator, the university often seems like a gigantic conspiracy to turn him into an office holder . . .[7]

If there seemed to be a gigantic conspiracy to turn administrators into office holders in the 1940s, we in academic librarianship thirty years later are almost tempted to conclude that the conspiracy was totally successful and that office holders allowed the creation of the personnel systems which now constrain us.

In his classic essay Hutchins tells us what *not* to do: "The temptation, of course, is to bury yourself in routine. There is so much routine—so many reports, so many meetings, so many signatures, so many people to see—all of some value to the institution, that you can conscientiously take your salary and never administer at all."[8]

He also prescribed a practical program for his own (and our own) day:

The essential points are that the administrator should not want to administer, but should be forced to do so for the public good; that he should have a long period of education, culminating in profound speculative study; that he should undergo a great variety of practical experience to form his character and develop the habit of practical wisdom; and he should serve for a limited term, after which he should resume his studies, if he expects at some later time to have another. This is the kind of scheme which is called for if the administrator is to have the moral and intellectual qualities which the times demand.

You will say that even this reduced and denatured version of the Platonic program remains utopian still. It is sufficient reply that our situation is so desperate that nothing not utopian is worth trying.[9]

In 1978 the personnel systems in academic libraries are so complex and constraining that it is time to make a simple demand of all would-be leaders: Be a courageous, just, and prudent administrator with the strength and fortitude to make decisions. Anyone can be an office holder and allow us to continue on our current convolted path.

REFERENCES

1. Jerrold Orne, "Future Academic Library Administration—Wither or Whether," *The Academic Library: Essays in Honor of Guy R. Lyle*, ed. Evan Ira Farber and Ruth Walling (Metuchen, N.J.: Scarecrow Press, 1974), p. 91.
2. Assocation of Research Libraries. *ARL STATISTICS, 1976-1977* (Washington, D.C.: Association of Research Libraries, 1977), p. 20.
3. University of Illinois, "Policy and Rules—Non-academic, Revised May 1, 1976," Preface, v.

4. Robert M. Hutchins, "The Administrator," *Journal of Higher Education* 17 (November 1946): 395–407.
5. *Ibid.*, p. 396.
6. *Ibid.*, p. 396-7.
7. *Ibid.*, p. 398-9.
8. *Ibid.*, p. 400.
9. *Ibid.*, p. 406.

John R. Yelverton

Georgia State University

WIN SOME, LOSE SOME: WRITING BYLAWS FOR AN ACADEMIC LIBRARY

The drafting of an internal governance document for an academic library is described. The effect of the university's administrative environment in shaping the document is discussed, and a personal assessment of the final document is given. Central to the discussion is the ambiguous role of librarians as faculty within the structured hierarchy of this particular academic library. Though the governance document omits a clear formulation, the issue is resolved in specific instances and a large part parallels the ACRL/AAUP definition of faculty.

In the fall of 1975, the University Librarian at Georgia State University appointed a committee charged with the responsibility for drafting an internal governance document— bylaws—for the library's professional staff. The membership of the committee was as follows: two reference librarians; two catalog librarians, including the Head of the Catalog Department; the Chief Bibliographer, as chairman; and the University Librarian, ex officio and non-voting.

The Bylaws Committee began work October 14, 1975. A final document was approved by the library faculty on December 9, 1976. It was approved by the University Librarian on December 14, 1976, and forwarded to the University administration for approval as required by the *Statutes* of the University. In all, we labored somewhat longer than a year. This paper is a personal assessment of that labor, and of the effect of the University's administrative environment in shaping the final product.

Georgia State University is an urban university, located in Atlanta, serving a student body of around 20,000. The William Russell Pullen Library houses close to 600,000 volumes, and has a professional staff of 27. There are no branch libraries.

The chief administrative officer of the University is the president, in whom the Board of Regents invests all executive power. The deans of the various academic colleges or schools are similarly the chief administrative officers of those units, serving under the Vice President for Academic Affairs. The recently approved *University Statutes* assign to the University Librarian the powers and duties of a dean.

Librarians at Georgia State have enjoyed faculty rank and status since 1959, with provisions for tenure. One of the results of this has been the development of a strong collegial relationship between teaching faculty and librarians. (For example, librarians serve on all major campus-wide faculty committees. I serve on the University Committee on

Statutes and Bylaws, the University Senate, and I am a member of the executive committee of the AAUP.)

In the early Spring of 1975, when new statutes for the University were nearing completion, a successful effort was undertaken to incorporate into these statutes a statement affirming the faculty status of librarians, and affirming their right to organize as a library faculty, in a form appropriate for the internal governance of an academic library. Both statements were thought to be necessary, since no official clarifying statement existed at the University level. And though library faculty governance had been implicit in Georgia State's statutes prior to 1975, no formal organization, outside of administrative procedures, had existed in the library. In contrast, several of the academic units (colleges) had governance structures of varying complexity.

As an outgrowth of these events, a study committee was appointed by the acting University Librarian for the purpose of studying governance in academic libraries. The charge of this study committee was as follows:

> To investigate methods for internal governance currently in existence in other academic libraries for the purpose of making recommendations to the Library administration for changes, as appropriate, in the internal governance of the Georgia State University Library. Since the University Library is not an academic school, the form of internal governance should apply to that of an academic library rather than to that of an academic school.

The last sentence of this charge makes apparent the issue which was, to me, central in the writing of the library's bylaws: that is, what does faculty rank and status for librarians truly mean in the particular setting which I have described?

The ACRL statement on *Standards for Faculty Status for College and University Librarians* states in part that "college and university libraries should adopt an academic form of governance;" that "librarians should form as a library faculty whose role and authority is similar to that of the faculties of a college, or the faculty of a school or a department." The formulation of the AAUP is that "as members of the academic community, librarians should have latitude in the exercise of their professional judgment within the library. . . ." The AAUP *Statement of Government of Colleges and Universities* (Section V, The Academic Institution: The Faculty) reads: "The faculty has primary responsibility for such fundamental areas as curriculum, subject matter and methods of instruction, research, faculty status, and those aspects of student life which relate to the educational process. . . . Faculty status and related matters are primarily a faculty responsibility; this area includes appointments, reappointments, decisions not to reappoint, promotions, the granting of tenure, and dismissal." The statement goes further and calls for faculty participation in decisions on salaries, budget, and retention of administrators. The statement, reasonably enough, gives recognition to the fact that limits may exist to the full exercise of these prerogatives.

As we have seen, the deans, and the University Librarian, are at Georgia State University the chief executive officers in their respective units, and are assigned final responsibility for the functioning of those units. Nevertheless, the University Senate of Georgia State University, which acts for the entire faculty, exercises legislative functions dealing with the general educational policy of the University. The faculty of each college or school is empowered to exercise, in general, jurisdiction over all educational matters within the college or school.

There can be little doubt that librarians at Georgia State perform as members of the faculty. They instruct students both formally and informally; they assist in research tasks and conduct personal research; they serve, as I have mentioned, on campus-wide bodies through which much educational policy is formulated. It is a fact of life, however, that these same librarians exist in an administrative hierarchy, subject to various levels of supervisory responsibility, with ultimate decision-making power residing at the top (in the person of the University Librarian). This is an arrangement considerably more stratified than that in which teaching faculty exist, and one which must, in some way, be reconciled with the view of librarians as a faculty, acting as a body, with policy making powers in library matters. Stated another way, are there matters within the library over which librarians, as a faculty, can assume jurisdiction, as can, presumably, teaching faculty in regard to educational policy? Though the sides were never so sharply drawn, we may imagine the library faculty on one side wishing to assume rights similar to those of teaching faculty, while the University Librarian, for his part, and for very good reasons, wishes to maintain clearly the locus of final authority. Whatever the hopes of individual members of the library staff for a "participatory" form of governance, it seems clear, in retrospect, that only a "consultative" solution was possible. In order to determine the degree to which the ideal of a library faculty—as faculty—was attained in our situation, we must look more closely at specific aspects of the completed library bylaws.

The study committee in its final report had merely recommended that the professional staff organize as a library faculty, and that bylaws be drawn up. The Bylaws Committee, of which I was chairman, was then appointed by the present University Librarian for that purpose. Briefly, the document which emerged contains the following major elements:

(1) A definition of the function and status of the library within the University;
(2) A description of the appointment, duties, and responsibilities of the University Librarian and the administrative staff;
(3) A description of the Library Administrative Council, a body advisory to the Librarian in administrative affairs;
(4) A definition of the library faculty, and in particular, of its powers;
(5) A description of the various standing committees:
    (a) Bylaws and Elections;
    (b) Communications and Public Relations;
    (c) Faculty Development and Continuing Education (charged with the responsibility for development of guidelines for leaves, released time for personal research, etc.);
    (d) Appeals and Grievances; and
    (d) Faculty Personnel (whose primary responsibility lies in the area of promotion in academic rank and tenure);
(6) A definition of ad hoc committees;
(7) Procedures for amendment, interpretation, and implementation;
(8) A statement on standing rules.

During the course of the committee's deliberations, much of the discussion was of necessity devoted to issues in which no major philosophical differences existed—for example, the document had to be brought into accord with University and University System regulations. Much time was spent in precise wording. Occasionally, items were included to clarify points which were clarified in no other document. We found it necessary, for example, to state that the library functioned neither as a college or school, nor as an academic department as defined in the University's *Statutes*, but that it had characteristics of both. In the case of the Grievance Committee, it was necessary to do careful research in order to adhere to the elements of due process. Other cases existed in which desirability was never an issue, though degree and extent were. Periodic review of the performance of administrative officers—including the performance of the University Librarian—was one such case.

When faced with the task of defining library matters which are of general concern with the library, and over which librarians as a body, might exert primary control (and through which they might secure a true faculty identity), the committee was unable to reach a satisfactory consensus. What, in fact, should these matters be? Cataloging policy? Public service? Equipment? Book selection policy? Are "library matters" equivalent to such "educational matters" as curriculum, subject matter in courses, methods of instruction, etc? Rather than risk an explicit formulation, and place the library faculty and administration in a position open to the possibilities of conflict, the committee chose ambiguity. This can be seen most clearly in a comparison of the first and final drafts of the section describing the overall powers of the library faculty. The first draft reads in part as follows:

[ARTICLE IV.]

Section 2. *Duties and Functions.* The faculty shall exercise legislative functions dealing with general library policy. It shall take a comprehensive view of the library's objectives, its resources, its problems, translating educational goals into library programs.

General responsibilities:

A. To adopt resolutions on matters of concern to the library and/or university;

B. To initiate proposals on matters relevant to the general welfare of the library and its staff;

C. To elect representatives to the University Senate;

D. To carry out functions authorized by the University Senate when within the scope of the library's operation;

E. To request action from other agencies of the university when such action affects the concerns of the library or its faculty;

F. To elect standing committees which shall be concerned with library development and welfare.

The final draft reads:

[ARTICLE IV.]

Section 2. *Powers.* The library faculty shall take a comprehensive view of the library's objectives, its resources, its problems, translating educational goals into library programs.

Its powers shall be:

A. To adopt resolutions on matters of concern to the library and/or university;

B. To initiate proposals on matters relevant to the general welfare of the library and its staff; and to make recommendations on these proposals when initiated by the university librarian;

C. To elect representatives to the University Senate;

D. To carry out functions authorized by the University Senate when within the scope of the library's operation;

E. To request action from other agencies of the university when such action affects the concerns of the library or its faculty;

F. To elect standing committees which shall be concerned with library development and welfare.

Note that the statement relating to legislative functions has been omitted. The power to initiate proposals (but not action) has been retained, and added to this is the power to make recommendations on proposals when they are initiated by the University Librarian. In this same article (Section 3) we find in the final draft the statement that "any action [i.e., proposal] passed by the library faculty shall be subject to review by the University Librarian." The first draft read: "The University Librarian shall have the right to veto any action of the library faculty. . . ." In an attempt to avoid an adversary relationship between the library faculty and the University Librarian, the word "veto" has been changed to "review," but as a consequence the limits of power of both parties has been blurred.

In spite of this blurring, and the absence of a firm theoretical basis, the relative strength of the library faculty vis-á-vis that of the University Librarian does emerge from the document as a whole in specific, concrete situations, and in fact parallels the ACRL/AAUP definition of faculty.

Concessions are made to the authority of both the library faculty and the University Librarian throughout. For example, the approval of the library faculty is consistently implied: "[The University Librarian] shall have primary responsibility, *in consultation with the library faculty* (emphasis mine) and through his administrative officers, for initiating and implementing policy and for planning library development." "*After consultation with the library faculty*, [the university librarian] shall prepare annually a budget request for presentation to the vice president for academic affairs." Administrative officers—the Associate University Librarian, Department Heads—are appointed only after consultation with library faculty. The Faculty Personnel committee may advise the Librarian on initial assignment of rank and credit towards tenure. Major documents produced by standing committees—such as criteria for promotion and tenure—must be presented to the library faculty for approval. Though the University Librarian is the final authority for the interpretation of the bylaws within the Library, the faculty is provided the means to communicate its judgment to him before he acts.

As with most groups of this kind, regular functions are carried out through a committee structure. All standing committees, however, (with the possible exception of the Committee on Bylaws and Elections in its routine business) are advisory to the University Librarian, whether this is explicitly stated or not. Proposals of certain committees—for example, those of the Faculty Development Committee—must be forwarded to the University Librarian for his review. He in turn makes recommendations to the faculty for their discussion, though not necessarily for their vote. In such cases implementation is specifically delegated to the University Librarian. Recommendations on tenure and promotion, and on the resolution of grievances, are only advisory recommendations.

But then again, the performance of the University Librarian is subject to periodic review by the library faculty as a whole, with reports forwarded to the Vice President for Academic Affairs. Furthermore, procedures for appeal to the University Administration are stated throughout the bylaws, should irreconcilable differences arise between the University Librarian and his faculty.

It seems evident that in drafting bylaws the authority of the University Librarian for overall planning and execution has been left virtually unchanged. On the other hand, our role as faculty has been enhanced and more adequately defined. A sense of ourselves as colleagues with common concerns beyond the level of administrative assignments may grow out of this structure (perhaps through an agency such as the Faculty Development Committee), even though the bylaws fail most visibly at this point. We chose to develop an administrative document, rather than a theoretical (or philosophical) one.

The library faculty has ensured for itself, for the present, the right to be consulted in important decisions, even though in many instances—budget-making and appointments, for example—the degree of consultation has not be spelled out. (The sentence quoted earlier: "[The University Librarian] shall have primary responsibility, in consultation with the library faculty . . . for initiating and implementing policy and for planning library development," is followed by the statement that "when these matters affect the library as a whole, he, *at his discretion*, shall consult with and seek the recommendations of the library faculty as that body is constituted and empowered in Article IV.") Interestingly, the role of the library faculty is most explicately detailed in those areas in which the concerns can easily be seen to be identical with those of teaching faculty—that is, in the areas of tenure, promotion, and grievances. Nevertheless, built into the document is a mechanism—not to be used lightly—for redress should consultation become an empty gesture. The bylaws state that a full review of the University Librarian's performance shall be undertaken in the library at each five year interval following his initial appointment. However, if two-thirds of the library faculty petitions in writing, an earlier review must be carried out.

It is clear from my remarks, I think, that as chairman of the committee I am disappointed that, as a committee, we did not face with more courage the ultimate questions which bear on the nature of our profession as it exists in the academic world. Rather than creating an adversary relationship, I feel such an attempt would have strengthened the partnership between administration and faculty. The document itself is flexible enough to allow for many styles of management. My only real concern is that, as written, it may allow the chief administrator more discretionary, or interpretative, power, than we at first intended. It is quite possible, should circumstances change, for an administrator who wishes very little faculty participation to justify his action statutorily. It is realistic to conclude that success of these bylaws requires an interested and alert library faculty, willing to participate, and a library administrator willing to share in the formulation of policy.

Joseph W. Barker

Virginia Polytechnic Institute and State University

THE DUTCH-DOOR CIRCULATION DESK

The usual circulation desk which dominates the entrance to most libraries can be abolished. Users can be routed to problem-solving centers staffed by professionals trained in references and other research supports and equipped with circulation terminals, and can fill in forms to request recalls and searches by a small, behind-the-scenes circulation staff, whose public service counter would only need to be a Dutch-door leading to their office. Economy, surer access to the collection at hand, improved public relations, and broader use/control of a circulation system are among the arguments for thus re-designing this area of library service.

There is a well-worn path in most libraries from the card catalog to the stacks to the circulation desk and from there to the exit or back to the card catalog where the cycle begins again. People confident in their ability to make use of the catalog to find the call number for what they want proceed either to find the volume where it should be, or to experience frustration. They then go to the circulation desk, either for checkout or help. it is rare that librarians are encountered along this path. Libraries, like budget department stores, seem to believe that clerks stationed at checkout counters can provide sufficient assistance once they are armed with rainchecks, complaint forms, and a suggestion box. Librarians are relegated to a corner where they will not be needlessly interrupted by the public, or they are assigned to public service a little like floor clerks; but, their public exposure is restricted by attachment to a collection of reference tools whose link to bookfinding is virtually nil and whose appropriateness in research is known only by a savvy elite.

Meanwhile, inexperienced users, unable to find what they are looking for, are told at circulation desks that the item can be held for them when it is returned or that it is currently missing but will be searched for and held if found. There is no mention of alternative sources of information which may be on hand, such as other editions of the same work or similar publications on the same topic. No one has a chance to explain the possible benefits of a search strategy embracing more subject headings or to suggest use of special subject bibliographies, encyclopedias, or journal indexes. Unless a library instruction course has already gotten through to the user, there is a good chance he or she will leave the library empty-handed and a little more confirmed in the belief that libraries are inefficiently set up and designed to be frustrating to use.

153

Experienced researchers, while they may be saved such dejection, find the well-worn path at best tiresome. Any elimination of steps and stairwells is welcomed. They would like self-service querying of circulation files or at least contact with personnel trained to grasp some of the consequences of their frustration. These users may have worthwhile suggestions to offer on collection development or there might be a new reference aid or one they could stand to be reminded to invoke. But rather than trek to the reference desk in addition to the circulation desk, they often exit—taking with them their advice and their disgruntlement.

I certainly am not the first to suggest that libraries alleviate the plight of frustrated users. The problem is central to the issue of access to library collections on a local scale. Paging and delivery systems are related to it as, to a lesser degree, are bibliography services. Acquiring multiple copies and adjusting loan periods to fit user demand are proposals that would help along this same line by increasing availability of heavily used materials.[1] Library methods instruction could also help by making users alert to basic alternative research strategies and to the value of seeking professional help.

A remedy more directly aimed at the problem would make the circulation staff consist of professionals.[2] This plan would succeed at increasing the probability of contact between users and professionals and therefore would provide for early diagnosis of user pain, but it would leave unmodified the library floorplan and the catalog-stacks-circulation-desk cycle—one of the *causes* of the pain. Temporary relief of symptoms would be the most that could be hoped for. Users would still have to congregate all in one place to inquire about circulation records, and the librarians armed with needed research tools and trained to teach how to find alternative, related titles would remain off the user's usual well-worn path.

To alleviate the cause of user pain, the gap needs to be closed between the *physical* process of tracking down a particular book in a particular library and the *intellectual* process of exploiting librarianship's tools to access ideas in interrelated books, articles, and other information sources. To do this, I submit that the circulation desk should be taken out of its prominent location and reduced in size to a Dutch-door behind which is office space for a small circulation staff. Then, through terminals placed at prominent service points attended by reference personnel, users could talk directly to librarians about both intellectual problems and physical bookfinding problems. Support services, such as recalls, holds, searches for missing items and the tracking of overdues, would be performed by the behind-the-scenes (or, behind-the-Dutch-Door) circulation staff.

* * * * *

We are working at a time when automation of the circulation process is not only a reality—it is an eventual necessity mandated by the size of our institutions and collections and by the cost of labor to service large manual files accurately and quickly. At the ISAD/LAD conferences in Dallas and Philadelphia this last year, about half the 500 or so librarians present were actively shopping for systems, and another quarter to a third already had computerized circulation. The question is not "whether" to automate, but "how."

Online circulation makes the immediate status of all loanable items available in snazzy, modern-looking terminals that can, theoretically, be placed anywhere. Providing the system one develops or buys meets three criteria, there is no need for its use to be restricted to a specialized circulation staff. The first test is privacy: the identity of the person to whom an item is checked out must be masked or blocked from general public knowledge. The second criterion is ease of use: the system should provide instructions and help, relieving users of the need to be initiated to system use and to remember the rites of passage. The third requirement is the means at remote terminals to request a hold for a checked-out item or a search for an item that is unaccounted for. If these tests are satisfied, independence of the circulation desk is possible, and the well-worn path can be redirected to reference desks, to information desks, to staffed or self-service terminals near the site of origin of user frustration among the stacks.

At Virginia Polytechnic Institute and State University, where development and implementation of the Circulation and Finding System (the CFS) have been in progress for three years, there exists a test environment with much that seems transferable to other libraries.[3,4] The library has over 1.2 million volumes, not including holdings in microform, to serve a borrowing population of about 30,000. VPI&SU's is a rapidly growing research library that continues to serve a large undergraduate clientele. Annual circulation totals about one-half million items. The professional staff numbers 54, clerical support 106.

The procedure at VPI&SU goes like this. Three terminals linked to the Circulation and Finding System are at reference-staffed desks near the stacks on three different floors. A fourth is at an information desk near the card catalog. When users approach these service points because an item is not on the shelf, the circulation data base may be queried by call number, author, title, or author-title combination. The CFS is sufficiently interactive and fields are clearly enough labeled that only a brief introduction to the system is required. If an item a borrower needs is checked out, the CFS will recall it and trap it upon its return. It will be held for that borrower's use. If the availability status of the item is undetermined, a form is completed to initiate verification of the request and an inventory of all copies of the item. Forms and returned books to be held are batched and processed several times daily by circulation staff. Items initially reported missing but later found to be in circulation are held as if first identified as checked out.

Referral to the circulation is thus obviated completely in bookfinding. To so outfit a library with terminals and service points, however, is still not enough to get users off the well-worn path to the circulation desk. It is necessary to get the circulation desk itself out of its prominent site and to strip it of its welcoming appearance. The records at VPI&SU[5] indicate that at least three out of four users who cannot find books for which they already have call numbers will walk right past reference desks, no matter how conveniently located, to head for the circulation desk down at the entrance. They have been accustomed to trouble-shooting circulation desks since their first dealings with libraries, and the presence of a ready-to-serve-you desk at the entrance tends to reinforce this habit.

It is not a minor change to move most circulation desks because they provide various desirable user services. Decentralization, however, greatly enhances the efficiency with which these services are performed. Book checkout is an exit-based event, just as checkin, walk-in requests for renewal, and picking up books being held are entrance-based. Since online circulation liberates these services from bulky, slow manual files and provides a high degree of accuracy, well-trained student help can perform these tasks at terminals near library doors. Returned books may be checked in and routed to the shelves by a casual staff at the return bin. The circulation system puts on account any fines for late return and traps items requested by another user as they come through checkin.

Discussions of fines, overdues, lost books, and the status of requests for holds are quite properly a job for a specialized staff. These are housekeeping chores evolving solely from the nonreturn of circulated library materials. Discussing these operations is time consuming and requires a thorough grasp of the procedures followed in each case, plus, often, a degree of backtracking to get to the bottom of a delinquency that is disputed.

This is an area of considerable human intervention in machine operation, and consequently one prone to error. As a result of errors and accountability requirements, and because users are often impatient with the library's circulation policy and routine bookfinding procedures, a need remains for a place in the library where the public can confront the people responsible for enforcing circulation policy and for locating unavailable books. Without this, the reference staff would be burdened by circulation-related questions they should not answer. What is *not* needed, however, is a focal point where people with finding problems mingle with others checking out or picking up books and still others inquiring about circulation activities proper. A Dutch-door opening to the public from a work area which remains essentially hidden would give the circulation staff a degree of public contact. without allowing circulation to dominate the library's problem-solving services. Here again, the department store model is useful.

The handling of overdues, fines and such, may be compared to discussions of delinquency of one's charge account at a department store; and a recall or a missing-book search (from the *user's* viewpoint) has much in common with a special order for an item temporarily out of stock. Having borrowing privileges can be seen as analogous to having a charge account. (The difference is that you are supposed to return the merchandise rather than pay for it when the time is up; "cash and carry" is not allowed.) Only in libraries where it is policy to block borrowing privileges or take other censuring action at checkout time for unreturned materials or unpaid fines and if a block happens to be in force, is there a reason for the status of a customer's account from prior transactions to come into play every time he or she attempts to use his or her account. Usually there is no need for the circulation staff (the credit department) to be placed out by the checkout counters. And in libraries where it is policy for delinquency to interfere with checkout, as is the case at VIP&SU, referring delinquent customers from the checkout terminals to other terminals permits investigation of the problem without losing at checkout a certain "express line" quality.

By putting the credit department up front, a prominently located, traditional circulation desk seems to question users' charge privileges before allowing them to determine if they want to check anything out. To search for material on a subject and to take it out of the library are two completely different processes.

The economy of the Dutch-door circulation desk is bound to be considerable. Since complaints and inquiries into circulation record errors may often be handled over the telephone, since requests for recalls and searches are received by reference people, a staffed circulation desk is no longer the sine qua non for providing good library service. It becomes unnecessary for the circulation desk to be staffed all hours the library is open. Although firm data on staff requirements cannot yet be presented, there is a good basis in experience at VPI&SU to date for the following estimated savings in clerical staff. With circulation desk hours shortened from 107 to about 70 per weeks, the need for one of two supervisors and for one evening clerk would be removed. In addition, since the time required for certain circulation taks has been reduced greatly as a result of automation, one-and-one-half clerk-typists are released from preparing overdue and recall notices.

All this translates at VPI&SU into a staff reduction of 50% ($29,000 per year)—3½ out of 7 positions available for reallocation. The remaining staff could be used as follows: one clerk assigned to missings searches, holds and recalls, and the other two and one-half to supervising, handling complaints, and generally keeping things going. Present staff workloads bear out the adequacy of these estimates. Student assistant time is estimated to have to remain the same: although students may no longer be needed at the Dutch-door circulation desk, that savings would be consumed in covering checkin and checkout service points.

An increased professional staff to implement a program such as this at VPI&SU has not been fully explored but is not anticipated.

The Dutch-door circulation desk may necessitate the purchase of more terminals and electrical hookups than would a rigidly centralized desk. At VPI&SU the four circulation and four reference terminals now in use would probably have to be increased by two with the decentralization a Dutch-door circulation desk implies. A certain amount of shifting to create prominently located, professionally staffed service points with terminals is also unavoidable. But whatever individual library structure requires for implementation, the return on the investment would include significantly enhanced public relations for the library as a whole. Besides the greater logic in library service and the modern image gained from widespread use of terminals in public view, there are more occasions for the public to deal with professional librarians. As this brings about more effective use of the collection and of reference tools, increased user satisfaction is inevitable. A fringe benefit for librarianship and for each library is greater public awareness of what librarians really do—or at least more users aware that librarians really do something usable. The belief held by many that all that librarians do is check out books might finally be laid to rest.

Another fringe benefit is the availability of prime, high-visibility space no longer occupied by a traditional circulation desk—a good location for a library instruction center or a display of library holdings of particular interest to the public.

An online circulation system itself is a major budgetary consideration, but one that is, as I have said, inevitable for most libraries. The Dutch-door circulation desk concept helps ensure that this major investment is used not only to enable the circulation staff to get its work done more accurately and quickly; also, it places reference staff on the front line to deal with the public and guarantees subordination of circulation as a support function. Control of the system is not in the hands of just one group in the library. When recommendations and decisions on system use and growth must be made, a balance between the technical processing and public service aspects of—the building of a data base, searching it, and exercising custodianship—circulation and bookfinding tasks is more likely to be achieved.

A potentially troublesome area in implementing the Dutch-door circulation desk is obtaining the reference staff's continuing support for the program, because there is no denying that it would increase reference desk workload. Removing the circulation desk from prominence would create a vacuum that the public would expect reference personnel to compensate for. This means longer, more staggered hours for reference. It might necessitate training and supervising some graduate student assistants, depending on the present number of reference librarians. In some libraries, more professional reference staff would be required. In some, it might suffice to reallocate clerical staff no longer needed at circulation to reference, in order to free librarians from clerical responsibilities they had become accustomed to performing.

Thorough training in system use is of course imperative, so that it can be given a chance to yield all it is capable of yielding. It can be observed that most of those reluctant to approach the nearby terminal simply do not know how to use it well enough to feel comfortable. Once ease of use is achieved, librarians working at some distance from the card catalog often try to rely on the circulation data base to ascertain not only availability status but collection holdings as well. They discover that this saves them and users time and effort, and before long support comes from reference personnel to put more bibliographic records online.

VPI&SU has had circulation terminals at reference service points for over two years now, and there are virtually no feelings of condescension and imposition among the reference staffs about calling up circulation records at the terminals. Public enthusiasm for the increased service and convenience is a powerful aid, as is the simple fact that most people find it somewhat entertaining to use a terminal once comfortable familiarity is achieved. Many of us derive a measure of self-satisfaction from being able to follow through on a user's problem without having to send him or her elsewhere in the library for help. We have less doubt that the user will try to obtain the circulation staff's help when it is possible to respond to his or her needs immediately, without referral. Often, having the ability to help a user locate a book is the means to get him or her to articulate the need for more complicated reference service.

For times when reference work occupies librarians too much to allow attending to individual bookfinding problems, users could record their needs for searches on forms made available for this purpose next to a sign headed, "In a hurry?" which would explain the procedure and would supply the appropriate telephone number so that users could, if desired, speak to someone about their special needs. A more useful support here would be self-service terminals, but these must be so easy to use that all pertinent data is comprehensible and all useful search strategies are readily apparent to the user.

Both libraries in the market to buy automated circulation and those owning systems already may find it worthwhile to study the feasibility of instituting a Dutch-door circulation desk. System selection and system growth to have ease of use, privacy for borrowers, and a few extra terminals and cables are relatively minor, specific obstacles. More problematic could be spatial planning and obtaining the support of the library staff. Justification for this effort and expense already exists or will, I believe, exist before long.

The future of academic libraries appears to hold bigger and bigger collections, circulating materials to a clientele inflated not only by college and university growth but also by borrowing networks. Physical access to materials will rely increasingly on dependably accurate and efficient use of computers. Heavily used titles will get even heavier use. Access to ideas may be more sophisticated but the need for professional help to succeed at getting *to* what one needs and *through* what one does not need will be even greater in the future. More course subjects and more research topics will be interdisciplinary and more pieces of information will be available in every discipline. These will be harder to classify and therefore harder to access by subject. The cost of computer hardware will decline, but not so programming and connect time. The result of all this will be greater demand placed on the local collection despite networks and data base reference capabilities.[6] Reliance on a local data base with relatively low access and maintenance costs and powerful search approaches will be highly desirable to get the most out of the collection. If my crystal ball is right, programs, promoting circulation staff precision and user contact with librarians will be welcomed. The Dutch-door circulation desk facilitates movement in this direction.

REFERENCES

1. Michael K. Buckland, *Book Availability and the Library User* (N.Y.: Pergamon Press, 1975).
2. Betty Young, "Circulation Service: Is It Meeting the User's Needs?" *Journal of Academic Librarianship* 2 (July 1976): 120–125.
3. V. Chachra and R. R. Crockett, *Detailed Documentation of Library Circulation and Finding System* (Blacksburg, Va.: Systems Development, Virginia Polytechnic Institute and State University, 1978).
4. Virginia Polytechnic Institute and State University, Systems Development Department, *Library Circulation and Finding System* (Boulder, Colo.: College and University Systems Exchange, 1978).
5. Over a ten-month period operating with a traditional circulation desk, circulation staff compared the number of recall and search requests originating at the circulation desk with those from all reference service points. The results: 5168 requests made at the circulation desk (80%); 1326 referred from reference. *All* service points had identical access to the same circulation files.

6. CF., Richard De Gennaro, "Copyright, Resource Sharing, and Hard Times: A View from the Field," *American Libraries* 8 (September 1977): 430–435.

Ritvars Bregzis

University of Toronto

THE TECHNICAL SERVICES BUDGET—1980
AND BEYOND

The reduced budget support for academic institutions is drastically compressing the allotment for bibliographic management in academic libraries. Technical services and especially cataloging costs are high, largely because of the traditional "entry" based cataloging method which is retained by AACR2. Automation by itself cannot compensate for the imprecise nature and operational costliness of this method. The information seeker requires more powerful access mechanism to information resources which integrates a wider resource spectrum than books alone comprise. An approach is suggested that could extend cataloging beyond the "entry" system and could integrate access to information in books and other sources.

THE ECONOMIC SITUATION

The "new economic reality" of the 1970s has brought a profound re-orientation in some of the priorities of academic library services. The 1960 decade of the cultural renaissance in America provided ample support for our institutions. The emphasis in most academic libraries was on the building of library collections. This was acknowledged to be a nationally vital, academically prestigious and functionally important goal. By and large this endeavour was adequately funded. It was also normal to receive reasonably adequate funding for the organization and preparation, i.e. cataloging of the acquired materials. In this period technical services operations were made more effective, precision of bibliographic control was honed, and new methods and techniques were developed and introduced. Along with these developments budgetary support was sufficient also for the required user services. Here too new methods were developed and new technologies introduced. The need to choose priorities among these three, in a sense sequential, operations did not arise as a practical necessity.

The situation, however, has changed quite drastically during the past seven or eight years. The dwindling budgets of the academic libraries have forced them to re-assess their priorities of budget support. One now notes a marked difference in the priority pattern of the three major operations. Collection building has become more important than ever. After all, library is books, and basically one cannot quarrel with the importance of collection building, since in most cases materials not acquired this year may never be acquired. User services, however, have risen to the next most important priority level. Again, reasons for this are many and well known, not to mention extended dependence on inter-library lending services resulting from the general economic stringency. This has left the preparatory services, important as they are, in the last place.

One of the consequences of this reshifting of priorities is that budget cuts have tended to be sought first in technical services. Frequently that is also where they have been taken. The contribution of preparatory services is not conspicuous to the public, it is difficult to evaluate by the institutional management, and it appears costly. Technical services also appear to have large potential for economic innovation. The library's catalog as a file of cards does not readily disclose the monumental effort of analysis, interpretation and systematization that supports this structure. The user public by and large is not aware of the methodology on which the bibliographic organization and control of a library's collection rests, and still less can it appreciate the high cost of it. Witness the interchangeable use of 'cataloging' and 'indexing.' Nor is it only the user public which takes cataloging and all the related operations for granted. So often a similar assessment comes also from other service areas within the library.

In this environment of economic pressure, of the wisespread vague understanding of the purpose and value rendered by the technical services functions, and of the impending re-orientation of the whole catalog base to a changed cataloging code, it should be instructive to analyze the costs and benefits of cataloging operations and the tangible value of services obtained from them. In doing this, hopefully each library will have the fortitude to question the philosophy, the cost and the serviceability of the library catalog as we know it today and as it relates to the technology and service expectations, current and future.[1]

CATALOGING COSTS

Costs of traditional cataloging always have been high even with the available shared cataloging services. The process is judgmental in nature, and only the mechanistic aspects of cataloging work have been meaningfully responsive to mechanization, automation and economization. The quantitative shift created by cooperative cataloging has helped to reduce some subtotals on the cataloging budget sheet, but this has not and cannot significantly reduce the relative costliness of the work which still remains judgmental in nature.

In the current economic climate surrounding the academic institutions, the budgeted income of the academic library has dropped considerably as a proportion of the income of the academic institution. The analysis presented here indicates a drop of library support percentage from 10.4% to 6.9% during the last decade. Library money has become scarce (cf. Table I). In addition, the cost of an average staff position has increased during this period two and a half times due to inflation and the general trend of salary rise related to, among other factors, increased unionization of library personnel (cf. Table II). Thus, in effect two factors have been at work in this economic contraction: the continuous attrition and loss of staff positions, and the progressive rise in the relative cost of the remaining staff positions.

Under this pressure, the relative priority assignment of support for collection building (i.e. books), for the preparation and technical services, and for the user services has been adjusted to satisfy the most pressing needs first. Inevitably the technical services have been left in the third place, if even by a close margin. This has placed technical services operations under a particularly concentrated pressure. The result now is that on the time scale of the last decade, the total impact of the economic pressure on technical services budgetary support amounts to a loss of about one half of the total aggregate dollar value calculated at 1977 salary levels (cf. Table III). At the same time, on the other side of the

TABLE I

Library Expenditure as Percent of University Expenditure

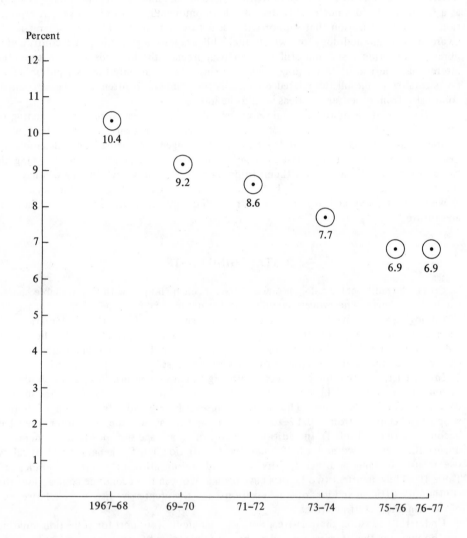

TABLE II

Nominal $ Value Average of a Technical Services Position

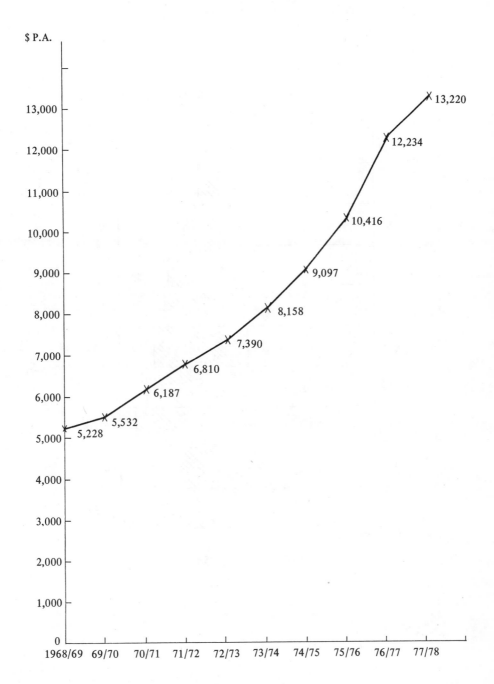

TABLE III

TECHNICAL SERVICE STAFF

Attrition of FTE's and Salary Cost Increase

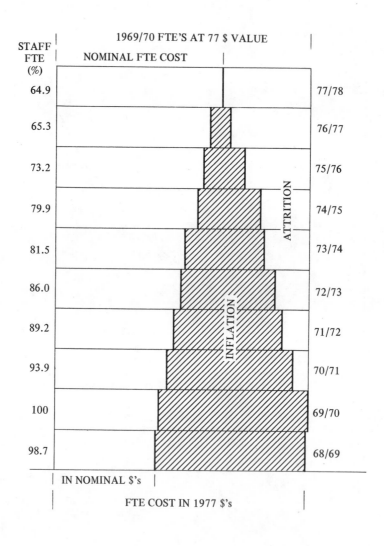

balance sheet, the level of work load and production during the same period has not decreased correspondingly. The decrease of the cataloging load has not reached more than about 16%, the number of serial units serviced has increased, and so has the requirement for binding.

Following through the components of the cataloging expenditure for staff and computer services (cf. Table IV), it is interesting to note that 20.3% of the total cataloging cost is spent on bibliographic identification of materials before acquisition and prior to cataloging. This may be read as a significant commentary on the level of effectiveness of the traditional catalog mechanism. Another 29.2% of the total cataloging cost is taken by the maintenance of the catalog, and catalog records, and almost two thirds of this latter cost (18.0%) goes toward the maintenance of the description of these items. One may conclude that the labor intensive nature of the descriptive conventions seems to call for detailed scrutiny.

Viewed in another way, the practice of the traditional cataloging method consumes 29.4% of the total cataloging cost for the bibliographic description, while only 19.6% go toward subject analysis. The maintenance of the entry system for the traditional cataloging method constitutes 35.2% of the total cataloging cost, with almost one half of this (15.8%) being expended for bibliographic identification of entries.

These summary observations which can be made from the presented cost distribution raise a number of fundamental questions—about the economy of the traditional methods of bibliographic description and its maintenance; about the relatively limited support expended for subject analysis; about the areas where automation may yield some further economic gains; about the efficiency of the catalog as finding device, especially for entries; but in particular, about the large proportion of resources expended for the practice of the entry system on which our traditional catalog is based.

THE THEORETICAL BASIS

The information service mandate to provide information as basis for our cultural activities has three principal dimensions which are not always clearly focused in their total context: the accumulation and maintenance of information resources of various levels of specificity; the generation and maintenance of mechanisms to identify and to control the intellectual aspects of these resources; and the methodology for the provision of the linkage between the needed information and the integrated totality of the existing information resources, through the intellectual mechanisms for satisfying the stated need for information.

Traditionally the library has always endeavored to serve this complex objective fully. And it has done this admirably within the existing limitations. The traditional catalog technique over the past century had evolved into a harmonious and mutually complementary co-existence of the catalog technology (cards, standardized printed record displays) and the corresponding intellectual mechanisms (entries, subject headings, descriptive conventions). Recently, the technology has begun to change, and quite dramatically. The card and fixed display technology is being replaced by flexible and very powerful computer controlled recording. The intellectual mechanisms, however, so far have remained in their traditional definition of entries and descriptive conventions. The traditional equilibrium of technology and intellectual mechanisms has been disturbed, but a new equilibrium accounting for the characteristics and capabilities of the new technology has not yet been established.

The AACR2 is only a new version of the traditional intellectual mechanism for bibliographic control to facilitate location and correlation of information units. In this scheme

TABLE IV

Distribution of Cataloging Cost 1977

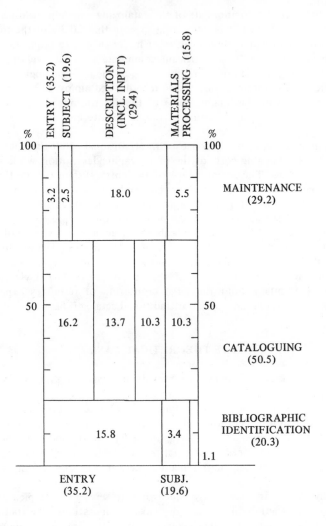

the correlation function employs the method of physical collocation of like forms, a combination ideally suitable to the technology of the catalog card and physically fixed display of record images. It presumes a common denominator form—the entry—that is to be generated through interpretation and human judgment. This is an increasingly costly process, besides being also less than precise and systematic. Because of the costliness and the demanding nature of this scheme the application of the entry system on a universal scale to all types of information resources is not feasible, and therefore practically it has been limited only to description of book type entities.

THE OBJECTIVE OF INFORMATION SERVICE

The information service mandate and the information seekers, however, have no reason to recognize this limitation as legitimate. Information resources are taken to be an integrated and coherent spectrum, and access is assumed to be available to any portion of this information spectrum, and at any reasonable depth, be the required information unit a book, a document, or a journal article.

The recent advent of the computer has changed radically the character and the power of the available and affordable information technology. Findability of information has become possible on a massive scale. Correlation of identificatory and descriptive characteristics of information can now be achieved through computer control in extensive arrays of relationships. The price of this process is now becoming competitive with the labor intensive, paper and print based methods. It has now become realistic for the information service providers to take advantage of this new technology on a large scale.

In the mid-sixties it appeared that a breakthrough in the area of information services was around the corner, and that the traditional library would be able to realize fully its avowed ideal and potential through the new technology. Excitement and the greatest of hopes greeted the imaginative research of the project INTREX. The potential of the new technology in service to information appeared to be unlimited. However, little has materialized yet for the user public.

A NEW APPROACH TO INFORMATION MAY EMERGE

In the immediate context, the likelihood to advance a systematic development of the intellectual mechanisms to match the level of current technological power does not appear promising. Now more than ever there is less time and less resources to do fundamental research. Nor is there a widespread recognition that something is basically amiss. Above all, there is only two years time for libraries to find a way to accommodate the AACR2, regardless of its long term practicality. In this task libraries will have basically three alternatives to choose from for the perpetuation of the traditional scheme.

Alternative one, to accept the new cataloging rules, with the benefit of entry economy to be gained in future, and with the burden of reconciling all existing entry precedents with the new forms. The costs and benefits of this alternative can be approximately calculated; they amount to a massive investment in return for questionable improvement in the effective gain for the information user.

Alternative Two, to ignore the new version of the cataloging rules, and to incur no burden of retrospective reconciliation, but to accept a burden of continuous retro-orientation of all future work, thus mortgaging technical services efficiency for a long time. (The Library of Congress has estimated that up to 11% of entries may have re-interpreted AACR2 forms at variance with those of AACR1).[2] For the information user this solution likewise does not promise a significant gain.

Alternative Three, to do what amounts to a betrayal of the classical entry system; i.e. to use both forms, the existing one as well as the new AACR2 form with the necessary convenience linkages, thus breaking the single-form entry principle. On the surface this sounds economically preferable, although functionally questionable and professionally so far unacceptable. On closer examination, however, this untidy appearing alternative may hold the key to the evolution of a more versatile and less interpretive mechanism, logically complementary to the character and power of computer technology.

Acceptance of this path of evolution could accommodate a logical and also operational separation of the *findability* of information sources from the *correlation* of information sources bearing cognate elements. The mechanical union of these two fundamental elements in the traditional catalog structure and technology is the main cause of the imminent breakdown of the large scale traditional catalog. The separation of the functions of findability and correlation can more naturally facilitate the application and use of different technological mechanisms to the two tasks. Findability then becomes amenable to handling of information sources on a massive scale and without the necessary traditional restriction of uniform entry formalization. This capability would answer the majority of information searches in the library catalog. Correlation, with the help of computer technology can be linked with findability, without both being integrally united, yet being practical and affordable. Two types of such linkage are available: linking records directly through imbedded codes; (pre-correlation); and, linking records at the time of searching, through the application of various combinatorial techniques to selected data elements in the records (post-correlation).

Thus behind the seemingly untidy conglomerate of 'entries' (or any other access points, for that matter) could gradually emerge a different system of information source management closer to the unrestricted needs of the information user. A system which could accept information units at their face value and their original form. Such approach would have the advantage of addressing and finding information sources as they present themselves, as they are cited, and as they are commonly referred to. Correlation would be possible through machine maintained linkages of cognate elements, through the records these elements belong to. The concept of 'entry authority' would be replaced by an invisible network of a multitude of pre-connected relationships without the requirement for identical form of these elements. Many types of such relationships can be automatically established through elements of common origin in the information sources. Others can be indicated at record generation stage, but without the necessity for the common normalized form. The establishment of such relationships once and for all would be a task for bibliographic utilities.

The concept of bibliographic integrity would remain the ultimate measure of validity. The characteristics of completeness, theoretical and functional soundness, and harmonious integration would be upheld. But the specifics would change. Normalization would be replaced by a multiplicity of linkages. Guidelines would become mandatory rules. Interpretation would be replaced by more literal acceptance of existing factors. Emphasis would shift from judgmental activity to enforcement of consistency. Selectivity would be opened up to the level of maximally practical universality. The machine would be given a more demanding role to handle larger quantities more systematically. The human intellect would be freed from a great deal of drudgery and detail and given to manage structures and patterns in a wider conceptual universe.

On the immediate practical level such approach permits the continuation of the traditional catalog system with normalized entries, while permitting also the use of free form access elements. The gradually emerging new bibliographic environment would accommodate the traditional normalized interpretive elements as well as the free form elements of bibliographic units. To attain this immediate objective it is necessary to set some conceptual goals, to do some planning and design, and to begin implementation. The nature of the process fortunately is such that it can accommodate a gradual shift from the old to the new. This factor would permit to begin such shift with relatively minor invest-ment, as well as it would permit relatively early easing of the burden of entry normaliza-tion. But it requires committed conceptual acceptance.

The fascinating aspect of such transformation is that it could be elected now as a planned objective, and that in the absence of such planning it may be forced on the li-brary by the sheer pressure to cope with the AACR2 imposed burden. It thus may become both the obligation as well as an opportunity to give to this development the intellectual direction which has so far been conspicuously absent from the planning agenda of the information service profession. The economic pressure and the AACR2 dilemma may point a forced direction toward a major turning-point in information management for the 21st century.

REFERENCES

1. Herman H. Fussler and Karl Kocher, "Contemporary Issues in Bibliographic Control," *Library Quarterly*, v. 47 (July 1977): 242.
2. U.S. Library of Congress, *Freezing the Library of Congress Catalogue.* (Washington, D.C., Library of Congress, January 16, 1978) p. 3. This document is further updated by the LC document *AACR2 Impact* [n.d.] distributed by the Association of Re-search Libraries, August 4, 1978.

Elizabeth J. Furlong and Karen L. Horney

Northwestern University

THE FUTURE IN OUR GRASP: AN ON-LINE TOTAL INTEGRATED SYSTEM FOR LIBRARY SERVICE

This discussion focuses on the importance of developing a comprehensive system in which all of the pieces mesh to produce on-line computer records which will serve the various needs of library staff, library management, and most especially library users. Drawing upon Northwestern University library's "total" systems approach, this paper looks at and beyond automation of "housekeeping" data control aspects of library operations to self-service public use applications of a fully integrated support service system. The emphasis is on the challenge of providing new methods of access to the library's information with services not possible in the past.

What does automation offer for the library's future? Will it be panacea or plague? Views covering a wide spectrum have been heard through the last ten years. Basing our opinions upon Northwestern University Library's experience throughout this period, we view the future of computer support systems with enthusiastic optimism. In particular, we see a remarkable potential already materializing for improved service to the library's user.

What should a library user expect when he comes through the door? Ideally, he should find a quick and easy method of identifying the library's holdings in his area of interest and a ready means of locating and actually putting his hands on the items. Naturally there are many questions about identification of and access to materials not in the local academic or research collection, but this discussion focuses on the immediate problem of facilitating full use of the academic library's own extensive holdings. This is the context in which a total integrated on-line system of computer support offers a quite astonishing potential for improved library services.

A "piecemeal" approach to library automation, effective as it has been for individual applications such as card production, falls far short of even the existing technology's true potential. Few institutions have been as fortunate as Northwestern University Library in having the full acquisitions process, including serials issue-by-issue check-in and claiming, operating as a part of a computer support system which encompasses cataloging and physical processing and interfaces with an on-line circulation control module. But, as crucial as processing efficiency is to the library's mission, automation of "housekeeping" functions is merely the beginning of improved service through total systems operations.

From a sound management perspective, it is axiomatic that a library should be expected to offer the maximum relevant information in the quickest time and at the lowest possible cost. Obviously this means fully utilizing a limited number of available staff. Cost-conscious administrators have long been contemplating automation as a means of eliminating repetitive manual tasks which the staff itself views as drudgery and, by avoiding useless duplication of work, freeing personnel for assignments at higher intellectual levels. In processing activities some of these savings have already been realized, although many librarians have now found themselves focusing even more clearly on the significant intellectual demands of the cataloging process.[1] Staff reallocations aside, important improvements in direct user service are now possible through automation. The opportunity lies in multiple use of the bibliographic data created or captured during processing. The challenge is in providing the user not just with a card catalog substitute but with a superior means of access.

Multiple use of bibliographic and holdings data is the essence of the integrated system which has been operational at Northwestern for over six years, and the official name, "Northwestern On-line Total Integrated System" (hence the acronym NOTIS), conveys this emphasis. How does this multiple use integrated system actually work? Ideally, data is input just once, as early as possible in the processing flow, and is used in building block fashion for all subsequent activities. If a library has on-line display and transfer access to a large data base from an external source such as LC/MARC or OCLC, keying is minimal, restricted for a large proportion of cases to local data such as call number and copy relevant information. The most desirable method of obtaining bibliographic information will be, of course, on-line transfers directly from the data bases maintained at the Library of Congress. Organizations such as RLG and the Network Technical Architecture Group are working toward this objective. At the present time, however, Northwestern must input sufficient, if minimal, data to identify a record and to create immediate on-line access to that record by its indexed title and author and then wait for at least a day before data can be captured from MARC tapes. A considerable amount of provisional keying now is necessary which will not be required in the future. Despite this current but temporary handicap, the basic principle of multiple uses of data holds. The record created, either by keying or by transfer from MARC tapes, is used to generate a purchase order, to record the receipt of monographs and periodical issues, and to produce claims, temporary catalog slips and worksheets. It is this same record with which the cataloger works, furnishing necessary additions or corrections to data. When this record is in fully cataloged form, catalog cards are generated as are the punched cards used for inventory control and the automated circulation system. Data fields in the record generate the terms used in the on-line index access system and in the brief bibliographic data displayed on holdings screens and order screens; they are also the basis from which a user's version of a bibliographic record is being developed. The logic of a single record serving multiple uses is inherently appealing and satisfactory to staff who either consciously or unconsciously abhor the multiplicity of files maintained in manual systems. The ultimate goal of an on-line catalog for library patrons is, of course, the logical end result of eliminating costly and "unnecessary" files.

Northwestern's experience indicates that the on-line catalog is a realistic goal and that the current planning at LC and many other institutions will result in fairly widespread use of this type of successor to the card catalog within the next decade. We must now face the challenge of insuring that this new access tool is in fact superior.

Returning to our hypothetical, but actually very real and all too often frustrated, users, what would ideally meet their needs? Several thoughts spring immediately into the minds of most librarians: a more responsive and more readily browsable tool than the conventional card catalog; access which is less dependent upon an understanding of filing rule complexities; a wider range of subject access than that possible through cards filed under LC subject headings; some kind of printed selection of items self-tailored to the individual's interest; and a method of determining the existence and availability of titles, volumes or issues wanted. (Has the latest issue arrived? Is a volume on reserve? Are all copies charged out? When are they due back? Has someone else already requested the next use?) Our user ought to have a high level of confidence not just about having identified the relevant materials but also about the likelihood of being able to find them when one goes to the shelf. Very little is more frustrating than a wildgoose chase through extensive levels of stacks simply for lack of the knowledge that the book has already been checked out.

Having identified some "ideal" service elements, let's consider how automation can affect each of them. giving our attention first to an improved successor to the conventional card catalog. Most librarians, deploring the general unresponsiveness of the card catalog in a large library, are aware of the pitfalls awaiting its unwary user. The exclusion of items, the type of alphabetic filing sort, and the various hierarchical arrangements are not self-evident and tend to mislead anyone who is not thoroughly familiar with the rules which are followed. These problems, as we all know, are compounded as catalogs get larger and larger. How often have patrons and librarians wished for the magical machine which would minimize or eliminate such problems and instantly deliver responses to an inquiry? With the advent of on-line catalogs we are coming very close to this magical response; indeed, at Northwestern we have much of the magic already at work for an enthusiastic staff. A pilot project at Northwestern's Science-Engineering Library is now putting it to work for faculty and students, testing the on-line author/title catalog in an operational user mode.

In meeting the challenge for a superior means of access which is easy to use, and effective, and economically feasible, Northwestern has developed an on-line field index access system. In this system, an author's name or a title or a series is typed, in natural language, on the keyboard of a cathode ray tube terminal. The computer responds immediately with a screen display of the item requested or with a message that the item is not found in the machine readable data base. If an author, whether personal or corporate, whether main entry or added entry, is represented in the data base by only one work, a bibliographic record is displayed, as are copy and volume holdings data when requested. If, however, an author is represented by more than one work, all titles by the author are listed on a display screen for browsing and selection. Similarly, a title wanted can be keyed and an immediate display of a bibliographic record or a list of identical titles, and associated main entries, results. Each of the displayed index listings also includes a place or date of publication so that immediate differentiation can be made between serials and monographs and among various editions.

At present all entries found in a traditional author/title card catalog can be accessed but so can entries not normally found in a card catalog. These include generic and common word titles, variant forms of serial titles, the lowest body in the hierarchy of a corporate entry, and the International Standard Serial Number. This index access system is not only instantaneously responsive to the request of a user, but readily permits several different approaches to a search with a minimum of time and effort. The rules are few and easily comprehensible. Listings are in a simple alphabetic sort ignoring punctuation and diacritics; there is no hierarchical array to worry about and no titles are excluded. Many spelling variations can be avoided since the user has the option of typing only the first few characters or words of a title or author's name. A user can key a request which will produce a displayed list of works by one author, or by authors with identical or similar names, or of identical titles, of series titles or uniform main entries. These lists are easily browsable, as much so as a comparable listing on a printed page, and much more so than flipping through cards in a catalog. Attachment of a printer to a terminal makes it possible to get a hard copy which can be used for various purposes. This is a tremendously provocative feature of the on-line index.

At Northwestern we are excited and enthusiastic about the present and potential capabilities of the index for not only is it easy to use but it provides access to all on-line records from the time of their original creation even if this was at the pre-order stage. We are confident that student and faculty users will be equally enthusiastic. We also recognize that a computer system should do far more than merely mechanize the traditional access points in a card catalog. Some non-traditional access points have already been furnished, as noted earlier. Others can be fairly easily provided and several are now being developed. Patrons will have, in the near future, infinitely better bibliographic access to library materials than has been possible with the card catalog as the primary tool.

Improved subject access is, of course, an exceedingly important component of an on-line successor to the card catalog. At Northwestern we have not directly tackled this complex problem but our many preliminary discussions have taken into consideration the inadequacy of LC assigned subject headings as the only, or even the primary, means of subject approach to the monographs in a large library. Obviously, the potential of computer manipulation of data affords a very real opportunity to go beyond present subject cataloging practices and provide in-depth subject analysis of the materials in a library collection. We have been following PRECIS developments with intense interest. However, LC contends that PRECIS strings offer no substantive gain over LC subject headings when they are used in combination with computer searchable terms from other fields in MARC records.[2] So perhaps PRECIS is not the answer. At the present time we feel that Pauline Atherton's Subject Access Project now underway at Syracuse University has great potential for the future.[3] Converting the tables of contents and the subject indexes of books into machine readable form has long seemed to be a logical approach to machine controlled subject access and now this process appears to be economically feasible. In our view, Pauline Atherton's study is indeed "pointing the way to the next definitive improvement in the art of bibliographic access."[4] Until such an approach can be implemented Northwestern will probably settle for a subject access system similar to that used by BALLOTS, that is, subject word or phrase access using Boolean logical connectors. This is one area, however, in which we at Northwestern cannot rely on our own experience for a vision of the future and therefore our expectation for improved subject access is tentatively optimistic rather than positively confident.

Forseeing major improvements over the types of access provided by the conventional card catalog, we should also look to various other extensions of service. One of these, already mentioned, is the ability to attach a printer which can produce hard copy of a self-tailored bibliography created by and for the user in response to his inquiry. This is a type of service not previously available or expected from the card catalog. Having identified items of interest, the user has generally been expected to take his chances on treking to the shelf, perhaps at a considerable distance, in hopes the book will not already be checked out. This problem no longer exists at Northwestern and its solution does not require staff assistance in obtaining circulation information. A self-service video display terminal is available with the instructions for its use program-generated to appear on the screen at all times. The user enters the call number of the item in question and receives a message informing him or her of the status of the various copies: on the shelf, checked out, in a carrel, on reserve, etc. Information as to date due and any request for next use also appears, although naturally the program will not reveal the identity of the user to whom an item is checked out. Assuming the book is available, our user retrieves it from the shelf and proceeds to one of the self-service check-out terminals located on the various stack levels, where they use a punched plastic University ID card and the punched book card automtically generated by the processing operations, to check out the item. It is no surprise that circulation rose a dramatic 30% since the computer-supported circulation system was introduced with the opening of the new building in January 1970.

Current programs for circulation information will, of course, be interfaced with the developing programs for public access to the bilibographic data base. In the not too distant future, terminals will be wisely available in stack areas and other public services locations, and probably in academic offices as well. With these terminals users will be able to find out, quickly and easily, what is in the collection, down to the latest issue of a periodical; where any particular title normally is; and whether it can be checked out immediately. Thus will we move toward full realization of the concept of a total integrated system.

The successful experience which we have had over the years with NOTIS, a dynamically evolving system, has raised our expectations to a level which may seem incomprehensible to some. Much of what we have briefly described here must sound like "blue skying" to many librarians. Yet so much is already reality, and most of our speculations are based on the evidence of present experience. The potential for dramatic improvement in user service is now within our grasp.

REFERENCES

1. Frances Ohmes and J. F. Jones, "The Other Half of Cataloging," *Library Resources & Technical Services* 17 (Summer 1973): 320–329.
2. [The Library of Congress, Processing Department] *Freezing the Library of Congress Catalog* (January 16, 1978), p. 4.
3. Pauline Atherton, *Improved Subject Access to Books in On-Line Library Catalogs* (Paper distributed at ALA Midwinter Meeting, January 1978).
4. *Ibid.*, p. 4.

Jean L. Graef

C L Systems, Inc.

INTERFACING INDEPENDENT AUTOMATED LIBRARY SYSTEMS: A SAMPLING OF EXISTING ATTEMPTS

Libraries which have postponed their automation plans or are using out-moded batch processing systems now find a growing number of commercially available systems for various applications. Librarians who have several independent systems wonder whether there are ways to interface them. Vendors, while working to develop new applications, are seeking ways to interface their applications with those of other suppliers. This paper describes some of the existing attempts at interfacing the automated systems of autonomous suppliers in the areas of acquisitions and circulation. The paper also describes some of the problems encountered by people who have successfully linked systems. These problems may be hardware related or may arise because different organizations have different administrative and legal requirements.

Introduction

The ideal of every systems analyst is an integrated data processing system, where information is entered only once and then used for several interrelated applications. The ideal is especially attractive to librarians, who want to perform the complex and time-consuming task of entering bibliographic data only once, then use it for acquisitions, cataloging, circulation, and accounting. But few libraries, except for perhaps the largest, have the financial resources and specialized staff necessary to develop integrated library-wide systems.

Libraries which have postponed their automation plans or are using outmoded batch processing systems, now find a growing number of commercially available systems for various applications. Since none of these systems include all of the applications, libraries are acquiring several independent systems. For example, a library might participate in a large network for cataloging, use a turnkey system for circulation, use a third system for acquisitions, and have access to a time-sharing service for abstracting and indexing data.

Librarians who have several independent systems wonder whether there are ways to interface them. Could they use the output of one system as input to another, use the same terminal for two or more applications, share some tasks with a local computing center, or convert a first-generation library system to a more modern one?

Librarians, impatient for vendors to produce systems with a full range of applications, are forging ahead in their attempts to integrate existing systems. Vendors, while working to develop new applications which will interface with their existing products, are also actively seeking ways to interface their applications with those of other suppliers. In the eyes of some systems analysts, these are crude, stop-gap measures. However, the attempts of both librarians and vendors indicate the great interest in the interface issue and the unwillingness of some librarians to wait for one vendor or supplier to develop a full range of automated library applications.

This paper describes, in Section I, some of the existing attempts at interfacing the automated systems of autonomous suppliers and, in Section II, mentions several kinds of problems encountered. The work done by some organizations such as the University of Chicago and Stanford University to achieve internal integration of automated applications is omitted here, since these efforts are already well documented.

SECTION I: EXAMPLES

Acquisitions-related Interfaces

Librarians have devised a wide variety of acquisitions interfaces, ranging from using hard copies of screen displays as purchase orders to directly linking one computer system to another by dial-up facilities. In addition, a project among publishers, vendors, and libraries to transmit orders on computer tape will have significant impact on the book ordering process. The list which follows is by no means exhaustive.

BATAB

BATAB, a batch processing book ordering and accounting system, is an example of how the machine readable files of a book vendor can be interfaced with the machine readable order files of a library. BATAB is marketed by the Baker and Taylor Company, a leading book vendor. The system consists of about twenty-five COBOL and assembly language programs which can be run on a variety of hardware configurations. Source listings for the programs (listings of the COBOL and assembly language instructions) are made available to the customer when the system is installed.

BATAB will prepare purchase orders to Baker and Taylor and other vendors. The orders to Baker and Taylor may be sent on computer tape, and shipments from Baker and Taylor to the library may be accompanied by a computer tape containing receipt and invoice data. Orders and receipts to and from other vendors must be entered into the BATAB system via keypunched or key-to-disc transactions. Thus, using the order data from Baker and Taylor on tape saves the library staff a great deal of time over the alternate method of keyboarding. The system works particularly well for Baker and Taylor approval plans, since librarians do not need to enter either the bibliographic, order, or receipt data. Any books returned to Baker and Taylor on approval, however, must be deleted from the BATAB system with a keypunched transaction.

Baker and Taylor will code on the approval plan tape records, certain library-specified data, such as fund number, library code, and a code for the location or subject area. This permits the BATAB system to post expenditures to the proper funds automatically and places the titles on the correct open order and fund reports.

BATAB/Faxon

As mentioned above, transactions with Baker and Taylor may be entered into the BATAB system without the time-consuming and error-prone step of keypunching. Other vendors offer similar automated services. For example, the F. W. Faxon Company, one of the nation's largest subscription agents, offers libraries invoice information on computer cards or tape for the titles placed with Faxon. The problem is that the Faxon data was not designed to be input into the BATAB system. Librarians at the University of Kentucky, however, developed programs that automatically translate the machine-readable Faxon invoice information into BATAB format, thus eliminating the keypunch step for 3,000 periodical titles.

Like BATAB, the Faxon card or tape service allows a library to have certain local data coded for each title. Each title on a library's annual Faxon invoice has the equivalent of two 80-column punched cards. The cards duplicate information on the annual invoice, including any additional charges or invoices for new items or any credit memos issued during the year. The library may request Faxon to code fifteen columns of local data on the second card. These columns on Kentucky's Faxon cards contain the library's title-specific control number, the branch library code, and the subject area code. This data provides the means of interfacing the Faxon cards with the BATAB system. The library specified this data for each title as it was added to the Faxon subscription list.

Kentucky uses the following procedure to convert Faxon invoice data into BATAB format:

1. Process the Faxon records (which Kentucky receives on tape) through an edit programs at the university computer center. This program eliminates any records in which the value of the invoice amount is zero and checks the library's local control number for validity. The outputs of this program are a list of errors and a disc file of edited Faxon title records, sorted on periodical name.

2. Process the above disc records through a second program which compares them to the BATAB master bibliographic file. This program creates full BATAB transaction records including periodical title for those Faxon records that do not match a BATAB record. For the Faxon records which do match, the program creates abbreviated transactions with only the accounting data. During this process, the local title control number becomes the BATAB control number, thus providing continuity with records of serial payments made before the library acquired the BATAB system.

3. The output of the program in the previous step is a disc file of transactions in BATAB format and a hard copy list of these transactions. After the list is checked by library staff, the disc file is input into the BATAB job stream along with other BATAB input.

CLSI/Book Vendors

A case can also be made for linking circulation and acquisitions systems, especially when the circulation record is the library's only machine-readable bibliographic data. Under these circumstances, the library can obtain on-order and in-process information along with the availability data provided by the circulation system.

The Boise Public Library and other libraries use the CLSI LIBS 100 system for circulation control to print a three-part "purchase order" to publishers and vendors. CLSI is a major vendor of automated library systems. Using the program by which new titles and items are added to the circulation master file, an operator can perform a preorder search on the computer console printer (which has been loaded with 3-part paper), add the requested title to the file, and produce a hard copy "purchase order." The following procedures are used:

1. Using the appropriate program, the operator enters an author/title search key for the book ordered. If the system finds a record which matches the search key, it prints the

record's bibliographic data. If another copy of the title is to be ordered, the operator adds a bar code label number (which uniquely identifies each book) in the field called "item" and changes the price if necessary. A clerk then performs step three below.

2. If the system cannot locate a record which matches the search key, the operator enters bibliographic data in the appropriate fields (such as "author"), the number of copies ordered in the "addata" field (a field for descriptive or additional information in the circulation record), the vendor in the call number field, and bar code numbers in the "item" field.

3. After all the data necessary to order a book has been entered into the system, the operator instructs the LIBS 100 to add the title or copies to the master file. The "purchase order" is removed from the console printer and distributed. (See Fig. 1). The first copy of the three-part form is sent to the vendor, the second copy to the reference

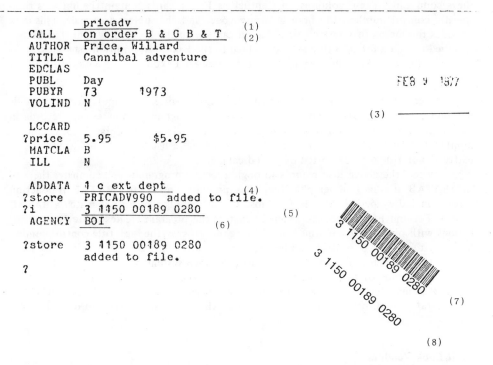

```
           pricadv
CALL       on order  B & G  B & T      (1)
AUTHOR     Price, Willard               (2)
TITLE      Cannibal adventure
EDCLAS
PUBL       Day                                          FEB 9 1977
PUBYR      73        1973
VOLIND     N
                                              (3)  —————————
LCCARD
?price     5.95        $5.95
MATCLA     B
ILL        N

ADDATA     1 c ext dept                (4)
?store     PRICADV990   added to file.
?i         3 1150 00189 0280              (5)
  AGENCY   BOI                (6)

?store     3 1150 00189 0280
           added to file.
?                                                        (7)

                                                         (8)
```

(1) author/title search key
(2) on order for the Boys and Girls section from Baker and Taylor
(3) Library purchase order number
(4) one copy ordered by the "ext" department
(5) item number corresponding to the bar code number (7)
(6) Boise Public Library is the agency that added the record
(7) bar code label that will eventually be attached to the book when
     it is received
(8) shelf list label used as accession number

Figure 1. Purchase order produced on the CLSI circulation system at Boise Public Library, Boise, Idaho.

department, and the third copy is filed in the order department. A bar-code label with a number corresponding to that which the operator entered in the circulation record is affixed to the third copy of the order form.

4. A clerk "checks out" the ordered items to the vendor by passing a light pen over the vendor's "patron card" and over each of the bar code labels on the third copy of the purchase order. Each vendor is assigned a bar code number and is given a "patron card." The ordered books are checked out for a 90-day "loan period" so that the system will notify staff when it is time to claim missing copies.

5. When the books are received in the library, they are matched with the bar-coded copies of the order filed in the order department. Then a clerk "checks in" each book by passing the light pen over the bar code label on the purchase order copy.

6. If the book has been requested by a user through the place-a-hold feature of the circulation system, the system notifies the operator of that fact immediately when the book is received and "checked in" from the vendor. The book is then expedited through technical processing and sent to circulation. Otherwise, the book is processed normally.

OCLC/Book Vendor

The University of Michigan/Dearborn has devised another method of using the hard copy of a bibliographic database for ordering materials.[1] The library obtains cataloging and holdings information and catalog cards from OCLC, Inc., a nation-wide shared cataloging network. Library staff use the OCLC terminal for preorder searching and then print the contents of up to two OCLC screen displays for records found as a result of this search. The paper copy of the OCLC screen display, produced on a printer attached to the OCLC Model 100 terminal, is mailed to vendors as a purchase order. (See Fig. 2). The library uses the following procedure for ordering books:

1. An operator searches each book order request in the OCLC on-line union catalog. If acceptable cataloging copy is found, the operator prints the contents of up to two OCLC screen displays on a printer attachment (by pressing the PRINT button on the OCLC terminal). If no usable copy is found, the operator creates a book order by using the printer attachment's keyboard.

2. A clerk then highlights the author and title fields of the OCLC record on the print-out.

3. The supervisor of the ordering section assigns the fund, vendor, and purchase order number. This data is written in an "information block" stamped to the right of the OCLC record on the print-out.

4. The four part print-out is burst and distributed as follows: original to the dealer; second and third copies filed in the order department; fourth copy in a fund activity file.

5. When the book is received from the vendor, the second copy of the order is retrieved and sent along with the book to the catalog department. The actual price (as opposed to the encumbered amount) is recorded on the third copy of the order and used for accounting.

CLSI/Brodart

A more direct way of interfacing circulation and acquisitions systems has been developed cooperatively by CLSI and Broadart, a major book vendor and also a supplier of an on-line ordering system. Using a CLSI circulation terminal, librarians at North Suburban Library System in Illinois can dial up Brodart's automated ordering system, search the Brodart master title file, place an order for the title, transfer the machine-

```
 Screen 1 of 2
 OCLC: 2188989        Rec stat: p Entrd: 760420          Used: 771114
Type: a Bib lvl: m Govt pub:    Lang:  eng Source:    Illus:
 Repr:    Enc lvl:    Conf pub: 0 Ctry:  nyu Dat tp: s M/F/B: 00
 Indx: 1 Mod rec:    Festschr: 0 Cont: b
 Desc: i Int lvl:    Dates: 1976,
  1 010        76-12586
  2 040        DLC c DLC
  3 020        0841902313. a 084190233X b pbk.
  4 050 0      HT1521 b .R235
  5 082        301.45/1/042
  6 090          b
  7 049        EYDX
  8 245 00     Race and ethnic relations : b sociological readings / c edited
by Gordon Bowker, John Carrier ; introductory essay by Percy Cohen.
  9 260 0      New York : b Holmes & Meier, c 1976.
 10 300        400 p. ; c 24 cm.
 11 504        Bibliography: p. [377]-382.
 12 500        Includes indexes.
 13 650   0    Race problems x Addresses, essays, lectures.
 14 650   0    Ethnic groups x Addresses, essays, lectures.
 15 700 10     Bowker, Gordon.
 16 700 10     Carrier, John.
```

Purchase Order No.
00239

Date 1/18/77 **Fund** 57

Requester
Rand

Price 14.50 **No. of copies** 1

Dealer
B&T

Additional information
Browsing

Univ. of Mich. - Dearborn
LIBRARY
4901 Evergreen Road
Dearborn, Mich. 48128

Figure 2. OCLC Record as "Purchase Order."

readable title data to the circulation database, and print a 3″ X 5″ "tracking slip" for the library's use as a record of the transaction. Brodart receives the order electronically; no hard copy purchase order is necessary.

Librarians may order titles which are neither in the circulation nor the Brodart files by simply entering the necessary bibliographic and order data and instructing the system to transmit an order. Addition of ordered items to the circulation file and printing of the tracking slips are optional processes.

Both the CLSI circulation system and the Brodart IROS ordering system are available separately to libraries as turnkey systems (self-contained systems which need only be plugged in and operated). However, the advantages of interfacing them are several. Users of the circulation system have access both to the bibliographic and "book availability" data in the Brodart files. This saves users from having to key in bibliographic data for new titles to be ordered. There is a further time saving because users can then transfer this bibliographic data to the circulation system without additional keyboarding. The CLSI/ Brodart Interface also makes instantly available data that previously was hard to come by and often out of date: the in-print and in-stock information for ordered titles. Another advantage of the interface is that electronic transmission of orders is faster than that of the U.S. Postal Service.

Book Vendors and Publishers

Some members of the information marketplace participating in the ordering process, such as book vendors, publishers and librarians, are working on a faster, more efficient method of order transmission. Representatives from some of the largest of these organizations have formed the Book Industry Advisory Committee, which has developed a standardized machine-readable format that will be used to send orders on computer tape. The fixed field format, now in its second version, uses the ISBN (International Standard Book Number) as the key data field. As long as the ISBN is present for a title, other bibliographic information is optional. Titles may be ordered without the ISBN, but this slows down processing of the order. The format is patterned after a list purchase order (but each title will have its own book number).

The format has been submitted to the membership of the American National Standards Institute Z39 Committee for comments and has been referred for consideration to the Z39 subcommittee developing a standard order form. The format is currently in use by Brodart, Random House, Doubleday, Wiley, Prentice-Hall, Baker and Taylor, Litton Educational Publishers, and B. Dalton.

OCLC/Book Vendors

Another interface of interest to librarians is the participation of OCLC, Inc. in the work of the Book Industry Systems Advisory Committee. OCLC has prepared a test tape in the above format and has sent it to the Baker and Taylor Company. OCLC is exploring a similar test with other vendors. If the test tape can be processed satisfactorily, OCLC will send a "live" order from its corporate library to the Baker and Taylor warehouse in Momence, Illinois. Eventually, titles ordered by individual libraries using the OCLC acquisitions subsystem may be sent on computer tape to the library-designated vendors that are capable of processing them. If vendors are not equipped to handle machine-readable order, they will receive regular paper orders.

OCLC/Bell Labs

Bell Labs Libraries and Information Systems Center in New Jersey uses records from the OCLC on-line catalog as input to an in-house acquisitions and cataloging system. Terminal operators search OCLC files either at the time the book is ordered or at the time it is received. If the operator locates a record, the record is transmitted without editing to the cassette-tape recorder built into a nearby teleprinter (which is attached to the OCLC Model 100 terminal). At appropriate intervals during the day, the contents of a given tape are transmitted through the teleprinter to the Bell Labs computer system where programs developed by Bell Labs staff extract certain data fields from the OCLC record and format them into records which can be input to the Bell Labs on-line acquisitions and cataloging system. When a book is received and is ready for cataloging, the system generates a cataloging worksheet containing the converted OCLC data for editing by a cataloger. Editing changes resulting from this process are input to the Bell system and the final edited record is then used in the production of a printed book catalog.

Circulation-related Interfaces

The following four examples of attempts at interfacing automated systems have the circulation application in common. The first two examples show attempts by individual libraries to input catalog records from the OCLC on-line catalog into circulation systems. The third example illustrates how this may be done commercially. The fourth example shows how one automated circulation system may be converted to another.

CLSI/OCLC

New York University uses its OCLC archive tapes to input single volume monographic titles into its CLSI circulation system. An operator cataloging an item enters the holding library code (where the book will be housed) and bar code label number of the book on the OCLC screen. This data appears on the OCLC record on the archive tape (a tape of NYU's cataloging transactions during a period of time) which OCLC periodically sends to NYU. At the university computing center, the OCLC archive tapes are read into a program which converts the OCLC records into a format acceptable by the CLSI circulation system. The resulting tape file of records is then mounted on a tape drive attached to the CLSI computer in the library and read into the circulation master file.

The procedure works like this:

1. During cataloging, an operator enters the four character holding library code, which represents the library in which the book will be located, and the last seven digits of the book's bar code label number (circulation control number) into the 049 field of the OCLC screen display. If there is more than one copy of a title, NYU staff enter the additional bar code label numbers later, after the OCLC archive record has been converted into CLSI format and is available for access through the circulation system terminals. Since few duplicate copies are ordered at NYU, keyed entry of additional copies in the circulation system is not a problem.

2. After a week or so, NYU receives the OCLC archive tape and processes it through conversion programs at the university computing center. This process first converts the tape from ASCII to EBCDIC code (more will be said of this in the section on problems), extracts certain fields from the OCLC record, formats the data into CLSI records, and then reconverts the records to ASCII code. Part of the process of formatting the CLSI records is deriving a search key (or index entry) for each title. The fields extracted from the OCLC records are:

008 (fixed field) – OCLC control number and year of publication

050 (LC call number assigned by LC)
090 (LC call number assigned by another agency) } one of these fields
099 (Locally assigned call number)

049 (holding libraries and bar code label number)

100 (personal name main entry)
110 (corporate body main entry) } one of these fields, only the first
111 (conference name main entry) } name listed

245 (title) truncated after a certain number of characters. Index entries
are constructed prior to truncation

3. An operator loads the CLSI tape records into the circulation system using the CLSI tape drive facility.

OCLC/Systems Control

The San Jose Public Library has devised a more direct way to enter OCLC bibliographic data into its circulation system, which is not yet completely operational. A microprocessor with a light pen attachment is connected to the OCLC terminal between the keyboard and the body of the terminal. The light pen/microprocessor device enables an operator to enter quickly the holding library code and bar code label number of an item being cataloged on the OCLC terminal. When the library receives its weekly archive tape from OCLC, the tape can be input directly into the SCICON circulation system. A technician employed by the city of San Jose built the microprocessor device. Programming for the interface was done by the supplier of the circulation system.

The interface works as follows:

1. An operator searches the OCLC on-line catalog with a bar code labeled book in hand. When the operator locates a matching OCLC record, he (she) passes the light pen across the book's bar code label.

2. The microprocessor then supplies the first three characters of the OCLC holding library code in the 049 field of the OCLC record on the screen.

3. The operator then adds the fourth character of the holding library code via the OCLC terminal keyboard.

4. The system supplies the bar code label number in brackets, followed by a space and another subfield delimiter and code. See below:

▶ 9 049   SJPA ≠ c [bar code number] ≠ a SJPB ≠ c [bar code number] ¶

5. The operator may then add the bar code numbers of other copies by scanning another copy's bar code label.

6. The operator finishes editing the OCLC record for cataloging and transmits the transaction to OCLC.

7. When the OCLC archive tape arrives, it is mounted on the SCICON circulation system. The OCLC records, which include the bar code numbers of cataloged items, are added to the circulation fields.

CLSI/OCLC/LISI

It is also possible to convert an OCLC archive tape or a manual shelf list into a format suitable for another automated application, such as a COM (Computer Output Microfilm) catalog or a circulation system, using a commercial service. Autographics, Blackwell North America, and Brodart are among the firms that perform such services for libraries. For example, CLSI works with LISI (Library Interface Systems, Inc.) to perform several types of conversion services for libraries using the CLSI circulation system:

1. Conversion of OCLC archive tape records to CLSI format, using either the periodic archive tapes or the OCLC retrospective tapes.

2. Matching circulation records against a bibliographic data base to retrieve records suitable for such applications as book or COM catalogs.

3. Shelf list conversion, where manual catalog records are converted into machine-readable records in CLSI circulation format.

CLSI/SYSTEM 7

Some librarians are reluctant to automate for fear that a system they purchase will become obsolete and will be difficult to get rid of. Change is inevitable in data processing, but once data is in machine-readable form, it is much easier to convert it into another machine-readable form than to start from manual records. The popularity of the OCLC archive tapes and of those services which perform shelf list conversion attests to the interest of librarians in making the first step toward the automated evolution of libraries.

In an effort to make it easier for librarians to convert from one type of automated circulation system to another, CLSI has developed a conversion station terminal which is capable of reading circulation records on punched cards and coded patron badges. The software developed by CLSI allows an operator either to add another copy to a title already in the CLSI database, add a new title, or add a patron. The system first reads the data from a punched card or patron badge. For title conversions, the system extracts an author/title key from the data and searches the CLSI database for a matching record. Then it displays the data it has read from the card along with the first matching record it finds. The operator decides whether the match is a good one. If it is, the operator indicates that the system should add another copy to this title. If the match is incorrect, the operator examines all other matching records. If the operator does not accept any of the records, or if the system fails to locate any records which match the search key for the title on the punched card, the system automatically creates a new title record in the CLSI master file.

For patron conversion, an operator enters a bar code label number and inserts a patron card in the conversion station device. The system reads the patron's name or other identifier from the card and attaches it to the label number entered by the operator. Later, the operator can enter full patron data from a CLSI keyboard terminal.

Copies of titles already in the system and new patrons may be added to the CLSI circulation files using the "pop zebra" facility. Instead of reading a bar code or OCR label number with a wand or entering the number via the keyboard, an operator can instruct the system to display automatically the next available number. By saving the operator a step, this speeds up the process.

The conversion station is currently in use at American University and University of Pennsylvania. American uses bar code labels; Pennsylvania uses OCR labels. Both originally had IBM System 7 circulation systems.

Books for College Libraries/IBM 357 Circulation System

Another kind of machine-readable bibliographic file interfaced with a circulation system is in use at Stockton State College in New Jersey. Under a grant from the Council on Library Resources, the Stockton College Library obtained a 40,000 record file of titles in MARC (machine-readable catalog records from the Library of Congress) format which represent a suggested core collection for college libraries. The first edition (in printed form) of *Books for College Libraries* (BCL), has been available for several years.

Programmers at Stockton wrote a program which matches records on the BCL tape against the library's machine-readable database which is used in conjunction with its IBM 357 circulation system. The program matches records from the two files by examining LC class number (but not the Cutter number) and the first ten characters of the title. If both data elements match, the programs add a tag to the machine-readable record indicating that the title is on the BCL tape. If a title on the BCL tape has no matching record in the circulation file, the program produces a list of these items for ordering purposes.

Each year, the IBM 357 system produces lists of items circulated and the number of times each item has been checked out. One list is in call number sequence, the other in title sequence. The BCL project makes it possible to indicate on these lists whether each title has been recommended for a basic college library collection. The list in call number sequence permits a rough subject analysis of these titles for collection development purposes.

SECTION II: PROBLEMS

Most of the problems encountered by people who attempt to interface two automated systems are a result of hardware requirements or administrative and legal constraints. Some of the hardware-related problems discussed below are variations in coding machine-readable data, incompatibility of terminals, and variations in the ways computer systems assign check digits (uniqueness digits) to record control numbers. Among the administrative and legal problems are the difficulty of using the outputs of some automated systems for accounting, variations in library conventions for call numbers and title keys, differences in the way vendors and libraries view purchase orders, and the matter of liability for incorrect machine-readable data used by several organizations.

Hardware-related problems usually require the services of specialists, particularly engineers and programmers, who are not likely to be on the library payroll. Administrative and legal problems, on the other hand, must be resolved by librarians and/or managers in cooperating organizations, usually not without much soul-searching and some compromise.

Varieties of Machine Codes and Recording Media

There is a variety of media for recording machine-readable data. Data can be represented on punched cards, bar code labels, magnetic strips, optical character recognition (OCR) labels, computer tape, disc and so on. Moreover, one cannot assume that all bar codes or OCR codes are alike, nor that a device to read 800 bpi (bits per inch) computer tape will read data on cassette tapes. This variety in recording media means that one cannot use a light pen to read OCR labels or mount a cassette tape on a regular tape drive. Nor is it possible to use a computer terminal connected directly to a local computer to access a remote data base via the telephone lines unless a modem is used. The modem is a device which translates the digital signals issuing from the computer into signals suitable for transmission over telephone lines. Thus, it is sometimes not possible to make one terminal do "double duty" for two different applications. Even when the manufacturers of computer equipment insist that two devices can be easily linked, it often takes tinkering by an engineer to achieve a successful interface.

There are also several ways of arranging the bits (binary digits) in a computer to represent numbers and characters. For example, the equivalent for the letter Z in the ASCII (American Standard Code for Information Interchange) code is 1011010, where the 1 is the presence of electrical current and the 0 is the absence of current. The corresponding code in EBCDIC (Extended Binary Coded Decimal Information Code) is 11101001. Although the ASCII code is widely used, large IBM computers use EBCDIC, thus making it too a kind of standard. This creates a problem for subscribers to the OCLC archive tapes who have large IBM computers; before processing the tapes, the data on the tapes must be translated from ASCII to EBCDIC.

Check Digits

Different types of check digits make it difficult to use the control numbers of one automated system in another system. The check (or uniqueness) digit is a number assigned to the end of a record control number to insure that records are updated accurately. The use of check digits is standard procedure in data processing, but there are several ways of assigning the digit. A computer assigns check digits by performing a mathematical calculation on the control numbers of newly created records (e.g. adding up the numbers in the control number and dividing by a constant). The result of the calculation (normally a one-digit number) is the check digit. Every time an update is performed on a record, the system recalculates the check digit of the master record. If the check digit of the update record does not equal the check digit of the master record, the system does not perform the update. In order to make the Faxon transactions mentioned previously acceptable to the BATAB programs using the library's own control number, the programmer had to locate the check digit calculation routine among all the BATAB programs and put it into the conversion program for the Faxon records.

Acceptance of Computer Output

In addition to the numerous technical problems, there are administrative and legal requirements which can make it difficult to interface automated systems. Among libraries there are wide differences in accounting, purchasing, and bibliographic control procedures.

In some universities, for example, the hard copy output from the BATAB ordering and accounting system (Invoice Summary Report) is acceptable by the university business office for the purpose of paying invoices. In others, library's bookkeepers must laboriously type vouchers for every invoice, even though the data on the vouchers is already in machine-readable form in BATAB.

Variations in Bibliographic Control Conventions

Local variations in bibliographic control conventions also pose problems for interfacing automated systems. Libraries using the Dewey classification system, for example, find cataloging using the OCLC/MARC records somewhat more complex and time-consuming than libraries which automatically accept LC call numbers. Even libraries that use the LC classification system have different ways of formatting the call number. This is one reason why the programs developed at New York University for converting OCLC archive tapes into CLSI circulation system format will not automatically work for other libraries using OCLC and CLSI. Another problem encountered by the NYU programmer is that libraries have different conventions for creating the author/title keys by which CLSI records may be retrieved. For example, to construct an author/title key for the book "1001 Ways to Grow Beans," many CLSI users would first convert the numeral 1001 into words, One Thousand and One. The CLSI system does not automatically derive keys from titles unless the conversion station is used. To do this kind of conversion from numerals to words on the computer proved to be so complicated the NYU ignores such titles on the OCLC archive tape and enters them manually into the circulation system.

Two Conceptions of a Purchase Order

These are some of the reasons why librarians view programmers as obstinate, and programmers view librarians as silly. When different types of organizations attempt to interface automated system, however, even larger problems emerge. For example, libraries over time have evolved a unit purchase order with only one title per order number. This allows a single 3″ X 5″ multiform slip to be used as temporary cataloging, purchase order, tracking slip (for monitoring a book's progress through technical processing units), accounting record, and a number of other purposes. Book vendors, on the other hand, regard all the titles ordered at the same time by the same library as one "purchase order." Libraries press vendors for individual treatment for each title (this one "rush," that one ship only if we have no standing order, another one only ship if the ninth edition has been published). Vendors press for standardization of instructions among titles to speed up the ordering process. These differing concepts must be reconciled if one is to develop a standardized order transmission format for automated systems.

Discounts

Another interesting problem, faced by at least one publisher, was the matter of discounts. For example, if a tape order contains records for 100 titles, 75 of which have ISBN's while 25 do not, the tape records must be split into two groups. The titles without ISBN's must be processed by hand using time-consuming procedures. The other titles can be processed rapidly using the computer. If a publisher normally grants a discount on copies for 100 or more titles, he is faced with additional costs for processing the 25 titles without ISBN's and is hard pressed to maintain the discount.

Liability for Program Changes

There are also legal issues involved in interfacing various systems. How shall each party be compensated for its role in the cooperative effort? What are the liabilities and responsibilities of each party if the cooperative venture develops problems? Many vendors of computer software refuse to maintain the systems they sell if customers modify the programs without the vendor's knowledge. It is almost impossible to diagnose and correct problems under these circumstances. Similarly, librarians who import software from another institution often find it extremely difficult to make the programs work satisfactorily on the local computer, even if the hardware is the same brand. Even if a library has a staff member who succeeds in making a successful modification to a program written elsewhere, that person may leave without having written down the changes that were made. One of the biggest problems of interfacing automated systems is the difficulty of maintaining and updating them.

Liability for Erroneous Data

Another legal issue is the question of which party is responsible for erroneous data. For example, if a library orders a book using an incorrect ISBN, who is to blame if the vendor supplies the wrong book: the library that ordered it, the vendor that sent it, the agency that assigned the ISBN, or the computerized library catalog from which the citation came?

Given such problems as these, it is remarkable that so many instances of interfacing exist. Librarians are impatient to link their automated systems, and some of them have enough ingenuity and cooperation from local technicians to succeed. Suppliers of automated systems, aware of the need, are also working to interface independent systems as well as add new applications to their product lines. An important by-product of such activity is that both librarians and vendors are becoming more knowledgeable about the needs and capabilities of one another. The problems that librarians encounter in their own interfacing attempts to make them more sympathetic to the delays and problems they experience in dealing with vendors. The experiences of vendors in their attempts to link systems make them more aware of the complexity of library data processing applications. The range of activity in both the public and private sectors is a symptom of the healthy evolution of library automation.

REFERENCE

1. Katherine J. Schreiner, "A New Use of the OCLC Cataloging Subsystem-Book Acquisitions." (Unpublished paper, January, 1977.)

Charles Martell

University of California, Berkeley

ERASING THE PAST: TECHNOLOGICAL SHIFTS
AND ORGANIZATIONAL RENEWAL

The introduction of computer-related technologies has begun to affect the staffing and service patterns of academic libraries. The impact of OCLC is a prime example. With a significant reduction in the size of technical processing units and with the resulting need for resource reallocation, libraries have the opportunity to shift their traditional technical core to boundary-spanning and information transfer oriented activities. (Technical core is defined as the area in which the primary task occurs.) To move in this direction the academic library world needs to consider new roles for librarians and new organizational configurations. There are serious reasons for believing that the opportunity for significant reorientation may be missed and that academic librarianship may, instead, adopt a course geared toward incremental changes in past technical processing practices.

This paper deals with two contrasting views of the effects which technological developments in automated cataloging and in related by-products, e.g., the on-line catalog, will have for the future of academic librarianship. These views may exist simultaneously in the same institution with colleagues entirely unaware of the deep, underlying divergencies in philosophy which their respective views signify. Let me illustrate this with a parable.

Two librarians are sitting together on a railroad train. The librarian on the right is looking out the windows on the right side of the train. The countryside fades into the distance. This librarian is musing in a fashion typical of the group of librarians who, in the words of the National Commission on Libraries and Information Science, call for the "remodeling" of the librarian's thinking and a willingness "to change [one's] notion of librarianship."[1] The librarian on the left is looking out the windows on the left side of the train. The city is close at hand. Towering buildings are in full sight. This librarian deals with everyday work problems related to cataloging and the card catalogs. Some of these problems are small. Many are subtle. But in the everyday context, they have meaning.

Very likely both librarians will infer the direction of the train in terms of those perceptions gained from limited side observations. In fact, the future may portend an entirely changed landscape. This paper can be considered in the context of these two travelling librarians.

For years, off in the distance, we have heard the cry, the plea, for new roles for librarians, for new more responsive library organization structures, and for a new service orientation based on information-transfer concepts. Critics have cited the routine and largely nonprofessional activities embedded in most professional positions. Critics have deplored the hierarchical, bureaucratic model on which most libraries are structured. They note that this model, borrowed from industrial organization, has failed to be responsive to the implied service orientation of libraries. They also note that the era of post-industrial society with its dynamic and uncertain environments and with its great stress on the creation, production and dissemination of knowledge has heightened the dysfunctional attributes of the traditional library organizational pattern. Quite simply, they say it is outmoded.

The critics, qua visionaries, suggest that it is not enough for libraries to concern themselves with the building of collections and with providing access to those collections. Rather, they suggest, it is imperative that libraries begin to concern themselves with the wider range of information services required by client groups. Information-transfer is one concept that is frequently emphasized by these critics. In this process, one is concerned not only with the artifact itself, but with the contents of that item and its meaning and utility to the client. Today, we even hear, in the language of Daniel Bell, a call for a knowledge-transfer orientation among our institutions.[2]

To these critics and other observers, recent technological developments in the library community imply far-reaching opportunities which, if seized, would allow libraries to move aggressively into a more service-oriented mode. Two specific developments can be cited. First, the introduction of computer-related technologies which are beginning to affect the staffing and service patterns of libraries. The impact of OCLC is a prime example. Second, the plans of the Library of Congress to freeze its card catalogs in 1981 and "to rely primarily on automated data to provide access to the collections."[3]

The growth of OCLC has been a phenomenon which some view as a milestone in the history of librarianship. The latest OCLC annual report shows that the percentage of items cataloged by using catalog records "already in the system rose from 72% in 1972/73 to 92% in 1976/77."[4] Although the evidence remains sketchy, simple productivity calculations lead to the inescapable conclusion that the diffusion and implementation of OCLC-type technologies have the potential to cause a significant diminution in the staff size of technical processing units. In his analysis of the 47 original OCLC members, Hewitt found that "original cataloging had been all but eliminated for the smaller libraries, and reduced to well below 20 percent of the total cataloging effort for other types. The time required to catalog books and to produce sets of catalog cards had been reduced in 91 percent of their libraries."[5]

With a significant reduction in the size of technical processing and with the resulting likelihood of resource reallocation, libraries have the opportunity to shift their traditional technical core to boundary-spanning and information-transfer oriented activities. The technical core is defined here as the area in which the primary task activity occurs. Charles Goodrum, Director, Office of Planning and Development at the Library of Congress states that "the collections of the Library as a research tool are on the threshold of dramatic change in the way they are retrieved, controlled and analyzed . . . our approaches to our research tools are new, unprecedented, wide-open. How we shape them suddenly is back in our hands to use them as we see fit, not simply 'how it's always been.'"[6]

The vast majority of all libraries are organized by function, i.e., acquisitions, cataloging, circulation and reference. This functional design facilitates the processing of materials and access to these materials. The linchpin in all these activities has been the card catalog. It is not unreasonable to suggest that the support and maintenance of the card catalog has become, from a historical perspective, the primary task of librarianship. To many, the investment, both human and material, which libraries have devoted to their catalogs, has greatly exceeded the utility of those catalogs to the user. The symbol of the card catalog as an albatross around the neck of the library as an institution has been used. Some have observed that the card catalogs absorb valuable resources that could be used elsewhere for improving direct services to clients or even to reorient the profession itself. Current technological developments have led some to conclude that the resources which might be released because of the adoption of these technologies could be used to further service goals.

In the July 1977 issue of *Library Quarterly* devoted to bibliographic control, Fussler and Kocher examine the card catalog as a technology. They note the growing reservations about the large card catalog. "Put more bluntly, the requirements are not simply to change the form of the card catalog or the technology by which it has been created and maintained, but rather to begin to build an essentially new and more responsive biblio-graphic system or systems."[7] These expressions concerning the opportunity for wholesale change must offer comfort and hope to those critics who have long sought new roles for librarians and new organizational configurations. To those who feel uncertain because of these developments, who feel a sense of threat, the words of French Field Marshal Foch might offer direction. "My center is giving way, my right is falling back, the situation is excellent, I attack."

The comforted and the hopeful should beware. Although the opportunity for erasing and correcting some of the constraints of the past exists, the opportunity may be short-lived. Indeed, although it is possible to shift the core of librarianship into a more inter-active and personal mode with the users, and to create the organizational forms to facilitate this interaction and to engage in information and knowledge-transfer roles, traditions may be a strong inhibiting factor. Stafford Beer finds that social institutions fail to respond effectively to changes in their environments. They simply shift "the internal position of equilibrium very slightly, thereby offsetting the environmental change that has occurred."[8] To many, the technological developments now on the horizon do not herald new departures and new roles and new orientations. Rather, they see the opportunity to improve the quality of traditional activities and traditional bibliographical tools. Widespread support exists for this position. During an Associated Colleges of the Midwest meeting dedicated to the topic of management issues in automated cataloging, one participant suggested that ". . . the administrator should see in automation the opportunity, not to do the same imperfect job more cheaply via mass production, but as the opportunity to create the kind of a catalog and the level of cataloging which would truly exploit the resources of a collection and make it as fully accessible as possible . . ."[9] To many, this thought is tremendously attractive.

In his technological analysis, Anderla, author of *Information in 1985*, states that "In terms of numbers and processing capacity, the electronic information systems created to meet the varied needs of the knowledge industry will in 1985–87 be almost a hundred times those of today."[10] He concludes, however, on another, far different note. "The revolutionary changes between 1980 and 1990 will . . . be only a prelude to the main spectacle."[11] By looking down the railroad tracks and not only out the side windows it is possible to conclude that improving on the past, e.g., the old wine in new bottles approach to organizational change, will not be an adequate response to future developments. Perhaps it is not too early to begin to make critical choices which might, in fact, be hard choices, but which will lead us in necessary directions.

Improving on the past or challenging the future—it is unlikely that the two somewhat dichotomous perceptions about what is preferred will live comfortably together. It is quite likely that the opportunities and expectations which excite the imagination of one group will be dashed by the success of the other group. For those who look for new roles, new organizations and new service orientations, success will probably rest on how they can remain true to the traditional activities of librarianship expressed in the area of cataloging and yet seize the probably fleeting moment when librarianship can be grasped, and moved with vision into post-industrial society.

REFERENCES

1. *A national program for library and information service* 2nd Draft (Revised, [Washington, D.C.: U.S. National Commission on Libraries and Information Science, September 15, 1974], p. 12.)
2. Daniel Bell, *The Coming of Post-Industrial Society: a Venture in Social Forecasting* (New York: Basic Books, 1973), p. 175.
3. "LC to Freeze Card Catalogs," *Library of Congress Information Bulletin* (November 4, 1977), p. 743.
4. Ohio College Library Center, *Annual Report* 1976/77, p. 5.
5. Joe A. Hewitt, "The impact of OCLC," *American Libraries* 7 (July 1976): 272–273.
6. Charles Goodrum, "Change at the Library of Congress," *Library of Congress Information Bulletin* (June 17, 1977), p. 428.
7. Herman H. Fussler and Karl Kocher, "Contemporary issues in bibliographic control," *Library Quarterly* 47 (July 1977): 242.
8. Stafford Beer, "Managing modern complexity," in *The Management of Information and Knowledge*, A compilation of papers prepared for the eleventh meeting of the panel on science and technology (Washington, D.C.: McGrath Publishing Co., 1970), p. 47.
9. Quote by Sanford Berman cited in *LJ/SLJ Hotline* (December 5, 1977), p. 5.
10. George Anderla, *Information in 1985: a forecasting study of information needs and resources* (Paris: Organization for Economic Cooperation and Development, 1973), p. 85.
11. *Ibid.*, p. 120.

Susan L. Miller

Ohio State University

THE EVOLUTION OF AN ON-LINE CATALOG

The development of an on-line computer-based circulation system into a remote on-line catalog for The Ohio State University Libraries is described. The original circulation system included call number, author/title, and title access to short bibliographic records. Changes to the system since 1971 including shelflist position search, author access, subject search, full bibliographic records, and public use terminals are discussed.

INTRODUCTION

In November 1970, The Ohio State University Libraries implemented the automated Library Circulation System. This circulation system was designed to control the circulation of holdings in all the Libraries which report to the Director of Libraries and to provide remote access to the University Libraries union catalog which is housed in the Main Library. Since 1970, several changes have been made in the system which have increased the capabilities, and gradually the system has acquired the name Library Control System (LCS).

A number of papers on the development and implementation of LCS have appeared in the literature. Subjects of previous articles include the economics of the circulation system,[1] batch mode subject access to LCS,[2] Technical Services use of LCS,[3] and the development and implementation of LCS.[4]

This paper intends to document the evolution of the Library Circulation System to the Library Control System which includes an on-line catalog. Although written in February 1978, the paper discusses capabilities planned for LCS implementation in June 1978. The programming for these changes is proceeding on schedule. The implementation may be delayed as a result of financial considerations. The Library Control System includes a Serial Holdings File, a Circulation file, and a Randtriever file; however, this paper is limited to the bibliographic description in an on-line catalog.

Author/Title On-Line Catalog

When LCS became available in 1970, the Libraries received a limited author/title on-line catalog. It was limited in that the short bibliographic record included only call

193

number, main entry, short title, edition statement, publication date, Library of Congress card number, and a holdings statement for each copy and volume. There were also indicators to specify serial, monographic set, oversized volumes, and language. (Figure 1.) The holdings statements include copy number, volume number where applicable, library location, and circulation condition code.

```
DSC/HN17.5T64

HN17.5T64      TOFFLER, ALVIN.      FUTURE SHOCK.   67-12744

            791445      1970        10

01       001        MAI

02       004        SOC

03       005  3WEEK UND

04       006  1WEEK EDU

05       007  3WEEK WCL

06       002  WTHDN BRW

07       003  3WEEK UND

08       008  WTHDN EDU

PAGE 1 MORE ON NEXT PAGE.   ENTER PD2
```

Figure 1. LCS Short bibliographic record retrieved using a detailed search by call number (DSC).

These short bibliographic records could be retrieved at computer terminals in all of the Libraries locations by a call number, by a title record accession number, by an author/title, or by a title. In the case of both the author/title and the title searches, LCS could be used to search only the main entry author and/or the title as it appeared on the cataloged item. Since 1970, two types of author search and a shelflist position search have been added.

Author/Title Access

The author/title, title, and one of the author searches use nine character search keys. For the author/title or ATS search, four characters are taken from the first significant word of the author and five characters from the first significant word of the title. For example, to search Toffler's *Future Shock*, the search key entered is TOFFFUTUR. (Figure 2.) A title or TLS search includes four characters of the first significant word of the title and five characters of the second significant word of the title. Thus, *Journal of Medical Ethics* is entered at MEDIETHIC. "Journal" and "of" are both considered non-significant words in LCS. The AUT author search key is composed of six characters of

```
ATS/TOFFFUTUR

PAGE 1              3 MATCHES        0 SKIPPED      (ALL RETRIEVED IN 1)

01 TOFFLER, ALVIN.      FUTURE SHOCK                      1971

02 TOFFLER, ALVIN.      FUTURE SHOCK                      1970

03 TOFFLER, ALVIN.      THE FUTURISTS $1st ed.            1972
```

Figure 2.   The display of the retrieved records from an author/title search.

the first significant word of the author and three characters of the second significant word. For example, Linguistic Society of America is entered in the AUT author search as LINGSOCIE. (Figure 3.)

The AUS author search allows full entry of the author's name. But at the same time, it requires exact entry up to the point that the user chooses to truncate the entry. Exact means that every character including spaces and punctuation must be correct. All author main entries which match the entered search up to the point of truncation are retrieved. (Figure 4.) shows an example of an AUS author search on the Linguistic Society of America.

The author/title, title, and both author searches are considered general searches. A general search retrieves a list of titles which match the entered search. With an author/title search key, ninety percent of the LCS records display on a page of ten or fewer matches.[5] With an AUT author search, eighty-three percent of the authors are displayed on three pages (fewer than thirty-one records). The information for each title displayed in a general search includes the author, title, and publication date. If the author or title is longer than the allocated space, they are truncated.

Shelflist Access

The shelflist position search (SPS) is another type of general search. In this search, the list of titles displayed are in shelflist sequence. (Figure 5.) The call number which was searched is displayed in the correct shelflist position. On the same line, the call number is followed by 10 characters of the author, a portion of the title, and the publication date. The same information is displayed for the other call numbers, which are retrieved. If the requested call number is not present in the shelflist index, it is included in the proper sequence in the display followed by a blank line. The OSU Libraries Automated Processing Division uses the shelflist position search when adding new titles to the Libraries holdings.[6]

Until June 1978, the shelflist position search was the only on-line subject search available on LCS. After June 1978, the shelflist position search continues to be the only subject access for titles cataloged before January 1977.

LSC Short Record Retrieval

In the general search displays, each title is listed on a separate line which is identified by a line number. This line number is used in a detailed search by line number (DSL) to retrieve the short bibliographic record and circulation data. The short bibliographic record can also be retrieved by a detailed search on call number (DSC) or a detailed search by title number (DST) in addition to the line number search after a previous general search. Figure 1 is an example of a detailed search by call number.

LSC On-Line Catalog

For several years, the OSU Libraries have been talking of closing the card catalogs. The schedule for this event, July 4, 1976, was based on an assumption that OCLC, Inc. would have a subject search available by that time. Although OCLC was working on subject search during 1975/76, they had not made schedule promises as to implementation. In May 1976, when it became apparent that OCLC would not have a subject search available in the summer, the specifications for an LCS on-line catalog were drafted.

AUT/LINGUISOC

PAGE 1   3 MATCHES   0 SKIPPED   (ALL RETRIEVED IN 1)

01 LINGUISTIC SOCIETY OF AMERICA   BULLETIN   1926

02 LINGUISTIC SOCIETY OF AMERICA   LSA BULLETIN   1970

03 LINGUISTIC SOCIETY OF AMERICA   MEETING HANDBOOK, FORTIETH ANNUAL MEET 1965

Figure 3. AUT author search and display.

AUS/LINGUISTIC SOCIETY OF A

PAGE 1   3 MATCHES   0 SKIPPED   (ALL RETRIEVED IN 1)

01 LINGUISTIC SOCIETY OF AMERICA   BULLETIN   1926

02 LINGUISTIC SOCIETY OF AMERICA   LSA BULLETIN   1970

03 LINGUISTIC SOCIETY OF AMERICA   MEETING HANDBOOK, FORTIETH ANNUAL MEET 1965

Figure 4. AUS author search and display.

```
SPS/HN17.5T64

11 HN17.5R61969/ROSZAK, TH THE MAKING OF A COUNTER CULTURE/1969

12 HN17.5R8/RUBINGTON,/THE STUDY OF SOCIAL PROBLEMS/1971

13 HN17.5S51974/SILVA, ANT/HIPPIES, DROGAS, SEXO, POLUICAO $2. ED./1974

14 HN17.5S75/STEIN, GEO/THE INDIVIDUAL AND EVERYBODY ELSE/1973

15 HN17.5T5/THOMASON, /THE PROFESSIONAL APPROACH TO COMMUNITY WORK/1969

16*HN17.5T64/TOFFLER, A/FUTURE SHOCK./1970

17 HN17.5T641971/TOFFLER, A/FUTURE SHOCK/1971

18 HN17.5T681/TOURAINE, /THE POST-INDUSTRIAL SOCIETY/1971

19 HN17.5U44/UNITED NAT/POPULAR PARTICIPATION IN DECISION MAKING FOR DEVEL/1975

1A HN17.5U45/UNITED NAT/POPULAR PARTICIPATION IN DEVELOPMENT: EMERGING TRE/1971

1B HN17.5V57/VIRILIO, P/ESSAI SUR L'INSECURITE DU TERRITOIRE/1976

PAGE 2   INPUT:HN17.5T64
```

Figure 5.   A display of the retrieved records in response to a shelflist position search (SPS).

The specifications identified the following capabilities, available in June 1978, to augment the LCS author/title catalog previously described:

1) display of full bibliographic records
2) access to the Libraries' holdings by subject
3) expansion of the author/title access to include secondary name and title entries
4) provision for adding subject cross references at a later date

Initially, these capabilities are available only for titles cataloged through OCLC since January 1, 1977. When the OCLC–MARC retrospective tapes are available and interfaced with LCS, the on-line catalog will include retrospective OCLC cataloging through January 1, 1974.

Full Bibliographic Record

Although the University of Toronto Library has reported that only an average of 7.74% of their COM microcatalog use is in the full bibliographic record file,[7] the full bibliographic record (FBR) is viewed as a desirable component of the LCS on-line catalog.

The FBR display contains all elements which are included on an OSU Libraries catalog card. (Figure 6.) The format was designed for a compact display without loss of information. The call number appears on the first line, the author on the second. Indented two spaces, the title paragraph includes title, edition statement, imprint, collation, and series note. All other notes are in a single paragraph, which is also indented. The subject headings are in a paragraph which begins "SUB:" and are numbered with arabic numerals. The secondary name and title entries are in a paragraph which begins "AE:" and also are numbered with arabic numerals.

Financial limitations resulted in a display which does not reflect current computer capabilities. The FBR display, as well as all other output, is in upper case alphabet only. Special characters, particularly diacritical marks, may be translated, deleted, spelled out, or retained. For instance, the Polish Ł is translated to L; the umlaut is deleted; and the flat sign is spelled out. In case the system is updated to process upper/lower case alphabet and all special characters, the OSU OCLC–MARC archive tapes are retained for future reloading of the FBR.

The full bibliographic record for a title, which has an FBR record in the file, can be retrieved by OSU call number (FBC), LCS title number (FBT) or by line number (FBL) after a previous general search.

Subject Access

The subject access in the LCS on-line catalog uses a subject index search (SIS) to display the subject headings available and also display the number of times each heading has been used. (Figure 7.) The entered subject displays in alphabetical computer sequence as line 11 at the top of the second display page, which displays first. After viewing the second page, the user may request page 1 or page 3 to view additional headings. This display is similar to an EXPAND display in the Lockheed Information System or to a NEIGHBOR display in SDC's Orbit.

A subject index search can be done on a Library of Congress subject heading or on any word or words which come to mind. The entered search displays on line 11 whether or not it has been used as a subject heading in a full bibliographic record. If the entered term has not been used, the number of items column is blank.

FBC/HN17.5T64

HN17.5T64

TOFFLER, ALVIN.

FUTURE SHOCK.   NEW YORK, RANDOM HOUSE   1970   XII,   505 P.   23 CM.   8.95

BIBLIOGRAPHY: P. 461-483.

SUB: 1. SOCIAL HISTORY--1945-   2. SOCIAL CHANGE   3. CIVILIZATION, MODERN--1950-

AE: 1. TITLE   &Q2741001

Figure 6. A display of the full bibliographic record in response to a full bibliographic record search by call number. This display may also be retrieved by a title number search or a line number search.

```
SIS/SOCIAL CHANGE

11*  361  SOCIAL CHANGE

12    52  SOCIAL CHANGE--ADDRESSES, ESSAYS, LECTURES

13    22  SOCIAL CHANGE--BIBLIOGRAPHY

14    24  SOCIAL CHANGE--CASE STUDIES

15    15  SOCIAL CHANGE--CONGRESSES

16   164  SOCIAL CLASSES

17    19  SOCIAL CLASSES--ADDRESSES, ESSAYS, LECTURES

18     7  SOCIAL CLASSES--AFRICA

19     1  SOCIAL CLASSES--BRAZIL

20     8  SOCIAL CLASSES--CHINA

INPUT: SOCIAL CHANGE

PAGE 2 of 3    FOR OTHER PAGES ENTER PS AND PAGE NUMBER

SBI/11
```

LINE NUMBER   NUMBER OF RECORDS   SUBJECT HEADING

Figure 7. The display of a response to a subject index search.

```
SBL/11

PAGE 1          361 MATCHES        0 SKIPPED        (NOT ALL RETRIEVED)

01 BT738E39/ELIAS, JOH/CONSCIENTIZATION AND DESCHOOLING/1976
02 HV41G185/GALPER, JE/THE POLITICS OF SOCIAL SERVICES/1975
03 HM101M54/MILES, IAN/THE POVERTY OF PREDICTION/1975
04 HN59L85/LUNDGORG, /FUTURE WITH SHOCK/1974
05 HN17.5M871974/MUSGROVE, /ECSTASY AND HOLINESS/1974
06 THESIS1973PHDP811/PONTING, J/RUMOR CONTROL CENTERS IN INTERMITTENT ORGA/1974
07 HN17.5T641971/TOFFLER, A/FUTURE SHOCK/1971
08 HM101M42;MEAD, MARG/CULTURE AND COMMITMENT/1970
09 HN17.5T64/TOFFLER, A/FUTURE SHOCK/1970
10 CB151R41957/REDFIELD, /THE PRIMITIVE WORLD AND ITS TRANSFORMATION/1957

FOR MORE TITLES, ENTER PG2
```

Figure 8.   A display of the retrieved records in response to a subject search by line number (SBL).

After the user has determined the subject in which they are interested, a subject search by line number (SBL) may be entered. (Figure 8.) This display is in inverse order by publication date and within date in alphabetical order by the first four characters of the entry. From this display a line number search for either the full bibliographic record or a short record can be entered.

Although subject cross references are not included in the current LCS on-line catalog capabilities, the subject file has been designed so that it can serve in the future as a subject authority file. The plan is for subject cross references to appear in the subject index display. When maintenance of the subject file is available, a single maintenance transaction can be specified to change a subject heading in all records in which it appears.

Secondary Author/Title Access

As of June 1978, secondary authors and titles for which full bibliographic records are in LCS are included in the author/title, title, and AUT author search key indexes. The nine character keys are created from the secondary entries in combination with the main entry and title as it appears on the piece when appropriate. However, when the retrieved title has a search key match on a secondary entry, the display for the record includes only the main entry and title. The secondary entries are not included in the terminal response for general searches. As mentioned, the secondary authors and titles display in the full bibliographic record.

Terminals

In 1970, the University Libraries had LCS terminals for staff use at circulation desks in the Main Library and Department Libraries. From the beginning, the LCS Telephone Center has used LCS terminals to provide library users, via the telephone, information regarding the Libraries holdings by title, author, and call number. Gradually, terminals have been added in both the Public Service and Technical Service areas until the system now has 80 terminals. Currently 15 terminals are designated public use terminals, at which library patrons may do their own searching of the LCS on-line catalog.

Closing of the Card Catalog

At this point in time, The Ohio State University Libraries have not determined when the card catalog will be closed. The development of the LCS on-line catalog is moving ahead under the assumption that the card catalog will be closed. In addition to cross references for subjects, we also have to provide name cross references, analyzed serials, non-roman titles, and retrospective serial titles in the on-line files. When the LCS on-line catalog has proved itself to be at least the equivalent of the tried and true card catalog, The Ohio State University Libraries will close their card catalogs.

REFERENCES

1. A. Robert Thorson, "The Economics of Automated Circulation," *Proceedings* of the 1976 Clinic on Library Applications of Data Processing (Urbana–Champaign, Ill., University of Illinois Graduate School of Library Science, 1977) p. 28–47.
2. Alice S. Clark, "Subject Access to a Data Base of Library Holdings," *Journal of Library Automation* 7 (December 1974): 267–274.

3. D. Kaye Gapen and Ichiko T. Morita, "OCLC at OSU: The Effect of the Adoption of OCLC on the Management of Technical Services at a Large Academic Library," *Library Resources & Technical Services* 22 (Winter 1978): 5–21.

4. *An Automated On-Line Circulation System: Evaluation, Development, Use.* Edited by Irene Braden Hoadley and A. Robert Thorson. (Columbus, Ohio, The Ohio State University Libraries, Office of Educational Services, 1973).

5. Gerry D. Guthrie and Steven D. Slifko, "Analysis of Search Key Retrieval on a Large Bibliographic File," *Journal of Library Automation* 5 (June 1972): 96–100.

6. Gapen, *op. cit.*, p. 14.

7. Valentina DeBruin, "Sometime Dirty Things are Seen on the Screen: A Mini-Evaluation of the COM Microcatalogue at the University of Toronto Library," *The Journal of Academic Librarianship* 3 (November 1977): 264.

John A. Bollier

Yale Divinity School

BIBLIOGRAPHIC INSTRUCTION IN THE GRADUATE/ PROFESSIONAL THEOLOGICAL SCHOOL

This paper presents context, components, and student/faculty evaluation of a three-hour credit, semester-long elective course on theological bibliography taught during the last three academic years at Yale Divinity School. Conclusions are that: (1) acquiring bibliographical sophistication requires studying bibliographic methods and resources directly; (2) there is room for both separate bibliographic courses and course integrated instruction in the same curriculum; (3) a separate course in subject bibliography produces a pool of students who may be used as reference assistants; and (4) teaching a course in subject bibliography and publishing scholarly bibliographies aid in the academic librarian's struggle for faculty status.

As bibliographic instruction becomes a topic of increasing concern in colleges and universities, so it is beginning to show signs of vitality also in the graduate/professional theological schools.[1,2] This paper will present the results of a three year experiment in a formal, three credit hour, one semester, elective course at Yale Divinity School entitled, "Theological Bibliography and Research Methodology." Its findings are applicable for both graduate and undergraduate subject-oriented bibliographic instruction in other areas of the humanities and social sciences as well as for theology.

THE CONTEXT OF THE COURSE

Yale Divinity School is one of the ten graduate professional schools of Yale University. The Divinity Library is a separate collection of over 300,000 volumes, but is a part of the total University Library system. The Divinity Library's primary clientele are some 425 master degree candidates from many denominations enrolled in the Divinity School, and approximtely 50 Ph.D. candidates in Religious Studies enrolled in the Graduate School. However, the Divinity Library, as with other libraries in the system, serves both the instructional and the research needs of the whole University.

After the Divinity Library developed staff-directed and self-guided orientation tours, library guide brochures, bibliographic hand-outs on a variety of subjects, and offered occasonal bibliographic lectures, the feeling persisted that there was still little opportunity or encouragement for the students who desired it, to develop sophisticated bibliographic skills.

Without ruling out the possibility of course-integrated bibliographic instruction at some future time, the Divinity Library administration decided to embark on the development of a library oriented, separate course on Theological Bibliography. With the encouragement of the Divinity School administration and the help of a grant from the Association of Theological Schools, this author proceded to develop a syllabus and write the necessary materials for a three credit hour semester course. The final proposal was accepted by the Curriculum Committee and approved by the Faculty for inclusion in the curriculum in the Spring Semester of 1976. It was taught then as well as again in the Spring and Fall Semesters of 1977. It is now being taught for the fourth time in the current Fall Semester 1978 and is scheduled to be taught regularly one semester during each academic year.

Enrollment in the first three semesters had been between ten and fifteen, whereas in the current semester enrollment has increased to twenty-four. Students electing the course include those who plan to enter the professional ministry, to teach in higher education, to become administrators, editors, or librarians. While over 40 percent of the Divinity School students are women, during the first three semesters the course was offered less than 10 percent of the students electing it were women. After discussing with women faculty and administration members the implications of the course for the Women's Movement because of its training students to become more independent in their study and research, I was curious to see whether there would be a change in the male-female ratio. For whatever reason, the male-female ratio has now shifted so that currently the nine women enrolled form approximately 37.5% of the class of twenty-four.

THE COMPONENTS OF THE COURSE

The course meets once a week for two hours during the twelve week semester. While the exact weekly class schedule and mix of components may vary from week to week, the course as a whole contains the following:

1. Weekly lectures of thirty to forty-five minutes on such topics as: the types and functions of bibliography; library theory and practice, e.g., classification systems, library catalogs, subject, author and title access to theological literature; forms of theological literature, e.g., reference works, monographs, serials, rare books, historical manuscripts and archives, and microforms; book publishers; government documents.

The comment of some librarians concerning this section is often, "But isn't that terribly dull and boring to the students?" But such a reaction is selling short the stock-in-trade of the library profession. For when these subjects are presented as means to better information retrieval, student motivation and attention continue. Of course, such presentations must be liberally illustrated with practical examples of the usefulness of library theory for doing a term paper in a current course or in pursuing professional practice after graduation.

This segment of the course also affords opportunity for the instructor to invite colleagues who have special expertise to make their contribution to the class. Asking a catalog librarian to speak about classification systems or subject access, or the acquisitions librarian to discuss book publishers and book dealers to help students develop their own personal libraries, or the archivist to present historical manuscripts, enriches both student and guest instructor alike.

However, a word of caution must be inserted here. Having a constant parade of guest lecturers with the regular librarian-instructor serving as only the coordinator will soon destroy any sense of continuity and will kill off student interest.

2. Weekly discussion of bibliographic and reference tools for thirty to forty-five minutes. This is a "show-and-tell" presentation, which one might think would be too

elementary for a class of graduate/professional students. But such is emphatically not the case. From the formal student evaluations discussed below, as well as from student attention during this period of each class session, it is obvious that the descriptive presentation, with most of the works actually present in class for the students to examine, is central to the course. The librarian-instructor should never underestimate the students' intelligence nor overestimate their knowledge of bibliographic tools. Even on the graduate/professional level, where a student may have read widely in the monographic literature of a particular field, one is constantly amazed at that same student's rudimentary knowledge of the bibliographic and reference tools in that field.

The degree of difficulty in preparing for this component of the course is dependent upon the availability of current guides to the literature of the particular subject field. In the case of theology, there is no adequate up-to-date guide. Consequently a bibliography was compiled of some 400 works, both general and theological, which might be considered essential for students to know for attaining bibliographic proficiency. This 70-page classified bibliography with author-title index was produced with the help of a part-time research assistant. It was reproduced by photocopy as class size required and sold to students as the basic text at cost. As a by-product of the course, this bibliography has now been revised, annotated, enlarged and will be published by Westminster Press on April 23, 1979 under the title, *The Literature of Theology: A Guide for Students and Pastors*, 208 pages.

As librarian-instructor, this author was responsible for making brief descriptive and critical remarks about the twenty-five to thirty-five works covered in class each week. However, two different students shared in these presentations each week by making ten minute oral reports on two particularly important works.

3. Seven sets of "case study" questions. Realizing that students would not really know a reference tool simply by hearing the instructor or fellow students talking about it in class, or even by examining it briefly during the coffee break or as it was passed around the table during the class period, seven sets of informational type questions were worked out which would require use of the works discussed in the previous class session. The Appendix contains one question from each of the seven sets to indicate the type of questions used. Each set, containing between six and ten questions, was assigned at the appropriate time throughout the semester. Answers were discussed briefly in class.

Again, when the course began it was feared that graduate/professional students might consider such assignments as mere busy work. But once again, the formal, unsigned student evaluation forms as well as informal personal feedback indicated otherwise. If questions were representative of the informational needs the students were currently experiencing in their course work or could expect to experience in later professional practice, these seven assignments were taken seriously and done regularly. As these assignments progressed through the semester, a growing bibliographic awareness and sophistication was observed in the students. They, too, found satisfaction in these newly developing abilities.

4. A bibliographic term project. By the fourth week of the semester students were required to choose a topic on which they intended to develop an annotated bibliography or write a bibliographic essay to be due at the end of the semester. Students were encouraged to select topics which related to term papers in another course they were currently taking or which was of special interest to them.

When this instructor did not feel competent to evaluate the subject content of a particular paper, faculty members with the required subject expertise to read the paper and give their opinion were called upon. Invariably faculty members cooperated willingly and responded promptly with in-depth evaluations to supplement mine.

The class was informed that the bibliographic term project assigned at the beginning of the semester, might be submitted to other faculty for second opinions. This probably inspires diligence in any students who may tend to laxness because they think they know more, or actually do know more, on a particular topic than the librarian-instructor. But not even a librarian can be an expert in all fields. And any librarian aspiring to teach a bibliographic course covering such a broad discipline as theology must be willing to take certain risks.

As a rule of thumb for students who felt they needed such guidance, a minimum goal was set of fifty works to be selected, annotated and arranged in the bibliographic term project. Papers varied in length from ten to forty pages. Topics also demonstrated a wide range of interests such a "Marriage Counseling," "English Deism," "Karl Barth's Theology," "The Book of Jeremiah," "The Parables," and "Indigenous Liturgies of the Caribbean."

Normally the three hours credit for the course was given in Area IV, which in the classical theological curriculum is Practical Theology. But if a student needed or wanted credit in Area I (Biblical Studies) or Area II (Historical Theology) or Area III (Theology and Related Disciplines, e.g. Philosophy, Psychology, Sociology, the Arts), such credit would be given if the term project were done on a topic in one of these areas.

During the last three class sessions as the bibliographic term projects were nearing completion, students made oral reports on their work. They were expected to share with the class such results as the search strategy employed, tools found most useful, bibliographic problems encountered, characteristics of the literature on their topic, and reasons for arranging materials as they did.

Further motivation for diligence in the project was the assurance that worthy papers would be copied and added to the Divinity Library's bibliography collection in the main reference room. Papers which the instructor deemed worthy of publication were so designated and as of this writing one has been published in a professional journal.[3]

5. Occasional visits to other libraries or collections within the University Library system for introduction to their materials relevant to the study of theology. Such field trips were made to the Beinecke Rare Book and Manuscript Library, the Historical Manuscripts and Archives Department, and the Government Documents Department where staff members lectured and exhibited materials. In addition, a class tour was scheduled in the main University Library, Sterling Memorial Library, where materials of special interest to theological students were pointed out.

In written evaluation forms one student made the rather astute observation that such field trips would be more valuable if actual assignments were made requiring the use of these various collections rather than just passing through them as tourists or hearing a staff member describe them.

6. Assigned readings. Specific readings from books, journals and encyclopedias were required only seven out of the twelve weeks of the semester. Those readings which were assigned dealt primarily with the nature and function of bibliography generally and with the present state of theological bibliography specifically. Required readings were purposely kept light in order to permit the student to concentrate on gaining mastery of the some 400 works discussed in class through using them in the case study question sets and in the bibliographic term project. It was assumed that a student develops sophisticated bibliographic skills by actually working on bibliographic problems rather than by extensive reading on the theory and practice of bibliography.

EVALUATION OF THE COURSE

Student reaction, even more than faculty opinion, will determine whether a new elective bibliography course becomes a permanent offering or is dropped as just another experiment in curricular reform which did not make it. The Divinity School encourages student reaction to courses through the use of a three page evaluation form which is returned to the Dean's Office. About 80 percent of the students in the Theological Bibliography course completed evaluation forms. While these unsigned forms invariably contain suggestions for improvement, many of which are incorporated into the course the next time it is taught, they have been unanimous thus far in their positive evaluation of the course as a whole.

Two questions on the first section of the evaluation form are: "Would you recommend to a fellow student that he or she take this course?" and "Would you recommend to a first year student that he or she take this course?" Without exception in all three semesters the course has been taught, both of these questions have been answered in the positive, usually with strong supporting comments.

Another part of the questionnaire asks students to indicate what the course seemed to foster and on a scale of one to five to indicate how well the course did what it seemed designed to do. Almost invariably students indicated "Acquisition of new knowledge" and "Acquisition of personal skill" and usually gave both of these the top value of five, but never lower than four. Occasionally they also indicated "Broadening of perspective," again with a value of five or four. With this kind of "consumer report" information which spreads automatically through the student grapevine, a bibliography course instructor need not rely on sympathetic faculty advisors to promote enrollment.

However, faculty reaction has been favorable, and while there is no formal instrument for measuring faculty opinion of the course comparable to the instrument used for measuring student opinion, individual faculty members have volunteered positive and encouraging comments. Many are strongly recommending the course to their advisees. Those who served as second readers for individual bibliographic term projects in their field seem to have a special appreciation for the course based on the results which they see it has produced. In at least three instances faculty members have employed students who took the course to do bibliographic research for them in connection with their teaching responsibilities and research projects. The fact that the course has become a part of the regular curriculum and is listed in the catalog as such indicates both faculty and administration approval.

CONCLUSIONS

1. Even on the graduate/professional level it cannot be assumed that students have developed bibliographic skills or mastery of the reference and bibliographic tools basic to their discipline without the formal study of bibliography as such. The first semester the Theological Bibliography course was taught, enrollment was divided almost equally between first, second and third year Master of Divinity students. In the second semester there were more first year students, but also one Ph.D. candidate in American Studies who was at the dissertation stage. The third semester class was almost all first year students. Evidence seems to indicate that even with a wide diversity of students the level of bibliographic sophistication, which was almost uniformly low at the beginning of the course, does not depend upon the number of years enrolled in graduate/professional studies, but rather upon a conscious effort, or lack thereof, in studying bibliographic methods and resources. In this sense, the study of bibliography is comparable to the study of Greek, Hebrew, pastoral counseling or preaching. The student does not acquire proficiency in any of these skills obliquely through studying only in other fields but directly by studying and practicing in the discipline itself.

2. In the on-going debate between course integrated bibliographic instruction versus a separate subject bibliography course, this author concludes that, on the graduate/

professional level at least, it is not a question of either/or but rather both/and.[4] To some extent Yale Divinity School already has some course integrated bibliographic instruction in the area of Biblical Studies. Each semester professors or their teaching assistants spend one class session per section on the basic bibliographic tools needed for writing an exegesis paper. With enrollment in these lecture classes running from fifty upwards to two-hundred students, this course integrated bibliographic instruction reaches far more than the couple dozen students enrolled in my course on Theological Bibliography. But while such instruction is helpful for doing the particular exegesis paper required by the course, it cannot begin to introduce the student to the wide range of bibliographies and reference tools in the whole area of Biblical Studies, nor does it attempt to teach search strategies. To perform these tasks satisfactorily requires a minimum of six class hours in the Theological Bibliography course. Such a large block of time simply would not be available in any of the Biblical courses. Thus, for those students who feel the need for going beyond the rudiments a separate course on subject bibliography should be offered.

3. One of the by-products of an intensive course in subject bibliography is the development of a pool of trained reference assistants who can serve their fellow students either formally or informally. This is especially important in a branch library of a larger university library system which often cannot provide professional reference service on evenings or weekends even though it is open for use during those periods. In hiring part-time student employees as public services assistants to aid the regular staff during such periods as well as during peak day-time hours, preference is given to students who have taken the course in Theological Bibliography. Moreover, several students who have taken the course, but have not sought such employment, have indicated that fellow students have often sought them out for bibliographic assistance.

4. Establishing one or more solid courses in subject bibliography and research methodology benefits not only the students and the institution, but also improves the image of the library and the status of the librarians. In the struggle for faculty status librarians can promote their cause by functioning as faculty in teaching bibliography and publishing scholarly bibliographical studies in the various disciplines. Without neglecting the time-honored roles of acquiring, storing and retrieving information and documents, the academic library, with its increasingly complex collections and information networks, must assume a more active, aggressive role in teaching users how to exploit these rich resources.

After demonstrating to faculty and students alike that bibliography is an essential discipline in the theological curriculum, this author was appointed by the faculty as "Lecturer in Theological Literature." Thus, it might be concluded that academic librarians with masters degree level subject competence, M.L.S. degree level professional qualifications and also a solid commitment to quality teaching, have a distinctive instructional contribution to make to their institutions which generally cannot be performed by anyone else.

REFERENCES

1. Two complete issues of the *Drexel Library Quarterly* 7 (July, October 1971): 171–378 are devoted to articles on, "Integrating Library Instruction in the College Curriculum."

2. For a selected bibliography on library instruction see John Lubans, Jr., ed. *Educating the Library User* (New York: Bowker, 1974), p. 423–435. However, one searches the literature in vain to find discussions of library user intruction in theological education.

3. G. Allison Stokes, "Bibliography of Psychology/Religion Studies," *Religious Studies Review* 4 (October 1978): 273–279.

4. For a discussion of both approaches by one who favors course related library instruction see James Kennedy, "Question: A Separate Course in Bibliography or Course Related Library Instruction?" in Sul H. Lee, ed. *Library Orientation.* Papers presented at the First Annual Conference on Library Orientation held at Eastern Michigan University Library, Ypsilanti, Michigan, by Pierian Press, Ann Arbor, Michigan, 1972, p. 18–28.

APPENDIX

Selected Questions from the Seven Sets of Case Study Questions

1. You are an advisor to a church youth group which is discussing sexual behavior. You want a half-dozen current books on this subject. What books would you select and where did you find them listed?
2. You are going to write a paper on New England theology. Where can you find a brief survey and bibliography for further study of this topic?
3. You are planning a series of sermons on the parables. Where can you find a bibliography to guide your study?
4. Where can you find a brief discussion of Origen's method of interpreting Scripture as shown in his commentaries?
5. Where can you find a bibliography on the ordination of women in a recent Catholic publication?
6. The Church and Society committee of your congregation wants to study the influence of lending institutions on the cost and quality of housing for the poor in your community. Where can they find relevant literature on this topic?
7. In your involvement with Jewish-Christian relationships, you want to find an extensive article discussing the "Holocaust." Where can you find such an article with bibliography?

Jean L. Graef and Larry Greenwood

C L Systems, Inc. and University of Kentucky

MARKETING LIBRARY SERVICES: A CASE STUDY IN PROVIDING BIBLIOGRAPHIC INSTRUCTION IN AN ACADEMIC LIBRARY

Libraries are similar to business firms in that both perform such functions as purchasing, production, finance, personnel management, and marketing. Unlike business firms, however, libraries have been largely passive with the marketing function. A program of bibliographic instruction at the University of Kentucky illustrates the successful application of modern marketing methods. The instruction librarian successfully created a "marketing mix" of price, product, promotion, personal selling, and distribution to meet the needs of students and faculty. Moreover, the Kentucky example demonstrates how one successful program can contribute toward marketing other library services.

INTRODUCTION

Libraries are similar to business firms in that both perform such functions as purchasing, production, finance, personnel management, and marketing. Unlike business firms, however, the marketing function in libraries has been largely passive. Librarians have directed most of their energies toward the purchasing and production functions of buying, cataloging, and circulating books. Meanwhile, librarians tend to neglect the marketing function of defining and anticipating the wants and needs of library users.

A program of bibliographic instruction at the University of Kentucky illustrates the successful application of modern marketing methods in libraries. Moreover, this example demonstrates how one successful program can contribute toward marketing other library services. The marketing function in businesses and libraries is discussed briefly below. The remaining sections of the paper will describe the bibliographic instruction program at the Universityof Kentucky, show how the program was successfully marketed, and illustrate the program's contribution to the marketing of other library services.

THE EVOLUTION OF THE MARKETING FUNCTION

The marketing function in the business world gradually evolved from a subservience to the production function around the turn of the century, through a sales orientation in the 1930's, 40's, and 50's, to the broader present day concept. During the first stage, most firms emphasized making a quality product and hiring people to sell it. In the second

212

stage, the emphasis was on the quality of the sales force, backed by consumer advertising and market research. Today, the marketing function has assumed a pivotal role in many organizations, marshalling all of their resources to translate an idea for satisfying a consumer need into a product and the product into sales. Thus, the needs of the consumer have gradually become the focus of marketing activities as time passed.

Many libraries still maintain a production orientation, in which they emphasize the technical processes required to acquire and catalog the collection. Librarians have borrowed techniques from operations research (the scientific analysis and evaluation of problems) and have applied automation to library processes in an effort to make production faster and more cost effective. Some libraries have moved into the second stage of marketing evolution where use studies and advertising are used to plan and promote library services. A few libraries have even undertaken the integrated approach which characterizes the third stage. These librarians have anticipated needs for services and products and then have marshalled resources both within the library and external to it to deliver the services and products.

Third stage marketing by a library would involve several components, which in business are sometimes together called the *marketing mix:*[1]

1. *Product* — the qualities, characteristics, design, and packaging of the product or service.
2. *Price* — In libraries, most services do not have a monetary price, but price may also be conceived as the user's time and trouble spent in finding information.
3. *Promotion* — The advertising and publicity used to make users aware of products or services.
4. *Personal Selling* — Librarians' face-to-face interactions with users during the process of making them aware of products and helping them choose among services and methods of delivery.
5. *Distribution* — The means used to distribute a product or service to users, such as delivery to faculty, who then distribute to students as opposed to delivery directly to students. Delivery to faculty would be called "wholesaling" in the business world because the library "sells" to people who in turn deliver to the end user; direct library delivery to students would be "retailing."

In addition to making the five types of marketing decisions described above, a firm or library must determine whether resources are available to produce and distribute a product or service. It must also calculate the demand for the product and determine whether other organizations are offering similar products in a cost effective manner, i.e., in a "competitive" manner.

ENVIRONMENT

The overall environment at the University of Kentucky was good for introducing a bibliographic instruction program. Other academic libraries were starting such programs; there was grant money available; the new director at Kentucky was innovative and service-oriented; and the faculty and administration of the university had complementary interests in the area of undergraduate instruction.

The bibliographic instruction programs at other colleges and universities across the country took several forms:

— Classroom presentations in which library staff, usually in the reference department, were invited by teaching faculty to talk about library services and resources.
— Credit courses for students taught by librarians, usually at the lower division level.

- Slide-tape and video-tape programs available for unaccompanied viewing by library users, sometimes at point-of-use.
- Orientation tours in which large numbers of students were conducted through the building by librarians, usually in the beginning of the school term.
- Full-fledged programs with all of the above activities, conducted either by a separate library instruction department, a well-defined section of the reference department, or even by the entire library staff.

The bibliographic instruction program at Kentucky was one of several funded by the Council on Library Resources and the National Endowment for the Humanities. Kentucky's proposal had been submitted during the first year of a new library administration and the funds began to flow in August, 1974.

Meanwhile, a third-stage marketing program was implemented at Kentucky shortly after the arrival of a new director in 1973. The new director emphasized both identifying new groups of library users and improving services to those people who were already using the library. He had initiated a year-long study of library management practices (The Management Review and Analysis Program, MRAP, sponsored by the Association of Research Libraries) in order to improve the ability of the main library and its twelve branches to provide services and to identify areas for new services. The resulting report pointed out that the entire campus was moving in the direction of improving existing educational services and extending services to new groups of clients. In addition, the report recommended that the library staff periodically survey users to determine their satisfaction with library services.

At about the same time, a university-wide task force on improving undergraduate education recommended the establishment of an Office of Instructional Development that would provide support, information, and consulting services for faculty. The recommendation was evidence of faculty and administrative concern over the quality of undergraduate teaching at the university.

THE PROGRAM IN BIBLIOGRAPHIC INSTRUCTION

The C.L.R./N.E.H. grant proposal specified a program of undergraduate instruction in the social sciences and humanities. Within the general guidelines provided by the project's objectives (Exhibit 1), library staff designed a program with the following components:

1. A sequence of three instructional units for the freshman English classes. The first unit described the card catalog, the second the periodical indexes, and the third the reference collection (Exhibits 2–4). The units were self-instructional materials in printed form, written by library staff and presented to the classes by graduate student instructors in the English department.

2. A printed, self-instructional unit for history students which introduced reference materials of potential interest to historians (Exhibit 5).

3. Orientation tours to acquaint new students with the facilities and services available in the campus libraries.

4. Directional signs and self-guided tours. The signs were both painted on library walls in bright colors and posted above service points.

5. Guidebooks to the library, suitable for students, faculty, staff, and visitors (Exhibit 6).

6. Bibliographic instruction materials printed in the student newspaper.

7. Talks and bibliographies for individual classes on library facilities appropriate in a certain subject area, such as journalism.

EXHIBIT 1

Objectives for Instructional Program

1. Expand the reference and instructional capacity of the University Libraries through programs that bring specialized library resources and services to students and academic staff.

2. In cooperation with the teaching faculty, relate library resources to University instructional and research activities through educational programs directed toward the effective use of the Libraries' resources.

3. Promote the provision of direct assistance to students and academic staff through in-depth reference work applied to specific research and instructional projects

4. Increase the effectiveness of reference service by coordinating the utilization of library personnel for in-depth reference services to undergraduates and the instructional staff in the social sciences and humanities.

5. Develop the capability among students and academic staff to make effective use of library resources in general.

6. Increase the awareness of bibliographic tools and research techniques among students and academic staff.

7. Increase the familiarity of students with Kentucky's library collections.

8. Aid students and staff in a systematic way to keep up with the literature in their fields of interest.

9. Allow selected faculty to receive regularly, materials of potential value in their instructional work.

(From: Appendix A, Proposal to the Council on Library Resources.)

EXHIBIT 2

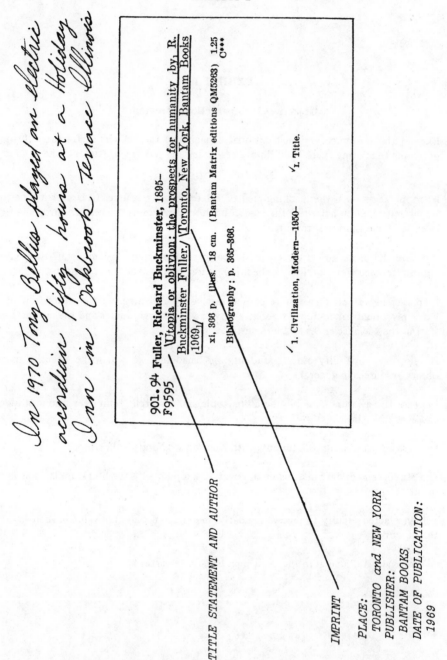

901.94 **Fuller, Richard Buckminster,** 1895–
F9595   Utopia or oblivion: the prospects for humanity ,by, R.
            Buckminster Fuller. /Toronto, New York, Bantam Books
            ,1969,

            xi, 366 p. illus. 18 cm. (Bantam Matrix editions QM5263) 1.25
            Bibliography: p. 365–366.   C***

            1. Civilization, Modern—1950–   I. Title.

TITLE STATEMENT AND AUTHOR

IMPRINT

PLACE:
TORONTO and NEW YORK
PUBLISHER:
BANTAM BOOKS
DATE OF PUBLICATION:
1969

In 1970 Tony Bellus played an electric accordian fifty hours at a Holiday Inn in Oakbrook Terrace Illinois

From: <u>Taming of the Dinosaur, Unit I: The Card Catalog</u>

EXHIBIT 3

THE TAMING OF THE DINOSAUR:
A KEY TO LIBRARY RESOURCES

UNIT 2...SOURCES OF CURRENT INFORMATION
LOCATING PERIODICAL AND NEWSPAPER ARTICLES

EXHIBIT 4

Reference sources which contain actual articles may be, as previously stated, universal in scope or limited in some way. Universal biographies are those which do not limit their entries by geography or profession. Rather, selection of entries is based upon sufficient fame or notoriety. CURRENT BIOGRAPHY and WHO'S WHO IN THE WORLD are in this category.

CURRENT BIOGRAPHY articles begin with an address through which the person may be reached.

STEWART, ELLEN

Theatrical producer
Address: La Mama Experimental Theatre Club, 74A E. 4th St., New York 10003

The course of contemporary theatre has been irrevocably changed by a handful of daring companies in that theatre's noncommercial avant-garde, known as Off Off Broadway. The contributions of such groups as The.... ludson ...morial Church, the C....

They end with references for further study......

...ut in fact he is ... developed sense of humor as an expert teller of deadpan jokes." In *Time* (December 6, 1971) his wit was characterized as "refreshingly acerbic." For recreation he turns to music, reading, the theatre, and an occasional game of golf.

References
Bsns W p76 D 4 '71 por
N Y Post p22 D 4 '71 por
N Y Times p30 N 25 '71 por; p20 F 18 '69
Time 98:25 D 6 '71 por
U S News 65:10 D 30 '68 por
Washington Post C p7 Ag 27 '68 por
Who's Who in America, 1972-73
Who's Who in World Jewry (1965)

Mr. and Mrs. Benjamin Nottingham announce that the marriage of their daughter MARY KATHERINE to Mr. Jerrold Atherton will not take place

From: Taming the Dinosaur, Unit 3; Reference Material

EXHIBIT 5

EXHIBIT 6

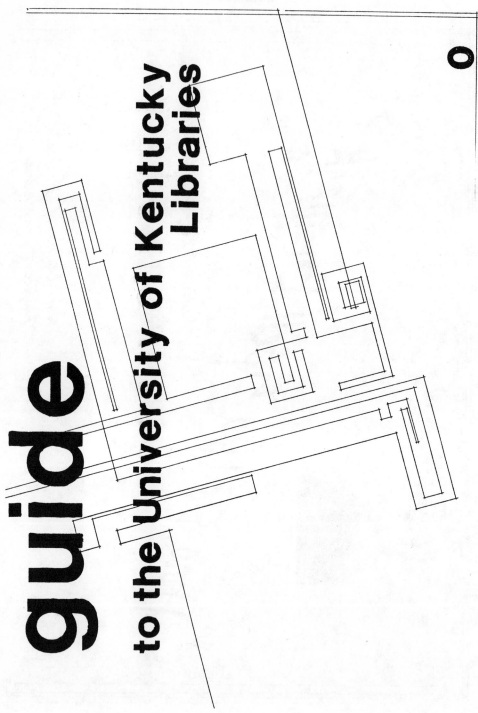

guide to the University of Kentucky Libraries

Exhibits 7 through 9 show the numbers of students served in various academic areas and at various levels of sophistication. Subject areas ranged from the theoretical (anthropology, English, history) to the practical (social work, merchandising). Levels of sophistication ranged from freshman composition classes to graduate and professional students writing theses or dissertation.

EXHIBIT 7

Comparison by Month of the Total Students Involved in Instructional Activities with the Previous Grant Year

1974/75 Number of Students	Month	1975/76 Number of Students
0	July	50
230	August	165
435	September	300
40	October	2415
230	November	971
0	December	0
125	January	358
700	February	2187
315	March	500
75	April	40
0	May	0
59	June	60
2209	TOTALS	7046

From: Second Annual Report to the Council on Library Resources

EXHIBIT 8

Breakdown of Students Involved in Instructional Activities in 1975/76 by Levels

Numbers of Students	Level	Description
2966	Orientation	Tours to acquaint new students with the library, regardless of class level.
3452	I	Freshman composition classes; emphasis on term paper writing.
246	II	Beginning work in students' major subject area
344	III	Advanced (junior/senior) students writing documented papers in major subject area
38	IV	Graduate and professional students writing theses or disserations.
7046	TOTAL	

From: Second Annual Report to the Council on Library Resources

EXHIBIT 9

Colleges and Departments with Course Numbers and Descriptions
Served by the Instructional Program

Colleges	Departments	Course Numbers and Descriptions
Architecture	——	ARC 810, Architecture Studio; ARC 820, History of Architecture and Urban Forms; ARC 830, Structures and Environmental Controls; ARC 850, Professional Practice. (Student takes these courses during his/her senior year.)
Arts and Sciences	Anthropology	ANT 605, Seminar in Method and Theory in Anthropology.
	English	ENG 101, Freshman Composition; ENG 102, Advanced Freshman Composition; ENG 105, Advanced Freshman English, Writing on Special Topics; ENG 203, Writing for Business and Industry.
	History	HIST 105, History of Europe, 1713 to the Present; HIST 316, Junior Seminar, Historical Method and Literature.
	Human Communication	SP 181, Basic Public Speaking; SP 288, Oral Interpretation; SP 488, Interpretation of Poetry.
	Journalism	JOU 203, Principles of Newswriting; JOU 204, Writing for Mass Media; JOU 501, Newsreporting.
Home Economics	Textiles, Clothing and Merchandising	TC 592, Special Problems in Clothing and Costume Design: Bicentennial Dress—Research, Design and Construction of Dress of the American Revolution.
Social Professions	Social Work	SW 124, Introduction to Social Services; SW 222, Development of Social Welfare; SW 322, The Social Work Profession and Social Welfare; SW 630, Social Welfare Policies and Services.

Course Numbering System

100–199 Open to freshmen
200–299 Prerequisite sophomore classification
300–399 Prerequisite junior classification
400–499 Prerequisite junior classification
500–599 Prerequisite junior classification
600–799 Open only to graduate students
800–999 Open only to professional students in professional colleges

From: Second Annual Report to the Council on Library Resources

These products were produced by the Instructional Services (IS) department in the library, newly created in August 1974. The department consisted of a full-time librarian and several part-time graduate students in library science, law, and communications. The librarian designed the program, made campus-wide contacts, edited and supervised the work of the students, and "sold" the instructional program to the faculty. The students both wrote the instructional units described above and conducted library tours. In addition to the regular students, other people helped on special projects, for example:

1. The teaching assistants in the English department distributed and presented the three instructional units to their freshman English sections concurrently with instruction in term paper writing. These instructors could demonstrate the relevance of specific library resources to those topics selected for the students' papers.

2. To produce signs and graphics for the printed materials, the Instructional Services department hired architecture students for short periods of time or paid them lump sums for specific projects.

3. Staff from other library departments volunteered their time (sometimes during their off hours) to give talks and prepare bibliographies for classes and to lead general library tours for new students.

THE MARKETING MIX OF THE BIBLIOGRAPHIC INSTRUCTION

The bibliographic instruction program met the needs of students for learning to find information by successfully combining the five components of the marketing mix.

The product of self-instructional printed materials was designed to reach large numbers of students at low cost and to provide a method of instruction which could be continued after grant funds ceased. Each unit was divided into sections that provided students with information necessary to conduct library research on a topic of interest. Unit I covering the card catalog was divided into four sections: Parts of the Card Catalog, Location of Material, Subject Card Catalog, and Basic Filing Rules. Each section was followed by a series of questions that when answered summarized all relevant knowledge that the student needed about the card catalog and the organization of material in the main library building. Unit 2 followed the same format, but covered the use of periodicals, periodical indexes, newspapers and newspaper indexes, and so on.

The "price" of bibliographic instruction to the instructors and students until January of 1978 was the time and trouble of acquiring it. After that date, students had to purchase the 70-page units in the university bookstore for 72¢ each. For the instructors, the price consisted of two class periods spent covering the units. A third period was devoted to a library tour led by library staff. The price for students (prior to January 1978) was not much more time than they would have spent attending English class. Furthermore, the students' effort on library work was an "investment" in their term paper grade.

During the first two years of the grant period, the library budget paid for printing all instructional materials except those printed in the student newspaper. However, because the library did not have enough money in its 1977–78 printing budget to pay for the instructional units, the library director arranged for the campus bookstore to pay the 57¢ per unit printing costs and sell the units at a 15¢ mark-up. Thus, the price became concrete in monetary terms. None of the library preparation costs were included in determining the selling price, and the library received no money from any sales. (See Exhibit 10 for a breakdown of costs for the freshman English program in 1976.)

There was no need for promotional activities for the bibliographic instruction program, since the students (consumers) were a "captive" market. They could not avoid taking freshman English and thus required no advertising or displays to lure them into obtaining bibliographic instruction. The program succeeded by using personal selling to gain the cooperation of the faculty.

EXHIBIT 10

Costs of the Freshman English Instructional Program as Implemented in Spring 1976[1]

I. Development Costs[2]

Library staff salaries

Professional (¾ year @ $14,300 per annum)	$10,725.00
Part time staff (3240 hours @ $2.26/hour)	7,290.00
Total development costs	$18,015.00

II. Operational Costs

Initial preparation

Professional and student staff time for packaging units and scheduling tours (320 hours @ $4.69/hour on the average)	1,500.00 est.

Printing

Instructional units (4,000 copies of each unit @ 17¢/copy)	2,000.00
Pretests/posttests (4,000 copies of each test @ 2¢/copy)	24.00
Total printing costs	2,024.00

Tours

Staff time for leading tours (218 hours @ $2.26/hour)	490.50

Evaluation

Staff time for compiling results of tests and questionnaire (39 hours @ $4.69/hour)	182.91
TOTAL OPERATION COSTS	$ 4,197.41

OPERATIONAL COSTS PER STUDENT	1.62
OPERATIONAL COSTS PER CLASS	40.50

1. Includes the following: Distribution of three instructional units and guided tours for 13 freshman English classes (325 students).
2. Does not include volunteer assistance from the Director of the freshman English program and nine English instructors.

It was the IS department head who "sold" the faculty on the idea of a partnership in improving bibliographic instruction. He developed a peer relationship with faculty members on several university-wide committees, to which he had been appointed through the influence of the library director. Examples were the Advisory Council on Continuing Education and the Freshman Year Committee. Through such committees, the librarian met one man who authored the instructional unit for history students and another who provided free audio-visual services to the instructional program. The librarian's collaboration with the Chairman of the Freshman English program, whom he met by simply paying a "sales call," was so successful that not only did the English professor offer guidance on the bibliographic instruction units, but he later requested the librarian to review a chapter on the library in one of his textbooks for freshman English students.

The bibliographic instruction units were distributed through the English instructors rather than directly to the students. In addition to making the units accessible to more students than if the librarians had taught them, this method allowed the instructors to present the material in their own way and avoided the need for a promotional effort. Thus, the librarians were viewed as consultants rather than as competitors, aiding and supplementing the English program rather than offering an independent course on term paper research.

In addition to developing a successful marketing mix for the bibliographic instruction program, the IS librarian mobilized resources within the library and on campus to produce and deliver the program successfully.

The Bibliographic Instruction Program as Part of the Library's Marketing Effort

As part of the total library effort to expand services under the new director, the bibliographic instruction program influenced new products and services, provided publicity, and helped identify new resources for producing services. Some examples of the role of the IS department and its program are given below:

1. New Products and Services
   - Because of his involvement with the university Advisory Committee on Continuing Education, the IS librarian prepared a grant proposal to involve the library in support for university continuing education programs.
   - Staff in the IS department prepared a guide to microfilms in the main library because staff members themselves found the collection difficult to use.
   - When the library director offered study space in the library for the athletic teams, the IS staff gave introductory tours to the players.
   - In collaboration with the university media services department, IS staff prepared video tapes of periodical indexes to be used by the library reference staff.
   - IS staff advised the library director on how to set up a library unit which would disseminate information on university academic services, such as tutoring.
2. Improving Existing Services
   - Under the direction of IS staff, brightly colored directional signs were painted on the walls of the main library.
   - IS staff provided feedback from library users to the circulation department. The English department instructors and students, as well as people who participated in general tours and classroom presentations, told the IS staff that the circulation desk personnel could be more responsive and that books should be shelved more quickly.
   - IS staff also made suggestions to the collection development department regarding purchase and replacement of widely used material. The English instructors and students researching term papers reported the need for duplicate copies.
   - IS staff worked with the reference librarians to develop a list of popular term paper topics so that when students complained to the reference staff about lack of materials on a topic, the librarians could steer them to other topics.
3. Publicity
   - The IS department became heavily involved in general publicity for the library. The "dinosaur" logo (Exhibit 11) developed by IS staff for the instructional units helped to counteract the dull, stodgy image of the library. The theme of "taming the dinosaur" was apt. The library system with its 1.3 million volume

EXHIBIT 11

Dinosaur Logo

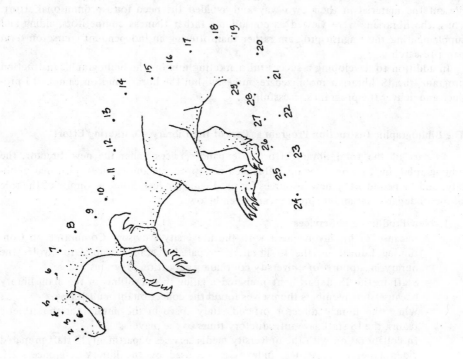

the end

collection, twelve branch libraries, and multiple sets of regulations, was both large and formidable.

— Since the main library, having just undergone a major expansion and renovation, was unusually large and confusing, there was a pressing need for directional signs, guidebooks, floor plans, and favorable publicity. The IS department was extensively involved in providing materials and services designed to tame this monster. Because of its graphics and writing expertise, the IS department was for two years the main provider of newspaper articles on the library and guidebooks for library users. For example the IS staff prepared guidebook material on the library for the information packets given to all new students. Some of this material was published in the student newspaper.

4. New Resources

— Because of its contacts all over campus, the IS department identified and used campus resources not normally available to work on library projects. For example, history department faculty and communications department students both served as writers for the instructional units. The former was free, the latter for nominal wages.

— Technical aspects of the video-taping project mentioned above were carried out free by the university media services department.

— Architecture students were recruited for nominal wages to design and paint directional signs.

— Library science students worked part-time in the IS department performing a range of tasks including typing, paste-up, writing, giving tours, compiling the results of evaluative questionnaires.

THE FUTURE

Based on the criterion of repeat business, the bibliographic instruction program was successful. The freshman English programs were repeated each year, and other disciplines became involved at various levels until in its third year the program reached 8500 students in more than eight departments. Positive comments from both students and instructors on questionnaires at the end of the bibliographic instruction sessions also revealed that the program was well received. One of the English graduate instructors became so involved and enthusiastic about the program that she maintained ties with IS staff even after she graduated and took a permanent position at a college nearby.

By the above criteria, then, the program was a success. However, to determine whether the program had lasting and significant impact on the ability of students to find information, the IS department would have had to do a longitudinal study on the students' college and professional careers. Unfortunately, a study of this sort is beyond the means of most institutions.

After three years, bibliographic instruction is firmly established at Kentucky. As a result, when the C.L.R./N.E.H. grant ended, the library director was determined to carry on the program. In the process of disbanding the IS department, he transferred the bibliographic instruction program to the reference department and the IS librarian became head of the circulation department.

The pace of change in the library has slowed. One wonders whether the lack of personnel whose specific responsibility and talent is in stimulating library-faculty partnerships will cause the program started by the IS department to slide back into the old passive marketing mold. With bibliographic instruction assimilated into the reference department (where librarians have desk duty and are being encouraged to write professional papers), the recruiting, training, and encouragement of an instructional "sales force" will take low priority. However, since the value of bibliographic instruction and other marketing devices have been demonstrated at least in the business sense, both will probably continue in some form.

REFERENCE

1. David P. Kollatt, *et al. Strategic Marketing.* (New York: Holt, Rinehart and Winston, 1972).

Patricia Senn Breivik

Sangamon State University

THE NEGLECTED HORIZON; OR, AN EXPANDED EDUCATION ROLE FOR ACADEMIC LIBRARIES

The potential contribution of academic libraries in meeting the challenges facing higher education today are enumerated with suggested activities for libraries. The problem in libraries' making this contribution is largely attributed to the lack of leadership on the part of library directors and their inability or unwillingness to reallocate from traditional functions to newer ones.

Most of us have known of lost horizons for many years; and, of course, this conference's theme is "New Horizons for Academic Libraries." For the next few minutes, however, I would like to direct our attention to a neglected horizon—a horizon which leads to an expanded educational role for academic libraries.

There are many changes occurring in higher education today. They are ones which colleges and universities find difficult to meet. They are ones for which academic libraries have a definite contribution to make but which, for a number of reasons, they have been neglecting.

What are these changes and the resultant problems? First, there is the problem of the variety in students who come to our campuses today. For a number of years we have known that the range of academic ability among college freshmen varies by 13 years. Many students today are non-readers, but they do come to college with an experience of 50,000 hours of television viewing—an amount significantly higher than the number of hours they have spent in classrooms. More women are returning to college; more people are interested in retooling for second careers.

Patricia Cross, nationally know authority on learner-centered education, sees the decentralization of learning as one of the major trends in higher education today.[1] We are already familiar with both the commuting faculty member and the commuting student, and it is clear that the needs of the commuting student are complicated quite often by the fact that they are older, work full time, and have family responsibilities. There is, in fact, today an almost bewildering spectrum of humanity included under the term "college student."

This spectrum is made even more complex by the variety in learning styles of students. Students learn best at different rates, and they learn best in different ways. Some learn best by listening, some by reading, some by seeing, and some by doing.

This is also much confusion as to what the undergraduate degree should be. A Carnegie Commission report recently "called for an end to 'neglect' of the undergraduate curriculum and urged colleges and universities to develop new, convincing rationales for a general education that would be shared by all students."[2] As part of this general education, there is the need for students to acquire lifelong learning skills. Educators have been saying for a long time that we should not concentrate on the teaching of facts but rather concentrate on the process of learning. This particular need has even been popularized in Alvin Toffler's *Future Shock*.

This need, of course, brings us to the information explosion—a cliche that is, nonetheless, very real. Today's graduates are going to be confronted throughout their personal and professional lives with an increasing and bewildering amount of information from which they must choose and manipulate.

Besides these more recent problems, other needs are of longer standing. There is still a need to train people to actively and effectively participate in a democracy. There is still the search for quality in one's personal life in the midst of a very chaotic world. There is a continued need for people to be able to advance themselves in society. The problems facing higher education today can be summarized as:

(1) the great variety in student abilities and learning needs
(2) the need to strengthen undergraduate education
(3) the need to prepare people for life-long learning
(4) the need to prepare people to participate in a democracy
(5) the need to provide people with an opportunity to improve their lives

What do libraries and librarians have to offer their institutions' answering of the problems and questions which these changes create? Unfortunately, surveys show that not much in the way of change has been happening in academic libraries. Undergraduate libraries have been created. They are getting easy-to-read materials. Collections are continuing to get larger. Libraries are somewhat grudgingly moving to encompass information in all of its formats. Some orientation to library materials is being done.

Of course, we all work feverishly networking, automating and closing down card catalogs, but these changes do not directly address the educational problems confronting higher education today. I suppose that whereas in the past librarians have been known as paper pushers, *now* we'll be known as terminal operators. But don't we really want to be known—quite apart from seeking faculty status—as educators?

Our lack of interest in actually seeking to help provide quality education amidst all these changes might not be so surprising except that as early as 1937 the Association of American Colleges commissioned Harvie Branscomb to investigate how the college library could better be coordinated with a college's educational and recreational programs. The outcome of this study was the publication of *Teaching with Books*,[3] the first major investigation of the library's educational effectiveness and the extent to which the efforts of the library are integrated with those of the institution as a whole. Is it not surprising that our profession has built so little upon this foundation since then?

What can we do? Our institutions talk about preparing people for life-long learning. This goal is probably stated in the catalog of every college and university represented here. Yet, very few places have a plan for achieving this goal or even know where to begin. There is one very clear way to proceed if the library is ready, i.e., to provide learning experiences whereby young people can develop an awareness of the literature of their fields, how to access it, how to evaluate it and how to effectively utilize it.

There are two main reasons for pursuing this goal: the rapid obsolescence on information and the fact, as most studies show, that 50–80% of what is learned in courses is forgotten by students within a year.[4]

We can also help make education more learner centered. Our campuses now have the skills to do cognitive mapping to find out how individual students learn best, and we know that no one single approach to learning can ever be maximally effective for all students. The vast multi-media resources of our collections can be organized to provide multiple approaches to learning. What isn't there can be bought or produced. All this is possible if there is an effective teaming between the librarian, i.e., the resource expert, and the classroom faculty.

Can we do anything for the academically disadvantaged college student? Have we ever questioned, for example, what good it does to have remedial reading and writing programs on our campuses if students are not also learning how to acquire and utilize information which provides them with something worth speaking or writing about?

As an aside, because I think it so important: Some work I did with educationlly disadvantaged students a number of years ago at Brooklyn showed that the gaining of information handling skills positively affected retention.[5] This would have been good news except for another even more interesting conclusion that emerged from that study. In the group that got traditional library instruction, (i.e., the orientation tour, the lecture on the card catalog and the basic indexes, done as we best know how to do it) the students did less well than the students who had no library exposure what-so-ever. Now, that is a bit frightening, because that type of library instruction is what most of our libraries are doing. We must proceed but we must proceed carefully.

Libraries *can* make a difference in the quality of people's living and their job performances because, for effective decision-making, it is crucial to have the skills to locate and evaluate all of the pertinent information before making a decision. As public accountability becomes more and more important in government, information handling skills are going to become even more valuable. It has been predicted that in the future occupational effectiveness for an increasingly greater variety of jobs will depend more and more on the utilization of information and that people trained in the application of information resources to their work will maintain a competitive edge in all types of employment.[6]

One of my librarians got a letter last year from a man who works for the Price Waterhouse in Washington, D.C., and he said,

> I cannot begin to tell you how many times I've followed your teachings to find some buried article or lost statute which later proved to be the key difference between success or failure on a project. Without a doubt, the fact that I can work my way through a library—per your instruction—has been a substantial contribution to my career.

What does it mean to effectively participate in a democracy? Again, libraries have something unique to offer. In an article, by New York State Senator Major Owens, he warns:

> . . . information literacy is needed to guarantee the survival of democratic institutions. All men are created equal but voters with information resources are in a position to make more intelligent decisions than citizens who are information illiterates. The application of information resources to the process of decision-making to fulfill civic responsibilities is a vital necessity.[7]

In truth, libraries have much to contribute to higher eduction today, and librarians are not the only people who think so. In its 1972 report entitled *Reform on Campus*, the Carnegie Commission on Higher Education made the following recommendation:

Libraries are usually looked upon as rather passive centers on the campus, places where books are kept and where students can study. They can, and in some places do, play a more active role. Librarians, in their subject-matter fields, can supervise independent study projects, teach seminars, give courses on research methods. They can be viewed as members of the instructional staff. The library can become the center for use of the new technology, such as computer-based instruction and videocassettes, and for self-instruction. It can also serve as a center for obtaining credit through standard testing mechanisms. To take a more active role, the library will need more than the standard 3 to 4 percent of the budget for "general and instructional" expense—perhaps as large as 6 to 8 percent. In many cases, librarians would also need a more aggressive orientation toward the distribution of information rather than the traditional great attention to the retention of books.[8]

Closer to my home base, in his 1977 annual fall address to the faculty, the Vice President for Academic Affairs at Sangamon State University spoke on academic quality. The following two quotes are taken from that speech:

We know too, that quality in education is neither sterility, nor narrowness, nor parochialism, nor facility, nor superficiality. That's why library skills are important.[9]

When anyone looks for quality at SSU, a most prominent example is the library. *The teaching library concept* works so well here that we take it for granted, but it has become a nationally recognized model, attested to by librarians from around the country who met here last June. As programs increasingly stress library skills requirements, we have the teaching faculty in the library to provide training in those skills. We must all realize what we have and use it to best advantage.[10]

Now I don't mean to imply from my title, "The Neglected Horizon," that no one in academic libraries is actively pursuing and supporting an expanded educational role for libraries. Indeed, the whole library instruction movement which has surfaced in ALA and state library organizations, is a grass roots effort of largely reference librarians directed at one aspect of this horizon, and ALA now has standing committees on bibliographic instruction. Yet, all of these activities are almost exclusively run by and participated in by public service librarians.

To date there has been little support from library administrators or from library schools. Library instruction is really not quite respectable enough for library schools yet. So, we are not training people for expanded educational roles. They are learning on the job, and they are learning in spite of the fear involved in venturing into new areas. Fear not only because of lack of training but because they are already overworked and their libraries are already under-budgeted. So how can they take on new kinds of service roles? And where library directors aren't particularly supportive, then what rewards are there? Moreover, the educational challenges being suggested in this paper obviously go beyond library instruction as commonly defined.

Why aren't the great majority of library directors aggressively seeking an expanded role for their libraries? The answer is obvious: tight budgets and an amazing number of matters demand their attention. Surely, no one other than the president of the institution has to grapple with such a variety of concerns of both an academic and business nature than the librarian.

An Illinois colleague of mine, Beverly Lynch, pointed out in a recent issue of *College & Research Libraries:*

> Few colleges or universities and few libraries within them define their goals and objectives with any precision, despite the direction given by those who say that without carefully defined goals and objectives an institution cannot evaluate its performance, allocate its resources wisely, plan for the future, motivate its members, or justify its existence.[11]

The lack of such objective setting, I believe, makes it almost impossible in a time of limited financial support to move into major new service patterns. Unless an expanded educational role is a clearly stated priority of the library, it is unlikely that considerable funds will be reallocated to undergird the effort or that much can be accomplished. There are too many library instruction programs that will only start if new, i.e., usually soft, monies are availalbe.

If we were really convicted that libraries could and should be actively involved in the teaching/learning process, a major part of the responsibility would rest with us to reallocate internally and start doing the kinds of research, the kinds of projects that can demonstrate on our campuses what libraries have to contribute to the challenges facing higher education today. Library directors and department heads must let their staffs know that they are supportive of library-based instruction.

Perhaps the single most effective way to support an expanded educational role for the library and the single activity which holds the most promise for insuring the success of the instructional program is to give staff time and encouragement to do serious planning. This is particularly difficult when staffs are already overworked. The sitting still long enough to think and plan for a new endeavor can be excruciatingly difficult if the cataloging backlog is building up by the second. But planning by the staff is as necessary as is the commitment on the part of the library director to the realization of an educational role.

We understand this in other curriculum areas. No one would start a college-level program in paralegal education, for example, by saying, "Well, let's have a tour of a law firm for the students; then we could give a lecture on such and such and sort of ad lib as we go along. No need for evaluation." Who would support an academic program like that or give credit for it? Our library instructional programs are largely hit or miss because we don't block the time to sit down and do serious curriculum planning.

We have got to look at the goals of our individual institutions (they do vary), look at our clientele groups and their needs (they vary) before starting to plan how most effectively to meet those needs. Then we must begin setting instructional priorities and honoring them, making sure, if we say that for this year we are going to accomplish a certain project in our instructional program, that nothing is allowed to interfere.

Assuming a fairly static budget situation, such priority setting will require a careful rethinking of staff utilization patterns and a reallocation of some amount of professional staff time from administrative to instructional activities. Some figures from a study of the utilization of professional staff time at the SSU Library for the 1976/77 academic year will illustrate this point. It showed that the minimum average direct contact hours for the eight librarians was 23.25 hours per week. This included reference work, instructional workshops and student advising. An additional average 7.75 hours were spent on curriculum and governance committees throughout the campus and in professional development activities. In addition to this resource, guides were developed and one librarian team-taught a demography course. It might also be interesting to you to know that during this period, the librarians gave one hundred workshops involving 2,708 contact hours and 1,680 people. Obviously, to make this possible, nonprofessional staff have administrative responsibilities beyond the norm.

Since I am director of an academic library known to be innovative and committed to library instruction, you have every right to expect me to be prejudiced in my viewpoint. Therefore, let me quote from some comments made by Warren J. Haas, who until he assumed directorship of the Council on Library Resources late in 1977, was Vice President for Information Services and University Librarians at Columbia University.

> It is obvious that library services must actively contribute to the substance of the academic program. By their very nature, libraries cost far too much to be permitted a passive role, and good librarians have too much to offer both students and faculty to permit them a life of splendid isolation. For libraries and librarians alike, the real risk is in setting sights too low rather than too high and expecting too little rather than too much.[12]

To avoid this risk, library directors must actively support expanding the educational role of their libraries through providing moral support and planning opportunities, and internally allocating resources to support the instructional program. Finally, library directors must be effective advocates for an expanded educational role for libraries and they must gain supporters among key administrators on campus to ensure the success of the program and perhaps eventually gain additional funding for the instructional program as it grows. Without this level of participation on the part of library directors, there is little hope for academic libraries' assuming their proper educational role in meeting the needs of higher education either today or tomorrow. Without this level of commitment on the part of library directors, the educational potential of academic libraries will remain a neglected horizon.

If I may paraphrase from G. K. Chesterton, who said "The Christian ideal . . . has not been tried and found wanting; it has been found difficult and left untried," academic libraries have not be tried and found wanting, expanding their educational role has been found difficult and left untried.

REFERENCES

1. K. Patricia Cross, "The Fourth R: Resources," speech given at the annual fall meeting of the Illinois Library Association, Springfield, Illinois, October 26, 1977, p. 8.
2. Malcolm G. Scully, "General Education: 'A Disaster Area,'" *Chronicle of Higher Education* 15 (December 19, 1977): 7.
3. Harvie Branscomb, *Teaching With Books* (Chicago Association of American Colleges and American Library Association, 1940).
4. Howard R. Bowne, *The Chronicle of Higher Education* 15 (November 14, 1977): 13.
5. Patricia Senn Breivik, *Open Admissions and the Academic Library* (Chicago: ALA, 1977).
6. Major Owens, "State Government and Libraries," *Library Journal* 101 (January 1, 1976): 27.
7. Owens, *op. cit.*, p. 27.
8. The Carnegie Commission on Higher Education, *Reform on Campus: Changing Students, Changing Academic Programs* (New York: McGraw-Hill, 1972), p. 50.

9. John H. Keiser, "Academic Quality at SSU," seventh annual welcoming address, Sangamon State University, Springfield, Illinois, 1977, p. 2.
10. *Ibid.*, p. 7.
11. Beverly P. Lynch, "The Changing Environment of Academic Libraries," *College & Research Libraries* 39 (January, 1978): 13.
12. Warren J. Haas, "Library Dedication Keynote Address," unpublished speech given at dedication of Ramapo College, Ramapo, New Jersey, November 17, 1977, p. 3-7.

Michael John Haeuser

Linfield College

CURRICULUM REFORM: A ROLE FOR LIBRARIANS

There is a growing consensus among educators that the open curriculum of the last decade has led to fragmented curriculum today. A re-emphasis on general education—those concepts and values we commonly share—appears to be in the ascendant. Academic librarians were beneficiaries of the open curriculum but should not fear its demise for they are well qualified—by tradition and training—to represent general education. College librarians must assert these affinities to be included in those groups that refashion curricula. Thus they can ensure that curriculum reform includes an increased emphasis on library services.

The curriculum of a liberal arts college proclaims its uniqueness. It is the area where concerns about educational philosophy and pedagogical techniques are frequently resolved. And, since the curriculum reflects current as well as traditional educational ideas, it is subject to change.

College librarians must not only be aware of curricular changes, they must anticipate them with a view of influencing the outcome. We must now recognize that significant curricular reform is underway and that it presents a new opportunity for librarians to contribute to undergraduate education. I am speaking, of course, of the reawakened interest in general education, that part of the curriculum that ensures, through institution-wide requirements, that all students obtain some knowledge of the ideas and culture of their common heritage.

Some of us might view the rekindled interest in general education as a threat to gains made by librarians during the last decade of experimentation with open curricula. Individualized instruction, independent study, the discarded textbook, the harried professor casting about for help on topics his or her students wished to research all combined to increase the need for more involvement of librarians in the teaching-learning process. The open curriculum brought demands for new materials and new forms of materials, and the budgets of the period produced the wherewithal to acquire those aids. The open curriculum gave impetus to the development of the library-college concept where the librarian became the teacher. It also encouraged the establishment and growth of programs of bibliographic instruction in our colleges and universities including, for example, the library-integrated innovations developed by Pat Breivik and her colleagues at

236

Sangamon State University. And, finally, the open curriculum lent legitimacy to our claims that we should be considered faculty because we shared many of the responsibilities of classroom teachers. Indeed, as academic librarians we owe much to the educational philosophies and teaching techniques that have been in fashion for over a decade.

Today, the efficacy of the open curriculum is being questioned and alterations are sure to follow. In an article entitled "The Changing Environment of Academic Libraries" which appeared in the January 1978 issue of *College & Research Libraries*, Beverly Lynch warned academic Librarians to be ready for change.[1] This conference is exploring the future of academic libraries and the changes we will make to deal with new situations. What can the college librarians do to ensure that present and future curricular changes enhance, not diminish, the role we play in the educational enterprise?

We can begin by recognizing that general education is increasingly back in vogue at liberal-arts colleges and the arts and sciences colleges of public universities.[2] Last year, for example, institutions as disparate as Harvard, Marist College, Stanford, Amherst, Middlebury, Berkeley and the State University of New York concluded that its undergraduate curriculum had lost a sense of essential unity that had prevailed when phrases like "foundation courses," "a core curriculum" and "distribution requirements" defined a generous amount of a college's offerings.

Last winter, in an important book, *Missions of the College Curriculum*, the Carnegie Foundation for the Advancement of Teaching concluded that it is necessary to further strengthen, indeed broaden, the general education component of the nation's undergraduate institutions.[3] They noted that ". . . fortunately, we are better able now than we have been for many years to offer effective general education programs."[4] Other leading educators, among the most recent Ernst Boyer and Martin Kaplan in a book they called *Educating for Survival*, point out it is time we refashion our core curriculums to present the commonality of our experiences as well as the "common" freedom of self-determination.[5]

Academic librarians should sieze the opportunity to help return general education to the center of the curriculum, not only because it belongs there, but also because we are uniquely qualified—by tradition and training—to represent general education.

Consider, for a moment, the history of academic librarianship. Early librarians were often liberally educated members of the faculty.[6] The importance of general education to professional librarians was confirmed by the Columbia University Trustees in 1911 when they granted academic rank to their library staff. The statement issued at the time emphasized the need for librarians to possess an adequate general education.[7] That has not changed. Most librarians recognize the best undergraduate preparation for librarianship is a solid grounding in the liberal arts. In an environment of sometimes mindless specialization, a librarian is frequently the engaging generalist that appears knowledgeable on a wide-ranging number of topics. Our professional experience, our exposure to many disciplines and problems, and the disparate needs of our academic constituency demands broad general knowledge and the on-going ability to learn as the varied disciplines themselves develop. The generalist librarian may, indeed, be unique in the specialized academic environment. Some years ago, the director of the Columbia University office of Placement and Career Planning wrote:

> General education is the most formidable unsolved problem hanging over our colleges and universities. He who does most to accomplish the academic, social and spiritual broadening, now being thwarted by specialists, will become the student's best friend. The librarian may be the one—for in training, in role, and often in temperament he is the only pure generalist left in academia.[8]

Even those of us who specialize in a particular service or discipline must be able to comfortably deal with others' specialities. This is second nature to us, it is in our blood. Indeed, the same critic adds:

> Today a good librarian is the only type of professional with the encyclopedic scope of a Franklin or a Jefferson—just the person to start rebuilding the curriculum.[9]

During the years of the open curriculum, however, librarians did not do much curriculum-building. George Whitbeck found, in a 1972 study entitled *The Influence of Librarians in Liberal Arts Colleges in Selected Decision Making Areas,* that librarians have only a minimal role in the committee structure of the college. Although many librarians were on a committee (the library committee) only one of thirty-one surveyed was on the curriculum committee.[10] It should be mentioned, parenthetically, that Whitbeck also found that librarians appear to have a very minimal role in the mainstream of events at most colleges he surveyed.[11]

We are in a good position to change both observations. I would like to describe briefly, curriculum revision at one college and the very substantial role the academic librarians played and are playing. In early 1977 Linfield College, a small private liberal arts school in Oregon's Willamette Valley, began an evaluation of its core curriculum. Linfield had undergone significant curricular reform some nine years earlier. The faculty had recognized the necessity to reconcile the students' needs for some choice (and the faculty members' need for some autonomy) with the need for a common core of knowledge that all Linfield students would share in. A broadly liberal core curriculum was fashioned with this in mind.

Sixteen paired courses were offered with each student required to choose eight. The humanities were emphasized but there were two social science options and students had a choice between Environmental Science/Biology or Environmental Science/Geology. Totaled, the core courses were to be fully one-third of classes taken by Linfield students— a very respectable general education program. Moreover, the courses were to be interdisciplinary and, in most cases, team-taught. Thus, for example, The Arts and Modern Man, a course designed to explore the development of and relationship between the arts and music, was to be staffed by a music professor and a colleague in the art department.

The library, which at Linfield includes the media center, looked forward to the change. To enable wide-spread individualized instruction to take place in the cores, an extensive effort to build up the non-print holdings was undertaken. The interdisciplinary nature of the courses required faculty-librarian cooperative efforts in fashioning the collection to meet the demands of the new curriculum. Finally, the structure of most courses offered a certain amount of room for independent study, an excellent area for student-librarian collaboration.

Over the course of nine years, however, the program had been weakened. It was leaderless. No provision for administrative direction had been developed. Key departments, history for example, had abdicated their responsibility for servicing the core. Personality conflicts had reduced some of the team-taught interdisciplinary general education cores to two separate courses. The textbook-lecture method again became the common form of instruction. A major re-appraisal was overdue.

The Dean of Academic Affairs and the Curriculum Committee chose the college librarian to head the Core Evaluation Committee. The balance of the group was composed of respected representatives of the college's four academic divisions and student leaders. The committee was charged with examining the philosophy of the core to determine if it was still valid, looking at the individual core courses to determine the current state of the core, and making recommendations designed to improve liberal arts education at Linfield. Six months later the group issued a report complete with specific recommendations to the Curriculum Committee. The faculty has subsequently accepted the whole report and the recommendations are being implemented.

Included in the suggestions was the need for a strong General Education Committee consisting of a part-time administrator, the librarian or his representative, and the division heads. Further recommendations were made that will result in strengthening the library's position in the curriculum. For example, the document called for increasing the use of instructional resources of all media. It recommended that a separate budget item for adequate library materials to support the core courses be established. The report emphasized the need to re-vamp the written communications portion of the core to include increased development of skills—including the formalized acquisition of library skills. And, finally, the document urged that the exercise of these skills become a key requirement throughout the curriculum. In sum, the reforms have enabled the library to become a fundamental element in the re-vitalization of liberal education at Linfield College.

The re-emphasis of general education at liberal arts colleges faces certain dangers. Chief among them, according to Trinity College President Theodore Lockwood, is a return to rigid requirements without analyzing why required courses collapsed in the first place.[12] Before we end up producing just another "eclectic muddle"[13] of requirements, it is best that each institution examine the objectives of its undergraduate program to discover and clarify basic convictions about the broader purposes of liberal education.

Academic librarians should take a leading role in this process. If those observers of academia are correct, there will be an increasing tendency for colleges to establish forums or committees in which institutional goals will be defined and ways to strengthen general education will be discussed. We librarians are, as I have suggested, uniquely equipped to represent general education in those discussions.

We should make ourselves aware of any future curricular change. Then we must approach and convince the president, the academic dean, or whoever we report to, that our inclusion on or leadership of a committee or task force will serve the interests of the college. There are several arguments we can use. (1) The academic librarian is a generalist with a broad, even interdisciplinary, approach to education. The staff of an academic library, although composed of generalists, boasts a cross section of major academic divisions or departments all of whose expertise can be drawn upon. (2) A librarian serves all areas of the curriculum so we have an awareness of the strengths and weaknesses of the college's academic program. At the same time, we are not limited by our discipline or profession to a single point of view. In other words, we have less of a personal vested interest in minor, or even major, curricular reforms. And because we represent no specific area (3) we can put ourselves forward as a non-political resource—something very important in the highly-politicized process of major curricular revision. (4) Equally important, we can apprise our colleagues of library resources at their disposal, of how much funding it will require to implement a program.

Once we have achieved representation on a group studying the curriculum, the librarian must begin to involve the library in any change. The development of library skills, for example, are closely related to the acquisition of writing and research skills. Course-related programs of bibliographic instruction are easier to bring about in the context of curricular change than in a static situation. Most importantly, the integration of libraries into the curriculum is less difficult to realize when the librarian is seen as being a part of curriculum development.

This, then, is our opportunity. It is a chance to identify a trend, to recognize the historical affinities our profession has with the concept of general education, and to involve ourselves in its rejuvenation. This will assure us and our libraries a chief role in the most important area of a college's operation—its curriculum.

REFERENCES

1. Beverly P. Lynch, "The Changing Environment of Academic Libraries," *College & Research Libraries* 39 (January 1978): 10–14.
2. "Many Colleges Re-Appraising Their Undergraduate Curricula," *The Chronicle of Higher Education* 13 (February 7, 1977): 1.
3. Carnegie Foundation for the Advancement of Teaching, *Missions of the College Curriculum: A Contemporary Review with Suggestions* (San Francisco: Josey-Bass, 1977), p. 264.
4. *Ibid.*, p. 166.
5. Ernest L. Boyer and Martin Kaplan, *Education for Survival* (New Rochelle, NY: Change Magazine Press, 1977). See also Sidney Hook, et. al. *The Philosophy of the Curriculum: The Need for General Education* (Buffalo, NY: Prometheus Books, 1975).
6. Robert B. Downs, "The Role of the Academic Librarian, 1876-1976," *College & Research Libraries* 37 (November 1976): 491–501.
7. Kenneth J. Brough, *Scholar's Workshop, Evolving Conceptions of Library Service* (Urbana: University of Illinois Press, 1953) p. 163.
8. Richard M. Gummere, "Toward a New Breed of Librarians," *Wilson Library Bulletin* 41 (April 1967): 812.
9. *Ibid.*
10. George W. Whitbeck, *The Influence of Librarians in Liberal Arts Colleges in Selected Decision Making Areas* (Metuchen, NJ: Scarecrow Press, 1972) p. 25, 34.
11. *Ibid.*, p. 122.
12. Theodore D. Lockwood, "The Rush Back to General Education," *The Chronicle of Higher Education* 14 (May 23, 1977): 32.
13. *Ibid.*

Edward R. Johnson and Richard D. Hershcopf

Pennsylvania State University and Colorado State University

THE UNDERGRADUATE LIBRARY AND THE SUBJECT-DIVISIONAL PLAN: PROBLEMS AND PROSPECTS

The concepts of undergraduate library service and the subject-divisional plan, both important movements in academic librarianship, are defined and their purposes, growth and development, and historical parallel are discussed. The present status of these concepts is presented, and it is asked whether or not they are appropriate models for quality library service given the problems of declining resources and shifting goals and academic directions. It is concluded that the prospects for the undergraduate library indicate decline but instruction programs may fill the gap, while there is a continuing need for subject-oriented collections and services in academic libraries.

INTRODUCTION

At a recent meeting of the administrators of several university libraries, the topic of library service to undergraduate students was the main theme. The head of a well-known undergraduate library began his remarks to this group by stating that "most university libraries overlook the needs of the undergraduate." The significance of this statement lies not in the content of the remarks, but in the fact that university librarians have been saying this for decades (although the speaker in question seemed to think his was a new and startling concept). Two fairly recent articles on undergraduate library instruction, for example, have addressed the perennial theme of undergraduate needs. "Students," we are told, "don't know how to use libraries."[1] We also read that "a need exists for undergraduates to learn independent study skills to cope with the expansion of information that faces them now and will continue to occur during their lifetimes..."[2] Nearly identical statements addressing the same themes in the same way can be found in the library literature of the 1940's and 1950's. This paper will examine past efforts to deal with these problems, considering the question of what an undergraduate library is, historical parallels between the undergraduate library and the subject-divisional plan, the present status of undergraduate libraries and subject-divisional plan libraries, and the future prospects of the undergraduate library and the subject-divisional concept as key elements of university library systems.

WHAT IS THE UNDERGRADUATE LIBRARY?

A. *Definition*

A discussion of the undergraduate library should begin by dispelling the widely-held notion that this is a new concept in library service. Billy R. Wilkinson in a 1971 article in *Library Journal* laid this myth to rest although the word still seems not to have gotten around.[3] There is an extensive literature on the subject of the undergraduate library and most discussions of definition of purpose refer to Irene A. Braden's excellent study in which she identified six ways in which this kind of library is different from the "traditional" university library. They include open access to the collection; centralized and simplified service to undergraduate students; carefully selected books "all undergraduates should be exposed to for their liberal education"; the concept of the library as an instructional tool; services in addition to those of the research collection; and a building with the undergraduates' needs uppermost.[4] Even Braden's definition, however, does not definitively explain the purposes of the undergraduate library. Librarians and laypersons alike could all point to libraries that meet most or all of the criteria listed above and yet do not call themselves "undergraduate" libraries.

In fact, there is no single definition of the undergraduate library that effectively explains its purpose. John Haak in a 1971 article in *Library Journal* noted that "the objective of providing additional services to those offered by the research library has often meant that undergraduate libraries have become a refuge for a mish-mash of special music, poetry, and art collections, most of which have only very tenuous roots in the undergraduate curriculum. And no undergraduate library has yet been allocated the staff and other resources necessary 'to make the library an instructional tool by planning it as a center for instruction in library use.'"[5] Haak, instead, believed that the "unique" function of undergraduate libraries should be defined in terms of two "basic capabilities":

1. The self-service potential—whereby the faculty member or student is encouraged to use the available physical facilities, including: a.) the library environment, b.) the book and periodical collection (usually duplicative of the "main" collection), c.) the reserve book, browsing, and special collections, d) the self-instructional devices, e.) the finding devices, f.) exhibits, g.) special facilities for the physically handicapped.

2. The active-service concept—which is based on the view of the librarian as teacher rather than technician, offering these services: a.) teaching undergraduates, formally and informally, b.) stimulating reading, c.) providing reference and reader advisory services, d.) serving the faculty in an advisory capacity, e.) working with the faculty to evaluate and improve teaching programs.[6]

B. *The Growth of the Undergraduate Library Concept*

The growth and development of the undergraduate library idea in the United States has been thoroughly examined and well-documented by other writers. This paper will not attempt to re-trace this history but will briefly summarize it in order to set the stage for later discussion. In 1949 Harvard University opened its Lamont Library as the first library in the United States dedicated solely to undergraduate library service. The effect of this event on the academic library world was dramatic. "Almost overnight," Wilkinson wrote, "Lamont became a beautiful legend. It was idealized. Many of us made pilgrimages to the shrine."[7] Although nine years were to elapse until other libraries began to follow Harvard's example, starting in the late 1950's and continuing for about a decade, some 24 to 30 universities (depending upon which author you want to follow) have adopted new and separate undergraduate libraries or extensively renovated existing buildings.

The University of Michigan's Undergraduate Library was the first in Harvard's footsteps and opened its doors in 1958. Others followed in rapid succession at the universities of South Carolina, Texas, North Carolina, Stanford, Ohio State, Pennsylvania State, Illinois, Tennessee, Cornell, UCLA, Washington, Wisconsin, Maryland, Berkeley, and Oklahoma. Other libraries endorsed the concept by setting aside collections or rooms, such as a "college library," for the use of undergraduates. By the end of the decade of the 1960's Warren B. Kuhn came to the conclusion that:

> . . . the undergraduate library would seem to be providing a number of effective answers for today's large universities. Removed from the immediate overwhelming shadow cast by the central research collection, spacious, attractive and offering as much individual privacy as possible under heavy enrollments, it represents not so much a lowering of limits as a more effective means of transition from the high school to the college library and ultimately to broader levels of learning.[8]

C. *The "Special Needs" of Undergraduates*

It has become almost an article of faith in academic librarianship that the undergraduate student has some special needs and that means must be devised by which to meet these needs. It is fascinating to trace the origins of this notion that has been propounded and debated by librarians for so many years. The problem of the unfilled needs of the unsophisticated student has been, and shows every sign of continuing to be, one of the major themes in the literature of librarianship. Down through the years, for example, librarians have been talking about ways to remove the "barriers" between students and books and organizing libraries so that students learned, almost in spite of themselves. Ralph Ellsworth addressed this issue in 1941, advocating a special reading room for undergraduates.[9] In 1959, Frank Lundy wrote that "it is probably no service to the typical undergraduate student to ask him to make himself at home among a million or more volumes in one continuous arrangement. In such a quantity of material there is so much that is purely of research interest, in contrast to the needs of undergraduate education."[10] Mary E. Anders, writing in 1961, discussed the need ". . . to bring undergraduate students into direct contact with a large number of books without exposing them to a possible frustrating experience of attempting to select their titles from the mass of materials available in the stacks. . . ."[11]

Discussion of the purpose and definition of the undergraduate library continues today. In the early 1970's Jerrold Orne[12] and Billy R. Wilkinson,[13] in separate articles, assessed the success of undergraduate libraries and it is interesting to compare their conclusions by way of illustrating the continuing differences of opinion concerning the role of the undergraduate library:

1. Environment—Orne concluded that one of the major successes of the undergraduate library was in maintaining the atmosphere of a "haven" for study and thought. It was his opinion that "it is not just a study hall; it is not a modified student union; it is not a snack bar; it is the library, a place to absorb, reflect, and grow." Orne admitted that the undergraduate library is primarily a study hall and Wilkinson agreed. "All undergraduate libraries," he wrote, "have been a screaming success as study halls." But, Wilkinson also noted that they have been "highly successful" (perhaps most successful) "as social centers."

2. Collections—Wilkinson cited the value of browsing collections but disagreed that the collections in general have been successful, or as Orne put it, that their success has been "assured." Wilkinson pointed to the heavy emphasis on the use of reserve services in undergraduate libraries and the fact that ". . . librarians are still gently receiving long, out-of-date lists from lazy, unconcerned faculty, and laboriously processing the volumes

to hide them away so that no one uses them. That submissive attitude perpetuates stagnant service." Wilkinson also criticized what he viewed as poor audio and visual services in undergraduate libraries.

3. User Assistance—Orne called this factor "guidance" and suggested that its use be applied in "subtle, unobtrusive ways." Wilkinson focused primarily on the reference aspect and, on the basis of his doctoral research, concluded that the record of performance was quite poor and "the job of undergraduate libraries has been only half done in the first 20 years."

THE PARALLEL BETWEEN THE SUBJECT-DIVISIONAL PLAN AND THE UNDERGRADUATE LIBRARY

A. *What Is the Subject-Divisional Concept?*

The traditional subject-divisional plan, first instituted in the early 1940's on a few campuses, implies the arranging of most library materials in a central building according to the broad subject content of those materials, and in association with other collections of a like subject nature, irrespective of format, i.e., books, periodicals, microforms, etc. Thus, in the conventional subject division library periodicals are cataloged and classified just as the monographs are, and they are interfiled on the same shelves with the latter. Core groups of the various types of items dealing with a broad subject field, such as the humanities, the social sciences, and the physical and life sciences, are separated from the rest of the collection and placed on shelves in large reading rooms. This is done after careful selection for their importance and usefulness by professionally trained subject specialist librarians.

> Factors such as available space, size of the library's collection, and the academic program determine the number of volumes shelved in these reading rooms. . . . Thus, the collection housed in the rooms must provide the best choice of those books likely to be of value in terms of undergraduate usage.[14]

Provision is made also for access to related lesser-used, more scholarly or esoteric titles in the bookstack area. Reference service in each of the subject divisions is given by trained staff to all patrons including undergraduate students. Moreover, all subject divisional libraries created the position and delineated the role of the subject specialists. These librarians, in addition to having the professional degree, also possess formal undergraduate or graduate training in a specific sphere of knowledge. They are experts in the bibliographical literature of these fields; they are expected to engage in collection development activities jointly with the faculty, and to furnish interpretations of the collections, especially to faculty and graduate students. However, in those libraries where a general reference department with its own cadre does not exist, the subject librarians are obligated to deal with the reference queries of undergraduates as well. Many of them also provide instruction to patrons in the effective use of the library.

B. *The Subject-Divisional Plan and the Undergraduate Student.*

Frank Lundy, former director of the University of Nebraska Libraries, and a strong proponent of the subject-divisional concept, believed that a separate undergraduate library either in the central building (as a "collge library" within the main research library) or in a completely separate facility, was in many ways an excellent solution to the problem of coping with and meeting the special informational needs of undergraduates. However, he pointed out that it was an expensive solution in terms of staff, physical plant, and collections, and that probably only the largest institutions could ever afford an additional building for this purpose. (Even to this day, Michigan State University's undergraduate library is housed within the main library.) Lundy wrote that:

> A majority of us must be content with one central library building to serve as well as it can all students at all levels of instruction, and all the faculty as well. When it is properly designed and managed, there is a great deal to be said in favor of the unified central library building. It is not always easy, actually, to draw such a clear line in the book collection between undergraduate and graduate materials as might seem to be implied in separate buildings, nor do all graduate students and faculty confine their reading at all times to what might be regarded as research materials.[15]

C. *Similarities of Concepts*

The divisional concept of library materials grouped by subjects in open-shelf reading rooms or in continuous open book stack areas, with specially trained staff stationed at logically appropriate points to assist patrons, is very similar to the separate undergraduate library idea wherein a core of highly selected titles is made available in an open shelf arrangement in an area of the central building or in a separate facility designated for that purpose. In the latter scheme also, a specially trained staff stands by ready to provide a variety of library services, including instruction in the effective use of the library, to undergraduates primarily but not necessarily exclusively. A principal difference might be that in the first instance all or most materials, regardless of form, are grouped by broad subject definitions while in the latter case there may be no such requirements at all, except for the boundaries prescribed by the classification system. However, in each plan there are several variations practiced in this respect, so the difference is often not as great as it might appear to be at first.

Thus, some libraries, usually the very large ones, in attempting to improve their services and the accessibility of desired materials to the exploding population of undergraduate students they found on their campuses in the 1950's and 1960's, developed and built undergraduate libraries. Fortunately, at the time they could afford it. This was the path taken by Harvard, Michigan, UCLA, Wisconsin, North Carolina, Berkeley, Cornell, and a host of others. The medium to large academic institutions: Colorado, Nebraska, Oklahoma, Oregon, Georgia, Utah and many others, with more limited financial resources and smaller undergraduate enrollments, attempted to meet the challenge through implementing a subject-divisional plan in a central building. It is interesting to note that while some libraries, such as Michigan State, abandoned subject divisions for the most part when their undergraduate library was established, others, such as North Carolina and British Columbia, continued the subject-division scheme in the main library after their separate undergraduate facilities came into being. Lundy's remarks in 1959 were prophetic:

> If I were to build such a building now, I can assure you that I would plan my divisional library for the undergraduates on two floors, distributing the undergraduate library according to local needs into divisional subject areas, and I would shelve the research collections on the floors above and below, or better perhaps out in the wings to the east and west, where they could grow into their millions of volumes as the years go by.[16]

PRESENT STATUSES—PORTENTS FOR THE FUTURE?

A. *The Subject-Divisional Plan Today*

Today, problems of growth, of increasingly restricted budgets in the face of a never-ending inflationary spiral, of a brake on the expansion of staffs and facilities, and of "campus politics", including tension and conflict between the teaching faculty and the administrators of the libraries, have led to skepticism among some library officials that the subject-divisional arrangement is an advisable or feasible one for the times.

> The subject divisional arrangement may be the ideal one for certain institutions at a particular period in their growth and development. Many of the smaller institutions may not be able financially to take advantage of the principles involved which produce the greatest benefits. Others, when they outgrow present buildings may be faced with the alternative of a separate undergraduate library, a separate Science library, or new departmental libraries.[17]

Sometimes this belief is shared by most members of their staffs, while in a number of institutions the staff is seriously divided on the current merits of the plan. Yet, at other libraries it appears that unanimity or near unanimity prevails regarding the retention of the essential features of the divisional plan, albeit the recognized necessity for certain modifications. A popular trend, even at the latter institutions, is the elimination of the arranging and display of periodicals, both current and retrospective, in the subject areas. Instead, they are consolidated either in a current periodicals room and/or stack area completely separate from the monographic literature. Under a strict definition of the subject division concept it is impossible to justify a current peridicals center. But practically, assignment of current periodicals to a central location offers the best patron-understood and accessible service pattern.

Differences of opinion on the issue of abandoning or retaining the subject-division scheme seem to revolve around the two key concepts of centralization vs. decentralization, and the changing character of information and knowledge. In this context, centralization often means the elimination of separate subject reference service areas and the consolidation of subject collections, staff, and space into one central location. Such a move is frequently favored by library administrators as an economy and space saving measure.

It is important to know the reasons given by supporters of the subject-division arrangement for their advocacy of its retention today and its continuation tomorrow. Some of these are: 1.) Subject-divisions foster and strengthen the crucial symbiotic relationship between user, materials, and specially trained staff, which results in better, more personalized service tailored to the individual patron's informational needs. 2.) The growing complexity of reference tools, abstracts, and indexes especially in the sciences, requires specialists in a special rather than a general setting. 3.) In a university research library a consolidated reference collection would be extremely large, unwieldy, and very confusing for the patron to use. 4.) Computer-assisted reference service and the development of search strategies require the talents of subject librarians. 5.) Subject-division organization allows for better instruction in the use of a large and complex library, and it also makes for more effective orientation and bibliographic training activities. 6.) Centralization of subject personnel in a general reference department would physically separate them from a large part of their collections and thus inhibit collection development activities. 7.) In the more traditional organization the subject specialists would soon lose their "expertise" and be "reduced" to generalists.

B. *The Undergraduate Library—Some Reconsiderations*

The undergraduate library became particularly popular in academic circles in the 1960's, in fact it was a veritable "rage" we are told, and its supposed benefits and virtues were widely extolled. The parallel with the subject-divisional plan is quite interesting and, like the divisional plan, even at the height of its popularity librarians began expressing some concerns and reservations about the undergraduate library concept. As John Haak worte in 1971, "for many undergraduate libraries the honeymoon period is now ending."[18] Another writer, Redmond A. Burke, called for the study of a fundamental question:

> It appears that the trend is toward a pattern of a separate college library operating within the framework of a university library system. . . The implied assumption is that the best situation for undergraduates is a separately housed undergraduate library. To what extent this is a valid assumption needs examination.[19]

Recently, at a conference on current problems in library organization, William J. Studer asked several questions that other university library administrators will be asking themselves as we approach the end of the austere seventies and prepare for the uncertainties of the eighties. "The twenty-six or so undergraduate libraries in the United States," he stated (in his yet to be published paper):

> . . . were almost all spawned during the affluent and expansionist late 1950's and 1960's. They are by definition virtually duplicate collections. Can we afford to maintain them as such? We need seating space, to be sure, but does that need justify maintenance of the status quo? I doubt that we shall see any more undergraduate libraries brought into being, and the premise of existing ones should be reexamined carefully.[20]

Whether Studer is right about no more undergraduate libraries remains to be seen but several university libraries have dropped their undergraduate libraries, some "separate" and some "in-house." For a survey of these changes, see Henry Wingate's recent article in *College and Research Libraries*.[21] The Pennsylvania State University's experience with the undergraduate library concept (which included both a separate library and an in-house collection) may not be typical, but it illustrates some of the problems facing nearly all institutions today that will undoubtedly have an effect on the future of undergraduate libraries. As a result of an extensive self-review conducted in 1974/75 as part of Penn State's Management Review and Analysis Program (MRAP), its undergraduate library was essentially eliminated in 1977 after ten or twelve years of existence. The reasons are rather complex but in summary they include:

1. Static or declining budgets in higher education. The days of growth are over for most academic libraries and, unfortunately, many institutions of higher learning are now planning for program cutbacks or elimination since they can no longer keep pace with inflationary pressures. Librarians all know the effect of inflation on monographs, and, especially, on periodicals and serials. The implications of this trend on undergraduate collections, which, in general, are essentially duplicative is clear. As the Pennsylvania State University tightened its belt, it was concluded that the library could no longer justify economically the continued duplication of monographs, serials, physical facilities, or staff.

2. Goals. Haak, commenting on the failure of "pious statements of purpose," concluded that "perhaps it is this failure to develop tangible goals which has contributed to the skepticism which a number of undergraduate librarians feel toward the intangible goals so often used to justify undergraduate libraries."[22] During the 1980's universities will be devising more sophisticated and demanding measures in order to force their units to justify their continued existence. Library administrators will probably need to explain the goals of the undergraduate library and its relationship to the other libraries on campus. The purpose of the collections, for instance, will need to be clarified and definitions of what librarians mean by less specialized or general versus advanced or research levels of collection development.[23] Service to users, especially reference service, will need to be analyzed carefully and program quality determined. The enrollment patterns envisaged at Penn State, for example, did not develop as projected in the mid-1960's. The university's graduate student population is rather small, somewhere around ten percent. So, in fact, the unversity is predominantly an undergraduate institution and most of its libraries, including those at the eighteen two-year campuses throughout the commonwealth, are also undergraduate in orientation. This fact, once recognized, meant that the problems of goals, definitions, and priorities in trying to reconcile an "undergraduate" library with this system became too difficult to resolve satisfactorily.

3. Academic directions. We have seen how the climate of the last decade affected library planning for undergraduate students and it is safe to predict that new directions in academia will continue to have an influence on university libraries. Besides economic problems there are other changes on the horizon that should be considered as well, although their scope is not yet clear. Enrollments are changing and universities, as they have in similar times before, are under pressure to be "more responsive" to the tight job market. Library collections and services, particularly those heavily-oriented to the humanities and the social sciences, may be harder to justify. Remedial education, graduate study, and research, all important academic functions, are in a state of flux and all that is certain is that their influence on library goals and staffing patterns will be influential. During the last several years the Penn State University administration has pressed its academic units to review their priorities and to assess their strengths and weaknesses, with an eye to eliminating "peripheral" programs. In such a climate, the decision was made to reassess the library's priorities and to reduce overlapping or duplicative functions. It was decided that a program of library instruction should meet the needs of faculty and students, especially the unskilled undergraduate, more effectively.

C. *The Undergraduate Library and the Subject-Divisional Plan: a Problem of Inappropriate Models?*

The eminent sociologist David Riesman once coined a term, which he called "isomorphic," to characterize the inclination of college administrators and faculties to take each other as models in what he described as a "snake-like procession."[24] Academic librarians are no less prone to this inclination, as a study of the subject-divisional plan in libraries has shown.[25] The growth and development of the undergraduate library probably was, in large part, due to such influences as well. The problem, of course, is that when modelling one's self after another or one's organization upon that of another institution, the good sometimes includes the bad. The subject-divisional plan was adopted by some libraries for the wrong reasons and certainly some undergraduate libraries came about because "X University has one and, therefore, we need one." As with the subject-divisional plan, undergraduate libraries have taken each other as models, perhaps inappropriately, but, even more inappropriately in this case, the number one model in the country has been Harvard University's Lamont Library.

The Lamont Library was created after several years of careful study and the implementation of comprehensive plans for the overall library needs of the Harvard community, which were: facilities for undergraduates, a rare books and manuscripts library (the Houghton), storage for little-used books (the New England Deposit Library), and relief of the pressures on the Widener Library. But the Lamont's influence quickly went beyond Cambridge. ". . . in the late 1940's, Mother Harvard had started something—in fact, she greatly influenced several ideas which are still very much with us in the world of university libraries."[26] The Lamont, then, was viewed by academic librarians as a good example, one to be emulated but not necessarily after the same careful evaluation of needs. However, as Orne has pointed out, Harvard is an "extreme" example, "one of the most thoroughly decentralized library systems of our time" and the development of the Lamont Library was merely another reflection of this situation. "In effect," Orne concluded, "this was fundamentally one more form of decentralization. There were two influences, then, which should be noted particularly; they are 1) the extent of decentralization, and 2) the size of the collection. We would add today one other important influence, and that is 3) the tremendous increase in the undergraduate student population."[27]

Orne's point is well taken: Harvard is not typical of American universities or university library systems; it is certainly not any more typical than, say, Columbia or Stanford for that matter. Yet, Orne seems not to question the fact that the development of the undergraduate library concept had as its "mother" the Lamont Library, surely a most inappropriate model for most academic libraries in the United States. During the 1960's, other universities were, indeed, facing tremendous enrollment pressures and this, coupled with the interesting concept pioneered by the Lamont, contributed to the spread of the undergraduate library to other universities. However, two other ingredients from the mix at Harvard are missing at most of these institutions; namely, very large collections and decentralized libraries. Now that the enrollment pressure has dropped off, some of these universities (particularly the medium-sized public institutions) are finding that they had little else in common with Harvard University and, thus, their undergraduate libraries may no longer stand the test when compared with their not-so-large and not-so-decentralized collections.

PROSPECTS

Predicting the future is a fascinating but highly inexact pastime. Uncertainty about library developments in the next decade or so is even more pronounced in today's depressed academic climate. However, our comparison of the undergraduate library and subject-divisional plan concepts has demonstrated that librarians have long had a propensity for re-inventing the wheel and a weakness for intellectual fads. With this in mind, an examination of the subject-divisional plan's development may give some indication of the possible prospects for the undergraduate library in the next ten years or so.

A. *Probable Future—Subject-Divisions*

The future of the subject-division concept and its practice is dependent on several factors; probably the chief one is economic. If, in a few years hence, there is a reversal of the present somber economic picture and academic libraries are once again the beneficiaries of a largesse of funds over a sustained period of time, we will undoubtedly see a revival of the popularity of the subject-divisional scheme in a number of university libraries.

Other factors operating in the present scene may also contribute to the strengthening of this idea tomorrow among university library staffs and administrators. For example, technological improvement in technical services, such as machine-readable catalogs and lists of serials, and the locating of data terminals in multiple physical areas of the library and on campus should facilitate strict subject arrangement of materials regardless of format. The recent innovative effort of OCLC, whereby it is cataloging U.S. government documents in the LC classification, could certaintly reinforce the subject-division approach. Moreover, the increasing automated integration of many public service and technical service functions which, together with resource sharing and networking, could result in the transfer of a substantial number of technical services personnel to the public service arena, and make possible once again the adequate staffing of subject divisions. Finally, the continued and heightened need for specialized reference service and for its practitioners could be viewed as being best conducted within the framework of the subject-division organization.

Edward Johnson declared at the end of his comprehensive survey of the development and decline of the subject-division concept that:

> Some of the essential features of the subject-divisional plan seem destined to survive but primarily as part of an overall philosophy of service which emphasized the needs of undergraduate students and the involvement of librarians in the learning process.[28]

B. *Probable Future – The Undergraduate Library*

It is not difficult to predict a further relative decline in the numbers of undergraduate libraries in middle-size to large universities. It is evident, in fact, that this decline is continuing. If the past experience of the subject-divisional plan is something like a clue to the future, then we will probably see some undergraduate libraries phased out, some added but, overall, a decline in numbers. How many is anyone's guess of course but this decline will undoubtedly be gradual and may not be as extensive as the one experienced by the subject-divisional plan. The factors contributing to this decline have already been analyzed: stable or declining enrollments, budgetary problems, and changing academic directions. Wingate, in his brief article on the undergraduate library concluded that the undergraduate library "bubble" has "burst," and suggests that the undergraduate library is "obsolete." In Wingate's opinion, the most important reason for this disenchantment is ". . . the realization that a separate facility works to deprive the undergraduate of a learning experience that only a large research library can offer."[29]

Wingate's prediction is probably too simplistic. The history of the subject-divisional plan indicates that it is fairly safe to predict that the undergraduate library concept at many universities will continue as an integral, important, and effective component of excellent library service. Those university libraries most likely to continue with successful undergraduate library services include the largest and most prosperous institutions. It probably will continue also, as the subject-divisional plan has continued, to function effectively at those institutions where extensive library service to undergraduate students coincides closely with overall library goals and is appropriate to general institutional objectives for the near future. However, the problem of declining resources will be a strong force putting pressure on library administrators to continue to justify the separate undergraduate library's existence.

C. *Variations on a Theme*

Two important aspects of academic librarianship—subject-oriented libraries and library instruction—have only been lightly touched upon but they should be viewed as possible alternatives or important factors in a discussion of the separate undergraduate library:

1. Subject-oriented departmental, divisional, or branch libraries have been on the academic scene almost from the founding of colleges and universities. The existence of these departmental libraries remains, in the view of Rutherford D. Rogers and David C. Weber, the "most persistent and difficult problem for the director of a university library" and continues to challenge library administrators today as it has for decades. Rogers and Weber have noted that under the present circumstances of proliferating academic departments and increasingly interdisciplinary research, ". . . the unbridled creation of branch libraries would be a disservice to users unless financial resources were to permit complete duplication of materials and service hours (but the resources never do)."[30] Nevertheless, the pressure for such proliferation will continue at most institutions of higher education.

The future may see an increase of more sophisticated subject divisions or, perhaps, more comprehensive subject area branch libraries in response to requests for more departmental libraries. Rogers and Weber predict a growing trend toward combining departmental libraries amidst clusters of teaching departments. They cite such possibilities as consolidated science libraries, social sciences libraries, health sciences libraries, or engineering libraries all located in central areas.[31] These ideas may prove popular or, probably more likely, unpopular with academic departments, and library administrators will need to be highly persuasive. In any event, the needs of undergraduate students will have to be balanced against the needs of other users, such as graduate students and faculty, who have a predominantly subject and research orientation.

2. The development of comprehensive programs of instruction for unsophisticated library users, especially undergraduate students, is rapidly growing in popularity in academic libraries. Librarianship has seen a veritable flood of articles, books, and workshops on the topic of library instruction. This concept, geared as it is to the extensive involvement of librarians in the formal educational experience of students, is a highly appealing one to many college and university librarians. In some respects it draws upon the fundamental tenets of both the subject-divisional plan and the separate undergraduate library. Administrators are beginning to look at it as a way of providing a high level of service in an innovative way but without committing the academic library to large investments in physical facilities and collections. However, we have seen that the subject-divisional plan and the undergraduate library also went through a period of popularity only to be, each in its turn, seriously questioned. Today, it appears that the undergraduate library trend, fad if you will, may be giving way to an emphasis on intensive instructional programs for library users. Whether library instruction will become the academic library fad of the 1970's and 1980's remains to be seen although it appears to be well on its way.

REFERENCES

1. Allan J. Dyson, "Organizing Undergraduate Library Instruction: the English and American Experience," *Journal of Academic Librarianship* 1 (March, 1975): 9.
2. Anne B. Passarelli and Millicent B. Abell, "Programs of Undergraduate Libraries and Problems in Educating Library Users," in: John Lubans, Jr. ed. *Educating the Library User.* (New York: R. R. Bowker, 1974) p. 117.
3. Billy R. Wilkinson, "The Undergraduate Library: a Screaming Success as Study Halls," *Library Journal* 96 (May 1, 1971): 1567.
4. Irene A. Braden. *The Undergraduate Library.* (Chicago: American Library Association, 1970) p. 5.
5. John R. Haak, "The Undergraduate Library: Goal Determination," *Library Journal* 96 (May 7, 1971): 1576.
6. *Ibid.*

7. Wilkinson, *op. cit.*, p. 1568.
8. Warren B. Kuhn, "Undergraduate Libraries in a University," *Library Trends* 18 (October, 1969): 206–207.
9. Ralph E. Ellsworth, "Colorado University's Divisional Reading Room Plan: Description and Evaluation," *College and Research Libraries* 2 (March, 1941): 103.
10. Frank A. Lundy, "The Divisional Plan Library; Origins and Development, Present Meaning and Future Potential," *Aspects of Librarianship* 18 (Kent, Ohio: Kent State University, Department of Library Science, 1959): 6.
11. Mary E. Anders, "Selection of a Divisional Reading Room Collection," *College and Research Libraries* 22 (November, 1961): 432–433.
12. Jerrold Orne, "The Undergraduate Library, *Library Journal* 95: (June 15, 1970), 2231–2233.
13. Wilkinson, *op. cit.*, pp. 1569–1571.
14. Anders, *op. cit.*, p. 430, 432.
15. Lundy, *op. cit.*, p. 4.
16. *Ibid.*, p. 7.
17. Archie L. McNeal, "Divisional Organization in the University Library," *University of Tennessee Library Lectures*, 12 (April, 1960): 50.
18. Haak, *op. cit.*, p. 1573.
19. Redmond A. Burke, "The Separately Housed Undergraduate Library Versus the University Library," *College and Research Libraries* 31 (November, 1970): 400.
20. William J. Studer, "From Cornucopia to Famine: the Impacts and Implications of Budgetary Decline," paper presented to the conference on *Emerging Trends in Library Organization: What Influences Change.* (Terre Haute: Indiana State University, October 21, 1977) proceedings in press.
21. Henry W. Wingate, "The Undergraduate Library: Is It Obsolete?" *College and Research Libraries* 39 (January, 1978): 32.
22. Haak, *op. cit.*, p. 1575.
23. Norah E. Jones, "The UCLA Experience: an Undergraduate Library—for Undergraduates!" *Wilson Library Bulletin* 45 (February, 1971): 585.
24. David Riesman. *Constraint and Variety in American Education.* new ed. (Lincoln: University of Nebraska Press, 1958): 14.
25. Edward R. Johnson. *The Development of the Subject-Divisional Plan in American University Libraries.* Ph.D. dissertation, University of Wisconsin, 1974.
26. Wilkinson, *op. cit.*, p. 1568.
27. Orne, *op. cit.*, p. 2230.
28. Johnson, *op. cit.*, p. 196.
29. Wingate, *op. cit.*, pp. 32–33.
30. Rutherford D. Rogers and David C. Weber. *University Library Administration.* (New York: H. W. Wilson, 1971) pp. 73–74.
31. *Ibid.*, 78.
32. Some of the material in this paper is based on a Study Fellow final report to the Council on Library Resources by one of the authors.

Thomas G. Kirk

Earlham College

COURSE-RELATED LIBRARY AND LITERATURE USE INSTRUCTION: AN ATTEMPT TO DEVELOP MODEL PROGRAMS

The Earlham run and NSF supported project which was designed to help institutions of higher education develop their course-related library instruction programs in undergraduate science education is described. In addition to the rationale for the project, the objectives and activities of the project are detailed. Special attention is given to the format and content of the project's workshops. The project's efforts to examine the nature and degree of impact on the participants' institutions are also described. The successes and failures of the project are outlined.

INTRODUCTION

Earlham College's program of course-related and course-integrated library instruction has been the subject of a number of publications in recent years.[1,2,3] One of these, Billy Wilkinson's *Reference Service for Undergraduate Students*, concludes its study of Earlham's reference and instructional services by saying:

> Library services for undergraduate students in liberal arts colleges—particularly the programs of library instruction and individual reference assistance at Earlham College's Lilly Library—should serve as archetypes worthy of imitation by undergraduate libraries on university campuses.[4]

Because of this attention, the members of the Earlham library staff are in constant demand to speak at conferences and library schools, and consult with individual institutions. More recently many persons have visited Earlham to study the bibliographic instruction program first hand.

One part of this bibliographic instruction program which has been of particular interest is the instructional services provided to science students. While a good deal of attention has been given in the past to the need to teach students library and literature use skills, it has been shown repeatedly that science students can not and do not make effective use of the library.[5,6,7]

Because there continues to be a need to find solutions to this problem and as a result of the keen interest in Earlham's library program, the Wildman Science Library submitted a proposal to the National Science Foundation for support of a project to export the idea of course-integrated library and literature use instruction to undergraduate science education programs in the United States. The project's objectives were three:

(1) To help individual institutions develop a library and literature use program.
(2) To develop models of such programs which could be distributed widely to the undergraduate science education community.
(3) To evaluate the project's impact on individual institutions.

What follows in this paper is a discussion of the activities undertaken to achieve each of these three objectives. In each case particular attention is paid to the activities of the project that were designed to achieve each objective. It is hoped this project review will be helpful to planners of workshops on this topic and to those concerned with the establishment of a course-related/course-integrated library and literature use instruction program for undergraduate science students.

TO HELP INDIVIDUAL INSTITUTIONS DEVELOP THEIR PROGRAMS

The NSF-funded project began in June of 1976 and for the first year was concerned primarily with the first objective (i.e., to help individual institutions develop their programs). The project staff developed a three-day workshop in which about half the time was devoted to an intensive examination of Earlham's course-related and course-integrated instruction program in the sciences, particularly in biology. The other half of the workshop provided the participants an opportunity to develop their own program under the supervision of the project leaders. In the design of the project and the workshop several decisions were made which in retrospect seem to have been important reasons for the success of the workshop and the project.

1. The workshops would be limited in size. The original concept called for four institution teams of a librarian and a professor, and while the first workshop did have four, the two held during the second cycle had five and six teams respectively. These small numbers made it possible to give adequate attention to the participants' individual programs.

2. The workshops would be designed for an audience who was already committed to library and literature use in undergraduate science education. The project was not designed to convince those who were only superficially interested or actively opposed to the idea. There are a complex set of interrelated attitudes which prevent librarians and teaching faculty from recognizing the importance of library and literature use training. These could not effectively be addressed by working directly with those who were not already interested. The project's second objective (i.e. to develop models) should be the mechanism for trying to convince those not already committed.

3. The workshop would be designed for a teaching faculty-librarian team which had already established a basis for developing a working relationship. At the foundation of the course-related and course-integrated library instruction idea is the assumption that most students come to appreciate the usefulness of libraries and learn how to use them best when the instruction is an integral part of the teaching faculty's course activities. From this perspective it is essential that the librarian and teaching faculty develop and plan their activities cooperatively. Therefore, the effectiveness of the workshop depends on the participation of a team.

4. The participant team had to have a specific program on which they wanted to work. This provided a practical reason for participating and made the committee more tangible.

5. The workshop would provide an opportunity to intensively study one course-integrated library and literature use model. This decision was based on the assumption that the participants needed models which could provide ideas for their work.

6. The workshop sessions would use a variety of formats to achieve the workshop's objectives. Each format should be suited to the specific purposes of the workshop. This variety would have the side benefit of enlivening the workshop.

7. The workshop would, in addition to studying one exemplary program, explore some of the general issues involved in implementing a course-related library and literature use instruction program. However this would not be done directly but as a by-product of the discussions about particular programs.

8. There must be an opportunity for follow-up and feedback, not only between the participants and the project leaders but also among the participants.

As the workshop plan developed, and the above decisions made, the project was advertised through a mailed circular. Eventually fourteen applications were received from which four were accepted. These four teams attended the three-day workshop at Earlham in October of 1976. This workshop, and the two held in 1977, were divided into seven units, each with its own purposes and format. They are:

1. Low-key social occasions to foster collegiality in the group.

2. Role playing, with the project leaders serving as teaching faculty and librarian and the participants as undergraduate students in their first year of college. This provided an opportunity not only to see from the inside how an instruction program works, but also what it is like for undergraduate students to face the task of researching a subject on which they are not an expert.

3. Short talks which describe specific details of instruction activities. These were able to convey specific informational efficiently.

4. A formal talk, with a question and answer period, to present the case for evaluating educational activities. The purpose was to raise awareness of the need for evaluation.

5. An unscheduled period in which the participant teams planned their work and did other things which individuals felt would contribute to the development of their own course-related library and literature use instruction program. If the participants were to get their programs off the ground they needed a block of time to plan their activities while away from the hectic everyday pace on their campuses.

6. Discussion of each program by the team with the workshop leaders. This provided an opportunity for the NSF-project leaders to share their experience as the participants developed their programs.

7. A reporting session in which participants presented their plans to each other.

In the development of the content for the workshop the project leaders assembled a complete set of documents associated with the Earlham course-related instruction program in science. In addition to the instructional materials and assignment sheets for introductory biology, there were examples of student work. Samples of instructional materials used in other biology courses, and in geology, chemistry, and psychology courses were included along with a series of documents associated with the efforts to evaluate the Earlham program. This notebook was given to project participants and was subsequently included in the first annual report of the project which is available from ERIC.

In addition to the initial workshop in 1976 this workshop pattern was used in the Fall of 1977. The concensus of the participants in the three workshops was that it was highly successful at introducing the idea of course-related instruction, of inspiring participants to work on their programs, and in providing a helpful setting in which to begin their work.

The major detectable weakness in the 1976 workshop was the failure to ask the participants for a written statement describing their activities. For the 1977 workshops the participants were asked to prepare for the interview sessions (see workshop part 6 above) a statement which explained three things: (1) the general objectives of their program; (2) a description of their program's planned activities, and (3) a statement of each team member's responsibilities in achieving their program's objectives. The participants in the 1977 workshops, as a result of this written statement, were better prepared to carry their programs forward when they left the workshop.

As a second part of the effort to help the institutions develop their programs the Project Director occasionally communicated by letter and telephone with the participants during the five months, November through March, following the Fall workshops. These contacts did not make a substantive contribution to their programs but were important in maintaining high motivation.

Upon completion of the first go-around of their programs, participants prepared a report on their activities. These reports included (1) a description of the institutional and curricular context in which the activities were carried out; (2) a description of the instruction and library-based assignment; (3) copies of all instructional materials used in the program; (4) examples of the students' completion of the assignments; (5) any formal evaluation results; and (6) the teaching faculty and librarian's subjective assessment.

Completed reports were due on arrival at Earlham for a one day follow-up workshop which was held in May. Portions of the reports were duplicated and all participants and workshop leaders were given a few hours to read the reports. Most of the workshop time was then spent discussing each program. The intent was to have participants share their experiences and for the project leaders to explore in detail the dynamics of the participants' activities.

As has been indicated above, the first year workshop was quite successful and the project therefore planned for a second workshop cycle. It was possible to advertise this second year activity widely and as a result the project received three hundred thirteen inquiries which led eventually to eighty-six applications. As a result of this overwhelming interest arrangements were made to take five teams into the project and those not accepted were invited to attend a special workshop under different ground rules. The project would not pay travel to the workshop site nor would an honorarium be paid for their completed reports. Despite these limitations twenty-six applicants indicated an interest and six were accepted. (See Appendix I)

TO DEVELOP MODELS, OTHER THAN EARLHAM, WHICH COULD BE DISTRIBUTED WIDELY TO THE UNDERGRADUATE SCIENCE EDUCATION COMMUNITY

Throughout the workshop the participant team and the Project Director thoroughly documented the activities of each team. The first year's annual report, mentioned earlier, contains excerpts from the participants' reports. A set of reports from thirteen institutions along with the Project Director's commentary, and an analytical index have been assembled and will be available later this Fall or just after the first of the year. These models represent a rich diversity of institutions, institutional objectives, and methodologies for teaching literature and library use. The institutions represented include large universities, both public and private, small undergraduate liberal arts colleges, and two year community and junior colleges. They are scattered throughout the United

States. The subject areas included range over the entire natural and physical science, including biology, chemistry, engineering, geology, and mathematics.

In addition, dissemination of information on these programs is being carried out through papers and talks.

TO EVALUATE THE INTENSITY OF THE PROJECT'S IMPACT ON INDIVIDUAL INSTITUTIONS

A consultant to the project, Dr. Steven Nelson, prepared a model of the diffusion of ideas (Figure 1) and suggested the possible points at which impact could be measured. He pointed out, as Figure 1 shows, that impact can come at several levels. The project's only direct impact is on the workshops' participants. Secondary impact comes from the influence the participants have on students and colleagues, and tertiary impact occurs when students and colleagues affect other students and colleagues both inside and outside the institution. The Project Director decided to examine only the primary and one aspect of secondary impact. However, it is hoped that follow-up on the project will be possible and therefore the other aspects of impact can be examined. The specific aspects of impact considered here include:

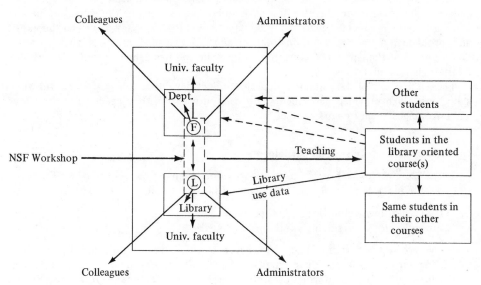

Figure 1. Model Project Impact Prepared by Dr. Steven Nelson, project consultant.

(A) Primary impact: Workshop evaluation

Evaluation of each workshop was undertaken at three points during the project. The first was immediately upon completion of the workshop. A questionnaire called for a quick judgment of the physical facilities and organization of the workshop and a general reaction to it. In conjunction with this participant evaluation the project's consultants, Dr. Steven Nelson and Dr. Gerald Bakker provided their evaluations. Both participants and consultants agreed that the workshops were well organized and the content effectively presented. They were especially pleased with the detailed inside examination of Earlham's program and the methods used in that examination. As they left the workshop they, by their own admission, were enthusiastic about what they had learned and about the activities they were about to undertake.

The second point of evaluation occurred at the end of the May 1977 workshop. In addition to the extensive discussions of each others' programs, the participants were divided into two groups to discuss and answer a prescribed set of questions. These groups were led by the project consultants and did not involve the Project Director or his teaching-faculty coworker. One of the questions asked participants was: "Given your recent experience how should the Fall workshop be revised?" Three conclusions can be drawn from the consultants' reports on the discussion of this question. (1) The participants continued to be enthusiastic about the general design of the workshop and its content. (2) The descriptions of instruction activities in psychology and political science should be dropped. (3) More specific information on techniques of evaluation should be included. In the subsequent 1977 workshops the sessions on psychology and political science were dropped, but little was done to change the nature of the session on evaluation. The Project Director felt it was not possible to do justice to the topic in the time allowed, and it didn't seem feasible to expand the session. The project had limited its objective to impressing upon participants the need for evaluation but could not tackle the large problem of techniques of evaluating teaching.

The third point of evaluation of the workshop came one year after the Fall workshop, and thus applies only to the 1976 cycle. A questionnaire sent to the workshop participants asked them to rate the workshop on whether (1) it adequately described the nature and problems of bibliographic instruction and (2) provided practical advice on the development of their projects. On a five point scale the participants rated the workshop a very high 4.8 and 4.4 respectively.

These three sets of data indicate that the project developed a highly successful workshop, one which provided participants with the information they needed and stimulated and encouraged them to work on their programs.

(B) Primary impact: Impact on participants.

To measure the impact on the participants a questionnaire was sent to the 1976 workshop group in December, 1977. On that questionnaire they were asked to indicate:

(1) whether they were continuing their projects:
(2) whether they were doing anything additional.

In every case the participants described how they were continuing, and in most cases improving and/or expanding their activities. A good example is the University of Arizona where the specific activity was to incorporate library use into one section of the English Department's course on technical writing for engineers. This past year, 1977–78, the library-use unit was included in all five sections which involved three different instructors.

(C) Secondary impact: The project's impact on the participants' colleagues.

As Figure 1 indicates there are a number of points at which the impact of this project can be measured. Many of them would require presence on the campus, or cannot validly be evaluated until several years have passed. Therefore, the Project Director had to make certain decisions on limiting the evaluation. The most important limitation was due to time. Because the project expired November 30, 1978 the participants or their institutional colleagues in the first year workshop (1976) could be questioned no more than one year later. (It is hoped that ways can be found to continue the project long enough to conduct "one-year-later" studies of the 1977 workshop participants, and perhaps "two-year-later" studies of the 1976 workshop group.) Because of the original design of the project, the Director could not get to the campuses, and because most measurements of impact would be premature it was decided to limit the measure of secondary impact to the participants' effects on colleagues in the library and in the teaching faculty.

The results of a "one-year-later" questionnaire indicated the participants were having an impact on colleagues. Each participant indicated specific individuals who were becoming interested or were undertaking library use instruction projects. In order to cross check the participants' impressions of their impact, the Project Director sent a follow-up questionnaire to key colleagues within the institution. During the May workshop the participants had been asked to list their supervisors and/or department chairpersons, top administrators, and colleagues who might have knowledge of their projects. Persons on these lists received the follow-up questionnaire in early February and within a five-week period there was a 54% return.

The results support the conclusion that each participant team was perceived by close associates as being enthusiastic supporters of the projects' ideas, and as having worked hard and done a good job. While the extent of the impact, in terms of the number of colleagues affected, varies, primarily because of the size of the institution, at least one teaching faculty and one librarian in each institution have been affected. The question which follows from these results is whether the impact will multiply in succeeding years. As has been indicated several times in this paper it is hoped that a follow-up on this project can monitor the continuing development of each institution's program.

In summary, while the project has been successful within its limited purpose, it has not been without its shortcomings. Below is a list of the most important specific successes and shortcomings.

SUCCESSES OF THE PROJECT

1. Of the 15 participating institutions, 13 have begun an instruction program of which their NSF Project is a part. This project has contributed to their program development by:
   a. providing information to the librarian/teacher team.
   b. motivating the team, which in turn has stimulated others to consider and/or implement the idea.

2. The project has resulted in the establishment of a group of people who have had experience with the idea of course-related bibliographic instruction in undergraduate science education.

3. The project has developed a number of models of such instruction which are included in the publication, soon to be released, *Course-Related Library and Literature Use Instruction; Working Models for Programs in Undergraduate Science Education* (8).

4. The project has not provided adequate help in the participants' evaluation of their projects.

5. The project has not had adequate time following the workshops, particularly those held in the Fall of 1977, to evaluate their impact. More importantly, there has not been time to assess the effects on students of the participants' activities.

FAILURES OF THE PROJECT

1. The project has not provided adequate help in the participants' evaluation of their projects.

2. The project has not had adequate time following the workshops, particularly those held in the Fall of 1977, to evaluate their impact. More importantly, there has not been time to assess the effects on students of the participants' activities.

UNFINISHED WORK

As was indicated earlier, assessment of impact at all points was neither feasible nor desirable during the first year of the project. In the second year we were able to carry out assessment of the first year participants' programs and the impact of the project on the participants' colleagues. Carrying out the same kind of assessment for the second-year institutions will require an additional three months. We believe this assessment would be useful for two reasons. First, it will give us more data and, therefore, will put our tentative judgments above on a firmer basis. Second, and more important, the second-year participants covered a greater variety of subject areas and a greater variety of types of institutions. The assessment, then, would help expand the applicability of the findings of the project.

The project did not address two aspects of evaluation. The first is the impact on students. Do students, in fact, have a greater sense of the value of libraries and literature and do they use them more because of the participants' work in their respective institutions? We can, through interviewing and a brief questionnaire, determine what differences, if any, exist between those who were in the project course and those who were not.

The second point is to determine what specific activities participants' colleagues have undertaken as a result of the project. Our results indicate that the participants' colleagues are sympathetic to the idea and give high marks to their colleagues for the work they have done. But does this positive feeling translate into action? By interviewing key colleagues already identified, we would itemize the specific activities that are spin-offs from the project.

A final reason for the extension of the project is best presented by the participants themselves in letters to the Project Director. The thread that runs through them is the conviction that the importance and meaning of what they themselves are doing would be more firmly conveyed to their colleagues if they had some outside help. This is consistent with the initial objective of the project: the development and establishment of models or examples that others can adopt.

The activities reported here were supported by the Office of Science Information Service, National Science Foundation under grant number DSI 76-10129. The opinions expressed herein are those of the author and do not represent policies of the National Science Foundation.

REFERENCES

1. David Harry Eyman, "The Use of Periodical Collections in Selected Liberal Arts College Libraries by College Seniors Majoring in History," (dissertation, University of Michigan, 1975).
2. Stuart Wayne Miller, "Library Use Instruction in Selected American Colleges," (dissertation, University of Chicago, 1976).
3. Bill R. Wilkinson, Reference Services for Undergraduate Students: Four Case Studies. (Metuchen, NJ: Scarecrow Press, 1972).
4. *Ibid.*, p. 348.
5. P. F. Fanta and I. M. Sydney, "Modern Techniques in Chemical Information; a new

graduate-undergraduate course at Illinois Institute of Technology," *Journal of Chemical Documentation* 11 (May 1971): 48–99.

6. John Lubans, "Nonuse of an Academic Library," *College and Research Libraries* 32 (September 1971): 362–367.

7. H. M. Woodburn, "Retrieval and Use of the Literature of Inorganic Chemistry," *Journal of Chemical Education* 49 (October 1972): 689–696.

8. Thomas G. Kirk, The Development of Course Related Library and Literature Use Instruction in Undergraduate Science Programs. Annual Report for 1976–1977 on NSF Grant DSI 76-10129. September, 1977. 4 vols. (Bethesda, Md.: ERIC Document Reporduction Service, Ed. 152 230; 231; 232; 233.

9. Thomas G. Kirk, Course-Related Library and Literature Use Instruction; Working Models. (New York, Jeffrey Norton, In Press.)

APPENDIX I: PARTICIPANTS IN PROJECT

Albion College (Albion, Mich.): William Miller (Reference Librarian) and John W. Parker (Geology Department).

Ball State University (Muncie, Ind.): James F. Comes (Department of Library Science) and Ruth H. Howes (Physics Department).

Central Arizona College (Coolidge, Ariz.): Glen Gordon Tiller (Assistant Director, Public Services) and Marion E. Cornelius (Department of Science and Mathematics).

Central College (Pella, Iowa): Robin Martin (Director of Public Services) and Kenneth Tuinstra (Assistant Professor of Biology).

Drew University (Madison, N.J.): Pamela Snelson (Reference Librarian) and Donald A. Scott (Professor of Chemistry).

Guilford College (Greensboro, N.C.): Rose Anne Simon (Library-Faculty Liaison Officer, Coordinator of Professional Information Services) and Frank Keegan (Biology Department).

Indiana University–Purdue University at Fort Wayne (Fort Wayne, Ind.): Mary Lou Stewart (Assistant Reference Librarian, Science and Health Science) and Phyllis Eckman (Assistant Professor of Nursing).

Johns Hopkins University (Baltimore, Md.): Lucie H. Geckler (Science Reference Librarian) and Warner E. Love (Biophysics Department).

Oregon State University (Corvallis, Ore.): Robert E. Lawrence (Head, Science/Technology Division) and Leo W. Parks (Department of Microbiology).

Penn Valley Community College (Kansas City, Mo.): Evelyn Staatz (Librarian) and Patricia A. Lorenz (Life Sciences–Biology).

St. Olaf College (Northfield, Minn.): Katherine Rottsolk (Reference/ILL Librarian) and Marland Madson (Biology Department).

San Jose State University (San Jose, Calif.): Cecilia P. Mullen (Acting Head, Science and Engineering Department) and Leonard Feldman (Mathematics Department).

SUNY, Potsdam (Potsdam, N.Y.): Jeanne Dittmar (Reference Librarian).

University of Arizona (Tucson, Ariz.): Joan Murphy (Science Reference Librarian); Dorothy Fuller (Department of English) and James P. McCormick (Department of Electrical Engineering).

University of Richmond (Richmond, Va.): Katherine R. Smith (Science Librarian) and W. Allan Powell (Professor of Chemistry).

Virginia Polytechnic Institute and State University (Blacksburg, Va.): Anatole Scaun (Assistant Science and Technology Librarian) and Charles J. Hurst (Department of Mechanical Engineering).

Anne Grodzins Lipow

University of California, Berkeley

TEACHING THE FACULTY TO USE THE LIBRARY: A SUCCESSFUL PROGRAM OF IN-DEPTH SEMINARS FOR UNIVERSITY OF CALIFORNIA, BERKELEY, FACULTY

Recognizing that few persons outside the profession of librarianship can keep up with the rapidly developing forms of bibliographic control and research methodology, a series of six to eight seminars for faculty on changing library tools and techniques is offered annually at the University of California, Berkeley, taught by librarian staff. The origins of this program, the make-up of the faculty participants, the changes in the program made over time, problems encountered and strategies for publicity are discussed in this paper. The author concludes that in offering in-depth instruction to faculty, librarians explode the myth that faculty won't admit their ignorance about using the library, that librarians have much to offer even the most sophisticated scholarly user, and that librarian instructors experience a new respect for the profession and a new confidence in themselves as professionals.

Perhaps future generations of faculty in colleges and universities will be more sophisticated library users than they are today because of the burgeoning of classes which teach undergraduates and even graduate students how to become library wise. But there remains, and will remain for some time, a population of faculty and researchers who have never had the opportunity to learn, to whom it never occurred that there was anything to learn, and who rely on methods they used years ago but which are no longer effective for research purposes.

The trouble is that they *think* they know how to use the library quite well—so that when they cannot find what they are looking for, they don't ask for help but assume we don't have it. (Asking for help from a librarian is anyway a difficult thing for faculty to do. It's not that we are such a fierce bunch—though some of us are; rather they fear they would be exposing an ignorance such educated people are not supposed to have.)

At the University of California, Berkeley faculty seminars on how to use the library for research in the social sciences and humanities have been offered since June 1976, with a success that surprises even the most optimistic of us, and these seminars are now a regular part of our public service program. So far, the seminars were given in June and September 1976, and in March and October 1977. But because the preparation of the seminars involves a tremendous expenditure of time and energy on the part of the librarian instructors, from now on the program is offered only annually, during the Fall Quarter.

Each program is a series of six to eight in-depth seminars covering general reference and bibliographic resources, with emphasis on interdisciplinary, recently published and difficult-to-use tools; shortcomings of the card catalogs and how to get around them; and reference sources in specialized subject areas.

There is no question that the program fills a need and is very much accepted by the faculty. Their attendance and written evaluations give the evidence for that. In the first series, a total of 26 faculty attended up to nine two-hour sessions each; in the fourth series 78 faculty participated, most attending more than one session, many attending 4 and 5 sessions and a few, 6 and 7 sessions. As one participant put it: "I found all of the sessions most enlightening. My only regret is that I hadn't the opportunity to have this particular look at the libraries long ago . . . This experience has been an eye opener." Another said, "I don't think I will ever feel uncomfortable again about asking for advice and assistance." One professor who had attended all seminars in an earlier series returned for all sessions of a later series. When we asked wasn't he bored the second time around, he said, "Heavens, no! You can't get too much of this." (He, by the way, is in charge of the course on "Library Methodology" for graduate students in his department.)

This paper will outline the content of the seminars and describe the changes that were made in succeeding programs based on evaluations by both the faculty participants and the librarian instructors. It will also discuss the publicity that was issued, the problems encountered, and about the faculty who attended. The effect of the program on the librarians who taught the seminars will also be discussed.

But first, a word about how the sessions got started. Back in February of 1976, this author submitted to administration an informal proposal suggesting the idea. It was met with support ("Sounds good; don't let it cost any money, and be sure you touch base with all relevant staff.") It then went before the body that would be the most important group from which to gain acceptance—the General Reference Department—because it would be from this group that the instructors would be drawn. This author was not a member of that body but rather part of another department and not considered to be a "reference librarian" in the formal sense, though everyone generally recognized that I "did reference." It was within this group that the reaction, as one might expect, was mixed. No one denied that faculty needed library instruction. All reference librarians in university environments have experienced "dumb" faculty members who don't know a journal index from an indexing or abstracting service; never heard of *LC List of Subject Headings*, can't decipher a simple library card—much less understand about citation indexes or computerized literature searching. And no one said out-and-out that classes for faculty was a bad idea. But nearly everyone was skeptical that we could pull it off. Responses ranged from "It's a good idea, but it won't work; we've tried it before in various ways" to "It's a good idea; we doubt that it will work for many reasons; but we're willing to give it a try."

The "various ways" it had been tried before were: (a) generic offers to faculty of our availability for consulting about library problems, and (b) offers to teach or help teach their classes about the library resources in the specific topic covered by the class. Too few faculty had ever taken us up on those offers. The reasons my co-workers gave for the faculty's rejection of our offers were: "Faculty can't admit they need us" or "Even if they could admit it, the last people in the world they would think would help them are librarians."

Not to denegrate the worth of my colleagues' assessment, I knew differently. I had been running a special bibliographic service for faculty where they could call a convenient phone number (BAKER—as the service has come to be called), ask for a book or journal article and have it delivered to their door. Since the service costs $1.00 per request, many come to us only as a last resort—after they have tried in vain to find what they want on their own. When we find it, we try to let them know where they went worng. So you see, *I* knew that *they* knew that I knew that there was a lot they did not know about using the library—and that knowledge somehow didn't matter to them.

We decided that "feelers" would be sent out to the BAKER service users, and that if there was interest by even a small number of faculty (10 was considered a lot) we would move ahead with confidence that there was some evidence of acceptance among the research community. A committee of four, including this author, would review the responses and plan accordingly.

Now here is where the first bit of deception was used. Since it was feared that even with the BAKER experience faculty might be reluctant to admit their need for this course in so public a way, this "feeler" or leaflet that was sent out had a few concessions to the Faculty Ego:

First, the announcement began with: "At the suggestion of many faculty members, the library will sponsor seminars on . . . " In fact, of course, no faculty member ever suggested anything of the sort.

Then, the program was titled "How to Use the Library for *Advanced* Research in the Social Sciences and Humanities" (emphasis mine), knowing full well that we would be covering very elementary library concepts. (For the last few series the course has been given a better title: "Library Update—Faculty Seminars on Changing Library Tools and Techniques.") The leaflet described the content of the course, and asked them to return an attached form expressing their interest in the seminars, commenting on their personal research work, and indicating preferred and undesirable times for scheduling the sessions. The leaflet promised that they would be notified of exact times and places.

Based on the responses to the leaflet, the following series of two-hour sessions was scheduled: one session would cover in a general way the catalogs, their supplements, and the sources in the General Reference Room. All enrollees would be encouraged to attend that one. Then they would have a choice of any one or more of sessions on Government Documents, Literature, History, Ethnic Studies, Social Sciences, Medical and Health Sciences, and Computerized Literature Searching. Two series of seminars were scheduled: one immediately following the Spring 1976 Quarter, the other just preceding the Fall 1976 Quarter.

A total of 78 interest forms were received, enrolling faculty in either the Spring or the Fall session. The enrollees came from 24 departments, representing the full cross-section of academic departments in the social sciences and humanities (for example, Anthropology, Asian American Studies, Classics, Psychology, Linguistics, Sociology). The departments with the highest number of respondents were English and Political Science, with 14 each. Also, they represented 11 academic ranks, including Research Assistants (numbering 13), who were recommended by the professors for whom they worked. Full professors numbered 20, and the rest came from the gamut of academic titles, including Associate and Assistant Professor, Lecturer and Instructor.

Of the 78 respondents, 57 actually attended classes: 26 in the Spring series, 31 in the Fall. Most of those who missed sessions took the trouble to send "regrets," an indication of how seriously they took this commitment.

At this point, for the sake of eliminating any ambiguity, let me henceforth refer to the faculty participants as "the students" and the faculty—that is, the librarian instructors—as "the instructors."

The seminars of the first two series were planned and taught by 16 instructors, under the general direction of the Head of General Reference, Sheila Dowd. In succeeding series, several other librarians have become involved in teaching the sessions. Before each series, we met twice as a group—once about one month before the first sessions to discuss and coordinate the content of the seminars, and again about a week before the first sessions to review final details. Within very general guidelines eliminating unwanted over-laps while consciously duplicating some sources for emphasis or to point up different ways to use a reference work, and keeping in mind numerous suggestions about teaching techniques, all of the instructors were free to develop their sections however they wished. In addition, an "official observer"—a librarian who knew our library system well and who would attend every session and take notes—was appointed. This was our way of getting a relatively objective overall evaluation of the course.

Preparation for the seminars turned out to be an enormous undertaking. As each of us worked through the organization and content of our sessions, we became reacquainted with reference works we had forgotten about, studied new ones we had never had time to use, and tried to articulate discrepancies and conflicts in library cataloging policy that until then we knew in our bones but never had to explain.

I should tell you that before our first live presentations, each of us, in our own way, got cold feet. Till now, we had openly laughed (among ourselves) at faculty ignorance about library tools. Now we were saying, "Dear God, what could *I* possibly have to tell Professor So-and-So, the world's leading expert on the subject of Russian emigration to France, 1810–1812? She's been through the Bibliotheque National, the Lenin Library . . . What could she possibly want from me?"

But our fears dissipated once the classes were underway. I, for example, knew we were doing right when, in my session on the catalogs, I was talking about subject searching, and flashed a catalog card onto the transparency screen. "Let's say, for instance (I said), that you liked this book you read on "drug therapy" and wanted to read more on the subject. Find the card for your book in our Author/Title Catalog, notice the subject headings assigned to the book (and here I pointed to the tracings), then go to the subject catalog using those headings." As I started to move on to another strategy for subject searching, my students detained me, wanting more detailed information about this catalog card which apparently held more information than they had realized.

As you can guess, the results of our labors were most rewarding. Student evaluations were most glowing ("All sessions were models of clarity and usefulness. Congratulations!" said one.) At the same time, they contained helpful criticisms and suggestions, most of which we were able to incorporate in later sessions.

Within the week following the last session of each series, while the experience was still fresh in everyone's mind, the instructors, the "official observer," and other librarians who attended some of the sessions met to appraise the program. The major conclusions we drew were the following:

- Overall, we felt the programs were excellent. Instructors gave competent deliveries and the students seemed to gain a great deal from them. Often enough, there were good give-and-take discussions.
- Our goal of increasing the researcher's ability to access our library's collections and services was met.
- Important basic information was imparted, as well as advanced and new reference sources and search techniques. Statistical sources were especially well received.
- The presence of a knowledgeable observer throughout the sessions was invaluable for two reasons. First, because it was important to have one person who could review the program in its entirety, and second, because when class discussions arose concerning reasons for certain practices or policies, the observer was able to supply the historical perspective that was required for maximum, or even sometimes adequate, understanding.
- We instructors were impressed with how much we had to offer the faculty, who, by and large, considered themselves sophisticated users.

With regard to changes we made in succeeding sessions, let me cite some important ones:

— Handouts of bibliographies (tailor-made to the sessions) and other written material improved the sessions immeasurably. They allowed greater flexibility in choosing titles to discuss, made following the lecture easier, and provided something the student could take home and consult.

— Publicity and coordination for the fourth series, in October 1977, was put in the able hands of Susan Craig, our Art History/Classics Librarian, who spent the greater part of her working life for a time preparing attractive announcements and getting them widely distributed. Her efforts clearly paid off: well over 100 signed up for the classes, and 78 participated—more than double any previous attendance.

— We stopped holding the sessions in the rooms where the books were shelved in favor of a large room that would seat everyone comfortably, where the ambiance was pleasant, where we would not be disturbing regular patrons nor would they be interrupting us, where coffee could easily be served and tables arranged to encourage maximum discussion. The problem with that—and we haven't yet solved it—is the difficulty of getting the books on to the trucks and over to the sessions, and later returning them to their shelves in a manner that least interrupts normal service. That requires extra and last-minute help so that it can be accomplished as close to the time the session is given as possible.

— In the fourth series, we divided the general session into two, devoting a full seminar to the catalogs (called "Developments in Bibliographic Access") and another to General Reference ("A Place to Begin"). Combining them as we had in the earlier series resulted in seminars that ran too long if we were to do justice to the topics, or if we held them to two hours, sessions that did not allow enough time to cover either topic adequately.

— Beginning with the second series, instructor attendance at the planning sessions was taken very seriously. In preparing for the first series, one instructor was unable to attend either of the two pre-seminar meetings, and without the benefit of the group discussions about direction, scope and purpose of the course, missed the point of the program and conducted a very different class than what was publicized.

— In the individual seminars we tried (and with each series got better at it) to avoid discussion of individual titles based on "how our library system is organized." Instead we worked toward a more bibliographically structured approach, trying to bring together titles, regardless of where they are housed, with bibliographic concepts. For example, in the first series, we offered two sessions in Social Science sources: one covering sources in our Main Library, the other sources in our Social Sciences Library (each session held in the respective library); we offered a third session on Government Documents (held in the Documents Library) and another on Computer-Assisted Literature Searching. By the fourth series, we integrated them all into one seminar, and maintained a separate session to demonstrate the capabilities of on-line literature searching that were discussed in all of the other sessions.

— In line with this, all seminars achieved a better integration of computer-assisted searching with subject lectures by the fourth series. Discussions based on handouts consisting of sample searches were quite successful.

— As series progressed we became more judgmental about the titles we discussed: when you'd want to use one title, when another; this is reliable, that is biased, etc.

— The seminar on "Literature" was narrowed in the fourth series to "English and American Literature" to make it more manageable.

— We did much more team teaching by the fourth series, and found that to be a more enjoyable way to prepare, and less demanding in that each instructor covered a smaller chunk of the topic. It was also easier on the students, who had more than one voice and style to listen to for two hours.

— Finally, we added to the evaluation form a place to indicate, on a scale of 5, how useful the sessions were to the participants. This helped us put their comments and suggestions about the individual sessions they attended in some context.

Finally, some generalities about what we have learned from this experience. I hope that the myth that faculty won't admit to their lack of library know-how is exploded. We now know that (1) many, if not most, faculty need an update course; (2) many faculty need guidance in elementary concepts and tools in addition to the more advanced ones; (3) if given the opportunity, faculty want to be educated about the library; (4) although it is true that most faculty may neither understand nor appreciate the crucial role of librarians in the information-retrieval process, faculty can be educated about this role, and no one but librarians can do that job.

Also, we have learned some truths about ourselves as professionals. Our experience has proven that librarians can reach the faculty in more than a casual way. In offering in-depth instruction, we come to realize how much, in fact we have to offer even the most sophisticated scholarly user. I think, too, that we now appreciate how difficult it would be for anyone outside the profession to keep up with the rapid changes in reference tools, forms of bibliographic control and research methodology. In a very real way, we have gained a new respect for our profession and therefore ourselves.

John Mark Tucker

Wabash College

THE ORIGINS OF BIBLIOGRAPHIC INSTRUCTION IN ACADEMIC LIBRARIES, 1876–1914

Many of the current concerns of the practitioners of bibliographic instruction originated in the years from 1876 to 1914. Books began to be used in different ways due to the rise of scholarly scientific research and its acceptance in universities as an equal partner with teaching. William Frederick Poole and William Warner Bishop, among others, broke fresh ground not by establishing comprehensive programs, but by articulating concepts of library instruction that are still alive today. They sought to make students independent learners and to clarify the role of the library in the university.

In 1953 Kenneth Brough wrote that "despite repeated insistence on the importance of teaching students how to use the library, and despite enthusiastic though sporadic attempts to reach this goal, the provision of effective instruction in bibliography and library mechanics for the great masses of university students—especially for the freshmen —remains an unsolved problem."[1] The birth and early years of bibliographic instruction in academic libraries took place in the 1876 to 1914 period, and my purpose is to look at its origins in light of Brough's observation. An appraisal of the early conceptions of this topic should inform current practice for, in fact, many of the major issues that now demand our attention were articulated in this period.

The early period is defined by two important publications of the U.S. Bureau of Education: the massive *Public Libraries in the United States of America* appearing in 1876 and a lesser known report, "Library Instruction in Universities, Colleges, and Normal Schools," published in 1914 and based on a survey of 880 institutions. These years mark convenient lines of demarcation for other reasons. One, as noted by Samuel Rothstein, is that bibliographic instruction is a theme closely related to reference work, notions of which, apart from "a few inconsequential antecedents," were not stated before 1875.[2] A second reason is that Arthur E. Bestor, Jr. identified this general period as the time when scholarly, scientific research attached itself to American universities, radically altering their structure and purpose.[3]

THE DEVELOPMENT OF THE EDUCATIONAL CONTEXT

In many academic libraries bibliographic instruction operates as an administrative unit of the reference department. The sources for constructing a history of bibliographic instruction are similar to those needed for a history of reference. The natural alliance between reference and bibliographic instruction is due to their common heritage as public services and, as noted by Rothstein, their emergence in the midst of fundamental changes in higher education in the latter part of the 19th century.[4]

In the mid-19th century the purpose of the American college was to train young men for the professions, using traditional methods (memorization and recitation) with traditional subjects (the *trivium* and the *quadrivium* of the medieval university). By 1876, however, a number of forces were working that were destined to alter the educational landscape. Prominent among these was the increasing acceptance of scholarly research as a necessary function of academia. American universities took German higher education as a model introducing the Ph.D. and establishing new programs by accepting into their curricula various recently developed scientific, technical, and professional disciplines.

A new kind of university was slowly emerging, featuring the graduate school dedicated to the task of educating men and women for the advancement of knowledge. "Graduate training attempted consciously to inculcate the ideal of the university: that the advancement of knowledge was as sacred a responsibility of any institution of higher learning and of any scholar connected with it as teaching itself."[5] The idea of the university as a community of scholars engaged in the equivalent activities of teaching and research owed much to its growing realization in institutions such as Columbia, Cornell, Harvard, Michigan, and above all the Johns Hopkins, founded in 1876 expressly for the purpose of graduate research.

Such fundamental changes in higher education ushered in newer teaching methods demanding that books be used in different ways. In 1886 Melvil Dewey wrote that "Professor after professor sends his classes, or goes with them to the library and teaches them to investigate for themselves and to *use* books, getting beyond the method of the primary school with its parrot-like recitations from a single text."[6] A number of professors corroborated Dewey's observation. For example, at the ALA conference in 1887, Johns Hopkins professor Herbert Baxter Adams described the work of several German-educated historians who fostered scientific historical research and employed seminar teaching methods.[7] Rothstein said that the "distinctive feature of the seminar was the first-hand investigation of original materials by the students under the close supervision of the professor. Preferably this process would take place in the library itself, where the group could discuss the students' work within easy reach of the materials cited."[8] In summary, research may be said to have suggested the necessity and value of bibliographic instruction.

In addition, academic libraries underwent a period of unprecedented growth. Between 1870 and 1890 the number of colleges and universities grew from 563 to 998.[9] Government reports show that between 1875 and 1891 several academic libraries greatly increased their book collections: Pennsylvania and Columbia quadrupled from 25,000 to 100,000 and from 33,000 to 135,000 respectively. Cornell jumped from 10,000 to 111,000.[10]

Equally significant was the concern of librarians to make collections more accessible. An excellent indicator of this is the number of hours per week a library is open for use. In 1876 Columbia was open 12 hours per week; 20 years later that had increased to 98 hours. Comparable data from Yale and Harvard show a change from 36 to 72 hours and from 48 to 82 hours respectively.[11]

Finally, universities were constructing new library buildings that claimed to emphasize a book-centered educational philosophy. A circular described the new building at Columbia as follows.

The aim has been to make use of the books by the professor and the student alike as easy and convenient as possible. If the library is peculiar in any respect it is in the emphasis which has been laid on this idea. The library is not so much a storehouse for books as it is a laboratory for those who are to use books.[12]

THE NATURE OF BIBLIOGRAPHIC INSTRUCTION

Nineteenth century librarians and educators interested in library instruction drew their inspiration from philosopher-author Ralph Waldo Emerson. In his essay on books, Emerson wrote that "the colleges, whilst they provide us with libraries, furnish no professor of books; and, I think, no chair is so much wanted."[13] Library authors referred to Emerson's comment at regular intervals throughout this period.[14] It is not clear that Emerson had in mind that college librarians, by virtue of either their training or personal inclination, should be his "professors of books." However unwittingly, Emerson encouraged librarians to think along these lines.

Formal college and university programs for training librarians were also in the formative stages during these same years; and thus the historian must differentiate education for librarianship from education of the library user. One who made such a distinction was Azariah Smith Root, Oberlin College librarian from 1887 to 1927 and professor of a three-course sequence in bibliography. Root said that his teaching was planned for the immediate benefit of "the student in his future college work...."[15] He considered the library training he was engaged in an instruction in library use, viewing it as a "valuable liberal arts field in itself, without regard to professional proclivities of the student."[16]

At the University of Michigan, Raymond C. Davis initiated courses that typified the content of library instruction. His classes were largely oriented to the history of books and printing; but they also included lectures specifically devoted to teaching students how to use the library, a process he termed "intellectual bibliography." Davis claimed to have "evidence every year that some individuals are helped by the lectures both in their ability to use books and in their appreciation of books."[17] His confidence and enthusiasm were shared by the Michigan Faculty and board of regents sufficiently for adoption of Davis's courses into the university curriculum in 1881.

Though George Bonn saw Davis as a pioneer, my purpose is to suggest something of his influence. (Indeed, Edward Holley has shown that Otis Robinson and Justin Winsor predated Davis's work in library instruction.)[18] In 1912 Joseph Schneider described instruction in bibliography as a movement owing more to Raymond Davis for its impetus than to anyone else, a sentiment echoed shortly thereafter in the Bureau of Education Report.[19] Kendrick C. Babcock recalled that Davis's lectures on bibliography were "excellent and stimulating," regretting only that they were optional rather than required.[20] Speaking at William and Mary, William Warner Bishop discussed the teaching of bibliography in relation to his own student days at Michigan.

In the German universities the professor usually lectures at the beginning of each course on the bibliography of the subject matter he is about to discuss before the class during each semester. Those lectures are generally the most highly prized and faithfully attended of the course. The custom has had some notable imitators in America, and I have always been profoundly grateful that most of my professors at Michigan have followed this practice as a matter of course.[21]

Bishop studied at Michigan during Davis's tenure as librarian. Davis's success teaching bibliography, and his ability to encourage his faculty colleagues to do the same, may deserve further inquiry.

THE EDUCATIONAL OBJECTIVES OF BIBLIOGRAPHIC INSTRUCTION

Library leaders in the 1876 to 1914 period succeeded in identifying some of the key issues educators and librarians wrestle with today. Otis Hall Robinson was perhaps the earliest to state succinctly the need to clarify instructional objectives. At the ALA conference in 1881 he said, "If the student reads, then . . . let it be for a purpose; let that purpose be definitely formed; and let the reading extend to as many good books relative to the purpose as time will permit."[22] Robinson did not draft statements on the order of those worked out by the ACRL Bibliographic Instruction Task Force, but he did clearly call for purposeful instruction.

The various objectives librarians cited fall into three general categories. First, they were concerned that students develop the art of discrimination, the ability to judge the value of books in relation to both their specific research needs and their education as a whole. William Warner Bishop said that a student should have:

> The ability to judge of the comparative merits of books both new and old . . . if the student has acquired some criteria for forming judgments on his own, he has gained from the college library, from his fellow students . . . from his earlier training, an attitude toward books which defies definition, but which may perhaps best be termed *discriminating.* [23]

As early as 1876 Samuel Swett Green had mentioned the value of library instruction in developing critical judgment, as did several other writers during the following decades, among them T. K. Davis of Wooster, George Little of Bowdoin, and Kendrick Babcock of the Bureau of Education.[24]

A second objective was that of training independent learners: teaching students to teach themselves. The importance of this objective was again noted by Green, also by Otis Robinson and William Warner Bishop who saw its implications for reference service: "The poise and balanced judgement of the true teacher who remembers that his business is, as had been well said, 'to make himself useless,' would be a great desideratum in a desk attendant."[25]

A third objective, known by the popularized term "life-long learning," encourages the college graduate to continue to read and study productively, thanks to his college-acquired facility to handle fundamental library resources. Edwin H. Woodruff discussed this objective at the ALA conference in Milwaukee in 1886.

> The practical duty of a college library . . . is to teach the student how he may, if necessary, at any time in his post collegiate years, seek out and use the books that have displaced or carried along the knowledge of his college days. It should reveal to him the fact that no professor's word is final. And he should feel that the college has done all it can for him when it has led him into the library, taught him . . . to use its contents.[26]

THE PLACE OF THE LIBRARY IN THE COLLEGE COMMUNITY

Perhaps no problems have been discussed more frequently than those involved in gaining the support of teaching faculty. Not only is faculty support usually needed for initial approval of a bibliography course, it is absolutely necessary if course-related instruction is to become a reality. In 1898 George T. Little of Bowdoin stated the ideal:

> College librarians have the advantage, in their respective college faculties, of a number of experts who are directly interested in the proper use of the library by students, and whose assistance in accomplishing this end can and ought to be obtained. Real, active, and continuous cooperation between professors and librarian is essential to successful work in this direction.[27]

Justin Winsor, Otis Robinson, T. K. Davis, and Edwin Woodruff had previously made similar remarks.[28] Seeing the need to work in harmony with teaching faculty led librarians to the next logical consideration—that of finding concepts for the role the academic library should play in its own community. William Frederick Poole sought to clarify the role of the library in the college curriculum in the Phi Beta Kappa address at Northwestern University in 1893. Poole surveyed educational and library trends in the previous two decades, demonstrating an awareness of the broad range of factors influencing the library's efforts in teaching students how to use its resources.[29]

A still much disputed question is whether bibliography courses should be offered for academic credit as part of the formal curriculum. Early leaders continued to be influenced by Emerson's dream of the "professor of books," and by the idea that instruction in library use should be combined with historical bibliography into courses accepted as part of the liberal arts tradition. The years from 1876 to 1914 being expansionary ones, many librarians saw courses in bibliography becoming a permanent fixture in academic curricula provided they, the librarians, could elicit support from their faculty colleagues. The successful and continuing work of Davis at Michigan and Root at Oberlin served as models for colleges and universities around the country. In their public statements library leaders occasionally alluded to course-related instruction, but few were successful in describing how it should work or in defending it as a worthwhile alternative to courses taken for credit toward graduation.

SURVEYS AFTER THE TURN OF THE CENTURY

In 1893 George T. Little reported that scarcely a dozen institutions of higher learning were offering systematic courses of library instruction, though we have no evidence that he conducted a careful survey. At the same time, he conceded that few colleges had "failed to make some attempt to give instruction in the use of libraries."[30] Little credited the Bureau of Education and its publications with stimulating colleges and universities to think about library instruction and to experiment with various methods. He may have had in mind the 1876 report and the *Circulars of Information* as well as annual reports. In 1912 William Warner Bishop said that college librarians and college professors alike were earnestly "studying methods" of bibliographic instruction and experimenting with "ways and means."[31]

Four months after the publication of Bishop's speech, the Bureau of Education began collecting survey data on the nature and extent of library instruction. In September 1912, George B. Utley, Secretary of ALA, wrote to Phineas L. Windsor, Librarian of the University of Illinois, asking for a critique of questions he had proposed sending to academic libraries. These questions included the following items:

1. Does your institution give any instruction in library methods and the use of the library?
2. Are the courses elective or required?
3. What subjects are taken up?
4. Is credit given for these courses, as for other regular courses in the college curriculum?
5. Remarks. (Please add any further information available as to exact nature of the courses, their scope and the method of instruction.)[32]

Windsor made substantive comments about the first question and the last one, indicating his concern to make a distinction between instructing library users and training librarians.

1. Does your institution give any instruction in (a) how to use the library or how to use reference books, (b) in cataloging, classifying, etc., (Library Economy), (c) in history of books and libraries, paleography, etc. I believe it might be clearer if these three subdivisions were brought out in your questionnaire.
2. Remarks. What is the especial purpose of the course in your institution? For example, are the courses intended primarily for school teachers? Are they intended primarily for students in English or History courses? Are they intended to train people for employment in libraries?[33]

The most striking aspect of these questions is their tacit recognition of the credit course as the appropriate vehicle for library instruction. Windsor's elaboration of the latter item sought to clarify the objectives of bibliographic instruction. He did not commit such work to the liberal arts curriculum, though that idea could be inferred from his reference to English and history courses. These questions, prepared by Utley and amended by Windsor, probably formed the basis for the October questionnaire sent out by ALA, though we cannot be sure to what extent Utley changed his questions to conform to Windsor's suggestions.

Results of the ALA questionnaire were summarized in the 1912 report of the Commissioner of Education. Of 200 questionnaires sent, 149 were returned for a rate of nearly 75%. Fifty-seven percent (85) of the respondents conducted instruction of some description. Of those 85 schools offering programs, 34 (40%) reported elective courses, 32 (37.5%) reported required courses, and 19 (2.5%) did not specify whether their courses were elective or required. Seventy-three (about 86%) of the respondents offering instruction taught courses "designed primarily to give greater skill in the use of books to the students as a whole and to teach the resources of the library."[34] The next annual report of the Commissioner of Education described results of a library instruction survey Willard Austen conducted for the New York State Library Association. Responses were generally similar to those of the ALA survey. For example, 49% of 165 responding institutions were engaged in organized library instruction.[35]

In his generally excellent historical article on library service to college students, Fritz Veit identifies a number of factors affecting the growth of a wide range of public services. In discussing bibliographic instruction, he cites the Bureau of Education report, "Library Instruction, in Universities, Colleges, and Normal Schools," compiled by Henry Evans and published in 1914. Veit notes that the Bureau had found that only seven of 446 academic institutions taught required courses and 19 taught elective credit courses in the use of libraries.[36] The view thereby conveyed, that only 6% of the institutions surveyed were actively engaged in library instruction, typifies the tendency of current literature to underestimate the scope and value of what was happening in this period. In fact nearly 20.5% (91) of the respondents described systematic attempts at bibliographic instruction (though not necessarily in the form of a credit course) and the bulk of the report consists of their narrative descriptions.[37] The data collected in the three surveys, published within a short two years, are not statistically comparable, but taken as a whole, indicate a considerably greater degree of interest and experimentation than we had previously thought.

SUMMARY

Bibliographic instruction for undergraduates in American colleges and universities from 1876 to 1914 occurred in the context of sweeping changes in higher education. The rise of research transformed the nature of the academic institution, gaining equal footing with teaching as a basic university function. Other trends included the decline of "textbook teaching" in lieu of seminars thus emulating higher education in Germany. The subsequent demands on academic libraries paralleled rapid growth in collections and in public services, stimulating discussion of the appropriate ratonale and methodology of library use instruction.

Library leaders paved the way in this field by defining and articulating ideas still active in the 1970s. They clarified persistent issues discussing instructional objectives, the role of the library in the institution as a whole, the need for faculty cooperation, the value of courses offered for credit, and ideas suggested by words and phrases such as "discrimination," "independent learners," and "life-long learning." The surveys, published by the U.S. Bureau of Education, indicate that, particularly after the turn of the century, more academic institutions experimented with the means and methods of bibliographic instruction than has been generally recognized.

REFERENCES

1. Kenneth Brough, *Scholar's Workshop; Evolving Conceptions of Library Service* (Urbana: University of Illinois Press, 1953), p. 158.
2. Samuel Rothstein, "The Development of the Concept of Reference Service in American Libraries, 1850–1900," *Library Quarterly* 23 (January 1953): 3-4.
3. Arthur E. Bestor, Jr. "The Transformation of American Scholarship, 1875–1917," *Library Quarterly* 23 (July 1593): 164–179. These major developments are treated in much greater detail in Jurgen Herbst, *The German Historical School in American Scholarship; A Study in the Transfer of Culture* (Ithaca, New York: Cornell University, 1965); Laurence S. Veysey, *The Emergence of the American University* (Chicago: University of Chicago, 1965).
4. Samuel Rothstein, *The Development of Reference Services Through Academic Traditions, Public Library Practice and Special Librarianship*, ACRL Monograph no. 14 (Chicago: Association of College and Reference Librarians, 1955), p. 14.
5. Bestor, *op. cit.*, pp. 170-171.
6. Melvil Dewey, "Libraries the True University for Scholars as Well as People," *Library Notes* 1 (1886): 49–50.
7. Herbert Baxter Adams, "Seminary Libraries and University Extension," *Johns Hopkins University Studies in Historical and Political Science* 5 (November 1887): 443–459.
8. Rothstein, *The Development of Reference Services*, p. 12.
9. U.S. Bureau of the Census, *Historical Statistics of the United States, Colonial Times to 1970*, pt. 1 (Washington, D.C.: GPO), p. 383.
10. Cited in Rothstein, *The Development of Reference Services*, p. 18.

11. Brough, *op. cit.*, p. 112.
12. Quoted in Ashton R. Willard, "College Libraries in the United States," *New England Magazine* n.s.17 (December 1897): 423.
13. Ralph Waldo Emerson, "Books," *Atlantic Monthly* 1 (January 1858): 344.
14. William Mathews, "Professorships of Books and Reading," in *Public Libraries in the United States of America* (Washington, D.C.: GPO, 1876), p. 241; Otis H. Robinson, "College Library Administration," in *Public Libraries in the United States of America*, p. 521; M. D. Bisbee, "The Place of Bibliography in the Equipment of a Cultivated Man," *Library Journal* 22 (September 1897): 429–430; George T. Little, "School and College Libraries," *Library Journal* 18 (October 1893): 432; Joseph Schneider, "A College Course in Bibliography," *Catholic Educational Review* 3 (March 1912): 216.
15. *Oberlin College Catalogue, 1903* (Oberlin, Ohio: Oberlin College, 1903), p. 91.
16. Richard Rubin, "Azariah Smith Root and Library Instruction at Oberlin College," *Journal of Library History* 12 (Summer 1977): 251.
17. Raymond C. Davis, "Teaching Bibliography in Colleges," *Library Journal* 11 (September 1886): 289.
18. Edward G. Holley, "Academic Libraries in 1876," *College and Research Libraries* 37 (January 1976): 28–32; George S. Bonn, Training Laymen in the Use of the Library," in *The State of the Library Art*, vol. 2, pt. 1, ed. Ralph R. Shaw (New Brunswick, N.J.: Rutgers University, Graduate School of Library Service, 1960), p. 28. See also, Robert E. Brundin, "Justin Winsor of Harvard and the Liberalizing of the College Library," *Journal of Library History* 10 (January 1975): 57–70.
19. Schneider, "A College Course," p. 217; Henry R. Evans, comp., "Library Instruction in Universities, Colleges, and Normal Schools," *United States Bureau of Education Bulletin* 34 (1914): 3.
20. Kendrick C. Babcock, "Bibliographical Instruction in College, *Library Journal* 38 (March 1913): 134.
21. William Warner Bishop, "Training in the Use of Books," in *The Backs of Books and Other Essays in Librarianship* (Baltimore: Williams, Wilkins, 1926), pp. 119–120. Reprinted from *Sewanee Review* 20 (July 1912): 265–281.
22. Otis H. Robinson, "The Relation of Libraries to College Work," *Library Journal* 6 (April 1881): 102.
23. Bishop, *op. cit.*, pp. 121–122.
24. Samuel S. Green, "Personal Relations Between Librarians and Readers," *American Library Journal* 1 (October 1876): 78; T. K. Davis, "The College Library," *Library Journal* 10 (May 1885): 100; Little, "School and College," p. 431; idem, "Instruction in the Use of Reference-Books and Libraries in Colleges," *Library Journal* 23 (August 1898): 92; Babcock, "Bibliographical Instruction," p. 134.
25. Green, "Personal Relations: p. 80; Otis H. Robinson, "Rochester University Library —Administration and Use," *United States Bureau of Education Circulars of Information*, no. 1 (1880): 21; William Warner Bishop "The Amount of Help to Be Given to Readers," *ALA Bulletin* 2 (September 1908): 328.
26. Edwin H. Woodruff, "University Libraries and Seminary Methods of Instruction," *Library Journal* 11 (September 1886): 221.
27. Little, *op. cit.*, p. 92.
28. Justin Winsor, "The College Library," *United States Bureau of Education Circulars of Information*, no. 1 (1880): 8; Robinson, "The Relation of Libraries," p. 101; T. K. Davis, "The College Library," p. 102; Woodruff, "University Libraries," p. 221; Holley, "Academic Libraries," p. 31.
29. W. F. Poole, "The University Library and the University Curriculum" *Library*

Journal 18 (November 1893): 470–471. Reprinted in *Landmarks of Library Litera-ture 1876–1976*, ed. Diane J. Ellsworth and Norman D. Stevens (Metuchen, NJ: Scarecrow Press, 1976), pp. 292–295.

30. Little, *op. cit.*, p. 432.
31. Bishop, *op. cit.*, p. 120.
32. Utley to Windsor, 12 September 1912, General Correspondence, ALA Archives, University of Illinois Library, Champaign–Urbana; also in Archives, Newberry Library, Chicago.
33. Windsor to Utley, 2 October 1912, General Correspondence, ALA Archives, University of Illinois Library, Champaign–Urbana; also in Archives, Newberry Library, Chicago.
34. John D. Wolcott, "Recent Aspects of Library Development," in *Report of the Commissioner of Education for the Year Ended June 30, 1912*, vol. 1 (Washington, D.C.: GPO, 1913), pp. 381–382. The text of the report states that the ALA distributed its questionnaire in October, 1912; the title page of the report claims to cover the year ending June 30, 1912. Apparently the title page is incorrect.
35. Mary E. Ahern, "Library Activities during 1912-13," in *Report of the Commissioner of Education for the Year Ended June 30, 1913*, vol. 1 (Washington, D.C.: GPO, 1914), p. 327.
36. Fritz Veit, "Library Service to College Students," *Library Trends* 25 (July 1976): 371.
37. Evans, *op. cit.*, p. 4, 6–23.

Anne C. Edmonds and Willis E. Bridegam

Mount Holyoke College and Amherst College

PERSPECTIVES ON COOPERATION:
THE EVALUATION OF A CONSORTIUM

This paper examines the climate in which consortia were established to share limited resources and to develop research collections. Today financial restrictions are forcing many libraries to re-examine the effectiveness and rationale of cooperative ventures. Against this setting the history of one such enterprise, the Hampshire Inter-Library Center, is reviewed, and a recent evaluation of its program to determine the future of library cooperation among its members (Amherst, Hampshire, Mount Holyoke and Smith Colleges and the University of Massachusetts) is examined. Observations on the process of evaluation and the initial effects of recommendations are discussed.

1976 marked the Bicentennial of this country, the Centennial of the American Library Association, and the twenty-fifth anniversary of the Hampshire Inter-Library Center, Inc., familiarly known as HILC.

HILC is a cooperative endeavor of five academic libraries and one public library. It is one of the oldest cooperative library consortia in the United States. At present it is undergoing a metamorphosis, changing from a physical entity with its own collections and staff to a conceptualized consortium within the framework of which cooperative activities will be developed.

This physical dissolution of the Center, with the dispersal of its collections, may seem to many like a step backward in the forward march to cooperation, so much a feature of today's library trends. Why should a long established center, regarded within the profession as a model and pioneer in cooperative endeavors, set within the framework of strong and prestigious collegiate libraries, and favored with the support of financially secure academic institutions, go out of business? In detailing the circumstances and developments relating to this change, the authors feel there may be a message here for others who are treading down the golden road of library cooperation.

This is not a history of the Hampshire Inter-Library Center. The documentation of its pioneering endeavors remains to be writtern. It invokes the names of Flora Belle Ludington, Newton McKeon, Margaret Johnson, Fremont Rider, Keyes Metcalf and a host of others.

For a background to the present situation though, it is necessary to give a brief description of HILC and its member libraries and to look at the national climate and factors in the library community out of which the movement for library cooperation grew. It is also necessary to understand the changing nature and interrelationships of each of the member libraries in this particular consortium. Finally, the manner in which the decision to change came about, the mechanism for handling the dissolution of the physical center and implication for the future will be spelled out.

HILC is located in the mid-section of Massachuetts. It is in the valley of the Connecticut River which cuts through the state travelling south from its origins near the Canadian border, and forming the boundary between Vermont and New Hampshire as it passes by Dartmouth College. The river continues South through Connecticut, giving a passing nod to Trinity and Wesleyan Colleges, until it emerges into Long Island Sound near New Haven and Yale University.

This segment of the state is known as the Pioneer Valley, and in it are clustered the five academic institutions which support HILC: Amherst College, founded in 1821 as an undergraduate liberal arts college for men, but which became coeducational in 1977; Mount Holyoke and Smith Colleges, both remaining colleges for women, one founded in 1857, the other in 1875; Hampshire College, a coeducational experimenting college which graduated its first full class in 1974; and the University of Massachusetts which began as a state agricultural college in 1876 under the Morrill Land Grant Act and is now a full fledged university with significant graduate programs in addition to its extensive undergraduate liberal arts major.

The Hampshire Inter-Library Center is one of the oldest cooperative library consortia in the United States. It was founded in 1951 by Amherst, Mount Holyoke, and Smith Colleges following a long period of informal cooperation among the three. Its goal was to be a center for a collection of little-used serials which would enhance the research resources of the three undergraduate libraries.

The University of Massachusetts joined HILC in 1954 and Hampshire College became the fifth member in 1970. The Forbes Library (the Northampton Public Library) has been an associate member since 1962. It might be interesting to keep in mind the present size of the library collections of each of the member libraries: Amherst 500,000, Hampshire 55,000, Mount Holyoke 400,000, Smith 800,000, The University 1,600,000. The combined library collections of the five academic institutions come to almost three million four hundred thousand volumes (3,400,000).

As a separately incorporated organization, HILC has had its own constitution, budget, and staff. The five colleges contribute equally to its maintenance and growth. The 1977/78 assessment from each of the five full members was $20,000, The Forbes Library contributed $10,000, providing a total budget of $110,000. A Board composed of five faculty representatives (one from each institution), the five Librarians, and the Five College Coordinator directs its activities.

It should also be noted that overlaying this library cooperative has been a long history of strong interinstitutional cooperation among the five academic institutions in the Valley which was formally incorporated as Five Colleges, Inc. in 1966.

Although HILC and Five Colleges, Inc. have been among the longest established and the strongest of cooperatives, cooperation has not been easy to maintain. Cooperation is one of those plus words, like Motherhood and the Flag. It is grandiose. It crackles with nobility. It conveys self satisfaction, generosity of spirit, the conferring of benefits But it is not always wealth that is being shared. As Ralph Shaw, that master of the trenchant phrase, used constantly to reiterate, "There is no point in cooperating just to spread the poverty." This has been too frequently the case. When one looks into the reality behind many of the listings of cooperative projects, one finds that they may range from a group of three libraries which have exchanged their lists of periodical subscriptions numbering in all 200 titles, to the Center for Research Libraries serving the needs not only of the ten universities which were its founding members, but also many additional members throughout the country, and having transatlantic access to the collections of the British Library Lending Division in Britain.

One should not decry any of these bridges, though, whether as local as a one lane New England covered bridge or as heavily trafficked as San Francisco's Golden Gate. For too long too many libraries have been overprotective of their resources and services, jealously afraid that they will be depleted by sharing. But too often bombast has taken such movements out of scale and created a facade about cooperation which makes for a sense of false promises and hopes and then bitterness when success is not realized.

A review of the literature on library cooperation over the past twenty years shows a dismal picture of efforts at cooperation in academic libraries. Interestingly enough, aspects of library activities which had potential for cooperation had been articulated in the early days of librarianship and haven't changed a century later: union lists of serials, interlibrary lending, cooperative processing, acquisition agreements.

But as Eileen Thornton pointed out in her review of "Cooperation among Colleges" in 1958, the small size of most collegiate library collections and the minimal staffing and funding provided them made effective cooperative endeavors virtually impossible.[1] Eleven years later, B. E. Richardson found very little to be sanguine about.[2]

The panic over education triggered by the launching of Russia's Sputnik in 1957 focused national attention on access to information and on libraries. Academic institutions proliferated and financial resources available to them and their libraries seemed limitless. However, even the infusion and seduction of foundation grants and government funds, whose guidelines attempt to enforce cooperative ventures, had little success.

As Ruth Patrick points out in *Guidelines for Library Cooperation: Development of Academic Library Consortia*, a 1970 Office of Education study showed that more than 90 per cent of the then existing 125 academic library consortia had been established since 1960 and over 75 per cent since 1965.[3] The 2nd edition of the *Directory of Academic Library Consortia*, published in 1975, lists 350 operating consortia, but the definition of consortia has been extended to include any consortium which has at least one academic member.[4]

The key change in cooperative development in libraries came with the breakthrough in the development of electronic data bases when the Library of Congress developed MARC I and MARC II. With the introduction of this new technology, a whole new dimension of size entered the cooperative picture. The scene was being shaped by systems such as OCLC (the Ohio College Libraries Center); regional groupings such as NELINET, SOLINET, AMIGOS; large inter-institutional groupings, such as Columbia, Yale, Harvard, and the New York Public Library in the Reserach Libraries Group; a recently announced union between the Standord and University of California/Berkeley Libraries; supra-organizations such as the Council of Cooperative Library Networks; and finally, at the national level, legislation such as "Networks for Knowledge," a part of the Higher Education Act of 1965 and its amendments; and the National Commission on Libraries and Information Services. The expense of the technology required for these networks implies that economies are only possible through cooperation on a large scale.

An excellent overview of this whole picture is presented in David Weber's article on a "Century of Cooperative Programs."[5] But there are cautions. Boyd R. Keenan writing on "The Politics of Technological Forces in Library Cooperation," in the context of the Arab oil embargo, warns that these types of electronic based cooperative activities are dependent on high energy consumption.[6]

These then were the external forces shaping the decision on the future of HILC. What were some of the internal forces at work?

Space was one element. Mount Holyoke, the University of Massachusetts, and Amherst had in turn provided free space for the HILC collections and staff. If the HILC collections were to continue to grow, a building of its own would have to be considered and its cost justified.

Money was another. HILC had started as a bootstrap operation. Its initial funds came from pooling backfiles and selling the duplicates. This money then made possible the purchase of new serial subscriptions. In the initial days Mount Holyoke provided cataloging services. Gradually institutional funds were allocated. However, as the financing of higher education became critical, the administrations of the five colleges were scrutinizing more closely the extent to which they were financing two library activities: their own home institution and an additional resource in the collections of HILC.

The changing nature of the University of Massachusetts shifted the balance of relationships. In 1960, the University was the smallest of the collections in the Valley and relied heavily on the collegiate libraries and HILC. As the University and its collections grew it developed its own research collections and resources to which the colleges began to turn. HILC became less important.

The development of closer inter-library relations among the five institutions also added a new dimension to the situation. In addition to the daily inter-library delivery service, students and faculty from each institution, beginning in 1973, could borrow in person from any of the libraries.

And last, but not least, there was a shift in that intangible quality that personal leadership and commitment bring. To quote from Ruth Patrick's *Guidelines* again, her studies found that successful consortia were established because of the commitment and driving force of an individual or individuals.[7] This was certainly true of HILC's beginnings. Of the three librarians who started HILC in 1951, the first to retire was Flora Belle Ludington in 1964. Retirement followed fairly quickly for the other two. Since then, Smith and the University have had three Librarians; Hampshire and Amherst have had two; and HILC itself has had three Librarians and one Acting Librarian. This past instability in the top administrative levels of the member libraries has made it difficult to maintain a steady commitment to a cooperative endeavor and to chart its future with any singleminded purpose.

The future of HILC has really been under discussion for several years. Several reports have been prepared on it. In 1969 library cooperation was one element in the report of the Five College Long Range Planning Committee.[8] A series of other investigations and studies, among them one by Lieberfeld Associates, and a limited study by the five present Librarians, came to no resolution. Finally, in the fall of 1976 four library consultants, Richard DeGennaro, Director of Libraries at the University of Pennsylvania; Donald B. Engley, Associate University Librarian at Yale University; David Kaser, Professor in the Graduate Library School of Indiana University; and Louis Martin, Librarian of Harvard College, were invited to survey HILC and five college library cooperation. They visited Amherst on January 9–12, 1977 and submitted their report titled "A View of HILC and its Future" on March 16, 1977. The substance of the consultants' report and the Librarians' recommendations in response to it provide the framework for a new and critical look at consortia, particularly those attempting to build and maintain cooperatively an independent, physicially separate, research collection.

The four Presidents and the Chancellor of the University (hereafter referred to as the Presidents) charged the consultants and the Librarians with considering seven basic questions:

1. To what extent can existing duplications in periodicals be reduced without serious detriment to the quality of holdings and user services?

2. To what extent should HILC expand its holdings to help reduce duplication? Are there viable alternatives to the expansion of HILC?

3. What are the long range needs for HILC's physical facilities and staffing? Is a separate building justified?

4. Is a common storage facility needed for little-used monographs?

5. Should we expand the Valley's union list of holdings, and how? What are the cost-benefit implications?

6. What automated library systems should be employed by all or some of the Five College Libraries on a cooperative basis?

7. How and at what point should Valley libraries join with other libraries, regionally or nationally, to maintain or increase the quality and variety of services and holdings? Should HILC be a focal point for regional cooperation?

Many academic libraries through the country have had to reduce their periodical holdings, whether they had close ties with other institutions or not. The proximity of the Five Colleges, the privilege of in-person borrowing, and 24-hour delivery service provided an even greater imperative to examine existing subscription lists for unnecessary duplication. Fortunately, this process was facilitated by the existence of the *Pioneer Valley Union List of Serials*, a computer produced publication, which listed not only the titles, but also the complete serial holdings of the Five Colleges and the Forbes Library. Not all duplication was found to be undesirable, however. The consultants warned, "Rather than permitting subject specialization, the high degree of commonality among the offerings of the five institutions to the contrary warrants a substantial incidence of duplication in the collections of the several libraries. Duplication is not necessarily bad; some is essential."

When the HILC collection of periodical titles was examined, it was found that about one-third of the titles were duplicated at one of the five college libraries. A use study by the HILC Librarian revealed that the number of five college loan requests for HILC material was surprisingly low. Of HILC's 598 current subscriptions, 326 had been requested on loan from HILC less than once a year over the last five years. The total cost of these 326 subscriptions for 1976 was $14,390. Not tabulated with the HILC loans, however, were periodical issues circulated to the area libraries for current awareness purposes and the in-house use of HILC. Current awareness use could not be measured, but HILC's in-house use was found to be an average of less than two registered visitors per day for the 1975–77 period.

In addition to justifying the cost of duplicated and little-used journals, it was necessary also to consider the major expense of housing the jointly owned materials. When the University Library was no longer able to provide quarters for HILC, Amherst College agreed to provide this space until July 1981. An expanding HILC collection, however, would require costly new quarters with at least 10,000 sq. ft. by 1981, plus an estimated $3. per square foot annually for overhead, maintenance, and depreciation.

To improve the Libraries' ability to respond to the research needs of their users, and as an alternative to the costly development of HILC as a research library, the consultants suggested membership in the Center for Research Libraries for each of the five libraries. Better yet, a National Periodical Library would, as John McDonald pointed out in the 1976 Pittsburgh Conference on Resource Sharing in Libraries, "greatly assist resource-sharing by freeing the existing system of much of its present traffic,"[9] but unfortunately, this development must be awaited. However, the important realization was that a consortium of limited size, serving just a few institutions, did not have the necessary economy of scale to justify operation of an independent research collection for its members. Instead, reliance on a national periodical bank, which could spread the cost among many institutions, was recommended. Since the consultants could not justify on a cost effective basis the maintenance of the HILC collections as an independent library, they suggested that "HILC should rationalize, reduce and decentralize its stored materials . . . and each remaining title should be articulated over the next five years into the collection of whichever member library seems to have the greatest need for it."

The five Presidents discussed the consultants' report with them and with the HILC Board, which also included the Librarians. They then made the report available to interested faculty and staff and asked the Librarians to prepare a response to the consultants' report and to make their own recommendations for the future of five college library cooperation. In their reply the Librarians concurred with the consultants that HILC should shift its emphasis from a physical collection to new consortial responsibilities and relationships. They also identified a number of steps necessary to achieve that change. The consultants' and Librarians' recommendations were accepted by the Presidents after consultation with their faculties in October 1977.

Approximately 425 HILC periodical titles were selected for immediate cancellation, and the remaining 175 more useful titles were renewed for one year while they underwent further evaluation. A few teaching faculty were distressed to see so many periodicals cancelled, but the documented lack of use over a considerable period of time made it difficult to argue responsibly for continuation of most of the HILC titles.

The question then became one of determining how to disperse the HILC collection among the five college libraries, a process that will engage representatives from each of the libraries for the next two to three years. The relative strength of existing academic programs, the research needs of faculty, and the availability of space in each library will be key considerations in this process.

Having rejected the idea of a central research collection, the Librarians decided to evaluate the benefits of merging some of their bibliographic records through various automated systems. By 1974 all of the four colleges had joined the Ohio College Library Center network through NELINET. The University Library, meanwhile, processed the MARC tapes independently to produce its catalog records. The consultants recommended that the University examine the cost benefits of participating in the OCLC system in order to make available on one system the cataloging records of additions to the five book collections.

A feasibility study for a Five College automated circulation system backed by the existing 24-hour interlibrary delivery service was proposed by the Librarians. Also of interest was a cooperative automated acquisition system which might provide the five libraries an opportunity to coordinate the purchase of research materials. It is by no means certain that these automated systems will be acceptable and beneficial to all of the Libraries, but the joint study should be of great value to each Library in making these determinations.

As part of the consideration of the Libraries' interrelationships, Hampshire College, which has always placed a greater emphasis on audio-visual services, agreed to conduct a feasibility study for a Five College Non-Print Materials Center. Joint acquisition of films, a central film repair and cleaning service, and possibly joint purchase of expensive equipment will be considered.

In addition to the recommendations for access to resources, plans were made to strengthen and formalize the mutual relationships that had been developing over the years. The Librarians Council, the name for the five Librarians meeting as a group, began to meet more frequently and to deal with critical issues facing the five libraries. The charge to the HILC Board was revised to include responsibility for advising the Librarians and Presidents on all aspects of college library cooperation, not just the activities of HILC. The HILC Selection Committee, comprising the Reference Librarians or a Bibliographer from each of the libraries, received an expanded charge to include dispersal of HILC materials and the exchange of information concerning proposed additions to and deletions from the five periodical collections. Other groups, such as the Circulation and Inter-library Loan Librarians found that occasional meetings helped them coordinate their policies and plan together for the future. The Presidents also agreed to meet at least once a year with the Librarians to review progress and to establish new goals.

To return to what was stated earlier, cooperation may seem grand, noble, and right, but some forms of cooperation may prove to be wasteful and inefficient when analyzed fully. The process of self-examination is difficult and sometimes traumatic. Those selected to help in the process must be carefully chosen and thoroughly briefed. Care must be taken to consult the faculty and staff and to keep them fully informed, a process that often opens valuable new channels of communication. Most important, librarians and others are foced to commit a considerable amount of time and energy to long-range cooperative planning, an aspect of cooperation that is too often ignored or given lip service.

Keyes Metcalf, in his survey of HILC in 1957 stated that "A major asset of the Center—and the best possible omen for its future—is the good judgment shown by its Directors."[10] As HILC responds to new conditions and changing requirements determined by the scrutiny of the past two years, those who have been involved in this study hope that a similar future judgment can be made of those who have made decisions during this crucial period in HILC's history.

REFERENCES

1. Eileen Thornton, "Cooperation among Colleges," *Library Trends* 6 (January 1958): 309–325.
2. Bernard E. Richardson, "Trends in Cooperative Ventures among College Libraries," *Library Trends* 18 (July 1969): 85–92.
3. Ruth Patrick, *Guidelines for Library Cooperation: Development of Academic Library Consortia* (Santa Monica: System Development Corporation, 1972), p. 1.
4. Donald V. Black and Carlos A. Cuadra, *Directory of Academic Library Consortia* (2d ed.; Santa Monica: System Development Corporation, 1975).
5. David Weber, "Century of Cooperative Programs," *College and Research Libraries* 37 (May 1976): 205–221.
6. Boyd R. Keenan, "The Politics of Technological Forces in Library Cooperation," *Library Trends* 24 (October 1975): 183–190.
7. Patrick, *op. cit.*, p. 25–27.
8. Five College Long Range Planning Committee, *Five College Cooperation: Directions for the Future* (Amherst, Mass.: University of Massachusetts Press, 1969), p. 140–147.
9. John P. McDonald, "Problems Needing Attention: Reactions," in Conference on Resources Sharing in Libraries, Pittsburgh, 1976, *Library Resource Sharing* (New York, M. Dekker, 1977), p. 169.
10. Keyes D. Metcalf, *The Hampshire Inter-Library Center: a Survey of its Background and its Problems with Recommendations for the Future* (South Hadley, Mass., Hampshire Inter-Library Center, 1957), p. 17.

Beverlee A. French

University of California, San Diego

THE FOURTH GENERATION: RESEARCH LIBRARIES AND COMMUNITY INFORMATION

The role of the academic library in cooperation with other types of libraries as well as with non-library information agencies is explored. Forms that such "fourth generation" cooperation can assume are described. Benefits to be realized for the community and for academic libraries from such efforts are identified and related to social forces affecting academic libraries. It is asserted that academic information services can be performed most accurately and efficiently when library staff members are completely aware of the information roles of non-library organizations and that academic libraries should assume leadership in establishing networks of the "fourth generation."

It is tempting to depict a bleak future for academic libraries and especially for access to them by those outside the academic community. In fact, significant sentiment for *decreasing* access to academic libraries was exhibited two years ago at a New York Metropolitan Reference and Research Library Agency (METRO) workshop-seminar entitled, "Personal Access: Myth or Reality?"[1] It was noted there that libraries which serve professional schools are developing effective barriers to access and many participating librarians felt that new access barriers are necessary if academic libraries are to meet the needs of their own constituencies.

In spite of this apparent trend, I will explore the role of the academic library in the community, in cooperation not only with other types of libraries, but with non-library agencies engaged in information transfer as well. While recognizing institutional and social pressures that influence service in college and university libraries, I will describe the forms such cooperation may assume and identify benefits to be derived for the community and for the academic library from this cooperative effort.

SOCIAL TRENDS

Providing the background for this discussion are a number of conflicting trends. Academic libraries are social institutions and, as such, feel all the diverse social forces affecting modern institutions. It scarcely needs repeating that dwindling resources and rising costs are forcing academic libraries to attempt to function more efficiently and to continue to focus on meeting the needs of the primary clientele. Budgets are normally based on enrollments and educational programs. Every minute of service extended outside the institution, usually without financial compensation, detracts from the library's primary mission. At the same time, in this era of accountability, the parent institution may indirectly promote library service by its own public service and community relations as it attempts to portray the publicly-supported university as relevant to taxpayers' interests. In fact, some citizens may harbor the idea that the principal purpose of the university is direct service to the state. While citizens who explicitly or implicitly subscribe to this philosophy are not demanding to enroll in classes without paying tuition, people have traditionally expected free service from libraries.

The demand for increased access to information that has emerged in recent years is a societal pressure affecting academic libraries. In the *Goals and Objectives* adopted by the American Library Association Council in 1975, we find that total access to information is a major concern of librarians, as the first stipulation calls for:

> Provision of library and information services and resources for all the people of the United States of America in order to increase their opportunity to participate in society, to learn . . . and to obtain information needed for research.[2]

Similar opinion is expressed by the National Commission on Library and Information Science in its report which states that:

> . . . the total library and information resource in the United States is a national resource which should be developed, strengthened, organized, and made available to the maximum degree possible in the public interest.[3]

In response to convictions such as these, the Association of College and Research Libraries has adopted a set of "Access Policy Guidelines" to assist academic libraries in developing and expressing their policies on access by individuals outside the institutional clientele.[4]

In the information environment by these national goals, users do not care where their information resides. They do not discriminate among libraries with different missions. Nor are they being exhorted to do so. Unfortunately, this enthusiasm for access is not accompanied by sufficient understanding by the public or by state and federal government of the financial requirements of a system of information dissemination to all citizens.

Another social trend that is currently attracting attention is that of "consumerism." The idea that people ought to be able to obtain information to enable them to make their own intelligent decisions is spreading, perhaps because it appears that decisions that are made for consumers are not always in their best interests. Information in fields such as law and medicine is no longer considered sacred and the appropriate domain only of chosen individuals and institutions. Competencies of professional practitioners are being questioned and trust in revered institutions is waning. Trust is being replaced by an increasing awareness of the need for information about matters affecting personal lives.

Finally, political priorities constitute part of a library's millieu. The example I will use in this examination of the academic library's response to societal pressures is the improvement of health care. Similar analysis could focus on environmental quality or the energy crisis. As the medical profession's emphasis on treatment reaps diminishing returns in improving the nation's health status, attention is shifting to prevention. A major component of the preventive movement is increased public demand for medical and health information. The federal government has begun to stress health education, although the effort is fragmented by the involvement of several agencies and the exclusion of others, such as the National Library of Medicine. In the face of the health care cost escalation, people themselves are seeking justification for all medical expenses. The health care system's failure in its information and communication roles has perhaps spawned the self-care movement.

COMMUNITY INFORMATION NEEDS AND ACADEMIC LIBRARIES

The relationship to libraries of this increased demand is manifested by such phenomena as the establishment of the Center for Medical Consumers and Health Care Information in New York and the nature of interlibrary loan activities reported by METRO (New York) for 1976. METRO's records revealed that medical science titles headed the list of most often requested items.[5]

At least some of what the public needs or wants is scholarly material typically found only in academic medical or hospital libraries. First, it should be recognized that medical and scientific consensus is increasingly elusive. There are no straightforward answers to many medical problems. Therefore, patients and practitioners must often make decisions on the basis of inconclusive and conflicting data. Conflicting scientific data contribute to the confusion surrounding energy, economic, and environmental problems as well. Material aimed at the lay public does not routinely represent these conflicts and, at any rate, in the form of trade books, is published with the purpose of making money. The public is constantly deluged with misinformation as well. Much of the public's so-called medical information is disseminated via television commercials.

Perhaps because of this situation, many responsible organizations engaged in health education are suggesting that the widest possible range of informed opinion be available to the public. The consumer publications of the Center for Medical Consumers and Health Care Information refer readers to articles published in professional medical journals. The newly established National Center for Health Education aims to assist people in making judgments when they are confronted with conflicting medical and scientific information, while participants at a recent international symposium on the role of the individual in primary health care concluded that the lay person should have increased access to high-quality, current information *and* technology.[6] In order to help the layperson to identify misinformation, a consumer health guide offers criteria for evaluating health information. One question to consider is whether the information has been published in a professional medical or health journal.[7] The guide offers no suggestions as to where the consumer is to obtain these journals.

Finally, a case history may serve to dramatize the public's need for scholarly scientific materials. Some years ago, a woman who suffered from a cluster of debilitating symptoms and whose diagnosis had eluded twenty-two physicians, decided that her only chance was to find the answer herself.[8] She began at the Biomedical Library of the University of California at Los Angeles. She returned many, many times, using books in the library, studying and taking notes. One day she came across a book called *Toxicology of Industrial Metals*. Ultimately, she correctly diagnosed that she had been suffering from lead poisoning.

There are two other undercurrents which are significant to a discussion of access in academic libraries. One is the reported trend toward client-centered service—the movement of libraries from an archival to an informational role. Another is the philosophical climate that pervades academic libraries. Both contribute to inadvertent expansion of service to outsiders. As librarians, we have a commitment to fulfilling informational needs, regardless of patron status. Last year, the American Library Association meeting provided the forum for a significant debate on free access to information. Each day, as the public's questions inevitably come to academic reference desks, librarians feel a moral obligation to help. Even so, medical librarians were recently chided at a University of Iowa conference on Public Access to Health Information Through Library Service, when health planner John Proe admonished, "To abrogate this responsibility is to deny your role as a professional librarian. . . . Health is too important for us not to become involved in it personally, as a community, a society, a professional."[9] These are strong words and yet, such dedication represents time and resources taken away from students and faculties. As academic librarians, we also have a commitment to serve our institutions.

FOURTH GENERATION COOPERATION

The challenge in this context is for academic libraries to increase access to locally unique and certainly expensive resources to those who legitimately need them without detracting from service to the primary clientele. Structures must be created that will enable academic institutions and individual librarians to fulfill this social obligation and to fully accomplish institutional objectives.

In order to address the dilemma successfully and imaginatively, we must look beyond the two options of erecting more formidable barriers or allowing service to deteriorate because of the encroaching public demand for academic services and resources. A first step is to explore the information universe that exists in any community. It includes more than libraries. It is comprised of government agencies, special interest groups, voluntary organizations, and even commercial ventures. Health information, especially, is disseminated from a variety of public and private agencies with little coordination of effort. Although informal networks of information referral exist in any metropolitan area, academic and public librarians generally have little knowledge of the information resources in the community, unless a formal community information and referral program has been established.

Several years ago, in comparing the evolution of library cooperation to that of computer technology, John Cory traced the development of the former through four generations of library organization.[10] The first generation of organization is a single library working in isolation. The second is a network of libraries of a single type. The third level is a cooperative system encompassing a variety of types of libraries—public, university and college, private. The fourth generation, a cooperative combination of various types of libraries and non-library agencies engaged in related activities, is still embryonic.

Academic libraries should play a leadership role in establishing cooperative fourth generation community networks. A university library's prestige will increase the political power of such a network and its leadership will assure that the arrangements made are in its best interest. A network, which is defined as a set of elements related to one another through multiple interconnections, should of course be tailored to the local situation and, very importantly, take into account the legitimate aspirations of its member institutions and agencies.

NETWORK ACTIVITIES AND BENEFITS

There are several kinds of activities that such a fourth generation network can undertake to the mutual benefit of its members, including the academic library with its hard-pressed information services.

1. A network may be able to support a librarian or information specialist to seek sophisticated information and materials for the public. People could ask their questions at any of the network nodes and when the resources of the community have been exhausted, the information specialist would personally use the academic library resources, answering questions and obtaining materials when necessary, thereby reducing the public's direct impact on the academic reference service (although possibly increasing interlibrary loan transactions).

2. The individuals involved in the network can assess the type and quality of information dissemination in libraries and other community organizations. Improving the community resources should remove some of the demand for academic resources. Medical librarians are in a position to assume leadership in evaluating material that is written for the lay public and are well acquainted with materials written for health professionals which may be useful to the lay public. At the same time, other members of the network will be more knowledgeable of non-traditional resources.

3. A major opportunity of such a formal arrangement is that of working cooperatively to improve community information service. Agencies and libraries share some of the same service philosophies and have much to offer one another in terms of knowledge, technique, contacts, and information sources. Members can explore common communication problems. Individuals working in the network, the information providers, must be acquainted with one another in order to be fully aware of community resources and the channels that will gain access to them. Cooperative, systematic training efforts should lead to better sharing techniques and improved information and referral service. In the area of health and medical information, such sessions may weaken some of the myths that exist about ethical and legal aspects involved in disseminating medical information. There is still considerable reluctance in many public library circles to deal with medical questions. The recent scattering of library programs addressing the issue of medical information in libraries suggests that this uneasiness is a major concern of librarians. The participants in such programs usually indicate that the public librarian should play a much more active role in dispensing medical and legal information.[11] I have been told that, even in a medical library for patients associated with a major health facility, patients may not see standard pharmaceutical reference works. Academic libraries, whose librarians adhere tenaciously to intellectual freedom principles, have apparently often been the only places where the public is free to examine some types of materials.

4. Library cooperation that includes community agencies and organizations enhances the creation and maintenance of current community service directories.

5. Improvement of the resources and skills in the community will promote the accuracy and efficiency with which information is disseminated. And, very significantly, academic libraries can perform services more efficiently and dispense more accurate information—in short, perform broad services—when staff members are completely aware of the information roles of non-library community organizations.

The results of a survey conducted in San Diego to identify the information needs being met and not being met in the community and to explore the value of fourth generation cooperation serve to support this assertion.[12] The survey revealed weaknesses in the information dissemination system where improvement could probably be made through cooperation. All types of libraries and non-library information agencies were asked anonymously the same twenty-nine questions, one-third of which were health-related. Libraries were found to have a tendency to bend questions so that they could be answered through printed sources when referrals would have been more appropriate. Information agencies seldomly referred people to libraries even when confronted with questions best answered by the types of resources that libraries possess. A similar situation was reported in a Canadian survey on legal information.[13] Law organizations exhibited the greatest tendency to answer questions from personal knowledge, a practice which normally resulted in inaccurate information. Lawyers were found to be no more reliable than the information centers, usually "ad libbing" the answers. The survey also discovered that librarians did not refer questioners to outside agencies and did not know which were appropriate. However, librarians are conditioned to avoid giving answers from personal knowledge, especially in law and medicine, and their responses reflected this background.

Full knowledge by academic reference librarians of the community resources will enhance referrals, educating the public and the information community as to where many information needs can best be met. In turn, the burden resulting from attempts to meet all demands through use of academic collections can be reduced. In other words, academic librarians will be in a better position to identify when use of their services and collections is unnecessary and inappropriate.

6. A cooperative network that is striving to meet some of the public information needs that have been identified as national priorities (e.g., health) and which is visibly improving local community information dissemintion can develop its own political power. Such influence may indirectly benefit the university library. Ideally, a network would develop enough community support to obtain the state and local resources necessary to adequately meet community needs without unduly intruding on the mission of academic libraries or of any other agencies. The cooperative system would be able to support "community librarians" to use research collections for the public. Schemes may even be developed to compensate the "net lenders" for use of their services and collections.

THE FUTURE: COMMUNITY INFORMATION AND INSTITUTIONAL GOALS

In the field of health information, it is promising to note the recent birth of several third generation cooperative projects involving hospital libraries and public libraries—specifically the Community Health Information Network in Cambridge, the Consumer Health Information Program and Services in California, and the Health Information Sharing Project in upstate New York. Although all types of health information providers recently participated in a Health Information Networkers Conference in San Diego, California, academic libraries are just beginning to be involved in third generation activities with other types of libraries and it has barely been predicted that these networks will include non-library agencies and institutions.

More than twenty years ago, when the Medical Library Association first held a session on library service to the layman, it was suggested that greater librarian awareness of information sources would lead to more cooperation among agencies dealing with the public.[14] The fourth generation concept was suggested nearly ten years ago. And five years ago a Karl Nyren editorial encouraged the coordination of the library's resources with all members of the "information community."[15] The movement apparently needs direction. Now is an appropriate time for academic libraries to assume leadership in establishing cooperative networks of the fourth generation. Such networks can help the university demonstrate its relevance to society by administering to community information needs and by responding to pressure for increased access, especially to sophisticated scientific and legal materials. With suitable cooperative arrangements, the academic library can accomplish these goals without compromising its primary obligation. Improvement of information resources and services outside the university—in the public libraries and in community agencies—should actually lessen the daily infringement upon academic resources. Finally, all information providers—librarians and individuals in other public agencies and organizations—can fulfill their own institutional objectives more successfully if they are completely aware of each other's roles, purposes, dissemination techniques and resources.

REFERENCES

1. Noël Savage, "METRO Meet on Access: Curse or Cure?" *Library Journal* 101 (December 15, 1976): 2532-2535.
2. American Library Association, *Goals and Objectives of the American Library Association*, as adopted by the Council of the American Library Association, January 24, 1975.
3. National Commission on Libraries and Information Science, *Toward a National Program for Library and Information Services: Goals for Action* (Washington, D.C.: The Commission, 1975).
4. American Library Association. Association of College and Research Libraries, "Access Policy Guidelines," *College and Research Library News* 36 (November 1975): 322-323.
5. "Interlibrary Loan, New $$ Constraints and Fees," *Library Journal* 102 (January 1, 1977): 24.
6. Lowell S. Levin, Alfred H. Katz, and Erik Holst, *Self-Care: Lay Initiatives in Health* (New York: Prodist, 1976).
7. Harold J. Cornacchia, *Consumer Health* (St. Louis: Mosby, 1976).
8. William H. Crosby, "Lead Contaminated Health Food: Association with Lead Poisoning and Leukemia," *JAMA: Journal of the American Medical Association* 237 (1977): 2627-2629.
9. "Librarians as 'Gatekeepers' of Medical Info," *Library Journal* 100 (November 15, 1975): 2094.
10. John MacKenzie Cory, "The Network in a Major Metropolitan Center (METRO, New York," *The Library Quarterly* 39 (January 1969): 90-98.
11. "How Much Should We Tell? Some Implications of Medical-Legal Reference," *Bay State Librarian* 64 (December 1975): 12-13.
12. John R. Haak, "The Information and Referral System in the San Diego Region." Mimeographed. (San Diego, Calif.: University of California, San Diego, 1976).
13. Linda Jewett, "Libraries and Access to the Law," *Ontario Library Review* 59 (December 1975): 220-225.
14. "Service to the Lay Public," *Bulletin of the Medical Library Association* 43 (1955): 241-262.
15. Karl E. Nyren, "Information Communities," *Library Journal* 98 (May 1, 1973): 1417.

Virginia Gillham and Margaret Beckman

University of Guelph

INDIVIDUAL AUTONOMY AND SUCCESSFUL NETWORKING: A CANADIAN EXPERIENCE

In view of the economic constraints and technological developments of recent years there can be little doubt that effective library service will best be accomplished through interlibrary cooperation and the judicious use of networks. Experience has shown that while network standards are essential, rigidity, extreme uniformity, and excessive central control are not desirable. The ideal is a loosely organized network wherein members are aware of one another's holdings and can benefit from them or from the bibliographic records that describe them, while at the same time a significant degree of independence and autonomy can be maintained within the various in-house operations.

INTRODUCTION

Financial restraints, or the 'new reality' of reduced funding and an inflationary resource market have compelled many academic librarians, certainly in Ontario, to have second thoughts about the efficiency of library networks or consortia. Originally seen as a way of making limited resources more readily available to all members of the Ontario academic community, and at a reduced cost through the implementation of common automated systems, these networks are now being challenged. As Richard deGennaro suggested recently, "Regional consortia may actually be costing their members far more than the benefits they derive if one includes the very substantial cost of staff time needed to make them work."[1]

Technological change is also impacting on the network environment. The concept of a huge central computer (or computers) with massive stores of data has been superseded, as mini and micro computers and mass storage equipment make it possible to reduce dependence on a central facility for maintenance and processing of a data base.

Without negating the benefits that have accrued and can be anticipated from continuing expansion or development of library networks, recent experience in the Ontario academic library network can be used to illustrate the concerns identified above.

THE ONTARIO NETWORK

The concept of networking is not a recent one for the university libraries in the province of Ontario. As early as 1968 the Presidents of the 15 Ontario universities established objectives for a library network which included in its description two propositions:

1. That each university be prepared to commit itself to participate in an Ontario Universities' library system, the principal features of which would provide for the various libraries to be essentially self-sufficient in the provision of service for undergraduate use, and to be effectively interdependent in the provision of service for research and graduate use.

2. That with such system development it would be anticipated that there would be appropriate coordination and centralization of technical processes, that library automation would be introduced where appropriate, and that there would be appropriate centralized storage of less frequently used library materials.[2]

Although it was five years before these concepts were formally recognized with the establishment of the Ontario Universities Library Cooperative Systems (O.U.L.C.S.), informal arrangements were initiated with an inter-university transit system in 1965. This was followed, in 1970, by the development of the cooperative use of two automated systems, for serials and documents, designed and operating in individual libraries in the province. These 'cooperative use' systems were characterized by an agreement among the participants to use the same programs and coding format (freely supplied by the originating libraries) to record data so that a simple merging of the files on an agreed schedule produced effective but economical union lists. These lists were used in the participating libraries to speed interlibrary loan transactions, to eliminate duplicate purchasing, and to make a larger (i.e. shared) resource available to faculty and students at each university. At the same time this concept allowed several libraries to enjoy the benefits of automation through the reduction of processing costs, with no investment in the original design or development of a computer based system.

It was these first cooperative systems which formed the basis for the establishment of O.U.L.C.S., in July 1973. Responsibility for directing or coordinating the existing projects and for developing and managing new ones was assigned to the Office of Library Coordination, which reported to the Council of Ontario Universities, (C.O.U.), a body representing the Presidents of the 15 universities.

Based on the experience with the 'cooperative use' systems, and cognizant of difficulties which were apparently occuring in emerging American networks, the participants accepted the following principles as requirements for operating the O.U.L.C.S. network. These still obtain, to a greater or less degree, in 1978:

1. Participation in any project is voluntary;

2. The members of each project own and operate that project consistent with overall O.U.L.C.S. objectives;

3. The Office of Library Coordination is a coordinating agency only and as such has limited powers;

4. Costs and benefits of the network should be distributed as equitably as is feasible, (no member should be penalized because of size or distance);

5. Responsibility for efficient and economic use of any system within the network rests with the individual participant;

6. Standards or formats, etc. developed for each system must be accepted and maintained by each participant. Flexibility in application of a system is desirable if it does not conflict with any of the objectives or principles of the network.[3]

By 1973 the O.U.L.C.S. network encompassed seven systems or projects, some with only six Ontario university libraries participating, some with all 15. Quebec university libraries and several federal government libraries were also members of some of the projects, and the general concensus in the province appeared to be satisfaction with the success that had been achieved by the network. A more detailed description of one of the systems in the network, CODOC, serves to illuminate the inaccuracies in this perception.

CODOC

CODOC, which stands for Cooperative Documents, is a cooperative computer based system for processing and retrieving government documents. Originally designed at the University of Guelph in 1966 it was and still is a highly efficient method for processing government publications.[4] It is not now and was not ever intended to be a cataloging system, and the cataloging rules or standards which might in any way hinder the speed and ease of coding documents were not incorporated in the original design.

After three years of successful use, this documentation system was shared by the University of Guelph with two other nearby university libraries, becoming the basis for the 'cooperative use' concept which underlies the Ontario network. In an informal agreement these institutions accepted the basic codes and corporate authors established by Guelph, as well as the record format, file structure and system products. All three libraries agreed to minor modifications to accommodate the idiosyncracies of the other two collections, providing alternatives if conflicts arose.

The purpose of the cooperative activity, the merging of the holdings files, created a 'quick and dirty' union list of documents, indexed by title, whose key elements were the unique document code and the corporate author of each document. This list, which was produced in COM/fiche, was entirely adequate to enable all three institutions to identify and retrieve records from one another's input, whether for expanding access to other collections, or for internal processing purposes. The original objectives of the consortium were being met.

Problems began after the system was incorporated into O.U.L.C.S. in 1973, as participation grew from the original three to 15. When additional libraries joined the group an attempt was made to share the workload by assigning areas of coding responsibility to each. Despite the entreaties of the original participants, new members, assigned an area of coding responsibility, felt called upon to reorganize the file even though many institutions had large bodies of material already coded in the system in a fashion incompatible with the reorganization. There was more and more pressure to create a clean, central data base, a goal which could only be accomplished if the original member institutions made extensive changes in their retrospective files. What was being suggested was the necessity for identical records in all fifteen institutions.

Such a goal, while perhaps impressive, was entirely inconsistent with the original and accepted design philosophy of the system. Its pursuit necessitated the expenditure of a great deal of staff time for recoding, relabelling and rearranging documents, and for telephoned and written exchanges among coding supervisors in the various libraries to ensure that new material was coded identically no matter which institution added it to the union file first. Meetings were also a necessary adjunct as Document Department Heads and Chief Librarians met frequently in attempts to reduce the growing dissatisfaction. Finally, an additional staff member was added to the Office of Library Coordination staff for the specific purpose of handling changes to the CODOC system programs necessitated by the constant restructuring which was taking place.

Needless to say, all this activity in pursuit of a 'clean' central file more than negated the economic benefits of a shared system. In addition, the level of system sophistication being sought required a significant amount of expensive programming time, and the direction in which the system was headed was producing a system more expensive to run and maintain. At the University of Guelph Library, for example, it was estimated that the costs for processing documents, while still less than they would be if cataloged, were double what they had been prior to the formal constitution of the network.

After three years of growing unrest the CODOC group was forced to step back and survey its accomplishments, progress, and goals, and to reassess the possible methods of achieving them. In doing so the members realized that they had lost sight of the philosophy of both the original Guelph system and of CODOC, which was the fast, efficient, inexpensive processing and retrieval of government documents through the cooperative use of a system whose effectiveness had already been proven. In truth, the modifications to the system which were being urged by some of the users would have made it a facsimile of the several cooperative cataloging support systems that were already in existence. If that was what was wanted, why not simply catalog the documents? Furthermore, in their zeal to 'perfect' the system, some CODOC participants were asking other libraries to forego the economic benefits of cooperation and the in-house benefits afforded by a flexible system, in favor of rigid adherance to guidelines intended to create a monumental, centrally controlled and maintained data base.

What is the answer? Cooperative systems will break down equally rapidly in the total absence of standards and controls. Other networks have been criticized for allowing too much autonomy. What is the compromise point which allows adequate economic benefit to be combined with reasonable flexibility and individuality among members of a network?

With the O.U.L.C.S. network the answer was to reformat the CODOC file structure so that the key element for each record became the title rather than the document code or corporate author, both of which were suceptible to varying interpretations. This allowed the libraries which had the most to lose if standardization continued, (e.g. Guelph, with more than 350,000 documents coded in the system), to stop making expensive changes to their records, but at the same time satisfied to a large extent the concern about a useful union file created by a large number of diverse contributors.

The CODOC union file remains a simple merge. If two slightly different versions of a record are entered simultaneously in the same listing they will file one under the other in the alphabetical title sort, causing little grief or searching for other group members who wish to extract the record for their own file. This version allows local flexibility, requires only minimal conformity among users, and still produces an extremely usable and cost effective union product. Individual systems have six points of access, including key word, to any document from any level of government, in any country. In addition, the COM/ fiche catalogs which display both the local and union files provide a breadth of access and retrieval denied by a card catalog.

CONCLUSION

The implications of this Ontario network experience are several. There would appear to be a function of size beyond which the advantage of cooperative system sharing may be negated by the costs of coordination. As the numbers of participants grow the role of the coordinating office assumes greater importance, and decisions may be made which impact adversely on some members of the network. Refinements in services appropriate to a few users may have to be funded from the operating budgets of all.

It may be that networks are not effective when dealing with systems which are intricately related to the files and policies established and maintained in the individual library. If this statement is true of document processing, it is even more valid for systems such as acquisitions and circulation which are much more susceptible to local requirements. It may also be that new models of network governance are necessary.

Fortunately it is now evident that recent technological changes, if accepted, can solve many of the network problems illustrated above. Mini or micro computers and on-line systems can allow individual libraries to process their own records for their own data base, providing their own variety of local services. These local files can continue to be contributed to a network and form part of a centralized union file as long as a minimum of standards and compatible procedures is maintained. Instant access to each other's data bases will in itself be the union file. The connections of a distributed network are virtually transparent to the user and the central facility, with its attendant costs and imposed coordination, no longer assumes such importance.

It would therefore seem that the ideal network may well be one that is organized with a minimum of control, wherein members are aware of one another's holdings and benefit from them or from the bibliographic records that describe them. At the same time such a network would allow a significant degree of independence and autonomy, responsive to the particular requirements of the local academic community.

REFERENCES

1. Richard DeGennaro, "Copyright, resource sharing and hard times: a view from the field," *Americal Libraries* (September 1977) p. 434.
2. Margaret Beckman and Ralph E. Steirwalt, "The Ontario Universities' library co-operative system and implications for regional and national networks," *Canadian Library Systems and Networks, Their Planning and Development* (Ottawa, CLA, 1974) p. 29.
3. Council of Ontario Universities. *Brief to OCUA* (Toronto, COU, 1978) p. 27.
4. Margaret Beckman, S. Henderson, and E. Pearson. *The Guelph Document System* (Guelph, The University of Guelph, 1973).

Barbara B. Gordon

University of Washington

THE UNIVERSITY OF WASHINGTON'S PARTICIPATION IN PACFORNET AS A CONTRACTOR

PACFORNET, a library-based information network, provides Forest Service personnel with the Monthly Alert, *an announcement of current literature which is coupled with document delivery, reference and literature searching, and the filling of general citation requests. In fiscal year 1977, PACFORNET delivered 49,128 documents at a total cost of $315,617; the estimated cost per user in fiscal year 1978 is $70.00. The University of Washington, as a contractor, operates PACFORNET North in its Forest Resources Library and works in liaison with PACFORNET South in Berkeley. Resolutions of some of the problems encountered are discussed.*

This paper is about an unusual library-based network called PACFORNET. Both the forestry subject matter and the rapid growth and extent of its services make it unique, but it is also composed of libraries that are not usually network bedfellows. PACFORNET, an acronym derived from 'Pacific Forestry Network,' combines a government field library and a distant academic library to inform and deliver documents to researchers, practitioners, and wildlife managers of the U.S.D.A. Forest Service.

A brief overview of the structure of the Forest Service should help clarify PACFORNET's parentage and working relationships. There are three sectors of the Forest Service: research, national forests, and state and private forestry. Research is conducted at the Forest Products Laboratory, the Tropical Forestry Institute, and eight regional forest and range experiment stations, and there are ten national forest regions. PACFORNET is funded by and serves two of the experiment stations and three national forest regions, because these administrators, as well as the entire forestry community, have been concerned with professional foresters working in outlying areas and hence cut off from technical information flow.

In a pilot outreach program in 1971, the Pacific Southwest Experiment Station library sent its accession list to the Klamath National Forest to encourage borrowing by mail. Other national forests were added to this program and in 1973, the California Forestry Network (CALFORNET) was born with the inclusion of the remaining national forests in California. Then in 1975, after the Pacific Northwest Experiment Station closed down its own library and bought into CALFORNET service, the network name was changed to the Pacific Coast Forest Research Information Network, or PACFORNET.[1]

There are now two service centers for PACFORNET; the Pacific Southwest Station's library, as PACFORNET-South, supplies California and Hawaii, while Washington, Oregon, and Alaska are serviced by PACFORNET-North, through the University of Washington as a contractor. The original accessions list has become more sophisticated, is coupled with document delivery, and is the basis of PACFORNET services. It is now titled, the *Monthly Alert*. Each issue averages 200 citations to literature pertinent to Pacific coast forestry. Included are: monographs, monographic series, reports, symposia, environmental impact statements, theses, and legislative documents. There are both key-word and species indexes. The *Alerts* are computer produced. The *Monthly Alerts* cumulate into the PACFORNET database, which is maintained on a FAMULUS program at the library of the Pacific Southwest Experiment Station or PACFORNET-South. Forest Service users return the *Alert* cover to their respective PACFORNET service center, listing the items they want to receive by number. Retention copies are sent, whenever possible, but published books and similar items are loaned on a queue basis.

Forest Service users of PACFORNET may utilize all four levels of service provided, with *Monthly Alert* responses as the first level. Other service levels are: the filling of any general literature request, reference and referral, and literature searching—including on-line searching of computerized bibliographic data bases. Statistics on PACFORNET service show that there were 36,000 documents delivered as *Monthly Alert* requests in 1977; this was a 65% increase from 1976, the first year of PACFORNET operation. The heaviest use was from the national forest personnel. There were also 13,000 non-*Monthly Alert* requests filled in 1977, up from 11,500 in 1976. In the *Evaluation of PACFORNET* these figures worked out as 50 non-*Monthly Alert* documents alone or 150 combined *Alert* and non-*Alert* documents supplied every working day of the year.[2]

In 1975, when the University of Washington Libraries signed the Forest Service contract to deliver documents and service to PACFORNET, there was some apprehension in the library system. It was feared that the collections might be diverted from the prime users—the students and faculty. Library unit heads were reluctant to loan books for the three month high-use period of the *Monthly Alert* for it was felt that the books would not be as readily available to their own clientele. Loss of books in the loans-by-mail program was also a threat.

Many of these problems have been resolved. In the budget the Pacific Northwest Station allocates $500 each year to replace lost books. However, only one book has ever been charged against this—and even that one showed up later. Careful statistics were kept of books borrowed from each library unit for the general requests during the first year, 1975/76, from the 23 branches or identifiable units. From 1–14 books were borrowed from each of 14 units, from 15–115 books were borrowed from the next 6 units, and the top three units varied even more: 205 items borrowed from the Fisheries/Oceanography Library, 916 from the Science Reading Room, and 2391 from the Forest Resources Library. These figures led to several new procedures being adopted. First, all loans other than for photocopy are submitted to the interlibrary loan office and treated like any other off-campus loan. Secondly, no books are borrowed for the *Monthly Alert* except from Forest Resources. Instead, two copies of all books to be listed on the *Monthly Alert* are purchased by PACFORNET-South with funds for the PACFORNET-North copy paid from a fund established by the Pacific Northwest Experiment Station. It turns out to be easier to shift monies within a federal agency and is, in fact, impossible to transfer a lump sum of money to a state university for book buying because of property and accounting restrictions. PACFORNET-North could have bought each book as it was needed and then applied for reimbursement through Forest Service channels, but it has proved less expensive to buy the two copies simultaneously.

One might ask whether or not there are any benefits to the University of Washington, because obviously non-profit institutions cannot reap profits. But there are many bene-fits. The loaning of books from the Forest Resources library is counterbalanced by the incoming flood tide of *Monthly Alert* materials that can be cataloged into the University collection after the period of intensive use is over. Students and faculty alike have bene-fited from the *Monthly Alert* service and the readily available current publications acces-sible via their *Monthly Alert* numbers until cataloged. Since the bulk of the Forest Resources library's series are not analyzed, the computer-produced keyword and species indexes of the PACFORNET data base provide needed analytics. The printouts are heavily used. Other assets are the PACFORNET librarian's on-line search training in-cluded in the budget and the thoughtful proviso of the PNW Station for allocation of money for the necessary office furniture and supplies to do the job. the PACFORNET-North staff is thus able to be highly service oriented, a state which causes envy among other college and university librarians.

Each of the PACFORNET service centers has institutional constraints and different operating climates. There are differences in funding, methods and responsibilities, yet it has been possible to work together harmoniously. Each service center utilizes a major research library: the University of California at Berkeley and the University of Washing-ton. PACFORNET-South purchases all *Monthly Alert* books and prepares the *Monthly Alert* citations and indexes. Suggestions for inclusion in the *Alert* are sent from the Forestry Library at the University of California–Berkeley and a small Juneau, Alaska library of the Forest Service as well as from PACFORNET-North.

PACFORNET-South is funded as part of the budgeted operations of the Pacific Southwest Experiment Station and is considered a field library of the National Agri-cultural Library. It has a working collection, but relies heavily on the University of California's Forestry library. In contrast, PACFORNET-North has no collection but is housed in and freely uses the collection of the Forest Resources library of the University of Washington. The bulk of the defunct Pacific Northwest Station library has filled gaps in holdings or extended the collection of the Forest Resources library, where the PNW Station's journals are sent after routing. Collection sizes differ at the University of Cali-fornia–Berkeley and at the University of Washington, but in the subject areas tapped they are about equal. The two university collections together total about 7,000,000 volumes.

PACFORNET-North sends unfilled requests to the Pacific Northwest Bibliographic Center to search regional holdings in its main entry catalog of over four million cards. This makes an extra step in the document delivery process, but PACFORNET-North has to work a little harder at times to locate materials. Both PACFORNET-North and South service centers also use the National Agricultural Library land grant college document delivery system through, respectively, Washington State University or the University of California at Davis. At times, borrowing is done directly from NAL, itself.

PACFORNET-North's contract is funded jointly by the Pacific Northwest Experi-ment Station and Region 6 of the National Forests; this continues the pattern of R-6 helping to fund the PNW Station's library. The University of Washington Libraries provide PACFORNET service under a basic contractual agreement with amendments added for each budget update or other specific points. Our contract for the 3-month start-up phase was for $19,000, with the first full year's follow-on contract for $67,000. The Fiscal Year–1978 contract was for $130,000. The total budget for the entire PACFORNET operation for FY–78 was $315,617. The cost per user is estimated at $70.[3]

PACFORNET was evaluated by a team of top managers of Forest Service experiment stations and national forest regions in 1977. Conclusions were: that PACFORNET provides needed technical information services not provided by any other government agency; that it is widely accepted and used; is cost effective and compares favorably with budgets for library service at other Forest Service units. Recommendations were made to expand PACFORNET into WESTFORNET after detailed analysis of possible service center locations, staff needs, potentials for contracting, costs, and potentials for financing by multiple users.[4] By February, 1978 the Intermountain Region had already drawn up plans for joining in with PACFORNET but with its own service center.

There has been some talk about forestry networks abroad. In 1973, the Food and Agriculture Organization of the United Nations recommended establishment of specialized information networks, with forestry one of the prime targets.[5] And in 1976, the International Union of Forestry Research Organizations recommended establishment of a uniform and readily accessible international system for storage and retrieval of research information.[6]

Dr. Robert Z. Callaham, in a speech given at the 1976 ALA Annual Conference for the ACRL Agriculture and Biological Sciences Section summarized a 1980's goal of the Forest Service as a Renewable Resources Technical Information System (RRTIS). He envisioned a bibliographic and textual scientific information system as an integral part of a worldwide forestry information network.[7]

One might speculate on the future of PACFORNET, WESTFORNET, or even possibly a national forestry network or NATFORNET. I'll be glad to leave the speculation to you—for I think I will be too busy delivering documents!

NOVEMBER 1978 UPDATE

In May 1978 PACFORNET expanded and changed its name to WESTFORNET—the Western Forestry Information Network. WESTFORNET now serves forestry professionals in 17 western states. There are 90 national forests or 65% of all the national forests in the United States, 7 national forest regions, 4 experiment stations, and over 30 major research locations and laboratories. Selected cooperating agencies, companies, and universities are also served.

There are now four service centers. The additional two centers operate out of Forest Service field libraries. The Rocky Mountain Experiment Station in Fort Collins, Colorado, supplies complete WESTFORNET services and the Intermountain Station in Ogden, Utah, delivers *Monthly Alert* items but contracts with Utah State University at Logan for filling all other requests.

The University of Washington's Forest Resources library continues as the service center for the Pacific Northwest states. The WESTFORNET-Seattle staff now consists of 2 librarians, 3 technicians, and 2.5 FTE hourly student employees. And due to the increased workload put on the library collection 1.5 FTE technicians are funded by the contract to work in the Forest Resources library. The budget for the current fiscal year is $169,738.

REFERENCES

1. Theodor B. Yerke, "Pacific Coast Forest Research Information Network (PACFORNET)," *Agricultural Libraries Information Notes* 2 (December 1976): 3, 5–7.
2. Robert Z. Callaham and Theodor B. Yerke, "An Evaluation of PACFORNET (Pacific Coast Forest Research Information Network)'" U.S.D.A. Forest Service, Pacific Southwest Forest and Range Experiment Station, Berkeley, CA (Sept. 16, 1977; 2nd corrected printing Nov. 1977), p. 18–21.
3. *Ibid.*, p. 75.
4. *Ibid.*, p. 3, 29–32.

5. Food and Agriculture Organization of the United Nations, Seventeenth Session, Rome, 10–29 November 1973. Item 12(a) of the Provisional Agenda. Conference (paper) C 73/18 (Sept. 1973).

6. International Union of Forestry Research Organizations. IUFRO World Congress, 16th, Oslo, Norway. Congress Recommendations, IUFRO World Congress (1976), p. 2.

7. Robert Z. Callaham, "A Renewable Resources Technical Information System," *Agricultural Libraries Information Notes* 2 (December 1976): 1–3.

Glenn W. Offermann

Concordia College, St. Paul, Minnesota

PARTICIPANTS' VIEW OF AN ACADEMIC LIBRARY CONSORTIUM[1]

Based on questionnaires circulated to library staffs and a sample of faculty members and students of participating institutions, the attitudes and opinions of these groups of consortium participants were examined relative to consortium establishment and activities as well as expectations of library coopera-tion in general.

Library staff members emphasized the importance of people and commu-nication in consortium establishment and implementation. All respondents were very positive in their overall attitudes toward the consortium and cooperation and were supportive of strategies which linked their library with others in the community, state, and nation.

Especially since the rather steady organization of library consortia in the 1960's and 1970's, much has been written in the literature about cooperation—mostly in the form of announcements of new ventures and descriptions of cooperative efforts. The objective of this study was to identify the attitudes and opinions of the faculty, students, and li-brary staffs on the institutions making up a library consortium toward cooperation and resulting activities and programs of the consortium several years after its establishment and operation.

FACTORS IN THE ESTABLISHMENT AND IMPLEMENTATION OF THE CONSORTIUM FROM THE VIEWPOINT OF THE MEMBERS OF THE LIBRARY STAFFS

A questionnaire was circulated to ninety-five staff members of the eight libraries making up Cooperating Libraries in Consortium (CLIC), the group which was studied. Included was a set of ten questions designed to elicit respones which would identify characteristics and activities which: (1) promoted successful cooperation, (2) hindered cooperation or made it more difficult, and (3) were common experiences in the develop-ment of the consortium.

Respondents totaled sixty-three or 66 percent of the library staffs. Each of the ten questions is shown in Table 1, with the actual responses given more than one listed in rank order following each question. All responses are summarized in the table although not all will be included in the discussion.

TABLE 1

Responses of Library Staff Members to Questions Regarding the Establishment and Implementation of a Consortium (Numbers in Parentheses Indicate Respondents to Item)

1. What factors do you feel have encouraged cooperation in your situation? (55)
   a. Needs of patrons (18)
   b. Good rapport among librarians; willingness to cooperate (17)
   c. Excellent service; past success (10)
   d. Economic situation (9)
   e. Physical proximity (7)
   f. Similarities among participants (5)
   g. Leadership; attitudes of administrators (4)
   h. Realization of resources available (3)
   i. Desire to provide good service (3)
   j. Outside funding (2)
   k. Publicity given cooperative activities (2)
   l. Establishment of a union catalog (2)
   m. Lack of storage space in member libraries (2)
   n. Other cooperative activities by member institutions (2)

2. What factors have hindered cooperation? (52)
   a. Reluctance of staffs to share; selfishness (10)
   b. Personalities; people with differing philosophies and practices (9)
   c. Costs of cooperative activities; inadequate budgets (9)
   d. Delivery system problems (8)
   e. Fear of lower standards; change; loss of autonomy (4)
   f. Pressures of local work; user demands (3)
   g. Poor communication (3)
   h. Unawareness of services, resources (3)
   i. Abusers of the system (3)
   j. Lack of standardization regarding procedures (2)
   k. Existing union catalog comprised of only main entries; remote location of union catalog (2)
   l. Not knowing other members; insufficient informal contact (2)
   m. None (2)

3. What have been the three most significant occurrences as far as your consortium's development is concerned? (41)
   a. Establishment of a union catalog (21)
   b. Courier service (16)
   c. Union list of periodicals (10)
   d. Inter-campus borrowing (8)
   e. Initiation of a conversion project to establish a microfilm union catalog (8)
   f. Cooperation with MINITEX (7)
   g. Grants: federal and private (7)

    h. Centralized interlibrary loan service; communication system (3)

    i. OCLC participation (3)

    j. Exchange of ideas and problem sharing; more contact with other staffs (3)

    k. Access to a broad range of materials (3)

    l. No-charge copying service (2)

    m. Esprit de corps among consortium staff members (2)

4. Do you feel that all consortium activities should eventually be paid by member libraries in contrast to grants and outside agencies? (57)
   a. Yes (21)
   b. No (17)
   c. No, grants should be sought where appropriate and available (8)
   d. Yes, insofar as possible; maybe for general expenses, securing grants for special projects (6)
   e. Both (3)
   f. Not necessarily (2)

5. How have individual users of your library been helped by consortium membership and activities? (53)
   a. Enlarged collection of resources; increased access (31)
   b. Obtain materials in their library at limited or no cost (10)
   c. Better service in filling needs; able to complete papers and projects (6)
   d. Library staff tuned to up-to-the minute developments (2)
   e. Heightened awareness of community resources (2)
   f. Reference questions answered better (2)
   g. Audiovisual materials available from other colleges (2)
   h. Greater understanding (2)
   i. Yes (2)

6. How have individual library users been hindered by consortium membership and activities? (48)
   a. Definitely none; none I can think of (23)
   b. Materials may be out to another school when needed (13)
   c. Staff time devoted to consortium activities that could have been spent for more local purposes (3)
   d. Students have learned to expect too much–they want everything and want it immediately (3)
   e. Consortium operation inefficiencies cause delays, non-delivery (3)

7. How has consortium membership affected collection development in your library? (50)
   a. Not much or not at all (19)
   b. Some influence by identification of specializations; purchasing has been more in depth if our specialty, and less if specialty has been assumed by another library (16)
   c. Coordination, pre-checking on major purchases (7)
   d. Don't know (4)
   e. A little cooperative buying (3)
   f. Yes, it has enhanced it (2)
   g. Cooperative retention of serials (2)

TABLE 1 *(Continued)*

8. In you opinion, should the consortium expand in size by taking in additional member libraries? If so, why and along what lines? If not, why not? (51)
   a. No, not now (30)
   b. Yes, providing access is increased and service maintained (9)
   c. Depends on kind and type; whether consortium can accommodate (3)
   d. Only if present problems can be resolved (2)
   e. Only in geographic area; should not become too diverse (2)
   f. Only if it can maintain its efficiency (2)

9. Which consortium activities would you eliminate last? (46)
   a. Reciprocal borrowing; interlibrary loan (19)
   b. Union catalog service; centralized searching (18)
   c. Delivery service (12)
   d. Photocopying of periodical articles (6)
   e. None (3)
   f. Union list of serials (2)
   g. No opinion (2)

10. What advice would you give to a group of librarians interested in forming a consortium? (44)
    a. Read all you can about groups already functioning; study other consortia. Personally interview participants of some systems, if possible (7)
    b. Plan; determine extent and kinds of service needed and how to implement; have definite goals (6)
    c. Enter arrangement with a cooperative spirit; be committed (6)
    d. Have lengthy and detailed discussions; get to know each other well (6)
    e. Try to find a benefactor; have adequate financial resources (5)
    f. Don't attempt to do too much too soon; be patient, but build optimistically (5)
    g. Do it! (5)
    h. Sell idea to all the library staffs; have open lines of communication with staffs (4)
    i. Think of advantages to all, not just your library; be generous; can't be viewed strictly as a "balance sheet" operation (4)
    j. Train staff and student personnel well; adequate orientation (4)
    k. Agree on standardized routines and policies (3)
    l. Follow our plan—it is good; study our consortium (3)
    m. Expect increased costs, but greater service capability (2)
    n. Open communication and frankness is a must; honesty (2)

The first question asked was: "What factors do you feel have encouraged cooperation in your situation?" It is apparent from reviewing the responses that library staff members viewed people and their attitudes and relationships as the most significant aspect in library cooperation. An open attitude and a good rapport among librarians were frequently mentioned as encouragements toward cooperation. The needs of patrons and the success with which these needs had been met in the past were also very important.

The second question related to hindrances to cooperation. People were also identified as significant hindrances. The reluctant staff member or the personality problem were frequently named as factors having a negative influence on cooperative efforts.

Just as the people involved can be either helps or hindrances to cooperation, so can economic conditions, according to the views of the respondents. On the one hand, co-operative activities seem necessary for survival and of the highest priority. On the other hand, it is very difficult for some to allocate funds out of already stringent budgets for cooperative projects.

When asked to identify the three most significant occurrences in question three, re-spondents identified things that facilitated intercampus borrowing such as the union lists and catalogs, grants, and delivery service. An interesting observation made by several people was the significance of timing with related events.

The fourth question dealt with who should pay for consortium activities. Most re-spondents felt it appropriate that members of the consortium should pay for routine operations out of regular budgets. At the same time, grants were widely held to be accept-able, and necessary.

In discussing how individual users have been helped by consortium membership in response to question five, respondents specified that such activity greatly increased the resources and services the patron had available.

For the most part, respondents could not see that consortium activities hindered the individual library user when asked this possibility as question six.

Few staff members could identify any great influence of consortium membership on collection development in response to question seven.

The eighth question asked if the consortium should be expanded in size. Most re-spondents did not feel the consortium was ready to be expanded and those who did were careful to qualify their positive response.

Activities respondents would eliminate last, in answer to question nine, would be reciprocal borrowing, the union lists and catalogs, and the delivery service.

Finally, among the frequently mentioned items of advice shared with potential con-sortium initiators were lengthy discussions to get to know participants, patience to pro-gress slowly, research and reading about functioning consortia, careful planning and goal formation, a committed and cooperative spirit, the engaging in action and activity as soon as possible, even if meager, and the securing of adequate financial resources.

Time and again respondents brought out the importance of people in consortium establishment and implementation. Open communication and the involvement and commitment of all staff members were pointed out as crucial for success. Increased staff development and satisfaction was also identified as one of the benefits of a successful cooperative program.

ATTITUDES AND EXPECTATIONS OF MEMBERS OF THE LIBRARY STAFFS, FACULTIES, AND STUDENT BODIES TOWARD THE LIBRARY CONSORTIUM

The questionnaire distributed to the ninety-five library staff members also included a set of seventeen statements pertaining to the consortium and library cooperation in general. These were a form of the same questions asked of a sample of 551 students and fifty-four faculty members of the seven colleges participating in the consortium. The sample represented 5 percent of the student body and 6 percent of the faculty members on the alphabetical lists used to obtain the sample. Replies were received from 204 students and forty faculty members. With the sixty-three replies from the staff members, a total of 307 replies were received. The first nine questions to the faculty-student group were unique to that group, dealt with respondent characteristics and other matters not asked of the library staff members, and are not included in Table 2.

The respondents were asked to indicate their opinion relative to the statements given on an agree–disagree scale of one to five, with a no opinion position in the middle. The

TABLE 2

Responses of CLIC Library Staff Members, Faculty Members and Students to Statements Descriptive of Attitudes and Opinions Regarding Library Consortia

Questionnaire Statement	Group	Strongly Agree N	%	Generally Agree N	%	Disagree Somewhat N	%	Strongly Disagree N	%	No Opinion Don't Know N	%
10. Whenever I have used the CLIC association . . . I have generally been pleased	Lib	30	47	28	44	1	2	1	2	3	5
	Fac	22	55	11	28	0	0	0	0	7	17
	Stu	44	22	55	27	11	5	5	2	86	42
11. I have been inconvenienced when materials from our library have been checked out to other CLIC libraries.	Lib	3	5	3	5	25	40	13	21	18	29
	Fac	0	0	1	2	7	18	15	38	16	40
	Stu	6	3	11	5	43	21	40	20	103	50
12. Our library ought to save the money it costs to belong to CLIC and use it to develop its own resources	Lib	0	0	1	2	9	14	52	82	2	3
	Fac	0	0	0	0	7	18	25	63	7	18
	Stu	8	4	19	9	65	32	67	33	43	21
13. Our college library is able to provide me with materials in an adequate variety of formats . . .	Lib	4	6	0	0	15	24	43	68	1	2
	Fac	6	15	22	55	8	20	3	8	1	2
	Stu	26	13	100	49	29	14	7	3	41	20
14. Our college library is able to provide me with an adequate depth of access . . .	Lib	3	5	7	11	17	27	33	54	2	3
	Fac	6	15	25	63	8	20	1	2	0	0
	Stu	20	10	106	52	42	21	7	3	27	13
15. Our college library is able to provide me with appropriate levels of materials . . .	Lib	4	6	9	14	15	24	33	52	3	5
	Fac	5	13	26	65	5	12	3	8	1	2
	Stu	27	13	108	53	32	16	7	3	29	14

16. Our library stands to gain as much or more than it gives by belonging to CLIC.	Lib	38	60	16	25	3	5	1	2	5	8
	Fac	18	45	17	43	0	0	0	0	5	12
	Stu	50	25	88	43	6	3	3	1	56	27
17. CLIC libraries ought to share audio and visual materials . . . as well as books . . .	Lib	29	46	21	33	4	6	3	8	6	10
	Fac	16	40	14	35	4	10	1	2	4	10
	Stu	56	27	78	38	16	8	6	3	48	24
18. A catalog in our library . . . of all the materials in other CLIC libraries . . . would be very useful to me	Lib	45	71	11	17	3	5	3	5	1	2
	Fac	19	47	11	28	3	7	0	0	7	18
	Stu	94	46	86	42	5	2	4	2	15	7
19. If I had available to me . . . a *card* catalog of just our library's materials and a *microfilm* . . . catalog . . . of the other CLIC libraries as well as our own, I would prefer to use the microfilm catalog . . .	Lib	20	32	11	17	15	24	8	13	9	14
	Fac	6	15	9	22	5	13	3	7	17	43
	Stu	50	25	56	27	31	15	6	3	61	30
20. The Minnesota Union List of Serials . . . is a valuable resource for me	Lib	47	75	11	17	0	0	0	0	5	8
	Fac	9	23	9	23	1	2	0	0	20	50
	Stu	12	6	30	15	18	9	22	11	122	60
21. Our library has some responsibility to help meet the information needs of the broader community . . .	Lib	30	47	24	38	5	8	1	2	3	5
	Fac	11	28	15	38	4	10	3	7	6	15
	Stu	36	18	85	42	27	13	8	4	47	23
22. It is desirable for a library user at our library to have access . . . throughout the country	Lib	26	41	27	43	4	6	1	2	4	6
	Fac	16	40	15	38	3	7	0	0	6	15
	Stu	30	15	82	40	29	14	0	0	61	30

TABLE 2 *(Continued)*

Questionnaire Statement	Group	Strongly Agree N	%	Generally Agree N	%	Disagree Somewhat N	%	Strongly Disagree N	%	No Opinion Don't Know N	%
23. Having a catalog showing . . . a statewide or regional basis would be of even greater value to me than . . . only materials in CLIC libraries	Lib	14	22	20	32	15	24	4	6	8	13
	Fac	7	17	14	35	7	17	1	2	11	28
	Stu	22	11	35	17	58	28	16	8	73	36
24. It is appropriate to utilize funds to support cooperative services that could otherwise be used for . . . materials	Lib	21	33	23	37	6	10	3	5	9	14
	Fac	13	33	15	38	3	7	0	0	9	22
	Stu	22	11	82	40	24	12	7	3	69	34
25. I believe our library should purchase duplicate materials	Lib	16	25	40	63	3	5	1	2	2	3
	Fac	11	28	24	60	2	5	0	0	3	7
	Stu	71	35	113	55	8	4	3	1	9	4
26. It makes little difference to me whether our library owns a specific item . . . as long as it is available	Lib	12	19	33	52	12	19	2	3	3	5
	Fac	14	35	17	43	8	20	1	2	0	0
	Stu	52	25	79	39	37	18	16	8	20	10

questions were designed to measure attitudes toward the need for cooperation, the effectiveness of current cooperative practices, and some of their expectations for cooperative library development in the future.

Responses to the statements by each of the three groups is shown in Table 2. For each category from the questionnaire the table shows the number of responses (N) and the percentage (%) those responses represent of the total number of respondents. In some cases, the entire statements which appeared on the questionnaire have been shortened to save space in Table 2. In all cases, however, the sense of the statement can be determined.

All categories of respondents evidenced a very positive attitude toward the library consortium and cooperation in general. There was 70–90 percent agreement with statements favorable to the consortium such as "Whenever I have used the CLIC association . . . I have generally been pleased," or that much disagreement with unfavorable statements.

The strongest support as determined by subtracting the percentage of disagree responses from the percentage of agree responses was ascribed to the suggestion of an author, title, and subject catalog of all consortium holdings in each library in statement 18 and to the concept that the libraries stand to gain more than they give by belonging in statement 16.

Several statements received a large number (over one-third) of "No Opinion; Don't Know" responses. One that received 83 percent and 91 percent agreement from library staffs and faculty was number 10, dealing with being pleased whenever the respondent utilized the consortium. Only 49 percent agreement was received from students because 42 percent had "No Opinion." Undoubtedly the "No Opinion" group was constituted of those who had not used the services of the consortium.

Fifty and 60 percent of the faculty and students were somewhat unknowing about the value of the statewide union list of serials (statement 20) whereas library staffs were 92 percent sure of its usefulness.

Considerably more mixed response was given to the concept of a statewide or regional data base (statement 23) rather than merely a consortium based catalog. In addition to the sizeable number of "No Opinion" responses—especially among the students—disagreeing replies were made by 19–36 percent of the respondents.

Although a majority of staff and faculty members disagreed that they had been inconvenienced by materials being checked out to other members of the consortium, (statement 11) 50 percent of the students, 40 percent of the faculty and 29 percent of the staffs didn't know. From a total consortium viewpoint, 10 percent or less of each group agreed they had been inconvenienced.

The statement dealing with preference for a consortium level microfilm catalog over against a local card catalog (Number 19) brought a spread of responses. Interestingly enough, although there has been concern in the consortium over *patron* acceptance of a microfilm catalog, *library staff* members registered the largest percentage of disagreements (37 percent). Twenty and 18 percent of the faculty and students, respectively, disagreed that they would prefer the microfilm catalog. However, 49 percent of the staff members, 37 percent of the faculty and 52 percent of the students agreed that they would prefer a consortium level film catalog. Fourteen, 43, and 30 percent of the staffs, faculty, and students did not offer an opinion.

Marked disagreement occurred between the library staffs and the faculty–student groups in responding to three statements regarding the adequacy of individual collections as to variety of format, depth of access and appropriate levels of materials. (Statements 13, 14, and 15) The staff *disagreements* accounted for 92, 81, and 76 percent of the responses. The faculty–student group offered 62–78 percent of their responses in *agreement* with the concept of adequate collections.

One of the initial group of questions asked of the faculty and student respondents dealt with response time required for requests. The data seems relevent to this discussion of consortium expectations. One hundred fifty-six, or 64 percent, of the respondents felt they needed their materials in one or two days or less. Fifty-seven, or 23 percent, expressed three or four days as an acceptable response time. Only thirty, or 12 percent, expressed one to two weeks as acceptable.

REFERENCE

1. Based upon part of the research done for "Relationship Among Minnesota Academic Library Consortia, Their Staffs and Their Clients," Ph.D. dissertation (Southern Illinois University, Carbondale, 1977).

Elizabeth J. Yeates and Laurie E. Stackpole

National Oceanic and Atmospheric Administration

MANAGING FOR RESULTS–A CASE STUDY IN COALITION BUILDING

Libraries, traditionally reactors to change, must now become instigators of change. New organizational structures are needed to offset current economic and political pressures. Greater sharing of resources, although technologically possible, is frequently blocked by lack of common interest or even by direct conflict. In the National Oceanic and Atmospheric Administration, library and information services are provided by several centrally administered centers and by more than 30 geographically scattered field libraries under diverse direction and control. A promising start has been made toward coalition building for resource sharing. The areas of cooperation have centered on the development of an Automated Library and Information System, which will permit direct access to the central research collection for both NOAA and non-NOAA users Nationwide.

The primary objective of this paper is to describe and comment on the development of a coalition or cooperative of the individual libraries and information centers of the United States National Oceanic and Atmospheric Administration (NOAA) as a contribution to the study of this management issue of our field.

A derivative objective is to record and communicate the nature of the library and information resources of NOAA, which in their scope and longevity appear relevant to academic institutions in those subject fields. The reason for presenting the resource at this time is that the library and information services component of NOAA has, during the past three years, embarked on programs, including a computer network, to make capabilities more widely and reliably available. These resources and programs perhaps should be accounted by academic libraries as they move toward the "new horizons" in the title for this meeting.

Creating organizations flexible enough to adjust to changing needs is a challenge that faces most libraries, regardless of type. We are in a period of financial retrenchment coupled with unprecedented demands created by heightened user expectations of what information technology can deliver and perhaps also by the psychology of the affluent society. Consequently, some long-standing decisions are having to be rethought, and the organizational structure that was best, or at least acceptable, as late as five years ago may not suffice now or two years from now.

Federal libraries have acquired a great deal of experience in the art of dealing with change. Over the years, we have been involved in dramatic organizational alterations as various attempts to restructure or streamline government service affected library operations.

NOAA is a classic case in point, and its libraries are examples of responders to, and more recently, initiators of change. NOAA was formed in 1970, the successor of another agency, the Environmental Science Services Administration, which had existed for about five years. This agency had been created by combining two completely separate predecessors: the U.S. Coast and Geodetic Survey and the U.S. Weather Bureau. Both of these agencies had considerable histories and libraries created over the years that reflected their roles as important national research organizations. The Coast and Geodetic Survey was the earliest scientific or technical agency in the Government, having been founded in 1809. The Weather Bureau was established in 1870, but its library collection included material dating from the 1820's when the Surgeon General's Office was responsible for weather observations. When NOAA was formed eight years ago, the functions of these two and several other agencies, in whole or part, were merged.

One large component brought into NOAA was the Bureau of Commercial Fisheries, which had, since 1940, been part of the Fish and Wildlife Service in the Department of the Interior. As a result of this earlier amalgamation, the Bureau library had been absorbed into the Interior Library. When the Bureau came into NOAA as the National Marine Fisheries Service, it came *sans* library materials in the Washington, DC, area, although with the small but important collections developed by 19 libraries connected with individual laboratories throughout the United States. NOAA also acquired several other operational and research programs related to the atmosphere, oceans, and other environment. Several of the programs absorbed dealt primarily with the collection and maintenance of data, and these were brought together to form a new unit within NOAA called the Environmental Data Service, recently renamed the Environmental Data and Information Service. Through an intermediate level of organization, the Environmental Science Information Center, what was initially envisioned as a temporary expedient for providing library services was adopted.

The two older libraries, those of the Weather Bureau and Coast and Geodetic Survey, were brought together administratively, but each continued to operate as a separate entity, collecting in its own field and serving its own clientele. A new collection was built to serve the fisheries interests in the Washington, DC, area and made a part of what had been the Coast and Geodetic Survey Library but housed in a separate location. The libraries in the field remained administratively under the control of their respective NOAA subunits, but a Field Libraries Coordinator within the library proper provided some functional direction. In 1975, a technical information division was added, resulting in the Library and Information Services Division (LISD). Restructuring service to meet NOAA-wide needs became apparent.

There comes a time in the life of an organization when it must stop reacting to outside forces and take charge of its own destiny. Many libraries in the wake of budget cuts, staff shortages, and political pressures have reached this point in the last few years. In 1977, LISD had another reorganization, this one planned and executed by the Division itself. (Fig. 1). It resulted in the integration into a service branch of what had become the Atmospheric Sciences Library, the Marine and Earth Sciences Library (with a fisheries subset), and two LISD-administered centers in Florida, as well as one being developed in Seattle. Services are now provided by six centers located where NOAA personnel are concentrated, backed by a central facility in Rockville, MD. Collections to serve local needs are maintained in the centers, and information services, including computer literature searching are provided. Material from other centers or older material housed in

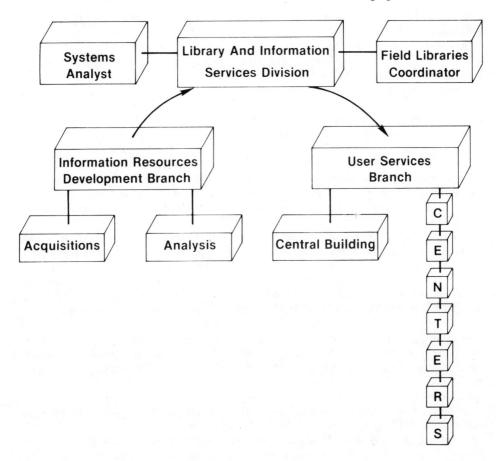

Figure 1.   LISD Organizational Structure.

the Central Building are immediately available. All interlibrary operations and distribution of NOAA publications, as well as information service for personnel distant from libraries, are also performed centrally.

By academic standards, we are a small organization. Our staff, counting both the Washington area and Miami, is about 50—this includes managers, technical processing, and services personnel; about the same number is found in the field. Our research collection consists of over 500,000 volumes. When the holdings of the field libraries are added, the resource approaches a million volumes. We offer a full range of services, which are available to all. The only service for which we charge, and then only to non-NOAA users, is computerized literature searching.

Federal libraries, except perhaps for the national libraries, have in the past been somewhat a world to themselves. They have been inward-directed, interested primarily in serving their own communities, and have made limited attempts to make themselves or their resources known. This situation is changing, particularly in organizations such as NOAA, which, under the present new administration, are becoming more publicly oriented. The present stress on NOAA's mission to provide environmental information to all those who are involved in the exploration or use of oceans and atmosphere coincides with trends in the library community toward more sharing and cooperation. We are therefore in a fortuitous position with both the professional and the political realities in some synchrony.

As NOAA moves more aggressively into the area of policy formulation and national and international regulation setting and enforcement, LISD is expanding its services to provide what the new NOAA administration needs and what the public will expect from the new NOAA in the way of information resources. The current stress is on legislative, socioeconomic, and current affairs information as well as the scientific interests which the NOAA libraries have traditionally served. Because our staff includes subject specialists, we have been able to move rather quickly to meet anticipated demands for new services. We are, for example, actively involved in a new program to produce issue briefs or overviews on high-interest and sometimes controversial topics, backed up by a selected annotated bibliography. Such briefs will meet the needs of our own administrators, State and Federal legislators, other government agencies, the academic and research communities, and the public for concise, unbiased discussions of provocative environmental issues.

To meet the challenges of making our resources and services more accessible, we are going in other directions new to us. Although for years we have been active participants in the Federal Library Committee, recently we have become part of a local consortium in which academic, public, and special libraries are represented as well. A major concern for us, as we strive to improve the availability of library and information services within NOAA, is the compatible and realizable goal of helping to meet the information needs of the academic and research community as well. As a unique national resource for information on the ocean and atmosphere, it is incumbent upon us to develop ways to share our materials and services. This is mandated not only by the widespread acknowledgment by the library community that resource sharing is essential but by our own position as a publicly supported institution with a commitment to the dissemination of environmental information.

The fact that library services are not centrally administered is a fact with which we are actively dealing. The National Maine Fisheries Service controls 19 libraries in its laboratories, and several other administrative units control one or more libraries. These libraries, a total of 33, are scattered geographically from coast-to-coast with facilities in Alaska and Hawaii as well. (Fig. 2.) Many are very small and may be staffed by only one person, not necessarily a librarian. LISD, through its Field Libraries Coordinator, provides these libraries with a number of products and services to help them streamline their operations and share their resources: (Fig. 3). They are given technical assistance, such as in acquisitions, cataloging, and the borrowing of material on their behalf when they have exhausted their resources. They are provided with access to the main LISD collection through a printed book catalog and monthly accessions lists. Duplicate resources are used to help them develop strong regional collections. LISD supports in entirety their use of computerized services for literature searching.

However, like academic institutions with historically decentralized administration of libraries, we concluded that there is only so much that can be done in the organizational arrangement that has prevailed in the past, even with the technology that is available to us. Parallel to the academic experience, we saw that the benefits of closer ties among the NOAA libraries and information centers would be improved and more cost effective library services nationally for the NOAA and NOAA interest communities, in part through formally planned sharing of resources.

We have gone into some detail about our situation because it has all the classic problems—geographic scattering, competition among administrative units, historical independence, territorial rights, and differences in subject orientation and focus. An additional problem is that the personnel who might be best qualified in terms of both

Figure 2. Geographical Distribution of NOAA Library and Information Centers.

- Resource Sharing

- Reference Assistance

- Book and Journal Selection Purchasing Help

- Cataloging Assistance

- Information Products

- On-Line Database Access

- Training

Figure 3. Assistance to Field Library and
Information Centers.

professional training and personal abilities are often not sought for library positions in
the field. This stems from the fact that those doing the placement are not particularly
involved with libraries and do not realize what effective library/information service
entails. Salary then becomes the paramount consideration with the result that some field
libraries have been staffed with personnel whose library experience is limited.

The problems we have identified, what we have done is our efforts to create an
efficient and economic structure out of independently dispersed units, and the successes

we have had may help others faced with the challenge of creating information systems for the 80's.

From our experience, we have identified five interrelated conditions that appear essential to the successful voluntary integration of discrete library units in an organization such as ours.

The first is that the participants must be able to identify with some common elements. These elements must be sufficiently discrete and specific to be both intellectually and emotionally meaningful and manageable and to outweigh the appeals of autonomy. Within NAOO, library/information center personnel are moving from identification with a local community toward affiliation with a region and with the concept of service to the environmental community. We believe that this alteration in attitude is resulting from: (1) Realization of economic constraints versus user demands and the potential benefits of pooling resources. These trends in the library field as a whole are influencing individuals, reinforced by specific advantages offered within NOAA, which will be detailed later. (2) Introduction of the regional concept, which appears to give a better span of control than a network radiating directly from Washington, DC. (3) The increasingly interdisciplinary nature of the environmental sciences. (4) Planned, improved communications and other interactions among the scattered library units.

A second major condition for consortium development is placement of effective personnel.

Our specific experience with these two factors, identification with common elements through regionalization and the effect of personnel, is shown in Florida, where we administer two centers. (Fig. 4). An extensive search for a new head identified an individual, incidentally a former academic librarian, with both library and scientific credentials and the enthusiasm and creativity to lead change. Potential areas of cooperation have been seen among the NOAA southeastern area libraries. The advantages of regional co-

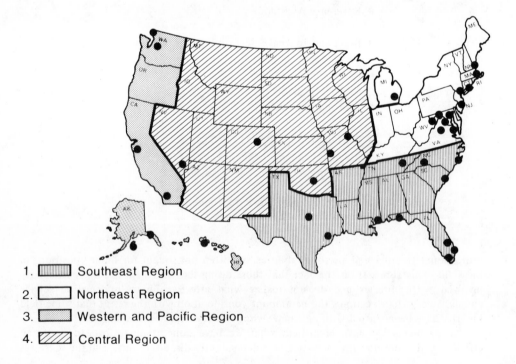

1. ▨ Southeast Region
2. ☐ Northeast Region
3. ▨ Western and Pacific Region
4. ▨ Central Region

Figure 4. Regional Coalition of NOAA Library and Information Centers.

operation have been recognized, and the field librarians from that part of the country have organized into a NOAA Southeastern Area Resources Cooperative (NOAASARC). This group has met and has begun work on documenting goals and objectives, such as collection development and common storage of lesser used materials.

A third condition, we believe, is that the participants be in a predominantly exchange relationship, rather than a dependency relationship. That is, each participant should be recognized as making a significant contribution to the cooperative effort. Such recognition becomes a reality as we move from a philosophy of size of holdings as the chief indicator of library value to one of including nature of holdings and level of service as important indicators. For example, within NOAA, many field libraries have collection segments that are unique in NOAA and perhaps in the country. A peer relationship among consortium participants seems to increase confidence in the system and reduce concern about loss of autonomy.

However, a fourth factor is that the leaders in consortium development must "market" not only to their colleagues but also to the top policymakers in the organization, who control the funds and the overall directions to be taken. The arguments to this audience must stress cost savings (or control) and other quantifiable effects such as reallocation of personnel to functions that can be perceived as more valuable. Within NOAA, over a year of educational efforts is resulting in involvement of decisionmakers from library and nonlibrary management on working together on such issues as governance and technological applications.

Finally, the benefits of cooperation must be highly visible. Ideally the cooperation probably should directly involve people in work of a technical nature where the benefits are immediately identifiable. The application of computer and telecommunications technology can provide a feasible framework for participation with valued fruition in an acceptable time period.

With NOAA, an Automated Libary and Information System is being developed to help link LISD and the field libraries and to provide products and services that will be beneficial to the users. (Fig. 5.) This system will provide the NOAA libraries with shared

- **expanded resources through sharing**

- **reduced duplication of material**

- **reduced duplication of work**

- **improved quality of access to books, journals, data, other resources**

- **greater speed and availability of access**

- **heightened currency of information**

- **reduced unit costs (e.g., 35% saving in cataloging)**

Figure 5. Advantages of Automated Library and Information System Network.

bibliographic access, reduce duplicate efforts, and facilitate technical processes. These are identifiable desirable goods. We have as an initial step accelerated our work with the libraries that are not administered by us to try to enable them to use existing computer capabilities already extensively used by LISD, such as the Ohio College Library Center (OCLC), and thus lay the foundation for further resource sharing. This topic is also one of the priority issues to be brought to the advisory council mentioned earlier.

The functions to be automated (Fig. 6) are the standard library unit operations, including production of microform catalogs, authority file maintenance, and management statistics. To this we add inventory control of the NOAA publications we distribute and information retrieval from the catalog data base. A requirements and feasibility study determined that the most cost effective way for us to automate is to use a minicomputer system that will interface with computer utilities for some operations, such as data construction and maintenance.

- **Acquisitions**
- **Serials**
- **NOAA And Sea Grant Publications**
- **Binding**
- **Cataloging**
- **Authority Files**
- **Circulation**
- **Information Retrieval**
- **Management Statistics**

Figure 6. Future Computerization; Fully Automated Library and Information System.

Because of the long process involved in procurement and the associated development and software implementation, initial steps toward automation have been taken that will both give us products now (or soon) and also feed into the long-term automation. (Fig. 7). A machine-readable bibliographic data base is being created from our records in OCLC and an earlier computer system and will represent our holdings cataloged since 1972, with monthly updates initially. Its main product, scheduled for early 1979, will be microform catalogs, thus giving users in remote locations, such as in our own field libraries, direct access to our holdings information. As we did with our first printed catalog published last year, prior to our full-scale automation plan, we are as far as possible making copies of our catalog freely available to other libraries.

The data base will provide not only the bibliographic information and location for our monographs and serials but will also list serials holdings by the end of 1979. The holdings information, captured in machine-readable form during input to the OCLC serials check-in module, will enable us also to cooperate more easily in the production of union lists. Its availability will allow us significantly to improve our input to one such list—an on-line serials file. This is an experimental effort in which several government agencies with related interests have been participating. The serials file is on-line with a commercial vendor. Other products of the data base will be authority file control, including subjects NOAA has added to L.C. headings and names; and a new, user-oriented version of our accessions list.

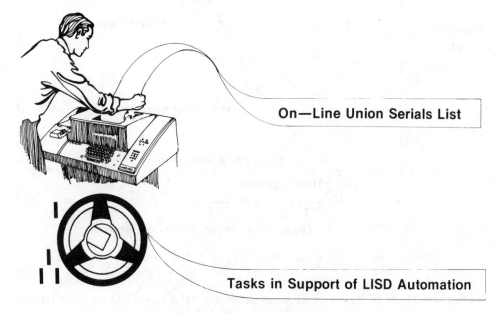

On—Line Union Serials List

Tasks in Support of LISD Automation

   ✔ **Bibliographic Data Base**

   ✔ **COM Catalog**

   ✔ **Serials Bibliographic Data Base**

   ✔ **Serials Holding Data Base**

   ✔ **On—Line Authority File**

   ✔ **Improved Accessions List**

Figure 7.   Computerization In Process.

A five-year time frame has been projected for the Automated Library and Information System. (Fig. 8.) It is scheduled to be fully operational in two years in our Rockville, MD Central Building, in three years at our other facilities in the DC area and Miami, and after then will be implemented in the field libraries. The success of cooperative efforts already begun in the southeast indicates that this would be a good choice as a pilot area.

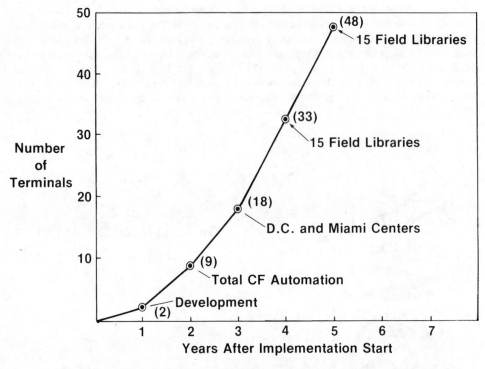

Figure 8. Automated Library and Information System—Planned Growth.

In these efforts to extend its resources nationally, LISD brings a history of success in computerization for information sharing. (Fig. 9.) In addition to our OCLC support, we have participated actively in building the *Government Reports Announcement* data base of the National Technical Information Service, providing for the public availability of NOAA-published material both as a hard copy listing and as an on-line service through commercial vendors. We have supported early efforts to make information in NOAA's areas of interest accessible by sponsoring the development and on-line availability of data bases such as *Oceanic Abstracts*, *Meteorological and Geoastrophysical Abstracts*, and *Aquatic Sciences and Fisheries Abstracts*.

Our past computerization efforts have provided us with printed products such as the *NOAA Scientific and Technical Publications Announcement*, which we can provide on request to facilitate the sharing of NOAA research results, and a cumulative listing in microform of our input since the early 1960's.

The atmospheric sciences part of our collection will be made more widely available through the G. K. Hall publication, *Catalog of the Atmospheric Sciences Library*. It covers the subject areas of meteorology, climatology, hydrology, physical oceanography, and air chemistry. It includes many books with pre–1870 imprints, 19th century weather records from France and England, Russian narratives and observations from the Tzarist weather station at St. Petersburg dating back to 1838, photostats of captured German and Japanese weather observations made during World War II, surveys, explorations, and many eye-witness records of historic sea voyages.

We have a substantial background in providing on-line search services and about a year ago extended this activity by publishing *Packaged Searches* on high-interest topics.

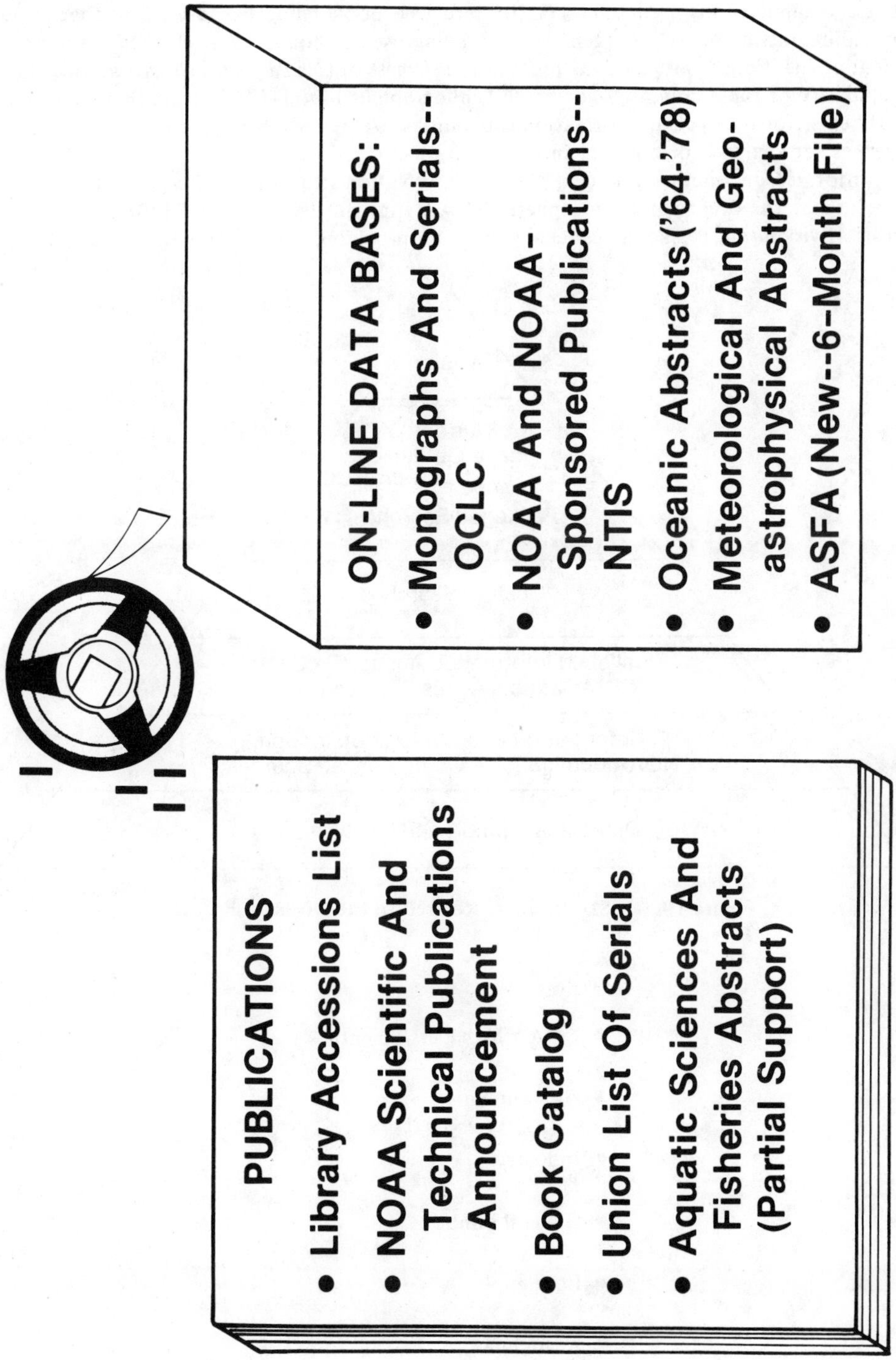

ON-LINE DATA BASES:

- Monographs And Serials--OCLC

- NOAA And NOAA-Sponsored Publications--NTIS

- Oceanic Abstracts ('64-'78)

- Meteorological And Geo-astrophysical Abstracts

- ASFA (New--6-Month File)

PUBLICATIONS

- Library Accessions List

- NOAA Scientific And Technical Publications Announcement

- Book Catalog

- Union List Of Serials

- Aquatic Sciences And Fisheries Abstracts (Partial Support)

Figure 9.   Current Computerization.

These computer-generated bibliographies are free upon request, and we find that more are going outside of NOAA even than are being used in-house. (Fig. 10.) Our issue brief program mentioned earlier has its roots in the success of this *Packaged Search* service. The popularity of these computer-generated bibliographies has made us aware that a demand does exist for our special information capabilities. We believe that there is an even greater market for analyzed or digested information on current environmental concerns that call for informed decisionmaking. (Fig. 11.) As the Nation's focal point for promoting effective use of the oceans and atmosphere, NOAA through its library and Information Services Division must take a leadership role in providing such assimilated information.

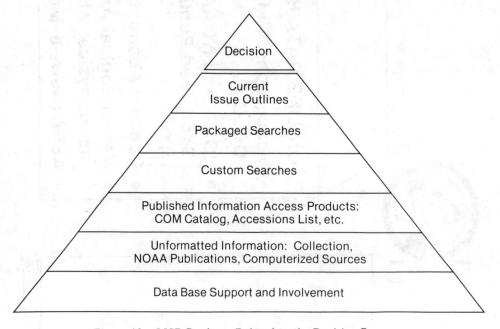

Figure 10.   LISD Products Related to the Decision Process.

- NOAA Managers/Scientists

- Government

- Industry

- General Public

- Foreign

- Academia

Figure 11.   Users.

As we implement our Automated Library and Information System, we hope to strengthen the direct ties that exist already between our field libraries and the academic community. (Fig. 12.) Some examples of the current cooperative efforts point up the possibilities of further sharing when the field libraries are tied into the total resources of the Library and Information Services Division. In North Carolina, the National Marine Fisheries Service library at Beaufort cooperates with the Duke University Marine Laboratory and the University of North Carolina Institute of Marine Sciences, for example in the production of a union list of serials. In Miami, the LISD administered libraries work closely with the Rosenstiel Institute and the University of Miami School of Atmospheric Sciences in collection building and resource sharing. In Princeton, the NOAA Geophysical Fluid Dynamics Laboratory makes its collection available for the use of graduate students. Similar instances of cooperation exist, particularly with some other institutions involved in Sea Grant programs. Cooperation between our National Marine Fisheries Service library in Seattle and the University of Washington and between our National Marine Fisheries Service library in Honolulu and the University of Hawaii are examples.

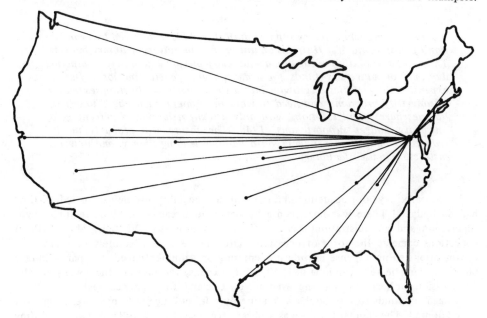

Figure 12. Nationwide Network of NOAA Library and Information Centers (Alaska and Hawaii not shown).

Finally, as our attempts to take control of our environment and build cooperation among our many independent units yield results, we hope others may benefit from our experiences. Finding out what works and what doesn't in building library coalitions may help others in their own efforts to develop cooperatives or networks at the many levels at which they are needed.

Arthur T. Hamlin

Temple University

A BACKWARD GLANCE INTO THE FUTURE OF UNIVERSITY LIBRARY SUPPORT

*A survey of academic library support until the 1940s is followed by examina-
tion of post World War II strains on university and university library budgets.
There was a revolution in the disgraceful salary picture and in new, competing
demands on university funds for academic and general purposes. Despite
expensive complexities of growth, increased scholarly publication, extension
of university programs, and need to work in unfamiliar languages, university
libraries have found solutions with only a slight reduction in percentage of
university budget support since 1946. The future will probably involve
reductions in staff, dependence on a national lending library, and universal
instruction in use of a library.*

In the early days our academic libraries had no budgetary problems, for indeed they
had no budgets! There was no expense for personnel because the chore required slight
supervision and administration was delegated to a professor. Virtually all growth of
collections came in the form of occasional gifts. There were absolutely no journals or
continuations so no expense in ordering, entering or claiming. Indeed, as separate library
buildings were erected beginning in 1840, utility expense was nil since there was generally
no provision for heating or lighting, even in New England, for some decades!

A need for funds to buy books was naturally felt, and ingenious measures of support
were adopted. The standard form was a library fee, usually of a dollar or two. In writing
of southern libraries Powell commented "In some of the institutions, the library fees
were placed in the general funds of the university and spent for other purposes. None
exceeded ten dollars per student, and the average was about two dollars . . . . Only
Virginia and North Carolina were aided substantially by endowments, and these came
after 1900."[1]

Trustees did find ingenious ways to raise a few dollars to buy books. In 1869 the
Delaware legislature established a fine for selling, "spirituous, vinous or fermented
liquors" within two miles of Delaware College or "procuring the same" for any student.
One half of any fine was to go for library support. A few institutions charged students
for each book borrowed, usually on a sliding scale, dependent on the size (folio, quarto,
octavo, etc.) of the volume. For a short while from 1752 the University of Pennsylvania
supported library acquisitions by fining trustees for absence from meetings and by

324

charging students for holidays taken. Departments of instruction frequently charged students a library fee informally, and banked the money in the name of the chairman. This has been done surreptitiously in the United States as recently as the 1950s. Historically this has precedent in the long established practice of the German institute to support its special research library with fees. The amount is determined by the professor who heads the institute; he collects the money and controls its expenditure.

By the middle of the 19th century only four colleges could claim incomes of over a thousand dollars for library purposes—Harvard, Yale, Brown and South Carolina. Many had no annual support of any kind.[2] And by 1876, the annus mirabilis of American library development, only seven are listed as above the thousand dollar income mark.[3] For most library purposes the only income was the occasional windfall from the legislature or trustees, a rare fund drive, the gift of a private library. The principal redeeming feature in this otherwise bleak picture is the literary society library, funded and operated by students, which flourished in the first half of the 19th century and went into decline shortly after the War Between the States.

With few exceptions it was only at the beginning of the present century that state legislatures recognized a responsibility for regular appropriations to their universities. An outstanding exception to this was South Carolina, which made regular appropriations to its South Carolina College, and provided a respectable library budget, from 1836 until the Civil War. Benjamin Powell's study of southern state university libraries states that "regular financial support from the states was not available to all of the universities until about 1900. The coming of regular support for the libraries coincided with the state appropriations to the universities."[4]

By the turn of the century the few institutions with research programs, the infant universities, were budgeting funds annually for their central libraries with specific provision for staff and equipment as well as for books and journals. Still, none by 1920 had so much as $200,000. and only nine had six figure budgets.[5] However modest these sums may seem, the support of libraries over the period from 1900 had kept pace percentage wise with the support of faculty salaries at most universities.[6] By 1938, the birth year we celebrate, the number with budgets of $100,000. or more had doubled to at least nineteen institutions. Even so, only eight expended more than $200,000. and only one is excess of a half million.[7]

It is not the purpose of this paper to trace the growth of library expenditure through to the present day when budgets of several million are commonplace and a few run in eight figures. The sums are meaningless without corresponding detailed interpretation of purchasing power. Suffice it to say that the Consumer Price Index increased almost exactly fourfold in the period from 1938 to 1976.[8] Rather, the subject in hand is the examination of a few forces which have influenced library support over the past fifty years and particularly since World War II.

The first point to recognize is the revolution that has taken place in regard to library salaries. For far too many decades the salary picture in virtually all university libraries was basically as disgraceful as anything in the garment trade of New York or the slaughter houses of Chicago. Essentially the same, the only differences in the library sweat shop were the elevated purpose, the general tone, the working environment. Salaries of $50. a month were not uncommon for college graduates in our best institutions in the late thirties. Fifty 1938 dollars equates roughly with two hundred 1976 dollars. I well recall a distinguished clergyman friend speaking of his several years in the library of his Ivy League alma mater at that salary in the thirties. He was a remarkably benign man of peace but his voice would rise and his face flush with anger whenever he spoke of his years in the library. Wilhelm Munthe, the deTocqueville of the library world, commented on this in 1939:

I leave it to the reader who is more conversant than I with living expenses in America to decide how many of the whole army of American library workers are paid more than a minimum required for a decent living by a single person with certain cultural interests. And how many are paid enough to support a family? I do not find it hard to believe that librarianship is actually "the worst paid profession in the United States." At any rate it seems to be based on the idea of celibacy.[9]

The distinguished library director and bibliographer, Margaret Stillwell, revered General Hawkins who formed the Annmary Brown Library over which she presided. However her hero worship was not entirely blind. "He sincerely believed I had the highest salary of any woman in the United States," she wrote in her autobiography. "He was wrong. He was subconsciously thinking in terms of the past, of my income as compared to that of the local seamstress in the Vermont village where he was born in 1831. He also told me that all I needed 'for maintenance and enjoyment' was rice pudding and just a little milk, three times a day. He was wrong on that count, too." Many a library trustee and director apparently thought "rice pudding and just a little milk" sufficient for his faithful female staff and, unfortunately most female staff accepted it, however resentful they might feel. It was only a few years ago that two superiors told me, "She doesn't need a raise. Why, her husband at —— university is a hot property!"[10]

Women were of course the principal victims of the salary picture partly because they were passed over for administrative posts and partly because of the universal prejudices then prevalent. This discrimination, existing as it has until relatively few years ago, is too well known to require elaboration. However the general administrative practice seems to have been one of paying as little as possible to anyone, in the interest of husbanding funds for books. Consider a case from my own experience. A long time staff member of an Ivy League library was jubilant when his immediate supervisor was made the acting director. Now at last he would get a raise from the $75. a month salary on which he had to support his wife and three children. The interview took over two hours. The boss was extremely sympathetic, put aside all work to show Jimmy how to budget so as to get along well on his present salary. And until the 1950s it was not at all unusual for the second in command of a major library to be paid less than half as much as the chief. In short it was the rule, rather than the exception, for highly competent professional librarians to spend a lifetime without acquiring a salary adequate for anything more than the modest expense of a single person unless, of course, the title of "director" was achieved. The sun shone at the top of the mountain.

In retrospect it is clear that great wrongs were worked, great bitterness engendered in otherwise devoted, selfless, able staff. It is ironic that the worst offenders were some institutions which took great pride in the importance of their libraries, indeed considered them central to basic functions, and as policy paid top salaries to faculty.

Change came rapidly in the fifties because of the rapid expansion in the job market and consequent shortage of professionally qualified personnel. It was a case of pay, or close shop.

An equally important factor was the gradual move to faculty status for professional librarians. The winning of academic recognition on a par with the teaching faculty has been a long, hard struggle, by no means won at this time. It was not until 1944 that a major university library, that of the University of Illinois, achieved full faculty status and rank for the entire professional staff. Other universities followed in the 1950s and 1960s and by the early seventies the majority of universities had swung over to recognition of most, if not all, of the professional library staff as members of the faculty, often with faculty rank and titles.

As library directors as a whole faced up to the salary picture, either as responsible leaders or forced to do so by union organization or the labor market, they also became concerned about the library's share of institutional funds available for all academic purposes. On the one hand most library operations were becoming increasingly expensive with growth, collections were required to meet ever widening and deepening graduate and research programs, staff competent in Slavic and oriental languages were required, yet the complexities of the post war world brought our universities new, important needs which required very large sums. A glance at the modern budget of a complex university will normally show appropriations running close to a million or more, often of several millions, for a number of activities entirely missing, or very minor, in a budget of the 1930s. Among them: computer activities, multi-media resources, measurement and research, campus security. Other expenses which date from an earlier period have mushroomed in cost, among them insurance for liability and unemployment, communications and travel, fringe benefits, vandalism, taxes, and, of course central administration. Consider then the library administrator of the late forties has he looked to the future. The picture obviously held great increases in collections and services; at the same time he could only see an increase in unit costs with any such growth for virtually every operation, whether acquisitions, cataloging, shelving, or circulation. Yet these increased unit costs must somehow be restricted because of the major new demands on the university budget, just mentioned.

Principal spokesman for this cloud on the horizon was Keyes Metcalf of Harvard. At the bicentennial celebration of the University of Pennsylvania Library in May 1951, he spoke on "the ever expanding demand for library materials and the threatened decline in support: how shall the gap be filled?" After noting the growth of libraries as "a terrifying thing, even if it becomes arithmetical rather than geometrical," he went on to state that "so long as a library grows more rapidly than the rest of the university to which it is attached, the situation will be serious because the library will tend each year to take a larger percentage of the total resources of the university. It will mean taking money from another part of the university and giving it to the library." Among the several courses of action suggested by Mr. Metcalf in recognition of the importance of the library was "each year one or more professorships or some other part of the university's works will be dropped and funds transferred to the library." This suggestion that each year the library, like the Cretan Minotaur, devour its annual tribute of a few professors, was publicized in other writings and gained little favor in academic circles. Nor did librarians relish the designation of "magpies" and their libraries as "rat holes" as Mr. Metcalf went on to say "that one of the greatest handicaps that librarians face today is the fact that they have the reputation for using more than their share of university appropriations. They are accused of being magpies who collect anything and everything, not because the things will be used, but simply because they are magpies. The library is considered a rathole down which any amount of money may be poured without, alas, drowning the rat!"[11]

Dr. Metcalf's fear that the library might take an ever increasing share of university funds has, of course, proved groundless. The library has nearly held its ground financially in the percentage of "academic and general funds" applied to its support. A recent study showed that for 24 large and medium large university libraries covering the period from 1946 to 1970, the median percentage of funds applied to library purposes went down from 3.9% to 3.35%. The mean percentage went down from 4.1% to 3.7%.[12] These declines are slight indeed in the light of needs which developed over that period for computers, security and similar expenses previously mentioned. For the decade from 1960 there was no decline in percentage applied to library support.

What, then of the future? This future for the library, as for most activity, is shrouded in mists but a few points seem relatively clear. The expansion of higher education, which brought the recent great increases in university support, has long since disappeared and there is no hope of similar expansion in the near future. Coupled with this is every expectation of inflation in publishing for some time and a seemingly inevitable spiral in personnel and other costs that accompanies inflation and the rise in the cost of living. In this situation institutions can hope for little more than remaining level with inflation, and libraries are unlikely to receive a larger share of the institutional dollar. In fact some slight shrinkage is anticipated.

There will undoubtedly be special pressures on library budgets which will require substantial changes. The cost of books and journals has risen much more rapidly than the cost of living and shows no signs of tapering off. The volume of publishing, world-wide, has doubled in the last two decades and this growth may continue. Meanwhile there continues to be a spread in research interests as our colleges assume university status and our universities take on new programs. Individual faculty will always be promoting new studies, demanding research facilities for special interests, and these bright, eager, often selfish pressures can be well nigh irrestistable.

To offset these costs our libraries certainly cannot plan on a return to the disgraceful personnel policies of the first half of this century; rather, a partial answer lies in reduction in number of staff. Modest reduction in number need not necessarily involve reduction in service. To date the computer has provided increased services to libraries and not the major economies that were predicted two decades ago. But the economies will come, although they may not be dramatic. Certainly a decade from now considerable savings will be possible in our technical service operations and in record keeping of all types.

And while university libraries will continue to grow in size, this growth should be considerably slowed by at least two developments now on the horizon. The first is the prospect of a national lending library of lesser used material, similar to that of Great Britain. Such a library for journal literature is well along in the planning stage. Once firmly established it should extend its coverage to all serials and monographs. A second development is the increasing interest in scientific publication not via journals, but of individual articles publicized and furnished, in one form or another, only on demand. This type of so-called publication becomes more practical with the extension of reference service with data bases.

A third development, for which I can provide only a forlorn but emotional hope, is universal recognition by our colleges and universities of the importance of required instruction in the use of libraries which emphasizes how knowledge is organized and made available. More than a century ago Ralph Waldo Emerson promoted this in his essay "Books" in which he stated "Meanwhile our colleges, whilst they provide us with libraries, furnish no professor of books; and I think no chair is so much wanted."[13] We have made precious little progress with this in most institutions. Of course a major requirement is recognition of this as instruction which produces income, just like any other classroom instruction. It is ridiculous to think we have to sell the concept that some modest sophistication in the use of reference works, bibliographical apparatus and library collections is basic to education. Such instruction should reduce the present necessity of using expensive personnel to give individual tutoring in the use of materials, which is all to often the case for the Reference staff today.

One thing is very clear, the critical role of the library must be forever emphasized with top university administration and librarians must be receptive to radical changes of emphasis despite the traditionalism of faculty and university administrators.

REFERENCES

1. Benjamin E. Powell, *The Development of Libraries in Southern State Universities to 1920* (Ph.D. dissertation. The University of Chicago 1946) (mf), p. 158.
2. C. C. Jewett, *Appendix to the Report of the Board of Regents of the Smithsonian Institution, containing a Report on the Public Libraries of the United States of America*, January 1, 1850 (31 Congress 1st session, Senate Misc. Doc. #120. Washington, 1850).
3. U.S. Dept. of Interior, Bureau of Education. *Public Libraries in the United States of America, Their History, Condition and Management.* Washington, 1876 (Dept. of Interior, Bureau of Education, Special Report. #1).
4. Powell, *op. cit.*, p. 158.
5. Princeton University Library. *College and University Library Statistics 1919/20 to 1943/44 Compiled from Figures Furnished by the Participating Libraries...* Princeton University Library, 1947. Statement is based on figures reported for "appropriations" and for "salaries" for 1920/21 and also for 1937/38. It is noted that the data covers only selected institutions and also that figures supplied may not cover all expenses.
6. George Alan Work, *College and University Library Problems, a Study of Select Group of Institutions Prepared for the Association of American Universities* (Chicago, American Library Association, 1927) See pp. 19–21.
7. Princeton University Library, *op. cit.*
8. Data on the cost of living is taken from *Historical Statistics of the United States, Colonial Times to 1970.* U.S. Dept. of Commerce (1957) Pt. 1, p. 210 and from *Statistical Abstract of the United States*, U.S. Dept. of Commerce, 1976, p. 439.
9. Wilhelm Munthe, *American Librarianship from a European Angle* (Chicago, American Library Association, 1939), p. 165.
10. Margaret Stillwell, *Librarians are Human: Memories in and out of the Rare Book World* (Boston, Colonial Society of Massachusetts, 1973), p. 101.
11. Keyes D. Metcalf, "The ever expanding demand for materials and the threatened decline of support, how shall the gap be filled?" In *Changing Patterns of Scholarship and the future of Research Libraries, a Symposium* (Philadelphia, University of Pennsylvania Press, 1951) p. 27–36. For quotations see pp. 28 and 31.
12. Herman H. Fussler and J. L. Simon, *Research Libraries and Technology, a report to the Sloan Foundation* (Chicago, University of Chicago Press, 1973) p. 19.
13. Ralph Waldo Emerson, *The Complete Works* (Boston, Houghton Mifflin, 1903-4), vol. 7, p. 191.

K. Suzanne Johnson and Joel S. Rutstein

Colorado State University

THE POLITICS OF BOOK FUND ALLOCATIONS: A CASE STUDY

Since 1972 the libraries at Coloardo State University have been using a formula to allocate the book budget. The formula was the result of the political atmosphere during the early 1970s during which time two significant events occurred which influenced the allocation of book funds. These were the demise of the Abel approval plan and a cut in book funds. This resulted in a perceived maldistribution of the remaining monies by the faculty and a desire on their part to see allocations made more objective and more equitable. Strong pressures have been applied from various groups to abolish the formula that was devised or to change it significantly. So far these pressures have been resisted but often at the cost of establishing contingency funds to "bail out" areas with reduced funding. The formula is still operational and is constantly monitored and re-evaluated to maintain its credibility as a viable distributor of book funds.

> Fund allocation is fundamentally a statement, translated into dollars, of the position of the Library on the relative importance of one subject to another. In other words, the very fact of allocation sets a large part of the collection development policy. Giving Forestry more money than English, for instance, says that we consider Forestry more important.
>
> [Memo from Moran to Anderson, July 16, 1971.]

This statement epitomizes the political controversy surrounding the allocation of book funds by formulae. CSU Libraries uses one such formula in apportioning its book budget by subject. This paper will discuss the implementation and utilization of the formula and its repercussions. First, it is necessary to place the formula within the context of the university library setting.

Colorado State University, founded in 1870, is the land grant institution of Colorado. The school is primarily known for its technical programs in veterinary medicine, agriculture, engineering, forestry and water resources. The planned expansion of the University coincided with the great post-Sputnik boom in higher education, during which CSU grew from a relatively small campus of 6,000 in 1960, to a large university of 17,000 by 1970. Although the sciences certainly did not suffer, the greatest visible effect of the boom was the growth and development of the programs in the liberal arts, which before 1960, emphasized undergraduate service programs. In the halcyon decade of the 1960s, most humanities and social science programs, expanded into the graduate arena. Some, such as psychology, initiated doctoral programs. The bulk of the Ph.D. programs remain, however, in the sciences.

The Libraries also benefitted during this period from the influx of funds. In the early 1960s, an approval plan was initiated which greatly enhanced the liberal arts areas and brought a degree of well-roundedness to the collections. The sciences faculties and their advocates complained about the situation as they saw the liberal arts getting, what appeared in their eyes, more than their fair share of the book budget.

Because of CSU's long polytechnic tradition, there has never been total agreement on the role the liberal arts elements play in the university. Indeed, many science faculty consider the liberal arts as interlopers, drawing upon and diffusing the hard-pressed resources of the University into less worthy activities.

Three advocacy groups were very much involved in the development and implementation of the allocation formula and should be explained at this time. The first is the seven subject librarians. Collection development is the sole responsibility of these librarians. Each works from his or her own book budget. Each subject librarian is a loyal, sometimes fierce representative of his or her disciplines. They are defenders of the faith, the campus in microcosm.

Two groups have similar names and should be carefully identified. The first is the Library Council which is a standing committee of the Faculty Council, CSU's deliberating body. The Library Council advises the Director of Libraries on policy and collection development. Although it is primarily an advisory group, its recommendations and opinions do carry weight, sometimes considerable weight. We might also add that this committee is composed of one faculty representative of each college of which five are science oriented and four are liberal arts.

The second group is the Library Faculty Council, or LFC. This is the deliberating body of the Libraries. All professional members of the staff (who incidentally also hold faculty rank), are automatically members. The LFC is also strictly advisory to the Director. The LFC has standing committees and task forces which deal with specific issues and report back to the LFC. One of these is the Collection Development Committee, also known as CLOD. It began as a task force and is now a standing committee. CLOD will be mentioned frequently since it was formed specifically to design and monitor the allocation formula.

One other group deserves mention. This is the Library Committee of the College of Humanities and Social Sciences, the largest college in the University in terms of student enrollment. Although each of the nine colleges has a library committee, this particular group, in the case of the allocation formula, has served as the representative and communicator for the faculty in the liberal arts and has been more vocal than other college committees. We will call this group HSSC.

With the onset of the present decade, a draconian cut in book funds occurred which resulted in the cancellation of the approval plan. With so little money available, the Director of Libraries chose to allocate the book funds evenly for each of the seven subject areas. Such action was received with consternation by the liberal arts faculties. After all, the approval plan had given these areas a very definite advantage in the allocation of funds. They feared a return to the old days with its great emphasis on the technical and scientific areas of the collection.

In the summer of 1971, HSSC sent a strongly worded memo to the Director. They requested that instead of equally subdividing the reduced budget, the allocations should reflect proportionately the actual expenditure of the previous year, which happened to be the last year of the approval plan. In other words, there may be little to share, but let's keep the liberal arts in their proper place under the sun.

A delegation from the College and the Associate Dean met with the Library Council to press the issue. Although their case was not accepted, the point was made. To quote from the Library Council minutes:

> . . . considerable concern was evinced regarding the need to develop formulae in a continual effort to distribute equitable annually available monies for books, serials, binding and other materials.
>
> [LC minutes, July 29, 1971.]

It was voted unanimously to request that the Libraries staff prepare and present to the Library Council an allocation formula. As will be seen the Libraries treated the problem most seriously and designed a working plan that is still in operation.

Many people have written about allocation of book funds in college and university libraries. Years ago, the generally accepted practice was to allocate funds to departments, in effect, giving the academic departments the responsibility and authority for deciding which items to purchase. In many cases, funds were allocated evenly to all departments.[1] In other cases, libraries developed formulae which could include one or several factors ranging from the average cost of books in each subject[2] to circulation figures.[3]

In the 1960s, this pattern began to change. It was felt that allocation was resulting in unbalanced collections. The responsibility for collection development became the library's. Interest in formulae was revived in the 1970s with the publication of McGrath et. al's paper on factor analysis.[4] Jasper Schad published an excellent paper in the January, 1978, issue of *Journal of Academic Librarianship*. He reviewed the historical development of formulae and the problems inherent in using them.[5] Rather than reiterate what he has written, we would rather refer you to his paper.

The literature on allocation formulae is remarkable in one respect—the absence of any discussion on the implications of implementing and using them on a continuous basis. With the exception of the broad statement that formulae were devised to prevent monopolization of book funds by particularly active or aggressive members of the faculty,[6] no one has published information on whether this in fact happens. Our experience is that while contentions on actual dollars may cease, the arguments are simply transferred to the factors and methodology in the formula.

Let us turn now to the mechanics of formula development and an explanation of the unique plan finally adopted and implemented at CSU.

Our formula is shown in Table 1. Note that it is divided into fourteen columns which consider seven factors, or criteria.

The original task force considered many criteria to be included in the formula. These are listed in Table 2. As you can see, a wide range of items were considered. As you can also see, all but seven were rejected for reasons from "too vague" to "not quantifiable" to "not relevant." Rather than discuss all of them, we have singled out three due to their continuing controversy.

We have included both "Enrollment X Credit" and number of courses because it was felt the former represents the depth of a program while the latter represents the breadth.

The length of time a program has been offered at CSU was discussed at length. At issue was the problem of maintaining existing collections versus building new ones at their expense. The criterion was finally rejected for two reasons: an existing policy statement which gave the Libraries veto power over new degree programs if we determined the library's collection in that area at the expense of tearing down another. However, this question points out what could be a major problem with the formula. It simply cannot reflect growth until after the fact. As an example, the first year veterinary medical class was increased 50% last year, but this was not recognized until this year's formula which in turn could not be used to decide allocations until the budget of 1978-79. The formula as presently constructed is incapable of anticipating new programs or filling gaps. Fortunately or unfortunately depending on one's point of view, CSU is in a stage of non-growth. We have a ceiling on registrations, and no new Ph.D. programs have been approved in several years.

There was and is general agreement in CLOD that research is significant in relation to the library. Agreement stops there. How to measure it was a bone of contention in 1971 and continues to be the thorn in the side of the liberal arts advocates.

The task force came up with three numbers: the dollar amount of sponsored research, numbers of faculty publications, and numbers of on-going projects. The dollar amount was eventually rejected because it ignored non-sponsored research. We finally accepted the number of on-going projects but this also has problems. Simply counting projects ignores the impact on the library. How can one equate the $800,000 annual contract which funds the Collaborative Radiological Health Laboratory which is studying the long term effects of low-dose radiation, and a $500 grant to an English professor to edit the letters of a local author? Counting faculty publications also has serious drawbacks. Faculty publications, at least at CSU, are almost impossible to tally. And how can types of publications be equated? Should a four-volume treatise on the biochemistry of hemo-globin be given the same weight as a review article or poem? If not, on what basis can we assign "value"? The inclusion of research as measured by numbers of on-going projects and faculty publications was approved by CLOD, LFC, and the Library Council but the decision was far from unanimous. More about research later.

Once the criteria were decided, the next problem was to weigh them. Unfortunately, the documentation on the assignment of weights is not as complete as on the selection of criteria. Even staff members who were on the committee at the time disagree on the exact rationale. The weights for lower and upper graduate levels appear to be based on a use study published by Fearn[7] and on a statement of costs of the three levels of education made by the president of CSU. In the first case, the ratios were 1:3:7; in the second, they were 1:3:8. Three in-house studies on 1) cost of materials, 2) time spent on reference duty, and 3) items circulated were also supposed to have been factors in the weighing.

After much discussion (but little rationale), the weights were set as you see them on the formula.

As you can see from Table 1, Social Sciences ends up with the largest individual percentage. However, the sciences receive approximately 60% of the budget and the liberal arts 40%. This ratio seems to reflect generally the program emphasis of the University.

It should be emphasized that this formula is based on many assumptions which have never been proved or disproved. Our formula is the product of many subjective decisions on what is objective. This is the cause of our continuing battle over research. The science subject librarians accept one set of assumptions; the liberal arts librarians accept another.

The committee worked on the development of the formula for six months. It was approved by the LFC in March, 1972, and the Library Council in May, 1972. It was to become operational in the forthcoming fiscal year. Although the formula was weighted with an emphasis on the sciences, the faculty in the humanities and social sciences, as represented by HSSC, more or less accepted the plan, taking a wait-and-see attitude. The primary criticism rested with the methodology for research which will be discussed later. But by 1974, the liberal arts faculty had pretty much concluded the formula was not working to their advantage and saw a need for drastic alteration. Their main objection was the formula's emphasis on graduate programs, instead of concentrating on what they called a program's "actual needs" for books and serials. Their library committee, HSSC,

TAB

Colorado State University Libraries Bo
(Revised

	1 Enrollment x credit (lower div.)			2 Enrollment x credit (upper div.)			3 Enrollment x credit (graduate)			4 Courses (lower div.)			5 Courses (upper div.)			6 Courses (graduate)			7 Majors (undergrad.)		
SUBJECT	%	wt.	pts.	%	wt.	pts.	%	wt.	pts.	%	wt.	pts.	%	wt.	pts.	%	wt.	pts.	%	wt.	pts.
Biomedical Sciences	7.52	1	7.52	9.80	2	19.60	33.92	8	271.36	1.82	1	1.82	7.12	2	14.24	15.04	8	120.32	8.48	1	8.48
Business & Economics	10.37	1	10.37	17.00	2	34.00	6.79	8	54.32	6.23	1	6.23	10.50	2	21.00	8.17	8	65.36	15.05	1	15.05
Engineering Sciences	2.86	1	2.86	6.30	2	12.60	14.84	8	118.72	3.12	1	3.12	8.85	2	17.70	15.39	8	123.12	7.05	1	7.05
Forestry & Agriculture	6.05	1	6.05	16.08	2	32.16	11.18	8	89.44	10.65	1	10.65	9.29	2	18.58	13.83	8	110.64	22.33	1	22.23
Humanities	21.87	1	21.87	12.87	2	25.74	3.98	8	31.84	28.31	1	28.31	20.57	2	41.14	10.09	8	80.72	14.54	1	14.54
Physical Sciences	29.08	1	29.09	12.63	2	25.26	12.82	8	102.56	20.78	1	20.78	16.75	2	33.50	16.61	8	132.88	9.01	1	9.01
Social Sciences	22.21	1	22.21	24.30	2	48.60	16.46	8	131.68	29.09	1	29.09	26.91	2	53.82	20.87	8	166.96	23.64	1	23.64
TOTALS TS:99-77																					

LE 1

ok/Serial Allocation Formula, 1977–78
7/5/77)

8			9			10			11			12			13			14	
Majors (Masters)			Majors (Ph.D. etc.)			Faculty			Research & Publications			Cost of Published Books			Cost of Purchased Serials			TOTAL	
%	wt.	pts.	%	wt.	pts.	%	wt.	pts.	%	wt.	pts.	%	wt.	pts.	%	wt.	pts.	Points	%
14.95	5	74.75	19.35	8	154.80	16.00	6	96.00	16.17	8	129.36	10.7	10	107.40	16.93	10	169.30	1174.95	16.8
8.18	5	40.90	3.43	8	27.44	9.00	6	54.00	4.51	8	36.08	16.7	10	166.70	25.76	10	257.60	789.05	11.2
11.20	5	56.00	22.37	8	178.96	13.00	6	78.00	35.48	8	283.84	6.	10	61.80	15.64	10	156.40	1100.17	15.7
12.06	5	60.30	24.56	8	196.48	17.00	6	102.00	17.22	8	137.76	2.	10	27.00	8.60	10	86.00	899.39	12.8
11.04	5	55.20	0.00	8	0.00	14.00	6	84.00	4.83	8	38.64	24.	10	241.50	5.19	10	51.90	715.40	10.2
8.43	5	42.15	18.31	8	146.48	14.00	6	84.00	12.90	8	103.20	12.	10	128.10	17.22	10	172.20	1029.21	14.7
34.15	5	170.75	11.97	8	95.76	17.00	6	102.00	8.89	8	71.12	26.	10	267.70	10.64	10	106.40	1289.73	18.4
																		6998.	100.0

TABLE 2

Criteria Considered for Inclusion

University Criteria	Bibliographic Criteria	Administrative Criteria
Number of students	Necessity for duplicate copies	Aggressiveness of a department or college
Number of faculty	Costs of books	The way a department has spent its money
Number of graduates produced by level	Cost of serials	Capability of displaying bibliographic materials
Number of courses by level	Gaps in the collection	
Nature of the course	Rate of obsolescence	
Number of majors by level	Amount of publication in the field	
Amount of faculty publications	Library policy statements on commitments to excellence and priorities	
Length of time a program has been in existence	Amount of material available by gift and exchange	
University policy statement on excellence and priorities	Length of time the library has been collecting in a field	
National visibility of a college or department	Language capability of patrons	
Total budget or a college or department	Ease of acquiring materials	
Number of buildings	Cooperative agreements with other libraries	
Number of GTA's/GRA's	Office or reprint collections	
Number of Postdoc's or trainees	Amount of use of the collection	
Research	Interlibrary loan statistics	
Number of degree programs		
Number of credit hours		
Amount of dollars in contracts and grants		

pointed out that the buying power of established graduate programs, which are primarily in the sciences, is weighed heavily against liberal arts programs which have fewer graduate students but more undergraduate service areas. "We have come to the conclusion," said HSSC, "that the only rational basis for a library formula is the cost of materials necessary in each subject area weighted according to that subject area's relative importance in the University's mission." (Furniss memo of June 21, 1974 to Vice-President Neidt).

It was considerate of this committee to disclose an alternative to the existing formula, but their plan was highly impressionistic and fraught with intangibles. It is difficult enough to establish average costs of materials for various subject areas, but it is well nigh impossible to calculate mathematically the true value of one program compared to another in the universe of institutional objectives. The real force of their concern, however, was reflected by this statement:

> We would remind those making this decision of the North Central (accrediting agency) statement to the effect that even if an institution wishes to place its major emphases on applied and professional degrees, it cannot be an excellent university unless it has a vital, strong, and effective liberal arts core in its instructional programs. The applied and professional fields and the sciences cannot produce effectively educated graduates unless their own programs are supported by excellence in the humanities, arts, and social sciences.
>
> [Furniss memo of June 21, 1974 to Vice-President Neidt]

The reply from CLOD was less than sanguine. Graduate programs, they said, are the essence of this university, and it takes more money to develop and maintain material to support each such endeavor than it does to support undergraduate core collections. CLOD dismissed the attempt by HSSC to weigh the value of campus programs as "bearing little or no resemblance to reality" and impossible to implement.

Later that year, HSSC again attacked the formula, this time limiting their criticism to specific areas:

1. Since persons are users, a more rational criteria than credits would be enrollment.
2. Majors should be omitted because assignments requiring library use are a function of courses taken, not the major of the student.
3. Doctoral candidates should not be weighted more heavily than faculty members.
4. The research criteria is acceptable if the measurement covers referred journals or officially recognized presses.
5. A weight of 30% of the formula in the area of bibliographic criteria is not enough. The price of serials alone, without the numbers of serials in subject areas gives too much weight to the sciences.

The task force never officially replied to these criticisms, but at the same time, the Library Council was wrestling with the issue of a contingency or reserve fund to aid those areas having difficulty living within the formula. More on this later.

The column (#11) on research has been, and still is the most explosive issue in the formula, and remains a clarion cry of battle between the liberal arts and sciences. If one criterion crystallizes the differences it is this column.

As we have seen, CSU is basically a research oriented institution. One third of the University's financial support comes from funded contracts and grants, with the bulk of funded research in the sciences. When CLOD first deliberated on various criteria for the formula, there was general agreement that some credit must be given to this immense area, so vital to the University's goals and objectives. The result was the research column previously described. Because of its methodology, this column was so controversial that the entire formula was almost defeated during the debate in the LFC. After the formula was approved, ten professional librarians signed a petition to the Director requesting that it be removed from the formula. To quote from the petition:

> It is felt by these members that this is not a valid method by which to measure amounts of research taking place at CSU, and that it does not reflect the actual use of the libraries for either funded research projects or non-funded research projects.
>
> The discussion in LFC showed that the criterion for amount of research was felt to be more subjective, therefore weaker, in its application than the other criteria.
>
> [Memo to the Director, March 20, 1972]

HSSC did not minimize the value of funded research, or argue that funded research should not be supported by the Libraries. They did emphasize that the Libraries should support all research, that non-funded research is as important to the University as funded research. The Library Council was also unsure of the research column. It was suggested that the Council address itself to a further exploration of "research" in the budget formula.

The Director of the University Experiment Station, which is almost exclusively involved in research, expressed his concern about faculty publications in column 11. He stated that by this method, a report, a note, an article, an address, and a book all count the same. Merely enumerating entries results in "bean counting" and may encourage fragmentation of research results. Alternatives to "bean counting" are not encouraging, he added, because 1) the value of research is not finally determinable, 2) neither department chairmen or deans really know who is doing valuable research, and 3) the only one who frequently knows the value of research is the man doing it, but he, unfortunately is the most biased. (Memo from the Library Committee, College of Humanities and Social Sciences, Summer, 1972.)

Column 11 was discussed frequently and heatedly in the Library Council. In 1975, it was moved by the representative from the College of Humanities and Social Sciences to abolish the column. By this time, the data for faculty publications was becoming outdated, since the first and only compilation was done in 1971. But the scientists and their supporters had the votes, claiming the Libraries needed a relationship to research, and the motion was defeated. New data on faculty publications was later compiled, but the central issue of methodology persisted.

In 1977, column 11 again appeared on the CLOD agenda. The science librarian member argued that the column *is* a measure of research, that it supports what faculty are supposed to be doing, and money from research aids collection development. The liberal arts member contended that the data is difficult to update, the data is always incomplete, there is no way to measure library use resulting from research, and the quality of publications vary, so quantity alone is a poor measure. CLOD asked the Library Council for advice.

In the same year, the Library Council held eight consecutive meetings devoted largely to column 11. In a close (5–3) vote, they advised the Director to retain the column for another year. In 1978, CLOD voted to strike column 11 from the formula. Admittedly, the membership had changed to librarians who were more supportive of the liberal arts. To allay the objections of the science disciplines, CLOD raised the weights of the faculty column to offset somewhat the obvious gain for the liberal arts. By one vote, LFC rejected CLOD's recommendations and referred it back to the committee. After further discussion, CLOD reinserted the column, but the methodology was changed to dollar amounts only, and weight was considerably reduced.

The allocation formula has been operational for six years. One of the great underlying issues is a philosophical one. How honest are we in utilizing the formula? Are we manipulating the methodology so the results look "correct"? Should criteria be added, abolished, or modified because the results don't look the way we think they should? In other words, does the end justify the means, or should it? Since the formula was developed by people, and people are fallible, the formula could be fallible. An assumption like this allows room for tinkering. There are two cases of formula "manipulation," or as one sage put it, ". . . extenuating circumstances multipliers to be used for especially impacted areas."

In 1976, some subject areas showed large fluctuations from the previous year after the data were fit into the model. Concern was expressed in CLOD that the areas with significant reductions would have trouble adjusting to a sudden drop in funds. A "data smoothing technique" was proposed and accepted as a solution. This simply involved averaging three years data. Everyone admitted the formula had been compromised, but CLOD felt justified since the data received for several columns appeared suspect.

In 1974, a contingency fund was proposed by the Library Council to cope with "unforeseen expenses that may occur during the fiscal year." (Library Council minutes, May 3, 1974.) The Council also noted the problems of Humanities and Physical Sciences in meeting their obligations because of low credit in the formula. Somewhat later, the contingency fund idea was expanded to mean a reserve fund of three to five percent to correct "inequities in collection development." The contingency or reserve fund originated in Library Council. It was never really discussed or analyzed by CLOD. In a sense, a major policy decision regarding the operation of the formula was made without CLOD's input. In the Fall of 1977, the reserve fund amounted to 5% of the subject allocation. This was distributed to Humanities, Physical Sciences, and Forestry and Agriculture because they fared less well in the formula. It is only fair to mention that there have been some very significant changes in the methodology over the years. These have impacted the final results. We still have not had two consecutive years with the same methodology to evaluate the true impact of annual changes in the data.

The implications of the contingency funds are serious, perhaps ominous. Is this recognizing an inherent weakness in the formula? Are these political maneuvers to keep the results "correct"? Will the fund actually grow or rival the monies allocated by the formula? This is the stage we are in and the issues are as vital as when the formula was developed.

What does our experience show? It is probably an understatement to say that the allocation of the book budget is one of the most political problems libraries have within the context of the university setting.

Our discussions on the formula reflect the concerns of the University. The sciences feel they are the top priority of the University. The liberal arts do not think an institution can be a true university without strong programs in their areas. Some faculty even think CSU should return to the polytechnic institute it once was. CSU's further expansions into the liberal arts have been curtailed by the state legislature which has ruled that new programs must not be duplicated in the state and that CSU will concentrate on the sciences while the University of Colorado at Boulder will have more support in the liberal arts. If the academic faculty cannot agree on the relationship of the sciences and liberal arts at CSU, is it reasonable to expect that the library can escape the controversy? We not only participate in the discussions, we are also a focus of the controversy. Although the formula was devised as a solution to the controversy, it has become a part of it.

So far, the formula has worked despite some very strong pressures to abolish it or change it significantly. We have attempted to make fund allocation objective, but considering it is based on subjective opinions and assumptions, its philosophical basis is constantly open to attack and criticism.

We do not necessarily recommend our formula to all university libraries. It was developed in response to a specific problem in a specific institution. However, we would recommend that libraries attempt to develop their own. Even if they are not successful, the experience is unique and immensely beneficial. It involves sitting down and examining almost every policy, procedure, assumption, fact, and belief in collection development. This examination can be considered more valuable than any resulting formula.

REFERENCES

1. Floyd W. Reeves and John Dale Russell, "The administration of the library budget," *Library Quarterly* 2 (July 1932): 268–278.
2. William M. Randall, "The college-library book budget," *Library Quarterly* 1 (October 1931): 421–436.
3. William E. McGrath, "A pragmatic book allocation formula for academic and public libraries with a test for its effectiveness," *Library Resources and Technical Services* 19 (Fall 1965): 356–369.
4. William E. McGrath, Ralph C. Huntsinger and Gary R. Barger, "An allocation formula derived from a factor analysis of academic departments," *College and Research Libraries* 30 (January 1969): 51–62.
5. Jasper G. Schad, "Allocating materials budgets in institutions of higher education," *Journal of Academic Librarianship* 3 (January 1978): 328–332.
6. Jasper G. Schad, "Allocating book funds: control or planning?" *College and Research Libraries* 31 (May 1970): 328–332.
7. Robin A. C. Fearn, "An information center user study," *Proceedings of the American Society for Information Science* 6 (1969): 463–470.

David B. Walch

State University of New York, College at Buffalo

BUDGETING FOR NON-PRINT MEDIA IN ACADEMIC LIBRARIES

An analysis of costs for different types of non-print media was made. The selection of items for sampling was based on media reviewed in issues of Previews. *Average unit costs and rates of inflation for these media were established for the years 1972 through 1977. The year 1972 was used as a base year with an index of 100.0. The rate of inflation for the five year period ranged widely depending on the format of the media but in most instances was greater than the inflation rate of books as well as serials. It was also determined that the unit cost of non-print media was much higher than that of books.*

It is difficult for academic librarians to ignore or attempt to delay the inclusion of non-print resources in their libraries. The gospel of "audio–visual librarianship" as preached by Louis Shores during the past three decades is nearing fruition.[1] The revised *Standards for College Libraries*, published by the Association of College and Research Libraries (ACRL) in 1975, includes as one of its standards the following statement:

> The library's collection shall comprise all corpuses of recorded information owned by the college for educational, inspirational, and recreational purposes, including multidimensional, aural, pictorial, and print materials.[2]

Of course there have been those who decry the inclusion of such materials in academic libraries. Their position has been articulated by Harry E. Foster who does not regard "media" as a library necessity but rather as some sort of albatross.[3] Obviously a balanced philosophy regarding media is critical. Sterling McMurrin, the Chairman of the Commission on Instructional Technology, gave sound advice for those who would refrain from recognizing the value of non-print media as well as for those who may tend to go beyond sound reasoning in procuring more software and equipment than necessary. He cautioned against:

> ... two kinds of schoolmen who are likely to short-change their schools in the future; those ultraconservatives who refuse to believe that the new developments in educational technology have something genuinely important

to bring to the improvement of instruction, and those ultras at the other extreme who plunge too hastily into expensive investments without reliable knowledge of their value and without adequate competence to employ the equipment (and materials) effectively.[4]

The standards published by the Association of College and Research Libraries are by no means alone in advocating the inclusion of non-print media. The *Guidelines for Audiovisual Materials and Services for Public Libraries* published by the Public Library Association, the *Guidelines for Two-Year College Learning Resources Programs* (also published by ACRL) and, of course, the *Media Program: District and School* prepared by the American Association of School Librarians and the Association for Educational Communications and Technology all include statements relating to the importance of including non-print media in libraries. The trend has been established—the course is unavoidable. The responsibility now rests with the academic librarian to become as familiar with the ramifications of acquiring, processing, and circulating non-print media as he has been with similar problems surrounding print material.

One of the major concerns faced by academic librarians results from the lack of quantitative recommendations included in the *Standards for College Libraries* and an additional paucity of data relating to the cost of non-print media. The *Standards* readily confess this by noting:

> Higher education has thus far had too little experience with non-print library materials to permit tenable generalizations to be made about their quantitative requirements. Since consensus has not yet been attained among educators as to the range, extent, and configuration of non-print services which it is appropriate for college libraries to offer, no generally applicable formulas are possible here. It is assumed, however, that every college library should have non-print resources in a quantity commensurate with its print holdings and appropriate to institutional needs.[5]

The phrase "commensurate with its print holdings and appropriate to institutional needs" is a bit ambiguous for librarians who are accustomed to measuring their print holdings against so-called national standards and formulas. This problem is further compounded by the lack of cost data. There is no *Publishers Weekly* that announces with annual regularity the average cost of filmstrips, transparencies, slidesets, etc., nor is cost data readily available to measure inflation trends which frequently provide directors with rationale for requesting expanded budgets. It seems, therefore, that development of data relating to quantity and cost would enable academic librarians to more intelligently establish non-print collections as well as budget for the development and annual growth of such collections. Thus far there has been a near total absence of literature published that addresses these fundamental issues.

It is the intent of this paper to show unit average costs and cost trends for various types of non-print media since 1972. Hopefully this will assist librarians in budget preparation. It should be recognized that this is a tentative first step in identifying cost data that will be useful to academic librarians as they consider the cost for acquiring non-print media.

As previously noted one of the primary arguments for an expanded acquisition budget set forth by more than a few library directors is the ever-present inflation factor. Fortunately *Publishers Weekly* provides a rather detailed analysis of book prices on an annual basis. This information is summarized each year in *The Bowker Annual of Library and Book Trade Information*. In addition to this the series by Norman B. Brown in *Library Journal* does a superb job of presenting and analyzing cost trends and related information about periodicals and serials. Consequently the library director has information at hand which assists him in preparing a meaningful acquisition budget for books and periodicals. Yet similar information for non-print media is not easily attainable. Since the acquisition of non-print media is becoming a more important factor in academic libraries it would be beneficial to know their rates of inflation and unit costs. Such information would allow for improved budget preparation.

In an effort to determine such information a cost analysis of various types of non-print media was made. The sample included the non-print media reviewed in the September issue of *Previews*. For those who may not be familiar with this publication *Previews* was first issued in September 1972. It was published in response to several requests that librarians had made for a journal that would review non-print media for all subject areas from pre-school through college level. Since many academic libraries purchase non-print media for their so-called "curriculum" collections as well as materials prepared for advanced levels, it was felt that *Previews* would provide an appropriate sampling of non-print media for the purposes of this study.

The types of non-print media selected for analysis include 16mm films, filmstrips, multi-media kits, and recorded sound (discs and tapes).

FILMS

There are a number of things that should be noted about 16mm films—both in relation to Table I as well as other general observations. Although this particular format, i.e. 16mm film, is not purchased with great frequency by libraries in colleges and universities there are indications, particularly at the college level, that libraries may become more involved in their acquisition.

In 1971 Dwight F. Burlingame, using a random sample, made a survey of academic libraries across the country. The survey indicated that twenty percent of the responding libraries had film collections although some were relatively small. Thirty-one percent of the institutions responding indicated that films were handled by the audiovisual center on their campus.[6] When one considers that twenty percent of the academic libraries surveyed had film collections in 1971 and then recognizes that the trend in community colleges of incorporating library and audiovisual services under one administrative umbrella is now being seen with more frequency in the four-year colleges, then one may conclude that the responsibility for purchasing 16mm film (or its video-cassette cousin) may well become a commonplace reality for college libraries. With this in mind the following cost data represented in Table I may be of value as one considers 16mm film purchase as well as rental.

In conjunction with the cost data in Table I some observations relating to 16mm film are worth noting. For example, prior to purchasing a film one should always consider whether rental of films would be more economical than outright purchase. The permanence of film content, manner of treatment, the frequency with which it is used on the local campus, need for inspection and repair, are all variables that must be considered. In 1977 color films rented at an average cost of $27.23 ($1.23 X 22.24 minutes). This compares to an average cost of $308.85 ($13.95 X 22.14 minutes). In other words, an institution could rent a film eleven times before equaling the purchase cost. Another observation that is hardly worth noting since it is so obvious is that the production of black and white film is rapidly decreasing.

Discussion of 16mm film costs would not be complete without some consideration being given to the 8mm film loop and videocassette. In recent years it appeared that the 8mm film loop would become an important form of media in the academic community

TABLE I

16mm Films* (Index Base, 1972 = 100)

	1972 Price Index	1973 Price Index	1974 Price Index	1975 Price Index	1976 Price Index	1977 Price Index
Average Rental Cost Per Minute	$1.15 100	$1.34 116.5	$1.15 100	$1.18 102.6	$1.16 100.9	$1.23 107
Average B & W Purchase Cost Per Minute	7.32 100	12.40 169.3	7.44 101.6	7.10 97.0	— —	— —
Average Color Purchase Cost Per Minute	11.95 100	12.40 103.8	11.55 96.7	12.85 107.5	12.93 108.2	13.95 116.7
Average Cost of Color Film	241.39 100	257.92 106.8	277.20 114.8	282.70 117.1	253.43 105	308.85 127.9
Average Length per Film	20.2 min.	20.8 min.	24 min.	22 min.	19.6 min.	22.14 min.

*For this and the tables that follow the years listed do not reflect the year of production. For example, the vast majority of films reviewed by *Previews* in the September 1977 issue were actually produced in 1976.

due to its versatility and reasonable cost. In 1974 8mm film with sound experienced the highest growth rate of any non-print media, up 50 percent over 1973 sales. However, in 1976 it suffered a 60 percent decline in sales from its peak year of 1975.[7] One of the reasons for this may be the growing popularity of videocassettes which are becoming a more commonplace acquisition for many academic libraries than 16mm film. As noted previously the sample used in analyzing cost trends was based on the reviews appearing in *Previews. Previews* does not review videotape as such although some 16mm film producers make their films available in videocassette format.

In a recent survey of 25 large and small nontheatrical film distributors only three indicated outright opposition to the videocassette format although not all of the others are prepared to distribute and sell it at this time. For example, Coronet Instructional Media makes no 16mm titles available on videocassettes and plans to continue with 16mm until customer demand encourages a changeover. On the other hand Films Incorporated is beginning to market its films in videocassette format and has recently published its first video catalog. The Learning Corporation of America does not handle videocassettes at all and has no intention to, claiming the ease of piracy and especially the expense of maintaining a double inventory as the deterrents. Time–Life Multimedia enthusiastically endorses the videocassette format. They sell, rent, and preview on videocassette and stock full video inventories.[8]

The companies surveyed were divided on their pricing policies for videocassettes, either pricing cassettes lower than the 16mm format or pricing them at identical rates while a few reflect a higher cost on the basis that they do not keep videocassettes in stock. National Geographic Society, for example, offers short subjects at the same price on both formats, but their 52-minute documentaries are $100 cheaper on videocassettes. Time–Life Multimedia charges a 20 to 30 percent lower rate for video than 16mm film. A sampling of 27 programs available in both formats revealed the average cost for 16mm film was $428 and the average cost for these same films on videocassette was $334. This represents a 22 percent cost differential.[9]

FILMSTRIPS

In 1975 sound filmstrips became the most popular non-print format sold, overtaking 16mm film which had traditionally been the leader in dollar share of industry sales.[10] Increased emphasis on independent study in academic institutions has undoubtedly led to increased use of the sound filmstrip. Utilization of filmstrips in the classroom setting also remains high. Indeed, it is a flexible medium which makes its use appealing to a growing number of institutions. Improved technology has also led to more sophisticated and efficient listening and viewing units, many of which are designed specifically for library use.

It will be noted from Table II that the average expenditure for a filmstrip set in 1977 was slightly more than $76.00 which represents more than a 100 percent increase over 1972 prices.

For accompanying sound audiocassettes enjoy an increasing level of popularity over discs. A breakdown of sound filmstrip sales reveals that filmstrips with cassettes account for approximately 75 percent of all such filmstrips sold. This is in contrast to only 20 percent in 1970.[11]

MULTIMEDIA KITS

Multimedia kit sales experienced the highest growth rate of all forms of non-print

TABLE II

Filmstrips (Index Base, 1972 = 100)

	1972 Price Index	1973 Price Index	1974 Price Index	1975 Price Index	1976 Price Index	1977 Price Index
Average Cost of Filmstrip with Disc	$12.78 100	$14.14 110.6	$15.77 123.4	$15.63 122.3	$17.82 139.4	$18.28 143.0
Average Cost of Filmstrip with Cassette	12.95 100	16.11 124.4	15.94 123.1	17.19 132.7	17.18 132.7	18.60 143.6
Average Cost of Filmstrip Set (Cassette)	37.56 100	54.77 145.8	63.76 169.8	73.91 196.8	58.41 155.5	76.26 203.0
Average Number of Filmstrips Per Set	2.9 FS	3.4 FS	4.0 FS	4.3 FS	3.4 FS	4.1 FS
Average Number of Frames Per Filmstrip	63.3 Fr	64.1 Fr	57.6 Fr	66.3 Fr	62.8 Fr	64.2 Fr

media in 1973. In 1974 kits posted by far the largest single dollar gain in educational media sales—double the dollar gain of 16mm film and nearly double that of sound film-strips. In 1976 their sales declined somewhat yet more money is spent on this form of non-print media than any other kind except 16mm film and sound filmstrips.[12]

Multimedia kits are officially defined by the National Center for Education Statistics as "A collection of subject-related materials in more than one medium intended for use as a unit and in which no one medium is so clearly dominant that the others are dependent or accompanying."[13] They are characterized by a broad conglomerate of different types of materials and consequently their cost ranges widely. For example, the sampling of multimedia kits used in this study ranged from a low of $35.00 to a maximum of $325.00. Materials in one of the $35.00 kits included one filmstrip, two cassettes, one book, two costume patterns, two puppet patterns, one script, and one teacher's guide. The $325.00 kit included 120 books, ten pads of visuals, ten posters, one bulletin board display, four duplicating masters, and one teacher's guide. Since multimedia kits include such a wide variation of materials it is difficult to observe a great deal of consistency in their cost trends. Regardless, average cost of these types of non-print media are provided in Table III.

RECORDED SOUND

Of the different types of media analyzed records are the most common form of non-print media found in academic libraries. In April 1977, The System and Procedures Exchange Center (SPEC) conducted telephone interviews with 27 ARL member libraries in an effort to collect data on practices regarding the acquisition, processing, and use of non-print media. As one would expect, the interviews indicated that non-print materials are integrated into research libraries to a lesser degree than into two-year or undergraduate libraries. Yet most of the libraries surveyed did maintain record collections.[14] A survey of the 14 Colleges of Arts and Science at the State University of New York reveals that of all types of media phonorecords (including audiocassettes) compose the vast majority of non-print media holdings.[15]

Cost data related to sound recordings based on the reviews printed in *Previews* reveals the following: see Table IV.

In procuring and budgeting for sound recordings the library needs to consider a number of issues. If a rare reference collection is being developed then the use of tapes, especially cassettes, is preferable to that of discs since a tape can be played more frequently with less wear. It is also advisable to purchase in tape format rather than disc for a circulating collection although there are some problems including ease of theft, shelving, and inadvertently erasing the tape. Some libraries make it a policy to dub tapes from commerical records. Such a policy, however, may well be an infringement of the new copyright law.[16]

CONCLUDING OBSERVATIONS

In view of the growing interest in non-print media and because of the importance many institutions are placing on such means of communication, it is clear that academic libraries cannot long disregard them or consider their acquisition lightly. However, a major consideration is the level of funding that should be devoted to such acquisition. In a recent article written by Elizabeth A. Teo and published in *Choice*, the following observation is made:

TABLE III

Multimedia Kits (Index Base, 1972 = 100)

	1972 Price Index	1973 Price Index	1974 Price Index	1975 Price Index	1976 Price Index	1977 Price Index
Average Cost per Kit	$51.33 100	$111.66 217.5	$100.00 194.82	$140.25 273.2	$93.63 182.4	$93.65 182.4

TABLE IV

Sound Recordings (Index Base, 1972 = 100)

	1972 Price Index	1973 Price Index	1974 Price Index	1975 Price Index	1976 Price Index	1977 Price Index
Average Cost Per Disc	$6.10 100	$7.13 116.9	$6.63 108.7	$6.88 112.8	$5.85 95.9	$6.72 110.2
Average Cost Per Cassette	7.81 100	7.70 98.6	10.76 137.8	10.32 132.1	12.08 157.7	10.63 136.1
Average Cost Per Disc Set	12.20 100	16.40 134.1	13.26 108.7	8.94 73.3	22.23 182.2	8.06 66.1
Average Cost Per Cassette Set	19.53 100	17.11 87.6	24.75 126.7	30.96 158.5	44.70 228.9	31.89 163.3
Average Number of Discs Per Set	2.0 Disc	2.3 Disc	2.0 Disc	1.3 Disc	3.8 Disc	1.2 Disc
Average Number of Cassettes Per Set	2.5 Cassettes	2.4 Cassettes	2.3 Cassettes	3.0 Cassettes	3.7 Cassettes	3.0 Cassettes

In general terms the best yardstick for estimating the annual media budget might be a percentage of the yearly book-budget needed to purchase the number of volumes recommended in guidelines such as the "Standards for college libraries" for a growing collection. Precise recommendations for media allocations have not been set in the standards, but a range of 25%–35% of the amount appropriated for books appears reasonable, with the latter figure favored if the library anticipates frequent rental or substantial purchase of expensive formats such as films.[17]

Twenty-five to thirty-five percent of a library's acquisition budget is exceedingly high, especially when one considers that for many academic libraries thirty to forty percent (or more) of the acquisition budget is already committed to the purchase of periodicals. Statistics compiled by the R. R. Bowker Co. and included in the *Bowker Annual* indicate that 3.4 percent of college acquisition budgets are spent on audiovisual materials (excluding microforms).[18] This may be insufficient for many academic libraries, depending on whether or not a campus has an audiovisual program separately organized just as twenty-five to thirty-five percent may be deemed excessive by others.

An added dimension of this problem is the amount of non-print media on the market. A survey by the National Information Center for Educational Media showed that the number of titles available totaled approximately 30,000 a year in the following seven forms: 16mm motion pictures, 35mm filmstrips, 8mm film loops, overhead transparencies, videotapes, phonodiscs, and audiotapes. It is estimated that over 200,000 titles are presently available in the educational field.[19]

It is difficult to determine how many of these titles would constitute some kind of core collection for academic libraries. As already noted, the major share of non-print media is prepared for elementary and secondary schools. There has been a minimal amount of software produced for the post-secondary market. This fact is reflected in sales statistics prepared by the Association of Media Producers. According to their 1976 data, 58.3 percent of sales were to the elementary and secondary school market and only 10.7 percent to institutions of higher education.[20]

Another comparison that is undoubtedly made by librarians and is in many respects a viable consideration is the relative value of differing kinds of media. For example, if a color 16mm film is purchased by the library at 1976 prices then nineteen books must be rejected, or the purchase of one sound filmstrip means that four or five books will not be procured. These are the kinds of decisions an academic librarian must be prepared to make in the development of non-print media collections. One thing is clear from this study and that is that for the types of non-print media analyzed the rate of inflation has been as precipitous and, in many cases, more so than that of either books (25.6%, 1972 to 1976) or serials (35.7%, 1972 to 1976). Additionally, the unit cost for non-print media is much higher.

A final consideration that cannot be overlooked is the tangential costs for hardware, storage and shelving, and special seating accommodations such as that provided by "wet carrels". Consideration of these necessities are beyond the scope of this paper. However, a minimal budget for hardware alone for a relatively small institution was projected by Teo at a cost range of $11,395 to $18,605.[21]

In spite of such costs it must be emphasized that the academic library can make a valuable contribution to the teaching staff by becoming a source of comprehensive information regardless of format. A concluding observation by Louis Shores is worth noting:

Long before Marshall McLuhan suggested the decline of the print medium, Georges Duhamel wrote, in In Defense of Letters (1939) that the defenseless book would be supplanted by "Less laborious methods of information and recreation." Dissenting from the opinions of both Duhamel and McLuhan, I urged my librarian colleagues in colleges and universities, while I was chairman of the ACRL Audio–Visual Committee, to reject this defense complex and to recognize that all formats are part of the generic book. As such, they should be selected and acquired, as well as processed and disseminated, without condescension.[22]

The recognition of all formats as part of the generic book is an important concept. It presupposes, however, careful integration with the curriculum, a wise selection of materials, and very prudent management. Consideration of cost factors and cost trends such as that outlined in this paper is a critical first step in determining the extent to which libraries develop such collections.

REFERENCES

1. Louis Shores, *Audiovisual Librarianship: The Crusade for Media Unity, 1946–1969* (Littleton, Colo.: Libraries Unlimited, 1973).
2. American Library Association. Association of College & Research Libraries, "Standards for College Libraries," *College & Research Libraries News* 9 (October 1975): 277–279.
3. Harry E. Foster, "Media in Libraries: Luxury or Necessity?" *Vital Speeches of the Day* 41 (July 1, 1975): 563–565.
4. Sterling M. McMurrin, "Technology and Education," in Sidney G. Tickton, ed., *To Improve Learning; An Evaluation of Instructional Technology*, vol. 2 (New York: Bowker, 1971) p. 7–8.
5. American Library Association. Association of College & Research Libraries, *Ibid.*, p. 279.
6. Dwight F. Burlingame and Herbert E. Farmer, "Film," in Pearce S. Grove, *Nonprint Media in Academic Libraries* (Chicago: American Library Association, 1975) p. 128.
7. Association of Media Producers. *Survey and Analysis of 1976 Educational Media Sales* (Washington, D.C.: 1977) p. 3.
8. Judith Trojan, "Film and Video," *Media and Methods* 13 (May/June 1977): 48–49.
9. *Ibid.*, 60–61.
10. Association of Media Producers, *op. cit.*, p. 3.
11. *Ibid.*
12. *Ibid.*
13. U.S. Dept. of Health, Education, and Welfare. Education Division. National Center for Education Statistics, *Educational Technology: A Handbook of Standard Technology And A Guide for Recording and Reporting Information About Educational Technology* (Washington, D.C.: U.S. Government Printing Office, 1975) p. 74.
14. The Systems and Procedures Exchange Center. "Spec Flyer No. 33" (Washington, D.C.: Association of Research Libraries, 1977) Unpaged.
15. State University of New York, Office of Library Services. *Library Supporting Data* (Albany, 1977) Unpaged.
16. Association For Educational Communications and Technology. *Copyright and Educational Media; A Guide to Fair Use And Permissions Procedure* (Washington, D.C.: 1977) p. 17.

17. Elizabeth A. Teo, "Audiovisual Materials In The College and Community College Library: The Basics of Collection Building," *Choice* 14 (June 1977): 500.
18. *The Bowker Annual Of Library & Book Trade Information*, 22nd ed. (New York: Bowker, 1977) p. 263.
19. Thomas Risner, "NICEM Mediated Media Index," *Educational Screen/AV Guide* 49 (Jan. 1970): 15.
20. Association of Media Producers, *op. cit.*, p. 14.
21. Teo, *op. cit.*, p. 501.
22. Shores, *op. cit.*, p. 93.

Herbert S. White

Indiana University

BUDGETARY PRIORITIES IN THE ADMINISTRATION OF LARGE ACADEMIC LIBRARIES

Under a grant from the National Science Foundation and the National Enquiry into Scholarly Communication, the Research Center for Library and Information Science of the Indiana University Graduate Library School is extending an earlier study which covered the years 1969–73 through 1976, years which saw not only the heaviest impact of budget curtailments, but also the dawning recognition that these were long term and not temporary aberrations, and had to be dealt with. The paper reports and analyzes data gathered about budgets and budget allocations in large academic libraries.

In a study undertaken for the National Science Foundation, the Research Center of the Indiana University Graduate Library School originally investigated, for the years 1969 through 1973, the strategies and priorities implemented by American libraries in attempting to cope with increases in costs within their own budgets. This study, which has been thoroughly reported in the literature[1,2] has now been updated to cover the years 1974 through 1976, under a further grant from the National Science Foundation and the National Enquiry into Scholarly Communication.[3] This paper will examine value systems and priorities which have changed, and which have remained the same.

While the original study, and the follow-up effort examined not only academic libraries of varying sizes, but also public and special libraries, as well as domestic and foreign publishers of scholarly and research journals, this paper will be restricted to evidence gathered for "large" academic libraries. In the definitions used for the 1969–73 study, academic libraries were divided into six strata based on the number of periodicals held as reported by the Higher Education General Information Survey (HEGIS) tapes of the Office of Education for 1971. The largest group of academic libraries, those reporting the holding of 5000 or more periodical subscriptions, consisted, according to the HEGIS tapes, of 141 libraries. Of these, 120 were chosen to receive the 1969–73 questionnaire, and 77, or 64% responded.

In the design of the follow-up study, covering the years 1974 through 1976, and repeating 1973, it was considered important to resurvey the same population, to permit comparison of responses and the identification of trends and changes. We felt that, in particular, the years 1974 through 1976 should provide significant information about library perceptions and actions. The full impact of library funding curtailments did not become apparent until the latter part of the 1969–73 period. It was therefore entirely possible that many libraries had not yet had the opportunity to fully evaluate the significance of the grave situation they faced, to be fully aware of trends in publication costs, or to have enough time for the making and implementing of management decisions. The years 1974 through 1976, by contrast, were not only reported in the library press as particularly difficult years for library funding, but also came at a time when library directors were already well aware of the nature if not wholly the magnitude of their problems. It was therefore our belief that, by 1974 through 1976, management decisions for dealing with problems now recognized as more than temporary aberrations would have been reached and implemented, and we were anxious to determine not only what those decisions were and what priorities had emerged, but also to learn what impact the documented growth in interlibrary loan and in the formation of networks and consortia had on these decisions.

Questionnaires for 1973–76 were mailed to the same 77 libraries which had responded to the 1969–73 survey. Responses were received from 73 libraries, for a return of 95%, which must be considered excellent by any standards of measurement. We therefore feel confident that the responses for 1969–73, in this stratum of large academic libraries, can be related directly to the reported 1973–76 data.

SIZE OF BUDGET INCREASE

As noted in earlier reports, the overall budgets of large academic libraries responding to our survey increased at an annual average of 8.1%/year during the period 1969 through 1973. We had expected this level to decrease during the 1973 through 1976 period, because of widely reported cuts in library budgets, academic enrollments, and overall academic support. We found, by contrast, that large academic libraries actually did slightly better during this period, increasing their budgets at an annual rate of 9.0%. Larger academic libraries did considerably better than smaller academic libraries in this regard, and only special libraries were able to increase their budgets at a more rapid rate than the reporting largest academic libraries. Of course, it should be quickly noted that *none* of these increase percentages were adequate to match the increasing price of library materials, and particularly of library serials. Here, large academic, as well as special libraries, were particularly hard hit, because of their heavy reliance on foreign titles, impacted by both greater inflation rates in the country of publication and the continued weakening of the dollar on international currency exchanges. For the years 1969–73 large academic libraries had reported an annual average periodical price increase of 11.2% for all subscriptions, for 1973–76 this became an annual rate of 15.9%, a startlingly sharp increase. Moreover, it should be noted that even this amount would suffice only to maintain present subscriptions, a policy which, in view of the continued growth of the periodical literature, would result in a worsening of actual holdings as related to potential holdings.

We also sought to determine, in the 1973–76 survey, whether there were differences in rates of budget growth, either by funding source or regional location. For large academic libraries, we found a relatively sharp distinction between publicly and privately funded university libraries, with the former increasing their budgets at an annual rate of 9.8%, while privately funded major universities increased their library budgets at an annual rate of only 7.2%. However, the results, while interesting, cannot be considered significant by statistical measurements, at best, so our statistics advisors inform us.

Geographic dispersions, however, also indicate wide differentiations which *are* statistically significant. Using the geographic area definitions employed by the U.S. Bureau of the Census, we found that, at the one extreme, major academic library budgets in the

West South Central states were growing at an annual rate of 16.0%, those in the Mountain states at 11.5%, West North Central states at 10.7%, and Pacific states at 9.9%. By contrast, large academic library budgets in the Middle Atlantic states increased annually at only 6.8%, and in New England states at 7.0%.

SALARIES AS AN OVERALL PART OF THE BUDGET

Serious as these statistical implications are, they were compounded, for the years 1969–73, by further evidence that the materials budget was not growing as rapidly as the library budget as a whole. We are not suggesting that funds were transferred from the materials budget to pay salaries, although this is possible in individual instances. It is more likely that salary decisions are made independently within the institution, and the library salary budget adjusted accordingly. The library materials adjustments may be based on entirely different criteria. We found some libraries, but relatively few, in which there is total freedom, at least theoretically, to transfer money between labor and materials categories. Even where this freedom theoretically exists, faculty opposition might thwart any attempt to shift money from the materials to the labor budget, although faculty might welcome a transfer from labor to materials. In any case, salary costs for large academic libraries grew, during 1969–73, at a greater rate than the budget increased as a whole, and at a rate of 9.1%. This meant that, while in 1969 labor costs represented 56.9% of the total budget, in 1973 they were 58.9%, a trend which, if continued, could arouse faculty attention and opposition. We are not suggesting that all of these increases were attributable to salary increases for existing personnel. Some may have been caused by more staff, increased fringe benefit costs, upgrading of vacant positions, or a whole variety of factors. We simply don't know.

We were, however, interested in determining whether this increasing percentage of the library budget devoted to salaries had continued past 1973, and found that while a slight increase had occurred between 1973 and 1974, this had been reversed in later years, so that, by 1976, the relationship was back to where it had been in 1973.

TRANSFERS WITHIN THE MATERIALS BUDGET

Our 1969–73 survey had found dramatic shifts of funds from the monographs to the serials budget, as libraries sought to protect the continuity of their ongoing subscriptions. It could be surmised that some library administrators, whether consciously or unconsciously, were treating the funding curtailments as a temporary aberration, and holding back on monograph acquisitions during this "temporary" displacement on the premise that these books could be purchased more easily than serials at a later date when funds were again more plentiful. Incidentally, we had initially asked for budget differentiations between periodicals and other serials, but found that libraries were generally unable to supply these. We were, therefore, restricted within the materials budget to considerations of monographs, serials, and "other materials"

As indicated earlier, we found, during 1969–73, dramatic shifts from the monograph to the serials budget among large academic libraries. In 1969 large academic libraries were spending $2.02 on monographs for every dollar spent on serials, and by 1973 this ratio had changed to the point where only $1.16 was being spent for books for every dollar spent on serials. We speculated in our report about how long this trend could continue, and expressed the opinion that this transfer had to stop and that, in fact, libraries would have to start making more critical decisions in their serials management without simply propping up serials purchases artificially at the expense of books. A large number of administrators and collection development officers in fact assured us that the budget shifts were at an end.

Our statistics for 1973-76 indicate that, in fact, these shifts continued, although at a decreasing rate, in large academic libraries. By 1976 materials categories had in fact reversed their importance, and large academic libraries were spending $1.23 on serials for every dollar spent on books. Stated another way, the transfer had been so sweeping that a 9.4% annual increase in the overall materials budget between 1973 and 1976 was translated into a 12.8% annual increase for serials, as contrasted to a 3.0% increase in the book budget and, perhaps surprisingly, a similarly small increase in expenditure for microforms.

By contrast, smaller academic libraries, those with periodical holdings between 1000 and 2000 subscriptions, and for which books have historically been a more important part of the collection, stopped the fund transfers entirely after 1973. We have thought long and hard about why these shifts are so prevalent. At least one reason seems to be cosmetic and political. A cut in the serials budget affects *immediately* specific and identifiable titles not to be renewed. A cut in the monographic budget will affect specific titles, of course, but neither we nor the faculty know what they are yet, and if we are lucky, maybe we'll never know.

IMPACT OF CONSORTIA AND NETWORKS

Membership in consortia and networks continues to increase among all types of libraries, but most particularly large academic libraries. In 1973 90.5% of such libraries indicated that they belonged to at least one such organization, and the mean number of memberships was 2.3. In 1976 no large academic library indicated that it did not belong to any consortia or networks, and the number of memberships was up to a mean of 2.9.

At the same time, it is difficult to assess the significance of this increased membership in terms of actual operations. Borrowing by large academic libraries increased 26.9% from 1973 to 1976, and lending by 53.6%. This may be used to indicate a greater reliance, even by large academic libraries, on one another's collections.

At the same time, however, while 8.2% of large academic libraries reported, as a result of membership in consortia or networks, dropping "some" duplicate subscriptions, 19.2% reported dropping "some" unique titles, and 27.4% reported foregoing "some" subscription placements, these responses may relate only to relatively few instances and cannot be quantified. In the response to the perhaps more significant question "How has the availability of periodical material through various types of borrowing affected your library's periodical holdings over the past 5 years," 73.7% of large academic libraries which answered the question indicated that it had had no effect, with the remainder equally divided between those which reported that such availablility had caused a decrease, and those which reported an increase (presumably because it enabled the library to learn about titles for the first time). Smaller academic libraries also reported no impact by overwhelming majorities, and for these the libraries reporting that the number of subscriptions had increased because of memberships in consortia and networks outnumbered those reporting a decrease.

CONCLUSION

The above has been only a brief and highly selective extract from a large quantity of data. In summary, it may be fair to state that large academic library budgets, while increasing unevenly for various types of funding sources and geographic locations, are nevertheless increasing at a rate (around 9%) which is as good as the rate increase of academic budgets as a whole. Academic institutions are not turning their backs on their libraries, although they are unable to support the library at rates sufficient to match materials cost increases (particularly for foreign materials). Labor cost increases which forced that portion of the budget to grow more rapidly than the budget as a whole appear to have been checked, although we don't know if this affected monograph budgets. However, the tendency to protect the serials budget by transferring funds from the monographic budget continues, almost without interruption. Libraries still appear to be making relatively little use, at least through 1976, of their membership in networks or consortia for the purpose of collection re-evaluation, although there are a few publicized examples of coordinated decision making, and this may increase further. At present, however, increased borrowing appears to result from pragmatic need, either because the title is not owned or because the owned copy can't be located. There is little evidence of *planned* borrowing. Hard pressed though they are to keep up with the double serials cost impact of inflation and literature growth, academic libraries are, for the most part, still almost holding their own in this area. Cancellations are highly selective and are heavily oriented toward duplicates and foreign titles, not generally toward regionalization of collections. All of this is happening at the expense of the monograph budget and, if levels of acquisition up to 1969 represented reasonable monograph needs, serious damage to the balance of the collection is being done. This is true not only because the expectation of eventually "catching up" becomes more and more of a forlorn hope, but also because this cutback in library monographic expenditures may mean that some scholarly material of marginal profitability may not be published at all, and because cuts in monographic acquisition impact some discipline more heavily than others. Finally, of course, it must end at some point, although we thought we meant it when we said it before. At present trends, by 1990 there would be no monographic acquisition at all, and I dare say none of us can imagine that. It appears that, through 1976, the decision to forego monographs for serials may be part of a strategy, conscious or not, to spare faculty and administration from budgetary realities, or to disguise or delay their impact as much as possible. It is a strategy which may backfire, and which appears forlorn in any case.

REFERENCES

1. Bernard M. Fry and Herbert S. White, *Publishers and Libraries: A Study of Scholarly and Research Journals* (Lexington, Mass., D. C. Heath & Co., 1976).
2. Herbert S. White, "Publisher and Library Behavior in Times of Funding Retrenchment," *Library Quarterly* 46 (October 1976): 359–397.
3. Bernard M. Fry and Herbert S. White, *Impact of Economic Pressures on American Libraries and Their Decisions Concerning Scholarly and Research Journal Acquisition and Retention* (National Science Foundation Grant DSI 76-23592. June 1978).

Martha J. Bailey

Purdue University

COMPENSATION PLANS FOR LIBRARY
FACULTY MEMBERS

The author examines the literature concerning compensation programs for library faculty members and reviews some of the elements that comprise these plans. A salary program for academic libraries is suggested which covers those with and those without administrative responsibilities, and methods for determining annual salary increases are also discussed.

An examination of the literature concerning faculty status for academic librarians indicated that few authors have considered compensation plans for library faculty members.

> . . . The relationship between librarians' salaries and faculty status for librarians has not been subjected to sufficient study. . . .[1]

Compensation plans include not only salary but also pensions, vacations, sabbaticals, tuition for dependents, housing, research funds, or travel funds (Fig. 1). Dow recently surveyed seven elements which comprise faculty status; included in these were the availability of research and paid leaves.[2] Salary surveys are published on a regular basis by various groups such as the Association of Research Libraries,[3] the Association of College and Research Libraries,[4] The American Association of University Professors,[5] Association of American Library Schools,[6] and Special Libraries Association.[7]

There is little information available on how far the library faculty member's salary is determined by faculty responsibilities and how far by administrative responsibilities where these are combined in the same person.[8] Some authors suggest that the positions of library managers and professional librarians (or library faculty members) should be separate;[9] management is not a professional responsibility. Such a division of responsibilities often is not feasible even in a very large academic library which has many branches and departments.

> . . . many if not most professional positions in libraries increasingly tend to become administrative in the sense that they involve supervision of other people and responsibility for planning and on-going operations. . . .[10]

Salary	Free parking
Pensions	Health and hospitalization insurance
Vacations	Employee credit union
Sabbaticals	Discount at university bookstore
Tuition for dependents	Educational discount at local museum or zoo
Tuition for self	
Housing	Use of college swimming pool, gym, or library
Research funds	Paid holidays (for 12 month contracts)
Travel funds	Secretarial or graduate student assistance
Paid memberships	
Sick leave	Free photocopy or photography service
Discounts for concerts, athletic events, fruit from college orchards, etc.	Free computer services
	Office space and supplies

Figure 1.   Some Elements of Compensation Plans.

There are two questions to consider: 1) how to establish salary plans and 2) how to determine salary increases each year. The problem of establishing plans which are comparable to those of the teaching faculty

> . . . is . . . complicated by the contention that some institutions have no salary scale for the faculty; hence any attempt to compare the two groups would make no sense. To compound matters further, it can be shown that there exist wide variations in the compensation of faculty members, depending upon the subject they teach or the school they belong to. (For instance, professors teaching social work or music or education or journalism might receive a much lower average salary than professors teaching medicine, law, business administration, engineering, or science.) Comparisons are further complicated by the fact that differences in rank among faculty members are based on different considerations from those applicable to rank within the library system.[11]

Due to the implementation of the federal equal opportunity guidelines in colleges and universities, probably many institutions currently have salary scales. At many state institutions, such as Purdue University, the salary lists of virtually all employees may be examined.

There are studies of some factors which affect salaries. Massman indicated that librarians who published received more money than those who did not[12] and there was monetary advantage to a sixth year certificate or a doctorate, especially for men.[13] Traditionally men have been paid higher salaries than women at each professorial and administrative level in both library faculties and teaching faculties.[14]

In a study of the SUNY library system, the strongest predictor of salary was the person's rank, with professional experience and sex the next strongest predictors.[15] At the University of New Mexico, the salaries were based on academic degrees, experience, and rank.[16]

The first step in establishing compensation plans is to prepare a description for each position. There is information available on how to prepare library job descriptions, such as the work of Sergean[17] or Wilkinson.[18] Canelas[19] provides sample descriptions.

It is difficult to adhere to a strict classification of positions in any organization because there are unique conditions and constraints which are involved in each position.[20] Although people are chosen for a specific position, they are concurrently evaluated on how well they fit into the overall organization and how they might be available for future change.

It is difficult if not impossible to set minimum standards for faculty activities for a specific position. These activities are: teaching, research and publication, professional competence and activity, service to the university, and public service.[21] The teaching faculty are hired to teach but are evaluated on the basis of their publications. The library faculty often are hired to supervise or work in a library department but are evaluated on the basis of their publications.

Rogers, in establishing a salary for a beginning professional, specified as the requirement for employment two languages and a graduate degree in library or information science from an American Library Association accredited university.[22] Then the salary was adjusted upwards on such elements as:

- Master's degree in a relevant field in addition to master's
  degree in library or information science $400
- Reading knowledge of desired exceptional languages,
  e.g., Slavic or Arabic $200
- High grade point average for undergraduate degree $100
- High grade point average for graduate library degree $100
- Exceptional personal qualities $100
- Relevant experience, e.g., teaching at college level, $300 per year for
  subprofessional library experience, or business   equivalent fulltime
  experience   work

Some additional qualifications might be applicable for both beginning and experienced professionals:

- Licenses, registrations, or certificates held, such as, Medical Library Association certificate
- Special experience such as with online computer information retrieval services
- Doctorate in library or information field or another relevant field
- Continuing Education Units (CEU)[23]
- Membership in professional organizations
- Citations in biographical works
- Awards and honors

Other items which were included in the SUNY study were length of time within rank, administrative function, age, and mobility for job advancement.[24]

Most of the salary studies which were examined included categories for nonadministrative positions such as curators, specialists, and bibliographers.[25,26,27,28] Sample position descriptions also are available.[29] Some authors mentioned that the library faculty member who does not have an administrative assignment is at a disadvantage in the salary program.[30]

The textbooks on compensation for business and industry include information on the scientist who does not have administrative responsibility.[31] This position may compare to the library faculty member who does not manage. The texts use a "maturity curve,"[32] which is the number of years in level and number of years since the last academic degree, as bases for compensation. These schemes also include provisions for advanced degrees.

The author developed a salary plan for library faculty members, based on professorial rank, administrative responsibility and years of experience (Fig. 2). With a base salary of $10,000, the formula is

$10,000 + professorial rank + administrative responsibility + years of experience =

salary

Basic Salary $10,000

Professorial Rank (4 levels)

    4 professor
    3 associate professor
    2 assistant professor
    1 instructor
            $1,500 X level   _____

Administrative Responsibility (7 levels)

    7 director
    6 assistant and associate directors
    5 unit heads
    4 departmental librarians
    3 curators and specialists
    2 associate librarians
    1 assistant librarians
            $1,000 X level   _____

Years of Professional Library Experience (7 levels)

    7 25–30 years
    6 21–24
    5 16–20
    4 11–15
    3 8–10
    2 4–7
    1 1–3
            $500 X level   _____

                        Total   _____

Figure 2. Basic Salary Plan.

For example, the salary for a person who is an assistant professor at level 3 administrative responsibility and 8 years of experience would be computed as follows:

base salary	$10,000
professorial rank 2 (2 X $1,500)	3,000
administrative level 3 (3 X $1,000)	3,000
years of expereience level 3 (3 X $500)	1,500
	$17,500

In this program monetary amounts could be assigned to the qualifications listed above, such as $2,500 for a doctorate, $1,500 for a second master's degree, or $100 for each grant. Thus people in the "curator or specialist" category who had advanced degrees and language specialities would be brought up to the level of those people with higher administrative ranks.

Checking this against ACRL annual list,[33] the specialist category is $14,883 for twelve months and the assistant professor is $14,670 for nine months. Adjusted to twelve months, at $1630 per month, the latter would be $19,560. The suggested $17,500 is about midway between the $14,883 and the $19,560. The faculty members also may receive outside additional compensation for consulting, writing books, or giving lectures.[34]

A recent publication summarizes a number of studies concerning the relative importance of publication, teaching, and research in determining faculty salaries.[35] For example, in an economics department administrative responsibility increased the salary $5,000, one refereed paper increased it $350 while a monograph had no effect.[36]

Examining the second question—determining the salary increases each year—is complicated by the fact that salary is only one phase of the performance appraisal. The others are promotion, career development, and performance improvement.[37]

> . . . the requirements of appraisal for salary administration might be satisfied through a combination of objective, common criteria, a quick rating of performance level and a peer review process to relate all appraisals to a common standard. . .[38]

Appraisal for promotion and career development are handled by peer review while performance improvement is evaluated by a combination of peer review and supervisor's appraisal.

The New Mexico study indicated that raises were based on cost of living and merit.[39] Other items to be considered were gleaned from the performance evaluation forms which were obtained from five Association of Research Libraries member libraries (Fig. 3). One item which is not included in this list is that of "marketability," which is comprised of both the demand for a person's abilities and his/her job mobility in the library and information field. Points could be assigned to each item on the list, and the total points for each person could be translated into a monetary amount.[40]

In conclusion, a review of the literature provided some insight into developing salary plans and determining annual salary increases for library faculty members. These are

- Professorial rank and administrative level, based on published studies
- Master or doctor's degree in appropriate subjects or sixth year certificate in addition to the master's degree in library or information science

— Number of years since degree, or in professorial rank, or in administrative level
— Other certificates, such as Medical Library Association certificate or Continuing Education Units (CEU)

The author suggests a plan for establishing a salary program which includes determining the annual increase.

I. Performance within the Library
— Teaching credit courses
— Participation in course and curriculum development
— Preparation of instructional materials including textbooks, library manuals, handbooks, visual aids and bibliographies
— Experimentation in design, demonstration or implementation of library systems including catalogs, selected dissemination of information, indexing, information retrieval or other means of improving user access to information, materials or services
— Involvement in institutes, workshops, or special programs

II. Research and publications
— Publications in refereed journals, research abstracts or equivalent publications
— Other publications
— Unpublished works and works in progress
— Papers contributred at professional meetings
— Invited lectures/papers given at state, regional, national and international meetings and at other educational institutions
— Research grants and awards received
— Research projects in progress
— Editorships or memberships on editorial boards

III. Professional competence and activity
— Participation in major programs, such as institutes, workshops and short courses as chairperson, lecturer, administrators, coordinator, etc.
— Offices and committee assignments in professional associations
— Service in doctoral, masters or honors thesis committees

IV. Service to university
— University level committee assignments
— School and departmental level committee assignments
— Libraries committee assignments

V. Community service
— Professional involvement in public and/or governmental service
— Professional involvement in community service
— Consulting
— Professional activities such as research, publication, or participation in professional associations
— "Marketability"

Figure 3. Performance Evaluation.

REFERENCES

1. Robert H. Muller, "Institutional Dynamics of Faculty Status for Librarians." In Lewis C. Branscomb, *The Case for Faculty Status for Librarians* (Chicago, American Library Association, 1970) p. 34 (ACRL Monograph no. 33).

2. Ronald F. Dow, "Academic Librarians: A Survey of Benefits and Responsibilities." *College and Research Libraries* 38 (May 1977): 218-220.

3. Suzanne Frankie, "ARL Annual Salary Survey" (Washington D.C., Association of Research Libraries, 1976) 25 p. Gives beginning salary and median salary for each member library 1975-76 and 1976-77.

4. "Salaries of Academic Librarians 1975/76" *College and Research Libraries News* (October 1976): 231-234. Gives average salaries for librarians by administrative position and by professorial rank.

5. "Report on the Annual Survey of Faculty Compensation, 1977-78." *American Association of University Professors. Bulletin* 64 (September 1978): 193-266. Gives average salary and average compensation by academic rank.

6. R. B. Bidlack, "Faculty Salaries of 62 Library Schools, 1976-77" *Journal of Education of Librarianship* 17 (Spring 1977): 199-213.

7. "SLA Salary Survey 1976" *Special Libraries* 67 (December 1976): 597-624.

8. A doctoral dissertation currently in progress is examining salaries. This is Ung Chon Kim. "Factors Affecting Salaries of Librarians in Universities: a Multivariate Statistical Analysis" Indiana University Graduate Library School, scheduled for completion Spring 1978.

9. Ralph M. Edwards. "The Management of Libraries and the Professional Functions of Librarians." *Library Quarterly* 45 (April 1975): 155.

10. Muller, *op. cit.*, p. 37.

11. *Ibid.*, p. 34-5.

12. V. F. Massman. *Faculty Status for Librarians* (Metuchen NJ, Scarecrow Press, 1972) p. 172-3.

13. *Ibid.*, p. 167.

14. *Ibid.*, p. 165-73.

15. B. K. L. Genova and others. "A Study of Salary Determinants Within the SUNY Librarians Association Between 1973 and 1974" (State University of New York, February 1, 1977) 59 p. (ERIC document ED 134 189).

16. Rex C. Hopson, "A Study of Academic Librarians Salaries and Privileges." (Albuquerque, University of New Mexico, November 1974) 6 p. ERIC document ED 098 958.

17. R. Sergean and J. R. McKay, "Description and Classification of Jobs in Librarianship and Information Work." *Library Association Record* 76 (June 1974): 112-115.

18. John Wilkinson and others, "A Matrix Approach to Position Classification." *College and Research Libraries* 36 (September 1975): 351-363.

19. Dale B. Canelas, "Task Analysis of Library Jobs in the State of Illinois; a Working Paper on the Relevance of the Study to Academic Libraries." (1971) 203 p. (ERIC document ED 067 113).

20. Sergean, *op. cit.*, p. 112.

21. Carl W. E. Hintz, "Criteria for Appointment to and Promotion in Academic Rank." In Lewis C. Branscomb. *The Case for Faculty Status for Academic Librarians.* (Chicago, American Library Association, 1970) p. 28-9 (ACRL Monograph no. 33).

22. Rutherford D. Rogers and David C. Weber. *University Library Administration.* (New York, Wilson, 1971) p. 43.

23. Elizabeth W. Stone, *Continuing Library Education as Viewed in Relation to Other Continuing Professional Education Movements.* (Washington, D.C., American Society for Information Science, 1974).

24. Genova, *op. cit.*

25. "Salaries of Academic Librarians 1975-6," *op. cit.*

26. Peter Spyers-Duran. "1973-74 Interinstitutional Salary of Professional Librarians Employed by the SUS of Florida." (Boca Raton FL, Florida Atlantic University, December 1973). 26 p. (ERIC document ED 088 523).

27. David C. Weber, "The Place of 'Professional Specialists' On the University Library Staff." In Lewis C. Branscomb, *The Case for Faculty Status for Academic Librarians. op. cit.*, p. 71-3.

28. Anita R. Schiller, "Characteristics of Professional Personnel in College and University Libraries." (Urbana IL, Graduate School of Library Science, University of Illinois, 1968) 188 p.

29. Canelas, *op. cit.*

30. Peggy Heim and Donald F. Cameron, "The Economics of Librarianship in College and University Libraries 1969-70; a Sample Survey of Compensation." (Washington D.C., Council on Library Resources, Inc., 1970) p. i (ERIC document ED 043 354).

31. M. L. Rock, *"Handbook of Wage and Salary Administration."* (New York, McGraw Hill, 1972) p. 8-24 to 8-35; and R. E. Sibson. *Compensation* (New York AMACOM, 1974) p. 155-73.

32. Rock, *op. cit.*, 8-30 to 8-32.

33. "Salaries of Academic Librarians 1975-76" *op. cit.*

34. Beverly T. Watkins, "Outside Income on University Time: A Conflict for Professors" *Chronicle of Higher Education* 15 (February 21, 1978): 13.

35. Howard P. Tuckman, *Publication, Teaching, and the Academic Reward Structure.* (Lexington MA, Lexington Books, 1976) Chapter 2. "Determinants of Academic Salaries: Alternative Views." p. 19-36.

36. *Ibid.*, p. 31.

37. Larry N. Yarbrough, "Performance Appraisal in Academic and Research Libraries." (Association of Research Libraries. Office of University Library Management Studies. Occasional Papers vol. 3 no. 1 May 1975) p. 1 (ERIC document ED 129 221).

38. *Ibid.*, p. 6.

39. Hopson, *op. cit.*

40. Rock, *op. cit.*, p. 8-29.

Phyllis Dougherty

University of Tennessee Center for the Health Sciences

INTERDEPARTMENTAL SWAP-OFF BY THE BUDDY SYSTEM: REPORT OF A STAFF EXCHANGE PROGRAM

The staff relations and development committee of a university library devised a staff exchange program to promote understanding of library operations and service and to generate ideas to improve them. A brief review of management theory formed the rationale. The exchange was implemented by a "buddy-system" random pairing of individuals from the various departments. After the pairing a questionnaire was distributed for evaluation purposes. Most of the returned questionnaires indicated some benefit received from participation in the program. It was felt that understanding was improved, but that the generation of ideas could not yet be assessed.

The Staff Relations and Development Committee and the University Library Advisory Council met to explore possibilities for a Staff Institute for the following year. Questionnaires had been sent to the staff members the previous year. The results indicated a lively interest in library activities in which they were not personally involved. Drawing heavily upon this information, the Committee stated as objectives for the Institute:

1. To create a better understanding among library staff members of the totality of library operations and service.
2. To generate ideas which would improve services to the University.

This University is located in a large Southern city. It had an enrollment of 19,000 students, mostly commuters, and included residents of two other closely neighboring states. There were about 700 faculty and staff people, 104 of these working in the library. The library was a large main building on campus with a 12-story stack tower, and five departmental libraries. One of these was located off the campus. The Library collection contained 2.5 million items. These included, in addition to monographs and journals, microforms, phonodiscs, tape cassettes, kits, maps, models, and some musical instruments. The Government Documents collection was a selective depository. The extensive Mississippi Valley Collection was part of the Special Collections Department. In view of the diverse nature of the library holdings, many thought it would be more exciting to present a program to the staff members which would acquaint them with something different from their everyday expeience. A series of workshops was discarded as an idea, because of being rather dull, time consuming, and restrictive to those who could not be released from their work to attend at a set time. The consensus among Committee members seemed to be that intimate involvement in a job process would be more helpful and interesting than a lecture, or observation by a group, such as a tour arrangement, One comment was that while showing people what a particular job entailed, and what materials it covered, a remark about answering the phone properly might be included. This could be an individual contribution to the whole of library service.

Eventually the idea of a "buddy system" emerged, by which each staff member would be paired with one from another department. Each would have an opportunity to show his/her "buddy" the procedures of the job, and some of the problems encountered. Many felt that an objective view from the fresh eye of an outsider might result in constructive suggestions as to solutions to these problems. Some felt a sense of isolation in their jobs, and saw participation in such a program as a step toward inclusion in the mainstream of library activities.

It was noted, too, that individual pairing for learning and communication would probably avoid disruption of the library work schedule. The pairs could set up their exchanges during slack times in their respective departments as they fluctuate with the academic year. As the purpose was not a training session, but to present an overall view of the job only, exchanges should not take more than half a day, and, in most cases, considerably less.

The most difficult area of discussion concentrated around the method of pairing. Since some members wanted to learn what a particular job was concerned with, they felt that the individuals should have a choice. This turned out not to be feasible, as some jobs might seem so attractive to a large number of people that the person holding it would be swamped with pairing requests, while others not seen to be so interesting might be the very ones in which the staff members would have the greatest need to communicate the demands of the job. A random pairing plan was adopted, with the option that the staff might wish to set up a future program in which the pairing considered choice.

The rationale for this program was founded in current theories of management. A brief summary of the development of modern management theories is given below.

"Classical" management theorists thought that workers' satisfaction with their jobs came with the monetary rewards obtained. The organization was seen as a formal hierarchical one with downward communication only. Workers' productivity or effectiveness could only be increased by improving the physical working conditions. The Hawthorne Studies completed in 1932 indicated that these factors were negligible.[1]

Further studies to discover what factors did affect productivity if physiological and monetary ones were constant revealed the following:

1. The level of production is set by social norms, not by physiological capacities.
2. Non-economic rewards and sanctions significantly affect the behavior of the workers and largely limit the effect of economic incentive plans.
3. Often workers do not act or react as individuals, but as members of groups.
4. The importance of leadership for setting and enforcing group norms and the difference between informal and formal leadership
5. Communication between the ranks.[2]

These factors stressed the importance of an informal organization, not necessarily related to the formal hierarchical structure.[3] This theory was the basis for the "Human Relations" school of management.

Suspecting that this management philosophy was too simplistic, a third school emerged. The "Structuralists" leaned toward the Human Relations school, but sought a synthesis of both it and the Classical School. Its theory was based on the alienation that exists between the worker and his work, which is documented in studies cited by Herzberg[4] in 1975, and more recently in *Working*[5] published in 1974.

This alienation contributes to job dissatisfaction because the worker feels that no one cares how he does his job, which he sees as unimportant, not only to others but also in his own eyes. Changes in attitude can only come through communication upward, downward, and horizontally in the organization with equal ease. The blueprint for this type of communication, which evolved at "participative management," was largely laid out by Rensis Likert[6] in 1961, and reported by Marrow in 1967.

University libraries have been administered in the past by the authoritarian method embodied in the Classical management theories. The trend, however, is swinging increasingly toward the Structuralists. The real ground-breaker was the UCLA library which developed its program out of the "free speech" movement of 1965–67. This plan was the model for the Advisory Council and Committee of the library mentioned here.

In 1970 the first Micro-workshop on Staff Development was held at an American Library Association conference. The papers presented were edited by Elizabeth W. Stone[8] who, in her introduction, stated that they had special emphasis on approaching staff development through

1. Participation in decision making.
2. Management by objectives.
3. Motivation of library personnel.
4. On the job training.

Also in 1970 a study was made comparing managerial styles with staff satisfaction and performance in university libraries. In this study Maurice Marchant[9] found a positive relationship between staff satisfaction and good library service. Marchant used Likert's "System 1–4" to determine the managerial style, which was one of the factors that directly influenced staff satisfaction. As Likert's applications in business and industry noted improved performance as the organizations moved toward System 4 (communication in all directions), Marchant noted the same trend in university libraries.

The Staff Relations and Development Committee in this instance was not trying to recommend a permanent managerial style, but simply to show that staff involvement, a prominent concept in modern management theories, was beneficial. They believed that as a staff member's knowledge about the functions of the library increases, his efficiency in performing his job increases. With improved efficiency, the clientele of a library is better served.

Marchant's research into "university library performance . . . serves to confirm the optimistic theory that what is good for librarians is good for patrons.[10] While top management tends to think of staff involvement basically as a morale booster, in fact such involvement is a distinct asset to management by providing feedback from the faculty through the staff. As a result of staff involvement, the faculty is better satisfied with the library. In the libraries studied, this action appears to flow primarily through improved staff satisfaction."

DeProspo stated that "any individual within the organization has the inherent right to achieve his own level of self-actualization. . . . The end objective or goal, though, remains one of increasing the institution's capacity to serve. That is, only by allowing the individual to 'grow' or behave as an 'adult' do we increase the potential of the institution to achieve effectively its role in society. The development of people is the key issue in the health and success of any enterprise."[11]

The Committee members believed that personal involvement contributes to better communication between members of the library staff. Communication is important for motivation and for the elimination of the feeling of alienation. When staff members realize the importance of their position in the library structure as a whole and relate their functions to other parts of the library, there will be improved esprit de corps. To implement the ideas expressed above, they recommended a random pairing on all levels of the staff for the purpose of learning about another person's functions in the library.

The above rationale and procedures for implementation were sent to the Library Director and the department heads for their approval. The program was presented to the staff at a regularly scheduled meeting. The Committee chair explained the program and an endorsement was added by the Director. Ballots were distributed so that members of the staff could indicate whether or not they were willing to participate. The Committee contacted those who were not able to attend the meeting. 79 of the 104 staff members agreed to participate. This number was 76%. The returned ballots were separated by departments, and paired at random. Participants were given the name of their "buddy." It was the responsibility of the partners to decide upon a mutually agreeable time for the exchanges. This was to be cleared with the partners' supervisors, or their department heads. The exchanges took place in the summer. Due to problems such as vacations, departures and closings for air-conditioning failures, they covered nearly a three-month period.

Following the exchanges, the participants met as a group in their departments to discuss their feelings about the program. Questionnaires for the purpose of evaluation were distributed at that time. Twenty-nine questionnaires were returned—about 37% of the total number of participants. Of these, 27 respondents believed that they benefited from the staff exchange. Nine of these benefited both when learning about another position, and while telling about their own. Three said only while learning, three said only while telling. Sixteen said they benefited socially, were helped in their job, or all three. Additional comments included benefits from learning their partner's responsibilities, and other library jobs. A lack of benefit was indicated by one respondent who was already familiar with the parnter's job, and would have preferred to have been exchanged with another.

Twenty-four people thought it would be worthwhile to have another staff exchange. One disagreed.

When asked about improvements, nine suggested that a choice of person or department would be best. Others felt that there should be more exchange between related departments, or regularly scheduled general exchanges. One person thought that the discussion after the exchange should be more general—more people together—while one thought that no discussion was needed.

Two of the department heads found that the program created such interest between their members that they repeated the pairing, one of them with two different departments.

In conclusion, it would seem that the first objective: "To create a better understanding of the totality of the library operations and service," was amply met.

As far as the second objective was concerned, it may not be realized immediately, but the climate for the generation of "ideas which will improve services to the University" has been enhanced. The degree of this will be difficult to assess, but Richard Emery in *Staff Communications in Libraries* states:

> ... employees tend to develop the will to do when they understand the work environment and its relation to their own individual interests. ... Adequate information (and its perception) is necessary for the efficient performance of duties.[12]

and;

> ... frequent and extensive interaction, flexible interdepartmental contacts and organisational procedures tend to result in favourable attitudes in the working relationship. A work situation which requires extensive horizontal contacts and an organisational structure that facilitates this, will tend indirectly to create positive attitudes of helpful cooperation. This can be of immediate benefit to individual departments cooperating with each other. . . .[13]

Staff members reported that they enjoyed comments from their partners such as, "I didn't know you did all this!" and "I'll be more careful about how I send you things." In view of this, the Staff Relations and Development Committee was confident that evidence of attaining the second objective would be forthcoming; and recommended that succeeding Committees repeat the program.

Special thanks are due to Ms. Reletha Martin who chaired the Staff Relations and Development Committee; Ms. Clair Josel, President of the Advisory Council; and Mr. Ian Edward, Head of Acquisition, who supplied much helpful information.

REFERENCES

1. F. J. Roethlisberger and W. J. Dickson, *Management and the Worker* (Cambridge: Harvard University Press, 1939).
2. Amitai Etzioni, *Modern Organizations* (Englewood Cliffs: Prentice-Hall, 1964).
3. John M. Pfiffner and Frank P. Sherwood, *Administrative Organizations* (Englewood Cliffs: Prentice-Hall, 1960).
4. F. Herzberg et al., *Job Attitudes* (Pittsburgh Psychological Service: 1957).
5. "Studs" Terkel, *Working* (New York, Avon Books, 1974).
6. Rensis Likert, *New Patterns of Management* (New York: McGraw-Hill, 1961).
7. Alfred Marrow, D. B. Bowers, and S. Seashore, *Management by Participation* (New York: Harper and Row, 1967).
8. Micro-workshop on Staff Development. 1st. Detroit, 1970. *New Directions in Staff Development* (Chicago: American Library Association, 1971).
9. Maurice, P. Marchant, "The effects of the decision making process and related organizational factors on alternative measures of performance in university libraries." (Unpublished Ph.D. dissertation, University of Michigan, 1970).
10. Maurice P. Marchant, "Participative Management in Libraries," in *New Directions in Staff Development, op. cit.*
11. Ernest R. DeProspo, "Management by Objectives: An Approach to Staff Development," in *New Directions in Staff Development, op. cit.*
12. Richard Emery, *Staff Communications in Libraries* (London, Bingley, 1975), p. 17.
13. *Ibid.*, p. 49.

Joanne R. Euster

Loyola University in New Orleans

A WOMAN'S PROFESSION IN ACADEMIA: PROBLEM AND PROPOSAL

Definition as a "women's profession" has created the problems of low status and pay which librarianship generally has experienced. In the academic setting the norms for advancement in rank and salary conflict with the traditional service values of librarianship and further devalue the profession. The status of academic librarians is examined in light of sex-role stereotyping, and three potential solutions are suggested: academic librarianship as a library school area of concentration, a professional expectation of advanced education, and a mentor system to systematically encourage the development of entering librarians.

That librarianship is viewed as a women's profession hardly bears repeating, nor do the overt and covert discriminations against women which have historically militated against female advancement in the field. What I believe is less clearly understood is the effect of this sex stereotyping on the profession as a whole, and upon academic librarianship in particular.

Why single out academic librarians for special emphasis? The outstanding reason is that librarians in colleges and universities, struggling valiantly to attain and hold onto faculty status, are at the same time buying into a status and reward system which is established by men for the most part, and which frequently offers scant rewards to a discipline, or to individuals, who do not subscribe to the criteria for advancement of that system, namely research and publication.

A few background facts and figures: In the 1974 *Advances in Librarianship*[1] Anita Schiller documents the historical majority position of women in the profession, including the fact that when Melvil Dewey opened his—and our—first library school at Columbia University in 1887, with an entering class of twenty, seventeen of the students were women. That Dewey was subsequently fired and the school closed as a result of his feminist admissions policy is another matter.

In 1900 75 per cent of all librarians were women; in 1975, 84 per cent were women.[2] Women however are less well represented in academic libraries, where they hold 61.5 per cent of all professional positions.[3] Blankenship reported in 1967 that 51.45 per cent of college head librarians were women; however, he surveyed only four-year colleges with enrollments of fewer than 5,000 students.[4] Furthermore, even his limited data showed women as more likely to be in head librarian positions in the smallest colleges and in private colleges. In larger public colleges, one-third of the heads were women. Schiller, on the other hand, reported in 1974 that in large academic libraries, defined as those serving institutions with 3,000 or greater enrollments, the chief administrator was female only eight per cent of the time, although among large public libraries 39 per cent of the top administrators were women.[5]

Clearly, even in a profession where overall the rank and file tend to be women, and the administrators disproportionately men, it is academic librarians who work in the most sex stereotyped setting of all.

Librarians have worked long and hard to define themselves as members of a unified profession, with those attributes which define a profession: a distinctive and defined body of knowledge with a broad intellectual base; self-initiated research and study programs carried on by its members to extend the specialized body of knowledge; standards for admission and practice of the profession, established and enforced by the members of the profession acting as a body through a professional organization; and a humanistic emphasis on service to individuals and to society.[6]

This professional unity is expressed succinctly in the standard qualification for entry into the profession; the M.L.S. Library schools have taught public and academic librarianship, not as separate branches, but as a single discipline.

This is not to suggest that the profession be splintered into small type-of-library subgroups; nevertheless, a case can be made for academic librarianship as, if not a specialty, at least an area of concentration. There are obvious differences in publics served, in collection emphasis, and in administrative structure from school and public libraries. But more important are the expectations of professional behavior which are implicit in the academic milieu. Some comparisons with the status of women in other disciplines may be relevant as well.

The sex role stereotyping which librarians experience is compounded in the academic setting. Juanita Kreps, in her study, *Sex in the Marketplace: American Women at Work*,[7] points out that women Ph.D.'s in economics, history and sociology held lower ranks and earned less pay than men in the same fields. These fields, like others in the social sciences and humanities, and like librarianship, attract a disproportionate number of women faculty, as opposed to the sciences.

Whether there is in fact sex discrimination in rank and salary is a point of disagreement. It is agreed that women's salaries in these fields are lower than those of men, and lower than women's salaries in less usual fields such as the natural sciences. Some writers argue, however, that women are less "productive" than men, as productivity is defined by academic rank and tenure committees. Women, it is argued, tend to emphasize teaching and service at the expense of research, committee and organizational work, and publication, so that when those criteria are applied, women are less likely to have met the norms for advancement. Certainly librarians fall into the group which emphasizes service and direct patron interaction, which can be equated with teaching, over administration and research. It is doubtful that the profession would want it any other way.

It is further argued that married women, in particular, have a high incidence of interrupted careers due to family responsibilities, and consequently simply do not have as many years' dedication to their profession as do men or single women of the same age.

Kreps suggests an economic model which implies that women are, as a result of career interruption and low academic productivity, always lower on the supply-demand curve, and consequently doomed to lower rank and salaries. Gail Sheehy, in *Passages*,[8] would lead us to believe that the most significant life task of the twenties decade is to form couple bonds and to define the self in terms of family and stability. Hennig and Jardim likewise point out in *The Managerial Women*[9] that few women actually plan careers;

more often, they simply fall into them. While their discussion is pointed toward women in management in business and industry, their analysis of the lack of willingness or ability on the part of women to play the organizational game according to the established rules can be applied with some illumination to academic librarianship.

The implications for women are clear; what is also important is that in a so-called women's profession, the implications extend to men as well, and ultimately affect the entire profession. It is true that men have fared somewhat better than women in librarianship. Men hold most of the administrative positions, with concomitant higher salaries, and even within the same ranks, the 1975–76 ACRL salary survey showed women earning 3.2 per cent less than men at the entry level, but 23.3 per cent less at the director level.[10] However, librarians' salaries as a whole are lower than for other faculty at the same institutions; this fact makes "faculty status" have a somewhat hollow ring, however hard the profession works for it.

Now, it is of course possible to insist that librarians have their own set of values, which emphasize service and teaching, and that these are at least as valid as the research and publication norms which are applied to most college and university faculty. This argument is also made on behalf of teaching faculty in many liberal arts colleges which emphasize undergraduate teaching, and is certainly a valid response. Regardless, given that academic librarians find themselves within a functioning system which evaluates and rewards, and which assigns status, on the latter basis, the "library faculty," as they are referred to at my university, are at a distinct disadvantage. Furthermore, this is a chicken-and-the-egg problem; librarians do not do research and do not publish because by and large they have neither inclination nor training; they are paid and ranked accordingly; and the profession attracts those who have little interest in the rigors of research and writing.

What does all this have to do with effectiveness? My experience and observation says that the effectiveness of academic libraries is nearly as much a matter of image as it is of collections and buildings. This leads me to hypothesize that the inferior status of the professionals who organize and run the libraries has a direct effect on the uses to which the libraries are put. If the teaching faculty and students think of the librarians as essentially poorly paid clerks and warehousers, albeit with certain academic pretensions, they are unlikely to ask or allow that librarians advise on selection, course design, and student needs.

What, if anything, then do librarians need to do? There are forces working to alleviate some of the sex-typing problems. Affirmative Action has been held out as having great potential for eliminating, or at least reducing, outright discrimination. However, if Kreps and others are to be believed, in many instances the academic system has not been applied in a discriminatory manner throughout; rather, a large part of the problem lies in the incongruity between the reward and status system as it presently operates and the goals and values of a service-oriented profession. Certainly the impact of Affirmative Action cannot be discounted, particularly in opening up the supervisory and administrative levels to women.

Another positive force is the renewed emphasis on skill in teaching, particularly of undergraduates, as a criterion for advancement, as opposed to research and publication. This emphasis on teaching can also be applied to the service orientation of librarianship. On the other hand, good teaching is extremely difficult to measure, and the path to evaluation of teaching is fraught with anguished howls and grievance filings; it is likely that the more easily measured criteria for advancement will continue to predominate, particularly at the university level.

Yet a third force comes from a growing change in lifestyles. As men and women begin not only to talk about, but to act on, shared responsibilities for child rearing, careers, and the like, women's career emphasis is likely to change. This is a social force of which the effects will be felt but slowly, however.

There are positive steps which can be taken by the profession to upgrade the role of academic librarians. The advantages to the entire profession—school, public and special librarians, as well as academic librarians—of such upgrading must again be emphasized.

First of all, academic librarianship should be viewed and taught as an area requiring a degree of specialization. At minimum, a librarian in training should be encouraged to consider the type of library in which she/he might work, and take at least one course specifically designed to teach an understanding of the peculiarities of that type of library. More than a nod should be given to administration of academic libraries; a much closer look at the unique characteristics of academic library clientele, collections, and organization should be available to the entering librarian. One of the severest lacks of librarianship in the academic setting is the failure to participate in the so-called "academic game." Whether all librarians, or indeed many, choose to play that game, they should at least have an understanding of how it is played and what the rules, rewards and penalties are. Librarians who choose to do continuing research and publication should have knowledge and practice in research and writing for publication. I think it an all too obvious fallacy to assume that anyone holding a Bachelor's degree and an ALA-accredited MLS has been trained to do either.

Secondly, advanced education for academic, and no doubt for other, librarians should be more readily available, and more actively encouraged. If the MLS is considered an entry-level degree, what comes next? For all too many, nothing. Management of libraries is taught as part of the MLS curriculum; the next training ground for tomorrow's library administrators is the school of hard knocks, and following the example of others who came up the same way. What is suggested here is not the availability of continuing education but a professional point of view that expects substantial continuation of one's formal education, particularly after a period of working experience. Detailed study of management principles might be available at such a post-MLS level; so, too might guided research projects, or specialization in information technology.

The third proposal has less to do with library education and professional standards. It is a matter of individual responsibility. Established members of the profession need to provide a sort of professional sponsorship for new librarians, guiding and educating by both precept and example. Of course, this has always gone on; however, the expectation that senior members of the profession will take continuing responsibility for the growth and development of junior members is the point here. Hennig and Jardim, again, emphasized the crucial importance of sponsorship to the development of organizational executives, and the relative inability of women to avail themselves or to provide such sponsorship. Perhaps part of librarians' failure to see themselves in the mentor role has to do with perceiving the MLS as the terminal degree for practicing librarians, rather than the entry level degree. Whatever the causes, it is surely one of the hallmarks of a profession that it takes both collective and individual responsibility for the passage of the professional torch.

To recapitulate: Academic librarians appear to suffer more from the sex-role stereotyping of the profession than librarians in other types of libraries. The profession as a whole is affected adversely by the low status problems of academic librarians. While there are professional and social forces which are tending to place academic librarians on the same level as other faculty, there are deeply entrenched practices and norms which tend to suppress librarian status. Three areas have been suggested in which the profession, collectively and individually, can act to, if not solve, at least ameliorate these problems. First, library schools can help by providing specialized courses for academic librarians to help them better to understand and cope with the pressures of the academic game.

Second, both the professional organizations and the library schools can help by making advanced education more available, and by fostering the expectation that librarians, as conscientious and commited professionals, will avail themselves of it. Third, individuals can help by actively engaging in a mentor system to foster the professional development of new librarians. This activity can be encouraged by policy statements, workshops, special programs and the like, but the ultimate success depends upon the experienced librarians who are willing to devote time, risk exposure of their knowledge to the eyes of younger colleagues, and see that the metaphorical torch is passed, still lighted, to the next generation.

REFERENCES

1. Anita R. Schiller, "Women in Librarianship," in Melvin J. Voigt, ed., *Advances in Librarianship*, vol. 4 (New York: Academic Press, 1974). p. 104-147.
2. "Women in Librarianship, Status of," in *The ALA Yearbook, a Review of Library Events 1975* (Chicago: American Library Association, 1976), p. 349-350.
3. *Salary Structures of Librarians in Higher Education for the Academic Year 1975-76* (Chicago: Association of College and Research Libraries, 1976), p. 9.
4. W. C. Blankenship, "Head Librarians: How Many Men? How Many Women?" in Athena Theodore, ed., *The Professional Woman* (Cambridge, Mass.: Schenkman, 1971), p. 93-102.
5. Schiller, *op. cit.*, p. 114.
6. Dale Eugene Shaffer, *The Maturity of Librarianship as a Profession* (Metuchen, N.J.: Scarecrow Press, 1968), p. 18-20.
7. Juanita Kreps, *Sex in the Marketplace: American Women at Work* (Baltimore: Johns Hopkins Press, 1971).
8. Gail Sheehy, *Passages: Predictable Crises of Adult Life* (New York: Dutton, 1976).
9. Margaret Hennig and Anne Jardim, *The Managerial Woman* (Garden City, N.Y.: Anchor Press/Doubleday, 1977).
10. *Salary Structures of Librarians in Higher Education for the Academic Year 1975-76*, p. 6.

Soon D. Kim and Mary T. Kim

Ohio State University

ACADEMIC LIBRARY RESEARCH:
A TWENTY YEAR PERSPECTIVE

Articles published in College & Research Libraries *from 1957 to 1976 are analyzed for trends in authorship and research methodology. A comparison of the first decade, 1957–66, to the second, 1967–76, reveals an increase in number of quantitative studies published. Quantitative studies continue to be descriptive in nature, although some experimental/quasi-experimental studies appear in more recent C&RL issues. While library administrators are the dominant authors of the earlier issues, rank and file librarians contribute as frequently to later issues. Reasons for these changes are suggested.*

On June 26, 1971, the Association of College and Research Libraries (ACRL) and the American Library Association (ALA) jointly adopted standards defining faculty status for college and university librarians.[1] A portion of these standards outlined the rights of academic librarians to be granted tenure and to be promoted on the basis of their academic proficiency and professional effectiveness. Having adopted faculty privileges of tenure and promotion, many academic librarians are now expected to meet the same criteria for tenure and promotion as do regular teaching faculty, that is teaching, research and publication, and service.[2]

Surveys of academic libraries confirm the application of these evaluation criteria. In a 1968 survey of directors of seventy-one ARL[3] member libraries plus twenty-nine state university libraries, Hintz determined that 96 percent of those libraries granting faculty status emphasized the research, publication and teaching performance of their library staff.[4] In a 1975 survey of libraries in the SUNY system, Gavrych noted librarians were required to do research, publish, and generally function as scholars.[5] Finally Ryans, in a 1977 survey of seventy-five directors of medium-sized, academic libraries, found that over half utilized the same promotion criteria and procedures as regular faculty departments.[6] Logically this increased emphasis on scholarly pursuits, specifically research and publication, should alter the activities of academic librarians, the nature of their professional meetings and the content and methodology of their scholarly journals. It is this last point which this study examines, the research methodology of journal articles related to college and university librarianship.

The major purpose of this exploratory study was to detect changing patterns in the methodology and authorship of academic library research articles by examining the last two decades of articles published in *College and Research Libraries*, the principal journal of academic librarianship. Specifically the following research questions were posed:

1. Is there a trend towards the publication of more quantitative journal articles on college and university librarianship?

2. Is there a trend towards an increased number of journal articles being written by rank and file librarians?

3. Is there any change in the publication tendencies of academic library administrators, library science faculty members or regular teaching faculty members?

4. Is there a tendency towards the use of more sophisticated data analysis procedures by academic library researchers?

5. Is there any change in the basic methodological approaches used in quantitative studies of academic libraries?

METHOD

A content analysis was performed on articles published in *College and Research Libraries* (CRL) between 1957 and 1976. CRL was selected for two reasons. First, it is the recognized journal of academic librarianship. Second, it is the journal most suitable for tracing trends, it having been published longer than any other journal devoted to college and university librarianship.

Editorials, book reviews and regular features were excluded from the analysis. The following author information was determined for each major CRL article:

1. Occupation of author:
   a. Academic librarian,
   b. Non-academic librarian,
   c. Library school faculty,
   d. Regular teaching faculty,
   e. Library school student, and
   f. Other
2. Type position, if employed as a librarian
3. Subject area, if a regular teaching faculty member.

Articles of multiple authorships were classified according to the occupation, position, etc. of the first author listed. The biographical information provided in each article was the source of data for author classification (e.g., position, occupation, etc.). The completeness and clarity of this biographical data varied from article to article. Consequently, the equivalence of occupational and positional titles could not be determined exactly in all cases.

The following methodological information was also analyzed:

1. Type of publication
   a. Quantitative, or
   b. Non-quantitative
2. Method of data collection
   a. Available data,
   b. Surveys and questionnaires,
   c. Experiments,
   d. Quasi-experiments, and
   e. Other

3. Specification of hypotheses
4. Specification of research objectives
5. Sampling strategy employed
   a. Simple random
   b. Stratified
   c. Systematic
   d. Cluster
   e. Other or not specified
6. Instrumentation
   a. Interview,
   b. Questionnaire,
   c. Observation,
   d. Test, and
   e. Other or not specified
7. Method of data anlaysis:
   a. Frequency,
   b. Percentages,
   c. Mean and standard deviation,
   d. Chi-square,
   e. Correlation,
   f. Analysis of variance,
   g. T-test,
   h. Multiple regression,
   i. Factor analysis, and
   j. Multi-variate analysis.

Quantitative articles were defined as any articles involving counting or numberical procedures. All other articles whether theoretical or descriptions of current library practices were categorized as non-quantitative. Quantiative articles were further analyzed according to type of data collection, method of data analysis, etc.

To detect possible trends, the articles were divided into two ten year periods, 1957 to 1966 and 1967 to 1976. Frequencies and percentages were computed for each coding category for the total twenty year period and for each ten year period. Only the latter will be reported in this study.

RESULTS

Quantitative Methods

Four-hundred and thirty-two articles were published in *College and Research Libraries* between 1957 and 1966 (first decade), while 402 articles were published between 1967 and 1976 (second decade). Analysis showed that only 15 percent of the articles of the first decade were quantitative in nature, while 43 percent of the second decade articles were classified as quantitative studies. Survey research was the principal research methodology employed, 73 percent of the first decade articles and 62 percent of the second decade reporting survey studies. Questionnaires continued to be the primary data collection method, 38 percent in the first decade and 43 percent in the second decade. The second ten years show an increase in the use of interviews, however, 8 percent of the published studies utilized interviews as opposed to 1.5 percent of the earlier research studies. The second decade of articles also included more experimental and quasi-experimental studies, 9 percent of the later quantitative articles reported experimental/quasi-experimental studies as opposed to only 2 percent of the earlier articles.

Research studies published in the second decade also appeared to be more systematically designed. For instance, specification of research hypotheses and/or objectives was more frequent or perhaps more clearly stated during the second decade. Twenty percent of these later articles stated hypotheses to be tested or objectives to be investigated as opposed to 12 percent in the earlier period. Sampling designs also improved, or at least the details of the sampling strategy were more clearly expressed. Twenty-seven percent of the later studies specified the sampling strategy as simple random, stratified, systematic or cluster samples, while only 18 percent of the earlier studies described their sampling strategies as simple random, systematic, or cluster samples.

An increased sophistication in data analysis was also noted. Table 1 presents a comparison of the two decades. The first decade limited its analysis to descriptive statistics, reporting frequencies (47 percent) and percentages (47 percent) and occasionally means and standard deviations (6 percent). A small number of studies reported correlational data (3 percent), however, no inferential statistics or more sophisticated measures of relationship were employed.

TABLE 1

Percentage of Quantitative CRL Articles Classified by Method of Data Analysis: A Comparison of Two Decades*

	1957–1966 (n = 66 articles)	1967–1976 (n = 173 articles)
Frequency	47%	22%
Percentages	47%	68%
Mean & Standard Division	6%	16%
Chi-square		6%
Correlation	3%	8%
T-test	—	4%
Analysis of Variance	—	3%
Multiple Regression	—	2%
Factor Analysis	—	1%
Multi-variate Analysis	—	—

*Data analysis categories are not mutually exclusive, therefore total percentages will exceed 100 percent.

The second decade still relied on frequencies (22 percent) and percentages (68 percent) as the major data analysis; however, there was an increase in the reporting of means and standard deviations (16 percent) as well as correlational data (8 percent). The marked difference between the two periods was the reporting of inferential statistics. Chi-square tests of association were conducted in 6 percent of the studies while t-tests and analysis of variance tests were used to detect significant differences in 4 percent and 3 percent of the studies respectively. Multiple regression (2 percent) and factor analysis results (1 percent) were presented in these later articles as well. Neither period published articles employing more complex, multi-variate data analysis procedures.

Authorship

As described earlier, the authorship of CRL articles was analyzed by occupation, position, institutional affiliation, etc. Table 2 presents the results of the occupational classification. As can be seen, the proportion of CRL articles—quantitative and non-quantiative—written by academic librarians has remained fairly consistent (60.9 percent vs. 57 percent). School of library science professors have become more active in publishing, a jump from 7.2 percent to 15.4 percent being observed. Non-library faculty members also appear to have increased their study of library problems, progressing from a 5.1 percent to 9.2 percent publication rate. A comparison of departmental affiliation of non-library faculty authors suggested a change in the content of these articles. The earlier articles were written primarily by humanities professors while business and public administration professors were the principal faculty authors of the second decade.

TABLE 2

Percentage of CRL Articles Classified by Author Occupation: A Comparison of Two Decades

Occupation	1957–1966 (n = 432 articles)	1967–1976 (n = 402 articles)
Academic Librarians	60.9	57
Non-Academic Librarians	6.9	3.2
School of Library Science Faculty	7.2	15.4
Other Academic Faculty	5.1	9.2
Library Science Graduate Students	1.2	2.0
Other	18.7*	13.2*
TOTAL	100%	100%

*Other category includes authors for which classification information was unavailable, in addition to authors who did not fall into any of the categories.

Further analysis of the academic librarian publications suggests the aforementioned consistency is deceptive. Table 3 presents the academic librarian articles broken down by

TABLE 3

Percentage of CRL Articles Classified by Library Position: A Comparison of Two Decades

	1957–1966 (n = 277 articles)	1967–1976 (n = 232 articles)
Administration	65.7	47.2
Librarians	33	46.6
R & D Unit	.4	3.9
Other	.9	2.3
TOTAL	100%	100%

library position. Administration—defined as directors, assistant directors, and leaders of major library services—dominated the CRL issues of the first decade publishing 65.7 percent of the total articles. Rank and file librarians—defined as librarians, bibliographers, supervisors of reference, cataloging, or acquisition divisions—published only 33 percent of the earlier articles. Research and development personnel were virtually non-existent (.4 percent). The second decade showed a noticeable decrease in administration activity, top administration accounting for only 47.2 percent of the total articles. Rank and file librarians had increased their publication rate to 46.6 percent. Research and development personnel were also more active, writing 3.9 percent of the later articles.

Methodology Classified by Authorship

To determine if the shift towards more quantitative studies was a function of increased involvement by library school professors and/or non-library professors, methodology and author occupation were cross-tabulated for articles of each decade. Table 4 presents this cross-tabulation. As can be seen, the publication rates of each occupation group are relatively consistent with overall rates observed earlier (see Table 2). Academic librarians, and not library science or non-library professors, contribute the largest number of both quantitative and non-quantitative articles in both decades (Decade 1: 63.6 percent and 60.4 percent; Decade 2: 56.6 percent and 57.2 percent). The increased activity of non-library professors does, however, appear to be more quantitative, progressing from 4.5 percent to 11.6 percent of the quantitative studies published.

TABLE 4

Percentage of CRL Articles Classified by Author Occupation and Article Type: A Comparison of Two Decades

| | 1957–1966 | | 1967–1976 | |
	Quantitative (n = 66 arts.)	Non-Quantitative (n = 366 arts.)	Quantitative (n = 173 arts.)	Non-Quantitative (n = 229 arts.)
Academic Librarian	63.6	60.4	56.6	57.2
Non-Academic Librarian	6.1	7.1	2.3	3.9
School of Library Science Faculty	9.1	6.8	15.6	15.3
Other Academic Faculty	4.5	5.2	11.6	7.4
Library Science Graduate Students	1.5	1.1	1.2	2.6
Other	15.2	19.4	12.7	13.6
TOTAL	100%	100%	100%	100%

Table 5 presents further analysis of methodology by occupation. It is interesting to note that academic librarians prefer the survey as the method of data collection in both decades (73.9 percent and 60 percent respectively) while the professors, both library and non-library, rely on available data as opposed to survey questionnaires. For example, in the earlier articles library science faculty published 12.5 percent of the articles using available data and only 6.5 percent of the survey studies. Likewise for later articles, library faculty published 21.4 percent of the articles utilizing available data and only 13.3 percent of the survey studies.

TABLE 5

CRL Articles Classified by Author Occupation and Research Method*

	1957–1966			1967–1976		
	Avail. *(n = 16)*	*Survey* *(n = 46)*	*Expt. Quasi.* *(n = 1)*	*Avail.* *(n = 42)*	*Survey* *(n = 105)*	*Expt. Quasi.* *(n = 15)*
Academic Librarian	43.8	73.9	–	54.8	60	53.4
Non-Academic Librarian	6.2	4.3	100	2.4	2.9	–
School of Library Science Faculty	12.5	6.5	–	21.4	13.3	20
Other Academic Faculty Member	6.2	2.2	–	11.9	7.6	13.3
Library Science Graduate Student	–	2.2	–	–	1.9	–
Other	31.3	10.9	–	9.5	14.3	13.3
TOTAL	100%	100%	100%	100%	100%	100%

*Fourteen quantitative articles dealing primarily with mathematical models were not included in this table. Therefore, decade totals do not correspond with the totals reported in Table 4.

The most interesting finding presented in Table 5 is the high percentage of experimental and quasi-experimental articles published by academic librarians (53.4 percent). Library and non-library faculty members accounted respectively for only 20 percent and 13.3 percent of the experimental studies. The cross-tabulations indicate that the increase in more complex, quantitative studies is not solely related to an increased interest in library problems by library and non-library professors, but appears to be related to increased research sophistication of academic librarians. This point will be discussed further in the following section.

This content analysis of the past twenty years of *College and Research Libraries* has revealed certain trends. Publications on college and research librarianship have become more quantitative. While some experimental/quasi-experimental studies have been reported, descriptive research, specifically survey research, continues to be most prevalent. Frequencies and percentages are still the basic methods of data analysis, but higher level analysis has appeared in a scattering of articles.

These trends may be interpreted in several ways. A change in editorial policies may have increased the percentage of quantitative studies, CRL promoting more systematic investigations of library science policies. A recent survey by Grotzinger of ALA accredited library program curricula suggests another explanation.[7]

Grotzinger reported that 93.5 percent of the ALA accredited programs offered an introductory research course suitable for master level students. 39.7 percent of those schools with such courses required all master level students to complete these courses prior to graduation. Another 57 percent indicated master level students could elect these courses. Knowledge of basic research methods is therefore not restricted to only top administrators and faculty members with doctoral degrees. Rank and file librarians, especially those who have completed their degrees more recently, also are equipped with basic skills. Wynar cautions, however, that these introductory courses only scratch the surface, providing little discussion of the more complex research and statistical techniques required for studying the more complex problems faced by academic libraries today.[8] Perhaps this explains the continued reliance on descriptive techniques in collecting and analyzing data, as demonstrated in this study.

Not only did the methodology of these articles change, but changes in patterns of authorship were also observed. Specifically, publications by rank and file librarians almost equal in number those written by top library administrators. Although no cause and effect relationship can be determined in this study, it would seem likely that the newly acquired responsibilities of faculty status contribute to the observed activity by rank and file librarians. The criteria for promotion and tenure emphasize research as well as publication. Research funds are becoming more available to academic librarians.[9] Some institutions are granting libraries released time in which to do their research.[10] All of these factors collectively would impact on both the academic librarian's publication rate and the nature of that publication.

Schick, in a similar content analysis of the now defunct *Library Research in Progress*, noted that two-thirds of the library research funded between 1959 and 1964 was conducted by employees of academic institutions. Degree candidates performed 42 percent; library science professors, 10 percent; non-library faculty members, 8 percent; and college and university librarians, 7 percent.[11] While direct comparisons of these figures with this study's findings cannot and should not be made, it is permissible to conclude that academic librarians have always been involved in research activities and will continue to be in the vanguard.

Perhaps academic librarians are finally paying heed to warnings of earlier scholars, such as Williamson[12] and Goldhor,[13] that library science will never become a separate discipline unless it develops its own body of theory and knowledge. Theory building requires research; research which seeks more to predict and explain than merely to describe the complex issues of librarianship and library science. Academic librarians have performed well to date, conducting the descriptive studies which lay the groundwork for future research. Their role for the future is clear—to expand their efforts in experimental and causal research. Non-library professors, also awaiting tenure and promotion decisions, are just discovering that library science is a fertile field for research. It would behoove academic librarians to sustain and upgrade their research activities if they are not to be eased out by their new colleagues—the regular teaching faculty of American colleges and universities.

REFERENCES

1. American Library Association. Association of College and Research Libraries. Academic Status Committee. "Standards for Faculty Status for College and University Libraries," *College and Research Libraries News* (May 1974): 112–133.
2. "Model Statement of Criteria and Procedures for Appointment, Promotion in Academic Rank, and Tenure for College and University Librarians," *College and Research Libraries* (September 1973): 192–195: and October 1973): 243–247.
3. Association of Research Libraries.
4. Carl Hintz, "Criteria for Appointment to and Promotion in Academic Rank." *College and Research Libraries* 29 (September 1968): 341–346.
5. Jacquelyn Gavrych, "The SUNY Librarians Faculty Status Game," *Journal of Academic Librarianship* 1 (July 1975): 11–13.
6. Cynthia C. Ryans, "The Academic Status of the Professional Librarian," *Ohio Library Association Bulletin* 47 (January 1977): 6–8.
7. Laurel Grontzinger, "Characteristics of Research Courses in Masters' Level Curricula," *Journal of Education for Librarianship* 17 (Fall 1976): 85–97.
8. Lubomyr R. Wynar, "Place of Statistics in Library Science Curriculum," *Journal of Education for Librarianship* 11 (Fall 1970): 155–162.
9. Arthur M. McAnally, "Status of the University Librarian in the Academic Community," in Gerrald Orme, ed., *Research Librarianship* (New York: R. R. Bowker, 1971).
10. Susan L. Miller, and others. "To Be or Not to Be: An Academic Library Research Committee," *The Journal of Academic Librarianship* 2 (March 1976): 20–24.
11. Frank L. Schick, "Preface: Library-Related Research," in Harold Borko, ed., *Targets for Research in Library Education* (Chicago: American Library Association, 1973).
12. C. C. Williamson, "The Place of Research in Library Science," *Library Quarterly* 1 (January 1931): 10.
13. Herbert Goldhor, *An Introduction to Scientific Research in Librarianship* (Washington, D.C.: U.S. Department of Health, Education, and Welfare, Office of Education, Bureau of Research, 1969).

Christina Wolcott McCawley and Scott Bruntjen

West Chester State College and Shippensburg State College

LIBRARIANS AS RISK TAKERS: DESIGN FOR SELF-MEASUREMENT

This paper provides the individual library decision maker with a method by which he or she may measure his or her acceptance of risk as it relates to decision making. The study discusses some of the literature on risk analysis and utility theory. It describes the importance to the manager of an objective risk-taking assessment as an early and vital step in understanding the constraints inherent in the selection of a specific course of action. Future research possibilities, including a possible comparison of librarians' risk profiles with the profiles of decision makers in private enterprise, are mentioned.

In this paper we will discuss the importance of a risk assessment to library decision makers, and we will also present a method for determining an individual's risk acceptance or aversion in particular situations.

Imagine that you have the opportunity to select one of the two alternatives which follow:

1. You will receive an unrestricted gift to your book budget of $50,000 *or*
2. You may take that $50,000 to Monte Carlo and, in *one* gamble, either double it or lose it.

There are a lot of questions that you might want to ask before you made this decision. What are the odds of winning at Monte Carlo? How much does my library need that $50,000? What will happen to me if I win (or lose)? A guide through the maze that surrounds this decision may be found by studying the concepts of risk analysis and utility theory.

During a time of growth, decision-making often consists of selecting one or more of the best of several alternatives. Resources seem to expand faster than use; mistakes carry little consequence; and excess capacity, more than just being tolerated, is actually encouraged. Who knows, for example, how many "extra books" are kept just so that almost every demand can be satisfied immediately? Such an expanding environment typified American libraries in the 1960s and early 1970s. A library manager could try almost any new idea to any degree of involvement. Consider, for example, how many obsolete dial access systems, or special collections on minute topics were developed, paid for, and later discarded. The only risk involved in such an expanding environment was the one associated with not trying something new; with not spending every dollar available.

In times of financial adversity, however, decision-making is difficult. Basically, it involves making more from less. During times of funding uncertainty and constraint, each individual decision becomes irreversible. Each action uses a non-renewable financial resource. Each decision is a path taken and a number of paths not taken. If a manger had the benefit of a long adjustment period between unlimited resources and times of constrained funds, he or she might become conditioned to this new environment, but a rapid change from one financial condition to the other places the manager in unknown territory. Now each action seems filled with danger. What is required is a personal scale of values for the various possible outcomes of a problem and a means of determining the risk one is willing to take to achieve a desired solution.

Risk and utility are concepts with which we deal, although unconsciously perhaps, in the daily conduct of our personal lives. We purchase life and health insurance to offset large financial risks; we are likely to measure the value (utility) of education in relation to future employment opportunitites. Risk-taking is defined here as an individual's likelihood of taking chances where there is a possibility that failure will result. A person who is risk averse will tend to make conservative decisions even if the probability of failure is perceived as being relatively low; whereas a person who is defined as a risk-taker will tend to make decisions of the "go-ahead" type, even if there is only a remote chance of success.

Librarians of all levels must at one time or another make decisions which involve various degrees of risk. It is useful, especially if these librarians are to make decisions in group situations, to consider the individual's degree of risk acceptance, that is, his or her "risk profile," when predicting what types of decisions he or she is likely to make. A librarian who is risk averse and a librarian who is risk prone will tend to behave differently and thus make different decisions under what seem to be exactly the same circumstances. If these decision makers are to have all relevant information about a problem, especially if they are to work with others, they need to be able to understand their own and others' acceptance of risk.

It seems that for library decision-making, risk has not been well described or understood.[1] The literature on risk-taking is found primarily in the fields of social psychology and economics. In social psychology a number of research studies were completed in the late 1960s on a phenomenon termed the "risky shift." The research was occasioned by a Master's thesis written in 1961 by J. A. F. Stoner at the MIT Sloan School of Management.[2] In this thesis Stoner presented results of research that showed that groups are riskier than individuals. The "risky shift" is the phenomenon that an individual will make more conservative choices as an individual than he will as a member of a group. Social psychologists spent years trying to understand this "shift." Their theories are well summarized in a review article by D. G. Pruitt in the *Journal of Personality and Social Psychology*.[3]

Economists, too, have been interested in risk. Much of the literature in this field has related risk to utility theory, a relationship which the remainder of this paper will attempt to explain. Utility theory, also known as cardinal utility theory, was first proposed by John von Neuman and Oskar Morgenstern in 1947.[4] Ralph O. Swalm, writing in the *Harvard Business Review*, describes utility theory as follows:

> (Utility theory) proposes that each individual attempts to optimize the expected value of something which is defined as utility, and that for each individual a relationship between utility and dollars can be found. . . . According to the theory, each individual has a measurable preference among various choices available in risk situations. This preference is called his utility.

Utility is measured in arbitrary units which we will call 'utiles.' By suitable questioning we can determine for each individual a relationship between utility and dollars which is called his utility function. (Plotted on a graph, this utility function) offers a picture of his attitude toward taking risks.[5]

In briefer form, Rouse notes that "utility is a quantification of the relative strength of a person's preference for an alternative. A utility function . . . of some variable . . . maps that variable from its physical scale to the individual's preference scale.[6]

The simple fact is that exactly the same reward or outcome may have greatly different values for different individuals. For example, given the assignment of ranking from high to low the receipt of 1. an Appaloosa horse, 2. a used portable television set, 3. a set of Edsel hubcaps, and 4. a gain of five dollars, it is quite conceivable that 24 decision makers would bring 24 sets of values to the problem and would come up with 24 different rank orders. Furthermore, if the probability that any of these outcomes might occur were other than even, the order of these lists might change markedly. Consider yourself, for example, an avid hubcap collector without a television set. If the chance to win the Edsel hubcaps were only 1 in 100 while the television were given 3 chances in 10 you might see the TV as the better bet, even though as a collector you would give your eyeteeth for the hubcaps. If the odds changed to 1 in 10 for the hubcaps, you might choose them, even though they were still a long shot; whereas at 9 chances in 10, you would probably consider the hubcaps the best bet, given, of course, that you needed Edsel hubcaps. Before this is dismissed as not at all relevant to libraries, substitute the following "rewards" for those given above: 1. Acquire an additional OCLC terminal. 2. Hire a librarian in a new position. 3. Become a document depository. 4. Be forced to pay for the new staff member out of funds now allocated to the book budget.

Before we can begin to predict how you would select your first, second, third and fourth choices among these options, we need a way to assess the risk profile that you bring to this decision. For example, would you, under all circumstances not make a decision if the outcome included a possible loss of $10,000 from the book budget of your library? Other information needs to be taken into account. If you had only $10,000 in your book budget, you would probably not risk losing it; whereas if you had a book budget of $1,000,000 and a shortage of staff, your decision would probably be to risk losing the $10,000 in order to have a chance to hire a new staff member. The question becomes one of determining at what point between $10,000 and $1,000,000 you would accept risking money from your book budget in order to gain one of the other options.

Ralph Swalm[7] interviewed 100 executives in an attempt to determine their risk averseness or risk-seeking tendencies. In the interviews Swalm used an instrument based on utility theory. This instrument has been simplified for purposes of presentation here, and it is hoped that librarians can use the following procedure to test themselves on their tendency to take or not to take calculated risks.

In using this instrument for risk analysis we first need to adopt some sort of standard notation for picturing these possible decisions. There are any number of methods that could be used to outline the problem. One simple and fairly well-accepted method, called a "decision tree," is as follows: a square represents a decision point, each circle a chance point, and each line an event. If we were to picture a problem composed of an even (50–50) chance of the occurrence of one of two events, it could be represented as shown in Figure 1. If the decision were either this one path or another that represented a 60–40 chance of the occurrence of two other outcomes, it would appear as Figure 2. At the square the decision-maker selects the path to follow, but at the circle the outcome is up to chance based upon the probabilities of occurrence as noted on each of the event lines.

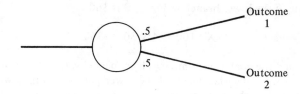

Figure 1.

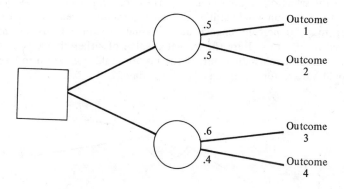

Figure 2.

With this notation we can begin to look at the selection of outcomes. If the goal were to maximize money, the selection would be fairly simple. Consider the problem posed by Figure 3. The "expected value" of the top branch is $50. This simply means that there is a 50 percent chance to win $100 plus a 50 percent chance to win $0. *Over the long run* one would receive as many $100 rewards as $0 rewards. The expectation (or expected value) equals the reward times the probability of winning the reward or:

$$.5 \times \$100 + .5 \times \$0 = \$50$$

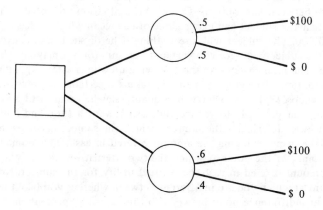

Figure 3.

The expected value of the lower branch in Figure 3 is $60.

$$.6 \times \$100 + .4 \times \$0 = \$60$$

If one had in mind the goal of maximizing the expected value; that is, if he or she were an "expected dollar value decision maker," the lower path in Figure 3 would be the one to choose, assuming that the decision could be made again and again. But what if the rules were changed and you could play but once? Here the path selected, much like real life, precludes the selection of any other. Now the decision maker has only one chance. In this example the selection would still be the same, for a 60 percent chance to win $100 is still superior to a 50 percent chance at the same outcome. Consider, however, the problem posed by Figure 4. Here the expected value of either choice is identical ($50), but the game is considerably different. If the player could not afford to lose $100, then he or she would have to forego the chance of winning $200.

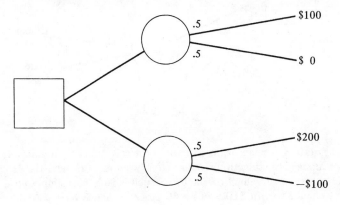

Figure 4.

Let us return to our modification of Swalm's risk assessment instrument. The instrument is in the form of a game, much like the situations above, in which the subject is asked to choose between two options. Consider the situation presented by Figure 5. The first option is that the subject can play a game of chance in which he has a 50–50 chance of winning $10,000. The subject will lose nothing if he or she loses the game. The other option is that the subject will receive a certain fixed sum for not playing. The subject can play only once. The interviewer asks the following questions after explaining the game: "You have the option of playing the game or taking a certain cash reward, say $7,000. Which do you choose?" The subject will probably say he or she will take the $7,000. The interviewer then proceeds to reduce the cash reward a thousand dollars at a time until the interviewer determines the point at which the subject becomes indifferent between playing the game or taking the amount offered in cash. This point is termed the "indifference point" or the point at which the two alternatives, that is, playing the game or taking the amount offered in cash, have equal utility for the subject. Now quiz yourself. The amount at which you are indifferent between whether you take the cash or play the game is your indifference point between, in this case, a 50 percent chance of winning $10,000 or a certain but lesser reward. Let us assume your indifference point is $3,000. You will play or you will take the $3,000 in cash; you are indifferent. For you the two outcomes are equal in value. We can express the utility of this $3,000 outcome as .5 $\times$

the utility for you of $10,000 plus .5 × the utility for you of $0. If we want to find the utility value of the indifference point of $3,000 we can arbitrarily assign utile values to the $10,000 and to the $0 and calculate the utile value of the $3,000 mathematically. Arbitrarily let us say that $10,000 equals 10 utiles and $0 equals 0 utiles. Thus we have the following equation:

.5 × 10 utiles + .5 × 0 utiles equals a utility value for $3,000 of 5 utiles.

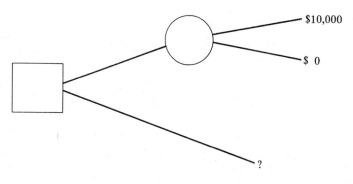

Figure 5.

As shown in Figure 6 we can begin a table and a graph using these amounts.

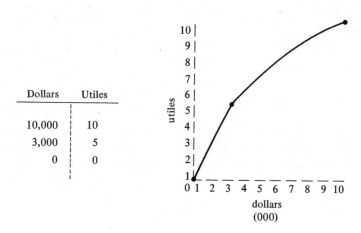

Dollars	Utiles
10,000	10
3,000	5
0	0

Figure 6.

Now we can play a second game to determine more information for the table and graph that we have just begun. The interviewer proceeds: "We will flip a coin and you will have a 50–50 chance to win $10,000 or $3,000 depending on which side of the coin comes up. However, you have the option of either playing this game or taking this $8,000 in cash. Which do you choose?" The subject in this example will probably say that he or she will take the $8,000. The interviewer then continues to reduce the cash award a thousand dollars at a time until the interviewer determines the point at which the subject is indifferent. He or she will play the game or will accept a certain amount offered in cash. Let us say that for this game the subject's indifference point is $6,000. When offered $7,000, the subject would rather have the money than play the game, but with a certain payment of $5,000 he or she chooses to play. At $6,000 the subject could go either way. Since we have already assigned $10,000 a utile value of 10 and have calculated that $3,000 has a utile value of 5 on this subject's scale, then our equation for this game looks like this:

.5 X 10 utiles + .5 X 5 utiles equals a utility value for $6,000 of 7.5 utiles.

We can now add this information to our table and graph first presented in Figure 6 so that it now appears as in Figure 7.

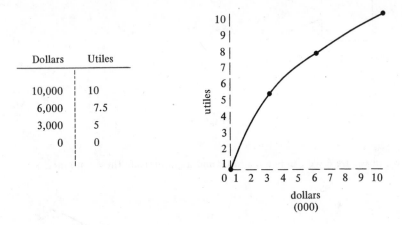

Dollars	Utiles
10,000	10
6,000	7.5
3,000	5
0	0

Figure 7.

Our third game is a new choice. The interviewer says to the subject: "We will flip a coin and you will have a 50–50 chance of winning $6,000 but you will lose nothing if you lose the game. You have the option, however, of taking this $4,000 in cash." The interviewer then proceeds to find the subject's indifference point. Let us suppose that it turns out to be $2,000. The equation for this game, considering that $6,000 has already been established in the game above as having a utile value for this subject of 7.5, is as follows:

.5 X 7.5 utiles + .5 X 0 utiles equals a utility value for $2,000 of 3.75 utiles.

Figure 8 presents the completed table and graph of this information.

We will return to Figure 8 but first let us suppose that a different subject plays these three games and his or her indifference point is always the expected dollar value of the game, that is, $5,000 in game one; $7,500 in game two; and $3,750 in game three. (The second and third games, of course, had to be modified as the subject defined a different dollar amount in game one.) This person would have a table and graph as shown in Figure 9. We would define such a person as "risk neutral" or an "expected dollar value player."

We can now define a risk-averse or a risk-prone person according to whether his or her curve plots above or below the straight line shown in Figure 9. A risk-averse person

Dollars	Utiles
10,000	10
6,000	7.5
3,000	5
2,000	3.75
0	0

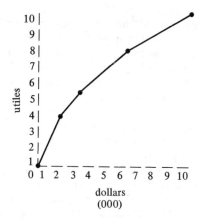

Figure 8.

Dollars	Utiles
10,000	10
7,500	7.5
5,000	5
3,750	3.75
0	0

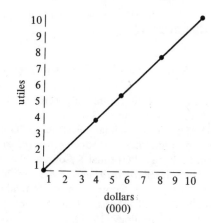

Figure 9.

accepts a certain cash payment which is less than the expected dollar value of the game (as in our subject of Figure 8). His or her curve will be above the straight line that represents the risk-neutral position. A risk-seeker will accept the certain cash payment only when it is more than the expected dollar value of the game. His or her curve will fall below the straight line of the risk-neutral position. In constructing a personal risk profile an individual may well find that at the upper limits he or she avoids risk, whereas with smaller amounts he or she may well be a gambler. With this technique, and with the areas of risk prone, risk neutral, and risk averse defined on the graph, you can now interview yourself, or your colleagues, to determine your own or your colleagues' risk profiles. A summary of the risk assessment game which we have describe to you appears in Appendix A.

A personal risk assessment has a number of practical uses for the library manager. A conscious understanding of personal feelings about how much each alternative is worth, depending upon what the options are, is valuable for the individual. More than just aiding the decision-maker, however, such an assessment may help superiors and subordinates understand each other. If a university library administration has an expressed policy of leading the state of the art, for example (consider the early development of OCLC on some campuses in Ohio), then high-level library decision-makers may be expected to take calculated risks in the acceptance of new technology. If a library director rules out a staff recommendation because he or she has assigned a different value (utility) to the possible losses inherent in the alternatives, then conflict may develop if the staff and the director do not know each others' risk profiles.

Swalm found in surveying 100 managers that some were risk-takers and others were afraid of risk. It seems that we in library science might now survey librarians to determine whether there are any significant differences between the general tendencies of librarians and of managers in risk situations.

The main objective of this paper is to introduce librarians to a simplified instrument that may be used to describe their risk profiles. It is hoped that librarians will administer this instrument to themselves and their colleagues in order to plot their own individual attitudes toward risk-taking. This information about oneself and one's colleagues should prove beneficial in calculating, describing, and understanding behaviors involved in specific decisions. Through this understanding of risk-taking, the decision-maker should be better equipped to deal with his or her attitudes and with the attitudes of others, and to predict his or her own behavior and the behavior of others in decision-making situations which involve risk.

REFERENCES

1. In recent library literature only three articles discuss utility and/or risk. They are: Robert L. Burr, "Library Goals and Library Behavior," *College and Research Libraries* 36 (1975): 27–32; William B. Rouse, "Optimal Selection of Acquisition Sources," *Journal of the American Society for Information Science* 25 (1974): 227–231; and William B. Rouse, "Optimal Resource Allocation in Library Systems," *Journal of the American Society for Information Science* 26 (1975): 157–165.
2. J. A. F. Stoner, "A Comparison of Individual and Group Decisions Involving Risk." (Unpublished M.S. thesis, Sloan School of Industrial Management, Massachusetts Institute of Technology, 1961).
3. Dean G. Pruitt, "Choice shifts in group discussion: an introductory review." *Journal of Personality and Social Psychology* 20 (Dec. 1971): 339–360.
4. John von Neuman and Oskar Morgenstern, *Theory of Games and Economic Behavior* (Princeton: Princeton University Press, 1947).
5. Ralph O. Swalm, "Utility Theory—Insights Into Risk Taking," *Harvard Business Review* 44 (1966): 123–136.
6. Rouse, "Optimal Selection of Acquisition Sources," p. 227.
7. Swalm, pp. 123–136.

APPENDIX A

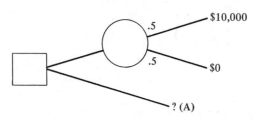

Game 1.

You have the option of playing the game or taking a cash reward. What cash reward would make you indifferent whether you took the reward or played the game? $6,000, $5,000, $3,000? Other? This figure, when you decide, is "A."

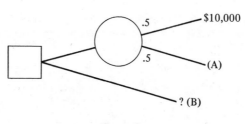

Game 2.

Plug in your amount for "A" from the last game. Now what cash reward in this game would make you indifferent whether you took the reward or played the game? $8,000, $6,000, $4,000? Other? This figure, when you decide, is "B."

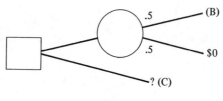

Game 3.

Plug in your amount for "B" from the last game. Now what cash reward in this game would make you indifferent whether you took the reward or played the game? This figure, when you decide, is "C."

Chart

Dollars	Utiles
10,000	10
B	7.5
A	5
C	3.75
0	0

utiles

10
8
6
4
2

2 4 6 8 10

dollars
(000)

Now substitute your figures for A, B, and C and fill in the graph to find your risk profile.

Robert J. Merikangas

University of Maryland at College Park

THE ACADEMIC REFERENCE LIBRARIAN:
ROLES AND DEVELOPMENT

The academic reference librarian needs a career perspective for personal decisions and to lead in service programs. An examination of reference librarian roles in three clusters shows how roles and personal development can be integrated. As subject specialist, the librarian is committed to lifelong learning. As a helper and educational counselor, the librarian exercises "heart" in caring. As a campus community change agent, the librarian expresses social concerns. These multiple roles can be seen as a cone of broadening competencies and responsibility. The apparent obstacle of limited resources finds its solution in the community and also in the social network concept.

Leadership in promoting institutional services to society will come, not from the institutions as such, but from the individuals who have a vision of service. Leadership for public services in academic libraries will come from those reference librarians who are able to integrate their professional careers with their dream of how they personally can serve the community. In order to provide this kind of "servant leadership"[1] the reference librarian needs a career-long perspective. The midcareer situation is especially critical, because it is then that the question of whether to advance by moving into management is faced. As Daniel Levinson has shown, in a midlife situation, one typically examines one's life structure to see how it fits with one's dream, and how it involves all of one's self.[2] It seems that when we examine the roles of the reference librarian, and how they can be integrated with self-development and personal growth, the future looks promising.

This paper offers one perspective on these roles, and suggests that they are challenging and at the same time not unrealistic. Career possibilities are open which can call forth the best one has to offer and invite what is not an impossible dream.

Librarian as bibliographer: subject specialist

The basic, traditional cluster of reference librarian roles revolves around the librarian as reference specialist, information specialist, and bibliographer. The librarian as teacher is based on these roles as well as on whatever scholarship the librarian has been able to acquire in and out of degree programs. The only reason the tasks of the librarian are not

395

impossible, of course, is that he is constantly learning from his patrons. A roughly hierarchical list of reference librarian roles at the core of expected professional activity might be these five:

1. Expert in the "second knowledge"[3] or that half of knowledge[4] which is knowing where to find it. The reference librarian stands forth first and foremost as an expert in retrieving information by means of the catalogs, indexes, and reference books. Identifying and using efficiently the great variety of reference books is one task that few besides the reference librarians will ever master. A "reference theory of specific information retrieval" has been expounded by Charles McClure,[5] which applies, it would seem, only to what is called "ready reference." Similarly, the "information" thrust of the policy statement, "A Commitment to Information Services" is too limiting,[6] as the roles listed next will indicate.

Orientation to the library for users flows from this basic reference librarian role. Tours, self-directed orientation materials, the signage system, and basic library instruction for new students and faculty are all based on the reference librarian's ability to deal with the question that asks, "where do I find information on . . . ?" Similarly, the librarian will normally prepare guides and point-of-use instruction materials for the most commonly used access points, such as catalogs and indexes, to supplement direct personal assistance.

2. Provider of information and referral service. The provision of community information and referral services in public libraries has developed widely and has been correctly seen as a natural extension of reference service. On a university campus the I&R files prepared by the reference librarian tend to refer primarily to campus information sources, but they may extend to resources in the larger community to meet the general information needs of students and staff. This service role differs from normal reference most in that it involves less emphasis on published sources and more on telephone contacts and material gathered and indexed by the staff.

3. Subject specialist librarian. The academic reference librarian as a subject specialist has been well described in a 1976 article by Thomas J. Michalak on library services to the graduate community.[7] The cluster of activities he identified as part of "an interactive, dynamic information service"[8] may also be extended, in general, to services based in an undergraduate library. The responsibilities include: selection and collection development, liaison with users and technical services, library instruction (including formal courses), current awareness and use of machine-readable data bases, research assistance and bibliographical services, and helping improve bibliographical control of the collections. To this list might be added the publication of guides to the literature.

4. Research service. Reference librarians may provide research service in an academic library, but it is not presently a common service. The best model for a complete research service is the Congressional Research Service. The CRS states its ideal service thus: "information is evaluated and selected for accuracy and authority, translated into terms of legislative issues, presented in a concise and orderly format, and delivered in as complete a form and on as timely a schedule as possible."[9] What can be done with a staff of 449 subject specialists with sophisticated retrieval systems at their disposal cannot be expected of a reference department, but a reference librarian may find himself going beyond the traditional preparation of bibliographies to a more complete research service, if the institution is willing to pay for such a service. Doing on-line searches for users is a move in this direction. Certainly we need to see how the preparation of a complete "package" of material or a complete research report differs from present policies, and ask whether there may be situations in which such a package is a more effective solution than repeated individual instances of research assistance.

5. Facilitor for self-directed learning. At the college level, the reference librarian will generally not see users unless they are in a self-directed learning situation to some degree. Even if a student wants only an alternative to her textbook, she has defined a deliberate learning project and is seeking a way to implement it. What is occurring now, however, is that such self-teaching is becoming more structured and embodied as the major feature of courses and programs, as in the external degree programs, the universities-without-walls, and the open university.[10] More academic library users will be midcareer adults and students in a variety of programs which expect the student to make a contract and carry out a series of learning experiences. The librarian's role in facilitating this learning is conceptualized and developed in public libraries as advisors to adult independent learners.[11] The best overall picture of this kind of learning activity in a general, not academic, context is still found in the studies of Allen Tough, especially *The Adult's Learning Projects.*[12] This role as learning advisor or facilitator is parallel to that of the subject specialist, but the content tends to be less curriculum and discipline based. The theory that underlies it is that of adult education rather than that of university education, but adult education is admittedly different more in emphasis and methodology than in substance.

Development of the librarian in these five roles which focus on communicating knowledge depends on these areas: (1) greater knowledge of the bibliographic structure of disciplines and information systems, (2) improvement in methods of interpreting them to others, individually and in groups, and (3) greater skills in program design and implementation. The cognitive base of these activities is thus shared with college faculty, adult educators, and instructional method experts, including media experts. The dynamic aspect of this cluster of roles in turn depends on a commitment to life-long learning on the part of the librarian and a continuing desire to share that learning.

LIBRARIAN AS HELPER: EDUCATIONAL COUNSELOR

After listing aspects of the reference librarian's role that primarily involve knowledge, I now want to describe a role which is not a separate activity, but one which adds more depth to the direct service relationships. It is evidenced particularly in the I&R services and in assisting in planning projects or learning episodes. Instead of the term "service," I want to offer the concept of "helping," and even use the terms becoming more common, helper and helpee. *Helping* gets us more into the personal changes that are involved in a person's search. The librarian's role as helper should integrate the tutorial and the guidance aspects of the reference interview. *Helping* focuses our attention on the counseling nature of much of the reference librarian's work, on which Patrick Penland of the University of Pittsburgh has long insisted.[13] The counseling of the librarian is educational, not therapeutic. Seeing the reference interview as counseling takes us closer to the real interpersonal situation than do more abstract communication models, and such concepts as "the reference interface."[14] The idea of counseling is even deeper and richer than that of advising, because it reminds us that the choices and decisions that the reader makes are more than intellectual. As a text states it:

> There is a vast difference between knowing and behaving. Knowing comes from getting more information. Change in behavior comes from the discovery of meaning. . . . Most people in the helping professions are very proficient in the information half of the learning equation. They know how to give people information very well. Most failures in the helping professions occur, however, not because helpers are unskilled at providing information, but because

of their lack of skill in helping persons discover the personal meaning of information for them.[15]

From the negotiation process of the reference interview and the subsequent search the patron learns methods but also learns how to make decisions, how to plan actions, and how to evaluate the results. In order to discover meaning and begin new ways of learning, the patron has to grow in both head and heart. He needs encouragement as well as data or technique.

The reference librarian who accepts and develops his role as counselor can integrate his own head and heart in a mode of service that deliberately includes *caring*. Caring for others is a mode of living that enables a person to integrate work life and home life, inner life and public life, in a unique way.[16]

By drawing attention to the counseling aspect of the librarian's roles, we stress the need to develop and exercise the heart as well as the head. Maccoby, in his study of executives, has found that in corporations the heart is usually undeveloped, as we might expect. Our institutions often seem to have the same effect. Maccoby defines the exercise of the heart in this fashion:

> The exercise of the heart is that of experiencing, thinking critically, willing, acting, so as to overcome egocentrism and to share passion with other people (justice-compassion) and respond to their need with the help one can give (benevolence-responsibility).[17]

A common enemy of the heart is careerism, which brings one to live in fear and anxiety over one's upward advancement.[18] Chris Argyris has drawn similar conclusions about the hostility of normal professional environments to true personal development. His Model I of professional action, the common practice, "is not conducive to cumulative personal development but instead tends to enable one to make use of only the more primitive aspects of the self."[19] He has described a new Model II, in which the professional "expects to be challenged by clients and by the organization on criteria that go beyond the criteria of the profession itself."[20]

Just as the basic knowledge-worker roles of the reference librarian are seen in more depth in a counseling framework, so the direct personal services may be seen to be limited by institutional and environmental constraints. This brings us to looking at the librarian as necessarily playing a role by using what Argyris calls second-order techniques: "first-order techniques are the arts and skills that comprise professional practice; second-order techniques are the techniques needed to create the institutional settings in which first-order techniques can function."[21] For the librarian this includes, but is by no means limited to, action to improve the organizational structure of the library itself. More generally, it means being a leader and change agent in relation to the whole community.

LIBRARIAN AS CHANGE AGENT: COMMUNITY LIBRARIAN

The role of the academic reference librarian is obviously interrelated with the role of the library as an institution. The efforts of an individual to broaden and deepen service roles will be frustrated in an institutional environment that does not allow "new dimensions for academic library service" (as the title of a 1975 collection by E. J. Josey described them).[22] It would be possible to search the literature and develop a matrix of possible new dimensions and options for institutional change. The wide scope of these possible directions, from new forms of information delivery to expanded library instruction, raises questions about the possible stance of an individual who is willing to be a change agent but uncertain of the meaning of such a role. A model that can help us to conceptualize a broader vision of service can be borrowed from the new field being called community counseling.

Counselors are developing new concepts and new roles to help them go beyond situations in which they help individuals to those in which they plan programs to affect whole communities. Not only do the approaches of the community-minded counselors offer good concepts for librarians, but the counselors themselves have been and continue to be natural allies as change agents on a college campus.

In a recent text, *Community Counseling*, Judith and Michael Lewis[23] have outlined a model of human services in which program planning can take place more systematically. Because of the general approach they take, "community counseling" can be translated into "community library service," and the community defined as the campus. The community aspect defines an approach, not a job title.[24] It embodies the *"human services concept*, which defines appropriate action in terms of the needs of individuals and the community, and never in terms of the helping methods with which professionals are already familiar and comfortable."[25] The stress is on developmental and preventive approaches, analyzed in terms of four facets: experiential and environmental, extensive and intensive. A broad perspective on possible library programs and interventions can be gained by using the facets, once it is realized that an interdisciplinary team will probably carry out the activity, and that the campus must be seen as a system of interdependent persons, groups, and organizations. How this counseling methodology can be applied to library service can best be seen by giving examples from each of the pairs of facets:

1. Extensive experiential programs (direct experiences available to the population as a whole):
    orientation to campus life and resources
    educational programs and clinics sponsored by the library
    participation in career information programs
    skill-building by self-instruction and open group methods
2. Intensive experiential programs (special experiences to individuals or groups that need them):
    desk reference services
    tutorial services
    class instruction, in and out of the library
    operation of satellite library locations (dormitories, etc.)
    programs for special groups: disadvantaged, honors, midcareer students, handi-
        capped, commuters, free university, etc.
    peer assistance programs
3. Extensive environmental programs (attempt to make the entire community more responsive to the needs of all its members; influence the climate on campus):
    participate in planning new academic programs and requirements
    participate in organizing an information services network
    use the campus media to raise awareness of information sources and services
    participate in applied educational research programs to improve instruction
    promote cultural programs
    advocate improvement of library facilities and services
    increase links to the resources of the larger community, including library networks
    advocate student rights and improved services
4. Intensive environmental programs (intervene actively in the environments of specific individuals or groups, so that their special needs can be met):
    consult with faculty in the planning of specific courses and assignments

consult with services on campus, to improve the information component: residence
hall staff, student government, counseling services, champlains, career and placement services, police, health services, student organizations
advocate provision of services for specific groups, such as handicapped.

This outline of areas of action seems broad enough, but of course the librarian has a
vision that extends beyond the immediate campus community he serves to the larger
community. Developments in the literature of reference, especially in what Shores calls
encyclopedics,[26] in networks, in the Library of Congress, in the publishing industry, and
in commercial indexing services, are all of concern. However, attention to these broader
professional concerns and other matters for which the American Library Association is
often the intermediary should not detract from attention to the needs of those closest
to home.

CAREER DEVELOPMENT IN MULTIPLE ROLES

The roles of reference librarians—subject specialist, educational counselor, change
agent—imply the need for a manifold continuing education or growth process. At the
First CLENE Assembly the adult educator Malcolm Knowles offered an assessment model
that we might use. To use his model we would first define roles, somewhat as we have
done, and then describe the competencies common to all librarians, the reference specialist competencies, and then the individual's personal stylistic competencies.[27] It is not
appropriate at this point to detail all the competencies, but we may add a graphic touch
by borrowing again from Lewis and Lewis; this time their image of a career *cone*, standing
on its point, as an ice cream cone.[28]

Instead of becoming more of a specialist to advance, the reference librarian remains a
generalist and moves up in responsibility because of more and broader competencies:
she moves up the cone. From the narrow base of reference interview helping skills, the
librarian expands in general competencies. This leads to an ice-cream top of the cone
composed of a sum total: helping skills (individual and group) + knowledge of resource
and information delivery systems + knowledge of academic community systems and
change strategies + ability in program development and administration + skill in consultation with other teachers and helpers + skill in education and training of assistants +
strong competency in research and program evaluation. This cumulative development
would enable the librarian to create new multifaceted programs and be a leader in the
campus community.

It is perhaps significant that the roles we have singled out as core areas for career
development correspond rather closely to the three categories described by Jerry G. Gaff
in *Toward Faculty Renewal.*[29] Corresponding to the knowledge of subjects and methods
of the reference librarian is the need of the faculty for instructional development. Corresponding to the role of counselor and the need to use self as an instrument is the
category called faculty development, which focuses on individual personal growth and
sensitivity. Corresponding to the librarian's role as change agent is the need of the faculty
for organizational development, which focuses on creating a more effective learning
environment. Gaff brings these competencies together by citing Harold Taylor, as we may
usefully do: "It is the richness and depth of the inner life of the teacher and the qualities
that he holds as a man of character and commitment that determine his students'
responses to his teaching. We, therefore, need to do everything in our power to arrange
the community life of our college campuses in such a way that its elements conspire to
produce stimulating and provocative effects in the intellectual and personal growth of
teachers,"[30] and, we may add, of librarians.

Multiple roles and limited resources

It is apparent by now that I have rejected the simple definition of reference work: giving answers to questions.[31] One reason that I reject it is that it is impossible to imagine enough resources to staff libraries to provide answers to all questions. To suppose that excellent "maximum" service will lead to sufficient funding to offer it to all users and nonusers is to engage in mythical thinking. As has been said, "one of the diseases of professionalism is the tendency to define a problem in a way so as to require only professionals for its solution, thereby rendering the problem unsolvable."[32] If only professional librarians can provide answers, there is no solution to people's information needs. But then how can I present multiple roles that go beyond even answer-giving and obviously require more staff time—the truly finite resource? Accepting others as providers of information and purveyors of library instruction is the obvious answer, but we need a conceptual approach that will help us develop action programs.

The *network* concept is useful here as it is in dealing with the other area of limited resources, funds for collections. A network is a system of people linked by agreements and expectations. Seymour Sarason has analyzed the problem of limited resources in providing services, and has shown how the network concept offers a promising direction in his 1977 book, *Human Services and Resource Networks.* Cooperation without the exchange of money and creation of a sense of community can lead to a deceptively simple relationship between those possessing resources: each is free to approach the other, to work for common purposes. Reference librarians should be able to approach their faculty and student service colleagues to exchange resources. The leadership required to create such a network goes beyond goal-setting exercises and use of communication channels. It requires even a kind of passionate vision. Expecting enough librarians to link users to resources is a fantasy; hoping for librarians who can assist in creating networks that link resources is a vision.

REFERENCES

1. Robert K. Greenleaf, *Servant Leadership: A Journey into the Nature of Legitimate Power and Greatness* (New York: Paulist Press, 1977).
2. Daniel J. Levinson et al., "The Psychosocial Development of Men in Early Adulthood and the Mid-Life Transition," in D. F. Ricks, A. Thomas, and M. Roff, eds., *Life History Research in Psychopathology*, vol. 3 (Minneapolis: University of Minnesota Press, 1974). See also Robert F. Pearse and B. Purdy Pelzer, *Self-Directed Change for the Mid-Career Manager* (New York: AMACOM, 1975); and Daniel J. Levinson, et. al., *The Seasons of a Man's Life* (New York: A. Knopf, 1978). Useful, also, is Harold L. Hodgkinson, "Adult Development: Implications for Faculty and Administrators," *Educational Record* 55 (Fall 1974): 263–374.
3. Eric H. Boehm, "On the Second Knowledge: A Manifesto for the Humanities," *Libri* 22 (1972): 312–323.
4. Louis Shores, "The Half of Knowledge," in *Reference as the Promotion of Free Inquiry* (Littleton, Colo.: Libraries Unlimited, 1976), pp. 91–98.
5. Charles R. McClure, "A Reference Theory of Specific Information Retrieval, *RQ* 13 (Spring 1974): 207–212.
6. Archie G. Rugh, "Reference Standards and Reference Work," *Library Journal* 101 (July 1976): 1497–1500.
7. Thomas J. Michalak, "Library Services to the Graduate Community: The Role of the Subject Specialist Librarian," *College & Research Libraries* 37 (May 1976): 257–265.

8. *Ibid.*, p. 257.
9. U.S. Library of Congress, *Information Resources and Services Available from the Library of Congress and the Congressional Research Service* (Communication from the Chairman, House Commission on Information and Facilities; Washington: U.S. Government Printing Office, 1976), p. 34.
10. See, for example, Union for Experimenting Colleges and Universities, *University Without Walls: a First Report* (Yellow Springs, Ohio: Union for Experimenting Colleges and Universities, 1972).
11. Office of Library Independent Study and Guidance Projects, *The Role of Public Libraries in Supporting Adult Independent Learning: An Interim Assessment* (New York: College Entrance Examination Board, 1974).
12. Allen Tough, *The Adult's Learning Projects* (Research in Education Series No. 1: Toronto: The Ontario Institute for Studies in Education, 1971), and Tough, *Learning Without a Teacher* (Educational Research Series No. 3; Toronto: The Ontario Institute for Studies in Education, 1967).
13. Patrick Penland, *Advisory Counseling for Librarians* (Pittsburgh: Bookstore, University of Pittsburgh, 1969), and *Interviewing for Counselor and Reference Librarians* (Pittsburgh: Bookstore, University of Pittsburgh, 1970), and "Counselor Librarianship," *Encyclopedia of Library and Information Science* (New York: M. Dekker, 1968-), 6: 240-54.
14. Bernard Frank Vavrek, *Communications and the Reference Interface* (Ph.D. dissertation, University of Pittsburgh; Book Center, University of Pittsburgh, 1971), and "The Nature of Reference Librarianship," *RQ* 13 (Spring 1974): 207-212.
15. Arthur W. Combs et al., *Helping Relationships: Basic Concepts for the Helping Professions* (Boston: Allyn & Bacon, 1971), pp. 95-96.
16. Milton Mayeroff, *On Caring* (New York: Harper & Row, 1971).
17. Michael Maccoby, *The Gamesman: The New Corporate Leaders* (New York: Simon & Schuster, 1976), p. 182.
18. Maccoby, *op. cit.*, pp. 189-209.
19. Chris Argyris and Donald A. Schoen, *Theory in Practice: Increasing Professional Effectiveness* (San Francisco: Jossey-Bass Pub., 1977), p. 154.
20. Argyris and Schoen, *op. cit.*, p. 155.
21. *Ibid.*, p. 149.
22. E. J. Josey, ed., *New Dimensions for Academic Library Service* (Metuchen, N.J.: Scarecrow Press, 1975).
23. Judith A. Lewis and Michael D. Lewis, *Community Counseling: A Human Services Approach* (New York: John Wiley & Sons, 1977).
24. Lewis and Lewis, *op. cit.*, p. 217-18.
25. *Ibid.*, p. 6.
26. Louis Shores, *op. cit.*, p. 164.
27. Malcolm Knowles, "Model For Assessing Continuing Education Needs for a Profession," pp. 82-98 in Continuing Library Education Network and Exchange, *Proceedings, First CLENE Assembly, Chicago, Illinois, Jan. 23-24, 1976* (Washington, D.C.: CLENE, 1976).
28. Lewis and Lewis, *op. cit.*, p. 313.
29. Jerry G. Gaff, *Toward Faculty Renewal: Advances in Faculty, Instructional, and Organizational Development* (San Francisco: Jossey-Bass Pub., 1975).
30. Harold Taylor, "The Teacher at His Best," in R. M. Cooper, ed., *The Two Ends of the Log* (Minneapolis: University of Minnesota Press, 1958), cited in Gaff, pp. 185-86.

31. See William A. Katz, *Introduction to Reference Work*, vol. 2: *Reference Services and Reference Processes* (2nd ed.: New York: McGraw-Hill Book Co., 1974).

32. Seymour B. Sarason et al., *Human Services and Resource Networks: Rationale, Possibilities, and Public Policy* (San Francisco: Jossey-Bass Pub., 1977), note p. 16.

Jean M. Ray

Southern Illinois University at Carbondale

THE FUTURE ROLE OF THE ACADEMIC LIBRARIAN, AS VIEWED THROUGH A PERSPECTIVE OF FORTY YEARS

Long-term trends in academic and research librarianship are indicated through personal recollections of the library scene at Amherst College in 1938, Yale University in 1948, Library of Congress in 1958, and Southern Illinois University at Carbondale in 1968. Facets analyzed include library education, duties performed, use of mechanized and automated equipment, salaries and fringe benefits, working conditions and hours, attitudes and objectives, staff participation in management, and status in the academic community. From the present situation predictions are offered as to what changes in policies, procedures, practices may be reasonably anticipated in the years ahead.

It seems appropriate that I should return to Massachusetts to take part in the first national conference of the Association of College and Research Libraries, since my own career in academic and research libraries is also forty years old; it began in this commonwealth at Amherst College Library in May 1938. Moreover, although this is the first paper I have presented before any part of ALA, I have been a member of it since I started training in librarianship here at Simmons College in 1935/36, have belonged to ACRL since its inception, and attended my first ALA conference here in Boston in 1941.

The only firm basis for predictions of the future would appear to be study of the past and present to observe, plot, and analyze trends. It is proposed therefore to compare conditions at ten-year intervals beginning in 1938, and project from these and the present scene what may be expected in 1988 or perhaps even in the year 2001. The survey rests on significant recollections as to (1) library education, (2) duties performed, (3) use of mechanized and automated equipment, (4) working conditions and hours, (5) salaries and fringe benefits, (6) attitudes and objectives, (7) staff participation in management, and (8) status in the academic community. The early years will be emphasized because few now remain active who can say of this period, "I was there."

Perhaps a few remarks on education for librarianship in 1938 would be appropriate. A bachelor's degree program, at the undergraduate or graduate level, was still the usual preparation. Courses were practically oriented, and cataloging exercises were recorded on P-slips in library hand. It is significant that Simmons had at this time the only approved library science program in all of New England, that it accepted only women students, and that the Library School's regular faculty was wholly female. In general the bachelor's degree in library science was regarded as terminal. From then on the new librarian was to concentrate on acquiring "good" experience, and there was almost no emphasis on further formal education.

AMHERST COLLEGE LIBRARY, 1938

Let us turn now to Amherst College's Converse Memorial Library, which in 1938 had a book collection of about 200,000 volumes. The staff numbered twelve, of whom only four were library school graduates. These were the head cataloger, who had both BA and BS, and three younger women, all in their twenties, all with Simmons undergraduate degrees, one working as assistant cataloger, one handling chiefly monographic orders, the third serials and binding. There was no reference librarian nor any reference service as such; requests for information were taken care of by two men who staffed the circulation desk and supervised student assistants. The administration of the library was in transition from the regime of its last "librarian" (son and successor to William I. Fletcher of Pool's *Index* fame) to the directorship of a young recruit from the English Department. Appointed director during the interim was an elderly and nearly blind professor of Greek; he was assisted by the executive secretary, a middle-aged woman, who had been trained by and served long years under both Fletchers. Finally there were three clerks, two in cataloging, another carrying out the bookkeeping aspects of the acquisitions process.

The year 1938 was back in the era of the typewriter and the adding machine (both non-electric), of duplicate hand-written or typed book cards (one filed under call number and one under borrower's name), of typing short-form original cataloging if LC cards were not available, when bill in duplicate for book orders was sufficient. Bibliographical resources of this period were also limited. Of the great national library catalogs in book form only that of the Bibliothèque Nationale, completed to the letter "R", offered much assistance in searching. The new edition of the British Museum *General Catalogue of Printed Books* had progressed only into the "B's," and there was no general record of Library of Congress's vast holdings except the depository catalogs or proof sheets found only in large libraries. One had to rely on *United States Catalog, Cumulative Book Index, Publishers Trade List Annual* and on national bibliographies of foreign countries.

Professional librarians then carried out many functions which were essentially clerical, but complained little and never in public. The work week of about forty-one hours extended through Saturday noon, but was mitigated by a last observance of "summer schedule," when the library was open only from 8:30 to 12:30 six days a week during the college summer vacation, and librarians could play tennis and swim every afternoon. A starting salary of $1200–1300 was considered adequate; there were no regular annual increases, and only by moving to a new position could one normally expect a higher salary figure. One received one's entire salary check each month then, however, with no withholding for fringe benefits or the miniscule income taxes of those days. Finally, the coffee break had not yet been invented; there were no authorized interruptions in scheduled work hours.

What of attitudes and objectives in 1938? Young librarians then, at least the Simmons variety, belonged to the generation with a "mission," and were also described as "adaptable, but with a fine feeling for form," to quote Charles Martel of Library of Congress as transmitted by Mary Elizabeth Hyde, Simmons cataloging teacher. But they did not talk much on the job about goals for library service, and certainly the library administration did not exhort in these terms. Most of the library staff's operations seemed to go on without concern for student use of its resources; there were no formal orientation sessions for anyone. Selection of books for purchase was carried out almost wholly by a relatively small corps of interested faculty, with no librarian taking responsibility for filling in the gaps.

In this age of innocence staff meetings, staff committees, any organized attempt at learning staff opinion—all were unknown. There was a sharp and unbridgeable gulf between director and staff, perhaps like that between officer and soldier in the military, epitomized by the door between director's office and the bibliography room, where some staff worked—this was noramlly kept closed but locked only on the staff side. In theory the director could burst through at any moment, though actually he seldom used it, and the staff could almost forget it. Any sort of faculty status for library staff below the administrative level would of course have been unthinkable. Contacts between faculty and librarians, except at the circulation desk, were strictly impersonal, mostly to locate books ordered and in process. There was no concern with membership or activities in professional associations. ALA seemed very remote, and a request to attend the annual conference of the New England College Librarians would be acceded to but not with any noticeable encouragement. However, there was a spirit of camaraderie among staff members, and a freedom to enjoy lectures, concerts, hikes, and picnics together outside working hours. To those who participated then and think back these were halcyon days indeed.

The decade between 1938 and 1948 besides encompassing World War II brought significant changes in academic librarianship. Dissatisfaction with old and agitation for new standards and procedures in library education was in the air, and resulted in complete transformation at the end of the 1940s.[1] It is said that wars do not create changes in society, but merely hasten changes already in motion. Perhaps then the alteration in sex ratio and marital status of librarians which became visible during the late 1940s was coming anyway. Many more men began entering the profession by the front door of library school, rather than a trickle through the side door of transfer from the teaching faculty. Simultaneously women librarians began marrying them or other males. This was to destroy, presumably forever, what had been the truth behind the legendary spinster librarians and "little old ladies in tennis shoes" (but the stereotype image would linger on in the public mind). Gone was the homeogeneous blend of unmarried females staffing academic libraries under a thin veneer of male administrators. The last of this generation of women however is only now moving up to the final years before retirement, causing the present extremely high average age of female librarians, and providing as they pass from the scene the chief hope of openings for the new crop of unemployed librarians.[2]

YALE UNIVERSITY LIBRARY, 1948

Sterling Memorial Library at Yale University was a great and inspiring institution in which to work in the year 1948. The staff was still largely female and mostly unmarried, except for a constantly changing corps of student wives who served as clerks and sub-professionals. There were some men librarians, though, of all ages and ranks. Further education was coming into favor, and the library would grant time and pay tuition for librarians to take courses in the graduate school after a year of service. Activity in professional associations was encouraged and might even be financially rewarded. Salaries for neophytes had climbed by perhaps $1000 a year, and small increases might be expected annually. Remuneration of $3000 for one with a decade of experience was only slightly below national average and compensated for by various intangible rewards inherent in being at Yale. By this time hospital insurance was available for all staff members; there was also a non-contributory pension plan benefiting those who remained there until retirement but not the transient. The working week had been slightly reduced, with coffee breaks generally accepted, but with Saturday morning hours still required.

Although the Yale Catalogue Department still prided itself on the quality of its subject cataloging, various sorts of experimental methods were being tried in an effort to cope efficiently with a floodtide of incoming material: production of cards by multilith machine; preparation of temporary records covering acquisitions for which cataloging was to be deferred; and development of the "W" collection of material expected to be little used, shelved by size and accorded minimal cataloging. It was a period of increased cooperation with other libraries, the heyday of the Farmington Plan with its input of foreign materials for which cataloging would appear as LC cards, as well as a substantial output of copy for LC's regular Cooperative Cataloging program. In addition a generous slice of the professional staff participated in an almost card-by-card review of the entire public catalog to select cards for possibly unique material to be photographed for addition to the National Union Catalog.

The typical library hierarchical structure still reigned supreme, but perhaps a few cracks could be observed. In a meeting of senior catalogers issues could be put to a vote, and the department head accede to the majority even if she did not agree. Staff members also had input through an active staff association which issued a monthly bulletin (subject to official approval) and sponsored professional forum programs. But Yale also had its undemocratic door, the only entrance on the west side of the building, kept locked except when administrators let themselves out to go to Morey's of Whiffenpoof fame across the street.

Morale was high at Yale in these years, nevertheless, though there was a difference in attitudes between old-timers who saw themselves as Yale employees who happened to be librarians and newcomers who were first and foremost professional librarians then working at Yale. In general new challenges and responsibilities seemed readily open to staff members who could qualify. Moreover Yale was "a great place to be from," and many of its staff went on directly to high-level positions elsewhere. But there were some who resisted elevation to supervisory status and clung insistently to duties with subject content and presumably more intellectual challenge. Faculty status, enjoyed by only a handful of administrators, was extended to all but beginning professional staff; that this step was possible was at least partly due to adoption of a position classification and pay plan throughout the library to replace unfair and inconsistent rank and salary arrangements previously in effect. The only benefits immediately apparent from this change, however, were the attaching of "research assistant" before one's title in the university directory and the opportunity to join the Faculty Club. One's social life still was built around one's library associates, and personal contacts with the teaching faculty were relatively rare. There was a well-organized staff orientation program, but no general concern with introducing students to the use of Yale's large and complex library system.

The 1948-1958 decade brought unprecedented expansion of programs and enrollments in the American academic world, with libraries sharing in the growth of the parent institutions. Librarians were in short supply, and active recruiting efforts were being made nationally. Meanwhile both the undergraduate and the fifth-year bachelor's degrees in library science disappeared as accredited degrees in the United States. A new program of basic training, initiated at Denver in 1974, adopted by all but the Canadian schools during the following years, pushed education for librarianship farther into the theoretical, and crowned it with a variety of master's degrees at the end of one graduate year (or a few months more).[3]

LIBRARY OF CONGRESS, 1958

It is not possible or appropriate to analyze activity at the Library of Congress in 1958 extensively, as has been done for Amherst and Yale. LC is not academic, and because of its size not even representative of research libraries either of the United States or of the world. Yet one merely reiterates the obvious to point to its leadership role and to state that new ideas and programs at LC may have universal impact on the libraries of academia, especially in the field of cataloging. During the late 1950s there were two such significant developments. The first was the abortive experiment with "cataloging in source," born again phoenix-like in the 1970s as "cataloging in publication." The other was the revolutionary new philosophy of corporate entries which Seymour Lubetzky was already sounding out in Descriptive Cataloging Division at meetings of section heads, and which would be incorporated into the *Anglo-American Cataloging Rules* of 1967, and should finally come to full fruition when "desuperimposition" goes into effect in 1980.

Although Library of Congress, viewed from a Washington perspective, was essentially a government agency which happened to be a library, it did have a nucleus of professional librarians, chiefly in Descriptive Cataloging Division and some other parts of the Processing Department. Nevertheless the line between clerical and professional activities was not always clearly established, and in-house training was frequently sufficient for upward mobility. While there was a flourishing Welfare and Recreation Association which brought staff together in hobby activities and in some educational programs such as language classes, the formalized small discussion groups which had operated earlier in the 1950s had been discontinued, and little staff participation in management existed. The LC work week conformed to the five-day, forty-hour standard of federal government offices. Salaries tended to be higher than those in academic libraries; one might increase income by 50 percent by a transfer to Washington, with probably less demanding duties. Fringe benefits included the generous government retirement plan and provision for life and health insurance, as well as access to nurses regularly on duty. Morale on the whole was high, except at times when a dreaded "reduction in force" might be pending.

The period 1958–1968 is close enough to the present to require little review. Higher education was booming, libraries included, fired by large government grants and a universal expectation of unending progress and expansion. An increasing number of accredited library schools were attracting more and more students for basic master's degree programs. Moreover substantial financial assistance was at last available for qualified librarians seeking further education at the doctoral level. American librarians were also serving worldwide on Fulbright grants, in Agency for International Development technical assistance programs, and in United States Information Service libraries.

MORRIS LIBRARY, SOUTHERN ILLINOIS UNIVERSITY—CARBONDALE, 1968

The scene shifts in 1968 to Morris Library, larger and older of the libraries of Southern Illinois University's two campuses at Carbondale and Edwardsville. A professional staff of fifty-two functioned in a centralized library with divisional reference service in a modular-type building. The work week had dropped to thirty-seven hours, while salaries had climbed to what would have been unbelievable heights two or three decades earlier, especially for the male half of the staff, who held all but one of the positions at administrative and department-head levels. The machine age had been accepted to the extent of automated circulation and multilithed catalog cards. But, except for a so-called "automation librarian" who was partly so occupied, the staff generally continued in traditional roles. Because of a very heavy commitment to student financial assistance few full-time clerical workers could be employed, and librarians were forced to carry out clerical functions when students were absent.

Staff participation in library management at SIU was still minimal at this time. Faculty status was accorded to all the professional staff, but for most, unless they had been granted tenure or were in the professorial ranks, it carried no voting privileges. Married women were just under 40 percent of the female half of the staff, several still saddled with the ambiguous lecturer rank left over from the years when anti-nepotism rules prevented them from receiving other than term appointments. At this time librarians at SIU, with a few notable exceptions, generally encountered only a somewhaat reluctant acceptance from the teaching faculty.

1978, PRESAGE OF THE FUTURE

The decade through which we have just passed has seen the birth and/or flowering of a number of developments which are undoubtedly the "stuff" of the future of librarianship. From conditions today one may deduce directions in which the profession may move in the last quarter of this century. Some bold guesses follow:

1. Education for academic librarianship will continue its expansive thrust from the early bachelor's degree programs to generally obligatory second master's degrees in subject fields and even a required doctoral degree for administrators. Library schools will attempt both to produce specialists and to provide graduates qualified for interdisciplinary work. Ability to use non-book media and computerized bibliographic systems will of course be essential. As long as the present overabundance of librarians lasts heightened selectivity in hiring will inevitably promote better preparation.

2. Emphasis and personnel in academic libraries will shift from simple ordering and cataloging books to providing bibliographical instruction for students and to sophisticated reference service employing on-line terminals, data retrieval through networks, computer output microforms, machine-readable shelflists, etc. Librarians will learn to live without the card catalog. Continuation of present funding shortages will require clearer distinctions between professional and clerical functions to achieve maximum utilization of librarians' potential.

3. Salaries will continue to rise slightly behind the cost of living, with increased fringe benefits a trend perhaps actively promoted by unionization and collective bargaining. As librarians' education and function approaches that of the teaching faculty the gap between average salaries for teaching and library service may close. Work-week hours probably will not decline much, but may become more flexible. Opportunities for sabbatical and other leaves for study and research should be more common, while retirement age maybe made optional at any point between sixty and seventy years.

4. Staff participation in management should increase as the faculty model becomes more prevalent in library personnel organization. There will be augmenting of present tendencies for committee rather than administrative determination of library policies, especially those dealing with staff selection, evaluation, tenure, and promotion. The women's movement seems here to stay, and this should be reflected in well-trained and motivated female librarians moving up to higher levels equally with their male colleagues.[4] In time perhaps the library's pyramidal organization pattern can be altered to allow more authority and compensation for a larger number of interested and qualified applicants for administrarive roles.[5]

5. Long-sought faculty status should be practically universal for academic librarians as they improve their campus image educationally, functionally, and through dedication to research and publications. As use of the library's complex new services becomes more difficult for patrons, the teaching faculty should be more appreciative of the librarian's interpretive role and more ready to accept the librarian as an equal in a knowledge

society. The need for more integration of library and classroom will come to be recognized.

With these gleanings and predictions from forty years of experience along the road from library handwriting to on-line computer terminals, I salute the new breed of academic librarian. We stand on the brink of developments which may change librarianship more fundamentally in the years immediately ahead than in all of the past century.

REFERENCES

1. Carl M. White, *A Historical Introduction to Library Education: Problems and Progress to 1951* (Metuchen, N.J.: Scarecrow Press, 1976), p. 224–68.
2. Michael D. Cooper, "An Analysis of the Demand for Librarians," *Library Quarterly* 45 (October 1975): 373–404.
3. C. Edward Carroll, *The Professionalization of Education for Librarianship, with Special Reference to the Years 1940-1960* (Metuchen, N.J.: Scarecrow Press, 1970), p. 144–82.
4. Beverly P. Lynch, "Women and Employment in Academic Librarianship," in Herbert Poole, ed., *Academic Libraries by the Year 2000, Essays Honoring Jerrold Orne* (New York: Bowker, 1977), p. 119–27.
5. Donald F. Cameron and Peggy Heim, *Librarians in Higher Education, Their Compensation Structures for the Academic Year 1972-73, a Third Survey* (Washington, D.C.: Council on Library Resources, 1974).

C. James Schmidt

State University of New York at Albany

FACULTY STATUS IN ACADEMIC LIBRARIES: RETROSPECTIVE AND PROSPECT

Since the earliest recorded granting of faculty status in 1911 at Columbia University, the number of institutions granting faculty status to librarians has increased so that in 1976 seventy-five percent of academic librarians have faculty status. Since 1966 the rate of increase has been fifty percent (from 51.2 to 75 percent). The claim to faculty status for librarians is based on the relationship between the functions of the university (to preserve, disseminate, and generate information) and the core activities of librarianship (selection of materials, organization of materials for use, interpretation of materials for users). After reviewing history and rationale, implications and problems of faculty status are discussed.

HISTORY OF FACULTY STATUS

The idea that academic librarianship "Ought not to be annexed to a professorship, but be itself a professorship," had its origins in the nineteenth century.[1] This vision was not to be realized for several decades because of several factors which impeded the professionalization of librarianship, such as the lack of adequate collections in colleges and universities, the qualitative and quantitative deficiencies in training for librarianship, and the serious understaffing which characterized most academic libraries. The Williamson Report and the creation by the American Library Association of the Board of Education for Librarianship to accredit library schools were developments during the 1920s which helped to make real the vision of the nineteenth century.

The earliest continuing grant of faculty status of which I am aware occurred at the University of Montana effective in 1902. In 1911, the earliest *recorded* granting of faculty status occurred at Columbia where it was provided as follows:

> ... the librarian shall have the rank of professor, the assistant librarian that of associate professor and the supervisors (with the grade of assistant librarian) shall rank as assistant professors and bibliographers(!) as instructors."[4]

This action of Columbia, while giving proper recognition to the role of its librarians, clearly related faculty rank held by a librarian to the level of a librarian's position in the hierarchical administrative structure of the library. The inability to separate the hierarchical structure of the library (or to radically alter that structure) from an individual's faculty rank is a problem which has persisted in many academic libraries. Holley had this problem in mind when he observed that:

> One puzzling aspect of the trend toward academic governance (in academic libraries) is that the organization charts remain the same. That follows logically from the concept which mandates that the staff makes policies and the administration carries out those policies. *However, can this be done realistically in a traditional hierarchical structure?*[3]

Axford made a similar point in 1974:

> While it is clear that increasing numbers of university librarians, including some of the top, are rallying to the position that a truly participatory environment can lead to a new birth of professional freedom, growth, and productivity there seems to be little clear understanding that achieving these goals will require a radical restructuring of the library, not just a cosmetic modification through a proliferation of committees and task forces.[4]

How widespread is faculty status? Since the Columbia action in 1911, the number of institutions granting faculty status has increased with most of this increase coming in the fifties and sixties.

By 1957, over 700 librarians had joined AAUP whose membership rules required that for a librarian to be eligible to join, he/she must hold faculty status and rank and have the right to vote at faculty meetings. Thus, *at least* 700 or approximately 10% of an estimated 8500 academic librarians in 1957 held faculty rank. The true figure was inestimably higher.

In 1966, Schiller reported that a bare majority, 51.2 percent, of her respondents held faculty rank: 20.9 percent were instructors; 16.5 percent were associate professors; 4.6 percent were professors.[5] Schiller noted certain kinds of institutions as more likely to grant faculty status than others. "Public institutions offer faculty rank more readily than do those under private control, but church-related institutions are even more likely to. do so than public institutions."[6] Holley arrived at a similar conclusion when he commented that "Resistance to faculty status has come largely from the older private universities and some of the more prestigious State (sic) universities in the past twenty years."[7]

In 1973, a committee of librarians at Old Dominion University conducted a survey of 245 academic libraries, public and private, large and small, in 48 states and the District of Columbia. The responses (79 percent) indicated that 60.8 percent of the institutions surveyed accorded faculty status to the professional staff of the library.[8] Thus, the percentage of librarians with faculty status appears to have increased from something more than ten in 1957 to just over half (51.2) by 1966, to just over three fifths (60.8) in 1973.

Early in 1976, ACRL's Academic Status Committee, supported by a grant from the Council on Library Resources, conducted a salary survey.[9] Included in the instrument was the following question: "Using the definition of faculty in your institution, do librarians have faculty status?" Seventy-five percent of the institutions responding said "yes." The respondents represented approximtely 13,000 academic librarians out of a total of approximately 19,900.[10] This percentage represents an increase of approximately half in the ten years since Schiller's survey. In 1966, one academic librarian in two held faculty rank; by 1976 the proportion was three out of four. It is worth noting that this increase occurred at the end of the period of growth and grandeur for American Higher education and that the increase continued in the seventies, a period marked by stable and/or declining support for higher education.

RATIONALE FOR FACULTY STATUS

Before discussing the implications of faculty status, it may be useful to review the rationale for faculty status for academic librarians. One begins with a model of university. The university is a conglomerate of different professions united by a common set of objectives which are to preserve, to disseminate, and to generate information. In his paper at the 1974 Annual Conference, Dwight Ladd called this a "congeries of interest."[11] Others have characterized this as a cybernetic model.

Those persons in university who teach, i.e., preserve and disseminate information are classified as academic, in other words "the faculty." Note that those members of the university community whose primary duties are the generation of knowledge—research— are more and more not classified as academic. Positions for research assistant or associate, junior and senior are becoming more common. There are many ulterior motives for this besides the integrity of position classification, but the effects of this trend are clear and relevant to the academic librarian's claim to faculty status.

The claim to faculty status for academic librarians thus turns on the degree to which academic librarians are preservers, disseminators, generators of information. A casual review of the core areas of librarianship—selection of materials, organization of materials for use, provision of assistance to patrons in the use of materials—reveals beyond reasonable doubt that academic librarians preserve, disseminate and generate information, and that the culmination of these activities is in the interface between librarian and patron, as is the case with others on the campus who teach.

If this rationale has validity then it implies a role for the library which is central to the objectives of the university. Conversely, if librarians reject faculty status, a different role for the library is implied.

IMPLICATIONS OF A FACULTY STATUS

What are or have been the implications of faculty status? *First*, academic libraries need to be organized and administered differently both to reflect the status held by librarians and to facilitate the activities and behaviors appropriate to that status. Fortunately, automation is proving to be a powerful force for reorganizing and for restructuring work.

Second, a library governance must be worked out, hopefully without myth or mayhem. A brief digression about governance is in order at this point.

"Governance, n. 1. The act, process, or power of governing. 2. The state of being governed."

"Govern, v. tr. 1. To control the actions of behavior of; guide; direct."

Thus is governance defined in the dictionary. However, as is too often the case, to discuss a word is to deal not only with the denotations of the lexicographer, but also with connotations composed of myth, tradition, perception.

In contemporary higher education, we can find a variety of patterns of governance. This variety has been cataloged and analyzed under the following three headings: bureaucratic; collegial; political.[12]

The first of these, the bureacratic mode, has its origin in the work of Max Weber. Weber attempted to describe bureaucracies in terms of characteristics which distinguished them from other kinds of organizations. Bureaucracies, he noted, were organized for maximum efficiency, were based on the principle of legal rationality, and used hierarchical structure tied together by formal chains of command and systems of communication. Stroup, among others, has argued that the Weberian model fits the university.[13] Indeed many aspects of university life such as appointments, tenure decisions, promotions, even the very chartering of the institution by the state are bureaucratic acts.

A second pattern of governance derives from the *collegial model* of a university. There is a substantial body of literature which consciously rejects the notion of a university as a bureaucracy. The Weberian model, it is argued, *may* account for *structure* and *formal* authority, but it does not speak to *process* or to *informal* authority in the university, and these latter two are at least as important, if not more so. At the heart of the collegial model is the concept of community, in this case the community of scholars.

> I do not believe that the concept of hierarchy is a realistic representation of the interpersonal relationships which exist within a college or university.

> The concept of community presupposes an organization in which functions are differentiated and in which specialization must be brought together, or coordination if you will, is achieved not through a structure of superordination and subordination of persons and groups, but through a dynamic of consensus.[14]

The collegial model is advocated as a practical, i.e., operable plan for the management of the university and it is argued that this model is consistent with the professionalization of the professoriate and with a minifest rebellion against the depersonalization of life as this occurs in a complex, urbanized, technological society.

A third pattern of governance has been identified which derives from a radically different model of the academic community. This pattern has been characterized as the political model in which governance is a process or instrument of conflict resolution.[15] In the political model governance is a process characterized by the exercise of power. What in the collegial model was called the "dynamic of consensus" in the political model becomes the prevalence of one group (or set of interests) over others, there usually being more than two contesting any given issue.

These three basic patterns of governance have been present not only in institutions, but also in libraries. Recall the 1911 action of Columbia mentioned earlier which related faculty rank to hierarchical position in the library—the Weberian bureaucratic model. Academic libraries continue to display a high correlation between level of hierarchical position and rank. This is reflected in the pyramidal structure of compensation for academic librarians which remains essentially unaltered since Heim and Cameron's first survey.[16]

Increasing numbers of academic libraries have reacted to faculty status by developing basic documents of governance, e.g., constitutions, by-laws. Some of these experiences will be described in papers presented during this conference. Governance documents have been variously legitimized—sometimes by consent within the library, sometimes in response to a campus governance system or administrative directive which requested each academic unit to produce a basic governing document, sometimes at the initiative of and through interaction with a faculty library committee. The scope of these documents varies as well—broad and inclusive, lengthy and specific, brief and general. Some of these documents provide a role for the Library Faculty and non-Faculty staff in the selection and/or evaluation of the Library's administrative officers (e.g., Minnesota). Occasionally, one finds that governance for the library is not in a separate document but is imbedded in a campus wide document (e.g., Ohio State). A common element in all governance documents is provision for handling personnel matters. In varying degrees of specificity, procedures, criteria, committees, and the like are established for recommending appointments, promotion, tenure, raises, etc.

So much for governance. A *third* implication of faculty status will be a dramatic change in the quality of academic library staffs. The most important aspect of this qualitative change will be evident in attitudes toward work. The academic librarian will view his/her job less in terms of time—hours a day or week—and more in terms of a commitment to a sense of responsibility. Faculty status will accelerate the professionalization of academic librarians.

A fourth point needs to be mentioned briefly here. How will the rationale for faculty status affect classification of other positions in the library? It may be heresy, but the fact is that all the professional positions in a contemporay academic library of any size are not appropriately classified as academic. Indeed, the library is the only unit on campus which has tried to advance the psoposition that professional is *ipso facto* academic. Consider the professional support staff in a dean's office. It is not classified as academic although the individuals in these positions may have earlier held academic positions and may, often do, return to academic positions. To continue to insist that all professional positions in the library should be academic not only defies logic and reality but also weakens the legitimate claim for those librarians whose positions are properly classified as academic.

PROBLEMS OF FACULTY STATUS

What problems remain? The most persistent problem is implementation. We must accept the responsibilities as well as revel in the benefits of full membership in the faculty fraternity. Among other things, this will require accepting the general standards of performance which are applied to faculty. But beware of false standards. Faculty performance standards are, to paraphrase Winston Churchill, myths enshrouded in a cloud and wrapped in secrecy. A healthy dose of scepticism is also in order. For example, how much real research is going on on our campuses at any given moment in time? Your provosts won't admit to answering such a question, nor should they since they must continue to press for more. My point is only that while we continue to press ourselves to be more productive and rigorous we should not delude ourselves nor allow others to be illusionary about what is going on around the campus.

However, in addition to scepticism, I think academic librarians need to be more self confident and less defensive—in the argot of our times "assertive." I am continually reminded by colleagues in two year institutions for example, that the Master's degree in Library Science is a level of education comparable to the norm of other faculty. I am also mindful of the myth of the doctorate as a uniform level of education in all faculties on a university campus.

Collective bargaining represents a unique aspect of implementation. In 1977 the smallest number of additional campuses organized for bargaining since the early seventies, in part because those sectors which have been most receptive to bargaining, i.e., public colleges and junior/community colleges, are saturated. As the spread of bargaining slows, its effect on librarians can be tentatively assessed. Kinnelly found no effect on faculty status. Those who had it before bargaining kept it; those who did not seem not to have gained it.[19] On the question of unit determination, the NLRB has consistently recognized an affinity of function between academic librarians and other faculty and has thus included librarians in the faculty unit, excluding only those librarians identified as super-visors.[20] In public universities which are organized, only Connecticut has not included librarians in the faculty unit.

Two other problem areas remain. The first of these is education for academic librarian-ship. It is easy to kick the dog, and library education is everyone's favorite canine. It shares this distinction with many other professional schools. What is clear however, is that library school graduates are insufficiently sensitized to the responsibilities of academic librarians holding faculty appointments. If three out of four of these graduates will hold faculty appointments, the process of socializing them to the responsibilities of these appointments, while not exclusively that of library schools, must at least begin with them.

Another problem of implementation I want to touch upon is technical services. The impact of automation in technical services is clear. Many technical services librarians are in a state of despair about faculty status. Having redefined "Librarian Work" through the use of computers in cataloging, those few librarians who are left are adding their voices to the chorus singing "What do we do now to be faculty." Some have replied that the jus-tification for faculty status has always been weaker for Technical Service librarians. My own view is that the province of the catalogers—bibliographic organization and control—is, along with the other two core areas of librarianship (selection of materials and pro-viding professional assistance to users of materials) directly analogous to the activities of other faculty in the academy, whose claim to status is the same as ours. We librarians and other faculty all share the common functions of preserving, disseminating and generating information. Thus, I argue that automation, rather than weakening the claim of catalogers to faculty status, strengthens that claim by restructuring jobs and releasing professionals for more appropriate tasks.

One final comment on implementation. Working out faculty status—in governance; in evaluation; in appointment, promotion, and tenure—must occur in each institutional milieu. Just as we may learn from one another, we must also adjust to the idiosyncracies of our environments. No single implementation plan can be devised by ACRL, or anybody else, which can be dropped into place on every campus. ACRL's Academic Status Committee has done a remarkable job since its creation as a standing committee in 1969 in developing model statements for implementation.[17] Most recently the commit-tee has completed and secured the ACRL Board's approval of a set of guidelines for search and screening committees.[18]

CONCLUSION

Robert Nesbit has observed that "while it is utterly impossible to predict the future, it is also impossible to resist the temptation to try." The increase in faculty status may or may not continue. It seems certain that there will always be institutions which will not grant faculty status to librarians and other institutions will change their policies, one way or the other. I can only say that we have hard work and stress and strain ahead. However, I believe that our problems will get worked out. I reject the notion that we should abandon the effort because, to quote another of this conference's speakers "I am ambitious for academic librarianship." In any event, the fact remains that with the great increase in faculty status since 1975 it is now clearly the prevailing norm. I prefer to believe this increase is in part at least, causally related to ACRL's activities.

REFERENCES

1. H. A. Sawtelle, "The College Librarianship." *Library Journal* 103 (June, 1978): 162. See also Arthur M. McAnally, "Status of the University Librarian in the Academic Community," in Jerrold Orne (ed.) *Research Librarianship: essays in honor of Robert B. Downs* (New York: Bowker, 1971), pp. 19-50.
2. W. E. Henry. *ALA Bulletin* 5 (July, 1911): 262.
3. Edward G. Holley, "Who Runs Libraries? The Emergence of Library Governance in Higher Education." *Wilson Library Bulletin* 48 (September, 1973): 47.
4. H. William Axford, "An Overlooked Cost of Achieving a Participatory Environment." *College and Research Libraries* 35 (January, 1974): 5-6.
5. Anita R. Schiller, "Characteristics of Professional Personnel in College & University Libraries." (1968) ED *L020-766, p. 65.*
6. *Ibid.*, p. 64.
7. Holley, *op. cit.*, p. 44.
8. Unpublished survey. Results available from this author.
9. Richard J. Talbot and Ann von der Lippe. *Salary Structures of Librarians in Higher Education for the Academic Year 1975-76* (Chicago: Association of College & Research Libraries, 1976).
10. *Ibid.*, p. 6, and U.S. Office of Education. "Preliminary data on college and university libraries for fall, 1976." (Washington: the author, 1977).
11. See also Dwight R. Ladd, "Myths and Realities of University Governance." *College & Research Libraries* 36 (March, 1975): 97-105.
12. Richard C. Richardson, Jr., "Governance Theory: a Comparison of Approaches." *Journal of Higher Education* (May, 1974): 344-354.
13. Herbert Stroup, *Bureaucracy in Higher Education* (New York: The Free Press, 1966).
14. John Millett, *The Academic Community* (New York: McGraw-Hill, 1962).
15. J. Victor Baldridge, *Power and Conflict in the University* (New York: Wiley, 1971).
16. Donald F. Cameron and Peggy Heim, *The Economics of Librarianship in College and University Libraries*, 1969-70 (Washington, D.C.: Council on Library Resources, 1970).
17. Academic Status Committee, Association of College and Reserach Libraries. *Faculty Status for Academic Librarians: a history and policy statement* (Chicago: American Library Association, 1975).
18. *College & Research Libraries News* (September, 1977): 231-233.
19. Jean R. Kennelly, "Current status of academic librarian's involvement in collective bargaining: a survey." In Millicent D. Abell (ed.), *Collective bargaining in higher education: its implications for governance and faculty status for librarians* (Chicago: American Library Association, 1976), pp. 74-90.
20. C. James Schmidt. "Collective Bargaining and Academic Librarians: a Review of the Decisions of the NLRB." *College and Research Libraries News* (January, 1973): 1-3.

Damaris Ann Schmitt

St. Louis Community College at Meramec

PROSPECTS OF COMMUNITY COLLEGE LIBRARIANSHIP

This paper explores the unique aspects of community college librarianship and its role in the American educational system. Traditional academic library services are contrasted with the specialized functions of the community college library; and projecting from current trends, the future training needs for community college librarians are outlined.

The community junior college is a reflection of American values, encouraging universal opportunity, furthering the dreams of the upwardly mobile. Correspondingly, the community junior college library, at the core of the institution, is a reflection not only of the general values but of specific library oriented values.

The two-year institution began to develop in educational thought during the 1890's when such leaders in education as William Rainey Harper and Henry P. Tappan[1] suggested that the German university model might be successfully applied to American public education. Because the first two years of university study are frequently generalized, it was thought that they might be more effectively administered on another level, possibly as a continuation of the secondary schools. The university would then deal primarily with the specialized upper division and graduate studies. William Rainey Harper was instrumental in the establishment of Joliet Junior College in Joliet, Illinois, generally acknowledged as the first public supported two year college opening in 1901. Several states adopted the innovation enthusiastically; most notably, California, which passed legislation enabling the establishment of junior college districts in 1921. By 1930 there were thirty-four junior colleges enrolling fifteen thousand students. The junior college movement gathered momentum in the early sixties, growing phenomenally from seven hundred and seventy-one colleges in 1965 to one thousand, two hundred and forty in 1977,[2] accounting for thirty percent of the students enrolled in higher education.

Throughout their history there have been three main philosophical themes that have differentiated two-year public colleges from the other types of institution, which indeed, have formed the basis of the community college philosophy. They are: the principle of open admissions, local control, and a broad-based relevant curriculum. Until the advent of the community college there was little opportunity for the lower and middle income and the lower and middle achievers. Before, they could not afford the tuition and board or could not qualify for admission. Yet life kept getting more complicated and job

418

requirements expected higher and higher levels of achievement. The public supported two-year institution offered accessible, economically feasible education. The two-year institution realized its value lay in its adaptability to its service area. Therefore it offered a broad-based curriculum: college parallel programs for those intending to save money on the first two years and then transfer, vocational–technical programs for those who need and seek career training or re-training for advanced technical skills, and finally enrichment and continuing education classes. Because of its efforts to serve its local supporters, the junior college often assumed the additional tag "community college." Community college in turn has become the popular term for the educational philosophy it represents.

Within those philosophies six major functions have evolved.[3] As previously mentioned, there are the functions of preparation for advanced study and career education. The third function, that of guidance, is one of the principal distinguishing marks of the community college. Open door policies and easy accessibility have encouraged more people than ever to attend college. Oftentimes they have never before been exposed to higher education. It has been observed quite accurately that it takes an education to get one; the guidance function of the community helps those students adjust and evaluate the options now available. The provision of developmental education is closely allied to the guidance function. Open door admissions mean a great deal to students who may not have "hit their stride" while in high school. It also provides opportunities for those who may not have had the advantages of formal education. However, once they are admitted they are tested and are then directed in developmental programs. Most developmental programs are designed to diagnose and evaluate the level of achievement and then lay out a plan to work up to the college level.

The final two functions reflect the involvement of the college with its community. The general education function of the college is intended to help the student, through the variety of its offerings, to orient him or herself within society. Finally, in coordination with the general education function, there is the community service function, providing enrichment courses intended to encourage the student in a life-long pursuit of education. Often, the flexibility and adaptability of the community service area of the college is an index to the sensitivity of the administration to the external environment. Ideally the college can adapt its offerings to serve the need or reflect the ambitions of its community. The functions outlined above are extensive and ambitious. The community college, it seems, would try to be all things to all people. In fact, the individual college can only strive to attain its objectives. If they are congruent with those of the community, the college can mean a great deal to many people.

The service efforts of the community college affect every facet of its operation but none so much as the library at the core of the institution. Traditionally academic library services have been important, but often passive. Teachers and students, even administrators did not need to be reminded of the role of the library in the preservation and dissemination of the cultural heritage. Services extended are part of a vast scholarly tradition, and, as such, are generally understood by the academic community. Community college libraries are not research-oriented, at most they only seek to train in research methodology, not to serve it. Their collections tend to be broad, introductory, and rarely range above one hundred thousand volumes. The emphasis is on comprehension and accessibility. Rather than serving the best collection of books, the intent is to serve the students and staff. In the traditional academic library, innovations are predominantly library function oriented rather than institution function oriented. Until the recent surge of interest in bibliographic instruction, there has been little interface between instructional programs and the academic librarians. Community college libraries tend to be more involved in the institution as a whole than four-year or university libraries, because of the interplay of the six functions of service. Open door admissions and guidance are probably the two most important factors in community college library philosophy. As mentioned earlier, a larger percentage of the student body is unfamiliar with the usages of higher education; developmental students may be afraid and intimidated in the bargain. While faculty members would seem to be the logical intermediaries for their students and the establishment, often it is the librarian who can work most effectively with the student. The librarian has the advantage of a one-to-one relationship in a less formal, less threatening, or grade-oriented environment. I personally refer to this phenomenon as the "performance affect." Occasionally, to capture the attention of the developmental learner, or to soothe the anxieties of a returning student, it is necessary to work in the mode of interaction analysis. The community college librarian may work more with the concepts of communication than with actual librarianship.

The community college librarian has the additional responsibility of the developmental and guidance functions. Many students simply cannot assimilate college level materials in their traditional mode of presentation; therefore, the community college librarian makes the effort to present the material not only on different comprehension levels, but in different formats. Community colleges are deeply involved with format interpretation, moving beyond the traditional monograph point of view. Their libraries are so involved with the instructional process and with multi-media presentation of information that they are commonly referred to in the professional literature as learning resource centers or instructional resource centers. The principal function of the learning resource center in regard to multi-media is the provision of commercially prepared materials; films, tapes, slides, videotapes, simulation games, etc. The librarian plays an important role in this area, since many of the media are not "mature" enough to have developed an extensive or readily identifiable literature. The librarian finds and facilitates. As faculty and students grow accustomed, even dependent, upon the wide range of media, the librarian and faculty member will often coordinate efforts to produce locally useful materials. One step further in the process is curriculum design—the librarian serving as consultant and coordinator as faculty members "package" entire course or sections in various formats, allowing the student to choose for his or her own best advantage. Community college librarians are pivotal in the development of Immediate Access and Self-Directed Learning programs where students can contract for a class at any point in the semester, and work through a program of media aides and readings with the advice and counsel not only of a faculty member in the subject area, but with a librarian as well.

Throughout this paper it has been repeatedly stressed that librarians must interact with the faculty in order to be effective on the junior college level. It is difficult to determine which came first, interaction or faculty status, but it is generally accepted that a higher percentage of community college librarians have full faculty status than do other academic librarians. The easiest explanation for this is degree parity. Community colleges stress teaching excellence and offer introductory level materials, or offer vocational-technical programs for which there is no doctoral level discipline. Therefore there is a tendency to hire the majority of the faculty at the Master's level, (64% in a recent survey[4]). Since the librarians have the same degree, and all faculty are more interested in instruction, and librarians are active within the instructional process, it is easy to justify faculty status for professionals.

Community college librarians also have a unique relationship with part of the teaching staff. It is easy to pursue the traditional academic role and stress college parallel and general education and enrichment courses. It is not as easy to provide instructional resource materials for the myriad vocational–technical programs. Many programs are in long established disciplines with traditionalized instruction and media; nursing, horticulture, criminal justice, hotel and restaurant technology, to name but a few. There are many offerings that are equally well-developed professionally, but they are not adapted to academic presentation. Often, it is the librarian who provides the interface, providing access to materials and adapting them so that they are useful on the introductory level. In addition, the librarian, through the preliminary faculty orientation process, is often the first contact for vocational–technical staff with the academe. Depending on that contact, the librarian and the instructional resource center can affect the teaching style of new faculty.

Like all other institutions, community colleges are affected by external trends and internal adjustments. Few institutions of any sort have been left unscathed by inflation. The tax-supported schools face inflation directly through lowered tax allocations, and indirectly through the effect on their service areas. As the college faces cutbacks, the instructional resource center, an easily identifiably four to six percent block of the budget, is often an attractive place to begin carving. In order to survive into the future, maintaining the same level of service, the community college librarian will have to cope not only with book prices that are moving into whole new frontiers of incredulity, but with the rapidly-rising prices of petroleum-based multi-media materials, and the rising utility prices for the energy to run the machines to make the materials accessible. Most colleges can justify risky financial status for a year or two based on rising enrollment trends, yet enrollments are dropping. The boom of the Viet Nam draft is over and the boom of the Viet Nam veteran is tapering off. The future community college librarian will be more actively involved in the public relations function, as he or she deals with the community users as part of the outreach program. The community colleges that mushroomed in the sixties are settling in now, assuming the characteristics of more "mature" institutions. They are past their pioneer days of small, closely-knit faculties, less-formal administration styles, and a general feeling of esprit de corps. The community college librarian of the future will have to take a leaf from the experience of the academic librarian regarding operations and cooperation within hierarchies and systems. All of these trends are affecting the entire higher education system of the United States. Other institutions seeking to stabilize enrollments as well as representing the needs of their communities are now offering programs in vo-tech and general education courses leading to the associates degree. As competition for students accelerates, there is the equally grave problem of the teacher and librarian glut. Perhaps due in part to the tremendous surge of interest in obtaining education, the surfeit becomes worse than ever since the community colleges have ceased to grow apace. Indeed, community colleges like other institutions are seeking ways to cut budgets. Before outright layoffs they often seek to cut faculty benefits and traditional privileges. Just as faculty members turn to professional organizations, so will the community college librarian of the future. Librarians, as small self-interest groups turning to unionization, may have far-reaching effects on their profession as well as their professional environment. In some instances all the trends and accompanying adjustments seem to lead inevitably to one conclusion—economics vs. service. Community college libraries priding themselves on their impact on instruction through the wide-ranging services are facing serious decisions.

Automation is more than a trend; it affects more than the community college; it has changed the character of American life and rearranged the traditional systems of organization. All community colleges use computers to some extent in their admissions and grading procedures; most colleges teach computers on one level or another; many colleges have their own systems. When the college has its own system, frequently the instructional resource center can piggyback on its services. The community college librarian of the future will be involved in programs and designs previously thought impractical or unwieldy for small collections or comparatively low circulations.

Automation affects every sort of library and librarians in all types of services. Library schools acknowledge computers as part of the future and are offering more and more programs geared to the usage of computer technology. Library schools are beginning to acknowledge the unique role of the community college—there are several courses now available in the area. Some elements in the future of community college librarianship might require specialized training; for example, curriculum design, coordination of vocational–technical materials, and working with the special educational needs of developmental students. However, most of the future of community college librarians applies to all accademic librarians.

Continuing education is the theme of the future, not only for librarians wishing to update their skills, but as the underlying principle of the educational establishment. The American public has accepted the philosophy of universal education and has developed vast myths about its own literacy level. Parts of American life require higher education. In many areas the effort is to make the process *fun*, but in doing so, they have removed the job of challenge, and the satisfaction of achievement. The community college seeks to reintroduce the public to its own education; to realize that it is a continuous process. The issue is to reconcile the philosophies of education with the newly perceived needs of the public. Community college librarians can and will play an important role in inculcating the continuing education process, its joy and challenge, through their services to their students.

REFERENCES

1. Charles R. Monroe, *Profile of the Community College* (San Francisco; Jossey–Bass Inc., 1975), p. 12.
2. Barbara Smith, "The Impact of the Community College on Academic Libraries and Librarianship," *Journal of Academic Librarianship* 3 (January 1978): 338.
3. Fritz Veit, *The Community College Library* (Westport, Connecticut: Greenwood Press, 1975), p. 7.
4. Kenneth Allen and Loren Allen, *Organization and Administration of the Learning Resource Center in the Community College* (Hamden, Connecticut: Shoe String Press, 1973), p. 9.

BIBLIOGRAPHY

Allen, Kenneth, and Allen, Loren. *Organization and Administration of the Learning Resources Center in the Community College.* Hamden, Connecticut: Shoe String Press, 1973.

Born, Jean S. "Do Community College Librarians Have Faculty Status?" Mimeographed. Mesa, Arizona: Mesa Community College, 1977.

Carnegie Commission on Higher Education. *The Open-Door Colleges: Policies for Community Colleges.* New York: McGraw-Hill, 1970.

Dale, Doris Cruger. "Questions of Concern: Library Services to Community College Students," *Journal of Academic Librarianship* 3 (May, 1977): 81–84.

Gleazer, Edmund. *Project Focus: A forecast study of community colleges.* New York: McGraw-Hill, 1973.

Medsker, Leland and Tillery, Dale. *Breaking the Access Barriers: A profile of two year colleges.* New York: McGraw-Hill, 1971.

Monroe, Charles R. *Profile of the Community College.* San Francisco: Jossey–Bass, 1975.

Peskind, Ira J. "The Junior College Library," *Library Trends* 23 (January, 1975) 383–391.

Smith, Barbara. "The Impact of the Community College on Academic Libraries and Librarians," *Journal of Academic Librarianship* 3 (January, 1978) 338–341.

Thomson, Sarah K. *Learning Resource Centers in Community Colleges.* Chicago: American Library Association, 1975.

Veit, Fritz. *The Community College Library.* Contributions in Librarianship and Information Science, Number 14. Westport, Connecticut: Greenwood Press, 1975.

Wallace, James O. "Newcomer to the Academic Scene: The two year college library/learning center." *College and Reserach Libraries* 37 (November, 1976) 503–513.

Wheeler, Helen R. *The Community College Library: A plan for action.* Hamden, Connecticut: Shoe String Press, 1965.

Mary H. Beilby and Glyn T. Evans

State University of New York

TOWARD AN INFORMATION SYSTEM FOR RESPONSIVE COLLECTION DEVELOPMENT

This paper describes the basic structure of an information system for library collection analysis which is under development. The system provides for the analysis of existing machine-readable data such as OCLC distribution tapes, computerized circulation records, enrollment records, as well as specially developed library management data. The system allows for an analysis of collections, enrollment, use, etc. by subject. It goes beyond the usual subject analysis in which each record is assigned to only one subject by allowing multiple assignment of records. Further, this system will be offered as a service by the developing agency permitting libraries to utilize the system without extensive staff involvement or access to computer facilities.

Fiscal constraints and social pressures are forcing higher education administrators to examine all campus operations in detail. A specific area of concern to academic libraries is the cost effectiveness of the acquisition/selection process. There is evidence that libraries may be purchasing, processing and storing volumes which will not be used in the foreseeable future.[1] A number of suggestions have been made to rationalize and improve the cost effectiveness of library acquisitions and selection. The basic requirements in this process are information:

> about what libraries have acquired in each subject;
> about what is being published in each subject;
> about the academic and research programs of the institution;
> about the use of the library collection in each subject; and
> about user satisfaction and dissatisfaction.

In a project administered by SUNY Central Administration and sponsored by the U.S.O.E. Libraries and Learning Resources for one year commencing October 1977, the writers have been concerned with developing methods of acquiring and analyzing the first three categories of information above. The project has not dealt with use and user satisfaction data, although they are a very important component in the library acquisition-selection decision.

This work can be viewed as the first stage in a long-range research effort to develop a management information system (MIS) for academic library collection development.

INFORMATION SYSTEM STRUCTURE

The basis of an information system is a set of well-defined data elements aggregated into useful and appropriate categories. These data are then manipulated by computer programs designed to produce reports useful to decision makers.

The primary effort has been to use data which exist in automated cataloging systems, acquisitions systems, academic program data bases and automated publishing records. This avoids the cost of separate data collection and provides a natural linkage to, and consistency with, other institutional systems.

One of the major concerns was to identify useful aggregations of the data elements. There is a strong case to be made for structuring library collection data according to subject because, historically, library collections have been developed on the basis of subject. One purpose of the library is to provide library collections to support the curricular and research interests of the institution.

It is apparent that one must define subject content in order to diagnose collection development problems. One cannot treat subject deficiencies or user frustration without identifying which subjects are deficient.

DEFINING SUBJECTS

Many libraries have defined the subjects which they intend to collect and the degree to which each subject will be collected. These subject profiles are specific to an institution and discourage comparison of collections among libraries.

In an attempt to provide national subject guidelines to evaluate and compare library collections, the ALA, RTSD Collection Development Committee adopted a "cut" of the L.C. Classification[2] based on an earlier one developed by Ortopan at Berkeley.[3] This division of the classification schedule makes sense as a device to describe subject strengths, monitor collection growth, and compare collections. However, the possibility of relating the subjects of library holdings to academic programs is almost nil. A simple cut of the classification does not take into account the interrelatedness of knowledge. For instance, Biochemistry would appear under Chemistry, and its relationship to Biology would be obscured. L.C. classifies statistics under QA (Mathematics), yet a simple cut of QA obscures the relevance of statistics to Biology, to Business Administration, Agriculture, etc.

Work performed at SUNY Central on a previous grant project[4] defined a procedure for collection analysis called 'component analysis' in which call numbers from any part of the classification schedule can be grouped together to define a subject. Computer programs count records allocated to each hierarchic subject description.

The subjects defined for 'component analyses' in the current project are intended to reflect the interrelatedness of knowledge, to be generalizable to a number of institutions, and to be compatible with the taxonomy used to describe instructional programs in higher education.

In order to allow comparison between the subjects contained in library collections, acquisitions, publishing output and instructional programs as well as to allow comparison among libraries the project has developed a translation or crosswalk between the L.C. Classification and the Higher Education General Information Survey Taxonomy (HEGIS).[5] HEGIS provides a taxonomy of approximately 450 instructional programs which is the basis of the national system of reporting enrollment and degrees granted at post-secondary institutions. The translation serves as a link between bibliographic records of publishing and library acquisitions (L.C.) and instructional programs (HEGIS). (See Figure 1.) In the project, 30 subject specialist librarians constructed machine-readable

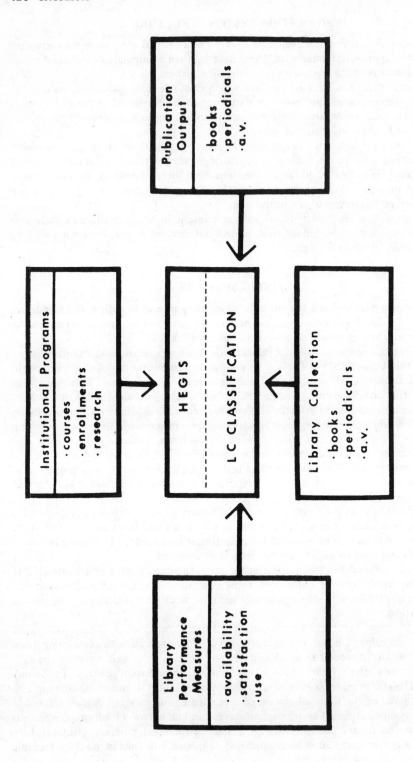

Figure 1.

tables of over 12,000 L.C. numbers and ranges of numbers through which bibliographic data could be sorted into the 450 HEGIS categories. These 450 groups can also be aggregated into any number of larger groupings.

It is also possible to correlate items acquired or held by a library with the demand for library materials expressed by such campus academic data as FTE students, student headcount, faculty FTE, sponsored research, student credit hours, etc. In SUNY, these data are available through the SUNY Central Course and Section Analysis (CASA) system, which records campus activity through use of the HEGIS Taxonomy.

Table 1 illustrates the use of the LC/HEGIS translation, library cataloging data, a campus CASA file, and the computer prgrams, to correlate newly cataloged titles recorded on the OCLC Distribution Tapes with student credit hours generated at one of the SUNY campuses. By correlating these two data elements it is not implied that there necessarily should be a direct relationship between student credit hours and titles cataloged. Rather, the purpose is to illustrate that it is possible to obtain and demonstrate such data analyses. Many correlations must be analyzed and interpreted before any conclusions can be drawn.

TABLE 1

Comparison of Titles Cataloged with Student Credit Hours in One SUNY Institution

HEGIS Group	Number of Titles	Percent of Titles	Number of Student Credit Hours	Percent of Student Credit Hours
Education				
08 Education	455	9.60	2,065	3.1
Math and Computer Science	369	7.80	13,179	19.8
07 Computer & Info. Sci.	112	2.30	3,563	5.3
17 Mathematics	345	7.30	9,616	14.4
Physical Sciences and Engineering	811	17.20	11,614	17.4
02 Architecture & Envirn. Sci.	161	3.40		
02 Engineering	376	8.00		
19 Physical Sciences	432	9.10		
Psychology				
20 Psychology	1,646	35.00	7,569	11.3
Social Sciences	3,066	65.20	31,994	48.1
Total	4,696	99.9	66,421	100.

Data: SUNY OCLC Distribution Tape, Jan.–Mar. 1977. Sc̄ted by Partial LD/HEGIS Translation, May, 1978. All subjects are not represented in this analysis. Student credit hour data from *SUNY Course and Section Analysis* file, Fall, 1976.

Table 2 illustrates the use of the LC/HEGIS translations to sort publication data into HEGIS subjects and to derive cost data. *The Book Publishing Record (BPR)* machine-readable tapes for 1975 through 1977 were used in this analysis.* All records were sorted

---

*The project is very grateful to R. R. Bowker and Co. of its kindness in making the tapes available for analysis by the project.

by imprint data and then by L.C. number. Soft cover prices were included if there was no hard cover edition. It should be noted that approximately 25% of the 1977 imprints will be found in the 1978 *BPR*, which was not included in this analysis.

TABLE 2

Analysis of B.P.R. Data by Four-Digit HEGIS (Social Sciences)

Subject	1975–77 Titles	Avg. Price	1977 Titles	Avg. Price	1976 Titles	Avg. Price	1975 Titles	Avg. Price
Social Sciences	24,610	$13.44	6,543	$13.40	9,543	$13.74	8,524	$13.40
General Soc. Sci.	446	$14.86	119	$14.71	183	$16.43	144	$13.00
Anthropology	2,694	$15.23	719	$14.87	1,056	$16.17	919	$14.45
Archaeology	849	$16.40	225	$15.62	324	$17.82	300	$15.44
Economics	6,665	$14.12	1,833	$14.05	2,546	$14.51	2,286	$13.73
History	10,326	$13.36	2,605	$13.56	4,006	$13.33	3,715	$13.25
Geography	1,373	$14.44	392	$14.71	526	$14.19	455	$14.49
Political Science	3,231	$12.52	872	$12.60	1,275	$12.97	1,084	$11.94
Sociology	3,509	$11.45	1,044	$11.02	1,333	$12.10	1,132	$11.09
Criminology	755	$12.68	252	$12.55	260	$13.02	243	$12.44
Internat. Relations	820	$15.37	193	$15.53	339	$16.31	288	$14.14
Afro Amer. Studies	217	$10.76	52	$12.44	88	$10.12	77	$10.35
Urban Studies	1,783	$14.22	539	$14.07	691	$14.71	553	$13.76
Demography	450	$16.70	133	$16.78	175	$18.01	142	$14.94
Womens Studies	1,120	$ 9.68	333	$ 9.11	425	$ 9.96	362	$ 9.87

The ability to analyze publication data according to HEGIS related subject categories may be much more relevant to collection development personnel than the data now published annually using 23 Dewey Decimal Classification-related groupings specified by an American National Standards Institute Standard.[6] It is anticipated that this type of data will be of use in planning and justifying acquisitions budgets. By matching the *BPR* data against the library OCLC tapes one could analyze the books purchased in contrast to those not purchased, identify missed titles, and, in a multi-branch or campus system, could identify the total coverage of the library system. Research and special libraries would also want to analyze the foreign publishing output since such data, although not available presently, may readily be incorporated. However, the majority of the currently cataloged titles in most academic libraries are English-language materials, and therefore the process has immediate applicability and utility.

The project recently completed demonstrates a means by which libraries can gather and correlate, at reasonable cost, information about the subjects of books already in the collection, the subjects of books being currently cataloged and books being published. It also provides the capacity to analyze university academic programs and relate these to bibliographic records. Additional data bases containing serial, foreign language, circulation and acquisitions records having L.C. classification numbers can be easily incorporated, as can additional campus management data.

PERFORMANCE MEASURES

Library collections should also be evaluated in terms of demand supplied (outputs) as well as in terms of total holdings (inputs).

Several collection-related performance measures have been suggested in the literature such as circulation, availability, document delivery capability, and user satisfaction. The preponderance of available research concentrates on circulation as a performance measure.

Circulation is an output measure which is highly dependent on the available collection, i.e. nothing can circulate which is not currently in stock. A number of circulation studies are available which analyze use by subject discipline. All found that distribution of circulation by discipline is somewhat predictable within a single library.[7,8,9] McGrath and Pierce attempted to explain the relationship between use, student enrollment, and disciplinary characteristics.[10,11] Pierce developed an acquisitions allocation formula based on the increase or decrease in circulation which could be predicted due to variations in enrollment. These studies focus on total circulation within disciplines and do not analyze the range of titles consulted or the multiple use of a core of titles.

Schad believes that the primary reason for considering enrollment in collection decisions is to determine need for duplicate copies as opposed to a larger selection of titles.[12] The proposed SUNY formula also takes this approach to the factor of enrollments.[13]

Availability is a second output measure which may help to define collection adequacy. Availability refers to the shelf availability of needed items. Availability may be frustrated by failure to acquire, by circulation to another library user, misplacement within the library or by user failure. Buckland conducted studies at the University of Lancaster in which he identified sources of unavailability.[14] Schofield conducted similar studies at Sheffield in which he categorized availability by discipline.[15] The availability measure does not have the major drawback which circulation has, in that it is not limited to measuring availability only of the existing stock of books; it can be extended to measure unavailability for reason of non-acquisition. Saracevic, Shaw and Kantor have developed a measure which is closely related to availability which they label satisfaction/frustration.[16] It is a refinement which allows analysis of the cause of frustration.

Availability, satisfaction/frustration and document delivery capability permit comparison of performance over time and among libraries since the measure is expressed in a percent of demands satisfied rather than as a gross number as is circulation. Comparison of performance at intervals allows a judgement on whether service is improving.

The information system developed in this project *can serve as the basis for future exploration* of the relationships among library performance, library collections, book production and academic programs, if library use is seen as the *feedback mechanism which informs and modifies the acquisition/selection decision.* Further work will pursue this relationship, which can be expressed through a modest realignment of the components described in Figure 1, as shown in Figure 2.

CONCLUSION

This paper reports some progress in a project to define library management data which describe the need for, and allocation of, library acquisition funds by discipline. It is recognized that the procedures described are not the total answer to library acquisition allocation and that further research is needed. In particular it is essential that the 'performance' components need to be refined and improved, and a way found to integrate the 'performance' data with the new acquisition/selection data in a closed systematic loop.

The advantages of the procedures proposed in the paper are that they rely on relatively inexpensive and universally accessible data and that the use of LC and HEGIS data as the basis for subject analysis make the process available to many academic libraries.

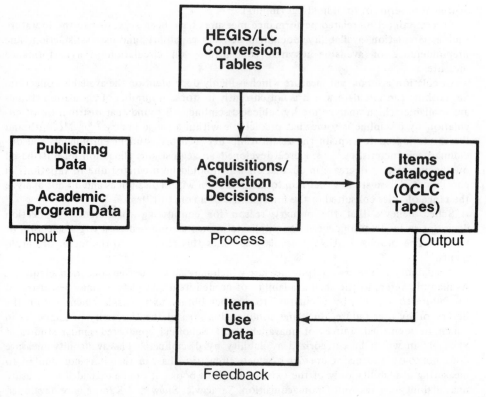

Figure 2.

The data and results embodied in the paper should be regarded as descriptive of the process, rather than definitive of subjects analyzed. The authors stress that although the LC/HEGIS tables evolve from core descriptions of subjects they can not be established as hard and fast definitions. In fact, they are open to evaluation and adaption at anytime. Institutions are different, and they are, as is knowledge, unique, dynamic, living organisms. It is the function of these programs to register and assess that essential vitality.

REFERENCES

1. *A Cost-Benefit Model of Some Critical Library Operations in Terms of Use of Materials: Final Report.* (Pittsburgh, University of Pittsburgh, 1977).
2. "Guidelines for the Formulation of Collection Development Policies." *Library Resources and Technical Services* 21 (Winter 1977): 40–47.
3. L. D. Ortopan, *Titles Classified by the Library of Congress Classification—University of California Libraries 1973* (Berkeley, General Library, University of California, 1974).
4. G. T. Evans, R. Gifford, D. R. Franz. *Collection Development Analysis Using OCLC Archival Tapes.* Final Report Project No. 475AH60088, Grant No. G007603346. (November 1977. ED 152299).
5. Robert A. Huff, *A Taxonomy of Instructional Programs in Higher Education* Washington, DC, U.S. Printing Office, 1970).

6. American National Standards Institute "USA Standard for Compiling Book Publishing Statistics, Z39.8-1968." (New York, ANSI, 1968).

7. W. E. McGrath "Relationships Between Subject Characteristics and Use of Books in a University Library." (Unpublished dissertation. Syracuse University, 1975).

8. Ching Chih Chen, "Applications of Operations Research Models to Libraries: A Case Study of the Use of Monographs in the Francis A. Countway Library of Medicine, Harvard University. (Unpublished dissertation. Case-Western Reserve University, 1975).

9. *A Cost-Benefit Model of Some Critical Library Operations in Terms of Use of Materials: Final Report* (Pittsburgh, University of Pittsburgh, 1977).

10. Thomas J. Pierce, "The Economics of Library Acquisitions: A Book Budget Allocation Model for University Libraries." (Unpublished dissertation. University of Notre Dame, 1976).

11. McGrath, *op. cit.*

12. Jasper G. Schad, "Allocating Materials Budgets in Institutions of Higher Education." *Journal of Academic Librarianship* 36 (January 1978): 328-332.

13. SUNY Office of Library Services, "Formula for Current Library Acquisitions: a proposal." (Albany, NY, SUNY Central Administration, 1976).

14. M. K. Buckland, *Book Availability and the Library User* (New York, Pergamon Press, 1975).

15. J. L. Schofield, A. Cooper and D. H. Waters. Evaluation of an Academic Library's Stock Effectiveness. *Journal of Librarianship* 7 (July 1975): 208-227.

16. T. Saracevic, W. M. Shaw, Jr., P. B. Kantor, "Causes and Dynamics of User Frustration in an Academic Library." *College & Research Libraries* 38 (January 1977): 7-18.

C. Roger Davis

Smith College

THE COMPLEAT COLLECTION DEVELOPER

Despite automation elsewhere, the future collection developer will still need to be human. Institutions are developing new modes of governance and co-operation, scholarship has become less discipline-oriented and more problem-oriented, and faculty have become restive and anxious. This requires that collection development have central direction. The old degrees are still needed, but with a degree of difference; the ability and willingness, through print, lecture, or association, to set goals, raise funds, involve satellite institutes, serve the faculty better by saving them more, and promote the liberal arts. Hardly the Snark as a Boojum, this new role, though fraught with chi-squares, involves a return to "Books, Ideas, People."

This author pleads guilty to semantic subterfuge in writing this paper; subterfuge of three sorts. First, by "the compleat collection developer" is not meant a new toy that one can look forward to—a massaging Barcalounger, a transforming Cuisinart, a marvelous custom-designed device in decorator colors and high-impact plastic for toning up flabby collections, filling them out where they're thin and making ugly fat disappear. Rather, we are talking about a person, not a machine. Second, this will not be about the person who develops complete collections, but the ambiguity has been left in to attract anyone who still thought that possible. Third, use of the word "compleat" is a shameless appeal to that which is most professional in us, historically: the desire for completeness. That is, the desire to be perfectly equipped or skilled; accomplished. The desire for this kind of completeness has become widespread; *Books In Print* lists 48 titles beginning with the archaic spelling of "complete," from *The Compleat Academic* to *The Compleat Were-wolf*. Probably none can compete with the best-known example of this type, though, Izaak Walton's *The Compleat Angler* (1653), and this author can't pretend to either. However, one can cast out some flies, bait a few hooks, and share thoughts on the future role of the collection developer.

In the recent *Festschrift* honoring Jerrold Orne, one writer states that the collection developer of the year 2000 "will deal with a world in which there is more of everything: more books and journals, more specialization, more inflation, more use of microformats, more access to everything, more federal and state governmental involvement, and more students," and he goes on to cover those points.[1] While this statement has a breezy

432

appeal, to describe the kind of person needed, we need to look more closely at the institutional setting. In it we see several tendencies among which are:

1. Some colleges are shutting down completely. Others are finding their independence eroded by the demands of their funding bodies or the dominance of larger, even more dependent institutions in their system or consortium.

2. The demand for courses in the traditional departments of the humanities is declining, particularly at the graduate level. Funds for faculty and library resources, if any, are being shifted to the social sciences, often to new programs of cross-disciplinary content and uncertain duration.

3. New, semi-autonomous inter-disciplinary institutes of an *ad hoc* but semi-permanent nature are being set in motion, like moons, by some universities, in the hope that the intellects thus orbiting will attract new interest to the main body of the institution.

4. This *ad hoc* fusion of disciplines into new programs and institutes is matched by a more permanent trend toward fission into subdisciplines. The kinds of anthropologists, for example, these days include biological, ecological, structural, semiotic, semiological, "etic," "emic," and ethno-[you name it].

5. Untenured faculty have become more transient and tenured faculty less mobile. Both are more restive and envious of the adjunct professors and the scholars of the first rank who now more visibly come and go like butterflies, sucking the nectar of prestigious visiting lectureships.

6. New federal, state, and institutional guidelines governing fair employment practices in interviewing, hiring, reassignment, reappointment, promotion, and dismissal, not to mention organizing and collective bargaining, have made committee work more time-consuming and tedious.

7. Belt-tightening in the form of "steady state" or "zero-based" budgeting has become institution-wide, with everyone who is bleeding grimly checking to be sure everyone else in the vicinity is bleeding just as badly.

Now into all this comes the collection developer, this reminds one of that 1969 publication *Naked Came the Stranger.* The term "collection developer" is meant to include bibliographers, book selection specialists, humanities librarians, assistant university librarians for acquisitions, and chiefs or directors or coordinators of collection development, by whatever name they are known.

One problem is that in many colleges they are not known at all, because selection is still done almost exclusively by the faculty. In some college and even large university libraries, much selection is done as a part-time assignment by reference librarians, catalogers, or the head librarian. Where faculty members have residual responsibilities for collection development, some few consider it a fair and honorable duty, as of old; others feel it their right (but seldom exercise it); others complain of being stretched by the factors already mentioned and view the library with annoyance and disaffection—partly because, like food in the Army, it is both an easy target and an unhappy reminder of an earlier Edenic state: the dinners Mom used to make; the library where I did my doctoral research and lived a life of pure reasons. Where selection is a secondary assignment for a librarian, it is often not evaluated as a part of job performance but thought to be an agreeable and harmless but often helpful hobby. In both cases, the library may develop fine collections in limited areas, but its overall holdings may be dangerously uneven.

One happy result of institutional belt-tightening in many places has been increased recognition of the fact that collection development deserves central direction. This fact must be made clear, or the "new horizon" for collection development will be a desert—drunk dry by the competing interests that do have full-time coordination and advocacy.

The skills needed to meet the tendencies mentioned earlier are as follows:

1. The ability to extract, shape, and understand the 5- and 10-year goals of one's institution and neighboring institutions, whether or not the head librarian is always out of town and the provost is said to be a congenital liar; and the willingness to help raise funds.

2. The ability and willingness to encourage collection use, through student instruction and public lectures on subjects central to the traditional departments in the humanities, and on the new programs where funds have been shifted and resources are now being acquired.

3. The initiative to seek out contacts at the new inter-disciplinary institutes and involve them in any discussions of overall collection development and financial support.

4. Awareness of the evolving divisions of substance and style and method within disciplines, and close monitoring of the kinds of research and publishing that each requires.

5. Acceptance of the role of trouble-shooter, lightning-rod, or ombudsman with respect to faculty/library relations of every kind, and student/library relations in collection development.

6. The efficiency and humility to serve the faculty better and save them more, by telling them of desired titles, research trends, grants, conferences, and institutional gossip that their colleagues or departmental secretaries used to provide but no longer do because of overwork, political estrangement, cynicism, or torpor.

7. The perseverance to maintain bibliographical control and quality control of the incoming acquisitions.[2] The ability to describe, through profiles, prose statements, or departmental or L.C. subject classifications what is being added, whether by purchase or gift, and why.

Skills like these, already routine for some of you, issue from a different world than that described by Robert Vosper just ten years ago. For an interview with Guy R. Lyle, he said,

> It's a whole new style of life. Tremendously exciting, you know! The librarians I really envy deep down in my green heart these days are those youngsters who have full-time jobs as book selection officers. If I were just smart enough and young enough to be the person who does nothing but buy books in support of medieval and renaissance studies at UCLA, it would be wonderful. Go off to Europe to visit the book shops, buy books, spend money, and not have to do anything else. I would spend my time talking to faculty and graduate students to learn what they need. It's a beautiful job, but you have to know something to do it . . . You must have a real knowledge of books, not just a vague love of books.[3]

Of course the last part is still true. The compleat collection developer would be well-advised to have a Ph.D. or have done significant research in a humanities discipline *and* have a good library degree *and* have solid library experience besides. Given the urgent work to be done and the candidates with these credentials in hand, it is hard to see why these matters are still argued. Phyllis Richmond made clear in 1957 why a Ph.D. needs a library degree, and Eric Carpenter stated in 1973 why a Ph.D. with a library degree is not enough either.[4] New horizons for academic librarians require building on this general subject knowledge, specific research capability, and library science skill.

What is being pointed to, overall, is an enlarged public role. In the past, a collection developer could pretty much sit with his catalogues and proceed. Accountability, common sense, and fulfillment, too, will soon require a lot more. Increasingly a collection developer will not really be "compleat" until he or she has had some kind of commerce with an Other: through publishing, through lectures, through association.

As for publishing, an old professor friend of mine, Robert Ralston Cawley, was a little puzzled by the "publish or perish" squawking in the '60s, because he saw publishing as a natural outgrowth of learning. He felt that what we learn—the grain that we gather—at great expense of time, effort and money, should not be stuck away in a silo somewhere, but spread out as on a seedbed, for others to work with and benefit from. In this view, it is selfish and wasteful *not* to write, and the recompense is the feeling of continual fulfillment of a natural process. Of course for a non-professor it isn't easy.

As for lectures, they can be an excellent way to stimulate student and staff interest in the collections and to make sure your circulation for the recently added titles is more than 56%, in case anyone is checking.[5]

As for association, one could quote from another of the "Compleat" titles, Henry Peacham's *The Compleat Gentleman*. It advises the university man, "Entertain . . . [those] whose conference and company may bee vnto you . . . a liuing and a mouing Library. *For conference and conuerse was the first Mother of all Arts and Science.*"

This year is an important one to enjoy all these activist roles. Harvard University's "Report on the Core Curriculum," its first major review of this subject since 1945, is expected to have widespread influence throughout American higher education.[6] The report of the "National Inquiry" on university publishing and scholarship is due this year; its conclusions could prove momentous for the future of scholarly works.[7] The Collection Development Committee of ALA's own RTSD is publishing its long-awaited guidelines on various aspects of collection development. It and two other groups in ACRL are now exploring ways of providing training for bibliographers in regional institutes.

The enlarged public role that has been envisioned should not be construed as "gadding about," which we sometimes accuse our faculties of, but as a direct way to increase specific job effectiveness, turning potentially vicious circles into virtuous ones. It's not just that to develop the seven skills already listed one needs to become adept at strategic psychological operations, or poker, or as Stephen Bailey has said, become "super managers: budgeteers, system managers, priority selectors, negotiators, compromisers, 'Dear Abbys,' and policemen."[8] It's not just that by writing you force yourself to think in disciplined ways, or that by lecturing you learn what your users think, or that through association you learn more about specific new subjects, treatments, methods, tools, dealers, or markets. It is that from this enlarged public role one can learn again to put the "why" before the "how."

"Again," because most of us learned about the "why," about the principles of library service, in school. But lately our profession has followed others in allowing some aspects of the "how" to dominate both the training period (whether at library school or on the job) and the work experience unduly. One thinks especially of a kind of battle that has been allowed to surface between the literates and the numerates, or, if you prefer, the debate about the proper place and contributions of quantiative methods and mathematical models. The literates, though concerned about classes and types, believe that these cannot be reduced to numbers or that science does not consist in accumulating "coefficients of correlation . . . without asking which theories lead one to expect what kind of a connection among which variables."[9] The numerates dismiss as mere hunches based on (inferior) "insight" the elaborate ruminations of their opponents. These in turn ridicule the costly calculations that say nothing about causes, and the endless correlations among variables lifted from their contexts that too often conclude that no conclusive evidence can be derived from them.

Happily, in the Orne *Festschrift, Academic Libraries by the Year 2000*, the chapter on operations research, by Herbert Poole and Thomas H. Mott, Jr., is a thoughtful, practical, and well-written essay that also helps bring these two sides together in a meaningful response to the problem of problem-solving.

What should concern us, to return to the "why" of what we do, is the progession of ideological triads observed during the last few years. No so long ago, the recruitment posters were saying, "Books, Ideas, People: Be a librarian!". In his piece for the Orne *Festschrift*, Edward Holley identifies what he terms "that triad so necessary for service in an academic library's operation" as "Books, Buildings, and Staff."[10] This author's experience suggests that the operative triad now is "Materials, Budgets, and Personnel." But what is worse, we have been accused of having as our standard, "Survival, Status, and Power,"[11] and there is some basis for this allegation.

If the desire for completeness is that which is most professional in us historically, service is a close second. One can foresee a future enriched by that commitment, a commitment to "Books, Ideas, and People," a commitment which in the end is a re-commitment to the liberal arts ideal.

Those who would lead colleges and universities to abandon the liberal arts ought to be told that these studies have great practical, *vocational* advantages. In many fields there is nothing more important than an understanding of fundamental principles, an ability to analyze, to weigh evidence, to listen intelligently, to argue persuasively, to write clearly, to learn new techniques and new approaches, to adjust to new circumstances. But more than preparation for a career, one thinks of the liberal arts as providing an enhanced capacity for developing one's own personal qualities, for enjoying things of beauty, for sympathetic understanding of other people, and for the development of constructive relationships with others.

One can only hope that we're buying books that promote this and that some of our students might look forward to a day, restoring the Golden Age, when in the words of Austin Dobson, "a book was still a Book / Where a wistful man might look / Finding something through the whole / Breathing—like a human soul."

One of the contributors to the Orne *Festschrift* enthuses as follows:

> Can't you just visualize the ultimate head trip for every collection development officer in the year 2000? Seated in front of his Hazeltine X-10,000, playing upon the keyboard like Lon Chaney at the pipe organ in "The Phantom of the Opera" totally engrossed in pounding out a bibliographic orgy of row upon row of exhaustive citations, punching out commands for printouts of these and film copies of those, until finally, exhausted but exhilerated, he whirls around to face the gathered crowd of wide-eyed patrons who spontaneously burst into frenzied applause at the performance![12]

That is one possibility. On the other hand, we might be satisfied with less, and more. Anthony Burgess begins his novel *Enderby* with the observation, "That man down below, whom that clatter of cheap metal has aroused from dyspeptic and flatulent sleep, he gives it all meaning." At the beginning and throughout this novel one is inclined to laugh at this. But at the end, after all the literate fun, it may be true. Burgess writes,

> Whatever the future was going to be about, things ought to be all right, namely not too good, with enough scope for guilt, creation's true dynamo. . . . Keep on. It will come out right, given time and application. . . . So away! Our camels sniff the evening and are glad. . . . And the words slide into the slots ordained by syntax and glitter, as with atmospheric dust, with those impurities which we call meaning.[13]

The collection developer in academic libraries of the future will need to think not only about "providing information" but about the advancement of learning. He or she will brighten the future by acting on these words of Justin Winsor, written in Boston exactly 100 years ago: "A collection of good books, with a soul to it in the shape of a good librarian, becomes a vitalized power among the impulses by which the world goes on to improvement."[14]

REFERENCES

1. William H. Webb, "Collection Development for the University and Large Research Library: More and More versus Less and Less," in *Academic Libraries by the Year 2000: Essays Honoring Jerrold Orne*, ed. Herbert Poole (New York: Bowker, 1977), p. 140.
2. See David L. Perkins, *Manual for Collection Developers* (Northridge, Cal.: California State University, 1975; ERIC ED 116 681), pp. 3–4.
3. Guy R. Lyle, *The Librarian Speaking: Interviews with University Librarians* (Athens: University of Georgia Press, 1970), p. 176.
4. Phyllis A. Richmond, "The Subject Ph.D. and Librarianship," *College & Research Libraries* 18 (March 1957): 123–126, 146. Eric J. Carpenter, letter, *College & Research Libraries* 34 (July 1973): 311. See also Eldred Smith, "The Impact of the Subject Specialist Librarian on the Organization and Structure of the Academic Research Library," in *The Academic Library: Essays in Honor of Guy R. Lyle*, ed. Evan Ira Farber and Ruth Walling (Metuchen, N.J.: Scarecrow, 1974), pp. 71–81.
5. See "Pitt Study Pegs Faulty Acquisitions Patterns," *Library Journal* 102 (July 1977): 1438.
6. Henry Peacham, *The Compleat Gentleman* (London: Francis Constable, 1622), p. 39.
7. Edward B. Fiske, "Harvard Is Debating Curriculum To Replace 'General Education'," *New York Times* (26 February 1978): 1.
8. David Mycue, "University Publishing and Scholarship: An American Confrontation," *Libri* 27 (March 1977): 31–53.
9. Stephen K. Bailey, "The Future of College and Research Libraries: A Washington Perspective," *College & Research Libraries* 39 (January 1978): 5.
10. *International Politics*, ed. Fred I. Greenstein and Nelson W. Polsby (Reading, Mass.: Addison–Wesley, 1975), p. 12.
11. Edward G. Holley, "What Lies Ahead for Academic Libraries," in *Academic Libraries by the Year 2000*, pp. 24–25.
12. Doris M. Timpano, *Crisis in Educational Technology* (New York: Gilbert Press, 1970), p. 13; quoted in Damon D. Hickey, "The Impact of Instructional Technology on the Future of Academic Librarianship," in *Academic Libraries by the Year 2000*, p. 46.
13. Webb, *op. cit.*, 44–45.
14. John Anthony Burgess Wilson, *Enderby* (New York: W. W. Norton, 1968), pp. 403, 406.
15. Justin Winsor, "The College Library and the Classes," *Library Journal* 3 (March 1878): 5.

Dennis W. Dickinson

University of Kentucky

SUBJECT SPECIALISTS IN ACADEMIC LIBRARIES: THE ONCE AND FUTURE DINOSAURS

This paper argues that for reasons of lack of substantive training, the necessity to cover multiple subject areas, lack of compatibility with library organizational structure, the questionable need for "balanced" collections, and declining resources, subject specialization in academic libraries faces an uncertain future. Several developments affecting libraries are suggested which make it appear as if librarian subject specialists may become increasingly redundant over time.

INTRODUCTION

Bearing in mind Peter Drucker's admonition that effective resource allocation demands periodic review of every activity of a public service institution in a constant effort to keep the organization lean, functional and efficient,[1] this paper will critically examine the rationale for installing and maintaining librarian selectors/subject specialists/bibliographers on the staffs of academic libraries—with special attention to the changing circumstances in which the latter find themselves today.

The terms "subject specialist, librarian selector, bibliographer," etc., are, in the finest tradition of library scholarship, never clearly and univocally defined, but it seems at least safe to say that there is considerable overlap in their respective referential sets, i.e., they sometimes mean the same thing—well, sort of. Therefore, although this author is principally interested in the collection development aspects of positions so designated, the terms shall be used interchangeably without, one hopes, loss of clarity.

COLLECTION DEVELOPMENT

There can be little doubt that, in library literature,

> . . . the bulk of the writing . . . seems to be more and more in favor of library staff selection, at least for the majority of library items and within the framework of larger academic libraries.[2]

438

The arguments advanced in support of book selection by librarians are, however, written almost exclusively by librarians, often less than compelling, counter-intuitive, alogical or even illogical, and, most important within the context of this conference, increasingly out-of-date.

One finds in the literature, for instance, explanations of the needs for bibliographers and subject specialists in libraries which cite factors such as: the growth of budgets and collections, the inception of area study programs, the need to assist and/or replace faculty selectors and "balance" the development of collections, the need to cope with radical increases in the amount of literature and specialized reference tools available in virtually all areas of scholarship, etc.[3] In spite of the alleged salutory effects of placing subject specialists on library staffs, however, there is evidence that library service is less than effective[4] and has been declining in quality precisely during the period in recent years when more and more responsibility for selection has been assigned to librarians, i.e., ". . . more people, more often cannot get the information they seek from the library."[5]

Ironically, a part of the decline in libraries' abilities to meet demands placed upon them may, in fact, be attributable to the very positions within the library specifically intended to enhance this ability. That is, positions such as subject specialist were not commonly found in American libraries until the late fifties and early sixties,[6] which coincides, albeit not coincidentally, with one of the most affluent periods in the history of education in general and academic libraries in particular. However, over the twenty years or so during which the presence of subject specialists in libraries has become more and more common, the economic situation in which libraries find themselves has changed[7] in such a way as to make these positions largely anachronistic.

For instance, a significant part of the original intent in having subject specialists in libraries was to have persons in these positions spend time evaluating the libraries' collection, strengthening any areas of weakness, filling obvious gaps caused by economic crunches or oversights in the past and/or deterioration of existing material, etc. But most libraries today find themselves in a fiscal situation that does not permit the acquisition of even a major fraction of materials being published each year which are appropriate and desirable for their collections. That being the case, there is little or no money for restoration and preservation of materials already held, let alone the expensive undertaking of retrospective buying in quantities sufficient to make up deficiencies in existing collections. It has been said with considerable justification that, for most libraries, collection development has given way to mere collection maintenance;[8] and even that may be an overstatement.

Therefore, an important aspect of the subject specialist's job as originally envisioned is simply rendered obsolete by prevailing economic conditions which will, in all likelihood, extend into the indefinite future. Today, if they are doing any evaluation at all, librarians are being paid to merely catalog lacunae in the collections with no real hope that there will ever be sufficient funds to set right the errors and accidents of the past and stem the ravages of time.

It may very well be, then that subject specialists are, at this point, at least as much a part of the problem as they are the solution, insofar as they require, in order to be effective, very substantial book funds on which to draw, and their relatively high salaries come from money which could otherwise be used directly for acquisition, restoration, preservation, etc.[9] Considered in this light, the maintenance of such positions on library staffs already appears, at best, of questionable utility; and the problem of justifying their retention will probably be further aggravated by future developments affecting libraries.

INTENSION/EXTENSION CONFLICT

A selector for a given discipline is, or should be, recruited primarily for his or her expertise in a given subject area and becomes, perforce, the library's nominal, resident expert in a particular field or fields. So-called subject specialists in libraries, however, are often laboring under more or less severe handicaps arising from the necessity to collect in a large number of fields.[10] That is, in the ideal case, "where bibliographers exist in adequate numbers, they assume responsibility for collection development in one subject area,"[11] but the ideal is rarely, if ever, realized, and, in fact, ". . . the real-life library selector is called upon to spread his efforts over more subjects than any professor would presume to teach."[12]

In explanation of this Danton points out that

> . . . not only the volume, but the specialization of scholarly literature produced by the many new subfields of knowledge, results in a situation unknown in the late nineteenth century when the system of subject specialists was developed. It is unreasonable to expect . . . (subject specialists) . . . to be experts in, or able to keep up with, the literature of four or more separate subject fields as is today often the case.[13]

Should any doubt exist that subject specialists are overextended in the manner just described, one has only to consider the possibility that every such specialist be assigned to teach at least one substantive course in each of the disciplines for which he or she is responsible. Contemplation of such a possibility would—in addition to producing a high incidence of hypertension and apoplexy among the population affected—quickly and unequivocally reduce to absurdity the notion that one individual can have any degree of competence in as many fields as most bibliographers are assigned.

For the foregoing reasons, individuals are frequently and of necessity assigned subject areas in which they have no academic preparation whatsoever; and it has therefore been suggested that it is more accurate to speak of "subject responsibilities" than "specialization;"[14] and that, in general, an indefinite number of so-called subject specialists would be hard put to meet even modest standards or professional qualification.[15] This concatenation of factors, then, makes ludicrous the notion of any real specialization in most libraries.

The problem of lack of subject expertise and/or over-extension on the part of library subject specialists appears the more significant when considered in the list of allegations that

> . . . very little serious study has been done on the decision-making process in book selection. A substantial part of the (library) profession is unprepared to mold collection goals, available materials and available funds into a workable selection model. . .[16]

Such an assertion, if true, leads to the conclusion that librarians have no particular expertise in the mechanics of collection development as such which would compensate for their lack of substantive knowledge in the fields for which they select.

STRUCTURAL AND ORGANIZATIONAL PROBLEMS

Yet another type of problem associated with the employment of subject specialists in libraries arises from the fact that it is necessary, in order to fully exploit a selector's knowledge and to translate that knowledge into an excellent collection, that individual selectors be given considerable independence in their collection development activities.[17] It is, perhaps, just exactly this requirement which often results in subject specialists being indicted for elitism by other members of a library staff—i.e., it is often charged that subject specialists are "prima donnas." In any case, there is necessarily a rather high degree of freedom required for a subject specialist *qua* selector to function effectively, and the problem arising from this is that while such freedom is required for effective collection development activity, virtually no one on a library staff has just and only that responsibility; and the combination of duties assigned to a subject specialist may and often does have disadvantages for the library.[18] That is, there is very often a kind of consciously cultivated halo-effect from a given individual's selection activities, to which independence is appropriate and necessary, to other activities assigned that same individual to which an equivalent degree of autonomy is inappropriate and, moreover, frequently inimical to the best interests of the library considered as a system.[19] An individual who is and must be granted a great deal of freedom in the prosecution of some of his duties will very likely insist on at least as much freedom in carrying out other duties assigned to him, in spite of the fact that the collateral duties may and probably will be such as to require substantially more standardization, coordination and control that is desirable or possible in collection development activities alone. As the latter become more and more restricted by shrinking acquisition budgets, the amount of subject specialist participation in other aspects of library operations can reasonably be expected to grow and occupy more and more of the specialist's time, with the result that the potential for mischief arising from the freedom/determinism conflict will increase concomitantly. Most, if not all, library jobs require considerably more control and coordination than does collection development,[20] and the increasing automation of library systems along with growing participation in library networks is already and will increasingly enforce routinization and regimentation within libraries.[21] Indeed, this ". . . dysfunctional aspect of subject specialization"[22] and the "incoherence, disunity and confusion which can result from a library operating as a series of . . . uncoordinated subject libraries" have already caused some libraries to abandon subject specialization altogether.[23]

THE NEED FOR "BALANCED" COLLECTIONS

Another of the reasons often given for placing bibliographers on library staffs is the need to develop "balanced" collections. Conversely, it is argued that selection by faculty is inferior, in large part, because it ignores this need and allows some areas of the collection to be developed at the expense of others.[24] But, quite apart from the usual lack of any attempt at a definition of "balance" by those who take this tack, it is not intuitively clear that, whatever a balanced collection may be, it is necessarily a *desideratum*. That is, as the buying power of academic library budgets continues to shrink, it may become increasingly necessary to rethink the relationship between relatively predictable, long-term research needs—presumably best served by a "balanced" collection—and highly predictable, immediate needs created by the academic program itself—presumably best served by a somewhat "unbalanced" collection.

Collections in American academic libraries, until very recently, were developed almost exclusively by faculty selectors[25] and do not now and did not at any period in their history, have "balanced" collections.[26] Rather, they would seem to consist of collections of great strength in some areas and something considerably less in others. That this situation should or even could have come about through the system of librarian selectors which exist in today's university libraries is extremely doubtful. The reason for this skepticism is stated succinctly in Marvin Scilken's "First Empirical Law of Library Science" which is that

> Librarians much prefer buying books nobody wants in preference to books they know everybody wants. or

> It's better to serve a possible future reader tomorrow than an actual reader today.[27]

A corollary to Scilken's law is, of course, that it is better to build a "balanced" collection which no one uses than an "unbalanced" one which will be used. Such a line of reasoning ultimately calls into question the concept of developing academic libraries as national resources at the expense of their local clientele,[28] and with it the notion that librarian selectors are necessary to develop and maintain "balanced" collections in libraries. In spite of these pregnant questions, however, librarian selectors, with their eyes fixed steadfastly on the future and both feet too often planted firmly in mid-air, get on with the very serious business of developing "balanced"—if unread—collections.

This rush to balance can only result, over time, in the production of uniformly anemic, homogeneous, mediocre and duplicative collections in most or all libraries during a period of declining resources such as the present and foreseeable future. The end result of such a strategy will be to create collections which do not have the resources to satisfy a majority of demands made on them by their primary, local clientele; and it will have the additional deleterious effect of making interlibrary cooperation less and less effective in compensating for the deficiencies in any given collection;[29] i.e., it will become increasingly true, as De Gennaro points out, that "all too frequently, cooperation is merely a pooling of poverty."[30]

CONCLUSION

Lest it be said that this author is a cynic in Oscar Wilde's sense of one who knows the price of everything and the value of nothing, let me hasten to add that I do recognize at least one seeming exception to the above. There will likely be a continuing requirement for librarian specialists to support area studies collections which present a complex of bibliographic, linguistic, acquisition and processing problems amenable to no other apparent solution. But while one may expect an area specialist to have some proficiency in several indigenous languages, knowledge of the bibliography, publishing practices, book trade and problems of procurement in a particular geographic area, it is patently ridiculous to expect that a single subject specialist will ever master the languages, let alone the logistics, required to extend these same capabilities over the entire publishing world.[31]

Finally, there are three developments which may begin to make it possible to move away from a system of librarian selectors and toward a more rational and effective means of building collections. The first of these is the developing capabilities of jobbers to adequately service blanket order/approval plans.[32] The second is an increasing interest in publication on demand—especially in the university presses.[33] The third is the nascent, but steadily developing, system of library cooperation. One may expect that these and related future developments will, someday, lead to a situation wherein a small number of resource centers, such as the Center for Research Libraries, will collectively acquire virtually everything, while academic libraries direct their resources to meeting what are coming to be recognized as more limited local needs.[34]

Few librarian subject specialists will be required in such a situation, since the resource centers would acquire materials comprehensively, and blanket order/approval plans with well refined profiles, along with patron requests and the long-term availability of a growing number of items through publication on demand, will free individual academic libraries from the necessity to select materials as is done today.

Thus, the various rationales for retaining subject specialists on library staffs would seem to be losing whatever validity they may once have had. Like the dinosaurs, then, subject specialists may be entering a period of environmental change wherein their specialization and voracious appetites will be maladaptive to a degree which will threaten the continued survival of the specie.

REFERENCES

1. Peter F. Drucker, "Managing the Public Service Institution," *College and Research Libraries* 37 (January 1976): 4-14.
2. David O. Lane, "The Selection of Academic Library Materials, a Literature Survey," *College and Research Libraries* 29 (September 1968): 364-372.
3. C. K. Byrd, "The Subject Specialist in a University Library," *College and Research Libraries* 27 (May 1966): 191-193; J. Periam Danton, "Subject Specialists in National and University Libraries, with Special Reference to Book Selection," *Libri* 17 (1967): 42-58; James F. Govan, "Community Analysis in an Academic Environment," *Library Trends* 24 (January 1976): 541-556; Eldred Smith, "The Impact of the Subject Specialist Librarian on the Organization and Structure of the Academic Research Library," in *The Academic Library*, ed. by Evan Ira Farber and Ruth Wallig (Metuchen, NJ: Scarecrow Press, Inc., 1974), pp. 71-81.
4. Miriam A. Drake, "The Management of Libraries as Professional Organizations," *Special Libraries* 68 (May/June 1977): 181-186.
5. Charles B. Weinberg, "The University Library: Analysis and Proposals," *Management Science* 21 (1974): 130-140.
6. George S. Bonn, "Evaluation of the Collection," *Library Trends* 22 (January 1974): 265-304; Byrd, *op. cit.*, 191; Danton, *op. cit.*, 49; Govan, *op. cit.*, 548; Lane, *op. cit*, 367; Smith, *op. cit.*, 72. The term "subject specialist" appears as an entry in *Library Literature* only since 1967-69 (and always as a cross-reference), suggesting that significant literature on the subject is a phenomena of the last decade.
7. Richard De Gennaro, "Copyright, Resource Sharing and Hard Times: a View from the Field," *American Libraries* 8 (September 1977): 430-435.
8. Brett Butler, remarks to the ACM Conference on Management Issues in Automated Cataloging, Chicago, IL, November 3-5, 1977.
9. Bury, "Subject Specialist," p. 193; Robert P. Haro, "The Bibliographer in the Academic Library," *Library Resources and Technical Services* 13 (Spring 1969): 163-169.
10. Danton, *op. cit.*, 42.
11. Goven, *op. cit.*, 549.
12. Robert Wadsworth, "Building Research Collections," *The University of Chicago Library Society Bulletin* 1 (Winter 1976): 13-19.
13. Danton, *op. cit.*, 52.
14. J. E. Scrivner, "Subject Specialization in Academic Libraries—Some British Practice," *Australian Academic and Research Libraries* 5 (September 1974): 113-122.
15. Danton, *op. cit.*, 44; Smith, *op. cit.*, 72.
16. Hendrik Edelman, "Redefining the Academic Library," *Library Journal* 101

(January 1, 1976): 53–56.

17. Smith, *op. cit.*, 77.
18. *Ibid.*
19. *Ibid.*, p. 76–77; James Thompson, "The Argument Against Subject Specialization; or, Even a Good Idea Can Fail," *ARLIS Newsletter* 22 (March 1975): 3–6.
20. Smith, *op. cit.*, 78.
21. William Axford, remarks to the ACM Conference on Management Issues in Automated Cataloging, Chicago, IL, November 3–5, 1977.
22. W. L. Guttsman, "Subject Specialization in Academic Libraries: Some Preliminary Observations on Role Conflict and Organizational Stress," *Journal of Librarianship* 5 (January 1973): 1–8.
23. Thompson, *op. cit.*, 5.
24. Danton, *op. cit.*, 55.
25. Bonn, *op. cit.*, 295; Lane, *op. cit.*, 365.
26. Helen Welch Tuttle, "An Acquisitionist Looks at Mr. Haro's Bibliographer," *Library Resources and Technical Services* 13 (Spring 1969): 170–174.
27. Marvin Scilken, letter, *Wilson Library Bulletin* 52 (October 1977): 130.
28. Edelman, *op. cit.*, 55.
29. Illinois State Library, Cooperative Collection Development Subcommittee of the Research and Reference Center Directors. "Toward Cooperative Collection Development in the Illinois Library and Information Network." Springfield, IL, 1977, pp. 8–9. (Mimeographed.)
30. De Gennaro, *op. cit.*, 434.
31. Danton, *op. cit.*, 51; Smith, *op. cit.*, 71; C. Steele, "Blanket Orders and the Bibliographer in Large Research Libraries," *Journal of Librarianship* 2 (October 1970): 272–280.
32. Kathleen McCullough, Edwin D. Pasey and Doyle C. Pickett, *Approval Plans and Academic Libraries: An Interpretive Survey* (Phoenix: Orix Press, 1977), pp. 1, 134–36.
33. Malcomb G. Scully, "On-demand Publishing System Weighed for Some Scholarly Works," *Chronicle of Higher Education*, (January 23, 1978): 9.
34. De Gennaro, *op. cit.*, 433.

Barbara J. Ford and Yuri Nakata

University of Illinois at Chicago Circle

GOVERNMENT PUBLICATIONS IN HUMANISTIC RESEARCH AND SCHOLARSHIP

Government publications in general have not been utilized to their fullest extent by academic librarians or users of academic libraries. Emphasis on the use of government publications has been in support of research and instruction in the social sciences. Virtually untapped are the vast numbers of government publications which can be used to explore the ideals and values in society, touching upon every facet of our life and culture. This paper discusses how government publications are applicable to humanities research and instruction and identifies some sources appropriate to instruction and research in the humanities.

Government publications in general have not been utilized to their fullest extent by academic librarians or users of academic libraries.[1] Emphasis on the use of government publications has been in support of research and instruction in the social sciences, not surprising since much of the data collected and published by governmental agencies is statistical in nature, providing valuable material for use in the study of social science issues. Little attention has been paid to materials provided by the government which could support research or course-related instruction in the humanities. Traditional sources in humanistic scholarship do not lead the researcher to government publications. Few can be found under subjects in the card catalog or in humanities indexes. Government publications are usually not thought of in the perspective of the humanities.

Many of the publications of government agencies, historically and currently, are relevant to research and instruction in the humanities. Virtually untapped are the vast numbers of government publications which can be used to explore the ideals and values in society, touching upon every facet of our life and culture.

This paper assumes that government publications supporting the social sciences and the sciences are well known to librarians. It will identify some sources appropriate to instruction and research in the humanities.

For our purposes we will adopt a definition of the humanities used by the National Endowment for the Humanities. The humanities include but are not limited to, "history, philosophy, languages, literature, linguistics, archaeology, jurisprudence, history and criticism of the arts, ethics, comparative religion, and those aspects of the social sciences employing historical or philosophical approaches. The last category includes cultural

445

anthropology, sociology, political theory, international relations, and other subjects concerned with questions of value and not with quantitative matters."[1] The emphasis is "to encourage understanding of ideals, values, and experiences which have been or will be formative in our culture, and to relate the study of the humanities to national concerns."[3] Unlimited government publications fall into thse aspects of the humanities.

In the traditional sense, humanitarians might consider only the publications of such agencies as the Library of Congress and the Smithsonian Institution and the great documents of our past such as the Constitution and the Declaration of Independence as truly supporting humanistic research and instruction. Government publications are primary sources and can provide information on what shaped our beliefs and attitudes and the possibilities and limitations of our society. This material will help us develop a critical sense which allows us as individuals to select and preserve the best of the human tradition and to decide the future course of our society. To exploit fully the extraordinary potential of these materials, we emphasize government publications which portray the ideals, values and experiences formative in our culture rather than materials that support specific subject areas. We will illustrate by way of examples.

Each year the reports and documents issued by Congress are gathered together into volumes which make up the Congressional Set (Serial Set). Buried within the Serial Set are materials little read and largely untapped by scholars—an example is the Pacific Railroad Survey.

By the mid-1800s several railroad lines that were already in existence connected the Mississippi River and the Atlantic Ocean. What was needed was a railroad from the Mississippi River to the Pacific Ocean. Congress, in March 1853, directed that topographical engineers be sent out to examine five possible routes. In addition to the topographical engineers who were in charge of the expeditions, the instructions for the survey read "competent persons will be selected to make researches in those collateral branches of science which affect the solution of the question of location, construction, and support of a railway communication across the continent, viz: the nature of rocks and soils—the products of the country, animal, mineral, and vegetable—the resources for supplies of material for construction, and means requisite for the operation of a railway, with a notice of the population, agricultural products, and the habits and languages of the Indian tribes."[4]

The "competent" persons included such specialists as an artist, an astronomer, a surgeon, a geologist and a botanist. The experts were directed to keep detailed journals and records and a report of the expeditions was to be made to Congress by a certain date. No secondary source can do justice to the richness of these original records and diaries which relate the battles with the elements and with the animals, tell of starvation and other hardships, and describe the beauty of the landscape.

These narratives are accompanied by scores of beautiful color drawings of the flora and the fauna and the landscapes which caught the artist's imagination while en route. Signatures of noted artists and engravers of the period are on the plates.

In this survey can be found materials to support various parts of the humanities, particularly descriptions of the Indians. Information includes: localities, numbers, modes of subsistence, residences, portraits of dress, traditions, supersititions, pictographs, antiquities and arts, vocabularies and history.

Reports on the Indians encountered by the expedition reveal the values and attitudes of the surveyors. Lieutenant A. W. Whipple observed that "the time is now arrived when we must decide whether they are to be exterminated; if not, the powerful arm of the law must be extended over them, to secure their right to the soil they occupy; to protect them from aggression; to afford facilities and aid in acquiring the arts of civilization and the knowledge and humanizing influences of Christianity."[5]

Another point of view expressed by Lieutenant J. Mullan of the U.S. Army was that should the Indians "continue to keep their pledges as faithlessly as they have before, that our military force should be sent among them, put every man, woman and child to the knife, burn down their villages, and thus teach the nation that since persuasion will not, force must and shall effect the ends that we have in view. . . . They had better by far be totally exterminated than left to prowl the mountains, murdering, plundering, and carrying everything before them."[6]

Because of the sectional prejudice of the times, the final report of the Pacific Railroad Survey was controversial and actually none of the routes was selected. Dee Brown states that "The government spent more than a million dollars in publishing over a period of five years the thirteen quarto volumes of explorations and surveys for a Pacific railroad, and although they contained little information that would have assisted a field surveyor in marking out a railway line, they were filled with an extraordinary amount of detail relating to geology, geography, land forms, American Indians, weather, trails, botanical specimens, birds, mammals, reptiles, and fish. Today the reports stand not as a guide for the routing of railroads but as a priceless compendium of the virgin West immediately before its despoilation by the Iron Horse."[7]

What we are suggesting is to use this enormous amount of information that was collected in a new light for humanistic research and teaching. Material to support the constituent fields of the humanities can be found here. Historians can be exposed to this primary source material. Students of literature can become acquainted with the surveyor's diaries from which poetry, stories and novels might evolve. There are passages dealing with comparative religions; art historians can benefit from studying the plates produced by noted artists and engravers; accounts of Indian tribes are important from the anthropologist's point of view. There is discussion of Indian languages and linguistics and the text itself serves as an example of the language used during this period. Through these documents we can also live vicariously the lives of various groups such as the Indians and the exploratory party, and become more aware of the total community of which we are a part and from which our society evolved.

There were many other expeditions in the early years of our westward movement and they are recorded in government publications. They contain material relating to the humanities and are particularly useful in illustrating values, attitudes and experiences.

Turning to more current times, the turmoil of the 1960s turned the nation toward a rethinking of values and a renewed social consciousness. Many recently formed agencies of the federal government have been concerned with humanistic values from their inception.

The Department of Housing and Urban Development is one such agency with its purpose to assist in the development of viable urban communities by providing decent housing and a suitable living environment and expanding economic opportunities, principally for persons of low and moderate income. In 1965 when the Department of Housing and Urban Development was created, Congress recognized that in our nation the city needed a coequal voice at the Cabinet level along with agriculture, defense and the other major concerns of the federal government.

Some other examples of recently formed agencies with humanistic concerns are the National Endowment for the Humanities, the National Endowment for the Arts, the Equal Employment Opportunity Commission, the Council on Environmental Quality, the Department of Health, Education and Welfare, the Environmental Protection Agency, and various groups concerned with consumer education. A perspective on the values and attitudes of our society could be developed from a history of the formation of government agencies and concerns. Examining the materials produced by these agencies should give us a good insight into the ideas, premises, rationale, logic, methods and values of our nation.

In the 1970s the problems facing the United States include the need for additional fuel to continue the growth of our economy. Alaska is one of the areas being explored to meet this need and environmental impact statements are the method of analyzing the effects on the environment of obtaining this fuel.

Environmental Impact Statements (EIS) came about through the enactment of the National Environmental Policy Act (Public Law 91-190) in 1969. This law specified that national policy would be enacted to "encourage productive and enjoyable harmony between man and his environment; to promote efforts which will prevent or eliminate damage to the environment and biosphere and stimulate the health and welfare of man; to enrich the understanding of the ecological systems and natural resources important to the Nation. . . ."

To achieve these goals, Congress directed federal agencies to include environmental concerns in their decision making. If an agency determines that an anticipated action (pipeline, highway, proposed Panama Canal treaties) would have a significant impact on the human environment, it must develop a formal statement on the environmental impact of the proposal, its adverse environmental effect, alternatives to the proposed action, the relationship between short-term use of the environment and maintenance of long-term productivity, and identification of any irreversible commitments of resources necessitated by project implementation.

"Among the earliest effects of the EIS process on federal decision-making was the Interior Department's second draft and its final EIS on the 800 mile Trans-Alaska Pipeline. Virtually all parties involved agree that the intensive environmental review of this project prompted important design changes and other improvements in routing and construction techniques."[8]

Impacts considered in this 1972 statement include a very wide scope: geologic resources, water resources, air quality, vegetation, freshwater fishery, mammals, birds, insects, recreation, fish and wildlife management, wilderness, archeology (historical sites), the Alaskan economy, native people, commercial fisheries, forest industry, and marine and nonmarine transportation.

Of particular interest in indicating the values and attitudes at this time is the consideration of adverse effects on native people. The report states that: "The result of all this could be a decrease in reliance on the subsistence economy and a subsequent alteration in the social institutions required under that system. Whether or not these changes could be considered adverse depends on the individual making the judgment; in any event there would be unavoidable changes in existing ways of life, cultural values, and attitudes."[9]

In 1976 the Alaska Natural Gas Transportation System Final Environmental Impact Statement was prepared. The following consideration of the impact on social conditions is included: "Many natives are unprepared to take advantage of opportunities brought by development. They lack the skills or competitive spirit, and fear the change. This leads to a feeling of insecurity, inferiority, and loss of identity; and thus to increased alcohol abuse, which has become a major social problem among the natives in the far north. If natives are hired for much of the work, social and economic disparities could be reduced. If not, they will be increased."[10] These considerations are particularly interesting in terms of values and attitudes at different times in our country when compared with observations made about the Indians in the Pacific Railroad Survey.

Both of these environmental impact statements on Alaska are accompanied by photographs showing some areas to be affected by the proposed fuel transportation systems. However, these reports do not include the varied information to support the constituent fields of the humanities that was included in earlier reports such as the Railroad Survey.

These examples are given to show how current government publications are applicable to research and teaching in the humanities. They also help relate the study of the humanities to national concerns.

Today there is increasing interest in the humanities on various fronts as researchers reconsider the humanities and educators attempt to make the university education more relevant to the students' life experience.

This is evident in the recent formation by scholars and educators of the American Association for the Advancement of the Humanities. In the past, humanities scholars and teachers have been perceived as uninterested in relating their expertise and experience to matters of broad public concern. The new association will seek to provide analyses of issues that concern humanists and will strive to provide a coherent voice for the humanities among scholars, policy makers and the general public.[11] As illustrated briefly in the preceding sections, government publications can contribute to such objectives.

A recent article in *Change* calls for a new core of educational experience to assure social continuity. The authors suggest that all students must be introduced to the events, individual ideas, texts and value systems that have contributed consequentially to human gains and losses. Boyer and Kaplan state that an "approach to heritage should be concerned with change, with shifts of historical paradigms, with sets of events viewed from different vantage points. One might study how the conventional wisdom about American involvement in Indo-China changed from 1950 to 1975. One might compare visions of Communism, or of time, in the 1920s and 1970s. One might trace how the ideas of empire, colonization, and 'manifest destiny' were born, implemented, and radically revalued. One might look at a particular historical moment from the perspective of black people, or of women, or of non-Western cultures."[12] This curriculum must also include a strong and forward look at the moral and ethical considerations that guide the lives of each person and must encourage searching discussions about the choices people and nations make.

Librarians must aggressively participate in this change by introducing government publications such as hearings of Congressional committees, Presidential proclamations, studies of commissions, and debates in Congress to researchers and in course-related instruction, and by teaching the use of specialized indexes to access these materials.

As illustrated by the examples in this paper, government publications can play a key role in humanities research and in the education of today's university students. As librarians we must sharpen our perspective on these materials and stretch our thinking and that of students and other faculty members to the utilization of government publications in new and different ways for humanities research and instruction.

REFERENCES

1. George W. Whitbeck and Peter Hernon, "The Attitudes of Librarians Toward the Servicing and Use of Government Publications; A Survey of Federal Depositories in Four Midwestern States," *Government Publications Review* 4 (1977): 183.
2. U.S. National Endowment for the Humanities, *Program Announcement, 1976–77.* (Washington, DC: National Endowment for the Humanities, [1976]), p. 1.
3. *Ibid.*
4. U.S. Congress, House, *Reports of Explorations and Surveys to Ascertain the Most Practicable and Economical Route for a Railroad from the Mississippi River to the Pacific Ocean;* Made under the direction of the Secretary of War in 1853-4, according to Acts of Congress of March 3, 1853, May 31, 1854, and August 5, 1854, Vol. 2 (1855), 33rd Cong., 3d sess., Ex. Doc. 91, p. 10.
5. U.S. Congress, House, "Report upon the Indian Tribes" in *Reports of Explorations and Surveys*, Vol. 3 (1856), 33rd Cong., 2d sess., Ex. Doc. 91, p. 7.

6. U.S. Congress, House, *Reports of Explorations and Surveys*, Vol. 1 (1855), 33rd Cong., 2d sess., Ex. Doc. 91, p. 438.

7. Dee Brown, *Hear That Lonesome Whistle Blow; Railroads in the West.* (New York: Holt, Rinehart and Winston, 1977), p. 36.

8. U.S. Council on Environmental Quality, *Environmental Impact Statements; An Analysis of Six Years' Experience by Seventy Federal Agencies.* (Washington, DC: Government Printing Office, 1976), p. D-1.

9. U.S. Department of the Interior, *Final Environmental Impact Statement-Proposed Trans-Alaska Pipeline*, Vol. 1 of 6. (Washington, DC: Government Printing Office, 1972), p. 217.

10. U.S. Department of the Interior, *Alaska Natural Gas Transportation System; Final Environmental Impact Statement, Overview.* (Washington, DC: Government Printing Office, 1976), p. 161.

11. "New Organization Aims to 'Advance' Humanities," *The Chronicle of Higher Education* 15 (January 9, 1978): 14.

12. Ernest L. Boyer and Martin Kaplan, "Educating for Survival: A Call for a Core Curriculum," *Change* 9 (March 1977): 25.

BIBLIOGRAPHY

The materials included in this bibliography are intended to provide a starting point for scholars, librarians and students who are interested in considering and examining government publications for their usefulness in humanistic studies. It is only a brief sample of some of the kinds of materials published by the government which have to do with humanistic inquiry. In addition, the aim is to promote use of government publications via novel modes of thinking about them; materials produced for one purpose can often be utilized in a new fashion. Re-examination of annual reports, environmental impact statements, catalogs, photographic materials and the classic documents of our past can reveal the imagination, values and ideals of society, and can offer rewards to the humanist who views government publications as source materials for research or instruction.

General Resources

U.S. Congress. Congressional Set or "Serial Set." 1817– . Over 13,000 volumes of Congressional publications printed in a collected edition and numbered serially. Senate and House Documents contain reports of special investigations made for Congress. Materials from executive and independent agencies ordered to be included in the series are also in the Documents. Invaluable source of materials includes results of explorations, surveys, annual reports of agencies and other items of interest. The recent *U.S. Serial Set Index* provides a means of access to students and scholars for use as a source for humanistic studies.

U.S. Congress. Hearings. Primary source materials in the form of testimony, exhibits and documents covering all aspects of American life. Indispensable source for humanistic scholarship.

U.S. Congress. *Congressional Record.* 1873– . (Title varies in earlier formats.) The daily "newspaper" of Congress covering its debates and reflecting the philosophical underpinnings of legislative activity.

U.S. Bureau of American Ethnology. *Bulletin* and *Annual Reports.* Includes information on all aspects of life among the Indians. The volumes in each of these series provide a wealth of linguistic, religious, aesthetic, historical and sociological information.

For index, see *List of Publications of the Bureau of American Ethnology with Index to Authors and Titles.* Smithsonian Institution Press, 1971. (Bulletin of American Ethnology no. 200)

Religion, Ethics, Philosophy

U.S. Bureau of the Census. *Religious bodies, 1936.* Washington, Government Printing Office, 1941. Information about the organization, doctrine and history as well as statistical information is provided.

U.S. Department of the Army. *Last Salute, Civil and Military Funerals, 1921–69.* Washington, Government Printing Office, 1972. Accounts of 29 funerals with photographs and diagrams.

U.S. Library of Congress. *Folklore of the North American Indians: an Annotated Bibliography.* Compiled by Judith C. Ullom. Washington, Government Printing Office, 1969. Selective bibliography of 11 Indian culture areas.

U.S. Library of Congress. *Philosophical Periodicals, an Annotated World List.* Compiled by David Baumgardt. Washington, Government Printing Office, 1952.

Language, Linguistics, Literature

U.S. Government Printing Office. *Specimens of Type Faces.* Washington, Government Prining Office, 1969. Include illustrations of various type faces.

U.S. Joint Publications Research Service. *Chinese-English Dictionary of Modern Communist Chinese Usage.* 2nd ed. Springfield, Va., CFSTI, 1965.

U.S. Library of Congress. *Metaphor as Pure Adventure.* By James Dickey. Washington, Government Printing Office, 1968. Text of lecture and bibliography of other publications on literature issued by the Library of Congress.

U.S. Library of Congress. *Sixty American Poets, 1896–1944: Selected with Preface and Critical Notes.* By Allen Tate. Rev. ed. prepared by Kenton Kilmer. Washington, Government Printing Office, 1954.

U.S. Smithsonian Institution. *The Great Tzotzil Dictionary of San Lorenzo Zinacantan.* By Robert M. Laughlin. Washington, Government Printing Office, 1975. Dictionary of Mayan-English, English-Mayan.

Arts and Architecture

U.S. Bureau of the Mint. *Domestic and Foreign Coins Manufactured by Mints of the United States, 1793–1970.* Washington, Government Printing Office, 1972.

U.S. Department of the Interior. National Park Service. *Historic American Buildings Survey: a Catalog of the Measured Drawings and Photographs of the Survey in the Library of Congress.* Washington, Government Printing Office, 1941. An attempt to build a permanent graphic record of American architecture.

U.S. Library of Congress. *A.L.A. Portrait Index: Index to Portraits Contained in Printed Books and Periodicals.* Ed. by W. C. Lane and N. E. Browne. Washington, Library of Congress, 1906. An index to portraits of 40,000 people with information about the subject and artist of the portrait.

U.S. Library of Congress. *Sousa Band, a Discography.* Compiled by James R. Smart. Washington, Government Printing Office, 1969.

U.S. Smithsonian Institution. *The Golden Door: Artist-immigrants of America, 1876–1976.* Text by Cynthia Jaffe McCabe. Washington, Government Printing Office (Smithsonian Institution Press), 1976. Presents biographical descriptions of American artist-immigrants with color reproductions of their works.

U.S. Postal Service. *Postage Stamps of the United States.* 1927– . (irregular). Washington, Government Printing Office.

Selma V. Foster and Nancy C. Lufburrow

State University of New York, College at Potsdam

DOCUMENTS TO THE PEOPLE IN ONE EASY STEP

The key to increased use of government documents is uniform bibliographic access, not physical organization. Using Government Printing Office cataloging copy now available in the OCLC data base, student employees produce catalog cards directly from shipping lists. Early results show a decline in the total cost of administration of a U.S. depository collection and a dramatic increase in documents circulation.

Underutilization of government documents is the traditional complaint of those concerned with the administration of documents in libraries. Much of the response to that complaint has centered on the question of physical location: should documents be segregated, fully integrated, or selectively mixed with the library's general collection? This paper describes a new, relatively inexpensive method for increasing document use, one based not on location but on access. It is our thesis that uniform bibliographic access through the library's catalog, be it COM, on-line, or the traditional card catalog, and not physical arrangement, is the key to full utilization of any collection.

Recent literature on the servicing and use of government publications indirectly supports our thesis. For example, Whitbeck and Hernon[1] noted that one of the chief reasons for the lack of use of documents was librarians' lack of familiarity with the bibliographic tools for accessing them. In reporting the results of another recent survey, Shearer[2] concluded that there was no consensus as to the "best system to promote the use of the documents collection." While 26% of his respondents thought it best to catalog all documents, only 3% actually did so. Another 42% reported that they catalog some but not all of their documents. It seems safe to assume for the first group of respondents and probably also for the second group that cost was the crucial factor in determining whether or not they catalog documents. The question then becomes not how documents are arranged, but what price are we willing to pay to increase their use. Our medium-sized undergraduate library decided to test its thesis and learn its price.

Our library has been a partial depository for U.S. government documents since 1964 and has selected about 1/3 of the currently available items; in other words we receive roughly 5,000 non-periodical documents each year. To make the fullest use of this free resource, our goal was to catalog all documents, Underlying our decision were two assumptions. First, we believed that the average undergraduate library user seeks information by subject. Second, we believed that access to library materials should be as simple as possible, that in fact, there is a correlation between the ease of access and the amount of use materials receive. We soon discovered that our intent to fully catalog all documents was impossible to realize; frequently, by the time acceptable catalog copy was available, a document was close to being out-dated. In reality, then, we found ourselves among that "pernicious" 42% whom Shearer scolds for managing a mixed collection.[3]

Not until the Government Printing Office announced plans to catalog documents in MARC format and make the cataloging available through OCLC, did it become apparent that we could at last marry our principles with our practice. While unabashedly retaining a physically mixed collection, we could now provide catalog access for all documents. In other words, documents of a relatively permanent nature would, as always, be integrated into the library's general collection; the remaining documents, as always, would be classed by SuDocs number in a separate collection. However, for the first time, they, too, would be fully accessible through the public catalog.

The actual procedure developed is relatively simple. As documents arrive, a clerk does the initial checking in, routing previously cataloged periodicals and serials to their respective places. The documents librarian, then, using her knowledge of both documents and user needs, sorts the remaining documents according to their seeming permanence. Those sorted into the SuDocs collection are primarily documents whose content, after 5 years, will either have become out-dated or have been incorporated into other published secondary sources: brief state-of-the-art reviews, descriptions of current government programs, forecasts, directories, grant information, and regulations.

Congressional hearings became a major exception to previous practice and present criteria. We consider them of long-term interest. However, since the Library of Congress classification does not disperse them by subject through the general collection, there seemed little advantage in integrating them. They, too, are now classed according to their SuDocs number.

For those documents that are to be integrated into the regular collection, only minor changes have been made in procedures; documents with cataloging-in-publication and monographic series which LC has classed as a series can be cataloged immediately, the latter using GPO cataloging copy. In neither case is any record of their presence in the library made before cataloging which usually takes place within three days of their arrival. The real streamlining had to take place in the procedures for handling the documents that were to remain in the separate SuDocs collection, since we wished to keep to a minimum the added cost of cataloging these documents. Our solution has been to have the depository shipping list which accompanies all documents act as a central control mechanism. It serves as both the search and produce record and can be used as a means of retrieving and listing documents for discard after the 5-year statutory period.

The new cataloging process works as follows. On the shipping list the documents librarian underlines in red the titles to be classed by SuDocs number. The shipping lists are then forwarded to the OCLC terminal where a student does all cataloging. Using the terminal on Saturday, the student searches the titles underlined on the shipping lists. When there is a perfect match between the title and the SuDocs class number of the document and the GPO cataloging copy on the screen, the student "produces" catalog cards and records the PRODUCE date in the right hand column of the shipping list for verification against receipt of cards. When there is no cataloging copy on the data base, the student records the search date in the left hand column; two subsequent searches are done at monthly intervals. After catalog cards have been received, the shipping lists from which the cards have been produced are filed by year so they can be used as a signal for discarding five years hence.

For documents in the SuDocs collection, no record exists until the OCLC shelf list card is filed. The time lag varies according to the speed with which records appear in the data base. A search after 2–4 weeks produces a 50% hit rate. After three months, we have an insignificant number of titles that have not been found in the data base, primarily those for which terminal search is not possible.

What is the price? Personnel costs appear to have declined. The documents librarian spends less time checking clerical work and more time making decisions at the time documents arrive. She now spends about half time on all aspects of documents work. Since most documents are quickly accessible through the card catalog, reference librarians spend less time explaining the *Monthly Catalog* and helping students find uncataloged documents. The catalog department does less original cataloging and fewer bibliographic searches, but its authority work has increased slightly. Since shelf lists are no longer typed, the document clerk's work load has been reduced by a third, more than off-setting clerical time needed for filing the additional cards in the public catalog. Student time has remained fairly constant since the student who formerly searched the OCLC terminal for LC copy now not only searches for GPO copy, but produces cards at the same time. (For those interested we calculate the labor cost for this search and production at 7–8¢ per title produced.)

Obviously, our OCLC charges have increased. However, we feel these have been more than cancelled out by the reduction in personnel costs. For a large percentage of our documents we have replaced our expensive LC search and cataloging process done by librarians and clerks with a quick cataloging process done by students.

What have some of the problems been? The primary problem has been the quality of GPO cataloging. A sharp increase in authority conflicts arose between the forms of entries established by LC and by GPO. Early copy was ridden with typographic errors, and SuDocs class number corrections have had to be dealt with. However, LC and GPO have been working together to resolve their authority conflicts, and GPO's quality control has improved considerably since the program began.

What are our results? First, we have achieved uniform bibliographic access for nearly all non-periodical documents through the card catalog before *Monthly Catalog* access is possible. Second, we have reduced the personnel costs of administering our documents collection. Third, we have scheduled and arranged for the orderly weeding of those documents whose shelf life is limited. Finally, the most important result is that documents which once languished unnoticed and little used, segregated by SuDocs classification in a separate collection, now circulate at a rate we never imagined possible. Less than one year after we began making catalog cards for our segregated collection, circulation of these documents had tripled.

Our limited observation might suggest that the age-old and seemingly endless controversy over how documents might best be organized to increase their use is moot. Our answer is clear. If documents are useful, and you really want them to be used, given them the same access you give the rest of the collection. It's the best way of getting "documents to the people!"

REFERENCES

1. George W. Whitbeck and Peter Hernon, "The Attitudes of Librarians Toward the Servicing and Use of Government Publications; A Survey of Federal Depositories in Four Midwestern States," *Government Publications Review* 4 (1977): 183–199.
2. Benjamin Shearer, "Federal Depository Libraries on the Campus: Practices and Prospects," *Government Publications Review* 4 (1977): 209–214.
3. *Ibid.*, p. 212.

Jeffrey J. Gardner

Association of Research Libraries

CAP: A PROJECT FOR THE ANALYSIS OF THE COLLECTION DEVELOPMENT PROCESS IN LARGE ACADEMIC LIBRARIES

In 1977 a process for analyzing and improving research libraries' collection development practices was developed. Using an assisted self-study methodology, the process was tested at three major American academic research libraries. This paper describes the issues faced by research libraries in the area of collection development, the conceptual model on which the process is based, the study methodology, and the operation of the pilot test studies.

In 1977 the Association of Research Library's Office of University Library Management Studies (OMS) received support from the Andrew W. Mellon Foundation to develop and test a self-study procedure for analyzing and improving research libraries' collection development practices. Called the Collection Analysis Project (CAP), it began in 1977 with a survey of all ARL libraries and site visits to a representative sample of twelve. This effort highlighted some of the collection development concerns of research libraries and provided the conceptual framework for CAP.

First among the issues of concern was the economics of building and maintaining research collections during a period when rising materials prices have outstripped increases in library materials budgets. A related concern results from the accumulated investment in collections and bibliographic records which greatly influences future options for collection development. It became clear that current collection allocation decisions are frequently closely related to the maintenance of past collection strengths regardless of university shifts in program emphasis.

This situation is particularly acute in connection with serials and journals. Continuing commitments for serial publications account for an ever-increasing proportion of libraries' materials budgets—up to 70 or 80 percent in some libraries—and there was concern that this is leading to an unplanned biasing of collections toward the sciences and away from the humanities.

One consequence of the growth of research library collections distinguishes them from instructional collections. While they have been developed primarily to serve local program needs, they have become—individually and in the aggregate—a national resource. This dual role has brought with it special responsibilities and pressures. Decisions to reduce specific collection commitments frequently have an impact beyond the particular campus and are difficult considerations of the impact of such decisions on the national scholarly community.

Other issues result from the political and program pressures coming from the university community. Many libraries reported that university administrators and faculty do not always appreciate the consequences to the library of program changes. For instance, they are reluctant or unable to provide the finances necessary to support the purchase or retrospective materials for a new doctoral program or for new national research interests.

Another complex issue involves the competing demands of research and instructional programs. While it is relatively easy to predict what level of holdings will satisfy the immediate curricular needs, individual research and faculty users specialize in quite narrow topics, and the probability is extremely small that any particular research book will be frequently used. Many libraries have been forced by extended economic stress to shift the balance away from the more speculative needs of present and future scholars and while this shift may be unavoidable for many libraries, there are some disturbing implications. The support of immediate needs frequently requires substantial expenditures for multiple copies of materials which have relatively limited lifetimes. These duplicate purchases do not add to a collection's richness and funds expended on duplicates are, of course, not available for acquiring unique research titles.

These generic problems have led to the design of the CAP self-study procedure. The intent of this procedure is to assist a research library in reviewing, describing, evaluating and analyzing its collection program in view of economic pressures and the changing role of research libraries in meeting the instructional and research needs of universities. The fundamental purpose of the procedure is to make the library's collection more responsive and relevant to this environment.

CAP is based on a conceptual model which illustrates the relationships among environmental forces, university needs, library programs and policies, and the research collection. At the heart of this model are the library's collections that support the university instructional and research programs. These collections are influenced by environmental factors such as user needs, student enrollment, faculty research interests, price trends, and new technology. While these environmental factors are generally beyond the control of the library, they have direct impact on its capability to perform successfully.

Libraries shape their response to university needs and environmental pressures by characterizing the scope, coverage, and intensity of collection development activities in formal or informal collection policies. In the CAP model, the library's acquisition program is viewed as the implementation of these collection policies by allocating resources, organizing and staffing, and maintaining the collection. The current acquisitions program in turn shapes and directs the growth of the research collection and research collection services.

The key components in the model then, are: university program needs, a collection development philosophy, collection development objectives, collection development policies, a program of acquisitions, and collection description and assessment. Examining and developing the relationships among these concepts is the heart of the program.

The Collection Analysis Project employs an assisted self-study methodology—representative library staff carry out analyses with resources and advice provided by the OMS. Past experience with this methodology indicated that it offers several advantages. It utilizes staff expertise and knowledge of the situation, develops their understanding of organizational realities, and typically insures commitment to the results. The process was tested in 1977/78 in the libraries at MIT, Arizona State University, and the University of California at Berkeley.

In the pilot test phase, the self-study methodology involved a systematic review of current collection practices leading to workable recommendations for change. The study was divided into two major parts. The first investigated library goals and objectives, environmental factors affecting collection development, and the historical development of the library collections. The goals and objectives review identified how objectives are prepared and used and assessed their suitability, particularly in the collection area. The review of environmental pressures for change examined trends in resource-sharing, scholarly publishing, higher education economics, and university programs. In examining the historical development of the collection, the study noted the strengths and weaknesses of the collection as well as its physical dimensions and major components. These introductory investigations led to an interim report which furnished background information for the second group of analyses and which defined the parameters for further investigation.

The second phase of the pilot studies included analyses of acquisitions operating practices, collection assessment, resource sharing, preservation, and materials fund allocations processes. The review of acquisitions operating practices looked at selection policies and practices and organizational staffing patterns. The collection assessment module investigated problems of assessment and available methods for such assessment, looked at the collection in terms of its overall description, and assessed portions of the collection. The project presented two basic approaches to collection assessment. The first treated the collection as a resource and focused on the intellectual breadth and depth of the collection. This approach responds to the concept that a research collection's value is intrinsically related to the unknown needs of future scholars. The second approach, client-centered assessment, focused on the utility of the collection to its current users. The pilot test libraries measured user perceptions of collection success in fulfilling needs in addition to measuring actual success via access and availability studies. The resource-sharing study investigated the impact of current and evolving national and regional programs on the library's collections programs. The final module examined current activities, needs, and future prospects in the area of preservation.

The study was carried out at each of the pilot test libraries by staff members appointed to a study team and a series of task forces. The study team was responsible for the overall conduct of the study at each library. It carried out the initial general analyses, coordinated and managed the work of the task forces, and produced the final report with recommendations for change. The task forces conducted the analyses in the second part of the study and reported results to the study team.

The library directors at MIT, Arizona State, and Berkeley played a critical role throughout the projects. After consultation with staff and university officials, the directors made the final decision to participate. They selected the members of the study team, and prepared a written charge to team members that presented their detailed expectations. The directors also provided their perspectives on anticipated problems and potential opportunities and communicated the project's intentions to university administrators and faculty.

University faculty provided the study team with information regarding their collection needs and assessment of the library's performance in fulfilling those needs. Much of this faculty input was generated during the collection assessment phase through surveys of faculty needs and satisfaction levels and joint evaluation of specific parts of the collection by faculty-bibliographer teams. Other input came from study team interviews with key faculty.

The OMS provided a series of resources to assist the pilot libraries in carrying out CAP. A self-study manual was drafted after considerable research and while the manual was prepared to be adaptable to a range of local differences among libraries, each library made specific adaptations. But the manual did eliminate the need for the study teams to expend large amounts of time on project design, in order to emphasize the actual review and analysis of issues and the development of recommendations for change.

The OMS also developed data-gathering instruments such as user surveys and interview guides, formats for analyzing and displaying data, and working papers dealing with such tasks as preparing the interim report, preparing the final report, and group decision-making.

Finally, the OMS provided direct assistance and training for the study team and task forces, mainly through a series of on-site work sessions where the OMS staff facilitated the definition and resolution of problems and the planning for the next study phases.

The three pilot test libraries assisted in the refinement and improvement of the project for future use by other research libraries. In this respect, their differences were important to the test.

MIT is an established research library that has traditionally emphasized development of scientific and technical collections maintained in a decentralized system. The university's more recent emphasis of social science programs and its development of strong interdisciplinary research programs offered interesting challenges. Arizona State is an emerging research library whose materials expenditures have increased dramatically in the last five years. The University of California at Berkeley is one of the five largest ARL members and provided a test in a very large, complex environment. Each of these participating libraries had worked on collection development projects in the past and was willing to contribute to the dual task of completing the collection analysis procedure and helping the OMS evaluate and improve its program.

The results of the pilot tests were within two general categories:

— First, the reports provided to each of the participating libraries an agenda for action. The need for specific changes was documented and specific strategies were recommended. These included changes in materials fund allocation processes, development of comprehensive preservation and conservation programs, the clarification of staff responsibilities in the collection development process and movement toward ongoing collection assessment programs. The MIT and Arizona State reports were completed in March, 1978 and their reports are being acted on.

— Second, the projects provided valuable insights to the OMS for the generation of a revised manual and methodology. The pilot tests re-emphasized the value of flexibility in the program and the need for a process which is adaptable to the varying requirements of different institutions. The magnitude of the initial studies led to a rethinking of the project schedule and each task force contributed to the OMS's understanding of the issues involved and the opportunities available for change. While the basic project methodology proved to be viable, many specific issues and project details were clarified. The project benefitted greatly from the research and experimentation carried out by the staffs and directors at MIT, Arizona State and Berkeley.

Barbara Haber

Radcliffe College

WOMEN'S STUDIES RESOURCES FOR COLLEGE AND RESEARCH LIBRARIES

*Women's Studies is a new field which has not yet received widespread atten-
tion from academic libraries. Its rapid development has created problems for
both college and research libraries attempting to collect in the field. By focusing on the impact of women's studies on the Schlesinger Library, a social
history library on American women, this paper will identify problems other
libraries may be experiencing such as the lack of comprehensive bibliographic
information. In offering suggestions for developing a research collection, it
is concluded that more is to be gained by collecting materials on a regional
basis than by attempting a comprehensive collecting policy.*

For the last seven or eight years the demand for courses focusing on women has become an issue at most colleges and universities in the United States. In addition, new
research on women has affected most academic disciplines in the humanities, the social
sciences and the biological sciences. The subject matter that is the result of this intellectual activity is generally known as "women's studies." While energetic debates about the
nature and the future of this new subject matter go on, and new courses continue to be
added to curricula, scarcely any attention is being given to library resources necessary
to support the new courses or the new research.

Among the problems facing book selectors in women's studies is the difficulty of
defining a field which by its nature is interdisciplinary. The absence of fundamental
bibliographic tools compounds the burden of determining the basis for a core collection
for college libraries, and even more difficult is the task of developing a research collection. How does one collect on half of the world's populaton? These are some of the problems we are dealing with at the Arthur and Elizabeth Schlesinger Library on the History
of Women in America at Radcliffe College. Although this institution may perhaps be
unique for reasons of its own history, it seems that certain problems that have been faced
and resolved in the recent development of the Library may be of interest to other
academic libraians who are shaping and developing women's studies collections.

Women's studies has its roots in the social movement for women's liberation which
began in the late 1960s in the United States. Almost from the start college students were
largely involved in its development. Some had worked in the civil rights movement and
others have been involved with anti-war activities. Women in both of these protest move-

ments had met with discrimination—been relegated to menial jobs—and became increasingly sensitized to the rights of women after their long concern with the rights of others.

Feminist groups sprang up all around the country and from the start their interest in current women's issues was accompanied by an intense interest in learning about women's history. Women's studies developed from these two areas of concern. What began as social protest has led to academic curricula and scholarly research which investigates issues raised by those in the women's movement. Thus, for example, feminist concerns with discrimination in education and employment have led to scholarly studies by historians, sociologists and economists. The new interest in women's history and literature has led to virtually new fields of study. Social historians are doing major studies which interpret women's history. Literary scholars are rediscovering important books by women and are constructing a feminist approach to literature—reevaluating past works and influencing the creation of new. All of these scholars are in pursuit of what can best be described as authentic female experience. To illustrate the effectiveness of women's studies one might consult a recent study by Florence Howe who evaluated the current status of women's studies courses in institutions across the country that was commissioned by The National Advisory Council on Women's Educational Programs (a body established by Congress in 1974 as part of the Women's Educational Equity Act). Howe reports in *Seven Years Later: Women's Studies Programs in 1976* that as of 1976 "more than 270 programs have been organized [and] some 15,000 different courses developed by 8500 teachers at 1500 different institutions."[1]

The relationship between all of this activity and the responsibilities of academic libraries is slow in developing. Generally, there is a suspiciousness of women's studies, charges that it is ephemeral, a passing fad like many of the other protest movements of the 1960s. But this does not seem to be the case. Fine scholarship is being produced and arguments which question the validity of the field now seem irrelevant. Fine scholarship, feminist or other, stands on its own merits. In the opinion of many, scholarship on women is revitalizing the humanities and social sciences. In addition, students are excited by this new approach to learning, having a sense of discovery about their work. Finally, it is my opinion that when the history of the 1970s is written, the changing role of women in America will be a major area of investigation for historians and social critics.

The Schlesinger Library, a special research collection on women in America, was founded in the 1940s when a Radcliffe graduate gave to the college the papers she had collected throughout her work in the suffrage movement. The Library might have remained a sort of shrine to that movement had not the college president, Wilbur Jordan, and Arthur Schlesinger, a professor of history at Harvard and the head of the Library's advisory board recognized the need for a social history library on American women. As early as 1922 Professor Schlesinger deplored the apparent assumption of historians that "one-half of our population have been negligible factors in our country's history." The purpose of the Library became the documentation of the contributions of all American women. Emphasis was on collecting primary sources, the papers of individual women and the records of women's organizations. Early additions to the Library were Beecher–Stowe family papers, the Blackwell family papers and the papers of the labor organizer, Leonora O'Reilly.

When this author began working at the Schlesinger Library in 1968, the collection of books and periodicals was considered a "companion-piece" to the primary sources collected by the Library. If the Library received the papers of a doctor or a labor leader, then books about women in those fields would be purchased. In general though, few books about women were written, and periodicals were limited in number so restrictions on purchases were not critical. Histories of women were generally about suffrage or other social reform in which women had participated. More frequently new books would be biographies of famous women or of the wives of famous men. The twenty periodical titles we received included standard women's magazines like *The Ladies Home Journal* and *Vogue* or government publications such as those published by the Women's Bureau in the Department of Labor. The Library spent less than $1,000 a year on printed materials. Those who used the Library were, typically, scholars beyond the Ph.D. whose interests were only temporarily in women's history. Almost no one specialized in the field.

The first indication of a new wave of feminism occurred in the academic year 1969–1970 when underground newspapers with titles like *Off Our Backs, Ain't I a Woman?* and *It Ain't Me Babe* appeared. They were published by women who were raising questions about sex-roles and the social and legal inequities between men and women. These challenges met with a response from women from all over the country including college instructors who began to organize course material that could begin to address the questions being raised. The Schlesinger Library was suddenly being visited by these young teachers who were astonished to find an entire library devoted to the subject of women's history.

The new interest created an unprecedented demand for materials and bibliographic information. Teachers who compiled syllabi were asked to leave copies at the Library which began to function as an informal clearinghouse for women's studies. The next problem for those teaching women's history was to fill the void of primary source material that was available in print. Instructors began searching through books for documents which could be used to teach women's history. Nancy Cott, a bright young graduate student at the time, compiled a selection of these previously obscure works for an anthology, *Root of Bitterness*,[2] which has since become a basic text in courses in women's history. Soon after, other anthologies based in part on the Schlesinger Library's holdings appeared, most notably Gerda Lerner's *Black Women in White America*[3] and Alice Rossi's *The Feminist Papers*,[4] works by mature scholars in search of documents by women for the purposes of classroom instruction.

Interest in women's studies accelerated and the Library, which had always been open to the public, became a center for college teachers in the area who used the resources themselves and then sent their students to do the same.

Numbers of academics were attracted to women's history. Some had worked previously in other areas of social history—urban, black and ethnic studies. The same impulse that had moved student activists from civil rights and other protest movements to women's rights seemed to be moving scholars and teachers in the same direction. The concerns that all of these people were bringing to women's studies were not only "historic" questions in the traditional sense of the term. They touched on literature and particularly on the social sciences, defining women's studies as interdisciplinary in nature. A recent succinct definition of what women's studies is in the Nov/Dec 1977 issue of *Heliotrope*, a publication of George Washington University.

> Women's studies seeks to revise the existing body of knowledge about women by including them in areas where they have been ignored in the past and by correcting sexist misinterpretation of their experiences, and to add to the body of knowledge by posing new questions about women from a feminist perspective.[5]

This definition raises interesting questions about how to shape and develop the collection of printed materials on the history of women.

No longer could the history of suffrage and other reform be considered an adequate definition of women's history. Teachers and students wanted to find out about average or anonymous women. They wanted to find out about women and the law, for instance, about imprisoned women, saints, prostitutes, and about the image of women in literature. The Library had no books on prostitution and no literary criticism. Looking back now, I recall how knowledge was so neatly compartmentalized. History was one thing and psychology, sociology, health, law and literature were areas for other libraries to collect. But when books in all of these fields came to be written from a feminist perspective, a new collecting policy had to be devised.

The Library had to give up old rules of thumb about what constituted women's history and had to respond to, indeed even anticipate, the directions in which the new research on women was going. Some retroactive buying had to begin in areas in which there was an existing body of literature—the psychology of women is an example. But the greater reason for shifting the scope of the collection was the appearance of books on women in fields which had previously ignored them. Suddenly there was a body of literature about sex-roles, women and health, and discrimination in employment and education. They were in fields never before considered to be within the scope of a history library, but their feminist perspective made them intellectual history. Their appearance was an effect of the women's movement and to ignore the work in these fields would constitute a failure to properly document women in the 1960s and 1970s.

Our ability to increase expenditures was due to a Library Resources Grant. Several other foundation and government grants have allowed the Library to expand and to increase its services. In 1972 the Rockefeller Foundation funded an oral history project to interview women leaders in the population control movement and is currently funding a black oral history project. Black women throughout the country are interviewing older black women whose lives may otherwise have gone unrecorded. Other grants are allowing the Library to publish on microfilm the records of women in the labor movement, to employ additional archivists to process primary material and to publish with a commercial press an important collection of letters (*The Maimie Papers*, Feminist Press).[6] Recently the Library has been awarded by the National Endowment for the Humanities a $400,000 challenge grant, and most recently we have received a Mellon grant to provide fellowships for scholars to use the resources of the Library.

Because the Schlesinger Library is a research collection our emphasis is on acquiring almost all books that are about American women, even books thought to be unsatisfactory by reviewers. It would be detrimental to future scholars if we collected only the feminist side of issues. Negative responses to the women's movement must also be documented. The movement is questioning values that have held a cherished place in American culture throughout most of the 19th century and for more than half of the 20th. The social model of women who are devoted to their homes and to the welfare of other family members is a concept that is difficult for many to give up. Men and women are critical of changes advocated by the women's movement. The opinions of Phyllis Schlafly and Right to Life proponents are all a vital part of the social history of these times. What feminists perhaps consider a temporary anti-feminist backlash might in fact be a reversal in feminist trends. There is, for instance, a restoration of traditional customs like the Sweet Sixteen party, high school proms and big church weddings. This, after couples have been writing their own marriage vows, leaving out the "obedience" clause and emphasizing equality within the marriage.

Apart from the staggering numbers of new books which have increased our expenditures at least by 1500%, the Library is acquiring unprecedented numbers of new periodicals. Standard titles like *The Ladies Home Journal* and *McCalls* continue, and new titles which had been the earliest herald of the women's movement have proliferated and grown ever more specialized. There are, for instance, two periodicals devoted to women and the martial arts: *Black Belt Woman* and *The Fighting Women News;* a newsletter for women alcoholics; and numerous titles devoted to women and the world of work. There are learned journals devoted to discussions of sex-roles, psychology, literature and art; and some prestigious journals like *Signs* and *Feminist Studies* which provide an overview of the various intellectual trends in women's studies. Whereas before 1969 the Library subscribed to around 20 periodicals, it now receives over 250.

In addition to books and periodicals, we collect and organize ephemeral material into subject, biography and organization files. Pamphlet material is cataloged and maintained along with articles about women clipped from newspapers and magazines, mailings from women's organizations, descriptions of conferences, etc. These files have existed since the founding of the Library. But since the advent of the women's movement we have maintained topical files holding the most current information which includes bibliographies, law cases, new federal and state laws, and information about issues. These current files are revised periodically and some of the material is absorbed into our established subject, organization and biography files.

What has proved extremely valuable to graduate students and teachers is our collection of bibliographies and reference works that describe research in progress. The rapidly increasing and intense interest in women's studies has created problems for those of us who worry about bibliographic control. In a new field which had few experts, there has been an inevitable lag between what existed and the tools which provide access to that information.

Clearinghouses on feminist publications appeared soon after the onset of women's studies. Two sources in particular have been invaluable to libraries and to individual researchers: Know, Inc., a clearinghouse in Pittsburgh which has distributed at minimal cost reprints of key articles and course syllabi in women's studies, and the Feminist Press[7] which has compiled bibliographies, reprinted books, and published for the first time some high quality feminist books.

College and research libraries concerned with developing women's studies collections would be well served by acquiring materials from these key publishers. Academic libraries can develop their collections in several ways. Many publishers are reprinting books. The most ambitious project to date is the series being offered by Research Publications, Inc. which includes microfilms of the pre-1920 holdings in books on women from major research collections which include the Schlesinger Library, Smith, Harvard, The Boston Public and the New York Public Libraries. The collection contains 1200 reels of microfilm and the guide to these reels is probably the most comprehensive list of books about women that now exists for the pre-1920 period. Other publishers are offering annotated bibliographies on women—Scarecrow Press, Garland and G. K. Hall.

College libraries that serve an undergraduate constituency mainly can now rely on some of these published guides for selective buying in women's studies. These institutions are no doubt already purchasing books in women's studies, but they are absorbed into the broad collection according to discipline and do not stand separately as a women's studies collection. Annotated bibliographies can help instructors of introductory courses locate appropriate books for their curricula.

The academic library interested in developing a research collection could acquire a large proportion of material on microfilm. Reprints of out of print books and periodicals for the pre-1920 period could be acquired at an estimated cost of $60,000. Merely keeping up with current published materials would probably cost $15,000 annually. But the cost of collecting materials for the years between 1920 and 1970 is inestimable. Nine-tenths of our printed material (20,000 books and pamphlets) falls into this category.

Perhaps a better plan for beginning a research collection on women would be to collect primary materials on a regional level. The task of collecting everything on the subject of women is impossible. At the Schlesinger Library we limit our scope to American women only. For manuscript collecting we tend to focus on individuals and organizations whose careers and purposes have national implications—Betty Friedan's papers and the records of the National Organization for Women are examples. Because we are in the Boston area we do some specializing in collecting on local individuals and groups within New England.

So much has been occurring on a community level throughout the country. Women have been organizing women's centers, involving themselves in continuing education in record numbers, seeking and receiving career counseling and becoming involved as candidates in local politics. These are visible examples of current activities, but social historians are convinced that women in the 19th and earlier part of the 20th centuries have also made contributions to their local communities—setting up schools, hospitals and other social services on a volunteer basis. As institutions succeeded, professional staffs took over and the initial efforts of large number of anonymous women have been obscured. Research libraries would provide unique services by collecting evidence of these achievements. Such collections would not duplicate the efforts of other libraries.

In presenting these thoughts and suggestions about library resources for women's studies, it is not intended to leave the impression that academic libraries other than the Schlesinger Library are totally ignoring the field. Smith College has maintained a special collection on women for as long as Radcliffe. Collections supporting women's studies programs have sprung up within large university and small college libraries all around the country. The Ohio State University Library, for example, has collected since 1970 and has published a bi-monthly newsletter that includes annotations of current books about women. Northwestern University has a special collection on women and so does Scripps College. The University of Wisconsin has the only state-wide bibliographer for women's studies. Probably numerous other institutions are quietly collecting in this wide-ranging, enormously interesting new field. One of the most important purposes of a professional meeting of this kind, no doubt, is to bring together those of us who share an area of interest such as women's studies and to acquaint ourselves with the efforts of one another's institutions.

Finally, mention should be made of a proposal we are working on. It is for a feasibility study to fund a library bulletin for women's studies, and hopefully a pilot issue can be developed under the terms of the grant. This publication would deal with problems in book selection, archival questions, news of new reference sources, works in progress, reviews, and miscellaneous information—notices of duplicate materials available at specific libraries, news of conferences, sources of funding. Anyone who is interested in such a journal should get in touch with this author.

Exchanges of information between women's studies specialists is necessary and important, but there are ways in which the awareness of the challenges of women's studies can be important generally to academic librarians. There are interesting possibilities for library school educators who might use problems of women's studies book collecting to illustrate the ambiguities of collecting within an interdisciplinary field, particularly one based on social history. In the largest sense, everything is social history. For instance, an example of an interesting selection problem is the subject of child-rearing. Child-rearing is a task long associated with the role of women. Should a research collection buy everything on that subject—baby-care books, manuals, how-to's of all sorts? After all, such materials reflect social attitudes of any given moment. The problem, of course, is that thousands of such books are written. Is it perhaps better then to acquire only books that deal with the history of child-rearing? That sounds safe, but unless the how-to books are collected, there will be no materials for future histories of what was.

There are other questions that could involve library schools. The bibliographic work in women's studies is still in its infancy. Students in reference, humanities and social science classes could be asked to compile bibliographic information that has never before been collected. This already has occurred in connection with Radcliffe College when the editors of *Notable American Women* asked library schools for student help in compiling initial information about specific women. The *Dictionary of American Biography* does this too.

For the librarian interested in scholarship, the new field of women's studies offers opportunities for publishing. The field needs directories, bibliographies, reference books of all sorts. But this in itself is a topic for another paper.

REFERENCES

1. Florence Howe, *Seven Years Later: Women's Studies Programs in 1976; A Report of the National Advisory Council on Women's Educational Progress.*
2. Nancy Cott, ed., *Root of Bitterness; Documents of the Social History of American Women* (New York: Dutton, 1972).
3. Gerda Lerner, ed. *Black Women in White America; A Documentary History* (New York: Pantheon, 1972).
4. Alice S. Rossi, ed. *The Feminist Papers: From Adams to de Beauvoir* (New York: Columbia University Press, 1973).
5. *Heliotrope* (George Washington University, Nov/Dec. 1977).
6. Maimie Pinzer, *The Maimie Papers* (Old Westbury, NY: Feminist Press, 1977).
7. Know, Inc., P. O. Box 86031, Pittsburgh, Pa. 15221; Feminist Press, Box 334, Old Westbury, New York 11568.

Richard G. Landon

University of Toronto

RARE BOOK AND SPECIAL COLLECTIONS LIBRARIES: HORIZONTAL CONSOLIDATION

Rare book libraries in North America developed historically in three forms: the subscription or society library, independent research libraries, and rare book and special collections departments in large general libraries. After a period of affluence, which witnessed a burgeoning of special collections departments in university libraries, a period of consolidation has arrived. The major problems faced today by rare book and special collections libraries are reliance on private donors for financial support, utilization of collections, security, and conservation and preservation.

Recently a number of articles have appeared (most notably in the Times Literary Supplement of Nov. 18th, 1977) which strongly suggest that far from seeking new horizons for rare book and special collections departments in academic libraries the librarians who practice in this slightly arcane field ought to be spending their time, talents, and energy seeking ways of shoring up the crumbling edifices that loom so formidably on the present horizon. The doctrine that 'more is better' (more institutions of higher education, with more graduate studies programs, which require more research libraries, with more books and manuscripts to fill more special collections departments) has come under the close and critical scrutiny of those who provide the funding for publicly supported institutions. The darkening twilight of the seventies has all but obliterated the last vestiges of the blazing noon-time of the fabulous sixites. Thus the new horizons for rare book and special collections libraries may well be circumscribed by consolidation, utility, security, preservation, and that dismaying phrase calculated to cause the rare book custodian to desperately fondle his First Folio: zero-base budgeting.

Rare book libraries, however, exist in an historical context and the problems which they face today can only be properly appreciated through an understanding of their historical development. In North America there have been three principal forms of the rare book library: subscription or society libraries, independent research libraries, and the rare book and special collections departments within large general libraries.

When Benjamin Franklin and his friends formed the Library Company of Philadelphia in 1731 the concept of a rare book collection would not have occurred to them at all. The purpose of their library was as eminently practical as their characters: to provide for the instruction and general education of themselves and their fellow citizens. That many of the books purchased by the Library Company and given to it by members have become 'rare books' (that odd definition of a book that combines intrinsic merit, desirability, and relative scarcity) is merely historical accident and the third edition of Catesby's *Birds* (1771) which was purchased by the Company in 1772 was acquired because it was considered a standard reference source. The first real collector of rare books in America seems to have been William Mackenzie of Philadelphia whose copy of the Jenson Pliny on vellum was surely purchased for the complex aesthetic reasons we associate with bibliophily. Mackenzie's library is happily preserved in the Library Company of Philadelphia, where, together with the collections of James Logan and others it forms what is one of the notable special collections libraries of the United States. The Library Company is, in fact, now an example of the second category of rare book library, the independent research library, and its transformation is part of one of the most notable collecting movements in North American history.

The independent research libraries developed directly from bibliomania, the passionate pursuit of rare books by wealthy collectors, and are essentially a twentieth century phenomenon. Although John Carter Brown formed his great collection of Americana in the nineteenth century it was formally institutionalized as part of Brown University in 1900. James Lenox, who brought the first Gutenberg Bible to North America in 1847 (and quibbled about the price of 500 pounds), incorporated his library in 1870, but the familiar rollcall of the names of the great American industrialists, who collected rare books on a scale which surpassed even that of the original members of the Roxburghe Club, begins with Henry Huntington. His collection was established as an independent research institution in 1919 and was followed by Clements in 1922, Morgan in 1924, Folger in 1930, and Clark in 1934. Of these, the brightest stars in the galaxy, only Brown, Clements, Folger, and Clark were formally associated with an institution, and even then their independence from the main university library was carefully preserved. Financed from endowed funds, given general direction by independent boards of trustees, housed in separate buildings, and presided over by a series of the most brilliant bookmen on the continent, these libraries flourished and continue to flourish to this day. Their influence on the development of rare book and special collections departments as part of the libraries of the major universities of North America was direct and profound, particularly regarding methods of acquisition.

It is, however, the rare book and special collections departments of academic libraries that most concerns this conference and their proliferation and growth parallels the growth of university libraries and the development of the universities themselves. The older, privately financed, institutions have always had substantial numbers of old books but even in 1876 the total collection of Harvard only numbered two hundred thousand, a figure easily surpassed by most of the major special collections departments today. Harvard's Houghton Library was established in 1942 with a substantial gift of books and money and has been followed by Beineke at Yale, Lilly at Indiana, and Fisher at Toronto, to cite only a few obvious examples. The development of these collections illustrates two essential attributes that these rather disparate institutions have in common; the presence of private collectors and the commitment of the parent institution to academic research at the highest level. Whether these universities, and the numerous other examples that could be cited, fully realized the implications of their commitment is debatable but it seems obvious, at the very least, that the large universities have been able, so far, to handle the commitment and hold their heads up in the company of the large independent research libraries.

In an exhilerating era of affluence, such as higher education in North America has just passed through, where the large and influential lead others are sure to follow. The University of California at Los Angeles opened what was said to be the first deliberately named 'special collections' department in 1950 and the library director became a pioneer in the wholesale methods of acquisition formerly indulged in only by the Morgans, Huntingtons and Folgers. Smaller universities and many colleges followed this lead and rare book and special collections departments sprang up in profusion. From Alberta to Florida, from Nova Scotia to New Mexico, it is difficult to go into a university library of any appreciable size and pretension and *not* see a collection of Anglo-Irish literature. The commitment made by these institutions has been exactly the same in kind (if not in scope) as that made by the 'big ten.' Whether these universities and colleges have fully realized and been able to support the commitment is very much debatable. What lies just over the horizon can be the subject of much gloomy speculation.

What exactly is the commitment to academic research at the highest level? In broad outline it implies acquisition of research materials of all kinds, from the 'rarissima' of printed books to the humble correspondence of a local weather observer; it implies housing with proper (and expensive) controls for temperature and humidity, security, and elaborate facilities for research; it implies a staff with special abilities and training who will be able to interpret and supply real access to the collections; it implies an effective conservation and restoration program that can at least make a concerted attempt to preserve the material for future use; it implies a program of support, whether financed internally or externally, which will allow the collections to be further developed and refined; and it implies a total institutional commitment to the concept of academic research. How many rare book and special collections departments in North America fulfill these criteria now? How many will be able to play in the big league in 1984?

In 1965 Gordon Ray, in a fascinating article on the world of rare books,[1] characterized the three great forces for change as affluence, institutional involvement, and the knowledge explosion. Affluence could be easily demonstrated, the most spectacular example being the University of Texas, who, between 1957 and 1965, spent twelve and one-half million dollars on books. It is worth noting that the most obvious manifestation of this expenditure, the Humanities Research Center, was established as an institution independent from the University Library and has remained so. Ray also pointed out that as an example of comparative affluence even this enormous sum does not compare with the expenditures of Morgan or Huntington during a similar period.

In 1965 Gordon Ray asked his correspondents (collectors, librarians, and dealers who supplied the information for his article) what they considered the number of 'significant' rare book libraries in the United States for the years 1945, 1965, and a projected figure for 1985. The average of the replies indicated that in 1945 there were twenty to forty-five, in 1965 thirty-five to fifty and that in 1985 there would be forty-five to one hundred. These knowledgeable opinions would convey the notion that during the twenty years between 1945 and 1965 the rich got richer but the charmed circle of 'significant' rare book libraries was not enlarged very much. The expectation, however, was that the next twenty years would see the development of a large number of new 'significant' institutions. From approximately a half-way point in the latter period has the predicted growth, in fact, happened? One would think not and whatever trend there might have been has probably been severely retarded.

The first ACRL Rare Books Preconference was held in 1959 with one hundred eighty-seven individuals representing ninety-seven institutions in attendance. Since then the number of conferrees has varied considerably but in 1965 the Rare Books Section of ACRL had four hundred fifty-three members. The 1977 membership was approximately eighteen hundred and the section has grown into one of the most active in ACRL. These figures, which are of dubious value in any absolute sense because they don't discriminate between active members and those who merely sign up, indicate that there are, at least, many more institutions which employ librarians who are interested in and concerned about rare books and special collections than formerly was the case.

In 1974 Gordon Ray again conducted a survey of the rare book world.[2] Where he had found the buoyant mood of affluence in 1965, by 1974 he could only conclude that affluence was gone and institutional involvement in the rare book market had diminished. What this statement really meant was that whereas ten years ago dealers in antiquarian books perceived that the pace in collecting was being set by institutions now private collectors and the dealers themselves have again taken the lead. This trend does not necessarily mean that the books and manuscripts do not end up in institutions. The presence of collectors has been previously mentioned as one of the chief common characteristics of the major rare book and special collections departments and the best institutional collections act as powerful magnets (helped considerably by liberal tax laws) toward private collections. The Tax Reform Act of 1969 has had a detrimental effect on the collecting of manuscripts by institutions in the United States but one is led to believe that there is still hope that the Act will eventually be re-reformed.

If the seventies can be called the era of consolidation, (and there seems abundant evidence that this is a mild expression of what is happening right now) what are the principal problems of the present and what prognostications can be made for the future? At the most extreme there is some indication that certain rare book libraries and special collections departments will disappear altogether. A substantial part of the Pforzheimer Library is now being offered for sale, Hofstra University has closed its Rare Book and Special Collections Department, and the rare books from the Franklin Institute have come under the auctioneer's hammer. The most important institutions are unlikely to have to resort to such drastic measures but it is worth noting the presence on the market of large numbers of duplicate copies and inappropriate books from institutional collections. Thus is partially affected a replenishment both of the supply of rare books and of shrunken institutional coffers.

The era of consolidation may even bring about some literal consolidation. Library cooperation, as it applies to collections, is more often talked about than acted upon but there are a few instances where small institutions with important collections that they are unable to care for properly have agreed to a transfer to a larger institution with better facilities. The arrangement worked out between Trinity College at the University of Toronto and the Thomas Fisher Rare Book Library is one example. We are, however, a long way from the 'Museum of the Book' mentioned by one of Gordon Ray's correspondents, which would amalgamate all the rare book collections in New York City.

Many of the important rare book and special collections departments have traditionally relied heavily on donors and friends groups for acquisitions funds. One can safely predict that their reliance will be even greater in the future, that many of the smaller institutions will form their own friends organizations, and that attempts will be made to utilize some of the money for purposes other than acquisition. It is an unfortunate fact of institutional life that whereas a donor will be gratified to have a collection, or even a room, named after him he will probably be less than ecstatic over the prospect of the John Smith Memorial Booklift. I can, however, provide a heartening example. The Thomas Fisher Rare Book Library has a large and important history of medicine collection, funded by a local foundation. The funding has provided not only for the books but also for the salary of a cataloger and the services of an expert restorer.

Rare book and special collections departments are now facing the problem of utilization, often, one suspects, for the first time. Embarassing questions about how certain collections fit in with the aims and objectives of the parent institution are now being asked with increasing frequency and the problems are sometimes compounded by the university adjusting its own objectives in the light of fiscal restraints. The independent research libraries have a considerable advantage in this area for they are able to formulate their own limited objectives and closely define their collecting interests. Many of the comparisons, often odious, drawn between them and university collections are neither very revealing nor very useful. The question of utilization is often put in the most difficult manner; that of cost justification. Has anyone ever dared apply the techniques of zero-base budgeting to a large, diverse, separately-housed rare book and special collections department? The resulting figures would, one suspects, require some considerable justification to many of the financial officers of our universities.

Security is a problem now and will become more severe in the forseeable future. Almost every major university in the United States and Canada has suffered a substantial theft at some time within the past five years and the number of stolen books on the market today is frightening indeed. New buildings tend to have specific, and sometimes satisfactory, arrangements for security but what about the special collections department that is part of a building that was designed for open access?

The foregoing problems are all serious and are guaranteed to provide a permanent headache for the director of a rare book and special collections library. They, however, pale by comparison with the most overwhelming problem faced by all libraries, and by special collections departments in particular: preservation and conservation. It has often been pointed out that the climate of a large part of North America, fluctuating as it does between below zero and one hundred degrees Fahrenheit and between less than five per cent and one hundred per cent relative humidity, is particularly damaging to the materials from which books are manufactured. When the instability of the materials themselves, particularly for the period after 1870, is taken into account the responsibility to provide research collections for future generations of scholars becomes awesome indeed. Some of the technology required to deal with the problems of preservation is available now and a great deal of research is being carried out, yet how many university special collections departments have coordinated preservation programs with qualified staff and proper equipment? Many institutions are caught in the financial squeeze (conservation is very expensive). When they had the money they were buying books not deacidification equipment and now they do not have the money for either.

Lest these observations seem to build to a crescendo of gloomy hysteria such that you might expect my next prediction to be that the world will disintegrate next Friday and that the only solution is to deftly slash one's wrists with an English leather-paring knife I will conclude with the observation that there is serious recognition of the problems and more work is being done now by more people to discover and implement solutions. Consolidation is a sobering experience but also provides its own exciting challenges. Metaphorically speaking we may never see the sixties again but will at least have the opportunity to describe to our successors, in the time honored tradition of the rare book world, the exhilerating excitement of the 'good old days'.

REFERENCES

1. Ray, Gordon N., 'The Changing World of Rare Books' in *The Papers of the Bibliographical Society of America*, vol. 59, no. 2 (1965) p. 103–141.
2. Ray, Gordon N., 'The World of Rare Books Re-examined' in *The Yale University Library Gazette* (July 1974): 77–146.

Diane C. Parker and Eric J. Carpenter

State University of New York at Buffalo

A ZERO-BASE BUDGET APPROACH TO STAFF JUSTIFICATION FOR A COMBINED REFERENCE AND COLLECTION DEVELOPMENT DEPARTMENT

Zero-base budgeting techniques can be used to anlayze reference and collection development activities. In Lockwood Library at SUNY Buffalo, subject specialists perform reference, computer searching, instruction, and collection development work. As part of a university libraries staff justification project, Lockwood administrators described discrete operations in "decision packages" which included quantitative measures and alternative methods of conducting each activity. Operations were ranked by priority. The study was successful in that it gave us complete and precise data immediately useful for our staff justification. It also raised many questions and forced us to re-examine some basic assumptions.

BACKGROUND

At the State University of New York at Buffalo, budgets are no longer as ample as they were in the 1960s, and a stalled building program for a new campus has created unexpected demands for library services. Because of the severity of competing needs for staff resources, the Library Administrative Council, which includes the Director of Libraries and the Heads of several library units, decided in fall, 1977 to conduct an extensive staff analysis and justification project. Each Unit Head was given the flexibility to use whatever methodology he or she wished for this project, and by spring, 1978 the results were still being reviewed.

For this staff justification project, Lockwood Library decided to use zero-base budgeting techniques to compile and analyze data about its staff. Lockwood is the graduate social sciences and humanities library. For years it also has been the 'main' library of the system. It has several departments, branches and special collections. By itself Lockwood is comparable in size to many medium size academic library systems. There were two reasons why Lockwood needed to analyze its staff in great detail. The first was that for years it has been perceived by other SUNY, Buffalo libraries as being overstaffed. In recent years Lockwood has had staff reductions, but some librarians still seem to feel instinctively that any operation so large must surely have excess staff. The second reason why Lockwood needed to conduct a thorough staffing analysis is that we are moving into a new, six-story building in May, 1978. To operate in this new building, we are consolidating and realigning services and staff. Our staff justification needed to serve as an explanation of present staff utilization. At the same time, it needed to serve as a plan for staff utilization in the new library.

ZERO-BASE BUDGETING

We chose to use zero-base budgeting methods because this approach has several advantages for us. By using it we developed an objective, detailed description of the way staff and other resources are used. This included the value of the results achieved. Zero-base budgeting eliminates historical justifications. The fact that we had certain staff and provided certain services a year or a decade ago is not adequate justification for having them today or in the next ten years. Zero-base budgeting is both a planning and a budgeting tool. In planning we identify the policies, goals and programs. In budgeting we identify the activities and resources needed to achieve our goals.

Zero-base budgeting consists of two steps. The first step is to develop "decision packages" which analyze and describe each discrete activity, current as well as new. I just used some terms I'd like to repeat for emphasis. "*Decision packages*" are developed to analyze and describe *discrete* activities. Discrete activities which are important enough to be described in detail have to be defined by the person analyzing the operation. Examples of discrete activities are reference desk service and book selection. After the first step of developing decision packages is completed, the second step is to rank them. The decision packages are evaluated and then ranked in order of importance. Priorities can be set either by subjective evaluation or by cost/benefit evaluation.

The key to zero-base budgeting is identifying and evaluating alternatives for each activity. There are two kinds of alternatives to be considered. The first is different *ways* of performing the same function. For instance, does an information and reference desk need to be staffed only by professional librarians, or can other types of staff be used to provide a good level of service? The second kind of alternative is different *levels* of effort of performing the function. For instance, should collection evaluation occur occasionally for some parts of the collection or constantly for all parts of the collection?

LOCKWOOD'S ZERO-BASE BUDGETING

Planning Lockwood's zero base budgeting project was relatively easy. A summary of principles gleaned from Peter Pyhrr's books on zero-base budgeting[1] as well as a form adapted from several given by Pyhrr were discussed by Lockwood department heads. The form was revised slightly, and then we all used it to describe our operations. That was the hard part! As a general rule both policy level and operational level managers must be involved in the zero-base budgeting process. Policy managers provide initial guidelines. For instance, it was decided that we would all describe our operations as we expected them to exist in the new library in 1978. Our unit head needed to give us information about anticipated changes and levels of staffing. Operational managers at the functional level (department and branch heads in our case) should do the detailed analysis, develop decision packages and rank them. Finally, policy level managers should review the analysis and initial rankings; they may decide to eliminate packages or reorder priorities. The planning forms we used are brief outline descriptions of each decision package. Additional documentation needs to be available for each package in case more thorough justification or explanation is needed. It was recognized by the Lockwood administrative staff that the project not only would give us a great deal of data, but it would also expose us to the scrutiny of anyone who took the time to read all the decision packages. Since we were trying to improve and refine our operations, it seemed preferable to set down all the facts for interpretation and discussion.

DECISION PACKAGES

Each decision package has a package name, a brief description of the activity, a statement of purpose as related to the department and to other parts of the library, a detailed description of operations, achievements from actions, the consequences of not approving actions, quantitative package measures (related statistics), resources required (staff, supplies, etc.), alternative levels of effort, alternative methods of performing the same function, and amounts and sources of funds. (See Appendix A for sample of form used.)

LOCKWOOD REFERENCE/COLLECTION DEVELOPMENT DEPARTMENT

Lockwood Library has a core of fifteen professional librarians responsible for providing reference desk service, computer searching of bibliographic data bases, library instruction, subject specialty reference work, collection development for the reference and circulating collections, and administration of all these services. In addition, five other librarians do some collection development work. 2.5 FTE classified staff and additional student assistants support the department's work. The Head of Collection Development coordinates and supervises selection activities. The Head of Reference supervises public service activities and has overall line responsibility.

The very first thing we discovered in analyzing department activities was that we would have to work together very closely. We also discovered that we would have to rewrite all eighteen job descriptions for the department. We needed to standardize our job descriptions and correlate them to staff allocation figures given in the decision packages. Let me use library instruction as an example of why we needed to rewrite job descriptions. Over the past five years, library instruction has become an important and integral part of our service. The gradual development of this service could be seen in our job descriptions. Some mentioned library instruction as part of reference work, some mentioned it as a major separate activity and still others included it as an after thought in a section called "other". Yet every subject librarian was equally responsible for library instruction as a significant part of their work. It was impossible to quantify. Before we could tell how much time each librarian and the staff as a whole was spending on library instruction, we had to rewrite job descriptions. This had to be done very carefully, and it took a lot of time. But we now have a standard job description for all librarians in the department. The percentages of time allocated are 45% for information service, 45% for collection development and 10% for other administrative and professional service activities. About half the librarians' job descriptions vary somewhat from the standard version, but all of them are closely correlated to the decision packages for the department. We cannot revise any of them without a corresponding need to revise our zero-base budgeting analysis. The only exception is language in the standard job description explaining the unique responsibilities of full librarians. (In SUNY, librarians have faculty status, and there are four ranks equivalent to professorial ranks: assistant, senior assistant, associate, and full librarian.)

THE REFERENCE DEPARTMENT

The work of analyzing *all* of the activities of an operation is the first of several hard steps in zero base budgeting. I'd like to emphasize the word "all". Most of us think about some of our operations in great detail, but how many of us give equal weight to scrutinizing all of them? I never did. It came as a surprise to me that I had set some of them aside for a rather long time. At this point, I learned that all parts of an integrated system need some regular attention.

Some Reference operations are easier to quantify than other professional activities. Our department has a regular desk and/or computer terminal assignment of eleven hours a week for each librarian. Given a standard job description, a standard work week and a standard work year, it was easy to calculate that each librarian spends 29% of his or her time at a schedule service desk. That left 16% to allocate to following up on reference questions, subject specialty reference or consultation, and library instruction. Allocations of time were based on a 37.5 hour work week and a 48 week work year. Hours per week were calculated to help the librarians understand how they might want to manage their time. However, for professional librarians it is more realistic to think in terms of hours or days per year. For instance, library instruction is more likely to be concentrated in some parts of the year and not given at all in others. The question is how much library instruction can the librarian give in nineteen days a year, not three hours a week. Librarians' activities not specifically allocated to collection development work were accounted for in the Reference decision packages. All of our librarians have 10% of their job descriptions allocated to "other". This includes administrative work such as consultation on service policies and attending department meetings. It also includes professional service work such as membership on Library Faculty, Library system-wide or University-wide committees. The amount of time allocated to a typical subject librarians' activities can be broken down as follows:

TABLE 1

Allocation of a Typical Subject Librarian's Time

	% of Job Description	Hours Per Week	Hours Per Year	Days Per Year
Schedule desk or computer hours	29%	11	528	70.4
Follow-up on reference questions	3%	1	48	6.4
Subject specialty reference or consultation	5%	2	96	12.8
Library instruction; in house publications	8%	3	144	19.2
Reference subtotal	45%	17 hrs.	810 hrs.	108 days
Collection Development	45%	17 hrs.	810 hrs.	108 days
Other—administrative	6%	2.0	108	14.4
—professional service	4%	1.5	72	9.6
Total	100%	37.5 hrs.	1800 hrs.	240 days

After reference operations were analyzed, they were described in twelve decision packages. Tables were developed to summarize staff allocations by package and type of staff, staff allocations by broad service activity and type of staff, and gross staff allocations by job descriptions for reference and collection development.

For simplicity's sake and because the professional component is the largest in our department, the reference decision packages with professional staff allocations are listed here in descending order of priority.

TABLE 2

Reference Activities (Decision Packages)

Package Name	Professional FTE*
1. Reference service—desk	3.43
2. Reference collection—selection	[.20]**
3. Reference collection—maintenance	.05
4. Reference service—subject specialization	.59
5. Library instruction; in-house publications	.85
6. Liaison; academic departments	1.13
7. Computersearch	1.17
8. Administration	1.71
9. Reference collection—vertical file	[.04]
10. Reference collection—telephone books	[.02]
11. Reference collection—corporate annual reports	–
12. Professional service	.71
Total	8.51 FTE

*FTE = Full time equivalent
**Figures in brackets were included in Collection Development FTE figures

When Lockwood's staff justification project was finished, it was made available to all the staff for reading. A few weeks later and before formal review began, the Reference and Collection Development Department met to review its portion of the project. Reference desk service and its supporting collections were reaffirmed as the highest priority. This was important since desk duty sometimes is seen as the activity that interrupts everything else. Library instruction, in-house publications, subject specialty reference and liaison with academic departments have second priority. They are all part of our continuing efforts to help students and faculty exploit our collections. Computersearch, our on-line bibliographic searching service, is third in priority only because it is not now as highly developed a service as we hope it will become. We have a good customized bibliography service, but we have not yet fully exploited on-line searching or OCLC for reference use. When our Computersearch service is more developed and integrated with reference desk service, it may become a first priority service also.

When we reviewed staff allocations in reference we found a few surprises. We reorganized the library five years ago and combined separate reference and collection development departments in order to enhance Lockwood's capacity to provide subject expertise. We have increased it, but that still means we have only .59 FTE specifically devoted to subject specialty reference service. (Of course these subject specialists also are available eleven hours a week at the desk.) Library instruction and in-house publications are considered an important part of our service program, yet they are allotted only .85 FTE. In contrast, and to our surprise, we learned that subject librarians account for .695 FTE or 40% of the administrative decision package. We decided that fairly heavy consultative administration is useful in an academic environment. Yet an old truism was reaffirmed. The more time we spend meeting, the less time we have to deliver service. The necessary meetings that we do have should be planned and conducted carefully so that the time spent does in fact improve library service rather than detract from it.

Secretarial, clerical and student staff time was distributed among various decision packages. When I first started thinking about the project, I envisioned a secretarial/clerical decision package. It wasn't very long before I realized that *support* staff is just that. People are needed to provide support for various service activities, and the time they spend doing this work should be accounted for in describing these activities.

How essential is administration? We spend 1.71 professional FTE on administration. That includes planning, training, evaluating staff and services, supervising support staff, etc. It also includes the .695 FTE mentioned above which is used in consulting subject librarians. Administrative work is important for supporting services and facilitating change, but it must have a lower priority than the programs it supports.

Professional service was ranked as the last priority not because it is unimportant, but because it is not a department service. It is not the activity that library users expect from us on a daily basis.

If our group discussion did nothing else, it helped us focus on priorities and reaffirm our commitment to a variety of service programs.

COLLECTION DEVELOPMENT

Collection Development within Lockwood Library is organized along disciplinary lines. Librarians select for disciplines related in most instances to particular academic departments. As in many other libraries, book selection is done within Lockwood by professional librarians who also work in various other capacities. The Heads of Acquisitions, Government Documents, Art, and Lockwood Library all serve as selectors, as does the Curator of the Polish Collection. The Lockwood acquisitions budget is allocated by the Head of Collection Development who acts as chief bibliographer and coordinates the work of the other fifteen selectors.

The first step in studying staff utilization consisted of revising job descriptions for the librarians working in reference and collection development. Four selectors in other departments were not able to provide full job descriptions, but they were able to say how many hours per week they spend on collection development. The time they spend was added to the number of professional FTE's in collection development.

The total amount of time available for collection development was calculated by adding the amount of time spent by each selector. This total was expressed as the number of FTE staff members allocated for work in developing collections.

Twenty discrete collection development activities were then identified and divided into broad areas of activity: liaison work, collection policy development, collection evaluation, searching, selection, ordering, budgeting, work with collections, and administration. Liaison activities were considered part of collection development, although they also are essential for library instruction and subject specialty reference service. These collection development activities were then arranged in one list according to the approximate order in which they are carried out by an individual bibliographer (Table 3). Note that liaison with patrons is developed before policies are formulated or materials selected.

TABLE 3

Collection Development Activities (Decision Packages)

Package Name	Professional FTE
1. Liaison with academic dept.	.662
2. Liaison with CTS and other LML Depts.	.397
3. Liaison with other libraries	.066
4. Writing collection policies	.198
5. Collection evaluation	.331
6. Bibliographic searching	.397
7. Choosing materials	2.325
8. File maintenance for selection	.133
9. Coordination of selection	.397
10. De-selection: cancellation and weeding	.066
11. Gift and exchange	.066
12. Preparation of order forms	.265
13. Budget justification and allocation	.198
14. Monitoring expenditures	.265
15. Transfers	.033
16. Collection maintenance: repair, replacement	.033
17. Policy preparation and implementation	.265
18. Personnel	.397
19. Design and monitoring of routines	.133
20. Clerical support for administration	—
Total	6.627

Each activity was then described and analyzed in a separate decision package using the standard form. The purpose of each activity, the description of actions performed, the consequences of not performing the activity etc. were all stated in as much detail as possible. All available quantitative measures were specified such as size of acquisitions budget, number of academic programs served, and the number of volumes acquired. Each activity was assigned a priority from one through four.

The crucial and most challenging part of this analysis for collection development was the determination of time actually spent by staff on each specific activity. The quantification of effort spent on book selection is a problem for which there does not appear to be a satisfactory solution at this time. It seems to many to be impossible to measure how long it takes a bibliographer to develop working relationships with faculty and students or to select a book. What was done therefore was to estimate the effort expended by the collection development staff *as a group*. A percentage of time spent by the total staff for each discrete activity was estimated in order to provide figures for the amount of staff used for each activity. The time spent by the one clerical and one student staff member on each activity was also estimated. These estimates were made by the Head of Collection Development and confirmed by the Head of Lockwood.

According to these estimates only 35% of the total effort expended by the bibliographers is being devoted to actual book selection, while another 10% is spent on liaison work. This can be explained by the fact that selectors spend about 12% of their time doing such non-professional work as searching, filing and typing or writing out order slips.

Because our selection is organized by discipline, we spend another 6% of our time insuring that needed materials of an interdisciplinary nature do not slip through our selection process. This can happen when a selector feels that he should not spend money on something his particular academic department may not want.

These and other facts discovered during this staff analysis will be useful in satisfying a number of short and long term planning and budgetary needs. An immediate goal of the project was to develop as accurate an assessment of present staff usage as possible, and this was accomplished. Since selectors are spending a significant amount of time on non-professional tasks, future budget requests may include larger amounts of support staff.

As each activity was closely scrutinized, progress was made toward another short term goal—the improvement of existing operations. The identification of alternative methods for each collection development activity has led us to implement some of these alternatives. Procedures are being written as needed and improved where we think it's possible. For example, the procedure for transferring titles within the collection has been simplified.

Long term needs and problems have also been identified and defined more clearly as a result of this analysis. It was mentioned earlier that a reference and collection development staff meeting was held to discuss this project. At this meeting questions were raised about the assignment of priorities for certain activities as well as the distribution of workload for collection development. The staff also stressed the need for careful interpretation and evaluation of the data.

When we discussed the present ranking of activities, for example, it was emphasized that this ranking is based on a fiscal reality—the need to spend our acquisitions budget by a certain date. This means that the actual selection of titles receives a higher priority than writing collection development policy statements even though policies are the foundation of good selection. In other words, the money must be spent or returned to the state, but writing policy statements can be delayed. Because many collection development activities are not as visible as public service activities and because they do not have to be conducted at rigidly scheduled times, it is easy to delay them or neglect them entirely. As a result of our staff discussion, a second ranking of activities in a preferred priority order was developed. This is the order in which activities would be conducted if a more adequate level of support staff were available to free the selectors from non-professional work and provide time for them to give more attention to such professional work as evaluating collections and writing policy statements.

Workload distribution is another fundamental problem that we have been able to define better, if not completely solve. Is our present distribution of workload among selectors effective and equitable? The analysis revealed discrepancies that raised still other questions. Do all areas of the collection require the same level of effort for development? Is it easier to spend a large or a small budget? Do junior librarians need more time for selection than their senior colleauges? Is it possible to define a minimum level of activity necessary to select materials for any given discipline? We have only begun examining these and other questions related to collection development, but we have defined the problems more clearly and developed data which at least indicate where we should begin to look for solutions.

CONCLUSIONS

What did we learn from this staff analysis project? First of all we accomplished our primary goal of developing as accurate a picture as possible of our present staff utiliza-

TABLE 4

Collection Development Activities—Preferred Priority

Activity	Priority
Liaison with academic dept.	1
Collection evaluation	1
Writing collection policies	1
Liaison with other libraries	1
Choosing materials	1
Coordination of selection	1
Liaison with CTS and other LML depts.	2
Gift and exchange	2
De-selection: cancellation and weeding	2
Collection maintenance	2
Monitoring of expenditures	2
Bibliographic searching	3
Policy preparation and implementation	3
Budget justification and allocation	3
Personnel	3
Design and monitoring of routines	3
Preparation of orders	3
File maintenance for selection	4
Transfers	4
Clerical support for administration	4

tion. In the process of doing that we examined our reference and collection development operations in great detail and found ways to make them more efficient. We also generated data that will be useful for short and long range planning and budgetary needs.

We also asked ourselves a more general fundamental question. Does our present staffing pattern, a combined reference and collection development department, provide the best possible service and collections for our patrons? When a single group of professional librarians is engaged in collection development, reference desk work, library instruction, and computer searching, can they perform all of these activities at an acceptable level of quality? If they can, how much clerical and student staff is needed to support their work? If they cannot, would it be more effective to divide staff between separate reference and collection development departments? We have been trying the combined approach for five years and feel the need to review it carefully. Other libraries with similar staffing patterns are beginning to ask the same questions. The times require it. As staff sizes stabilize or decrease, and as the demand for new types of library service increases, it becomes imperative that we examine our traditional patterns and review old assumptions. Using zero-base budgeting techniques can provide a framework for this necessary and demanding task.

REFERENCE

1. Peter A. Pyhrr, *Zero-Base Budgeting; a Practical Management Tool for Evaluating Expenses* (New York: Wiley, 1973).

APPENDIX A. FORM USED FOR ZERO-BASE BUDGETING

Lockwood Library
Budget Analysis & Planning

(1) Package Name (1 of)	(2) Department or Branch	(3) Activity	(4) Dept. Rank	(5) Unit Rank

(6) Statement of Purpose as Related to the Department or Branch

(7) Statement of Purpose as Related to Lockwood Library

(8) Description of Actions (Operations)

(9) Achievements from Actions

(10) Consequences of not Approving Actions

    (a) For the Department or Branch

    (b) For Lockwood Library

(11) Quantitative Package Measures	FY 1974/5	FY 1975/6	FY 1976/7	FY (projected) 1977/8

(12) Resources Required: Staff				Resources Required: Dollars Budgeted			
	1975/6	1976/7	1977/8		1975/6	1976/7	1977/8
Professional				OTPS Supplies			
Paraprofessional				Contractual			
Secretarial				Capital outlay			
Clerical				Travel			
Students				ACQUISITIONS			

Prepared by: _____ Title: _____ Date:_____ Page 1 of ____

Lockwood Library
Budget Analysis & Planning

(1) Package Name	(2) Department or Branch	(3) Activity	(4) Dept. Rank	(5) Unit Rank

(13) Alternatives (Different Levels of Effort) and Cost

Dept. Rank:

Unit Rank:

Dept. Rank:

Unit Rank:

---

(14) Alternatives (Different ways of Performing the Same Function, Activity, or Operation)

(a)

(b)

(c)

(15) Sources of Funds (in dollars)		FY 1974/5	FY 1975/6	FY 1976/7	FY 1977/8
Operational:	State				
	Federal				
	Other				
Grants:	State				
	Federal				
	Other				
Capital & Lease	State				
	Federal				
	Other				
Endowments:					

Prepared by: _____ Title: _____ Date: _____ Page 2 of___

Edwin D. Posey and Kathleen McCullough

Purdue University

APPROVAL PLANS ONE YEAR LATER: THE PURDUE EXPERIENCE WITH SEPARATE SCHOOL PLANS

In a 1977 survey of approval plans in academic libraries, it was suggested by the responses that individual school plans might serve decentralized library systems better than a single general plan. Purdue University's recent experience with school plans is reviewed and evaluated. Some problems—for example, provision of needed added copies—are solved by individual plans. A new question arises: that of the effect on the total collection of acquisitions plans geared to the specific interests of single libraries.

Studies of approval plans have indicated their increasingly important role in the acquisition process. Most of these studies have concentrated on the experiences of academic or large public libraries. One of the most recent[1] presents the experience of 101 academic libraries with approval plans, concentrating on their use as a collection-development device.

This survey reveals a wide variation in the approach to and the use of the plans. After the profile is established, some libraries with inadequate staff for conventional book selection allow the approval plan to add new books to their collection with minimal staff involvement. Others, again understaffed, allow the plan to monitor publishing, but the staff then screens the result carefully. In both groups, one with a frankly expedient approach and the other coupling convenience with evaluation and selection, there are librarians both satisfied and dissatisfied with the results. The reactions range from euphoric to appalled.

Because of the wide range of variables involved (institutional structure, funding differences, for example), one of the principal conclusions of the survey is that approval plans are an individual matter, specific to the institution, and generalization is unreliable if not impossible. It was suggested that the body of knowledge relating to approval plans is likely to be a collection of individual experiences that can be quantified but not applied as a standard or norm. Their utility is as models.

The survey also suggested that one of the causes of dissatisfaction is the application of a centralized plan in a decentralized library system, especially if the plan supplies one copy only of any title. Most libraries responding were in that situation, and most of these required that added copies as well as profile exclusions be purchased, when wanted, from funds other than those dedicated to the approval plan, most frequently these being departmental discretionay funds. Although most libraries said they had no problem with the arrangement because they had some arbitrary means for assigning the single copy, the problem for the remainder is obvious: it then becomes necessary to decide which departmental library gets the approval-plan copy and which has to expend its own funds if it also wants a copy. This arrangement can and does lead to disillusionment on the part of school and departmental librarians who feel that they are being treated inequitably. Factors such as this led to the suggestion that individual school plans would be a more satisfactory arrangement, both to deal with the added-copy problem and to allow more accurate profiles.

This report addresses these two points: local experience with the decentralization of an approval plan in a decentralized library system.

Since the survey was completed, the Purdue University Libraries discontinued the former one-copy approval plan serving the entire library system (twenty-five departmental libraries in nine schools), which was administered by a central acquisitions department. The reason for dropping the plan was the budget. Organized originally to permit unlimited added copies, it was found necessary first to eliminate added copies, then steadily reduce the number of publishers covered to stay within budgetary limits. As the plan became less productive, it was decided in 1976 to abolish it and redistribute the funds budgeted to maintain it. The money was divided among the nine schools of the university, part of it being used to establish school librarians' discretionary funds and the remainder returned to departmental discretionary book funds. The librarians and schools were then offered the option of establishing individual approval plans. Four schools elected to establish plans, although two departments, Education and Psychological Sciences, chose not to participate in their school's plan, and three others, Physics, Chemistry, and Geosciences, later dropped out of the School of Science plan.

The plans now in operation, for approximately a year, are those in the School of Humanities, Social Science, and Education (excluduing Education and Psychological Sciences); the Schools of Engineering; the Departments of Biological Sciences and Mathematical Sciences in the School of Science; and the School of Veterinary Medicine. The Schools of Agriculture, Consumer and Family Sciences, Management, Pharmacy and Pharmacal Sciencies, and Technology chose not to establish approval plans (see Chart I).

Each school or department developed individual subject profiles with the vendors. The mechanics remain essentially the same, although some of the services formerly provided by the central Acquisitions Department are now performed by the department or school library; books and invoices are shipped directly to the individual libraries, and the librarians are responsible for controlling them. Some centralized services continue, however; the Acquisitions Department still keeps accounting records, pays invoices, and handles returns, and the Cataloging Department catalogs all of the books. Bibliographic searching is done in the Cataloging Department for all except one school, which maintains its own bibliographic unit.

To determine the advantages and disadvantages the individual plans offer as compared with the former centralized plan, selection librarians[2] were polled as to their opinions. Those librarians who chose not to establish a plan were asked their reasons, and the Acquisitions Department staff was also requested to comment on the new procedures. Their responses are summarized in the following list.

The librarians adopting an approval plan for their individual schools or departments cite the following reasons for so doing:

1. Gives the librarian greater involvement in the selection process and, consequently, in collection development.

2. Facilitates book selection by permitting decisions based on examination of the actual book rather than depending on publishers' evaluations or later reviews.

CHART I

Purdue University School and Departmental Libraries, Reflecting Overlapping Structure and Academic Interests[3]

Schools	School Library	Departmental Branches	Serves Departments from Other Schools	Departments Served by Other School Libraries
oAgriculture	xoLife Sciences Library	oBiochemistry Library oEntomology Library	xBiological Sciences (from School of Science)	oAgricultural Economics (in Krannert Library)
oConsumer and Family Sciences	oConsumer and Family Sciences Library			
xEngineering (six schools)	xEngineering Library		oAviation Technology (in a branch; from School of Technology)	
xoHumanities, Social Science, and Education	xGeneral Library	oEducation Library oPsychology Library	oSchool of Technology (except Aviation Technology)	
oManagement	oKrannert Library		oAgricultural Economics (from School of Agriculture)	
oPharmacy and Pharmacal Sciences	oPharmacy Library			
xoScience		oChemistry Library oGeosciences Library xMathematics Library oPhysics Library		xBiological Sciences (in Life Sciences Library)
oTechnology				oSchool of Technology (except Aviation; in General Library) oDepartment of Aviation Technology (a branch of the Engineering Library)
xVeterinary Medicine	xVeterinary Medicine Library			

x – has approval plan   o – has no approval plan   xo – some departments do not have plans

3. Saves selection time and effort.
4. Books arrive sooner.
5. Blanet coverage of certain pubishers possible.
6. Broad coverage of the entire field of publishing.
7. Privilege of returning unwanted books, not always possible with firm orders.
8. Saves faculty time and effort; less input required.

Those librarians who chose *not* to institute approval plans gave these reasons:

1. Approval plans are too general, and their fields are highly specialized (cited by four respondents of six); subject is therefore difficult to profile.
2. Not enough money to implement a specialized plan successfully (again, cited by four).
3. The former approval plan was not producing the individual books wanted by the faculty or those expected by the librarian.
4. Approval plan is too slow; if it does not produce the book promptly, it may be too late to get by other means.
5. Inability of the plan to provide retrospective coverage.
6. Uncertainty factor; "cloud of unknowing"; lack of control over the ordering process.
7. Easier and more productive to claim a firm order; vendor is indifferent to specific approval-plan title requests.
8. Just enjoy conventional selections procedures; prefer scanning announcements.
9. Interdisciplinary problems and overlapping interests with other library units, making profiling difficult.
10. No saving in staff time or book funds.

The accounting section of the Acquisitions Department reported that, after an initial shakedown period, the individual plans are causing no problems. In fact, one advantage has emerged; processing separate, and therefore, smaller plans enables the clerk involved to fit the routines into the rest of her daily work. Formerly it required setting aside a day or two to process the large general shipments. Elsewhere in the department the only problem is that occasionally processing of approval-plan shipments in the outlying libraries is delayed, so that when they arrive in Acquisitions rush procedures are required to meet book-return and invoice-discount deadlines.

The arguments advanced in favor of approval plans have become a litany and require no further comment here. The dissenting opinions, however, perhaps merit some scrutiny.

The problem of not receiving some books and the subsequent difficulties in obtaining them seem to be related directly to (1) profile difficulties, (2) publishing patterns in certain fields, and (3) the performance of the vendor in covering the very broad spectrum of publishing.

Obviously, no approval plan can produce books that have not been published, and some fields produce very few new titles. Profile deficiencies may be caused by poor planning, but there are also problems inherent in the vendor's classification process. For example, when books are wanted that deal with immunological responses in animals other than man, most approval-plan thesauri do not have sufficient discriminatory power to produce so specific a title. Immunology books abound, as do books dealing with animals, but the problem is restricting the selection to those titles with both characteristics. This problem could be alleviated were the vendor computer software to incorporate some connective logic ("or," "nor," "and").

The problem of adequate funding is pervasive among those librarians not adopting plans. It is evident that there is a correlation between funding level and the espousal of an approval plan.

Two instances are the Schools of Pharmacy and of Consumer and Family Sciences. Both overlap heavily with other disciplines, Pharmacy with chemistry, biochemistry, plant science, retail management, pathological processes among others, and Consumer and Family Sciences with economics, management, retailing, consumer affairs, chemistry and biochemistry, art and design, psychology, sociology, and education among others. With a limited budget, one way to control the approval plan is to limit the number of publishers covered; in discrete disciplines appropriate publishers can be identified. The librarians for these schools contend that profiling an approval plan covering diverse subjects with a limited publisher list is impossible; publishers cannot be selected to supply everything needed, and the budget is too small to provide coverage of all subjects from all publishers.

The School of Management has a reverse problem. In trying to match publisher and subject coverage to budget, the question is how to select from an abundant publishing output. Business and economics publishers are identifiable, and they produce many books on management, for example. The librarian asks how he can justify returning one book and keeping another when both are very nearly the same in content and only one is needed, or how to construct a profile in the first place that will eliminate one and produce another.

The problem of timely production of a title is especially interesting since it is mentioned by both camps; advocates say approval plans are faster, whereas opponents state they are slower. It is suspected that these opposite opinions are based on the exceptional instance, rather than on the overall performance of the plan. Parenthetically, a formal study of this bibliometric topic would be of great value. One group of responses has been labeled the "cloud of unknowing," or the "uncertainty factor." It is assuredly uncomfortable to have to wait helplessly, hoping that a particular book will appear, as opposed to having entered a firm order for it. The book may not arrive any sooner if firm ordered, but at least the requestor has a piece of paper stating that it was ordered. Some respondents characterize this as "control." This uncertainty could be largely eliminated if on-line access to the file of titles treated by the vendor were established, and this service will probably eventually become available.

The remaining major objection to the approval-plan concept is perhaps the most difficult to answer rationally; that is, statements like "I just prefer to do it the old way; I like to read *Publisher's Weekly*, all the blurbs, and so forth." These respondents are usually librarians with a great deal of experience in book selection.

One of the features of the former centralized approval plan was the display of all books received for examination by librarians and others, and the loss of this capability is regretted by both groups of respondents.

Conflicting opinions as to relative staff time requirements were noted. Although less professional time is required for selection, more clerical time is needed since the individual libraries are now responsible for functions formerly provided by the Acquisitions Department.

The goal of the original centralized approval plan was to assure the acquisition of at least one copy of every book of scholarly content related to all fields of teaching and research at Purdue. Unrealistic at the outset, inflation soon made this goal unattainable. This expectation is probably served even less well by the decentralized plans, since they were not implemented by all schools and departments, and also because there is more duplication from overlapping interests (see Chart I and Reference 3), and because more books of peripheral interest may be rejected. Ideally, the university's library holdings are regarded as one collection; in actuality, they consist of a number of discrete collections. Even with overlapping academic interests, these collections exist to serve and are restricted to the teaching and research efforts of each school or department. Individual approval plans probably serve to strengthen these subunits at the expense of the overall collection. Since individual plans are more closely monitored by the supervising librarians, there is likely to be less peripheral material purchased, i.e., material of collateral but not basic interest. The hazard in this approach is, of course, that as institutional goals change, the collection may be unable to provide adequate support for new teaching and research activities if they veer very widely from the historical emphases. In a time of budgetary stringencies and inflationary spirals, this is probably unavoidable.

The overall effect of the decentralization of Purdue's approval plan has varied from school to school. The institutional setting of any approval plan is extremely important, and Purdue is no exception. Under either kind of plan, the same problems of interdisciplinary subjects and overlapping teaching and research interests still exist. Because unrestricted added copies are again permitted, in extreme cases there are four or five libraries building collections in the same field. On the other hand, if these institutional patterns are coupled to the fact that many research books do not have an immediate application, it can be inferred that a decentralized plan may not adequately serve the total collection needs of the university. Further, interdepartmental teaching and research,[3] which has no single library as its focus, may be better served by a single all-school plan with a broad profile. A book of adjunct interest, likely to be rejected by a school or departmental librarian with an eye on the budget, would have a better chance of being placed somewhere on campus under a general plan. At Purdue there is an *ad hoc* response to the problem. Individual librarians consult each other about interdisciplinary or peripheral materials. The process helps ensure that, if one library does not want a book, it can be made available elsewhere.

It does not necessarily follow, however, that conventional selection methods will remedy the danger of weakening the total collection. In fact, the very process of profile construction can help clarify the goals of each library unit, and the effect, if implemented by most library units, could well be to strengthen the collection. Until objective measures to evaluate collections are available, this must remain a philosophical proposition.

Finally, it should be emphasized that these responses and reactions are from human beings. It is certain that local personal and institutional factors will also affect the performance of approval plans elsewhere.

School and departmental plans will solve the problem of needed duplicate copies; they will not solve the problem of building expensive duplicate collections. They will not solve the problem of collecting collateral materials, unless formal procedures to offer the books to other campus libraries are established or the initiative of the librarians can be relied upon.

They will transfer many clerical details to individual libraries, increasing clerical time in the libraries and decreasing some of it in the acquisitions department. They will decrease professional time spent on book selection, but may increase time spent in managing and supervising.

Depending on the individual librarian's view, they are an aid or a hindrance to selection and collection-building. Whether school, departmental, or general plans, they are still very much a matter of individually varying needs, individual setting, and individual attitude.

REFERENCES

1. Kathleen McCullough, Edwin D. Posey and Doyle C. Pickett, *Approval Plans and Academic Libraries; An Interpretive Survey* (Phoenix, Ariz.: The Oryx Press, 1977).
2. The following persons generously gave time and thought to questions about approval plans:

Ruth Ahl, librarian, School of Agriculture and Life Sciences Library; associate professor of library science.

Theodora Andrews, librarian, School of Pharmacy and Pharmacal Sciences and Pharmacy Library; professor of library science.

Martha Bailey, librarian, Physics Library; associate professor of library science.

Richard L. Funkhouser, librarian, School of Science and Mathematical Sciences Library; associate professor of library science.

Mary Gibbs, librarian, School of Consumer and Family Sciences and Consumer and Family Sciences Library; assistant professor of library science.

Helga Graf, supervisor, fiscal account clerks, Acquisitions Department.

Coy Harmon, head, Acquisitions Department.

John Houkes, librarian, School of Management and Krannert Library; professor of library science.

Laszlo Kovacs, librarian, School of Humanities, Social Science, and Education and the General Library; associate professor of library science.

John Pinzelik, librarian, Chemistry Library; professor of library science.

Gretchen Stephens, librarian, School of Veterinary Medicine and Veterinary Medicine Library; assistant professor of library science.

Marjorie Zumstein, librarian, Education Library and Psychological Sciences Library; associate professor of library science.

3. In addition to overlapping interests from one library to another, there are many inter-school programs offered to students by the teaching departments, and there is interdisciplinary research, both independent and laboratory-sponsored, conducted by faculty and graduate students. This kind of interdepartmental organization will affect the administration of an approval plan, whether departmental, school, or university-wide. Examples are:

Laboratory for Applications of Remote Sensing, a semiautonomous, purely research organization affiliated with NASA and having faculty ties to the School of Electrical Engineering. Its purpose is to develop systems for the identification from the ground and from air- and spacecraft of vegetation, soils, hydrologic status, and general agricultural conditions. Among libraries involved are Engineering, Geosciences, Life Sciences, and Physics.

Food Science Institute, a unit for both teaching and research offering graduate and undergraduate courses under the aegis of the Schools of Agriculture, Consumer and Family Sciences, Engineering, and Veterinary Medicine. All these school libraries, and in addition, Krannert, Chemistry, Biochemistry, and Physics, are among those involved.

Cancer research, done independently without an organizational center by faculty members of the Department of Biological Sciences and the Schools of Pharmacy and Veterinary Medicine. Life Sciences, Pharmacy, and Veterinary Medicine Libraries are involved, and if sociological, psychological, nursing, or bioengineering aspects are to be considered, the Engineering, General, and Psychological Sciences Libraries as well.

A prelaw option offered to undergraduates by the Department of Chemistry (patent law), which suggests courses in chemistry, physics, mathematics, literature, history, philosophy, and oral interpretation. Libraries are the three in science and the General Library.

Jutta R. Reed

Massachusetts Institute of Technology

COLLECTION ANALYSIS PROJECT IN THE MIT LIBRARIES[1]

The purpose of this paper is to report on the Collection Analysis Project in the MIT Libraries. The project focused on (1) clarifying collection development philosophy and objectives; (2) determining the most effective use of resources for meeting objectives; and (3) improving the effectiveness of the collection development program. This report will emphasize the general characteristics of a rational collection management program and describe some of the specific findings of the project in the MIT libraries.

A series of problems and challenges face collection development programs in university libraries today. These problems result from the legacy of rapid growth in the size and scope of collections in the 1960s and the transition to limited growth in the 1970s. They are exacerbated by continued publishing and information output; and further compounded by increased specialization and diversification of university programs and user information needs. Most important, the combination of reduced or at least relatively stable budgets and the inflationary pressures on library materials costs has a powerful impact on collection development today. Although the forces at the roots of these problems are outside the control of university libraries, libraries are developing new responses and methods for ensuring effective collections. One key response is a growing awareness and recognition of the importance of the management of collections. Collection management is concerned with the basic functions of building, maintaining, and preserving collections. A rational management system provides the necessary tools to improve the effectiveness of these functions and to maximize available funds to meet user needs. The Collection Analysis Project (CAP) offers the opportunity for a rigorous self-examination of collection management. The purpose of this paper is to report on the results of this assisted self-study in one of the three pilot libraries—the MIT Libraries.

The CAP Study Team of six librarians, appointed by the Director of Libraries, began its formal analysis of collection practices of the MIT Library System in July 1977. In October 1977 the Study Team prepared an interim report that covered (1) the historical development of the collections and (2) the internal and external factors that have a major impact on the MIT Libraries—the economic situation, institute educational and research programs, interlibrary cooperative efforts, and publishing trends. In the interim report the Study Team identified a number of long-standing problems in the collection development

490

process and set the direction for further studies.

In November 1977 task forces were established in the areas of allocation of materials funds, collection effectiveness, staffing of the collection function, preservation, and resource sharing. Each task force was responsible for collecting and analyzing data in its field and identifying optional approaches to critical issues facing the Libraries.

The Study Team and the five Task Forces focused their efforts on the following goals:

— to clarify the collection development philosophy and objectives
— to determine the most effective use of resources for meeting the objective
— to improve the effectiveness of the collection development program

In reporting on CAP in the MIT Libraries, these three areas will serve as an overall framework. The report will emphasize the general characteristics of an effective collections management program and describe some of the specific results in the MIT Libraries.

COLLECTION PHILOSOPHY, OBJECTIVES AND POLICIES

Essential elements of a collection development program are a clearly stated collection philosophy, collection objectives, and policies. All three are critical tools in collection planning, decision-making, and evaluation and monitoring. While they will not eliminate problems and conflicts, the process of developing a written collection philosophy and objectives and policies provide the conceptual framework for directing decisions and setting priorities. The collection philosophy is the sum of values, beliefs and operating assumptions. "Collection objectives are statements of long-range, broad intent, which represent the component means to transfer the collection philosophy into action."[2] Collection objectives must be explicit, unambiguous, and operationally meaningful. Specifically, collection development objectives should relate collection development to university programs; delineate support for these programs; identify priorities among program needs; and specify the user populations served. Collection policies translate the broader collection objectives into more specific policies and define the scope and depth of the collections in various subject fields and for various types of materials. They enable "selectors to work with greater consistency toward defined goals, thus shaping stronger collections and using limited funds more wisely;"[3] they inform users "as to the scope and nature of existing collections and the plans for continuing development of resources."[4] They can also assist in defining collection responsibility within a library consortium or among cooperating libraries. Taken together a written collection philosophy, explicit collection objectives and a coordinated set of collection policies provide the basis for the examination and evaluation of the collection development program. During CAP we concentrated much effort on formulating a comprehensive collection philosophy and detailed collection objectives, and developed general criteria for written collection policies.

EFFECTIVE USE OF RESOURCES

A second major effort during CAP dealt with resource allocation. Planned and logical allocation of limited book funds to contending collection needs is a critical problem in university libraries. While many university libraries have shifted from a primarily incremental system, few have developed agreed-upon criteria and rationales for allocating book funds. An effective collection management system necessitates the development of an allocation method based on objective criteria. Such a method serves as a valuable planning and decision-making tool. Although each institution will need to develop its own method for allocating book funds, we identified the following two essential steps in the budget process for allocating book funds.

The first step is the establishment of specific subject accounts which correspond to collection policies. Our analysis indicates that the advantages of a subject-oriented budget allocation system are substantial. Such a system will closely relate budget allocation to collection development policies and goals. It will enable the library to integrate collection development activities with the university's educational and research programs. It will also enable the library to monitor progress in meeting collection goals and will identify a mechanism to identify expanding and contracting program needs. Finally, in a period of budgetary austerity it provides a process for planning and decision-making in accordance with the overall collection development program.

The second step involved in an effective collections allocation process is utilization of quantitative data and information. Analysis of these data will contribute to objective and equitable allocation of available funds to meet university program priorities and needs. Although the specific data elements will vary from university to university library, for the MIT Libraries they include some of the following elements: number of courses and course enrollment; number of students and faculty; size of subject collection; publishing statistics, and expenditure analysis.

These data elements will provide a mechanism for analyzing and coordinating information about various aspects of the university environment. They will enable us to monitor changes in educational and research programs, to assess their implications, and to respond by reallocating resources necessitated by shifts in university programs. While we recommend the use of quantitative data in formulating resource allocation decisions, we recognize that allocation decisions will not be exclusively based on quantitative criteria. Experience suggests that subjective factors or unique qualities of each subject are also important and that a single-minded focus on a rigid set of quantitative criteria is neither desirable nor justifiable. We believe, however, that the analysis of a set of quantitative data can lead to more equitable allocations and to a more articulated decision-making process. We also believe that the process of analyzing some of the variables affecting user demands on the collections and the availability of data to support collection needs will increase the effectiveness of budgeting in the collection development program. Finally, it will enable the university library to demonstrate more clearly to the university administration where funds are needed and how they are spent. These two steps do not eliminate difficult decisions in building collections, but they provide a method for planning and monitoring the development of the collections in accordance with stated priorities and recognized criteria.

EFFECTIVENESS OF THE COLLECTION DEVELOPMENT PROGRAM

In addition to clarifying goals and objectives and determining an effective allocation method, we focused our major efforts on improving the effectiveness of the collection development program. These efforts concentrated on the following 5 broad areas:

— Communication with the User Community
— Evaluation of the Collections
— Organization of the Collection Development Process
— Preservation of the Collections
— Resource Sharing

COMMUNICATION WITH THE USER COMMUNITY

For university collection programs the need to promote the communication between the libraries and the university community is a particularly critical concern. To meet this challenge, the MIT Libraries currently utilize a variety of channels to communicate with the user community. The acquisitions list is the most popular method of giving notification of additions to the collections to students and faculty. However, we found considerable concern among librarians for additional mechanisms which would augment already existing programs. One effective means which we used during the Project is a user survey. We surveyed a random sample of faculty, researchers and students entering the library. Although administering this opinion survey was time consuming, the carefully designed and distributed questionnaire survey provided useful feedback from users. We believe periodic user surveys will assist in determining community assessment of collection effectiveness and discovering service deficiencies. We identified a number of other mechanisms to promote effective communication. Among these are a formal outreach program wherein faculty members will be contacted and informed of current collection development policies and encouraged to participate in book selection; and a publicity campaign to promote library services.

EVALUATION OF THE COLLECTIONS

A second important area in collection management is the assessment or measurement of the effectiveness of the collections in terms of how well they meet users' information needs. Frequently assessments of collections are sporadic and they are based largely on subjective appraisals with little or no objective data available on a systematic basis to substantiate the conclusions. However, a well-designed and coordinated program of evaluating the quality and usefulness of the collections is essential in order to monitor collection development relative to university programs and the information needs of the user community. Toward this end, we identified the prerequisites and the essential characteristics of an effective evaluation program. Since achievements must be measured against clearly defined goals, the availability of collection policies and basic data on collection size, growth and expenditures; on circulation transactions; and on the user community are critical prerequisites for all libraries. The main characteristics of an evaluation program are that it must be on-going, coordinated and systematic. Equally important, a variety of methodologies and techniques should be employed so as to take advantage of the different kinds of information obtained from each approach. A number of approaches exist that may be applied to the evaluation of a collection. The available methodologies can be grouped under two headings: (1) Collection-centered—those methodologies which focus primarily on the collections themselves and (2) User-centered—those methodologies which focus primarily on the user community's interaction with the collections.

During the course of the Collection Analysis Project we conducted three studies which investigated user-centered aspects of evaluation. These studies were a survey to obtain users' assessments of the effectiveness of the collections; a utilization study to determine the circulation of the collections; and an access test to measure the capability of the MIT Libraries to provide the materials which library users need. Time does not allow to report on these studies in detail, however, all three reinforced our conclusion that assessment must be an integral part of the management of collections.

ORGANIZATION OF THE COLLECTION DEVELOPMENT PROCESS

Organizational structure is a critical component of the collection management system. From our analysis of current operating practices two important issues emerged. The most pressing problem is the need for effective coordination—the development of cooperative relationships between the subject specialists. In the MIT Libraries the increase in inter-disciplinary or multidisciplinary subjects has spurred efforts to coordinate selection on a system-wide basis. A number of our recommendations aim to strengthen the communication between the selectors, to clarify the roles, responsibilities, and authorities of all librarians involved in areas of collection development, and to provide mechanisms for integrated collection development.

A second important concern in our analysis of the organization of the collection development process was the role of the faculty in the selection of materials. In the MIT Libraries selection is the responsibility of literature and/or subject specialists. However, the Libraries actively seek to promote faculty participation in selection activities. Since MIT's research efforts frequently are at the frontier of tomorrow's fields, selectors must constantly anticipate and respond to shifting research interests. To meet this challenge, all selectors must depend on effective communication with the faculty. Although the selectors in the MIT Libraries maintain active contact with the faculty, we identified additional methods to supplement existing practices. Among these are the development of a "suggestion brochure" which will emphasize the MIT Libraries' openness to suggestions for purchase, and the previously mentioned outreach program to faculty.

PRESERVATION OF THE COLLECTIONS

Preservation of the collections is an integral part of the collection management process. However, traditionally university libraries have emphasized acquisition and maintenance of the collections and have concentrated preservation efforts primarily on rare books and special collections. But it is evident that the basic research collections also require strong and on-going preservation efforts to halt physical deterioration. As part of the CAP analysis of current preservation efforts in the MIT Libraries, we sent a questionnaire to all library units. Responses to this questionnaire identified the major preservation needs and concerns. To meet these needs, we sought to lay the groundwork for a preservation program at MIT. This program includes the following key characteristics. Most important is the creation of a staff appointment for a Conservation Librarian to provide the expertise and direction in implementing a preservation program. The second important requirement is stabilizing the physical environment for the collections. A stable environment with relatively constant temperature and humidity is the single most beneficial preservation technique. Unfortunately many improvements in the environment will require extensive renovation of existing facilities, but others can be achieved at relatively low costs. Finally, an effective preservation program must focus on the care of the collections. A wide range of factors affect the preservation of materials. These include: acquisitions policy, handling, in-house repair, commercial binding, maintenance and security. In many of these areas we identified the need for guidelines and procedures to ensure the long-term preservation of the collections.

RESOURCE SHARING

The final dimension of the management of collections concerns resource sharing. While economics have been the driving force in the development of cooperative arrangements among university libraries, resource sharing has become a necessary element of library activities. Although "resource sharing is essential, . . . it is not a panacea."[5] In order to make resource sharing arrangements successful, libraries will have to explore the possible benefits, costs, and disadvantages carefully. Some cooperative arrangements "may actually be costing their members far more than the benefits they derive."[6] Based on our study of resource sharing activities of the MIT Libraries, we believe the Libraries should carefully limit these activities, so that the Libraries can put maximum effort into those programs in which they participate. Consequently, we focused our efforts during the Collection Analysis Project on improving the accessibility of the resources available through cooperative agreements. Among our recommendations are an effective publicity campaign to promote the use of resource sharing activities. There exists an appalling lack of awareness of these programs among the MIT community. We also explored the feasibility of a telefacsimile system for interlibrary borrowing of materials, and recommend a dedicated delivery system for the Boston Library Consortium, the formal cooperative agreement among Boston libraries. Almost all of the most successful cooperative agreements in which the MIT Libraries participate provide passenger and document services, and we believe that such services would be the most effective means of increasing access to the resources of other Boston libraries.

SUMMARY

For the MIT Libraries the Collection Analysis Project has been one of the most critical and potentially far-reaching activities ever undertaken. Completing the project of this magnitude in seven months was difficult and demanded a major time commitment on the part of many staff members. But we believe the Project will strengthen the effectiveness of the collection development program.

The analysis and evaluation of the Libraries' collection development program have convinced us that some structural changes must be made and that some new mechanisms must be developed to ensure meeting the information needs of the MIT community. We have formulated recommendations toward a responsive collection development program which will have considerable impact on the future of the MIT Libraries. We also hope to have helped to modify the ARL self-study model in ways that will benefit other research libraries.

REFERENCES

1. This report is based on the final reports and recommendations of the CAP Study Team and the five Task Forces.
2. Jeffrey J. Gardner and Duane E. Webster, *The Collection Analysis Project: Operating Manual for an Assisted Self-Study for the Review and Analysis of the Collection Development Functions in Academic and Research Libraries* (Washington, DC: Association of Research Libraries, Office of University Library Management Studies, 1977), Section 2.2.3.
3. American Library Association. Collection Development Committee, "Guidelines for the Formulation of Collection Development Policies," *Library Resources and Technical Services* 21 (Winter 1977): 41.
4. *Ibid.*
5. Richard DeGennaro, "Copyright, Resource Sharing, and Hard Times: a View from the Field," *American Libraries* 8 (September 1977): 434.
6. *Ibid.*

George J. Soete

Arizona State University

THE COLLECTION ANALYSIS PROJECT AT ARIZONA STATE UNIVERSITY LIBRARY: AN EXERCISE IN STAFF DEVELOPMENT

In addition to producing recommendations which will profoundly affect the library's total collection development program for years to come, the Collection Analysis Project at Arizona State University library also proved to be a staff development exercise of considerable depth and duration. Staff partici- pation exercised leadership and group decision-making skills and gained practice in formal self-study, negotiation, and report-writing processes. Finally, CAP seems to have brought about significant changes in both staff and administration attitudes toward collection development and toward each other.

For six months, from August, 1977 to February, 1978, the Arizona State University Library participated in the Collection Analysis Project, a pilot self-study project spon- sored and assisted by the Association of Research Libraries and funded by the Andrew Mellon Foundation. As the project progressed, it became clear that, in addition to pro- ducing a report whose recommendations will profoundly affect our Library's collection program for years to come, the staff who participated in the project were engaged in a development program of considerable depth and duration. In short, *process* might in fact have been our most important product.

Assisted self-study projects of this sort are not new. ARL's own Management Review and Analysis Project provided a convenient prototype for the Collection Analysis Project. What is interesting to me is that the professional library literature, including material written about MRAP, gives little more than a nod to the notion that self-studies are valuable as staff development projects.[1]

Usually three major reasons are given for choosing a self-study project rather than, for example, a study done by outside consultants:[2]

1. The library staff, knowing more about the local situation, is better equipped to analyze it.

2. The product of a self-study is usually better than that produced by outside consul- tants or by the library administration working on its own.

3. Recomendations which come from the staff—even though they have been modified during negotiations with the library administration—tend to be more readily accepted by the staff when they are implemented.

I would add to this list a fourth, no less important reason:

4. A self-study project is valuable as a staff development project.

Recent professional writing on the developmental aspects of self-study projects acknowledge the important relationship that exists between *staff development* and *shared decision-making* (or *participatory management*, to use a term which has perhaps fallen out of favor).[3] The self-study project is essentially an exercise in shared decision-making. Recent articles on shared decision-making in academic libraries suggest that while it is not a magical cure-all, it can be a valuable consultative tool for management as well as a means of releasing organizational tensions.[4] Several writers have pointed out that shared decision-making can also function as an important component of an organization's total staff development program, particularly as a means for junior staff to gain administrative *savoir-faire*.[5] Yet it seems that, in the total staff development programs of most academic libraries, in-house development activities, such as self-study projects, have been largely ignored in favor of more traditional activities such as courses for credit and outside workshops and conferences—even though in-house projects are easier to initiate, less expensive, and probably most directly beneficial to the library.[6]

For this reason I should like to concentrate on the staff development aspects of the Collection Analysis Project at Arizona State University Library. I should warn you that I am rather high on the Collection Analysis Project: what follows might begin to sound like a recitation of the benefits of joining the Boy Scouts. Anyone with a low tolerance for euphoria might wish to leave the room at this time, although I can assure you that I shall mention one or two problems and disadvantages along the way.

Any educational experience ought to be describable in terms of new information, sharpened skills, changed attitudes, and enlarged perceptions. It is these "learnings" that took place at Arizona State that I'd like to describe in some detail for you now.

New information first—and briefly. We were constantly amazed at the information we turned up during the data-gathering phases of the project. For the staff, it was rather like rummaging through grandmother's attic. We unearthed collection policies, resource-sharing agreements, and statistical work-ups that no one remembered seeing before. In studying the history of our collection, we made the astounding, but finally not very surprising discovery that in 1959, when Arizona State achieved university status, approximately 50% of the book collection was made up of gifts. Talk about discovering your roots! In studying the University environment, we compiled a great deal of statistical information about academic programs, degrees granted, and research in progress: later the University Administration told us that they had never had all of this information together in one place before. I think it is safe to say that the twenty-five persons who participated in CAP came away with a great deal more information about the Library's history and its local and national environment when the project was over. And we had a sense of contributing to a much larger information system.

So many staff skills were exercised during the project that it is hard to know where to begin listing them. I think everyone got a healthy dose of the self-study process recommended by ARL which can be summarized in these steps: observe, analyze, recommend. During the observation or data-gathering phases of the project, participants were required to be objective, to construct survey and interview instruments which gathered the information that we needed without influencing the respondents to give us hoped-for answers. Sometimes we were forced to conclude that there simply wasn't enough information to make a point that we felt intuitively should be made. During the analysis phase, we were constantly reminded to consider strengths as well as weaknesses; to point out problems, but to point them out fairly with a view toward solving them. Under the terms of the project, we were constrained to deal with issues rather than with people. This seemed a disability on occasion, but finally made for a problem-oriented report remarkably free of bitterness. Finally, the formulation of recommendations, which constitute about 10% of our final report, seemed to take about 90% of our time. A number of important skills— entirely new skills, I'm sure, for some participants—were exercised here. Recommendations were taken out of the usual staff lounge bull session "Why don't they ... ?" context and elevated to high art. We tried to make each recommendation specific and do- able. In most cases we were able to assign responsibility to a specific person and to call for a specific product by a certain date. Perhaps a few examples will suggest the hard work and care that went into formulating the 58 recommendations which appeared in our final report.

Example #1: The Head of Acquisitions Service and the Chair of Reference should develop an expeditious procedure for the review by Subject Specialist Librarians of in- coming order request cards, with a view toward improving the Subject Specialists' oppor- tunity to monitor and complement order activity within their subject areas. Target date: May 1, 1978.

Example #2: The Collection Development Librarian for the Social Sciences should develop, in consultation with other monitors, the Head of Acquisitions and the University Librarian, a plan for applying uniform monitoring standards to all blanket order and approval plans. Target date: October 1, 1978. I cannot stress enough the value of staff participation in this kind of recommendation writing.

The skill of negotiation was practiced by all participants at one time or another. Nego- tiations went on within the Study Team, within the four Task Forces, between these two, and finally between the Study Team and the University Librarian, often simultane- ously. It is something like a small miracle in the history of organizations, I think, that we worked out all of our differences without a single minority report being filed and without any disclaimers in the University Librarian's introductory remarks to our final report. We were determined from the beginning to issue a report which represented the consensus judgment of both staff and administration forcefully, fairly, and constructively. I think we finally issued such a report. But again, the process proved to be at least as valuable as the product. We learned during those long grueling sessions that we could yield without surrendering. Sometimes we discovered that our conflicts were based in semantics rather than in truly substantial differences of opinion. For example, in negotiating with the University Librarian on the whole issue of communication, it was particularly difficult to negotiate a reasonable statement of our problems. He contended that he *had* communi- cated; we countered that the staff nonetheless felt that they were not receiving sufficient communication. As a result of our careful negotiations, I believe that we do now have a better communication system.

At least ten persons, to one degree or another, got a chance to exercise their leadership skills during CAP. Many of us held supervisory positions within the library or had chaired short-lived ad hoc committees, but few had had the long-term special project leadership experience that we gained in CAP. Emphasis was placed on the facilitation aspect of leadership: we were there to help rather than to give orders. For those of us who were used to assigning tasks and seeing that they got done, this was a bit of a strain at first. Eventually, however, I think we all adapted and were able to translate some of these new leadership skills into our daily work.

A few of the more quantifiable skills practiced during CAP include report writing and working against deadlines. I have already mentioned the effort expended on writing specific, doable recommendations, but of course there was also the extensive supportive material on which the recommendations depended. I wish I could tell you that our report writing went smoothly; it was in fact on the issue of report writing that the most conflict arose. Two problems surfaced early in the project: (1) virtually everyone—and I include myself—had a proprietary feeling about his own or his group's writing; (2) there developed a division—philosophical, aesthetic, or practical, depending on how you viewed it—between those who wanted to display our findings in full and those who wanted to condense, synthesize, and emphasize. Again, it is a small miracle that our final report doesn't bear too many scars from this conflict. As a learning experience, I think everyone profited from *encountering* the conflict, even though it was never truly resolved.

We had a bit more luck with meeting deadlines. Time was a problem from the beginning: as a pilot library, we had committed ourselves to completing the project in the recommended six months. By the time the Study Team issued the Interim Report in early November, 1977, we were veterans of the deadline war. But then the new Task Force members had to learn our hard-won lesson anew while they prepared their working reports against an early January deadline. Finally, the Study Team had to relive the experience in February, 1978, as we prepared the Final Report. The chief lesson we learned, I suppose, is that there is a point of diminishing returns. We began to understand that, for the purpose of achieving objective "A", you really need only so much information. I think it was a revelation to many of us that we could produce quality work within a practical time limit, that we could make workable recommendations based on *sufficient* findings, and that we could write a readable report without trying to rival Truman Capote.

Finally, the many skills involved in making decisions as a group are perhaps the most distinctive feature of this sort of project. Under the careful guidance of our ARL facilitator, Jeffrey Gardner, we learned to use the techniques of group decision-making which we'll be able to use throughout our professional work. I have already mentioned the negotiation process. Among other skills, we found *brainstorming* and the *consensus decision* to be particularly useful. During brainstorming sessions, which were particularly useful at the beginning of a new phase of the project, everyone was encouraged to come up with ideas on a particular subject, which were listed uncritically on flip-chart sheets. Later we sifted through these ideas, sorting out the unworkable, clustering near-duplicates and so forth. The important point is that *everyone* contributed to the helter-skelter of suggestions and so everyone shared finally in determining our course of action. Decision-making by consensus was an invaluable concept that we adhered to faithfully once we discovered its merits. *Consensus* means essentially that everyone in the group can live with a particular decision. During the whole course of CAP, we never—in several hundred hours of meetings—took a single vote. We pursued every decision until we could all live with it. While recommendations formulated by consensus occasionally lost a bit of their polemical flavor, I think they gained a great deal in terms of rationale and substance.

Surely one of the purposes of an intensive long-term self-study is to affect the staff at a level somewhere deeper than the pure skill level. At this point then we must enter the twilight zone of affective learning. How to describe changed attitudes and enlarged perceptions? Although it is difficult to prove that these changes took place, my conversations with participants and with our University Librarian convince me that they did, and so I'm going to tell you about them anyway.

First of all, I think CAP changed some attitudes toward staff-administration relationships. Those of us who participated in negotiations with the University Librarian frequently discovered, in the process of talking things out, that we held essentially the same positions but that we had simply approached them from different points of view. A similar phenomenon occurred among staff participants. One of the obvious problems inherent in a self-study is individual advocacy. You can be sure that the Head of Acquisitions will have a lot to say about a study of the organization of his unit, as will the reference librarian who's been having trouble getting his rush orders processed. Self-study projects such as CAP never dispel the advocacy problem, but they do provide a neutral forum where issues can be discussed in a problem-solving context. As a member of the CAP Operations Task Force in Phase II, a group which was pretty evenly balanced among technical and public service personnel, we had our problems with advocacy; and yet I remember most vividly those occasions on which we were able to lay down our axes and discuss a problem as something that affected the whole library. If we did not achieve perfect symbiosis, we nevertheless got closer to it than we had been before.

Finally, I am convinced that no one could have "graduated" from CAP without a clearer perception of the goals and objectives, the strengths and weaknesses, and the possibilities and limitations of our library and its collection program. One of the most important tasks in Phase I of the project was to gather together the Library's written goals and objectives statements and to relate these to University goals and programs. This was, of course, an enormously informative exercise. But beyond this formal data-gathering, which led eventually to the formation of an ad hoc committee on goals and objectives, the entire staff was given a chance to participate in an assessment of our goals and objectives.

During the analysis phases of the self-study, we always considered both strengths and weaknesses in the collection development program. We found some weaknesses, of course, but the CAP method forced us to cite strengths as well: a valuable exercise for all concerned.

Perhaps the most important but least tangible result of CAP was the greater appreciation of our possibilities and limitations. For example, we discovered that one reason for some of the quirks in our acquisitions system was that the University Comptroller would not permit the Library to carry book funds over from one fiscal year to the next, thus creating real work flow problems in the Library. It was important for the staff to recognize this significant external limitation. (Not only did we recognize it, by the way; we also wrote a recommendation that the Comptroller start taking our special problems into consideration). But this sort of discovery was not reserved for the staff alone. The University Librarian has told me that, while he knew from the beginning that the staff was capable of conducting such a study, he gained a new appreciation of staff abilities during CAP. He feels that he now has a more favorable attitude toward staff participation in decision-making, and he definitely plans to use the assisted self-study method again as appropriate problems arise.

I don't want to leave you with the impression that we enjoyed six months of unmitigated ecstasy during the Collection Analysis Project at Arizona State University. We had our ups and downs. The opening statement of the MRAP report issued by Case Western Reserve Libraries states that "self study is a painful process."[7] I think our experience might safely lie somewhere between pain and ecstasy. During CAP, we learned about our roots and our environment. We practiced valuable skills which have been translated into our daily work. We changed, perhaps in significant measure, our attitudes and perceptions. In short, while analyzing our collection development program, we were engaged in a staff development exercise of immense value.

REFERENCES

1. See, for example, "MRAP: the University of Tennessee, Knoxville Experience," *Southeastern Librarian* 24 (Fall 1974): 23, 32; Michael K. Buckland, ed., "The Management Review and Analysis Program: a Symposium," *The Journal of Academic Librarianship*, 1 (January 1976): 6.
2. Maurice P. Marchant, "Participative Management as Related to Personnel Development," *Library Trends* 20 (July 1971); 48, 57.

3. Marchant, "Participative Management," p. 55–56; Elizabeth W. Stone, ed. *New Directions in Staff Development: Moving from Ideas to Action* (Chicago: American Library Association, 1971), p. 48–50.
4. Louis Kaplan, "The Literature of Participation: from Optimism to Realism," *College and Research Libraries* 36 (November 1975): 478; "Participatory Management in Libraries: What Is Its Future?" *Library Journal* 101 (May 15, 1976): 1186–1187.
5. Amelia Breitung and others, "Staff Development in College and University Libraries," *Special Libraries* 67 (July 1976): 305.
6. Breitung, "Staff Development," p. 308–9.
7. Buckland, "The Management Review and Analysis Program," p. 10.

BIBLIOGRAPHY

Breitung, Amelia, Marcia Dorey, and Deirdre Sockbeson, "Staff Development in College and University Libraries," *Special Libraries* 67:305–10 (July 1976).

Buckland, Michael K., ed., "The Management Review and Analysis Program: a Symposium," *The Journal of Academic Librarianship* 1:4–14 (Jan. 1976).

Flener, Jane G., "Staff Participation in Management in Large University Libraries," *College and Research Libraries* 34:275–79 (July 1973).

Kaplan, Louis, "The Literature of Participation: from Optimism to Realism," *College and Research Libraries* 36:473–79 (Nov. 1975).

Kaplan, Louis, "On Decision Sharing in Libraries: How Much Do We Know?" *College and Research Libraries* 38:25–31 (Jan. 1977).

"MRAP: the University of Tennessee, Knoxville Experience," *Southeastern Librarian* 24:22–40 (Fall 1974).

Marchant, Maurice P. "Participative Management as Related to Personnel Development," *Library Trends* 20:48–59 (July 1971).

"Participatory Management in Libraries: What Is Its Future?" *Library Journal* 101:1186–87 (May 15, 1976).

Stone, Elizabeth W., ed., *New Directions in Staff Development: Moving from Ideas to Action*. Chicago: American Library Association, 1971.

Sandra Spurlock and Ellen Yen

Massachusetts Institute of Technology

APPLICATIONS OF AN OPERATIONS RESEARCH MODEL TO THE STUDY OF BOOK USE IN A UNIVERSITY LIBRARY: IMPLICATIONS FOR LIBRARY MANAGEMENT

The purpose of this study was to investigate patterns of use of mathematics and physics books in the MIT science library. The hypothesis was that these books would show higher frequency and volume of use than other books in the library, and that older books in these collections would be shown to be used more frequently. The method used was the Morse-Chen model of book use, which measures several variables of use based on books in circulation. Results of the study essentially confirmed the hypothesis. The usefulness of these results in terms of management of the collections is discussed.

INTRODUCTION

Librarians in academic libraries are becoming increasingly aware of the need for ways in which to gather meaningful quantitative information on the use of their collections. Their goal in collecting such information is to be able to make more rational decisions in collection building, in budget allocation, in weeding and storage of library materials, and in setting loan, renewal and duplication policies. The information used to make these decisions is most useful when descriptive statistics, which most libraries collect in some form or other, are used in a dynamic way in a model which allows patterns of use to emerge.

Investigators in a number of libraries have devised a variety of methodologies for conducting use studies. These are reviewed in a recent book by Lancaster.[1] The motivation for conducting a utilization study is that the measured use of materials is a direct reflection of expressed user needs, and is a measure of the number of successful transactions between the collection and the user community.

In a use study, one may look at either the circulation of library materials, or the in-library use of these items, or both. Use studies which examine the external circulation of materials are more well-defined and in general are easier to implement. This report describes the application of one such methodology in the MIT Science Library.

DESCRIPTION OF THE STUDY

The purpose of this study was to obtain information which would clarify patterns of use of mathematics and physics books, and to provide an index of use for this part of the Science Library's collection. In addition, the results of this study can be compared to the results of two previous studies done at MIT, one which identified patterns of use for life sciences books[2] and a second which established a behavior norm for all books in the Science Library.[3]

The specific question asked was, how does the behavior of mathematics and physics books compare with the behavior of other books in the Science Library? An operations research model is used to measure past and current use, and to predict the future use of mathematics and physics books as compared to other books in the library. Implications of the results of this study for making decisions for budget allocation, for evaluating the effectiveness of the mathematics and physics collections, and in assessing the effect of loan, renewal, and duplication policies on the use of books in these subject areas, are also described.

HYPOTHESIS

One of the benefits of using a quantitative technique to study book use is that results of such a study can verify the intuitive judgments which librarians have made about the use of their collections. It is difficult to support and justify such judgments without some form of data to back them up, particularly at a time when librarians are increasingly required to account for the collection management decisions they make.

On the other hand, sometimes the results of a use study will not support a previous assumption about the nature of book use in a particular discipline. This result is also useful to the librarian, because it focuses attention on an area of the collection which requires further study to clarify patterns of use.

Based on current assumptions about the nature of use of the literature of mathematics and physics at MIT, we anticipated that the results of this study would show:

1. That mathematics and physics monographs are used differently than are books in life sciences, both in frequency and in intensity of use.

2. That the active portion of the mathematics and physics collections will be larger than the active portion of life sciences monographs.

3. That a larger number of older mathematics and physics books (older than 10 years old) are in demand compared to older books in the life sciences.

4. That the values derived from this study for mathematics and physics books, when compared to average values previously calculated for the Science Library as a whole, will give meaningful information to the librarian for the management of the mathematics and physics collections.

DESCRIPTION OF THE MODEL

Circulation studies may be designed in a number of ways, depending on the type of information one wishes to gain and the time and personnel constraints under which one is working. Some of the elements of the design of the study reported here are determined by requirements of the model we used; others were set by us for various reasons.

The model used in this study is one developed by Philip Morse at MIT[4] and later modified and tested by Ching-chih Chen at the Countway Library of Harvard Medical School.[5] This model, derived from probability theory, is based on three assumptions: first, that the process of book circulation is a random one; second, that on the average, book circulation drops off exponentially with time; and third, that there is a time correlation from one time period to the next concerning the behavior of books. That is, a book may become popular after having been little used for several years; once such a book becomes popular, the circulation history from then on is as though it had been popular all along.

In his original study of book use, which was based on the circulation histories of a random sample of books from the stacks, Morse found that the average circulation of a *class* of books, N(m), during its t + 1 year depends on its circulation the previous year, year t. From this observation, he developed a linear model which predicts the probable future circulation of a class of books based on their present circulation:

$$N(m) = \alpha + \beta m$$

This model says that all books of a given class that circulate m times in one year should have an average circulation of N(m) the next year. The value of N(m) depends only on m, plus the parameters α and β.

He found that N(m) is smaller than m for most books, because on the average, the circulation of a class of books for a given year tends to be less than that of a previous year. Parameters α and β will be different for each class of books studied. Parameter α is a measure of the mean circulation which older books of the class will eventually reach with time. Parameter β measures the rate at which the "popularity" of a book of the class diminishes from year to year.

Chen's extension and modification of the model consists of a change in the method of collecting data, with a corresponding change in the predictive model itself. Morse's methodology used statistics gathered from a random sample of books on the shelf. This "collection sample" method is quite tedious and time-consuming to use. Chen changed the procedure to a "checkout sample" method, which uses statistics gathered only from the cards of books in circulation at the time of the study. This method is quick and easy to apply, requiring a minimum of staff time and effort. However, statistics collected in this way are biased toward the active books in the collection, and exclude books which do not happen to circulate during the sample time. Chen modified Morse's mathematical model to remove this bias, allowing one to apply the Morse model when data are collected from the active books in circulation. While the values thus obtained are less accurate than if a sample of books on the shelf were examined, the results obtained from such a study are accurate enough for making management decisions.

The corrected model is expressed as:

$$N(j) = M(j)/[1 - (1 - p)^j] \qquad \text{where } j = 1,2,3...$$

In this model,

N(j) = The expected (corrected) value of all books which circulated j times in the current year

M(j) = The number of books which actually circulated j times during the sample period

$$[1 - (1 - p)^j] = \text{The correction factor}$$

METHODOLOGY AND APPLICATION OF THE MODEL

The sample for this study consisted of all Science Library mathematics and physics monographs and monographic series (Library of Congress call numbers QA and Dewey Decimal call numbers 510–519 for mathematics; Library of Congress call numbers QC and Dewey Decimal call numbers 530–539 for physics) circulating in the sample period. The sampling period for mathematics books was eight days and eleven days for physics books. The number of days necessary for collection of data from about three hundred books determined the length of the sampling periods.

The data which were collected consisted of a record of the number of times each book in the sample had circulated each year for as many years as appeared on the book's charge card. Each due date represented one circulation. Since the study was conducted in February, 1978, the due dates of the books in circulation fell in March, 1978 (one month loan period). Therefore, a year was defined as March of one year to March of the next. The charge cards of all books in the sampled classes which had been borrowed each day during the sampling period were examined. A sample of the data collection forms which were used is shown in Figure 1.

Call No.	1977-78	Call No.	1977-78
	1976-77		1976-77
	1975-76		1975-76
	1974-75		1974-75
	1973-74		1973-74
	1972-73		1972-73
	1971-72		1971-72
	1970-71		1970-71
	1969-70		1969-70
	1968-69		1968-69
	1967-68		1967-68
Call No.	1977-78	Call No.	1977-78
	1976-77		1976-77
	1975-76		1975-76
	1974-75		1974-75
	1973-74		1973-74
	1972-73		1972-73
	1971-72		1971-72
	1970-71		1970-71
	1969-70		1969-70
	1968-69		1968-69
	1967-68		1967-68

Figure 1.   Sample of the data collection form.

The following data analysis steps are fully described in Chen's book.[6]

First, data were transferred from the data collection forms to a summary sheet. A portion of the summary sheet for QC books is shown in Figure 2. On this sheet, m is the number of times a book circulated in year t and n is the number of times that the same book circulated in the next year, year t + 1. The recorded circulation histories for all books in the sample are thus recorded in such a way as to show the pattern of use from one year to the next.

m	n
0	0, 1, 1, 0, 0, 0, 1, 5, 1, 4, 5, 1, 2, 1, 0 . . . .
1	0, 0, 0, 0, 0, 0, 1, 2, 0, 0, 8, 1, 3, 3, 0 . . . .
2	0, 1, 2, 5, 3, 1, 0, 4, 1, 5, 5, 1, 3, 3, 1 . . . .
3	4, 4, 3, 6, 3, 1, 3, 1, 0, 4, 1, 2, 0, 4, 1 . . . .
4	3, 3, 3, 4, 3, 4, 1, 2, 3, 4, 0, 3, 1, 1
5	2, 1, 5, 5, 0, 5
6	1, 1

Figure 2. A portion of the data summary sheet for QC books.

Next, the data from the summary sheets were totalled and displayed in a circulation distribution chart. The charts for the QA and QC books are shown in Table 1. In this table, m is the number of circulations in year t, and M(m) is the number of books which circulated m times in year t and n times in year t + 1. The N(m) column of figures consists of the mean (average) circulation during year t + 1 for books which circulated m times in year t.

TABLE 1

Circulation Distrubiton Chart—QA and QC Books

QA:

m	$M(m)$	0	1	2	3	4	5	6	7	8	9	$N(m)$
0	216	95	71	31	13	2	4	–	–	–	–	.930
1	223	73	59	40	27	9	10	3	–	1	1	1.53
2	133	34	35	26	18	6	7	3	3	1	–	2.10
3	70	10	16	13	19	8	3	–	1	–	–	2.20
4	22	1	4	4	10	2	1	–	–	–	–	2.50
5	10	3	–	2	2	2	–	–	1	–	–	2.50
6	3	–	1	–	–	1	1	–	–	–	–	3.33
7	1	–	1	–	–	–	–	–	–	–	–	1.00

QC:

m	$M(m)$	0	1	2	3	4	5	6	7	8	9	$N(m)$
0	132	58	42	21	1	3	6	1	–	–	–	1.02 1
1	172	48	43	30	27	10	9	4	–	1	–	1.75
2	107	17	28	16	19	11	6	2	7	–	1	2.44
3	65	9	15	10	14	6	7	4	–	–	–	2.46
4	13	1	3	1	6	2	–	–	–	–	–	2.38
5	6	1	1	1	–	–	3	–	–	–	–	3.00
6	2	–	2	–	–	–	–	–	–	–	–	1.00

The circulation distribution of all books in the sample were then represented visually by plotting the m values from the circulation distribution chart versus the N(m) values. Shown in Figure 3 are the plots of m versus N(m) for classes QA and QC. In these graphs, the circulation distribution for the sampled classes were able to be fitted to a straight line, a necessary requirement if the model is to be used. The slope of the line is parameter β. The point where the line crosses the y axis is equal to α_a, a parameter which needs to be corrected to account for books that did not circulate at all during the sampling period.

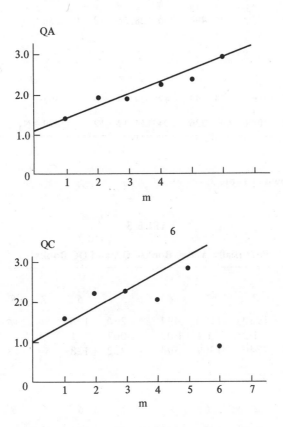

Figure 3. Plots of m vs. N(m) for QA and QC books.

At this point, a different circulation distribution is displayed. This is the circulation distribution for the current year, 1977–78, only. To obtain this distribution, we used the correction factor $1/[1 - (1 - p)^j]$. The circulation distribution for the current year for QA and QC books is shown in Table 2. In Table 2, the M(j) values indicate the number of books in the sample which circulated j times in 1977–78. The M(j) values multiplied by the correction factor result in the N(j) values which include the number of active books in the collection which did not happen to circulate during the sampling period. The value of N_a, the number of active books, is the sum of the N(j) values.

The N(j) values were used to calculate N_p, the number of potentially active books in the collection which were not active in 1977–78 but which will probably circulate in the future. We determined the N_p values by using another correction factor, $1/(1 - e)^j$.

TABLE 2

Circulation Distribution for 1977–78—QA and QC Books

QA:

j	1	2	3	4	5	6	7	8	9	Total	Total Circulation accounted for by N_a
M(j)	91	78	70	38	26	16	8	3	2	350	
$1/[1 - (1 - p)^j]$	50	25	17	13	10	8	7	6	5		
N(j)	4550	1950	1190	494	260	128	56	18	10	8656 = N_a	16690

QC:

j	1	2	3	4	5	6	7	8	Total	Total Circulation accounted for by N_a
M(j)	69	64	63	42	42	19	3	3	305	
$1/[1 - (1 - p)^j]$	33	17	11	8	7	6	5	4		
N(j)	2277	1088	693	336	294	114	15	12	4829 = N_a	10231

These values are shown in Table 3.

TABLE 3

Potentially Active Books—QA and QC Books

QA:

j	1	2	3	4	5	6	7	8	9	Total
N(j)	4550	1950	1190	494	260	128	56	18	10	
$1/(1 - e)^j$	1.6	1.2	1.1	1.02	1.007	1	1	1	1	
N_p	7280	2340	1309	504	262	128	56	18	10	11907

QC:

j	1	2	3	4	5	6	7	8	Total
N(j)	2277	1088	693	336	294	114	15	12	
$1/(1 - e)^j$	1.6	1.2	1.1	1.02	1.007	1	1	1	
N_p	3643	1306	762	343	296	114	15	12	6491

When N_a, the number of active books, is added to N_p, the number of potentially active books, the sum is N_ℓ, the number of live books in the collection:

$$N_\ell = N_a + N_p$$

$$QA: \quad N_\ell = 8656 + 11907 = 20563$$

$$QC: \quad N_\ell = 4850 + 6491 = 11341$$

The value of C is the fraction of active books to live books:

$$C = \frac{N_a}{N_\ell}$$

QA: $C = \frac{8656}{20563} = .421$

QC: $C = \frac{4850}{11341} = .428$

The value of C, when multiplied by the mean circulation of the active books, $\bar{R}_a$, gives the mean circulation of the live books:

$$\bar{R}_\ell = C \times \bar{R}_a$$

QA: $\bar{R}_\ell = .421 \times 1.93 = .51$

QC: $\bar{R}_\ell = .428 \times 2.12 = .907$

The value of C is also used to correct the α_a value derived graphically from the plot of m vs. N(m) values:

$$\alpha = C \times \alpha_a$$

QA: $\alpha = .421 \times 1.2 = .51$

QC: $\alpha = .428 \times 1.02 = .44$

Finally, the active and live fractions of the collections are calculated:

$$\% \text{ active} = \frac{N_a}{N}$$

QA: $\% \text{ active} = \frac{8656}{12990} = 66.5\%$

QC: $\% \text{ active} = \frac{4850}{13181} = 36.7\%$

$$\% \text{ live} = \frac{N_\ell}{N}$$

QA: $\% \text{ live} = \frac{20563}{12998} = 100\%$

QC: $\% \text{ live} = \frac{11341}{13181} = 85.3\%$

The values of N, the total number of books in the sampled collections, were calculated by adding together the number of volumes on the shelf, the number of books in circulation, and a number equal to the number of books in circulation to account for books which were not on the shelf because they had not been reshelved or were unaccounted for.

LIMITATIONS OF THE STUDY

As with all studies, there are limitations to this one which affect the usefulness of the results. One limitation is that the information we have obtained does not give a complete picture of the use of mathematics and physics materials. In order to fully evaluate the total use of materials, one needs to measure in-library usage of all forms of the literature, the use of serials, and the use of non-print materials such as technical reports on microfiche. Journals and materials in microform do not circulate in the Science Library, and the loan policy is different for standard serials than for other books, so the use of these categories of materials could not be measured in this study. In addition, the data we have obtained is quantitative data only, and does not take into account other variables which affect the value of a book to a particular patron and will affect use patterns, such as accessability (with corresponding user frustration), the quality of book selection in the past, availability of needed materials from other libraries in the area, etc.

This type of study also gives no information on who uses the collections which were studied, either according to academic departmental affiliation or by status of user. Such information is essential to a thorough evaluation of the user of a collection, and is information which is quantifiable. However, it was not possible to identify users in this study because users' names are illegible more than half the time on the charge cards. With an automated circulation system, such information would be easy to obtain. This type of study also does not tell us who does *not* use the collection, nor the reasons for this non-use.

Another limitation results from the fact that data were collected for eight (mathematics books) and eleven (physics books) days only, from only books in circulation. This will affect the accuracy of the results, although not to an unacceptable degree. Morse states that the model for removing the bias caused by using this procedure gives results sufficiently accurate to compare total circulation rates, and to assist in determining the need for change in policy.[7]

It became clear to us in the course of applying this model both in this study and in previous studies that a more meaningful way to look at the use of books in a particular subject discipline is to devise a system more precise than general class call number ranges to identify the books to be studied. Such general Library of Congress and Dewey Decimal call number ranges are just too broad to give specific information on the use of books in a particular subject area. One promising approach, which has been used by McGrath and others,[8] is to break down degree programs, course listings, and research programs at a university into groups of Library of Congress sub-classes, and then look at the use of all books in those specific groups of sub-classes.

A final limitation to the accuracy of our results is that we determined α and β graphically (although the α_a value determined for active books was corrected for bias). The fact is that we ended up with *estimated* values for the circulation of books, and *estimated* α and β values, all of which limit the absolute accuracy of the results. However, for the purpose of comparing the same values for categories of books, the information obtained is useful.

RESULTS

The results of this study are shown in Table 4. The total number of active QA books is estimated to be 8656. This active fraction represents 67% of the QA collection. When potentially active books are added to the active books, the total is 20563 live books, which represents 100% of the QA collection. The total circulation of QA books in 1977–78 is estimated to be 16690 (the product of multiplying $N_a \times R_a$).

TABLE 4

Circulation Characteristics of QA and QC Books

	N_a	N_p	N_ℓ	N	$\bar{R}_a$	$\bar{R}_\ell$	α_a	α	β
QA	8656	11907	20563	12998	1.93	.813	1.2	.51	.35
QC	4850	6491	11341	13181	2.12	.907	1.02	.44	.48

	% active	% live	C	$\bar{R}\,(t+1)$
QA	66.5%	100%	.421	.794
QC	36.7%	85.3%	.428	.872

For the QC books, the active fraction is estimated to be 4850 books, or 37% of the QC collection. The live QC books consist of 11341 books, representing 85% of the QC collection. The total circulation of QC books in 1977–78 is estimated to be 10231.

The mean circulation of active books in 1977–78 was 1.93 for QA books and 2.12 for QC books. The mean circulation for live QA books is .813 and .907 for live QC books. The model predicts that the mean circulation in 1978–79 for live QA books will be .794 ad .872 for live QC books.

The estimated values for α are .51 and QA books and .44 for QC books. The values of β are estimated to be .35 for QA books and .48 for QC books.

DISCUSSION

We were able to quantify a number of useful circulation variables for mathematics and physics books in this study. In addition, we can compare these values with similar ones which were previously measured for all books in the Science Library, and for books in the life sciences collection. Since we assume that the circulation behavior of a group of books represents one aspect of user demand, we now have some measure of the effectiveness of the mathematics and physics collections.

The central question which we asked was, are mathematics and physics books used differently than other books in the library, and if so, in what ways? We expected to find that mathematics and physics books are used more frequently and in larger numbers than books in the life sciences, and that older books in mathematics and physics are used longer than the average older book in the library.

These expectations have been partially confirmed in this study. For the purpose of discussion, the following information is shown in Table 5: circulation variables calculated for mathematics and physics books; similar variables calculated for life sciences books in a previous study;[9] and the same variables calculated for all books in the Science Library.[10]

TABLE 5

Circulation Variables

	N_a	% active	$\bar{R}_a$	N_ℓ	% live	$\bar{R}_\ell$	α	β
Mathematics	8656	66%	1.93	20563	100%	.813	.510	.350
Physics	4850	37%	2.12	11341	85%	.907	.440	.480
Medical	422	17%	2.02	747	30%	1.14	.328	.498
Other life sciences	1558	18%	1.79	3411	40%	.816	.547	.175
All books in the Science Library	15146	14%	1.83	36098	33%	.769	.382	.410

In terms of volume of use (measured by N_a and N_ℓ), mathematics and physics books do show higher use than life sciences and medical books. Together, these books account for about 80% of the circulation for books in the Science Library. However, the N_a number calculated for the Science Library in a previous study was derived during a low-use period at an atypical time of the year, final exam week during December 1977. Therefore, this number is approximate only, and is not directly comparable with the numbers derived for mathematics and physics books.

It should also be noted that the measured values for the active and live fractions for the mathematics books leads one to question the accuracy of these results. The live fraction has been estimated, using Chen's model, to consist of 20,563 books, a number of books which is larger than the total holdings in the mathematics collection: this would mean that 100% of the mathematics collection is live, that is, either active or potentially active. The active fraction of mathematics books, 66%, is also quite high, probably higher than is the actual case. The active and live fractions are derived by dividing N_a and N_ℓ by N, the total holdings in the collection. For this study, we estimated N by counting the QA and 510–519 books in the stacks, adding to this number the number of these books which were in circulation, and also adding a number equal to the number of books in circulation to account for books which were waiting to be shelved or were missing.

There are at least two possibilities which might explain why the measured N fraction is so unreasonably high. First, our estimate of the holdings may be incorrect; we can ascertain this by a more careful count. Second, it may be that the nature of the current circulation distribution of mathematics books is such that the requirements for use of the correction model have not been entirely met. One test of this is to plot, on semi-log graph paper, j vs. N(j), to see if the distribution results in a straight line. When this is done for mathematics books, a straight line is the result but the fit of the data is not entirely satisfactory, particularly when compared with the graph of the physics books (see Figure 4). The data point for j = 1 for the mathemtics books is far from the line. We think that had data been collected from a larger number of books, this distribution might more clearly show the proper pattern. In any case, we think that this study of mathematics books should be repeated with a larger sample to try to clarify why the measured values of N_a and N are so high and to carefully count the total holdings in the mathematics collection.

An examination of frequency of use gives some measure of the demand for books as measured by $\bar{R}_a$ and $\bar{R}_\ell$. In terms of mean circulation of the active books, $\bar{R}_a$, mathematics and physics books show a freqency of use above the norm for books in the Science Library and above the value for most life sciences books. Only active medical books show a higher mean circulation than mathematics books, while physics books have the highest frequency of use. In terms of the mean circulation of live books, $\bar{R}_\ell$, both mathematics and physics books again show higher use than the norm for all books in the Science Library, although medical books show a higher frequency index for live books.

The active fractions for both mathematics and physics books are quite high, well above the norm for the Science Library. The live fractions for both categories of books are also high. In spite of the ambiguity in regard to the accuracy of the high mathematics books values mentioned above, it is clear that more than 50% of the books in both of the collections studies are either active or potentially active.

The usefulness of the results discussed thus far may be summarized as follows. First, the N_a and N_ℓ values, and the estimated active and live fractions indicate that the mathematics and physics collections consist of predominantly live books. The "dead" or unused fractions are very small, which indicates that book selection has been consistent with the needs of users at MIT. This is further supported by the $\bar{R}_a$ and $\bar{R}_\ell$ values, which show that not only are the books used, but they are used more frequently than the average book in the Science Library. For the mathematics and physics subject librarian, this

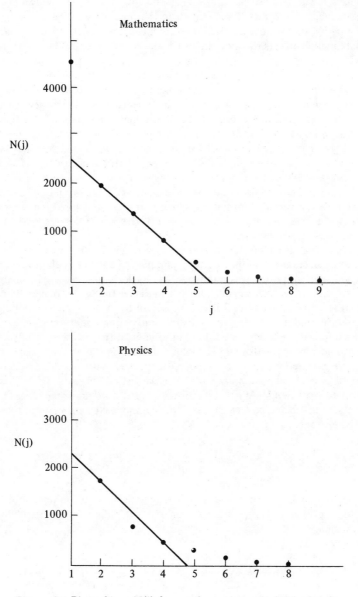

Figure 4. Plot of j vs. N(j) for mathematics and physics books.

information is useful in determining patterns of use of her collections.

The α and β values derived for mathematics and physics books also give one useful information. The α parameter is a measure of the average circulation which books of a class will reach with time; it is a measure of the long-term value of books in the collection. A large α indicates that books in the collection will continue to be useful for a long time. The α values for mathematics and physics books are higher than the norm for the Science Library, and higher than the α value for medical books. The α for other life sciences books is the highest. We think that the low α for the medical books may be partially explained by the fact that research in the medical sciences is relatively new but of rapidly growing importance at MIT; therefore, the demand for medical books is not in a steady state, which affects the measured variables for the medical books.

The β value is a measure of how rapidly books in the collection diminish in popularity from year to year. The smaller β is, the faster the mean circulation will drop from the previous years. The β value for mathematics books is lower than the β value for the average book in the Science Library, contrary to our expectations. We suspect that we would have derived a higher, more accurate β value for mathematics books if the size of the sample had been larger. The β value derived for physics books is larger than that for the average book in the Science Library. Taken together, the α and β values indicate that physics books are used longer, and lose their popularity less rapidly, than the average book in the library. We had anticipated that this would be shown to be true, although we expected that the margins of difference from the average book would be larger.

In addition to the useful information which is represented by the measured variables N_a, N_ϱ, $\overline{R}_a$, R_ϱ, active and live fractions, α and β, the results of this type of study have other implications for the librarian.

For example, the effect of a change in loan or renewal policies on the use of a collection could quite accurately be measured by conducting a study both before and one year after such a change in policy was implemented. By looking only at the change in mean circulation of the active fraction, $\overline{R}_a$, in each phase of the study, one could not find out how much more or less use of the collection resulted from the change in policy.

In addition, if this study was designed differently, one could determine a meaningful way to set a duplication policy based on operating data. In this case, a study of the use of mathematics and physics books would include measuring the mean, average, time a book is on loan, the parameter μ. Once μ has been determined, a different Morse model may be used if, in addition, α and β are known for each class of books.

As described by Chen,[11] Morse established that if a book circulated R(1) during its first year, its total single-copy circulation during the next ten years in the library was expected to be about:

$$R_{10} = \frac{10\alpha + \beta R(1)}{1 - \beta} - \frac{\alpha\beta}{(1 - \beta)^2}$$

The increase in circulation over and above R_{10} which would be produced by having a duplicate copy present from year 2 to year 10 is R. This can be calculated from the following formula:

$$R = \mu \left\{ \left(\frac{\alpha}{1 - \beta}\right)^2 \left(10 - \frac{1 + \beta}{1 - \beta}\right) + \left[\frac{\alpha}{1 - \beta} + \beta R(1)\right]^2 \left(\frac{1}{1 - \beta^2}\right) \right\}$$

One could then compare the additional circulation which result from a duplicate copy to the average circulation of a book of the class, and decide for each title whether the additional circulation would justify the purchase of a duplicate copy.

In summary, we have found our initial assumptions about the use of mathematics and physics books to be confirmed, for the most part, in this study. We do feel the need to repeat the study of mathematics books in order to clarify the use patterns.

At the same time that we were studying the use of mathematics and physics books in the Science Library, we also repeated the previous study of life sciences material, and found the initial results for those books confirmed. In the case of the life sciences collections, the life sciences librarian found it quite useful to compare the comparison of the data for medical and life sciences books to portions of her budget which were allocated for purchasing books in each category. She found that the proportion of her budget set aside for medical books matched the proportion of use represented by those books, thus indicating that the allocation of her life sciences funds was appropriate, based on the use of the collection.

Also, the information gained from this study could be used as an aid to library management decisions concerning weeding and storage. For example, once the live fraction of the collection is determined, one can decide whether the "dead" or unused fraction of the collection warrants weeding or removal to storage. A by-product of this study was that the subject librarian responsible for mathemtics and physics collections in the Science Library took the opportunity to examine the charge cards in the sample and thus identify monographic series which might be candidates for storage.

In conclusion, we think that the information gained from this study, which required a small amount of time spent in the collection of a relatively small number of quantitative data, is useful to both library managers and subject librarians. We recommend this type of study as a useful way to evaluate the use of subject collections.

REFERENCES

1. Frederick Wildred Lancaster, "Evaluation of the Collection," in *The Measurement and Evaluation of Library Services* (Washington, DC: Information Resources Press, 1977), pp. 165–206.
2. Sandra E. Spurlock and Ellen Yen, "A Study of Life Sciences Book Use in the MIT Science Library: Budgetary Implications," in *Quantitative Measurements and Dynamic Library Services* (Scottsdale, Ariz.: Oryx Press, 1978).
3. MIT Libraries, "Collection Analysis Project. Task Force on Collection Effectiveness. Final Report and Recommendations" (MIT Libraries, Feburary 1978).
4. Philip M. Morse, *Library Effectiveness: A Systems Approach* (Cambridge, Mass: MIT Press, 1968).
5. Ching-chih Chen, *Applications of Operations Research Models to Libraries* (Cambridge, Mass.: MIT Press, 1976).
6. *Ibid.*
7. Philip M. Morse and Ching-chih Chen, "Using Circulation Desk Data to Obtain Unbiased Estimates of Book Use," *Library Quarterly* 45 (April 1975): 179–194.
8. William E. McGrath and Norma Durand, "Classified Courses in the University Catalog," *College and Research Libraries* 30 (November 1969): 553–539. William E. McGrath, "A Pragmatic Book Allocation Formula for Academic and Public Libraries with a Test for Its Effectiveness," *Library Resources and Technical Services*, 19 (Fall 1975): 536–369.
9. Spurlock and Yen, *op. cit.*
10. MIT Libraries, "Collection Analysis Project," p. 50.
11. Chen, *op. cit.*, p. 117.

Stephen Wiberley

University of Illinois at Chicago Circle

SOURCES FOR THE HUMANITIES: MEASURING USE AND MEETING NEEDS

Citation studies in the humanities have usually overlooked use of primary sources. Because humanities publications tend to concentrate on a small number of primary sources, often referenced in embedded citations, it is worthwhile to measure use of humanities sources in units of paragraphs as well as in units of references. Paragraph analysis of sample of humanities publications reveals twice as much use of primary sources as of secondary. Academic and research libraries should strengthen traditional policies and adopt new strategies that meet those needs, particularly by striving for intellectual control over unique primary sources.

One of the ironies about our knowledge of the use of academic and research libraries is that there is general agreement that humanists depend on the library more than other scholars and yet studies of humanists' use of the library are far fewer than studies of use by physical scientists and social scientists.[1] Nonetheless, if librarians are to meet the future needs of their principal clinetele, they must study in greater depth the use of sources of information by humanists.

This paper discusses the citation study as a way of measuring the sources used by humanists, explains the paragraph analysis, an alternative to methods of citation study used heretofore, and suggests briefly ways of providing the materials and services humanists need most. But before entering into this discussion, a short general comment on the nature of the humanities and on their differences from the physical and social sciences is necessary.

The humanities attempt to understand, appreciate, evaluate, and explain the creative efforts of men and women. The term "creative efforts" here covers a broad range of endeavors from the artistic efforts of individuals to the collective efforts of societies. As students of human endeavor, humanists necessarily examine that which has occurred in the past whether it be a painting, a symphony, a scientific theory, or a national constitution. The essence of the humanistic enterprise is coming to terms with that which is unique and outstanding in human achievements. In this quest humanists do not feel bound by any single methodology or viewpoint, nor required to make their findings conform to earlier interpretations.[2]

Humanists always study either a document or an artifact that embodies human effort. When dealing with historical topics social scientists also use documents and artifacts, but when investigating current events and phenomena, they study groups of people directly. Physical scientsts, of course, study natural phenomena, not documents or artifacts. In methodological orientation humanists are individualistic, while social sicentists try to follow models and use methodologies that a number of their peers have employed. The physical sciences are paradigmatic: physical scientists' findings must come to terms with the dominant theories and contribute to scientific progress.[3]

Given the basic differences in objects of study, evidence used, and methodology employed by the humanities and by the social and physical sciences, it is surprising that citation studies in the humanities have differed little from those in the social and physical sciences. In particular, because the principal objects of study in the humanities are documents and artifacts that embody the creative efforts of people, it is hard to understand why most citation studies of the humanities do not measure the use of primary sources.

Interesting in this respect is Benny Ray Tucker's citation study of classical philology. Tucker counted only footnotes that referred to "secondary source material illustrating or supporting a point in the text." He rejected counting references to original Greek and Latin texts because such material is usually cited within the text and not in a footnote. He conceded that "the ancient texts and other primary source material represent the basis for research by classicists," but believed "that treating them on the same level with other material is improper."[4]

Tucker's decision to exclude primary sources from his count seems to conflict with his belief that primary sources are the basis for research by classicists. Yet, his position is not unique. David Broadus's investigation of the literature of speech, David L. Vaughan's citation study of musicology, and Wesley L. Simonton's analysis of sources used by art critics do not measure use of primary sources.[5]

Two citation studies that do measure use of primary sources are Edwin Gleaves's analysis of sources used by critics of American Literature and Charles Bolles's dissertation on sources for American studies. Gleaves employed an involved sampling procedure, not fully explained, to compile the group of citations he analyzed. Sixty percent of these citations were to primary materials.[6] Bolles used the straightforward method of counting all references in the first twenty-one volumes of the *American Quarterly*. He also analyzed in greater depth than the others, the references in volumes one and two, six, eleven, sixteen, and twenty-one. In contrast to Gleaves, Bolles found that at most 29 percent of all sources used were primary.[7]

The contrast between Bolles's and Gleaves's findings deserves extended criticism. But limitations of time and heuristic advantages of examining Bolles's work will force me to restrict comment to it. Gleaves does not fully explain his sampling method, and it apparently differs from other citation studies in the humanities. Bolles counts citations just as the Institute for Scientific Information does. (Of course, ISI does not analyze citations by class and form as Bolles did.) Comparison to Bolles of a new technique for counting sources of information like the paragraph analysis, suggests, in effect, how that technique relates to ISI's citation counts. Since ISI has the largest data bases of citations, now including one in the arts and humanities, the paragraph analysis should be related to it.

Strictly speaking, both Bolles and ISI count references not citations.[8] That is, when counting sources of a publication like a journal article, Bolles lists each distinct bibliographic entity cited only once; duplicate citations—*ibid.*'s and *op. cit.*'s—are ignored. This can lead to underestimating the extent to which an author relied on a single source. For instance, in an article in the *American Quarterly* on Alexis de Tocqueville's opinion of nineteenth-century America, Cushing Strout cited *Democracy in America* more than forty times, in sixteen different paragraphs. Yet, by his rules Bolles counted only the first citation.[9]

Bolles's decision to count references instead of citations is typical of many "citation" studies. Given the nature of much scholarship in the humanities, counting references is questionable. Because humanists investigate the creative efforts of men and women as embodied in documents and artifacts, they often devote entire publications to analysis of a single work or a small number of works, quoting from each or discussing each extensively. Furthermore, in such essays, some scholars do not use footnotes, but supply embeded citations within the text. Finally, some scholars are less careful than others in giving credit to their sources.

To compensate for these characteristics of humanistic publications, in addition to counting references, it is worthwile to measure the use of sources in units of paragraphs. This may be called paragraph analysis. In it the investigator determines class, i.e., how many paragraphs are based on primary sources, on secondary sources, on both primary and secondary sources; and then ascertains what forms—books, serials, newspapers, archives—of primary and secondary sources the scholar used. The investigator decides arbitrarily the forms of sources to be counted. For example, he may differentiate among published collections of manuscripts, literary works, critical editions, and Festschriften, or classify all these under the form books.

In measuring the use of primary and secondary sources, the investigator ignores the number of distinct primary or secondary sources on which an individual paragraph is based. He simply decides whether the paragraph derives from primary sources alone, from secondary sources alone, from both primary and secondary sources, or from neither. Thus, for instance, a paragraph based on a book and a manuscript that are both primary sources counts no more toward the total of paragraphs based on primary sources than a paragraph derived from a manuscript alone. Likewise a paragraph based on three primary source serials counts no more toward the total of paragraphs based on primary sources than a paragraph based on one primary source serial.

Tables 1 and 2 illustrate a paragraph analysis for a six-paragraph article. Comparison of the list of sources (Table 1) with the tally sheet of the analysis (Table 2) emphasizes the fact that when measuring use by class, each paragraph has the same value, regardless of the number of sources and variety of forms of sources on which it is based.

TABLE 1

List of Sources

Paragraph No.	Sources
1	None
2	One secondary book
3	Two secondary serials
4	One secondary book
	Two secondary serials
5	Three primary manuscripts
6	One primary manuscript
	Two primary serials
	One secondary book

TABLE 2

Tally of Analysis

| Paragraph No. | Class of Sources Used | | | |
	Primary	Secondary	Both Primary and Secondary	Neither
1				X
2		B		
3		S		
4		B, S		
5	M			
6	M, S	B	X	
Total	1	3	1	1

KEY: B–Book;   M–Manuscript;   S–Serial

As an experiment, I measured in units of paragraphs the classes of sources that were the basis of volume twenty-one (1969) of the *American Quarterly*. The analysis revealed that 503 paragraphs were based on primary sources alone (called P), 204 paragraphs on secondary sources alone (S), and 153 paragraphs on both primary and secondary sources (B). Including paragraphs not based on sources, volume twenty-one has 1105 paragraphs. Overall 59 percent (656) were based on primary sources; 32 percent (357) on secondary sources. To measure the relative reliance on primary (R_p) and on secondary (R_s) sources, one uses the simple formulae:

$$R_p = \frac{P + B}{P + S + 2B}$$

$$R_s = \frac{S + B}{P + S + 2B}$$

Applying these formulae one finds that the relative reliance on primary and secondary sources ($R_p:R_s$) is 65:35.

The contrast of these findings with Bolles's analysis of the same volume is striking. Bolles reports that only 29 percent of all references were to primary sources. This percentage is low not only because Bolles counted only references, but also because it is based on a very narrow definition of primary sources. Bolles restricts his definition to unpublished materials and newspapers, but primary sources include much more.[10] They may be defined as documents (1) embodying the creative effort(s) under study; (2) contemporaneous with the event or phenomenon under study, or (3) created by the participants in the event or by the makers of the phenomenon being investigated. Documents here means both verbal materials and artifacts. Besides newspapers and unpublished materials they can include monographs, serials, government documents, and art objects. Under its broader definition, nineteenth-century children's magazines like *Juvenile Miscellany* and *Youth's Companion* that are the subject of the first article in volume twenty-one of the *American Quarterly* are rightfully counted as primary sources.

A shortcoming of the paragraph analysis is that it sometimes involves more subjective judgments than the reference or citation count. The essential problem is deciding whether or not a paragraph is based on sources. Naturally, any paragraph that is footnoted or contains embedded page references is counted. For other paragraphs the general rule is to count only those that advance the argument with evidence and give new facts whose source can be inferred. Thus, introductory, transitional, and summary paragraphs normally are not counted.

While recognizing the difficulties involved in a paragraph analysis, it should be pointed out that determining what references should appear in a list of references in *Social Sciences Citation Index* or in any other reference count can sometimes be every bit as difficult as determining whether or not a paragraph is based on sources. It is particularly hard to sort out references in articles with dozens of footnotes to portions of publications like the *Congressional Record* or the *Patrologia Latina.* Such footnotes offen contain a myriad of personal named, *ibid.*'s, and page numbers that are extremely difficult to list consistently.[11] Also difficult to enumerate are references to manuscript materials. Does one list separately each citation to single items in a manuscript collection or does one just list the collection containing the items? To count the former may exaggerate the use of manuscripts, particularly when the scholar was meticulous in citing them. To do the latter can easily underestimate the importance of the manuscripts.[12]

The paragraph analysis, as a product of pure research, may become as useful in intellectual history as in library science. Its strength is in analysis of publications that tend to derive from one or a few sources and to give insufficient credit to these sources in footnotes. Even if paragraph analysis is primarily a research tool, its application to publications in the humanities reminds librarians of an important fact that demands practical action: primary sources are central to the work of the humanist and more important than secondary sources. Paragraph analyses of samples of journal articles in music and art criticism as well as in American studies given quantified evidence of this fact. In the first ten articles of volume fifty-seven of the *Musical Quarterly* (1971), 67 percent of the paragraphs draw on primary sources; 37 percent on secondary sources; the relative use of primary and secondary being 64:35. In the first ten articles in volume fifty-five of the *Art Bulletin* (1973), 72 percent of the paragraphs are based on primary sources; 34 percent on secondary; the relative use 67:33.

These data show why emphasis must be on primary sources when meeting the needs of humanists. In many ways traditional policies will meet these needs: in collection development librarians have always paid careful attention to published primary sources, such as literature, philosophical texts, religious tracts, and printed collections of manuscripts like the correspondence of artists, notebooks of writers, and papers of politicians.

While much primary material is published and generally available, a vast amount is not. Most archives, manuscripts, paintings, and sculptures are unique. To make these available both to scholars working at the institution that owns them as well as to the public, libraries should devote as much effort as possible to gaining intellectual control of these materials. The challenge here is tremendous since manuscript materials alone number in the millions. A library must create and disseminate finding aids to its own collections and collect as widely as possible the catalogs of unique primary materials that are held by other institutions.

Different from, but related to descriptions of the holdings of individual depositories, are directories of primary sources in subject areas that are held by a number of institutions. For example, the National Endowment for the Humanities has sponsored the Women's History Sources Survey conducted by the University of Minnesota Social Welfare History Archives. The project has produced a national guide to 20,000 manuscript descriptions from over 1,600 collections.[13] Librarians have obligations not only to respond to requests for information from compilers of these directories, but also to volunteer information when compilers overlook them.

The computer, of course, is an extremely important tool in current efforts toward bibliographic and intellectual control over documents. In an era of shrinking financial resources, librarians have to make hard choices about its use. At this point the basic choice seems to be between using the computer to retrieve citations to secondary literature or employing it to access listings of primary sources. Given the findings of paragraph analyses on samples of humanistic scholarship, the latter choice appears wiser for the humanities. This is not to deny the value of using computers to produce print indexes like *RILA* and *RILM*. But it is to question seriously the greater expense of obtaining data bases like these on-line. Rather libraries should explore the possibility of joining computer networks that may grow out of the efforts of groups like the Museum Data Bank Committee and of projects to put on-line the *National Union Catalog of Manuscript Collections.* At present there are major questions about the feasibility and economy of computerization of records about primary sources.[14] But the falling costs of computer system suggests that it would be foolish to preclude such projects.

Whether or not these visions of computer networks become reality, librarians will still be able to utilize traditional methods to meet the needs of humanists. With a new technique of measurement of the sources of information that humanists use and the resulting greater knowledge, it is hoped that librarians will employ either traditional or automated methods more effectively.

REFERENCES

1. Lois Bebout, Donald Davis, Jr., and Donald Oehlerts, "User Studies in the Humanities: A survey and a Proposal," *RQ* 15 (1975): 40.

2. Harcourt Brown, "Why This Book Was Written: An Introduction," in *Science and the Creative Spirit: Essays on Humanistic Aspects of Science*, ed. Harcourt Brown (Toronto: University of Toronto Press, 1958), pp. xii, xvii, xxvi; Ronald S. Crane, *The Idea of the Humanities, and Other Essays Critical and Historical*, 2 vols. (Chicago: University of Chicago Press, 1967), 1: 7–11; Karl W. Deutsch, "Scientific and Humanistic Focus of Attention," in *Science and the Creative Spirit*, pp. 3–8; D. J. Foskett, "Problems of Indexing and Classification in the Social Sciences," *International Social Science Journal* 23 (1971): 247: Walter J. Ong, "Crisis and Understanding in the Humanities," *Daedalus* 98 (1969): 617–618; and G. Jon Rousch, "What Will Become of the Past," *Daedalus* 98 (1969): 641.

3. J. M. Brittain, *Information and Its Users: A Review with Special Reference to the Social Sciences* (New Castle-upon-Tyne, England: Bath University Press in association with Oriel Press, 1970), p. 18; Deutsch, "Scientific and Humanistic Focus," p. 3; Thomas Kuhn, *The Structure of Scientific Revolutions*, 2nd ed., Foundations of the Unity of Science Series, vol. 2, no. 2 (Chicago: University of Chicago Press, 1970); D. J. Urquhart, "The Needs of the Humanities: An Outside View," *Journal of Documentation* 16 (1960): 121–2; and V. A. Winn, "A Case Study in the Problems of Information Processing in a Social Science Field: The OSTI-SEA Project," *Aslib Proceedings* 23 (1971): 81–8.

4. Benny R. Tucker, "Characteristics of the Literature Cited by Authors of the *Transactions of the American Philological Association*, 1956 and 1957" (Master's thesis, University of North Carolina, 1959), pp. 9–10.

5. Robert N. Broadus, *Research Literature of the Field of Speech*, ACRL Monograph, no. 7 (Chicago, 1953), p. 22; Wesley C. Simonton, "Characteristics of the Research Literature of the Fine Arts during the Period 1948–1957" (Ph.D. dissertation, University of Illinois at Urbana, 1960), p. 5; and David L. Vaughan, "Characteristics

of the Literature Cited by Authors of Articles in *The Musical Quarterly*, 1955–58, and *The American Musicological Society Journal*, 1953–56" (Master's thesis, University of North Carolina, 1959), p. 12.

6. Edwin S. Gleaves, Jr., "Characteristics of the Research Materials Used by Scholars Who Write in Journals in the Field of American Literature" (Master's thesis, Emory University, 1960), p. 37.

7. Charles A. Bolles, "Characteristics of the Literature of American Studies as Indicated by Bibliographic Citations" (Ph.D. dissertation, University of Minnesota, 1975), p. 61.

8. Nan Lin and Carnot E. Nelson, "Bibliographic References Patterns in Core Sociological Journals, 1965–1966," *American Sociologist* 4 (1969): 47.

9. *American Quarterly* 21 (1969): 87–99.

10. Bolles, *op. cit.*, p. 61.

11. Cf. *Social Sciences Citation Index, Sources*, 1975, s.v. "Benedict ML;" and Michael L. Benedict, "Preserving the Constitution: The Conservative Basis of Radical Reconstruction," *Journal of American History* 61 (1974): 65–90.

12. Cf. *Social Sciences Citation Index, Sources*, 1975 s.v. "Norton MB;" and Mary B. Norton, "Eighteenth-Century American Women in Peace and War: The Case of the Loyalists," *The William and Mary Quarterly* 33 (1976): 386–409.

13. "Research Collections," *Humanities: Newsletter of the National Endowment for the Humanities*, vol. 7, no. 7 (Oct., 1977), [p. 1].

14. Maynard Brichford et al., "Intellectual Control of Historical Records," *The American Archivist* 40 (1977): 307–313; David Scott, *The Yogi and the Registrar*, Museum Data Bank Research Report, no. 7 (Rochester, NY, 1976); and H. J. Swinney, *Characteristics of History Museum Activity and Their Influence on Potential Electronic Cataloging*, Museum Data Bank Research Report, no. 8 (Rochester, NY, 1976).

Charles Willard

Princeton Theological Seminary

MICROFORMS: CHANGING THE CONCEPTUAL POLARITY FROM NEGATIVE TO POSITIVE

The failure of librarians seriously to consider microforms as a major resource has resulted in substantial, unnecessary expenditures. The alternative model here advocated is not merely speculative, as it already works in a limited field whose structure may satisfactorily be extrapolated to large reserach libraries. The paper outlines an integrative system, covering areas in which libraries may apply the active model both individually and collectively. Among the former are interlibrary loan transactions and retrospective collection development. Cooperative programs include the design of large microform projects initiated by bibliographers and scholars rather than commercial agencies.

Although the deterioration of printed literature, especially from the mid-nineteenth century forward, is as inevitable as the eventual exhaustion of the world's oil reserves, the library response to this resource crisis is about as phlegmatic as the national response to the energy crisis. There are also elements of similarity in the causes, in the futility of individual efforts and the weak will to cooperate. The purpose of this paper is to counter this lethargy by outlining the characteristics of a coordinated national program for the microform preservation of our literary resources and by appealing to research libraries to act in their own self-interest. The program, moreover, is not merely conservative, inasmuch as the widening of access to the primary and secondary literature of the period under discussion is effectively an expansion of resources. The paper begins with a review of the program of the American Theological Library Association Board of Microtext, a successful but underknown model. The second part describes elements in an aggressive, national microform program, a program involving many facets of library operations, from acquisitions through cataloging to public services, including interlibrary loans.

The American Theological Library Association includes some 150 theological libraries and 400 individuals who are either theological librarians or are involved in theological bibliography. In 1958, an $80,000 grant from the Sealantic Fund established the Board of Microtext as an agency of the ATLA for the purpose of making available in microform, literature essential for theological and religious research that is accessible only in scattered, broken files, printed on deteriorating paper, or both, and that is unlikely to be attractive to commercial micropublishers or reprinters. In the case of serials or multi-volume sets, the Board seeks to bring together the most nearly complete file possible.

523

Cataloging and collation sheets are filmed in source; the Board's master negatives are filmed at a low reduction ratio and are processed, stored, and serviced following archival standards. Positive copies of titles in the Board's program are sold at a price that apportions the cost of the negative among five copies. In the two decades of its existence, the Board has filmed approximately 500 monographs and 300 serials, and capital reserves were $52,500 in 1978.

Recently, however, two additional factors have become evident. First, the Board's emphasis upon preservation rather than potential sales has resulted in fewer additions to the program likely to break even, that is, to sell more than five copies. Second, most material in the program will not sustain heavy use in any collection. In fact, the long term loan availability of titles in the program would support most research that can be envisioned with these primary resources. This fact, however, is in tension with the need of the Board to recover capital invested in master negatives, in order to continue to film more materials. In response, the Board has developed a program that, if successful, will deal creatively with both new factors. The program is the Cooperative Microform Project on Religion and Theology (COMPORT). For an annual subscription of $250, a participating library has long term loan access to any title in the program as well as a 30% discount on titles acquired from the Board. At the present time, COMPORT membership is limited to ATLA member libraries, but in principle, the Board is committed to widening the membership base. It is hoped, obviously, that the annual subscription income will offset both the probable decrease in sales and the cost of making the positive copies on demand for loan. The Board believes, moreover, that effective access to titles in its program must be available at the local level and achieves this through one or more of the following three mechanisms: (1) Cataloging for all titles in the program is added to the data base of the Ohio College Library Center, where these records are thereafter available on-line to OCLC members. (2) Cards representing catalog records of Board titles in the OCLC data base are available at cost to COMPORT member libraries in one of three formats: main entry only, main entry and all non-subject added entries, and main entry and all added entries. (3) Semi-annually, from January 1978, a fully cumulative, computer-output-microfiche, dictionary, union catalog is being compiled from OCLC archive records of the titles cataloged by Union and Princeton seminaries, the theological libraries of Yale and Harvard, and the Board of Microtext. The second cumulation of this microfiche catalog, which has been named CORECAT, has recently been produced, and plans are being made to offer this and subsequent editions on subscription. Any subscriber, therefore, will have full catalog access to all titles in the Board's program.

The reason for rehearsing in some detail the development of the Board of Microtext is the importance of recognizing that a group of concerned librarians in a relatively small, subject-isolated area can successfully design and initiate a program of microform preservation for the benefit of scholarship in general, without commercial motivation or intervention. Reflection will suggest that it is also possible for elements of the overall proposal offered below to be undertaken within single-subject fields or by a single-institution. Given the traditional conservatism of the library community, it is probable that individual initiative is the only way to begin. On the other hand, the total effect of the widely coordinated program is significantly greater than the sum of such individual parts.

The support that this proposal—or a similar one—will generate is directly proportional to the degree to which librarians and institutional administrators appreciate two facts: (1) that the books on shelves of every library throughout the country are deteriorating and (2) that the age of a volume, which is an accurate, although not absolute, indicator of the relative state of embrittlement, is also a highly reliable, inversely varying predictor of probable use.[1] These observations are almost commonplace, yet the first has failed to arouse the condition of alarm, even desperation, that it merits, and the second has not been sufficiently exploited, mostly for parochial reasons. It is the first that requires the development of the coordinated, national approach, advocated by this paper, and it is the second that makes the practical necessities of the program a realistic possibility within the responsibilities of American research libraries.

The proposal follows considerations already advanced by Gordon Williams and now a part of the National Preservation Program under the aegis of the Library of Congress, but it expands the scope of that program, as outlined to date, and it provides a greater number of avenues for exploitation.[2] The proposal is also informed by a nascent feasibility study for a preservation and storage program for ATLA libraries, undertaken by Andrew Scrimgeour. I do not here attempt to outline a detailed master plan, although I think that it is possible to identify three minimum and desirable characteristics necessary for success and wide acceptance: (1) There must exist a national standard for bibliographic control. (2) The system must invite a very high level of confidence with respect to quality control and permanent accessibility. (3) The design of the system must allow participation along a wide spectrum, from the individual library to a national cooperative. Let me briefly elaborate each of these elements.

Bibliographic control: Titles in the system must be available through one of the national, machine readable cataloging networks, although ideally, there would be a satisfactory interface that would make data in one accessible to users of the other. It is not entirely clear that a complete bibliographic record, in the MARC sense, should be required, and it is quite possible that an initial inventory of titles, cumulated prior to actual microfilming, would necessitate a truncated format capable of subsequent upgrading. Early agreement on these formats is important in order that institutions and cooperative groups may move ahead promptly.

Quality control: The standards and requirements for archival film and processing as well as appropriate layout and targeting sequences must be gathered in a single guide.

Permanent accessibility: There are two aspects to this element. The first, related to quality control, is physical access in the sense that the nature of the film, processing, and storage are such that the data will be preserved 300–500 years. The second has to do with legal access, where confidence means certainty that a preservation master for appropriate duplication will actually be available to the national library community 300–500 years from now.

The system: The mechanism for establishing the minimum and appropriate full bibliographic elements already exists in the National Preservation Program; the same mechanism could also identify the necessary characteristics and standards for proper quality control for film and processing. In order to insure that both concerns for accessibility are met, a preservation master storage and service center must be established. The purpose of this center would be four-fold: (1) to provide the environmental conditions required for the archival preservation of properly manufactured and processed microfilm, (2) to serve as the permanent depository for masters, (3) and to generate working masters as required by contributing agencies, and (4) to sell copies of masters where the right to do so has been transferred to the center.

Once bibliographic and archival standards have been set, the center would also monitor compliance by participating agencies. Individual institutions, cooperative groups, and commercial firms would be able to generate master negatives according to these standards. These negatives, certified as meeting film and processing standards, would be permanently deposited with the center. One option would be for legal title to be transferred to the center, in which case, the center would seek to recover the costs of storage through the sales of copies. The second option would be for the originating agency to retain legal ownership and distribution rights to the master, in which case an annual charge would be payable for maintenance of the master; default on such payments would cause title to pass to the center. Commerical firms, of course, would be able to transfer ownership to some other firm and to secure working masters at will. Such an arrangement, moreover, should respond to the distress within the library community over the growing trend toward non-silver distribution films, inasmuch as the existence of a silver master would be insured.[3]

I have intentionally avoided discussion of a book storage center, as I believe that the concerns for storage and preservation are quite distinct. At best I can imagine the circumstances under which a book storage center would be a desirable, although temporary expedient. Let us consider the instance that one or more libraries have come to terms with the problem of deteriorating paper, concluding that microform access is at least a preferable alternative to prospective no access. These libraries, however, are faced with immediate space problems to which the only present alternative is a building program. No present microfilming program can commit the necessary number of titles to microfilm within the limits of time. Under such circumstances, a regional storage center could serve a useful holding stage, providing the truncated bibliographic control earlier suggested. The cost of such a cooperative warehouse would inevitably be lower than ordinary library building space. The holdings of such storage centers would be reported on regularly updated COM catalogs, which would also be integrated with the catalog of the master storage center. Such a union COM catalog could, therefore, represent substantially and at an early date the record of most titles finally to be available through the national preservation program, records being updated to show availability in microform.

In addition, or as an alternative to low temperature control, a book storage center might find gaseous deacidification a cost-efficient means of stabilizing titles added to its collection. Parenthetically, let me observe that I cannot anticipate that widespread general gaseous deacidification is a satisfactory solution to the retrospective brittle paper problem of libraries, although it may be the only way that libraries can deal with a current and propsective problem, namely, the continued publication of most books acquired by most libraries on non-acid free paper.

Participating libraries may annotate their own catalog cards to indicate the location of titles available in the storage or master center, although patrons interested in such literature will almost invariably find a substantially larger selection of material in the storage/master COM catalog. The request for a center title takes no longer to fill than a recall of the same title from another user. If not already available on film, the title is recataloged, the machine readable data base record updated, and a reproduction—microform, microprint, reduced print, or full size copy, as requested—is delivered to the participating library.

Can we know the impact of such a system if it were already in effect? A careful analysis of the circulation patterns in Speer Library, based on a random sample of all books in the collection, showed that for the five year period 1971–75, books with an imprint of 1800–1919 accounted for approximately 12% of the circulation. The portion of the collection, however, from which this 12% was withdrawn amounts to 39% of all the monographs owned. Total annual circulation runs about 35,000 volumes, indicating that 4,200 volumes would have to be requested from an operational center, if all the volumes within this imprint period were sought there.

A further side benefit to large research libraries, the recipients of a disproportionate number of interlibrary loan requests, is that incoming requests for their titles available from the center would be immediately referred there for fulfillment on a cost-recovery basis. I am aware of no scientific study of the imprint pattern of interlibrary loan requests; however, since we began referring all interlibrary loan requests for pre-1906 imprints, presumptively in the public domain, to the Board of Microtext for microform preservation and reproduction as an alternative to circulation, the number of such requests appears to be disproportionately large compared to the general distribution of books in the collection according to imprint.

Although this simple proposal requires a significant reconsideration of traditional operating policies by potentially participating libraries, it is still shy of an aggressive program. These activities are essentially conservative, and provision for the research needs of the twenty-first century requires a further step, the much more deliberate assumption of control by librarians, bibliographers, and scholars of the microform programs serving research collections, which, after all, are both the primary source and virtually the sole market for most commercial programs.

First, the *ad hoc* microfilming program constituting the initial stage of the proposal must be significantly supplemented by a more carefully thought-through project, organized by subject areas, capturing initially the basic literature for each field and then increasing by coherent increments. One of the persistent difficulties that the problem of deteriorating paper poses is sheer immensity. The success of the Board of Microtext commends desirability of the subject approach, and it should be possible to assign subject responsibilities to research libraries along the same lines of the now abandoned Farmington plan. Such assignments have the advantage of appealing to the areas in which a particular library has great strength; these are the very areas in which the library is likely to have a substantial number of brittle books and thus a larger stake in both preservation and expansion.

It is possible that commercial firms might here sense profit, and the three parties named earlier must seize and hold the responsibility for assessing the potential scholarly need for particular microform projects as well as for insuring both the proper filming and cataloging of such collections and the permanent accessibility by the scholarly community to the master negative. Many more copies of some commercial micropublishing projects have been sold than a reasonable estimate of the probable research need indicates, which suggests to me that funds are not being responsibly spent. Some, perhaps many, current, commercial projects are not viable if predicated upon a realistic accounting of actual need. This is not purposely anti-entrepreneurial but insists that the micropublisher is usually only a broker—indeed, sometimes a creative one—between a source and consumers, consumers who for various reasons are often uncoordinated, unsatisfactorily informed, isolated, and subject to many cunning pressures. Our primary sources are too precious and the financial resources too limited to give over the field entirely to the merchant, and thus inviting needless duplication and acquisition, with the result that other, less attractive literature is left to deteriorate.

Finally, it is not necessary to await the program envisaged by this paper for individual libraries to make significant changes in current practices. The *National Register of Microform Masters* already lists many thousands of titles available in microform, to which may be added those in the *International Guide to Microforms in Print* and the cumulative catalogs of a number of micropublishers. Desiderata lists should regularly be checked in these resources; moreover, potential reprint, rare book, and ordinary out-of-print acquisitions should be screened against the same lists. Access to a good microfilm laboratory will make it possible to carry these proposals further. The NUC pre-1956 locates a substantial number of the titles appearing in ordinary desiderata files, and lost titles should be replaced promtly by film made from an original located in another library; furthermore, it is almost certain that original copies of out-of-print titles will be more expensive than a microform copy commissioned from a reported location.

In closing, let me make several observations about mass purchases. Recently, two block acquisitions by theological libraries have come to my attention, one running $40,000, the other, in excess of $1,000,000. The strength of both acquisitions lies in the mid-nineteenth to the early twentieth century. While portions of the latter collection are rare, for the most part these are quite ordinary, old titles. The point to be made is that very, very few of these titles are not already located in research collections in this country, and a much more sophisticated, comprehensive collection along the specialized interests of each of the acquiring libraries could have been brought together in microform for no more than was spent on the purchase of the originals. The result would have been a significant contribution to the long-term research needs of the scholarly community rather than merely the transfer of substantial quantities of brittle paper from one library to another.

The details of this proposal are necessarily sketchy, but the argument is predicated upon compelling need rather than attractive alternatives. Although it is clear that implementation, including action by many research libraries to take maximum advantage of the facilities, would bring change to some research patterns, the known use of the literature most seriously affected demonstrates that the impact would be disproportionately small and the gains would be more than commensurate. The most probable alternative to this proposal or something like it, of course, is that before the turn of the century, for all practical purposes, this literature will otherwise be totally inaccessible or altogether lost.

REFERENCES

1. Herman Howe Fussler and Julius L. Simon, *Patterns in the Use of Books in Large Research Libraries* (Chicago: University of Chicago Press, 1969).
2. Gordon Williams, "The Preservation of Deteriorating Books," *Library Journal* 91 (1966): 51–56, 189–94. See also "A National Preservation Program for Libraries" ([Washington]: Office of the Assistant Director for Preservation, Administrative Department, Library of Congress, n.d.) and Gordon Williams to Richard Sullivan (unpublished letter, 2 February 1976).
3. Pamela Darling, "Microforms in Libraries: Preservation and Storage," *Microform Review* 5 (1976): 99–100.

Raymond K. Fisher

University of Birmingham, England

ACADEMIC LIBRARIES AND
PART-TIME ADULT STUDENTS

An examination of the role of academic libraries in serving the needs of continuing education or extension students is presented. Comparisons are made with equivalent services in the United Kingdom. The library needs of adult students are defined and the effectiveness of the ACRL guidelines assessed. The various problems associated with non-credit and off-campus courses, extension centers, and non-traditional programs are described with reference to the maintenance of academic standards. It is concluded that university librarians have a direct responsibility for extension students and that special extension library services should be instituted.

This paper is concerned with library services to those students who are studying part-time on the continuing education or extension courses of universities and four-year colleges. An attempt will be made to define the role of academic libraries in serving the needs of these students. The problems are considerable, partly from a lack of clearly defined responsibilities in the past and partly because the number of students in this category, already large, is likely to increase further in the future.

The function of extension divisions is to extend the facilities and scholarship of the university to the community at large, and at once it is clear that this function has important library implications. Courses may be post-graduate, or for degree-credit, or they may be non-credit; they may be on-campus or off-campus; they may be day-time, or evening, or weekend. The main questions to be addressed are: (1) Do adults taking part-time university courses have special library needs, distinct from those of regular full-time students? (2) Are the academic standards of extension courses affected by the availability of adequate library services? (3) What is the responsibility of the university librarian toward these students? (4) How effective are separate extension libraries in providing the sort of services that are needed?

Universities are moving more and more into the field of continuing education and non-traditional degrees, and this growth is likely to continue in the 1980s following the fall in the number of young people entering higher education. This, then, is a new "horizon" for universities, and implicitly for university libraries.

I am approaching this problem from the perspective provided by my own experience in university adult education in England and by first-hand observation last year of several university main libraries and extension libraries in the U.S.A.[1] Two things in particular struck me on my visit. Firstly, the range of part-time studies and of learning-methods available to adults through universities is wider in the U.S.A.[2] than in the U.K., although recently the Open University has certainly extended the range in Britain. In the program of a British university extramural department you would never find traffic safety, for example, or wine appreciation rubbing shoulders with biochemistry or the theory of knowledge, as you may do here. Also in the U.K. there are far fewer part-time university course leading to qualifications (least of all degrees) than there are in the U.S.A.—the emphasis is still on liberal adult education or "special interest" courses. But then extension divisions in the U.S.A. are sometimes literally "extensions" on a part-time basis of a university's full-time activities, while this is not the case with any British extramural departments. Secondly, university libraries in the U.S.A. (especially those which are publicly funded) are more "open" than those in Britain, frequently offering their full range of services without extra charge to those members of the local community who ask to use them; so while it is rare in Britain for extramural students to be allowed to use their university main library, in the U.S.A. it is normal practice for a university to grant all its extension students (whatever courses they are doing) full library privileges.

Now this very fact often seems to have been regarded as solving the problem of library services to extension students: "open the doors of the library to them," it may be thought, "treat them in the same way as regular full-time students and there is nothing more to be done." However, the ACRL guidelines *Library services to extension students*[3] recognized that there were special considerations to take into account in providing for these students. Why is it that the guidelines seem to have had so little impact in the 11 years since they were published? To answer this we must first try to identify the library needs of extension students.

The first fact is that most adult students have full-time jobs and are busy people. Many are strongly motivated and often academically bright, bringing a mature approach to their subject. But for them part-time study takes up valuable spare time. Therefore, when they need books or information they want them available at the right time and in the right place. If their courses are on-campus they certainly have a great advantage, but even then, if they visit the campus only once or twice a week, they need to make good use of the little time available to them before their class meets—they need flexible loan periods for books on reserve and they need instruction in the evenings or on weekends on how to make the best use of their visits. Very few university libraries seem to have made allowances of this sort for their part-time members.

Many degree-credit courses in the U.S.A. are based on prescribed textbooks—students are obliged to buy these, and many university libraries make a point of not supplying them; in the U.K. there is less emphasis on the textbook approach—there will be certain books which students are "encouraged" to buy, but it is possible for them to survive without doing so as university libraries usually acquire them. This does not mean that the U.K. situation is any better than here—rather it is a diference of approach. But as a result it is sometimes said that in the U.S.A. credit extension students do not need libraries—they can do well enough if they get through their textbooks and absorb any learning packages that their instructors might give them. But it cannot be called university level work if a student is not stretched and stimulated to read beyond the set textbooks. How can one write a good term paper, or do a project adequately, if one is not willing to consider a number of different points of view on a subject—not just those of the instructor and the textbooks, however excellent they are? This applies particularly to the humanities and the social sciences, which are essentially reading-based subjects. So we are here dealing with academic standards—reading books cannot fail to educate, which is the main business of the university, and librarians should be alert to any opportunities to further the process.

In the context of extension studies, then, this question of reading and standards is particularly important, as it is so easy to regard part-time study or off-campus study as marginal or inferior and less demanding of students. But it is crucial that extension courses should be seen to be as academically demanding as regular full-time courses, and the existence of adequate library support is essential to this process. And yet it seems that this support is not at all easy to achieve. Very little progress has been made in this direction in the last 50 years. A statement on university off-campus credit courses made in an ALA report in 1926 is as true now as it was then: "For such classes access to books is essential, whether these be books required to be read as part of the work of the course, or reference books needed to satisfy the student's ordinary or occasional needs arising in the progress of his work. This is a mere truism. But at present the means of satisfying that need are extremely diverse and not infrequently wholly ineffective. This seems chiefly due to lack of clearly defined responsibility."[4] If this is still largely true, then with the recent rapid growth of continuing education, the problem is now urgent. What are the complications?

In the first place there are the non-credit courses, in which students study a subject "for its own sake," not working for any formal qualification. This tradition of "liberal" adult education is very strong in the U.K. For these courses library needs can vary enormously. A course in music may require very little formal reading, but if it is, for example, Greek tragedy or local history research then surely it must require a great deal. At several universities here it was reported to me that non-credit students on "academic" courses were among the best—highly motivated, critical, eager to learn, eager to read. Paradoxically some students are at their best when they are not tied to an examination syllabus or working for the "carrot" of an extra qualification. There is no reason why non-credit courses *per se* should be regarded as inferior or less in need of library support, just because they are non-examinable. The real problem is that many universities put on popular, "non-academic" subjects, and it is these which give non-credit work a poor reputation. Universities should concentrate on what they themselves can do best—in this way non-credit work would be *seen* to need adequate library services, which is rarely the case at present.

The second complication is the many courses that are held off-campus, often individual courses in isolated centers. In many ways this is the raison d'etre of extension work, providing opportunities for adults who for various reasons cannot attend on campus. But again paradoxically at some universities it is the very courses which are regarded as not needing library resources which are held off campus—this seems to be denying the main principle and further to reduce the academic respectability of extension work. In contrast, at some universities all the off-campus courses are post-graduate, and if this term makes any sense they must involve extensive reading. In these cases the library problems can be acute. It is often claimed that extension students rely heavily on their public libraries and on interlibrary loans, but for busy people with study schedules to keep to these are rarely adequate as main sources, especially in rural areas. A student may literally have no library to turn to within reasonable distance of his home or place of work; or if he has, the library will almost certainly not be geared to his special requirements in the way that university main libraries are geared to the needs of on-campus students and staff. Because of this instructors sometimes "tailor" their courses so as to make the minimum demands on libraries—hardly a desirable practice in educational terms. And so we have a vicious circle. Several university librarians said to me that the problem of library services to off-campus students was unresolved.

There is also an intermediate problem, where extension centers have been established by universities in places where there are regular concentrations of courses each year. These are often high schools or community colleges. Adult students are usually allowed to use the libraries of these institutions, but they are rarely adequate for their needs.[5]

A third complication is "non-traditional" study—the new course structures and learning methods introduced in recent years. Correspondence study is well established, but there is an increasing provision of external degrees involving self-directed learning and home-based study. Many of these are based on a one-to-one student-tutor relationship and involve individual project work, so that library needs are often unpredictable. Here it is a direct off-campus service to individual students that is needed. Several public libraries have shown a desire to help independent learners who are not attached to formal institutions, but it should not be forgotten that some universities have their own "independent" students, with their own special needs.

We now have an answer to my first main question: part-time adult students *do* have special library needs. On campus they need an immediacy of service because of shortage of time, and guidance to enable them to make the best use of this time. Off-campus they need an on-the-spot service from a library that is specially geared to extension work, this service to include collections of books for classes, a mailing service for individual students at home, and an information service based on the resources of the main library. And we can answer the second main question—the academic standards of off-campus courses *do* suffer where there is inadequate library support for them.

What, then, can university libraries do in this matter? What is the responsibility of the university librarian? One reason why so little has been done is that the question of responsibility has never been clearly defined. There has been a similar lack of definition in the U.K., with similar results. The general needs of off-campus students have usually been regarded as coming solely within the province of the dean of extension, and all too often these have been assumed to include library needs. And so the ACRL guidelines have been largely neglected. Guideline no. 3 is crucial: it recommends that before the teaching of a course off-campus is approved, an assessment should be made of the library needs of the course and the extent to which these needs can be supplied. Academic quality and library resources are therefore inextricably linked. So here we have a joint responsibility—that for academic standards lies squarely with the dean of extension, that for library services lies squarely with the university librarian. Collaboration between the two is therefore essential. The obvious first step is for the university librarian to appoint a member of his staff to be responsible for materials and services for extension and to ensure an effective collaboration with extension staff. A job cannot be done without somebody to do it, and it is quite clear that the university librarian should take the initiative.

Now some universities have all their extension courses on campus. What is needed in that case is a librarian to be given the task of liaison with the extension division, obtaining information about courses and library material needs well in advance, and ensuring that allowances are made for part-time students: special times for library orientation, flexible loan periods for overnight loans and books on reserve, and availability of professional help at unsocial hours.

Of those universities with off-campus programs some have made an attempt to provide a service from their main library collection. But all too often the onus is on the instructor himself to borrow some books or make some photocopies and take them to the class. In contrast, a small number of universities have made a conspicuous success of providing a direct service for extension programs from a library with this sole function, shipping collections of books out to class centers for students to borrow on the spot. Among the best of these libraries are those at the State University System of Florida, the University of Michigan, and the University of Wisconsin. In addition, the University of Rhode Island Extension Division has its own "campus" with a library serving only extension students.

The fourth main question is "how effective are separate extension libraries in providing the sort of services that are needed?" I have already anticipated my answer in referring to the "conspicuous success" of the best of these libraries, and this judgment is based on my own experience in England. In the U.K. most universities with extramural departments have established separate extramural libraries and the best of these have for the last 30 years or so been building up collections of books, periodicals and audio visual materials directly related to the course programs in their areas and directed solely at the needs of extramural students and their instructors. The demands are there: instructors can discuss their courses with the librarians, and students can borrow (at the meeting-place) the books they need when they need them and when their interest is at its highest. As the service improves, demands and expectations increase, and in the U.K. the best extramural libraries are now finding it difficult to keep pace. The inadequate libraries do an injustice to the system—by not being able properly to carry out their function they are thought by some to be unessential and so do not help to gain professional support for the activity as a whole. This U.K. situation is very similar in the U.S.A.—where there is a good extension library the evidence shows that instructors voluntarily make good use of its services. The Florida library, for example, now circulates over 40,000 books a year to off-campus classes and the loans to students is many times over this number. There can be no doubt that separate extension libraries are the best way of providing the services that are needed, and one can be sure that in terms of academic quality and the level of student learning these extension courses benefit a great deal from the availability of this service.

The message for the future, then, is clear. The growth of part-time continuing education presents a new challenge. University librarians should institute special library services to cater for this growth. No new technology is needed—rather an acceptance of responsibility and a realization that here is a new opportunity to show that the role of academic libraries is crucial in the maintenance of academic standards.

REFERENCES

1. Raymond K. Fisher, *Library services to university extension students in the U.S.A.: a critical survey.* (London: British Library Research and Development Department, 1978.)
2. See for example: Robert F. Ray, *Adult part-time students and the C.I.C. universities: a study of credit and degree earning opportunities for adults at eleven midwestern universities* (Iowa City: the University of Iowa, Division of Continuing Education, 1977.) Linda W. Gordon and Judy H. Schub (eds.), *On-campus/off-campus degree programs for part-time students.* (Washington, DC: National University Extension Association, 1976.)
3. Association of College and Research Libraries, Committee of Standards, "Guidelines for library services to extension students." *ALA Bulletin* 61 (Jan. 1967): 50–53.
4. American Library Association, *Libraries and adult education: report of a study made by the American Library Association.* (Chicago: ALA, 1926) p. 146–47.
5. See Ralph W. McComb, "The problems of extension centers." *Drexel Library Quarterly* 2 (July 1966): 220–223.

Edmund G. Hamann

Suffolk University

ACCESS TO INFORMATION: A RECONSIDERATION OF THE SERVICE GOALS OF A SMALL URBAN COLLEGE LIBRARY

The difficulties of research libraries in upholding their commitment to comprehensive collections in the face of declining material resources is mirrored in smaller college libraries which have accepted the conventional values of their larger cousins. One small urban college library of insufficient size, however, has reassessed its priorities and formulated collection development and service policies which stress access to rather than ownership of information. While recognizing that a collection must be maintained which fulfills most of the ordinary needs of its student clientele, the library is striving at the same time to meet extended needs for information by providing systematic access to other library resources in the city. The orientation to client needs rather than material ones should enable a small library with only modest means to improve significantly service to its clientele.

The library press has made it abundantly clear to all of us that research libraries are in trouble: the momentum of growth encouraged by the affluence of the 1960s is being slowed down by the cost-push inflation of the 1970s. For those of us who have so ardently courted the Alexandrian ideal of amassing in a single library all the resources for research in any branch of knowledge the dream is dissolving into a nightmare of running as fast as we can only to fall further and further behind. Then voices are heard urging us to awaken to reality. DeGennaro, for one, in his prize winning article for *American Libraries* warns academic librarians that they must expect to reduce their excessive commitments and expectations to match their declining resources.[1] The landmark "Pittsburgh Conference on Resource Sharing in Libraries" held in the fall of 1976 emphasized that librarians, administrators and clientele will have to make a profound reassessment of the goals of librarianship, to effect a change of attitude about the kinds of things librarians are responsible for doing.[2] A thesis of the conference is that academic librarians must move from a "materials orientation" to a "client orientation" and that, accordingly, the criterion of ownership must yield first place to accessibility. Preliminary evidence from a University of Pittsburgh study encourages this change of emphasis by substantiating the notion that the cost of collections is enormous and cumulative in terms of space and management and is not at all proportionate with its use.[3]

534

Clearly then, the problems of large research libraries are being addressed, answers suggested, and a degree of action taken, which the organization of resource sharing cooperatives such as the Research Libraries Group exemplifies. But what of small academic libraries? Serving a cleintele consisting largely of undergraduates and teaching faculty, are they exempt from the pressures exerted upon their big cousins? Unfortunately experience tells us that such is not the case. Farber talks about the "university-library syndrome," a pattern of attitudes which cause both college librarians and faculties to think of their libraries in terms of university libraries. On the one hand, college faculty are taught to perform research rather than to teach during their graduate training, and on the other, college librarians are constantly influenced by the outlook of university librarians quite simply because the latter are the chief spokesmen for academic libraries.[4] Accordingly, the cardinal responsibility of the college librarian has been to bring a maximum amount of funds to bear upon the development of the collection. Strongly encouraged by a faculty which assumes a proprietary responsibility for the collection, the librarian energetically pursues the chimera of comprehensiveness, which even if manifestly unobtainable, is nonetheless perceived to be "a good thing." The collection will surely grow larger, but it does not follow that service to the library's clientele will develop proportionately. In the worst case the library becomes an archive of miscellaneous books, many of them serving no purpose other than the satisfaction of the notions of individual members of the faculty, and ignores its teaching role in the college community.

Perhaps I may be accused of oversimplifying matters or of describing a pattern of management which is no longer true. However, I am persuaded by the few sensitive spokesment for the college libraries, people like Evan Farber and Guy Lyle, that this problem does in fact exist in the world of the small academic libraries. Their observations encourage me to describe a change in outlook that has been made in one college library with the expectation that my remarks may be instructive to other college library administrators.

The College Library of Suffolk University, a school of medium size in downtown Boston, has a substandard collection by any traditional criteria and insufficient space for housing a significantly larger one. Collection development has been controlled primarily by the faculty, many of whom are prey to impulsive book selection, the blandishment of publishers' advertisements, and the building of self-conceived mini-collections—or who ignore the needs of the collection entirely. To the bibliophiles among them weeding is a violation of the scholarly ethos; for others less ardent it is an onerous necessity. The result is a fragmented collection, dotted with eccentric and obsolete books unrelated to contemporary academic needs, and even worse, revealing embarrassing gaps in subject areas actively taught. Following the pattern of collection building and as a result of it, library service has been characteristically passive, reactive to rather than anticipative of client demands, and pessimistic, accepting the glib assumption that one of the several large libraries nearby can conveniently and charitably provide the book or information that a small one cannot. The end result is that the library fails to discharge its teaching role and is regarded as being little more than a study hall and repository of required reading materials.

How is it possible, then, for this small, insufficiently stocked library without the wherewithal to expand significantly to turn around such a unsatisfactory situation and make itself the first rather than the last resort for informational resources? Right away we have to abandon the notion of self-sufficiency and recognize the absurdity of our attempts to possess a range of resources sufficient to meet all needs, real, potential or imagined. We had to make a realistic reassessment of the library's mission to its clientele and decide what it could do to serve them effectively. Encouraged by the consensus of the Pittsburgh conference, the library committed itself to a philosophy of service which expresses itself in policies enhancing access to rather than ownership of recorded knowledge.

The concept of "access," tempting us to contemplate the heady goal of total availability, is, in its way, no less grandiose than that of ownership of a "comprehensive" collection, particularly when it ignores the mundane fact that for most users the first and only search is for what is held locally. Thus, formulation of new policies began with a hard look at our time-honored collecting habits. The result was the library's first written collection development policy, one based in its essentials upon the ACRL *Standards for College Libraries.*[5,6] The policy statement reminds us that the fundamental aim of collection development is the support of the school's current curriculum. Stressed are non-unique, basic undergaduate materials with emphasis upon defined areas of academic strength. Eccentric purchases, marginal or unrelated gifts, and special status collections are discouraged. The faculty is encouraged to base its selections upon reviews, particularly *Choice* for current books, *Books for College Libraries* for retrospective ones, and the common periodical indexes for new subscriptions. With few exceptions, no attempt is made to cover special requirements engendered by advanced studies or faculty research. A vigorous and continuous weeding process is endorsed in order to maintain the appropriateness of the collection. In this regard, the faculty has had to be persuaded that books are an expensive incumbrance if they are not used. However, a measure of reassurance is provided by the stipulation that items listed in the core bibliography, *Books for College Libraries*, are to be retained indefinitely.

The library is emphasizing the acquisition of reference tools which describe conveniently obtainable information. These include local union lists, printed library catalogs, and selected commercial services. Although the library has very few government documents, a wide range of them is accessible by subject in the *American Statistics Index.* Whenever a pertinent document is identified, the library will buy a microfiche copy and give it to the user assuming that, since it is unlikely to be requested again, it is not worth retaining. The point is that the goods have been found and delivered when needed.

Consistent with its new philosophy, the library scrapped its old habit of buying at random and cataloging popular fiction and non-fiction, material read a few times and quickly forgotten, and began leasing books from standard best seller lists. These are placed uncataloged on highly visible browsing shelves and removed as readership falls off. This modest program effectively takes care of recreational demands at very little cost and reduces distraction from academic collection development.

Our library, however, cannot achieve self-sufficiency in fulfilling the exponential demands of advanced study no matter how well it puts its own house in order. But it stands in the midst of a wealth of bibliographic resources, which easily extend beyond the needs of any individual small school. The problem for us was how could we fairly gain access to these resources and systematically channel our users to them? The solution entails three important assumptions. One is that a small academic library cannot impose its own clientele, undergraduates in particular, upon the charity of large research libraries, which are already straining to provide adequate service at their own level. Second, there exists the potential value of reciprocal services with the many nearby small libraries. Third, an effective program of outreach costs money.

The seriousness of our commitment is demonstrated by the radical decision to carve funds from an already meager materials budget and allocate them to operations which make these resources known and available. This speculative investment was made with the confident expectation that it would yield better results in bringing information to our clientele than a conservative one in the augmentation of our local holdings.

Six levels of access have been established with other libraries, most of which are within walking distance or reachable by metropolitan transportation. These levels may be categorized as network, formal cooperation, informal cooperation, individual membership, fee-based, and legal.

Membership in the New England Library Information Network (NELINET) is our largest single investment. The conventional justification of improved efficiency in technical processing, however, is secondary to the opening of a wide window to the world of bibliographical information and the potential for exploiting it. The interlibrary loan module in development is expected to be a breakthrough for small libraries, stimulating loans among themselves to a degree which I suspect will become tantamount to providing a new service to undergraduate users.

There is a clear correlation between the services of NELINET and a new local cooperative of eleven small libraries called the Fenway Library Consortium. The consortium is founded upon the agreement that students affiliated with one library may use the facilities and borrow materials from any of the others subject to ordinary local regulations. However, the lack of remote access to the bibliographical holdings of individual libraries, an aggregate of over one-half million items, severely limits their use. The production of a union list of serials is a first and obvious remedy for closing the gap between availability and access. Knowledge of individual monographic holdings will come initially via OCLC terminals, available now to one-half and eventually to all of the members. The ultimate objective is the production of a COM catalog of the consortium's combined holdings, dovetailing OCLC-produced records with older manual ones converted to a simplified MARC format. With the assistance of a computer-based network it becomes no longer an impossible dream to weld a group of independent libraries into an effective system.

Informal cooperation has been successfully pursued with several nearby commercial libraries which contain material relevant to several advanced study programs in the school. By the exchange of letters and personal visits it was agreed that students may make on site use of their materials and copying equipment upon identification of institutional affiliation. While it is understood that their own users may use our library, substantive reciprocity comes in a form which businessmen define as goodwill. Through this approach our modest collection of business publications, for example, is considerably reinforced by special collections of economic material held by leading banks in the city.

Either by paid membership or use fee the library offers systemtic access to other, non-commercial, special libraries. In the former instance, it is a member of a private library specializing in Latin American materials, providing extended support of the school's special Spanish/Sociology curriculum. In the latter, it pays an annual use fee to a large university library for the distinct purpose of supporting a measure of faculty research.

Finally, there is the traditional legal privilege of using the reputable Boston Public Library system, including its unique downtown business branch. While its eminence as a resource is not to be denied, it is no longer used as a crutch for our library. At the same time, however, as dependency upon it decreases, a greater effort is being made to make it a more effective source for our users through orientation programs conducted in cooperation with the public library's research specialists.

The policies and programs I have summarized reflect my conviction that a small, modestly endowed college library, confronted by rising expectations coupled with rising costs, need not resign itself to a chase after the status quo. What such a library should do is make a thoroughgoing reassessment of its service goals, one which takes into account both the actual mission of the college and the environment in which it operates, and develop objectives and policies of implementation which stress the utility of books and information. I believe that the fresh approach expressed at the 1976 Pittsburgh conference can move the small academic library away from the old rituals of acquisition and retention and toward a goal of giving better service to its student clientele.

REFERENCES

1. Richard De Gennaro, "Copyright, Resource Sharing, and Hard Times: a View from the Field," *American Libraries* 8 (September, 1977): 430–435.
2. Kent, Allen, and Thomas J. Galvin. *Library Resource Sharing; Proceedings of the 1976 Conference on Resources Sharing in Libraries, Pittsburgh, Pa.* (New York: Marcel Dekker, 1977). See also Karl Nyren, "Resource Sharing in Libraries; conference report," *Library Journal* 101 (November 15, 1976): 2336–2339.
3. Thomas J. Galvin and Allen Kent, "Use of a University Library Collection; a Progress Report on a Pittsburgh Study," *Library Journal* 102 (November 15, 1977): 2318–2320.
4. Evan Ira Farber, "College Librarians and the University-Library Syndrome," in *The Academic Library; Essays in Honor of Guy R. Lyle*, edited by Evan Ira Farber and Ruth Walling (Metuchen, NJ: The Scarecrow Press, 1974) p. 12–23.
5. Association of College and Research Libraries, *Standards for College Libraries* (Chicago: 1975).
6. Elizabeth Futas, ed., *Library Acquisition Policies and Procedures* (Phoenix: Oryx Press, 1977) p. 224–229.

Gail A. Herndon and Noelle Van Pulis

Ohio State University

THE ON-LINE LIBRARY: PROBLEMS AND PROSPECTS FOR USER EDUCATION

The evolution of user education for an on-line library catalog is discussed. Methods of "humanizing" and simplifying both the library and computer aspects of the system are highlighted. The authors point out key principles to be followed in developing instructional materials and programs. Hardware and software problems, as well as decisions relating to content and format of instructions, are considered.

BACKGROUND

The on-line library is no longer a thing of the future; it is here and now, and becoming more prevalent every day as more libraries plan for automating their card catalogs. The concept has been a reality at The Ohio State University since 1970, when its on-line circulation system became operational. The new system provided the staff in all our 25 libraries with direct author, title, or call number access to the libraries' shelflist and circulation records and allowed the establishment of a Telephone Center that patrons could call to locate, charge out, or renew items from the libraries when they could not come to the libraries in person. From the very start, the system proved its worth as a public service by improving the communication between all the libraries and by offering new and additional services that the libraries could not affer before.

During the next few years, new features were added and the system came to be known as the Library Control System (LCS). In 1974, the Libraries decided to let patrons try their own hands at using the on-line catalog and a public self-serve terminal was made available at the Catalog Information Desk in the Main Library. During the weekday hours that the desk was staffed, patrons could be given personal assistance in learning to use the system. This was important because use required knowledge of the search commands and keys, plus awareness of a stop-list of non-searchable terms. And, of course, the system had many idiosyncracies that in some cases only sophisticated staff users knew about.

Even simple as the system was in those days, it was still a bit of a challenge to produce simple printed instructions. Items used for staff training could not be used because of the circulation transactions and other features not appropriate for patrons. Also, the style and completeness of staff materials would not have encouraged novice users. For patrons, the first materials were large, colorful posters hung on the wall by the terminal. Since that first attempt, instruction in the use of on-line system has been playing a game of keep-up that only recently got near the prize.

After a year of practice, the Catalog Information Desk staff replaced the posters with a more permanent instructional tool that we called simply the "orange card." This 5 X 8 card with its simple listing of basic search codes and algorithms was an obvious reaction against the excesses of the large signs on the wall. It was furthermore clearly designed to supplement personal instruction at the terminal by serving as a quick reminder of the codes and basic steps for both the instructor and the students.

The card and the on-site assistance were the extent of the instruction for LCS until the implementation of a major new development in the system in June of 1977. At that time, the serial holdings were added to LCS and the public service station that had previously given serials information was closed. For the first time, patrons were left without a traditional alternative for finding material in the library and were forced to use the computer.

TASK FORCE FOR ON-LINE USER EDUCATION

In response to these new developments and the imminence of further changes, the Director of Libraries appointed three task forces, including one on Education for Patron and Staff use of On-line Systems. The creation of this Task Force was the first major effort at LCS instruction since the development of the orange card. Meanwhile, staffing at the Catalog Information Desk had diminished to a maximum of five hours per day during the quarter while the number of public use terminals in the Main Library had grown to eight; terminals had been installed in five other libraries on campus and were planned for all 20 others; the system's search commands and other functions had far outgrown the limits of a card; and finally, a series of major new developments were beginning to take place and would continue over the next several years. In other words, the Task Force on User Education had to plan a program that relied on minimal personal assistance, that would be used system-wide in a variety of physical environments and staffing patterns, and that could easily be adapted or revised as LCS changed.

THREE PRINCIPLES FOR INSTRUCTION

The Task Force quickly decided to concentrate initially on printed materials to explain the system. The members also agreed that these should be of two kinds: a short form and a longer manual. The experience of developing these tools and the input from both patrons and staff ultimately gave us three very important principles that came to be the guiding lights for our efforts.

First, if at all possible, begin at the beginning: start planning for public use of any computer system right along with the initial program itself. The impetus for increased automation comes from Technical Services, but the implications of it are the most far-reaching and long-lasting for Public Services. LCS was not designed for public use and this fact contributed to some of the difficulties in instruction. (This could also be a problem for libraries which make their OCLC terminals available to patrons.) Such matters as file order, search keys, display format, error messages and countless other points all have to be scrutinized carefully from the user's point of view. Simply making a shelflist, order file, or serial record available to the patron through the use of a computer terminal will not automatically solve his or her problems with the library. It may, in fact, create additional, and perhaps unnecessary, barriers.

To begin with, a computer display puts everything right out in the open. Patrons often confront and question for the first time items like LC numbers, title numbers, or designations such as MONO or SER. Very careful editing of the records is called for before librarians are bogged down in answering questions about things patrons have no need to bother themselves with. A more positive note is that the immediacy of a computer display may be useful for directing attention to the things we have never in the past been able to get patrons to look at.

Another barrier is raised by all the problems in simply "making the computer go." We found, for example, that trying to explain how to determine if there was more information on the next screen and how to "turn pages" to get there was taking up an inordinate amount of time and paper. In this case we finally realized that our problems were compounded by our own failure to take advantage of the computer's capabilities. We finally simplified the instructions by having displayed on the screen internal prompts that provided the necessary instructions, permitting us to leave this process out of the printed sheets. One of the great advantages of a computerized file is that it, unlike a book or catalog, can interact with the user. This interaction, however, is also governed by the rule about the increased impact of information viewed on a screen. A poorly worded message—such as "Illegal input field" or "Illegal input command"—besides being computer jargon and bad English can do a great deal of damage, in this case increasing the patron's fear of the system.

The message that the programmers chose to display for turning pages had even more implications for our user-education program. The programming staff settled on using the term "enter" (for example, "ENTER PG2") to describe the two-step operation of typing the required information and then sending the message. The Task Force adopted the same usage in its own materials to play up the similarities between our system and other public use computer systems, such as computer-assisted instruction terminals and 24-hour banking machines. This meant revising our materials accordingly and making the staff aware that they should try to use the term in their instruction to the public.

This kind of planning and systematizing could have been done from the very beginning. Decisions about search keys or alogorithms often cannot be changed. Even if they can be, re-educating the public may simply be bad publicity for the library and re-educating the staff may be asking people to perform the almost impossible task of breaking old habits and learning new ones

Our second major lesson was that the introduction of a computerized or automated system, no matter how well planned, forced us into some difficult decisions about how much we had to tell the patrons or how much we could assume they knew in order to operate the system. A whole set of problems was raised by the hardware itself. We may assume that people above the ages of five or six know how to pull out drawers and flip through cards. Can we assume so easily that all these people know enough about a typewriter keyboard to be able to operate a computer terminal? No one needs to turn on the card catalog, but we must be sure that patrons realize that the terminal must be turned on before they can use it. Even the most well-intentioned efforts can be thwarted by these human factors.

One intriguing example of the human factor is the apparent need most patrons feel to clear the screen before beginning their searches, despite our telling them that the step is not necessary. This is, again, a hardware problem. Clearing the screens is a different process on the two terminals we use now, and for one of them requires the use of four different keys in a timed pattern reminiscent of Lawrence Welk leading his orchestra. We hope this problem will be solved by posting operating instructions on each of the terminals and relying on the patrons to familiarize themselves with each one as they use it.

In addition to the newly introduced hardware problems, an automated catalog raises more clearly than ever before the difficulties patrons always have had in using the card catalog. For example, the fact that people use the card catalog and then proceed to the nearest circulation desk or the stacks seems to indicate that there is a connection between the information in the catalog and the volumes on the shelves. Exactly what is this connection? What is the throught process which makes this happen? One informal study done at OSU shed some light on user behavior. A few patrons were asked to speak into a tape recorder their thoughts as they used the card catalog. The transcripts showed an amazing jumble of luck, inspiration, and some knowledge, all of which was triggered by flipping through the cards that had authors, subjects, and titles with the key word in them. The computer version does not allow for such browsing and in fact demands fairly detailed knowledge before a patron can approach the terminal. As with all machines, the operator has to tell it specifically what to do. This raises again the old bugaboos of the differences between a main entry and an added entry, between a title word and a subject, between a call number with a date in it and one without, and between the volume and year on a serial record.

In some cases we may decide that the lack of one visible file is such a serious flaw that we will retain the more traditional book or card catalogs. Serial records may be a good example of this. Those who work with the public are well aware of the difficulties most patrons have in learning to look up the title of the journal instead of the title of the article. It may turn out that many more patrons than we suspect have this problem but correct it themselves when they look at whatever serial file is available in the library and see that the information there does not match the title of the article but does look like the second piece of information they have, the title of the journal.

Some of these questions the Task Force faced and answered. We omitted instructions concerning some features of the system. For example, we do not tell patrons about searches by copy number. This, in part, duplicates another search by library location, which is a concept more patrons understand; also, we could not be sure that patrons know what is meant by copy number. If you need to develop some empathy with the patron's dilemma, you might try someday to define "copy." Other questions concerning user familiarity with libraries we have ignored, as librarians have done for years, but we will not be able to do so for much longer. In all likelihood, cataloging practices will have to be adapted to the limits of both the computer and the patron, and we will most definitely need more public service personnel to interpret the system and to use it for the patrons who cannot or, understandably, do not want to learn it for themselves.

The third major lesson we learned was that any instructional materials or personal assistance for the computer would have to sell the system as well as explain it. The general assumption that this generation of students is the generation of the machine is like all generalizations, an exaggeration. Many shy away from the new technology and it is up to us to convince them to try it. In a rather interesting turnabout, we have found that patrons are not so afraid of what the machine will do to them as they are of what they will do to the machine. They seem to have visions of obliterating the computer's entire memory bank with one misplaced key. Encouragement to these patrons can be given both direction and indirectly. Directly, by making the instructions inviting and attractive. Indirect encouragement can be given by avoiding jargon. We have for years mystified patrons with terms such as "main entry," "classification," and "tracing," and how many know what a "corporate author" is? The on-line catalog adds yet another class of terms: "matches," "search keys," "enter," and "illegal input command." These add yet another level of obfuscation and should be avoided as much as possible.

The application of these three principles is apparent in the Task Force efforts. We developed a short form of instructions and the longer manual in formats that can be easily updated or supplemented. The different versions allowed us to experiment with the content and make sure that it was both correct and cogent. With each version, we actively solicited comments and suggestions from the staff and even polled them on certain questions.

Capitalizing on the patron's curiosity was our main goal with the short form of instructions. The revised and expanded versions of the orange card continued to carry out many of the functions of that first attempt. The short instructions were necessary for at least three reasons: (1) patrons don't want to, and should not need to, read a lot of information in order to use the system; (2) we needed to encourage "hands-on" experience with the terminals because actual use is the key to converting many patrons into supporters of the system; (3) patrons need "carry-out" instructions that they can take away and study or that the experienced user can use as a quick reminder. We also maintained the blocking or columnar character of the short instructions. This format seems to be the most effective for showing the construction of a search code that is made up of "building blocks" of information. Also, avoiding prose eliminated the confusion concerning punctuation needed for grammatical purposes and that required for using the system.

Other revisions were essentially a matter of placement of information. For example, a major flaw with the orange card was placing the instructions for sending the message on the back of the card. Many people did not realize that they had to look at the other side. Similarly, we moved the stop-list and location codes from the terminals to the instruction sheet. This freed space for instructions about use of the hardware.

In addition to the new version of the orange card, the Task Force realized that longer and more detailed instructions were necessary to explain the increasing complexity of the system and to help more sophisticated users take advantage of special features of the system. We also realized that we needed materials that could in some way stand in for personal assistance at those times when our reduced staff could not be available to give instructions. We chose a comb-bound book format because we could use one page for each kind of search and still revise it easily. The preparation of this "user's manual" has taken the largest part of the Task Force's time. Every line was checked for accuracy, readability and comprehensiveness. Choices of words and phrases were made carefully. We scrutinized the need for capitalization, underlining, color and indention, and tried numerous formats. After months of meeting and working, we produced two mock-ups, one of which we have placed near a terminal test run.

Having finally prepared the basic printed materials that introduce the patron to our system, we now are planning to move into other means of instruction, such as a computer-based education program, possible audio-visual programs, including slide-tape and/or cassettes right by the terminals, or, our great goal, tutorial program available on the same terminals used for LCS.

Despite the amount of time and energy already spent on these materials, we have not begun to develop a real substitute for personal assistance. Most libraries still have to help users with the card catalog and a computerized catalog will raise at least as many difficulties for the patron. Aside from being the best way to answer these questions, personal assistance is also the unquestionably best way to sell the system to the user. Finally, one of the greatest advantages of an on-line catalog is not that the patrons can use it themselves but that the library staff can use it for them and provide answers in a short time while the patron waits right there.

EVALUATION

While continuing to plan more methods of instructing patrons in the use of LCS, we will also be turning more attention to fuller evaluation of the instructing we already have done. From this re-telling of the means by which we developed our materials, you can see that we were actually evaluating at each step of the way. The feedback from the staff guided the revisions of the short instructions and the pooled wisdom of the Task Force members was essential to the development of the user's manual. Most committees are recognized as a means of slowing if not completely stopping any productive thought or work. In contrast, this Task Force redeemed itself in preparing these instructions by bringing together the staff who were most interested in and capable of assuming the patron's point of view. We recommend this method for anyone contemplating the development of instructions for a public on-line system.

We have had some indirect evaluation from the patrons themselves. We can judge how successful our short forms are by whether they are taken or not. They were slow to disappear until a staff member pointed out that patrons didn't seem to realize that the sheets had anything to do with the terminals. The additon of a drawing of a terminal on the instructions solved that problem. We also have observed peer instruction and faculty members or teaching assistants instructing their classes. We can document that terminal usage is up. The terminals themselves provide an evaluation tool of sorts as occasional walks past the public terminals give insight into patron knowledge of the system. A series of "Time out—reenter transaction" messages indicates that another patron has missed the instructions for sending messages. A screen with a series of nine zeros on it is the characteristic mark of the patron trying to log-in to LCS using the instructions for a nearby OCLC terminal available for public use. We've even found complete messages explaining in detail the patron's difficulties in using the system. For further evaluation, we will be doing surveys by the terminals and continuing to work with an internal university-wide poll.

Of necessity, most of what we have talked about so far is limited to our experience at OSU. It was offered with the intention of making the transition to public use terminals easier for any of you who are considering this move. We also thought it important to emphasize the need for librarians to consider the public service implications of the use of self-serve terminals for on-line catalogs. If cataloging practices cannot be changed or we cannot get additional staffing in public service areas to deal with the new demands of automation, we can at least begin to include in our plans for automated catalogs a national publicity campaign that will prepare patrons to encounter machines instead of or along with the usual card catalog. The unpleasant surprise afforded a patron who comes into a library expecting a card catalog but is greeted by perplexing and complicated machinery is not going to win us friends. As the ones who are supposed to represent the patron, we had best start preparing him for the new look in libraries.

Leila M. Hover

Suffern, New York

THE INDEPENDENT LEARNER AND THE ACADEMIC LIBRARY: ACCESS AND IMPACT

The increasing number of independent learners is causing two types of fall-out: the students' need for access to academic materials (which are not supplied for those enrolled in the various open university programs) and the reluctance of both private and public academic libraries to permit use by these "unaffiliated" students. Some plans, both in effect and suggested, to overcome this reluctance are examined; the long-range implications of this growing student body as they affect the academic library and librarian are discussed; and recommendations are made for improved service to this population.

The tradition of independent study is a long and honorable one in the history of British education. In the United States, however, it is only in the last decade that this concept has been deemed a serious alternative for the obtaining of an academic degree.

As this non-traditional road has become more widely known, and regarded with greater esteem, it has developed several second generation options toward the achievement of that goal. Among them are the Open University, the University Without Walls, and the External Degree Program. Regardless of name, they are more similar than not: the greatest similarity lies in the fact that this method tends to utilize no classrooms, no lectures, and frequently no formal textbooks, thus requiring students to make extensive use of the library in order to satisfy their needs for material and information.

The surge toward independent study has now reached the point where the number and needs of these students are beginning to be felt by the academic library and its librarians. Its corollary is the lack of access to this type of library from which many of these students suffer. But as their numbers continue to increase, so will their demands for this kind of access, and it behooves the academic library to respond in a positive fashion.

Indeed, Dr. James Groark asserts that "If such [independent learning] programs are to be viable alternatives and if the library is to actualize its potential, it is necessary that administrators incorporate into their planning and operation the characteristics of library use of the students they are educating."[1]

One problem, however, lies in the identification of these characteristics—although some studies have been made, they are few in number and small in size. Nonetheless, there is a difference, Marianne Nolan observes, in the library requirements of non-

545

traditional students as compared to those of campus based students. As an example, only infrequently are there prepared reading lists that might be helpful in readying a library to meet the curriculum needs of these students because "they often involve topics still on the fringes of the established body of published research."[2]

An additional stumbling block is that of time. "Learning contracts" generally run for a one- or two-month period. This requires the accumulation and reading of materials within a very short interval and, in addition, infers good library skills, either on the student's part or, since these students cannot be vastly different from all others in their knowledge of the library, the librarian's.

This suggests another aspect of the time problem arising from two areas: the previously mentioned brevity of the learning contract, and the usually even briefer circulating time of library material.

In a 1973 study of Empire State College (ESC) enrollees, the students' comments revealed the problems of not being able to keep a book the length of a contract, and difficulties in obtaining from the library "the right book at the right time,"[3] which resulted in their having to purchase books as the easiest way to solve these problems.[4]

This issue seems to crop up in all varieties of independent study programs. In their study of the Dallas Public Library Independent Student Program, Jean Brooks and David Reich make note several times of the dependence of this type of student on the library as the source of materials, and the frustration of study when a particular book was unavailable,[5] or, having once obtained the desired book, the inability to renew it because some other user had a reserve on it.[6]

In 1966, a survey of academic libraries which loaned material to non-members of the institution revealed that while most of them did not shorten the loan period to qualified outsiders (although generally that period is too short for the independent learner), a number of the libraries stated that they did not grant renewals to outside borrowers.[7]

Another facet of the time problem is that of library hours. In her study, *Library Service for Commuting Students*, Matilda Gocek outlines the multiple life-roles, which take their toll in time and energy, of the commuting student,[8] and, by extrapolation, delineates at the same time the independent learner. Both these groups suffer a shortage of time and have great need of *convenient* library use. This convenience may mean the content of the collection, or it may well mean the college library being open at a time when the student can make use of it—be that Sunday afternoon or 11 P.M. of a week-night.[9] Indeed, it has been asserted that "Early library closings are mentioned as environmental barriers to adults' entering of colleges and universities."[10] Therefore, the "failure of the colleges to conveniently provide library services" for the commuting student, and by extension, the independent student, "places the responsibility on other libraries . . . that are not really equipped"[11] for this type or level of service.

What, then, is this type or level of service? What are the library use traits and needs of the independent learner and how do these affect the academic library?

These students are fairly heavy library users who "are not served by any single library."[12] Moreover, this finding is not unique to the United States. It has been reported by W. A. J. Marsterson and T. D. Wilson, in their study of the British Open University student, that home-based students "have no library whose primary concern is to serve their needs."[13]

It is a commonplace, however, that students go where the books are, and it is difficult to say whether the phenomenon of the "library-hopper" is the result or the cause of having no primary library, particularly academic, concerned about their needs. This type of student has been characterized by David Kaser as a "mobile user" and "free-standing student" who requests and utilizes library service as needed, when needed, and in whatever locale is most opportune.[14]

This was amply demonstrated by the Empire State College (ESC) study of students in two widely separated geographic areas within New York State. In the first area, 72 students utilized 51 libraries, with one of the group accounting for 35 of them; in the second area, 45 students visited 56 libraries, with one student utilizing 23 of them. Cutting across all lines, these libraries included public, academic and special—up to and including the Library of Congress.[15] Kaser's observation that "an unaffiliated user is, first of all, a user, and in many cases it may also be assumed (because he made a special effort to get here) that he is a heavy user,"[16] certainly rings true.

Unfortunately, many institutions of higher education, public as well as private, are guilty of ignoring this burgeoning group. In 1966, E. J. Josey addressed himself to the overall problem of community use of the academic library, at which time he noted that if an individual is unassociated with the institution, he cannot gain access to the academic collection. This refusal is predicated upon the belief that the academic library's primary function is that of servicing the institution's students and faculty. But, he continues, harking back to the 1963 ALA conference-within-a-conference on the meeting of student needs, "Should not all libraries be moving to a pattern of shared responsibility for library service to all students. . . ?"[17] And adopting a less altruistic tone, he remarks pointedly: "Could not residents of the community argue that they had a right of free access to college and university libraries receiving generous support from state and federal funds to which their taxes had contributed?"[18] Indeed, he suggests that in the future federal monies may be withheld from those institutions which do not open their library doors to the community.[19]

Nevertheless, ten years later independent learners are still in much the same bind. In fact, they are in many cases not even considered students since, as Empire State College reports: "Borrowing privileges were not obtainable because the library was at an independent college or university that did not recognize ESC student needs as legitimate."[20] Indeed, one student noted that they are ". . . often not even allowed in-library reading privileges."[21] It is fortunate that this particular group of independent learners has open access to any of 35 SUNY libraries and 20 community college libraries (as does any SUNY student since February 1974). In fact, a study done between February and October 1974 indicates that ESC students were by far the heaviest users of this plan ("216 borrowers took out 651 items from 23 participating SUNY libraries").[22]

However, it is obvious that students are not always so ideally located geographically as to be able to take advantage of the access available to them in New York State, and in many other states there is not this availability in any case. At these times it has been incumbent upon ESC administrators, as well as those of other states with similar programs, to come to some sort of *sub-rosa* arrangement with private libraries to allow their students the use of those facilities. Even in this event, the privileges don't always include borrowing materials. Despite these arrangements, it is apparent that, with increasing numbers of non-traditional students, and library costs rising apace, such gentlemen's agreements will not suffice in the future.[23]

It should come as no surprise, therefore, that the Advisory Committee on Planning for the Academic Libraries of New York State has indicated that those associated with academic libraries must be aware that the emergence of independent study and external degree programs, and, in particular, "the freestanding student with at most a tenuous campus relationship,"[24] is of great consequence to libraries.[25]

If it is fear of spiraling costs that inhibit libraries, perhaps a longer and more serious look at Kaser's proposal of a library "credit card," which will permit the expense of serving the peripatetic scholar to be allocated to the user's "fund base,"[26] is warranted.

An additional fear that may be lurking—loss or damage of materials by the unaffiliated user—might well be alleviated by the system used in the SUNY plan. This requires the user's home library to be held responsible by the loaning library for any uncollectable fines or replacement costs. As of early 1975, it had not been necessary to invoke this clause.[27]

Thus far, the discussion has centered on the independent learner enrolled in a nontraditional, sometimes physically non-existent, college. However, independent study, once the hallmark of the graduate level in traditional schools, has filtered down to the undergraduate. Eldred Smith believes this to be the result of the growing impetus toward interdisciplinary study, which has in turn initiated a reassessment of standard educational methods.[28] As a result, one finds the concept of independent learning invading some of the staunchest "old school tie" institutions. For this reason they, too, are confronted with a problem which, although akin, has a slightly different orientation.

The problem is inherent in the increasing numbers of disciples of the interdisciplinary concept. As the lines between the disciplines grow fuzzier, it is obvious that more students will find independent study engaging their interest; when this occurs they will no longer be content with a few standard works. Rather they will begin to stretch both the library and the librarian to the capacity of their abilities in the search for more unique materials.[29] Indeed, there are those who believe that the distinction between the 'independent' and 'dependent' learner will disappear, and regardless of how or where independent study occurs, its effects will be felt by libraries of all types.[30]

The librarian will become more deeply involved in the student's work, and will undoubtedly find it a more challenging and professionally stimulating method as "Textbooks, reserved book lists, 'lectures to bunched herds of assembled hundreds' . . . vanish," and are "replaced by seminars, independent study, tutorials and special bibliographies."[31]

Education intrinsically means growth and change, usually as applied to the student. But the independent learner's evolution will act upon the library, which must be prepared for change.

First to be considered must be open access to the academic library, public or private, for the independent student. Perhaps in the case of the private institution, a fee might be considered, but not one so high as to effectively bar admission to all but the most affluent students.

For those colleges with restricted hours, additions to existing hours, or perhaps a change in the hours, will have to be made. Perhaps it could even be done on an appointment basis, so as to obviate the cost of full staffing.

Time limitations on the lending of materials must be made more flexible, and customized to fit the independent student's contract requirements.

One possibility worth some thought is the appointment of librarians as special consultants to a given number of independent students, to whom the students could turn for advice with their library problems. Some of these problems can be solved by the compilation of special bibliographies or study guides, or even by the development of special bibliographic instruction particularly suited to these students' needs.

Certainly other ideas will evolve in time as more attention is directed to this area.

Independent learning is not a fad, and independent learners will not just disappear if we ignore them. Rather, they should be considered as a challenge which "will demand total revitalization . . . of all types of libraries" as well as one which "provides an ideal opportunity for librarians to reach their full potential in terms of supporting the individual in his personal development."[32]

REFERENCES

1. James J. Groark, "Utilization of Library Resources by Students in Non-Residential Degree Programs," *Bookmark* (September–October 1974): 14.

2. Marianne Nolan, "Library Access for Students in Non-Traditional Degree Programs," *Drexel Library Quarterly* 11 (April 1975): 17.
3. A. Paul Bradley and Ernest G. Palola, "Empire State College Student Library Use," *Research and Review* 9 (April 1975), p. 6.
4. *Ibid.*
5. Jean S. Brooks and David L. Reich, *The Public Library in Non-Traditional Education* (Homewood, Ill.: ETC Publication, 1974), p. 59.
6. *Ibid.*, p. 87.
7. John E. Scott, 'Fees and Modified Privileges for Outside Borrowers?", In "Community Use of Academic Libraries: A Symposium," Moderator E. J. Josey, *College and Research Libraries* 28 (May 1967): 189.
8. Matilda Gocek, *Library Service for Commuting Students* (Poughkeepsie, NY: Southeastern New York Library Resources Council, 1970), p. 13.
9. *Ibid.*, p. 18.
10. Brooks and Reich, *op. cit.*, p. 164.
11. Gocek, *op. cit.*, p. 17.
12. *Ibid.*, p. 14.
13. W. A. J. Marsterson and T. D. Wilson, "Home-based Students and Libraries," *Libri* 25:214.
14. David Kaser, "Library Access and the Mobility of Users," *College and Research Libraries* 35 (July 1974): 281.
15. Bradley and Palola, *op. cit.*, p. 1–2.
16. Kaser, *op. cit.*, p. 284.
17. E. J. Josey, 'Implications for College Libraries,' "Community Use of Academic Libraries: A Symposium," Moderator E. J. Josey, *College and Research Libraries* 35 (July 1974): 281.
18. *Ibid.*, p. 201.
19. *Ibid.*, p. 202.
20. Bradley and Palola, *op. cit.*, p. 5.
21. *Ibid.*, p. 8.
22. Nolan, *op. cit.*, p. 22.
23. *Ibid.*
24. E. J. Josey, editor, *New Dimensions for Academic Librarianship* (Metuchen, NJ: Scarecrow, 1975), p. 323.
25. *Ibid.*
26. Kaser, *op. cit.*, p. 281–282.
27. Nolan, *op. cit.*, p. 22.
28. Eldred Smith, "Changes in Higher Education and the University Library," In *New Dimensions for Academic Librarianship* ed. by E. J. Josey (Metuchen, NJ: Scarecrow, 1975), p. 38.
29. *Ibid.*
30. Ivan L. Kaldor and Miles M. Jackson, Jr., "Education for Academic Librarianship," *New Dimensions for Academic Librarianship* ed. by E. J. Josey (Metuchen, NJ: Scarecrow, 1975), p. 194.
31. Brooks and Reich, *op. cit.*, p. 160.
32. Marvin W. Mounce, "The Open University and External Degree Programs," *Pennsylvania Library Association Bulletin* 28 (Jan. 1973): 35.

William J. Hubbard

Virginia Polytechnic Institute and State University

DEVELOPMENT AND ADMINISTRATION OF A
LARGE OFF-CAMPUS SHELVING FACILITY

In administering an off site shelving facility, the means for identification of materials location, maximum storage capacity, and an efficient delivery service are requisite. The unique two-level file structure of the mini-computer based VPI&SU circulation and finding system provides on-line location information for the 200,000 volumes recently moved off campus. This and two hour turnaround on delivery are features that have made this program palatable to a growing clientele. A major face lift and the addition of much needed reader space in the locations vacated by this move justify the decision to go off site.

Off-site shelving presents a set of unique problems in custodianship, access, and control of library materials. As a short range answer to growing collections and static building programs, more libraries are dealing with this in a variety of ways.

Due to the rapid expansion of Virginia Polytechnic Institute and State University in the last five years and the library's need to support the programs of a comprehensive university, space for the collection and readers was at a premium. Although a library addition had been planned since the early seventies, funding had not been available. The University was able to lease 20,000 square feet in an abandoned department store some five miles from campus, half of which was turned over to the library for temporary relief.

The first reaction was to move Technical Services off site, thereby freeing office areas which could be converted to reader stations. Several difficulties, including catalogers' access to the card catalog, were being investigated when it was learned that the sanitary facilities in the building were insufficient for the staff which was anticipated. In fact, the building could not be opened to the public due to this limitation. The only remaining alternative was to shelve library materials in this building, making them accessible through a delivery service. This decision was formalized and planning for the shelving, move, and servicing of the off site collection began in earnest.

Certain objectives for setting up and maintaining the off site collection were established. Since minimum growth was anticipated, shelves would be packed in order to allow maximum storage capacity. Access to materials and quick turnaround were considered essential, so student assistants were budgeted for coverage during hours the main library was open. It was also considered imperative that the move be conducted with no disruption of service. Materials had to be accessible before, during, and immediately after they were moved off site. All materials to be moved had to be identifiable and able to circulate through the library's recently developed automated circulation and finding system. Finally, in an effort to minimize paging and user inconvenience, anticipated use would be the main criterion for selection.

SELECTING OFF SITE MATERIALS

Selection of materials to be moved was the responsibility of the collection development librarians in the Reference Department. Some 74,000 volumes of Dewey classed materials were the first candidates for this move. Although no records were kept of previous circulations, it was felt that these would be lower use items as the library had been classifying in LC since the late 1960s, and most of the Dewey material had earlier imprints. The Dewey collection, if moved intact, would not require entry into the circulation and finding system for identification. The Dewey number, itself, would indicate that a volume was shelved off site. Another benefit of moving Deweys was that they could be reclassified according to use. As a book was called in from the off site area it became a prime candidate for reclassification. Although this would gradually reduce the number of volumes off site, it would through reclassification, bring together the more heavily used items in the main library where they would be more accessible.

Another group of materials that could be moved was a large collection of pre-1950 serials that had been located in packed shelving on the lower level of the library. These were originally placed in the basement as it was believed that they would be little used. Besides fragmenting the collection (post-1950 imprints of the same titles were shelved in the main stacks) accessibility was further hindered by the extremely narrow stack aisles in this collection.

It was agreed that long runs of serial titles were the preferred choices for off site shelving as a large number of volumes could be moved while only one circulation entry would be required to indicate location. The titles and ranges of volumes to be moved would be selected by subject specialists, and each subject division would have approximately the same amount of off site shelving allocated. To add incentive to move lesser used materials, the subject divisions agreed to add no new shelving in public areas. Thus space would be freed for new acquisitions and reader space would not be affected.

PHYSICAL FACILITY

When the decision was made to move library materials off site, the University administration budgeted funds to purchase new shelving. This gave the library considerable flexibility in preparing the site prior to the move. Certain restraints dictated by fire codes, existing walls, and fixed store shelving somewhat limited the amount of floor space available.

New shelving was erected in ine ranges with a total capacity of 429 double faced sections (Fig. 1). At seven shelves per face, a little over 18,000 linear feet of shelving was available. Although the built in store shelving was not ideally suited for library materials, it was determined politic to leave it erected and to utilize it as fully as possible. They added approximately 1,500 linear feet. Three ranges, including the store shelving, were allocated for the 74,000 volumes of Dewey materials, and the remainder was apportioned to the three subject divisions to fill within the agreed upon selection criteria.

When the selections were made, the linear feet required by each LC class and sub-class

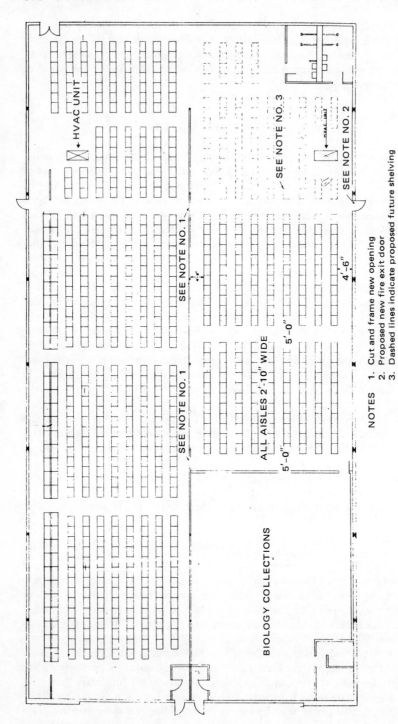

Figure 1. Floor Plan of Off-Site Facility.

were measured and the new shelving was marked accordingly. By predetermining where each sub-class would fall, flexibility was built into the forthcoming move.[1] It was not necessary to work from A to Z, but instead one floor or subject division could be moved without interruption, which proved to be beneficial in scheduling and supervision.

It was understood that the stacks would be filled, however every fourteenth shelf was left vacant in the Dewey section to accommodate books that were in circulation at the time of the move. This also built in a little freedom for necessary shifting when the Deweys were shelf read.

COLLECTION CONTROL

All materials that were to be moved out of the main library had to be marked so they would be retrievable. Catalog overlays were discussed as one means of identification, but the extent of the move and the fact that long runs of serials were selected prohibited this. Instead, the library's newly developed on-line circulation and finding system lent itself ideally to this use. Since bibliographic records were searchable at two levels, a title could be entered and volume holdings could be listed for different locations. When a particular volume was requested, it could be bar coded and entered in the system at the item, or specific piece, level while still associated with its original bibliographic, or title, level entry. Not only did this serve as a means of identifying materials that were off site, but it also allowed for circulation once they were called to the main library by a requestor.

When a book was circulated from off site, special bar code labels were assigned. These had been marked with a yellow highlighter for visual identification by the circulation staff and shelvers. Although the bar code portion of the labels was covered, the light pens read through the highlighter with ease, and the library staff was aware that any item with a yellow bar code was to be returned to off-site shelving.

After selecting materials to be moved, the subject divisions submitted their records to Serials for entry into the circulation and finding system. Call number, serial title, volumes to be moved, and linear inches required were included in these records. Serials verified titles in the shelf list and entered the complete bibliographic record in the circulation and finding system. A bibliographic note indicating the range of volumes located off site followed the complete holdings record. This type of entry allowed a number of volumes to be entered under one bibiographic record, thereby creating major economies in data entry labor and on-line storage.

MOVING

Several methods of moving were considered. Packing materials in cartons and transferring a complete truck load at once was suggested[2] but the length of time volumes would be inaccessible ruled this out. One of the requirements of the move was to avoid service disruption, and it was conceivable that books could be packed away for several days under such a plan. It was suggested that books could be strapped down and an entire shelf could be moved to the new site intact. Since new shelving had been erected off site, this plan was rejected. Due to the distance of the new shelving area, the bucket brigade method of moving was impossible.[3]

Finally it was determined that moving with standard three shelf book trucks would cause the least confusion while being relatively inexpensive.[4] The library had planned to purchase book trucks anyway, so twenty were ordered in time for the move. An additional ten trucks were borrowed from various sources throughout the library and reserved for moving. The plan was to work with two crews of student assistants and two movers with a closed van. The first crew of students would load ten book trucks in call number sequences and tape slips numbered 1–10 on the trucks as they proceeded. The students would line the trucks up inside the loading dock and the movers would wheel them from the dock to the moving van. The full book trucks were then delivered to the off site location where the movers would unload them from the van. A second crew of students would receive the trucks and transfer the books in sequence from the trucks to the pre-marked shelves. The movers would pick up ten empty trucks and return them to the library loading dock. By the time they returned, the first group of students would have loaded the third set of book trucks, so the movers would be able to make another trip immediately. In practice this worked quite well, and eight loads could be moved in each 8–5 working day.

Using the procedure, approximately 160,000 volumes were moved in sixteen working days. Materials were accessible at all times except for the hour they were in transit, and several times items were pulled off book trucks in response to a patron request. Delivery service was an immediate requirement as soon as the move began.

PAGING MATERIALS

Since the off-site materials were shelved in a closed stack, efficient paging and quick delivery was requisite. One full-time clerk was assigned to oversee the off-site operation. Responsibilities of this job include supervising student pages and maintaining the delivery schedule.

A step van was purchased for paging, and five daily delivery runs were instituted during the work week. Since the library has a shorter schedule on weekends, three and four runs are made on Saturday and Sunday, respectively. This schedule provides for two hour turnaround on most requests for off-site materials, and in many instances the delay is much less.

After materials are identified at one of the circulation and finding system terminals as located off site, delivery is requested at the circulation desk. A simple paging slip is completed and left in a pick-up box for the delivery person. On each run these slips are taken to the shelving area, the materials are pulled from the stacks, bar coded for entry into the circulation and finding system if needed, and delivered to holding shelves behind the circulation desk. Due to limited shelf space, borrowers are instructed to pick up off-site materials within 24 hours of requesting them. When taken from the holding shelves, materials are circulated in the normal manner, using a light pen to read the borrower's ID number and the bar code on the book. In the same manner, returns are checked in through the circulation and finding system and are placed on separate return shelves. On each trip off site, the page picks up these returned materials and reshelves them in their proper locations.

SECOND PHASE

After the off-site service had been in operation two months, the University provided another 10,000 square feet in the same building. The remainder of the new shelving was erected there, allowing room for another 40,000 volumes. Selections were made for this second shelving area and the volumes were moved in one week using the book truck method. No attempt was made to back shift and intershelve with the existing collection, but instead the area was designated as a separate shelving unit. Materials moved in this second phase were given a different location code in the circulation and finding system and a pink highlighter was used to mark bar codes on volumes that circulated from this section.

The second phase raised the total number of volumes shelved off site to approximately 200,000. Dewey volumes are being reclassified selectively as they are returned by requestors. Since they are being added to the main collection after reclassification, the off site Dewey collection is gradually diminishing. The off site collections are dynamic, though, and eventually shifting and intershelving must take place. Since the original moves, a number of titles have been sent off site and several others, after being identified as high use, have been reassigned to the main library. The ease of modification of the data base records allows for this flexibility, so as low use items are identified, the paging load should decrease.

Although the initial move caused a modicum of user dissatisfaction, the off-site shelving program soon gained general acceptance by library clientele. The fact that off-site materials could be quickly and accurately identified and that the delivery system actually worked, eased the dismay of first time users of this closed stack. Still, a major drawback to this arrangement is a lack of browsability. Occasionally patrons have gone to the off-site center by appointment, and arrangements are being made for scheduled opening on a very limited basis.

Perhaps even more important in the acceptance of off-site shelving is the use made of the vacated areas. Two floors of the library were completely rearranged, making the bulk of the collection more accessible and providing space for 160 additional seats. A general face lifting and interior repainting of the main library created a marked environmental improvement, and did much to ease the initial dissatisfaction with the decision to go off site.

REFERENCES

1. William H. Kurth and Ray W. Grim, *Moving a Library* (New York: Scarecrow Press, 1966).
2. Matt Roberts, "Some Ideas on Moving a Book Collection," *College and Research Libraries* 27 (March 1966): 103–108.
3. Barbara L. Feret, "Moving the Library at Dutchess Community College," *ALA Bulletin* 61 (January 1967): 68–71.
4. Kurth and Grim, *op. cit.*, p. 149–150.

Ward Shaw, Patricia B. Culkin and Thomas E. Brabek

University of Denver

THE QUERY ANALYSIS SYSTEM:
A PROGRESS REPORT

The query Analysis System is an on-line, interactive, computer-based system designed to assist library users in the perception and solution of information problems. In the Query Analysis System we have invented and implemented a technique for managing a large, complex "thesaurus" of terms, collected initially from a variety of sources, in a non-normative, empirical way. Users of the system interact with the thesaurus, supplying their own terms which the system learns and incorporates in its structure, modifying and enriching that structure under user direction, and yielding individually tailored guides to research. We have shown that it is possible to relate the terminologies of different sources and users productively and interactively, and have built a system which does that. Pilot development is in sociology.

In 1975, the University of Denver received from the Exxon Education Foundation a grant to develop the Query Analysis System. We would like to report on the status of that project.

BACKGROUND

Patricia Culkin developed at the University of Denver Library a computer-assisted library use instruction program that has been in use since November 1971. The CAI installation features a CRT terminal used on-line with the University's Burroughs B6700 computer. Twenty-one courses ranging from use of indexes and abstracts, to use of the card catalog, to how to do research for a term paper are available to the students, eighteen hours per day. The CRT terminal, located in the main information area in an unrestricted public access situation, allows users to select courses which meet pre-determined research needs.

The design and implememtation of this CAI project was prompted by two factors:

1. The need to devise a method of advertising the library's resources to patrons who were reluctant or unwilling to initiate reference interviews on their own.

2. The need to provide instruction in the use of these resources on a systematic basis, thus circumventing time limitations imposed by traditional reference interviews.

Statistical evaluations have borne out the validity of the premise that CAI was capable of accomplishing these functions, and CAI has become an intrinsic element of reference service at the University of Denver.

By 1974, we felt that the interface capability of the computer could be tapped to an even greater extent; that it could be used not only to meet the needs addressed in the CAI project, but that it could interact directly with the user in the perception and the solution of individual information problems. Specifically we decided to design, implement, and evaluate a pilot, computer-based information system that would translate user's questions into language to which traditional library tools would respond and then subsequently present to uers an indivdiually generated "Pathfinder," following the MIT design, to guide them in their research.

The Pathfinder, as developed at MIT, is a single sheet guide to research in particular subject areas or particular questions, organizing for the research in logical form an approach to a solution of a problem. The significant limitation of the approach was that the Pathfinders were developed for pre-defined research problems identified by librarians' experience concerning questions users frequently asked, and consequently were restricted to problems already researched. The approach is incapable of directly addressing the nuances and variability of the individual researcher's needs. We decided, therefore, to attempt a computer-based system that would identify those nuances and generate individual Pathfinders in response.

A description of the kinds of information access problems that users have experienced in the past and a look at some of the reference and library instruction aids that libraries have generated to counter them illustrates the need for this kind of system. The most universal problem encountered in assisting clients in the use of libraries has been the failure of libraries to provide adequate instruction in effective library research. The second most universal problem has been the language problem—the difficulties users have of expressing information needs in language to which traditional information tools can respond.

Attempts to control these query languages have met with varying success, from LC subject headings with the cross reference structure to the several thesauri developed for particular subject areas, notably in the sciences and social sciences.

Because we have failed to provide adequate library instruction and because these language control programs have met with varying success, both library CAI and library Pathfinders were designed to anticipate a whole range of library user needs, either in terms of general library use instruction or beginning search strategy related to specific topics. CAI provides a medium for instruction in the use of general reference tools such as indexes and abstracts, use of the card catalog, etc. Library Pathfinders are checklists of references which present a variety of forms in which information on a specific topic can be accessed. Both are intended to highlight basic sources of information which have been predetermined to be relevant to a user during the first few hours of library research and both can be utilized without the interjection of a library "instructor" into the research process. Yet neither allows for direct attack upon a specific information problem, and both by their very nature suppress the opportunity for education of the library user in the environment of specific problem solving situations.

THE SYSTEM

We have developed a computer-based system to address these last two problems. First, we use CAI technology to allow a user to interact personally with a query language, moving up, down, and across its hierarchical structures, examining alternatives of expression to better form his questions. Second, as the system and the user interact, the system, through a coordinated data base containing university information sources, generates a guide for attack of his particular question in its final form. The two system products are a better formulated, clearer problem and an integrated, individually-tailored Pathfinder, produced at the terminal in hard copy form.

THE PROCESS

Using a specific discipline—Sociology—as a pilot, and drawing heavily upon the University expertise existing within that discipline, we developed this on-line, interactive computer software system in several phases (with overlap).

Phase one was the selection of the specific discipline for the pilot project. We examined existing thesauri, research activity at the University, resources within the community, applicability to other disciplines, previous related research, University expertise, and other pertinent factors in selecting Sociology as the discipline to be studied. To be candid, there were also substantial political considerations here.

Phase two involved a careful examination of the nature of the discipline selected, including the kinds of resources which exist, the linguistic control available, and special limiting problems. To accomplish this, we hired as Project Associate a doctoral candidate

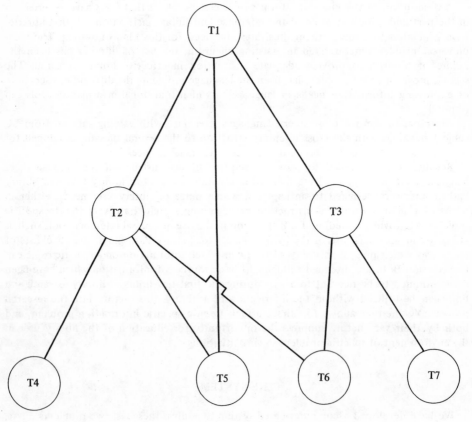

Figure 1.

in Sociology, familiar with the selected discipline. She was able to examine the resources available and supply us with an initial base of terms to function as the "start-up" thesaurus, incorporated from standard research tools (Sociology Abstracts, LC, etc.) and some 40 introductory texts.

This thesaurus became a representation of the structure of the languages Sociology uses, relating information resources to terms within the structure, and providing for user (broadly defined) interaction with the structure through a package of computer programs. Relationships between a set of terms were drawn as follows, assuming a hierarchy of specificity from top to bottom. The relationships we were immediately concerned with were "Broader Term"—T2 is a broader term to T5; "Narrower Term"—T3 is a narrower term to T1 and "Related Term"—T6 is a related term to T5.

Each term T1, T2 . . . Tn, is represented by a record in a computer file. Such a record would contain the term, and information concerning three categories of relationship: broader, narrower, and related. Each relationship is expressed by two implicit and two explicit pieces of information.

1. Relation from—implicit by the record it is expressed in.
2. Relation to—explicit.
3. Category of relationship—implicit by position in record.
4. "Value" of relationship—for the present, an expressed frequency of use count.

Such a record might look like:

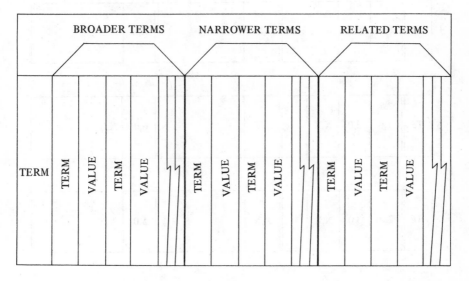

Figure 2.

The file containing the relationships specified in the sample above would contain seven records, as shown in Figure 3. X's are used to indicate the end of expressed relationships, and each relationship is expressed by a pair, the zeroes in the second number of each pair indicating that the paths have yet to be threaded. Addition of terms and relationships is easy—only the relationship indexes need to be updated, or, in the case of adding a new term, one record needs adding. Suppose, for example, T8 were to be added as a narrower term to T2. Record T8 would be added as shown in Figure 4.

	TERM	BT			NT					RT
1	T1	X,X			2,0	3,0	5,0	X,X	X,X	
2	T2	1,0	X,X		4,0	5,0	6,0	X,X	X,X	
3	T3	1,0	X,X		6,0	7,0	X,X	X,X		
4	T4	2,0	X,X		X,X			X,X		
5	T5	1,0	2,0	X,X				6,0	X,X	
6	T6	2,0	3,0	X,X	X,X			5,0	X,X	
7	T7	3,0	X,X		X,X			X,X		

Figure 3.

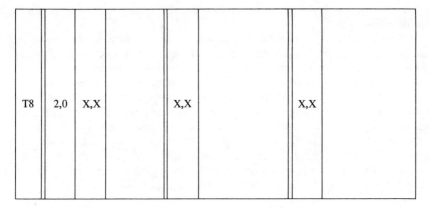

Figure 4.

and record 2 would be updated as:

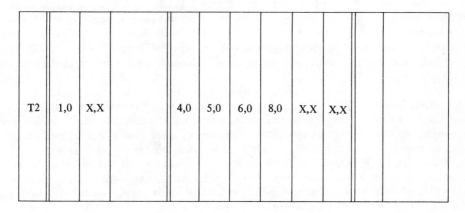

Figure 5.

All we did is tie each term to information sources—more like traditional library reference than indexing—and developed programs to help users place themselves within the term matrix.

We then devised a series of computer programs forming the information system, which coordinates two data bases, one consisting of a linguistic structure, and one consisting of the relevant resources within the community. The lay user uses the system to manipulate both data bases toward the stated objectives of better formulated clearer questions, and interrelated, individually tailored "Pathfinders" to help him answer those questions. Of course, the process and the structure are transparent to the user.

The interactive computer program we designed was of necessity most complex but can be viewed as having four major components: (1) preliminaries, including log-in and user identification data, e.g., name of student, course, etc.; (2) the interactive sequence wherein the focusing and exploration of the data base occurs; (3) library search guidelines, i.e., given a student's topic, a list of library resources that are appropriate, and (4) system growth input, i.e., new terms and new relationships that the student proposes for expanding the data base.

After considerable exploration of a wide variety of alternatives, we decided that the system should permit two very different forms of inquiry. Some students might approach the system with only very broad topics in mind and use the system to explore and identify increasingly narrow or related terms. In this sense by both focusing and confronting them with related terms, new research paper topic ideas might be stimulated. In contrast, other students might begin with a specific term and basically request that the system help them make connections to a range of descriptors under which related materials might be classified. As indicated above, this is desirable because each major reference tool uses somewhat different descriptors, i.e., each reflects a different taxonomy and there is no translation device to help students jump from one to another. The two examples which follow illustrate each of these processes.

HOW IT WORKS: TWO EXAMPLES

Let's assume that a student has logged in and has provided the requested information, e.g., course title, previous use, etc. The student wishes to explore a set of relationships which may lead to a research paper topic. Figure 6 presents the type of output such a student might obtain upon tracing through one of a multitude of potential paths. Note that each choice made took the student to a successively less abstract level, i.e., from "groups," as one level of social organizations, to types of groups, and so on. Careful study of Figure 6 will provide a more thorough understanding of the format and logic of the system.

Upon completing the exploration, work is summarized at the end, thereby ordering the various levels of abstraction, related terms under which relevant material might be indexed, and finally a list of source materials for each of the particular terms. In this way students begin to see the emergence of a structure—the theoretical structure of the discipline—initially as we organized it, and later as the users themselves organize it.

The examples presented as Figure 7, illustrate how the process unfolds when the student starts with a particular term. Two examples are presented—first, "alienation: and then "riots." Note that the system indicates that the search has started and then that the term has been found. Most students are surprised at the speed at which the computer completes the search process (typically a second or two). Note also that both broader, narrower, and several related terms are provided. These related terms can in turn be entered simply by selecting the numbers listed. At this point many students have suddenly started exploring new relationships and possible topics which they might otherwise never considered.

The system is designed to be both reflexive and heuristic in the sense that the structure is not imposed, but can change, develop, and grow as a result of interaction. As clients use the system, any terms not in the initial base are incorporated immediately and automatically into the linguistic base. Their place in the hierarchy is specified by the user, subject to review only for garbage data by a project employee at a later time. The addition and integration of these terms insures that the translation problems affecting coordination of laymen's language and diverse sociological lexicons become continually less broad, and that the utility of the products is tested and the products modified as a result of actual user experience. It is this "learning" feature of the system which distinguishes it from others which are bound by the precepts that generated them.

Students and faculty at DU have been using the system for about a year, and initial results of our evaluation procedures indicate that the use is educationally productive. The

SAMPLE OUTPUT: Tracing Through the Structure as a Means of Focusing

---

Enter Yes to search by major category: Enter No to search using your term
$\boxed{\text{Yes}}$ *Student Response:*   All user responses are identified in this manner.

The following are the major categories currently available to the program with a sequence preceding to aid in the retrieval:
- 01.   Social Science
- 02.   Social Theory
- 03.   Social Research
- $\boxed{04.}$ Social Organization
- 05.   Culture
- 06.   Mass phenomena
- 07.   Population
- 08.   Social Problems

Please enter index number of category of interest (ex. 02) $\boxed{04}$ ← *term selected*

Do you wish to list related terms corresponding to this category: Yes or No.
There may be other narrow terms associated with synonyms; these can be found by an examination of your term of interest. $\boxed{\text{Yes}}$ ← *request for related terms*

Listed below are the narow terms related to this category.
- 01.   Social Structure
- 02.   Social Processes
- 03.   Social Systems
- $\boxed{04.}$ Levels of Social Organization
- 05.   Fraternity

Choose index of term or phrase of interest and enter it (ex: 01 or 02) $\boxed{04}$ ← *term selected*

Listed below are the narrow terms related to this category.
- 01.   Individuals
- $\boxed{02.}$ Groups
- 03.   Complex Organizations
- 04.   Community
- 05.   Society

Choose index of term or phrase of interest and enter it (ex: 04 or 12) $\boxed{02}$ ← *term selected*

There may be other narrow terms associated with synonyms; these can be found by an examination of your term of interest.
Listed below are the narrow terms related to this category.
- $\boxed{01.}$ Types of Groups
- 02.   Group Characteristics
- 03.   Group Processes
- 04.   Children

Choose index of term or phrase of itnerest and enter it (ex: 04 or 12) $\boxed{01}$ ← *term selected*

Figure 6.

Listed below are the narrow terms related to this category.

    01.   Small Groups
    02.   Secondary Groups
    03.   Primary Groups
    04.   Age Group
    05.   Groups, Occupational
    06.   Pressure Group
    07.   Reference Group
    08.   Interest Group
    09.   Membership Group
    10.   Out groups
    11.   Disadvantaged Groups
    12.   Low Income Groups
    13.   Acquaintance Groups
    14.   Ingroup
    15.   Ethnic Groups
    17.   Status Groups

Choose index of term or phrase of interest and enter it (ex. 04 or 12) 03 ← *term selected*

There may be other narrow terms associated with synonyms; these can be found by an examination of your term of interest.

Listed below are the narrow terms related to this category.

    01.   Friends
    02.   Clique
    03.   Gangs
    04.   Primary Groups

Choose index of term or phrase of interest and enter it (ex. 04 or 12) 03 ← *term selected*

There may be other narrow terms associated with synonyms; these can be found by an examination of your term of interest.

Listed below are no narrow terms currently in this area.

       *****   Summary Associated With Chosen Category   *****

-----------Level 01

Social Organization

The following synonyms or use-fors are associated with this term.

                Organization, Social

Source materials that reference this term or synonyms.

           (Lists of source materials are given for terms at levels
               2, 3, 4, 5, and 6 in same format as above, e.g.,
                    Sociological Abstracts, etc.; Library
                    call number is included for each item.)

Figure 6. *(Continued)*

SAMPLE OUTPUT: Entering the System with a term

Example #1:   Student has the term "alientation" in mind and has logged in.

Enter Yes to search by major category: Enter No to search using your term ⌞No⌝← *student response*

The term or phrase should be in field of sociology. Please avoid suffixes and hyphens: hyphenated words are treated as one word.

Phrases should contain a maximum of five words, and only one space should separate the words. Terms or phrases of more than 48 characters will be truncated.

Enter term or phrase: ⌞ Alienation⌝← *term entered*

Search Started:

Your Term Found:

The following synonyms or use-fors are associated with this term.

The hierarchy table which follows will show broad term, narrow term and other related terms corresponding to the term you've chosen. After the hierarchy table is printed you will be allowed to enter other broad, narrow and related terms of your choice, and to examine further one of the terms in the table. Each term in the table is preceded by a number which will aid in selecting the table term you wish to examine further.

Press return key (CAR RET or XMIT)

          Broad Terms:
01 Attitudes   — — —

                Your Term: Alienation

          Narrow Terms:
01 Powerlessness   — — —03 Alienation, Organization

Related terms are on next page——please press return key (CAR RET XMIT)

                Your Term: Alienation

          Related Terms:
04 Social Adjustment   — — —05 Anomie
06 Deviance   — — —07 Socialization
08 Social Participation   — — —09 Social Isolation
10 Deviant Behavior   — — —11 Marx, Karl

(Student may pursue any of above terms by selecting number; if none are selected the sources for the original term are listed).

Figure 7.

Examples #2:   Student has the term "riots" in mind, has logged in and has entered term
in a format parallel to that listed above.

Enter term or phrase: |Riots| ← *term entered*

Search started:

Your term found:

The following synonyms or use-fors are associated with this term.
Riot, Social

The hierarchy table which follows will show broad term, narrow term and other related terms corresponding to the term you've chosen. After the hierarchy table is printed
you will be allowed to enter other broad, narrow and related terms of your choice, and to
examine further one of the terms in the table. Each term in the table is preceded by a
number which will aid in selecting the table term you wish to examine further.
Press return key (CAR RET or XMIT)

Broad terms:
01 Collective Behavior   — — —02 Social Unrest

Your term: Riots

Narrow terms:
03 Racial Riots   — — —

Related terms are on next page——please press return key (CAR RET XMIT)

Your term: Riots

Related terms:
04 Panic   — — —05 Suggestion
06 Contagion   — — —07 Protest, Social
08 Collective Excitement   — — —09 Race Problems
10 Revolution   — — —

(Student may pursue any of above
terms by selecting number;
if none are selected the
sources for the original
term are listed)

Figure 7. *(Continued)*

data base has grown by over 25% and has been broadly manipulated toward a wide variety of problem situations. Acceptance by users has been high, and the premise that CAI technology can be usefully incorporated into the research process has been proven. Though further enrichment and refinement must occur in each of the data bases for them to be totally effective, the model that will precipitate and encourage that process has been built, and needs only further use to become essential to the research process.

We have discovered, however, that the importance of the project is not in its specific application as a research aid in Sociology, or even its use as such in another discipline, but rather in its potential as an integrating mechanism for a variety of information access tools. We have built a system that relates terminologies of different users and resources responsively and interactively. It is one component that has been neglected in network research, the "driver" that effects the linking of the user with a variety of access tools, local and global, while enriching his conception of his problem and its locus in the discipline. We expect to do further research to test whether this system can accomplish this.

Aline Soules

University of Windsor

OFF-CAMPUS LIBRARY SERVICES: THOSE INBETWEEN YEARS

This paper discusses the library services that complement growing university and college off-campus programs and specifically centers on the years that fall between the start of such services and the final establishment of a physical satellite library. Suggestions are offered for the handling and future developmentof these library services; suggestions are drawn partly from the literature and primarily from experiences at the University of Windsor.

In the last few years, with decreasing enrollments and the threat of a continuation in this trend, universities and colleges have sought new ways to boost their flagging numbers. At the same time, there has been an upsurge in the "non-traditional" studies analyzed at length by the Commission on Non-Traditional Study in its report *Diversity by Design*.[1] One result of these two factors has been the geographical expansion of universities and colleges to points farther and farther removed from their main campuses. In some cases, as a natural outgrowth of the off-campus program, a satellite campus has emerged.

Academic libraries, in consequence, have had to go off-campus as well, and they have done so in a variety of ways, usually establishing a new "branch" or extension library if and when a satellite campus is formed. These extension libraries have different degrees of independence based on the size and nature of their operations. Between the two situations of no service and an extension library, however, there is still a need for *academic* library service and the most common denominator of all attempts at such service has been the involvement of the public library.

Joint ventures at non-traditional forms of a college education have been appearing on the scene with great regularity, but there are often indications that it is the public libraries that are taking a great deal of the initiative in providing the library service that goes with it. Indeed, in *Diversity by Design*, one of the recommendations of the Commission reads:

> The public library should be strengthened to become a far more powerful instrument for non-traditional education than is now the case.
>
> This recommendation is directed not only to public officials and public librarians themselves but also to *college and university faculty members and*

administrators who could work productively with them in developing non-traditional study opportunities at the post-secondary level.[2] (*italics are mine*)

The Commission goes on to expand on their conception of the role of the public library as a "college around the corner"[3] whose opportunity has now arrived. No specific mention of the academic library is ever made.

However, in 1967, when the Association of College and Research Libraries published its "Guidelines for Library Services to Extension Students," which included all extension students on- and off-campus, it was implied that the academic library was responsible for services to its own students regardless of where they were situated. Guideline 3 recommended that the librarian, who would be in charge of all extension activities, would assume responsibility for the provision of materials and service to off-campus students through an off-campus location if necessary.[4]

What has happened, unfortunately, in the intervening years is that the public libraries have "hustled" while the academic libraries have not. For example, in the September, 1973 issue of *American Libraries*, in discussing the use of the Memorial Hall Library, Andover, Massachusetts, as a college site, the Memorial Hall Library Director, Harry Sagris, is quoted as the one who saw the need for the service and performed a survey to determine how many would be interested.[5] In the November, 1972 issue of *Library Journal*, Larry Earl Bone, assistant director of the Memphis Public Library and Information Center is cited as the "prime negotiator" in a contractual arrangement between the public library and the nearby community college, Shelby State.[6]

This is not to imply that academic libraries and librarians are doing nothing, but it is our attitude that disturbs me and I think it is one of the reasons the Commission focussed on the public library to the exclusion of the academic one. In the preface to the Commission report, Samuel B. Gould wrote:

> Most of us agreed that non-traditional study is more an attitude than a system and thus can never be defined except tangentially. This attitude puts the student first and the institution second, concentrates more on the former's need than the latter's convenience . . . This attitude is not new; it is simply more prevalent than it used to be.[7]

It is my contention that while public libraries are undoubtedly invaluable to the types of programs being offered on an off-campus basis, academic libraries have often allowed public library enthusiasm and drive to do their work for them. Academic libraries have a responsibility toward their students no matter what their distance from the main campus. Our attitude has been lax and our efforts minimal. We have moaned about budget problems and our difficulties in meeting even the demands of on-campus students, instead of realizing our own role in providing service to what is essentially our own community —a role that may to a large extent be indirectly administered, but a role that we must fulfill if we are to accord our students the rights they deserve.

The most positive move in the direction of assuming those responsibilities has been shown in the study by Orton and Wiseman reported in *Canadian Library Journal* in February, 1977 under the title "Library Service to Part-Time Students." Dealing with both on- and off-campus students, once again, the authors sent questionnaires to part-time students at Trent and Queen's Universities and also surveyed libraries near their off-campus teaching sites. Of interest in terms of off-campus services are the qeustions they asked of the public libraries, which were:

1. Are your resources adequate without assistance from the university?
2. Do you rely heavily upon interlibrary loan services?

3. Who should provide library materials, the university or the public library?

4. Are you able to provide professional staff assistance for this category of reader?

5. If the answer to this last question is 'no,' would you welcome assistance from the university's professional library staff?[8]

The answers they received from these questions and their other surveys should finally lay to rest any doubts we may have about our responsibilities.

While the Orton–Wiseman studies have been directed toward part-time students as a whole, they have had to devote separate sections to discussions of on-campus and off-campus services. Yet, one of their conclusions is that a Coordinator could be appointed to handle services to part-time students—again as a whole.[9] While this dovetails with the original Guideline 3 of the ACRL guidelines on extension services that I mentioned above, this is where we part company, because the needs of on- and off-campus students differ greatly. At the University of Windsor, we separate the two in terms of library services, and my work as Coordinator of Extramural Library Services deals exclusively with our off-campus students, a few of whom, I might add, are full-time rather than part-time. In fact, across campus, every attempt has been made to treat students as students rather than separating them into part-time, full-time, day, evening, or any other category. Distinctions are made *only* when absolutely necessary. All academic aspects of students' programs are handled by the Deans of the appropriate faculties. There is no Dean of Extension. Instead, there is a Director of Part-Time Studies to handle any administrative problems specifically related to part-time students and a Coordinator of Extramural Programs to handle any administrative problems specifically related to off-campus students. I might add, also, that the Coordinator's office is located in our largest off-campus center, Chatham, rather than on campus.

The library, to complement this approach, also makes distinctions among students only when necessary. Our on-campus students naturally have the same access to the library whether they are in full-time, part-time, or special programs. Our on-campus library hours and reference service hours are extensive enough to satisfy any customer (we are open until midnight every night seven days a week with reference service until 8 P.M. during the week and from noon until 5 P.M. on Saturdays and Sundays). In addition, any services offered, such as library instruction classes, are similarly arranged to be available to *all* on-campus students.

With off-campus students, however, library services are another matter. Our eventual goal is the provision of materials and service of an equivalent *qualitative* degree to that provided on the main campus. We attempt to provide that service as closely as possible to the actual location of the students' classes in order to create a facsimile of the main campus where classes and library are obviously in close proximity. Consequently, in some cases, we use more than one library location in a given city. The accompanying map shows all the areas we are serving or have served in the past. We have two library locations in each of Chatham and Sarnia, one a public library and one a local community college library. The third continuous site is Leamington while the other sites are used either in conjunction with summer classes or with special study programs for individual students.

The number of students we serve in those areas is shown in Table I which covers only our three continuous service areas. These figures are taken from enrollments registered during the 1970/1971 through 1977/1978 school years and include (from 1974/1975 on) both graduate and undergraduate enrollments. As Chatham is obviously our largest service center, the second table shows only the number of courses offered in Chatham during the same period with the corresponding enrollments. In Chatham we offer library service through both the Chatham Public Library, our oldest and most used location, and the Thames Campus Library, open since January, 1977. The former serves those students

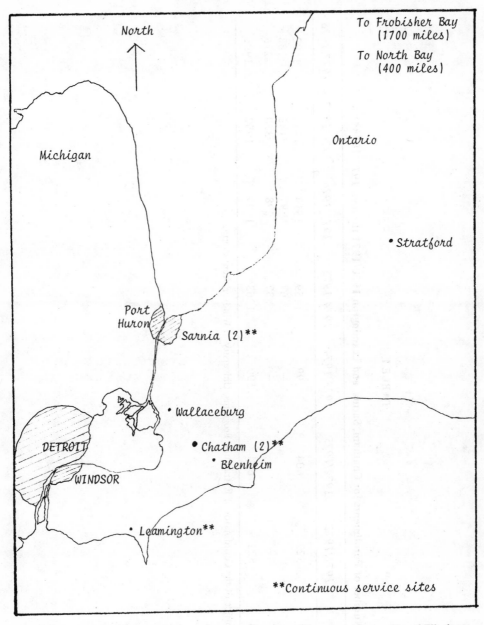

To Frobisher Bay
(1700 miles)

To North Bay
(400 miles)

North

Michigan

Ontario

• Stratford

Port
Huron

Sarnia (2)**

• Wallaceburg

DETROIT

• Chatham (2)**

• Blenheim

WINDSOR

• Leamington**

**Continuous service sites

Figure 1. Major Service Areas of Extramural Library Services, University of Windsor.

TABLE I

The Number of Enrollments for Chatham, Sarnia, and Leamington 1970/1971 through 1977/1978**

Location	1970/1971	1971/1972	1972/1973	1973/1974	1974/1975	1975/1976	1976/1977	1977/1978
Chatham	374	522	604	599	1159	1514	1477	1582
Leamington	–	–	–	–	67	97	185	188
Sarnia	–	–	–	–	37	298	320	226
TOTAL	374	522	604	599	1263	1909	1982	1996

**Figures supplied by the office of the Coordinator of Extramural Programs, University of Windsor, Kent Center.

TABLE II

The Number of Courses Offered in Chatham Compared with The Number of Enrollments, 1970/1971 through 1977/1978**

Year	Number of Courses		Number of Enrollments
1970/1971	13		374
1971/1972	20		460
1972/1973	16		604
1973/1974	24		599
1974/1975	32	undergraduate	
	2½	graduate	
	34½	total	1159
1975/1976	47	undergraduate	
	2	graduate	
	49	total	1514
1976/1977	46	undergraduate	
	2½	graduate	
	48½	total	1477
1977/1978	52	undergraduate	
	2½	graduate	
	54½	total	1582

**Figures supplied by the office of the Coordinator of Extramural Programs, University of Windsor, Kent Center.

taking classes at the high school about a mile away and the latter serves students taking classes at Thames Campus, which is a ten-minute drive away from the high school/public library area.

In all five of our continuous service sites, our first priority is to provide course reserve materials so that students will have the specific items they need to complete assigned readings and papers. Consultation with instructors determines the necessary titles and now that the demand has risen so much, we ship only up to 50 titles per course. The materials are housed in the libraries during the run of the course and shipped back when the course is completed. They are then kept on the main campus library shelves for use by on-campus students until they are required off-campus again. Often a book will see three different places in a given year.

For Sarnia and Leamington, this is currently all we require. Occasionally, we have sent a piece of audio-visual equipment for a course and any of our off-campus library sites can telex or telephone with a special request for materials which we try to supply as quickly as possible. In Chatham, however, it became apparent, by 1975, that we needed more. Discussions between the Chatham Public Library and ourselves resulted in the opening of a separate room for the University students in December, 1975, the provision of additional types of materials, and, beginning in 1976, the payment of a service fee.

The University Study Room has essentially become a mini-library with shelving for materials, a microfilm reader, desks and study carrels. In addition to course reserve materials, there is a slowly-growing small collection of materials housed permanently in the Study Room and these materials provide additional background reading and sources for major papers and projects. We have also bought materials that are housed with the

Chatham Public Library's collection. These consist primarily of reference titles which can be used in conjunction with other searching tools. Finally, the service fee secures us, in addition to the regular Chatham Public Library services, half the time of a professional librarian and of a clerical. This means more skilled reference service, on-the-spot supervision of the operation, and better lines of communication between the main library and our clients. The professional also supplies library tours or class visits if necessary, consultation on the selection of materials for the permanent collections, and assistance in the development of new policies and procedures. Between us, we attempt to fill in the gaps not handled by the standard course reserve materials or procedures.

At Thames Campus Library, we still provide just the course reserves; however, should it develop as the secondary school/public library arrangement has developed, we will build our services along the same lines as at the Chatham Public Library. As we now have our own permanent materials at the Chatham Public Library, we are free to shift them about at will should we ever need to switch our base of operations. When materials for our off-campus permanent collection are cataloged and processed, they are treated as if they belonged to an Extramural Library. This allows us the flexibility of maintaining our operations at their current size or growing with the program into our own library which will already have a basic collection to start it.

As for our other intermittent locations, we send course reserve materials to any local library or even a private home from which they can be circulated. In cases where a student is taking a special home study course, we send materials to his home on a long-term loan basis. What we attempt to do in all our services is to keep the level of that service compatible with our level of growth as dictated by enrollments, the number of courses taught, and the types of materials required.

In case this all sounds too good to be true, I must point out that we have had problems—many of them. I began by speaking of attitude and responsibility and how the public libraries have taken the initiative. A great deal of our attitude has been fostered by the Chatham Public Library whose Director was looking for help and turned to the University whose students she was trying to serve.

Another problem is that we have, to some extent, grown like Topsy, springing up in a variety of locations as courses have been taught. There is the distinct possibility that we will spread ourselves too thinly. We might be wiser to consolidate activities in Chatham, for example, in one location, rather than attempting to build two sites. However, so far, it appears that students, the majority of whom have severe time limitations, prefer and indeed require on-the-spot, quick service. Before the Thames Campus Library was available for use, when students still had to travel down to the Chatham Public Library from Thames Campus classes for materials, course reserve circulation dropped. There is every indication that although the Chatham Public Library offers more open hours and a more developed service, convenience is the key factor in the students' preference of location.

A third problem is communication. While having a half-time professional has alleviated a great many communication problems, there are still two areas we must conquer. One involves the professors, who still do not fully realize the importance of communicating their needs accurately and on time. We require at least two to three months advance notice of needed titles. This allows us the time to send what we already have and place rush orders for those items we must buy. As professors become more familiar with procedures, however, and gain experience with off-campus teaching, the importance of timing becomes more clear to them and the majority cooperate with us in seeing that students have materials as early in the year as possible. The second communication problem revolves around the various University offices. There are times when certain administrative offices forget or do not see the importance of conveying information to the library—usually information concerning course scheduling for an upcoming session or reports of on-campus procedural or policy changes that will affect off-campus activities as well. Again, it is a matter of familiarity and experience. As the program becomes more firmly established in the pattern of the university, these communication problems seem to lessen and with time and persistence, we hope to eradicate them completely.

A major problem, as might be expected, is the budget. When the program got under-way, funds were tight, but not impossible. They have subsequently become impossible. During the 1976/1977 and 1977/1978 budget years, we have had to scrounge for funds outside the basic library budget, which had no provision for off-campus expenses, and the money we have garnered has been in the nature of a survival amount only. In 1976/1977, we only had money for course reserves and none for any additional collection develop-ment which had to be suspended temporarily. In 1977/1978, funds eased somewhat, but we are still in serious difficulties. The problem stems from attitude, once again. While I worry about spreading ourselves too thinly among off-campus sites, my colleagues working in the main library worry about the same thing—only the relationship they worry about is between on- and off-campus services. In the past, I have been asked such ques-tions as "How can we support off-campus services when we cannot keep up with last year's serial subscriptions?" I have a great deal of sympathy with this, but cannot agree. If a university makes a commitment to off-campus teaching programs, then it must be pre-pared to carry that commitment to its proper conclusion and support the necessary attendant services that go with it. The library must not look on off-campus students as a group to be served after the others, but in conjunction with them. We must share the financial blessings and burdens equitably. Fortunately, we are slowly coming to accept this viewpoint and the program is now much more accepted as a part and parcel of our overall service offerings.

A great deal of our various problems and solutions are inextricably tied up with internal politics, and this has led me both to misgivings and to some optimism for the future. While we have had some difficulties getting fully airborne, we are nontheless sur-viving and our dramatic enrollment increases off-campus—increases that, incidentally, are not currently reflected on-campus—should result in the conclusion that our future market is beyond the confines of the main campus. As the competition for students be-comes keener and we try harder to attract and please prospective customers, our chances of solidifying off-campus library service will be there.

In the meantime, therefore, we must enter into a heavy period of self-assessment. Orton and Wiseman have begun with their study at Trent and Queen's, while the Adminis-trators of Medium-Sized Public Libraries of Ontario (AMPLO) are currently undertaking a follow-up study in our area. What I should like to see, however, is a consolidation of these studies so that we can develop an overview of the off-campus picutre. In 1973, the Commission on Non-Traditional Study analyzed non-traditional forms of education and provided recommendations for the future. In 1978, it is time to form a similar group to study existing non-traditional forms of academic library service and to provide recom-mendations far more specific and up-to-date than those currently incorporated in the 1967 ACRL Guidelines for Library Services to Extension Students. I challenge ACRL to recognize the special and separate needs of off-campus students and to be the catalyst for the development of new guidelines for this important and growing field of service.

REFERENCES

1. Commission on Non-Traditional Study, *Diversity by Design* (San Francisco: Jossey-Bass, 1973).

2. *Ibid.*, p. 82–83.

3. *Ibid.*, p. 83.

4. Committee of Standards of the Association of College and Research Libraries, "Guidelines for Library Services to Extension Students," *ALA Bulletin* 61 (January 1967): 1.

5. "Andover Library Becomes College 'Campus,'" *American Libraries* 4 (September 1973): 8.

6. "A Community and its College Share Library Facilities," *Library Journal* 97 (November 15, 1972): 20.

7. Commission on Non-Traditional Study, *op. cit.*, p. xiv.

8. Larry Orton and John Wiseman, "Library Service to Part-Time Students," *Canadian Library Journal* 34 (February 1977): 23.

9. *Ibid.*, p. 27.

T. Philip Tompkins and Gary D. Byrd

University of Missouri–Kansas City

THE URBAN UNIVERSITY LIBRARY: EFFECTIVENESS MODELS FOR 1989

The paper proposes that by 1989 the bulk of urban university library resources be directed to a deliberate expansion of information services. In modifying their organization, library managers should give primary emphasis to marketing of information services. The organizational changes required if a library is to market its services are sketched. Techniques for new program development in higher education are discussed. A model, similar to one developed at Pennsylvania State University, is mentioned because it includes community participation (academic and civic). Three new programs at the University of Missouri–Kansas City libraries similar to programs at other urban university libraries serve to illustrate the growth and change needed if these programs—and similar programs—are to survive and develop.

Some librarians feel that in academic libraries by the year 2000 there will be "more knowledge about information but less help for the user of that information." in this paper we suggest how successful urban university libraries should develop in the next ten years. We propose that the bulk of library resources be directed to a careful but deliberate expansion of information services. Some justification is based on summary reviews and predictions in the professional literature.[1] Clearly there is a need to transcend the housekeeping activities which have dominated library development in the 60s and 70s, especially automation projects.

We have made certain assumptions in writing this paper. Urban university libraries cannot be seen as independent information systems. Rather they must be seen as subsystems functioning within larger systems—within the university and within the metropolitan community of which they are but a single information center. As Glynn Harmon has suggested in a recent review, libraries are. . .

open systems models of professionalism vis-a-vis earlier static and prototypical models of professionalism. The information profession itself may be viewed as a system of functionaries who must progressively adapt their fundamental concepts, technologies and services to the demands and realities of their political and socioeconomic environments. The profession's survival and security are then dependent on its ability to anticipate the demands of its future operating environment, to render well organized, timely and concerted responses, and to get and use feedback.[2]

A corollary, Glynn Harmon suggests, is that urban university librarians can expect to encounter user groups which are

incorporating more and more information processing functions into their traditional roles. New information specializations appear to be emerging *within* user groups and user institutions and *outside* the stereotypical information processing areas. . .

such as libraries.[3]

To function successfully in an open environment, urban university libraries need to redesign their organization and programs to give primary emphasis to the marketing of information. Regional, state and national resource libraries are taking the steps through cooperative arrangements to bridge the gaps in metropolitan area library resources. State and federal governments are currently in the mood to support this kind of cooperation, but they are not in the mood to assist in underwriting the delivery of information services. This is and will be the work of the individual library, particularly its cadre of public service librarians.

If libraries are going to provide effective new outreach services to individuals and groups of users, two things must occur:

1. information professionals must develop new marketing *skills*, and
2. the *information requirements of users* in the sciences, social sciences and humanities must be more creatively identified, recorded and satisfied in a cost-effective manner.

In this context, it is clear from recent experimentation with the design of information systems that many more variables need to be incorporated in the planning of these services. The status of the information seeker has as much effect, for example, on the way in which an information need is formulated and satisfied as the subject matter of the problem itself.[4] The patron's time constraints, outlook and depth of need add factors which are often unnoticed as important variables. Studies show that the design of information systems is exceedingly complex.[5] How much more complex must the input and analysis be for an urban university library which has a mix of clientele within the academic institution it serves and an even more varied mix of actual and potential clientele within the community at large.

Library administrators frequently argue that budgets have been reduced and that even present levels of acquisition and service will be difficult to maintain. We would counter by saying that this attitude is self-defeating. Only by designing and marketing effective new services will urban university libraries secure the budgetary support they need to prosper. Cooperative planning with and for the broad cross section of users will be the only way to guarantee fiscal support. The users for whom and with whom we plan new services will themselves bring new support for new programs at budget time.

If we can agree that there is a need for the deliberate expansion of outreach information services from the urban university library, then we need to consider procedures for the development of specific new programs. Some useful models for this kind of program development have appeared in the management literature of higher education.[6] Lee and Gilmour have argued in the *Journal of Higher Education* that most post-secondary education program planning techniques such as *enrollment projection* and the *community needs survey* have dealt with marketing problems for *existing* programs. These procedures are not adequate for planning new programs. They then suggest that the principles used by marketing researchers in the development of *new* products would be useful in planning new academic and service programs. Their model consists of eight interacting states: (1) definition of institutional mission and service areas, (2) idea generation, (3) idea screening, (4) concept development, (5) concept testing, (6) costing, (7) estimation of program demand and (8) program evaluation. A pilot project using this model at Pennsylvania State University's York Commonwealth Campus appears to have been a success. A characteristic of this model which we find most attractive is the deliberate involvement of the user community in the development of new programs; we argue for a similar approach in libraries.[7]

Philip Kotler has written extensively on marketing techniques for nonprofit organizations. Kotler says that

> marketing calls for a new orientation of the organization. Marketing is more than a set of added activities. It amounts to a whole new attitude toward the organization's various publics and missions. It is a thorough-going adoption of this new orientation that produces the major benefits of better survival and growth for the organization and the satisfaction of its customers.[8]

Kotler calls this new orientation "responsiveness' and he suggests that organizations fall into four groups based on the level of their responsiveness. To move from a casually responsive to a fully responsive capability, urban university library managers need to break out of the current fascination with centripetal styles of management which emphasize internal relationships and activities (no matter how mechanized) and develop new centrifugal styles that include marketing methods, analysis, program development and application. We further suggest that these program development procedures should involve sectors of the user community from the very beginning.

We would like to use two new programs which have been developed during the past seven years at the University of Missouri—Kansas City and a third which is being developed in cooperation with public and health sciences libraries in the Kansas City area to illustrate the kinds of challenges urban university library managers will face as they seek to develop new outreach information services. The Bibliographic Instruction Program (BIP) of the UMKC General Library and the Clinical Medical Librarian Program (CMLP) at the UMKC Medical Library have both been well received by their user groups. The Kansas City Libraries Metropolitan Information Network (MINET) is a voluntary referral network for on-line bibliographic database searching through eight public, academic, and special libraries in the bi-state metropolitan Kansas City area. All three of these programs will need more active marketing support to continue to develop significantly. We have chosen these three programs because we think they are illustrative of outreach efforts in urban university libraries across the country. They represent the directions for new marketing efforts. What follows is a brief description of these programs and an indication of the new activities we feel are needed to help them and similar efforts to prosper and mature.

The University of Missouri—Kansas City is a medium size urban institution with an enrollment of about 10,500 students. Its libraries deliver services at seven locations for a College of Arts and Sciences, and Schools of Medicine, Dentistry, Pharmacy, Law, Music, Education and Administration.

The Bibliographic Instruction Program of the General Library and the Clinical Medical Librarian Program at the Medical Library both began in 1971. The Bibliographic Instruction Program (BIP) was developed from the model first deisgned and tested by Patricia

Knapp at Monteith College of Wayne State University in 1966[9] and predates the 1975 ACRL *Guidelines for Bibliographic Instruction in Academic Libraries.*[10] This program serves the sciences, social sciences and humanities in the College of Arts and Sciences as well as the Schools of Education, Administration and Pharmacy. The student enrollment of those units is equivalent to about 4650 full time undergraduates and 1045 full time graduate students. Ten professional librarians staff the program serving as *information officers* to the curricula of those departments and schools. The service is initiated by a reference librarian who contacts individual faculty members and offers to work with them as they plan courses. Each librarian seeks to participate in planning sessions, bringing information about potential resources which might substantially increase the quality of course achievement. Librarians also assume responsibility for the design of search strategies, the logistics of group use of information materials, and the presentation of information retrieval skills and techniques to students in the courses. About fifty such presentations are made each semester. Last year the General Library received a Council on Library Resources grant which will allow it to experiment with a more complete integration of library services for a unified science undergraduate curriculum.[11] Although the bibliographic instruction program involves the reference staff in regular outreach activities, the staff continues to provide the majority of its services in the General Library. In this sense the program is similar to much of the activity in other academic and research libraries across the country.

A more focused outreach information service at UMKC is the well documented Clinical Medical Librarian program (CLMP) at the Medical School.[12] In 1971 the Medical School had an enrollment of 76 students in its new six-year combined baccalaureate–M.D. program. By the fall of 1977 the number of students in this had risen to 440. The student body in the last four years of the program is divided into six units, each composed of four teams of 12–14 students. Each unit also includes four physicians/teachers call Docents as well as several hospital health professionals including residents, doctors of pharmacy, nurses, dieticians and others. Currently four Clinical Medical Librarians are serving the six units, although originally one CML was assigned to each docent unit. The CML concept, which originated at the University of Missouri–Kansas City, was funded during the first four years by a research grant from the National Library of Medicine. The first goal was to

> institute a new program in which medical librarians would become integral
> members of multi-disciplinary patient care teams in an urban teaching
> hospital. The second goal was to test a number of specific hypotheses about
> the ability of these Clinical Medical Librarians to search, select and provide
> documents to meet the information needs of other team members.[13]

Extensive data on the activities of the CML's were collected for a total of sixteen months during the two research grant periods. The major findings of this research have been described as follows:

> 1. CML's identify and state the information needs of their users with greater
> than 90% accuracy,
> 2. a high degree of correlation exists between judgment of the CML and that
> of the user as to the pertinence of the information selected by the CML,
> 3. a limited number of journals produce most of the documents pertinent to
> the users' information needs, and
> 4. documents appear in a different set of journals for each category of user;
> each subject category of information need and each clinical specialty or
> discipline.[14]

A follow-up study of graduates of the medical school in residency programs confirms the effectiveness of the program on the information habits of these young physicians.[15]

One of the most unusual features of the program is that the CMLs are part of the health care team making rounds in the teaching hospital. This arrangement has allowed the librarians to identify information needs as they arise in patient care. About one-third of the CML's time is spent on rounds or in the Learning Resource Centers which serve as their home base on each docent unit. Two-thirds of their time is spent in the medical library satisfying the information needs of the patient care team. As one might expect, these information services rely heavily on computer searching of MEDLINE and other on-line databases. Currently the CML program is undergoing further developmental scrutiny which should lead to additional programmatic and budgetary support. The marketing of these library services in a new medical education program which is experimental and expensive remains a challenge during a time of reallocation and retrenchment within the University as a whole. But successful information programs such as those described above must continue to be supported if we are to continue and increase innovative library services in higher education.

Since 1976 the Kansas City Libraries Metropolitan Information Network[16] (called MINET) has offered citizens throughout the metropolitan area access to on-line data base search services. The network has established a mechanism for training searchers in eight search site libraries (public, academic, health sciences) and formal referral procedures between search site libraries and all other area libraries. The training of searchers in the search site libraries has been a major joint effort of the network. To date most training funds have been provided by the Missouri State Library. Now after almost two years of operation, the MINET network has had to face a troublesome opportunity. The potential for offering on-line bibliographic search services to a larger number of user groups is recognized by all members of the network, but with present staffing levels, the eight search site libraries feel unable to handle the increasing workload.

To meet this challenge, MINET has taken a two-level marketing approach. On one level a jointly sponsored, community-wide publicity campaign gradually to increase awareness and use of these databases has been started. Another level being considered is a program to sponsor and support free lance searchers who can provide database search services to those user groups which our present library staffing cannot handle.

This marketing approach will stimulate and improve the level of service throughout the community without encouraging service to one user group and excluding service to others. This is in the best tradition of public library service to all sectors of the community. At the same time, the special services provided by free lance searchers under the sponsorship of the network can potentially satisfy having highly specialized needs and the money to pay the costs of searching services and the free lancer's time.

These three examples illustrate the types of marketing possibilities which are now a part of one urban university library's outreach program. Each program has its own unique set of challenges and opportunities. These programs share the characteristics of the programs of many urban university libraries. All have planned and developed new services in collaboration with their clientele and with other area libraries. As library managers reexamine critically the total structure of information services in light of particular needs of individuals and groups, there will be greater growth and positive change.

This growth and change will certainly involve a host of new considerations beyond those we have been able to touch on this paper. For instance, MacGregor and McInnis have designed an excellent model for the integration of classroom instruction and library research which has marketing applictions throughout an urban university library system and beyond.[17] New user studies in the social sciences and the humanities will surely add some other pieces to the puzzle. Some attempts have been made to study and design information systems based on the information requirements of practitioners (including teachers) in addition to the long standing interest in the information and communication habits of researchers.[18]

The training of librarians and other information professionals with the skills needed to develop outreach services will also be crucial for success. Clearly the information requirements of users can hardly be addressed by examining the quality of a library collection using standard quantitative formulae. Certainly redesigned information services in urban university libraries will require experimentation with new technologies. Also dialogues with accrediting agencies in higher education are needed which will introduce information services as a peer evaluation standard with volume count. But more importantly faculty and students will be motivated to reassess their information needs when they are included in the library team planning and designing new services. A major consideration in planning any new services, as Dougherty and Blomquist suggest,[19] must include a timely, efficient mechanism for moving *on demand* the documents users need out of the libraries and into the offices and laboratories where they can be put to use.

REFERENCES

1. Martha Williams, ed., *Annual Review of Information Science and Technology*, Vol. 11 (Washington, DC: American Society for Information Science, 1976), pp. 347–80; R. M. Dougherty and L. L. Blomquist, *Improving Access to Library Resources: The Influence of Organization on Library Collections and of User Attitudes Toward Innovative Services* (New York: Scarecrow, 1974); *The Responsibility of the University Library Collection In Meeting the Needs of Its Campus and Local Community: A Symposium in Honor of Melvin J. Voight* (LaJolla, CA: Friends of the University of California, San Diego, 1976); Herbert Poole, ed., *Academic Libraries by the Year 2000* (New York: Bowker, 1977), pp. 152–65; Michael Sanderson, "Coping with Turbulence," *Journal of Academic Librarianship* 4 (September 1978): 192–195.
2. Martha Williams, *op. cit.*, p. 348.
3. *Ibid.*, p. 348 354; Kriss T. Ostrom, "Public Libraries and Community I & R Agencies: Partners in the Same Business?" *RQ* 15 (Fall 1975): 25–28; Rosemary Magrill and Charles H. Davis, "Public Library SDI: A Pilot Study," *RQ* 14 (Winter 1974): 131–137.
4. J. S. Kidd, "On-Line Bibliographic Services: Selected British Experiences," *College and Research Libraries* 38 (July 1977): 285–290.
5. J. M. Brittain, *Information and Its Users: A Review with Special Reference to the Social Sciences* (Bath, England: Bath University Press, 1970) pp. 101–124; William F. Heinlen, "A Commitment to Information Services: Developmental Guidelines," *RQ* 15:327–30 (Summer 1976); Noelle P. Cooper, "Library Instruction at a University-Based Information Center: The Informative Interview," *RQ* 15 (Spring 1976): 233–240.
6. Wayne A. Lee and Joseph E. Gilmour, Jr., "A Procedure for the Development of New Programs in Postsecondary Education," *Journal of Higher Education* 48 (May/June 1977): 304–320; D. V. Leister and D. L. Maclachlan, "Assessing Community College Transfer Market: Meta-Marketing Application," *Journal of Higher Education* 47 (November/December 1976): 661–680; Don E. Gardner, "Five Evaluation Frameworks: Implications for Decision Making in Higher Education," *Journal of Higher Education* 48 (September/October 1977): 571–593.
7. Wayne A. Lee and Joseph E. Gilmour, *op. cit.*, p. 307.
8. Philip Kotler, *Marketing for Non-profit Organizations*, (New York: Prentice–Hall, 1975), pp. 37–38.

9. Patricia Knapp, *The Monteith College Library Experiment*, (New York: Scarecrow Press, 1966).

10. ACRL Bibiographic Instruction Task Force, "Guidelines for Bibliographic Instruction in Academic Libraries," *ACRL News* 36 (May 1975): 137–139, 169–171.

11. Kenneth LaBudde and Shirley Mickelson, *CLR Unified Science Project Quarterly and Final Reports*, University of Missouri–Kansas City General Library (Council on Library Resources Library Service Enhancement Program grant, 1978).

12. Virginia Algermissen, "Biomedical Librarians in a Patient Care Setting at the University of Missouri–Kansas City School of Medicine," *Bulletin of the Medical Library Association* 62 (October 1974): 354–358; R. K. Noback and Virginia Algermissen, *Biomedical Librarians in the Patient Care Setting* (Final Report, National Library of Medicine Research Grant No. NLM01574, May 1, 1972–April 30, 1975); R. K. Noback and Gary D. Byrd, *Developing Clinical Information Needs and Systems*, September 1, 1975–August 31, 1976 (Final Grant Report, National Library of Medicine, Research Grant No. 54008-1, June 1977; ERIC Clearinghouse Accession No. IR-005-347).

13. Carolyn A. Reid, "Clinical Medical Librarianship at the University of Missouri–Kansas City School of Medicine: Results of Research and Continuing Activities," (Unpublished report, 1977), p. 1.

14. *Ibid.*, pp. 4–5.

15. Gary D. Byrd and Louise Arnold, "A Long-Term Retrospective Evaluation of a Clinical Medical Librarian Program," submitted to the *Bulletin of the Medical Library Association*, October 1978.

16. T. Philip Tompkins, "An Online Network Serving a Multitype Library Cooperative in a Metropolitan Area," *LJ Special Report* 4 (January 1978): 38–46. "The Evaluation of an Urban Multitype Library Online Searching Network," (paper delivered at the ALA/Association of State Library Agencies for the ALA annual conference, Chicago, 1978).

17. John MacGregor and Raymond G. McInnis, "Integrating Classroom Instruction and Library Research; The Cognitive Functions of Bibliographic Network Structures," *Journal of Higher Education* 48 (January/February 1977): 17–38.

18. For example, Lois Bebout et al., "User Studies in the Humanities: A Survey and a Proposal," *RQ* 15 (Fall 1975): 40–45; John Muthord and Linda Crocker, "Rehabilitation State Supervisors as Knowledge Users," *Rehabilitation Counseling Bulletin, RQ* 15 (Fall 1975): 433–443; John W. Newfield, "What Are the Information Demands of Curriculum Supervisors?" *Educational Leadership* 34 (March 1977): 453–456, B. Skelton, "Scientists and Social Scientists as Information Users: Comparison of Results of Science User Studies with Investigation into Information Requirements of Social Sciences," *Journal of Librarianship* 5 (1973): 138–156; Steve Parker and Kathy Essary, "A Manual SDI System for Academic Libraries," *RQ* 15 (Fall 1975): 47–54; Paul D. Hood, "How Research and Development on Educational Roles and Institutional Structures Can Facilitate Communication," *Journal of Research and Development in Education* 6 (1973): 96–113.

19. Dougherty and Blomquist, *op. cit.*, p. 82–83.

ACRL WHO'S WHO

ACRL NATIONAL CONFERENCE

George R. Parks, Chair*
Diane Lutz, Deputy Chair*

Program:
Richard D. Johnson, Chair
Irma Y. Johnson, Deputy Chair*
Paula Corman
John J. Hawkins
John P. McDonald
Patricia Ann Sacks

Budget and Finance:
Willis Bridegam, Chair
Liam Kelly, Treasurer
Richard Talbot

Exhibits:
Joseph deBerry, Chair

Local Arrangements:
Carol Ishimoto, Chair
David Ferriero, Deputy Chair
Jennie Meyer
Thomas H. Cahalan*

Publicity:
Robert D. Stueart, Chair
Joy McPherson, Deputy Chair
Judith Blight

ACRL Liaison:
Julie A. C. Virgo
Hal Espo

ALA Liaison:
Chris Hoy

ACRL New England Liaison:
Sherrie S. Bergman

*Ad-Hoc Pre-Planning Committee member. Other members are: Beverly Lynch, Richard Olsen, and Joan Stockard.

ACRL OFFICERS

President:
Evan Ira Farber

Vice President:
LeMoyne W. Anderson

Past President:
Eldred R. Smith

Executive Secretary (ex officio):
Julie A. C. Virgo

ACRL PAST PRESIDENTS

1938/39	Frank K. Walter	1958/59	Lewis C. Branscomb
1939/40	Phineas L. Windsor	1959/60	Wyman W. Parker
1940/41	Robert B. Downs	1960/61	Edmon Low
1941/42	Donald Coney	1961/62	Ralph E Ellsworth
1942/43	Mabel L. Conat	1962/63	Katherine M. Stokes
1943/44	Charles B. Shaw	1963/64	Neal R. Harlow
1944/45	Winifred Ver Nooy	1964/65	Archie L. McNeal
1945/46	Blanche Prichard McCrum	1965/66	Helen Margaret Brown
1946/47	Errett Weir McDiarmid	1966/67	Ralph E. McCoy
1947/48	William H. Carlson	1967/68	James Humphry III
1948/49	Benjamin E. Powell	1968/69	David Kaser
1949/50	Wyllis E. Wright	1969/70	Philip J. McNiff
1950/51	Charles M. Adams	1970/71	Anne C. Edmonds
1951/52	Ralph E. Ellsworth	1971/72	Joseph Reason
1952/53	Robert W. Severance	1972/73	Russell Shank
1953/54	Harriet D. MacPherson	1973/74	Norman E. Tanis
1954/55	Guy R. Lyle	1974/75	H. William Axford
1955/56	Robert Vosper	1975/76	Louise Giles
1956/57	Robert W. Orr	1976/77	Connie R. Dunlap
1957/58	Eileen Thorton	1977/78	Eldred R. Smith

ACRL EXECUTIVE SECRETARIES

1947–49	N. Orwin Rush	1963–68	George M. Bailey
1949–56	Arthur T. Hamlin	1968–72	J. Donald Thomas
1957–61	Rihard B. Harwell	1972–77	Beverly P. Lynch
1961–62	Mark M. Gormley	1977–	Julie A. C. Virgo
1962–63	Joseph H. Reason		